W. H. Auden: A Bibliography
1924–1969

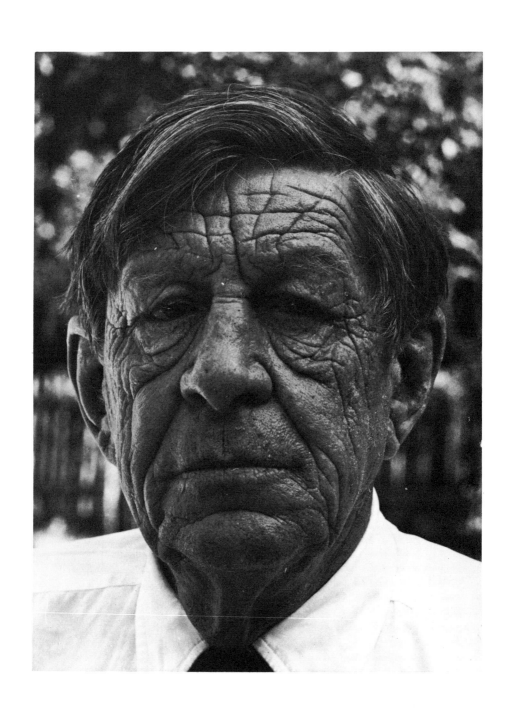

W. H. AUDEN

A Bibliography

1924-1969

Second Edition

B. C. BLOOMFIELD *and* EDWARD MENDELSON

Published for the Bibliographical Society
of the University of Virginia

by the University Press of Virginia
Charlottesville

THE UNIVERSITY PRESS OF VIRGINIA
Copyright © 1972 by the Rector and Visitors
of the University of Virginia

First published 1964
Second edition 1972

Frontispiece photograph is by Peter Mitchell,
Camera Press, Ltd., London.

ISBN: 0–8139–0395–5
Library of Congress Catalog Card Number: 71–77260
Printed in the United States of America

To

Wystan Hugh Auden

CONTENTS

INTRODUCTION

"Fresh addenda are published every day."—The Double Man

WHEN the first edition of this bibliography was published in December 1964 the introduction stated, "Hitherto there has been no full-scale bibliography of the work of W. H. Auden—one of the greatest living English poets—and the amount of relevant critical work is small." It appears in retrospect that the bibliography was published on the crest of a boom in studies of Auden's work, in the prices of his books in the sale room, and, last but not least, in the popularity of his poetry.

The reviews of the first edition were in general approving, but reviewers often complained that the terminus date of 1955 was set too early for a publication issued in the later part of 1964, and most complained that dust jackets were omitted from the bibliographical description. Some attempt has been made to meet both complaints in this revised and extended edition: the terminus date is now 1969, and mention is made of dust jackets. (However the reviewer who complained of the prolixity in the first edition will find no relief here; two compilers seem to make for even greater length.)

Following the publication of the first edition Mendelson wrote and suggested several corrections and improvements which might be made. This began a marathon correspondence, exhaustive if not exhausting on both sides, which has delayed the publication of this second edition by several years. Both collaborators have contributed to all sections of the bibliography, but the first half is principally by Bloomfield; the second mostly by Mendelson. We have evolved the present arrangement of the bibliography through much amicable if at times heated wrangling, and it clearly owes much to the work of other bibliographers, notably Donald Gallup and Emily Wallace; but the principal object remains as stated in the introduction to the first edition, to make the work as comprehensive, lucid, and useful as possible.

A. Books and Pamphlets by W. H. Auden

This section of the bibliography follows normal practice except in one particular. What is normally referred to, bibliographically speaking, as the "Contents note" is subjoined to the collation, whilst the heading "Contents" is reserved for the listing of the literary contents of the book being described, i.e., the word is used in its generally accepted sense.

Normal practice is observed when transcribing upper- and lower-case letters; italic is used for any of the modern sloping type faces; and coloured printing is indicated in square brackets placed before the relevant words or letters. No differentiation is made between small and large upper-case letters.

The first impression of the first edition is usually fully described, and only where notable differences occur are later impressions included or mentioned. The wartime differences in appearance of English editions of Auden's works owing to the War Economy regulations are ignored, since they caused no difference to the texts or the settings, although occasionally the shortage of cloth caused the colour of the casing to be changed. The first and last impressions of Auden's earlier works were checked on the Hinman collating machine in the British Museum to verify this. Where corrections in the text were made in subsequent impressions this is usually mentioned. Editions subsequent to the first are described in a briefer form.

A more systematic attempt has been made to describe the bindings of the books listed, and this is based on the proposal outlined by Professor G. T. Tanselle in "A system of color identification for bibliographical description" (*Studies in Bibliography*, XX [1967], 203–34), which, while not perfect, is demonstrably a great advance on any other system. A brief descriptive note has been included for any dust jacket.

Under the heading "Contents" an attempt has been made, as each poem is listed, to give its previous and subsequent printings. Thus, knowing the first appearance in collected form of any particular piece, one may glean some idea of its textual history. This attempt is now fraught with complication since in recent times Auden rarely reprints any piece without in some way or other revising it.

The listing of reviews is still not complete although we hope to have included any of importance, while excluding many minor notices. In the notes, in addition to the publishing information, an attempt has been made, where possible, to give information about the actual composition of the work. This proved in the case of the plays to be revealing and valuable. In some cases there is a conflict of evidence on the actual date of publication of a work; in such cases the date given first is that supplied by the publisher or another similar source, and the date following in square brackets comes from the Library of Congress Copyright Office's *Catalog of copyright entries*, referred to as *CCE*.

B. Works Edited, Translated, or Having Contributions by W. H. Auden

The plan of this second section of the bibliography follows that of the first except that the collations of the items included have been much abbreviated and no reviews are listed. For a variety of reasons the publishing information is not always complete. Some records have been destroyed, and some publishers preferred not to give this information.

C. Contributions by W. H. Auden to Periodicals

This third section contains the largest number of entries and is arranged in order of the date of publication, beginning with the earliest item and closing with items published at the end of 1969. Each entry is as full as possible, giving title, first line, the name of the periodical, the volume and part number, date, and page references. Some short notes are included in this section.

Other Sections

Since the modern writer's work can now be published in such a variety of ways we decided to include details of Auden's contributions to film, radio, television, sound recordings, and other work, and it seemed better to list these in separate sections. There are difficulties in arriving at satisfactory solutions for describing this material, and we do not pretend to have solved them, but we do hope to have made the listing of Auden's scattered work more exhaustive and complete.

The only thing of which we can both be sure is that our work is incomplete, but either of us will always be glad to have a note of any corrections or additions to the bibliography, which may be sent to us at the University Press of Virginia.

B. C. BLOOMFIELD
EDWARD MENDELSON

February 1971

ACKNOWLEDGEMENTS

THE compilers are very conscious of the great help which has been given to them during the past years. While it is somewhat invidious to single out particular persons, we want to pay especial tribute to Mr. Auden himself, Christopher Isherwood, Mrs. Janet Carleton, Perry Reed, Ruthven Todd, John Fuller, A. R. A. Hobson, W. D. Quesenbery, Jr., Alan Clodd, John Whitehead, Masao Nakagiri, and particularly to the publishing staffs of Random House (Marjorie Currey, Berenice Hoffman, and Jean Pohoryles) and Faber and Faber (Charles Monteith, Rosemary Goad, Sarah Cleaver, and Louisa Browne), all of whom have borne our enquiries with great fortitude; to booksellers Anthony Rota, George Lawson, Robert Wilson, Mrs. Marguerite Cohn, Philip Lyman, L. D. Feldman, James Carters, Andreas Brown, Timothy d'Arch Smith, Gerald Nairn, and John Rolfe; to librarians and scholars Samuel Hynes, Richard Macksey, Barbara Hardy, the late Professor Geoffrey Tillotson, Mardi Valgemae, I. J. Kirby, Franz M. Kuna, Donald C. Leavitt, R. H. Super, Daniel Hoffman, R. C. Johnson, Karl C. Gay, Hugh D. Ford, Lee Chang-bai, Kenneth Lohf, Herbert Cahoon, Mary M. Hirth, D. G. Neill, Warren Tsuneishi, Mrs M. Uding van Laarhoven; and also to Robert M. Agard, Robert Allen, Alan Ansen, Arno Bader, E. C. Baker, Kenneth Baldwin, Robert Bloom, J. M. Boykow, Dorothy Boyle, Neville Braybrooke, Michael J. Briggs, Benjamin Britten, William Bruehl, Glenn W. Bunday, B. N. Chaturvedi, Chen Tsu-wen, Margaret Church, Aurora Ciliberti, Cyril Connolly, Louis Criss, Robert W. Daniel, W. Stuart Debenham, James H. Dee, Charles Elliott, Richard Ellmann, Evan Esar, Donald Gallup, David Goldstein, James F. Govan, Frederic Grab, Helen M. Grady, Thomas B. Greenslade, Erling Grønland, Boksoon Hahn, E. T. Hall, Richard Hart, Catherine D. Hathaway, Horst Heiderhoff, Stephan Hermlin, Phillip Hodson, Grace B. Howes, Samuel Hynes, Carlo Izzo, Mildred L. Joy, M. W. Jones, Mirko Jurak, Hideo Kaneko, Anna Katona, Walter Kerr, László Kéry, Thomas Kilfoil, Kenton Kilmer, Sungha Kim, David K. Kirby, Aaron Kramer, Paul Kresh, Matsuko Kyoto, James Laughlin, Isobel C. Lee, Jay Levine, Alexis Levitin, Kenneth Lewars, William T. McKinnon, Charles Mann, Johanne Martens, K. K. Merker, Charlotte Morse, Donald E. Morse, M. Marquis Morse, Pablo Neruda, Fred J. Nichols, Frank Ochiogrosso, Robert T. Peterson, G. Philipsen, Martin Price, Aleksis Rannit, Pamela G. Reilly, Carolyn Riley, Edouard

Roditi, Raymond Roseliep, Marvin Rosenthal, Peter Salus, Vilas Sarang, Ernst Schnabel, Mark Schorer, Laurence Scott, W. Schürenberg, Walter P. Sheppard, Ellen Shub, Leif Sjöberg, Ted Slate, Milton Smith, Monroe K. Spears, Mrs. Seymour A. Steindler, Halldor Þorsteinsson, Dennis Todd, Güven Turan, John Updike, David Vaughan, Myron M. Weinstein, Ulrich Weisstein, Joseph A. Winn, Margaret Wolf, Anthony Wood-Corfield, and Mary Alice Wotring; to the staffs of the University of London and Yale University libraries and countless other libraries; and also to the staffs of the other publishing houses we have bothered and fretted with our seemingly endless enquiries.

Auden's letters to his American publisher are quoted by kind permission of Random House, Inc., and the Columbia University Libraries where the letters are now held.

The senior compiler also wishes to acknowledge his indebtedness to the School of Oriental and African Studies for three months' research leave and a grant from the Irwin Fund of the Central Research Fund of the University of London, both of which allowed him to visit libraries in the United States during the summer of 1968.

We offer our sincere thanks for the trouble taken on our behalf and hope the result will be considered worthwhile.

B. C. Bloomfield
Edward Mendelson

ABBREVIATIONS

Auden's principal works are listed below, with the abbreviations subsequently used in the bibliography. Substantially revised editions are listed on separate lines.

P (1928)	*Poems*. S. H. S[pender], 1928.
P	*Poems*. Faber, 1930.
P2	[Second edition]. Faber, 1933.
O	*The orators*. Faber, 1932.
	[Second edition]. Faber, 1934.
	[Third edition]. Faber, 1966; Random House, 1967.
DD	*The dance of death*. Faber, 1933.
AP	*Poems*. Random House, 1934.
DBS	*The dog beneath the skin* (with Christopher Isherwood). Faber, 1935; Random House, 1935.
AF6	*The ascent of F 6* (with Christopher Isherwood). Faber, 1936.
	[American edition]. Random House, 1937.
	[Second English edition]. Faber, 1937.
LS	*Look, stranger!* Faber, 1936; [as *On this island*], Random House, 1937.
LFI	*Letters from Iceland* (with Louis MacNeice). Faber, 1937; Random House, 1937.
LFI2	[Second edition]. Faber, 1967; Random House, 1969.
SP	*Selected poems*. Faber, 1938.
OTF	*On the frontier* (with Christopher Isherwood). Faber, 1938; Random House, 1939.
JTW	*Journey to a war* (with Christopher Isherwood). Faber, 1939; Random House, 1939.
AT	*Another time*. Random House, 1940; Faber, 1940.
SoP	*Some poems*. Faber, 1940.
DM	*The double man*. Random House, 1941; [as *New year letter*], Faber, 1941.
FTB	*For the time being*. Random House, 1944; Faber, 1945.
CP	*The collected poetry of W. H. Auden*. Random House, 1945.
AA	*The age of anxiety*. Random House, 1947; Faber, 1948.

CSP	*Collected shorter poems, 1930–1944.* Faber, 1950.
EF	*The enchafèd flood.* Random House, 1950; Faber, 1951.
N	*Nones.* Random House, 1951; Faber, 1952.
	The rake's progress (with Chester Kallman). Boosey and Hawkes, 1951.
SA	*The shield of Achilles.* Random House, 1955; Faber, 1955.
OMR	*The old man's road.* Voyages, 1956.
PA	*W. H. Auden: a selection by the author.* Penguin, 1958; [as *The selected poetry of W. H. Auden*], Modern Library, 1959.
HTC	*Homage to Clio.* Random House, 1960; Faber, 1960.
	Elegy for young lovers (with Chester Kallman). Schott, 1961.
DH	*The dyer's hand.* Random House, 1962; Faber, 1963.
SE	*Selected essays.* Faber, 1964.
ATH	*About the house.* Random House, 1965; Faber, 1966.
	The bassarids (with Chester Kallman). Schott, 1966.
CSP2	*Collected shorter poems, 1927–1957.* Faber, 1966; Random House, 1967.
SelP	*Selected poems.* Faber, 1968.
CLP	*Collected longer poems.* Faber, 1968; Random House, 1969.
SW	*Secondary worlds.* Faber, 1968; Random House, 1969.
CWW	*City without walls.* Faber, 1969; Random House, 1970.

W. H. Auden: A Bibliography

1924–1969

A

BOOKS AND PAMPHLETS BY
W. H. AUDEN

A 1   POEMS   1928

W. H. AUDEN | [long rule] | POEMS | [short rule] | S. H. S.:1928.

Collation: 2°. 4¾ x 3¾ in. [A² B–C¹⁰], pp. [i–iv, 1–2] 3–37 [38–40].
[i–ii]: blank. [iii–iv]: title, verso blank. [1]: 'TO CHRISTOPHER ISHER-
WOOD'. [2]: 'About 45 copies. [followed by the autograph number of the copy]'.
3–37: text. [38–40]: blank. A printed erratum slip bearing poem I(h) is loosely inserted between pp. 6 and 7.
  The Connolly copy, now rebound, which was displayed in the National Book
League's exhibition in 1947,[1] appears to have the following collation: [A²B–C¹⁰D²],
the last gathering of two leaves being blank. The new binding obscures the original
stitching, but traces of it are still evident between pp. 30 and 31. The last two leaves
are doubtless genuine and were not inserted by the binders, since one bears a wa-
termark found earlier in the book. In view of Spender's account of how the book
was finished, it would seem either that the binder made a mistake or that Spender
made up this copy himself. The absence of a copy number and the erratum slip
(which was probably printed by the Holywell Press), and the nature of the dedication may lend strength to the second explanation. It appears, however, that the
Columbia copy also has three final blank leaves.
Binding: Stitched in strong reddish orange (35) wrapper lettered across the front
cover in black: 'W. H. AUDEN | [long rule] | POEMS'. All edges trimmed.
Paper: Cream wove paper watermarked with a triangle bisected horizontally, the
letter 'T' in the upper division and the figures '831' in the lower. Paper supplied by
the Holywell Press is watermarked: 'ABERMILL | BOND | MADE IN GT.
BRITAIN'.
Contents:

I (a) The sprinkler on the lawn ...
  (b) Bones wrenched, weak whimper, lids wrinkled, first dazzle known ...
       Reprinted in P.
  (c) We saw in Spring ...
  (d) This peace can last no longer than the storm ...
  (e) 'Buzzards' I heard you say ...
  (f) Consider if you will how lovers stand ... First printed in *Oxford
       poetry*, 1927 ("Extract"), revised here, and reprinted by Isherwood
       in *New verse*, November 1937.
  (g) Amoeba in the running water ...
  (h) Upon the ridge the mill-sails glow ... On the printed erratum slip.

---

[1] National Book League, *English poetry: a descriptive catalogue* ... , compiled by John
Hayward (Cambridge: Cambridge University Press, 1947), no. 340. A description of the
Hayward copy was added to the 1950 edition.

The University of Cincinnati Library copy has a manuscript copy of the erratum slip in Spender's hand.

II I chose this lean country...
III No trenchant parting this... Reprinted in P.
IV Suppose they met, the inevitable procedure... Reprinted in P.
V On the frontier at dawn getting down...
VI Who stands, the crux left of the watershed... Reprinted in P, P2, AP, CP ("The watershed"), CSP, CSP2, and SelP.
VII Nor was that final, for about that time... Reprinted in P.
VIII The crowing of the cock... Reprinted in P.
IX Because sap fell away...
X The mind to body spoke the whole night through...
XI From the very first coming down... Reprinted with minor verbal revisions in P, P2, AP, CP ("The love letter"), CSP, PA ("The letter"), and CSP2.
XII The four sat on in the bare room...
XIII To-night when a full storm surrounds the house... Reprinted with revisions in P ("Paid on both sides"), P2, AP, SP, CSP, and CLP.
XIV Night strives with darkness, right with wrong... Revised and reprinted in P ("Paid on both sides"), P2, AP, SP, CSP, and CLP.
XV Control of the Passes was, he saw, the key... Reprinted with minor changes of punctuation in P, P2, AP, CP ("The secret agent"), CSP, CSP2, and SelP.
XVI Taller to-day, we remember similar evenings... Reprinted, with revisions, in P, P2, AP, CP ("As well as can be expected"), CSP ("Taller to-day"), PA, and CSP2, again revised.
XVII The spring will come...
XVIII The summer quickens grass...
XIX Some say that handsome raider still at large...
XX To throw away the key and walk away... Reprinted in PA ("The journey").

These last four poems are reprinted, with some small revisions, in the charade "Paid on both sides" in P, P2, AP, SP, SoP (except XX), CSP, and CLP.

Notes: "I spent the remaining part of the long vacation [1928] printing a little volume of the *Poems* of W. H. Auden, an edition of thirty copies which is sought after today" (Stephen Spender, *World within world* [London: Hamish Hamilton, 1951], p. 116).

Spender has no more exact memory of the number of copies printed, but it would seem likely that this lower figure is more nearly correct since the Ayerst copy, which has an inscription by Spender dated 1 February 1929, is "No. 24-About". The distribution of copies would presumably have been nearly complete by that date. The higher number quoted in the book itself may have been one which made no allowance for wastage in the machining.

The printing was done in Frognal, Hampstead, on "an Adana printing set price £7 for chemists' labels" (Spender in a letter to Bloomfield), and the "copy" was supplied by the Reverend A. S. T. Fisher and, probably, Auden himself. Portions of this "copy" Spender sold, shortly before the last war, to Miss Caroline Newton, and it is now in the Berg Collection at New York Public Library.

Normally, when this type of small press is used a complete dummy of the book is first made and the type set from it. Each folio sheet is then printed; two pages to the forme in the larger presses, or one on the smaller. That the former appears, at first, to be the case is indicated, in the Johnson copy, by the noticeably parallel misalignment of the impression on pp. 10 and 11 and pp. 8 and 13, and the thin, uneven inking of pp. 3 and 18. An examination of the Cincinnati copy, however, reveals the fact that pp. 6 and 15 were obviously not impressed simultaneously, for their alignment is markedly different, and the inking of p. 15 is heavier than that of p. 6. In addition, when setting what we may suppose to have been the first paged forme, the amateur compositor mis-set the page number "20" so that it printed in the gutter instead of the outer corner of the page. This mistake was repeated with the first sheet in which both pages were numbered—so that "18" came in the gutter—but never afterwards. When the printing is completed the sheets are gathered and stitched according to the make-up of the dummy. Stitching is visible between pp. 10 and 11 and pp. 30 and 31. The first gathering is tipped in. The quality of the printing improves in the last part of the book, *i.e.*, beginning with p. 23, "when I had broken the set and took the rest of the book to the Holywell Press Oxford who finished it and bound it for me" (Spender in a letter to Bloomfield). This, of course, accounts for the professional look of the finished booklet. It may also raise questions of format, but it would seem likely that this had already been settled by the advanced state of Spender's printing, and that the Holywell Press merely completed his work in the manner in which he had begun it. The press, unfortunately, no longer have any record of the transaction.

Copies traced are those belonging to: Christopher Isherwood (no. 2), H. Bradley Martin (no. 4), John Hayward's copy, sold at Sotheby's on 12 July 1966 and now in a private English collection (no. 10), John Johnson (no. 12), Professor E. R. Dodds (no. 15), University of Cincinnati Library (no. 17), Harvard College Library (no. 19), Durham University Library (no. 24), D. G. O. Ayerst ("No. 24—About"), Jack Samuels's copy now at Columbia University Library (unnumbered), Cyril Connolly, and George Rylands. Both the Connolly and Johnson copies lack the erratum leaf, and the Cincinnati copy has it supplied in Spender's autograph. The Johnson copy was used for the University Microfilms Xerox facsimile issued in 1960, and the University of Cincinnati Library issued a facsimile edition of 500 copies of its exemplar in 1964. This facsimile has a prefatory note by Spender.

A 2 POEMS 1930

a) First edition

POEMS | BY | W. H. AUDEN | LONDON | FABER & FABER | 24 RUSSELL SQUARE

Collation: 8¼ x 6¼ in. [A–E]⁸, pp. [1–6] 7–79 [80].
    [1]: 'POEMS'. [2]: 'To | CHRISTOPHER ISHERWOOD | [four lines of verse]'. [3]: title page. [4]: 'FIRST PUBLISHED IN SEPTEMBER MCMXXX | BY FABER AND FABER LIMITED | 24 RUSSELL SQUARE LONDON W.C.1 | PRINTED IN GREAT BRITAIN | BY TREND AND COMPANY PLYMOUTH | [one line]'. [5]–79: text; 36 blank. [80]: blank.
Binding: Glued in a white card cover with a light greenish blue (172) paper wrapper lettered across the front in black: '[all within a border of four red rules, title in hollow upper case] POEMS | BY | W. H. AUDEN | LONDON | FABER & FABER LIMITED | 24 RUSSELL SQUARE'. All edges untrimmed.
Paper: Cream laid paper watermarked 'FABER & GWYER'.
Contents:
    To Christopher Isherwood: Let us honour if we can... Reprinted in CSP2.
    Paid on both sides: a charade. First published in *Criterion*, January 1930. "I have sent you the new Criterion, to ask you to read a verse play 'Paid on both sides', by a young man I know which seems to me quite a brilliant piece of work.... This fellow is about the best poet that I have discovered in several years" (T. S.

Eliot in a letter to E. McKnight Kauffer in the Pierpont Morgan Library).[2]
There is an interesting sidelight by Isherwood on the circumstances of the composition of this piece in *New verse*, November 1937, pp. 5–6: "I once remarked
to Auden that the atmosphere of *Gisli the outlaw* very much reminded me of
our schooldays. He was pleased with the idea: and, soon after this, he produced
his first play: *Paid on both sides*, in which the two worlds are so inexplicably
confused that it is impossible to say whether the characters are really epic heroes
or only members of the school O.T.C."

Six sections of the charade first appeared in P (1928) as poems XIII, XIV, and
XVII through XX (see A 1). The whole charade is reprinted in SP, CSP, and
CLP, and excerpts are reprinted in SoP. The following six pieces are reprinted
separately in CP:

Not from this life, not from this life is any . . .   ("All over again")
Can speak of trouble, pressure on men . . .   ("Always in trouble")
The spring unsettles sleeping partnerships . . .   ("It's too much")
To throw away the key and walk away . . .   ("The walking tour")
Tonight the many come to mind . . .   ("Remember")
Though he believe it no man is strong . . .   ("Year after year")

The issue of *Criterion* in which the charade first appeared was reviewed by J. D.
in *Granta*, XXXIX (17 January 1930), 201–2, and in the following issue (24
January 1930), 218–19; the reviews are principally concerned with Auden's work.
There was a production of the charade at Briarcliff College, New York, by
Hallie Flanagan and Margaret Ellen Clifford, in March 1931, but Auden had no
part in it; and there was another production "conducted by Joseph Gordon
MacLeod" at the Festival Theatre, Cambridge, 12–17 February 1934.

    I Will you turn a deaf ear . . .   Reprinted in P2, AP, CP ("The questioner
       who sits so sly"), CSP, and CSP2.
    II Which of you waking early and watching daybreak . . .
    III Since you are going to begin to-day . . .   Reprinted in P2, AP, SP, CP
       ("Venus will now say a few words"), CSP, and CSP2.
    IV Watch any day his nonchalant pauses, see . . .   Reprinted in P2, AP, SP,
       SoP, CP ("We all make mistakes"), CSP ("A free one"), and CSP2.
    V From the very first coming down . . .   First printed in P(1928).
    VI To have found a place for nowhere . . .
    VII Upon this line between adventure . . .   Reprinted in P2, AP, CP ("Do
       be careful"), CSP ("Between adventure"), and CSP2.
    VIII Again in conversations . . .   Reprinted in P2, AP, CP ("Two's com-
       pany"), and CSP ("Never stronger").
    IX The crowing of the cock . . .   First printed in P(1928).
    X Love by ambition . . .   Slightly revised and reprinted in P2, AP, CP
       ("Too dear, too vague"), CSP, and CSP2.
    XI Who stands, the crux left of the watershed . . .   First printed in P(1928).
    XII We made all possible preparations . . .   Reprinted in P2, AP, CP ("Let
       history be my judge"), CSP, and CSP2.
    XIII Bones wrenched, weak whimper, lids wrinkled, first dazzle known . . .
       First printed in P(1928).
    XIV Sentries against inner and outer . . .   Reprinted in P2, AP, CP ("Shut
       your eyes and open your mouth"), and CSP.
    XV Control of the passes was, he saw, the key . . .   First printed in P(1928).
    XVI It was Easter as I walked in the public gardens . . .   Reprinted, with con-
       siderable excisions, in P2, AP, SoP, CP ("1929"), CSP, and CSP2.

---

[2] We are indebted to Herbert Cahoon for this reference.

XVII This lunar beauty... Reprinted in P2, AP, CP ("Pur"), CSP ("Like a dream"), PA ("This lunar beauty"), and CSP2.

XVIII Before this loved one... Reprinted in P2, AP, CP ("This one"), CSP, PA, and CSP2 ("This loved one").

XIX The silly fool, the silly fool... Reprinted in P2, AP, CP ("Happy ending"), CSP, and CSP2.

XX The strings' excitement, the applauding drum... Reprinted in P2, AP, CP ("Family ghosts"), CSP, and CSP2.

XXI On Sunday walks... Reprinted in P2, AP, CP ("Such nice people"), CSP, and CSP2 ("On Sunday walks").

XXII Get there if you can and see the land you once were proud to own... Reprinted in *Twentieth century*, March 1931, and, in a slightly revised form, in P2 and AP.

XXIII Nor was that final, for about that time... First printed in P(1928).

XXIV From scars where kestrels hover... Reprinted in P2, AP, CP ("Missing"), CSP, and CSP2.

XXV Suppose they met, the inevitable procedure... First printed in P(1928).

XXVI Taller to-day we remember similar evenings... First printed in P (1928).

XXVII No trenchant parting this... First printed in P(1928).

XXVIII Under boughs between our tentative endearments, how should we hear... Reprinted in P2, AP, CP ("When the devil drives"), and CSP.

XXIX Consider this and in our time... Reprinted in P2 and AP and, in a revised form, in CP ("Consider"), CSP, and CSP2.

XXX Sir, no man's enemy, forgiving all... Reprinted in P2, AP, SoP, CP ("Petition"), and CSP.

Notes: Published 18 September 1930 [*CCE* 9 October 1930] in an edition of 1,000 copies, at 2/6d. In a letter to Bloomfield, Frank Morley, then with Faber and Faber, suggested that some of the sheets were kept unbound and later issued in boards, but we have not been able to find such a copy, although a second impression was advertised.[3] Morley's suggestion might be explained by the changed appearance of the second edition. The title was advertised as out of print in *Criterion* for October 1933.

Faber and Faber issued other books of verse by new poets in this style, with the substitution of different-coloured wrappers. Auden's book was one of three published on 18 September 1930, the other two being *The ecliptic*, by J. G. MacLeod, and *Pursuit*, by P. P. Graves. However, the books were not given a series title.

John Carter says: "If it is true that more copies of W. H. Auden's *Poems*, published in London in 1930, were sold by one book-seller in New York than by all the book-sellers in what was then the author's own country, it [*Poems*, 1930] is probably now commoner in the United States than in England."[4]

The bookseller in question was Terence Holliday. In a letter to Bloomfield he says: "We wrote our London agent, Wm. Jackson, for fifty copies of Mr. Auden's first book, prose or verse. When 'Poems, 1930' appeared... we included a notice of it in our monthly bulletin; the immediate response was such that we wrote or cabled for another fifty copies, or possibly one hundred, and it became one of our most successful ventures into the poetry of the period."

Isherwood possesses the corrected proof copy of this book.

[3] *New verse*, 1 (January 1933), [20].

[4] John Carter, *Taste and technique in book-collecting* (Cambridge: Cambridge University Press, 1948), p. 144.

Reviews:

B. Dobrée. *Listener,* IX (14 June 1933), 958.
D. Fitts. *Hound and horn,* IV (Summer 1931), 625–30.
L. M[acNeice]. *Oxford outlook,* XI (March 1931), 59–61.
N. Mitchison. *Week-end review,* II (25 October 1930), 592, 594.
Poetry review, XXI (November–December 1930), 468.
D. Powell. *Sunday times,* 28 December 1930, p. 3.
J. M. R. *Granta,* XL (28 November 1930), 184.
M. Roberts. *Adelphi,* n.s. I (December 1930), 251–52.
Times literary supplement, 19 March 1931, p. 221.
M. D. Z[abel]. *Poetry,* XXXVII (May 1931), 101–4.

b) Second edition   1933

POEMS | BY | W. H. AUDEN | LONDON | FABER AND FABER | 24 RUSSELL SQUARE

Collation: 7¾ x 5¾ in. [A]–F⁸, pp. [i–ii, 1–6] 7–89 [90–94]. $1 signed 'A.P.', except A. [i–ii]: blank. [1]: half title. [2]: 'also by W. H. Auden | [star] | [two lines]'. [3]: title page. [4]: 'FIRST PUBLISHED IN SEPTEMBER MCMXXX | BY FABER AND FABER LIMITED | 24 RUSSELL SQUARE LONDON W.C.1 | SECOND EDITION NOVEMBER MCMXXXIII | PRINTED IN GREAT BRITAIN BY | R. MACLEHOSE AND COMPANY LIMITED | [two lines]'. [5]: 'To | CHRISTOPHER ISHERWOOD | [four lines of verse]'. [6]: blank. 7: 'NOTE | [six lines]'. [8]: blank. [9]–89: text; 38 and 40 blank. [90–94]: blank.
Binding: Bound in yellowish grey (93) cloth lettered down the spine in light blue: 'POEMS *by* W. H. AUDEN'. Top edge only trimmed. Pale yellow dust wrapper printed in blue.
Paper: White unwatermarked wove paper.
Contents: As the first edition, with the substitution of the following poems for those originally so numbered:

    II   Doom is dark and deeper than any sea-dingle... First printed in *New signatures* (1932) ("Chorus from a play"), and reprinted in AP, SP, SoP, CP ("Something is bound to happen"), CSP ("The wanderer"), PA ("Chorus"), CSP2 ("The wanderer"), and SelP.

    VI   Between attention and attention... Reprinted in AP, CP ("Make up your mind"), CSP ("Easy knowledge"), and revised in CSP2.

    IX   Its [*sic*] no use raising a shout... Reprinted in AP.

   XIII   What's in your mind, my dove, my coney... First printed in *Twentieth century,* November 1933, and reprinted in AP, SP, CP, CSP, and CSP2.

 XXIII   Look there! The sunk road winding... First printed in *Twentieth century,* February 1933, and reprinted in AP and, in a revised form, CP ("The bonfires"), CSP, and CSP2.

   XXV   Who will endure... Reprinted in AP, CP ("Better not"), CSP, PA ("No change of place"), and CSP2.

 XXVII   To ask the hard question is simple... First printed in *Criterion,* July 1933, and reprinted in AP, SP, CP ("What do you think?"), CSP ("The hard question"), PA ("The question"), and CSP2.

Notes: Published 2 November 1933 at 5/– (but we have seen a copy with a review slip giving a publication date of 16 November 1933). Faber and Faber have no figures for the first two impressions, so these are quoted from the printer's records. The first impression was of 1,000 copies, and the book was subsequently reprinted in September 1934 (1,500 copies), February 1937 (1,517 copies), June 1939 (1,500 copies), December 1943 (1,040 copies), January 1946 (1,000 copies), December 1948 (1,000 copies), and April 1950 (2,000 copies). Out of print in 1963.

Reviews:

D. G. Bridson. *New English weekly*, IV (21 December 1933), 234–35. See also D. Hawkins, IV (18 January 1934), 331.
F. C. *Granta*, XLIII (29 November 1933), 170.
F. R. Leavis. *Scrutiny*, III (June 1934), 70–83.
J. Pudney. *Week-end review*, VIII (16 December 1933), 668, 670.
Times literary supplement, 15 March 1934, p. 190.
A. D. W. *Cherwell*, XXXIX (18 November 1933), 142–43.
C. H. Waddington. *Cambridge review*, LV (1 December 1933), 147–48.
R. P. Warren. *American review*, III (May 1934), 221–24.

A 3 THE ORATORS 1932

a) First edition

THE ORATORS | AN ENGLISH STUDY | BY | W. H. AUDEN | LONDON | FABER & FABER LIMITED | 24 RUSSELL SQUARE

Collation: 8¾ x 5½ in. [A]–F^8G^{10}, pp. [1–8] 9–116. G2 is signed.
[1–2]: blank. [3]: 'THE ORATORS | AN ENGLISH STUDY'. [4]: 'BY THE SAME AUTHOR | [star] | POEMS'. [5]: title page. [6]: 'FIRST PUBLISHED IN MCMXXXII | BY FABER AND FABER LIMITED | 24 RUSSELL SQUARE LONDON W.C.1 | PRINTED IN GREAT BRITAIN BY | R. MACLEHOSE AND COMPANY LIMITED | [two lines]'. [7]: 'TO | STEPHEN SPENDER | [three lines]'. [8]: blank. 9–116: text; 10, 12, 40, and 84 blank.

Binding: Bound in black cloth lettered across the spine in gold: 'THE | ORATORS | *by* | W. H. | AUDEN | FABER | & FABER'. Top edge only trimmed, and stained dark blue. Cream dust jacket printed in blue.

Paper: Cream unwatermarked wove paper.

Contents:

To Stephen Spender: Private faces in public places... Reprinted in CSP2.
Prologue: By landscape reminded once of his mother's figure... Reprinted in AP, SP, CP ("Adolescence"), CSP, and, slightly revised, in CSP2.
Book I The initiates
 (i) Address for a prize-day. First printed in *Criterion*, October 1931 ("Speech for a prize day").
 (ii) Argument.
 (iii) Statement.
 (iv) Letter to a wound. Reprinted in CP.
Book II Journal of an airman
 Contains the following two pieces of verse reprinted in CP, CSP, and CSP2. The first is also included in PA.
  There are some birds in these valleys... ("The decoys").
  We have brought you, they said, a map of the country... ("Have a good time").
Book III Six odes
 (i) Watching in three planes from a room overlooking the courtyard... First printed in *Dope*, New Year 1932, and reprinted in a much revised version in CP ("January 1, 1931") and CSP ("1st January 1931").
 (ii) Walk on air do we? And how!... Dedicated to Gabriel Carritt.

(iii) What siren zooming is sounding our coming... Reprinted in SP and, in a revised form, in CP ("The exiles"), CSP, and CSP2 with further revisions. Dedicated to Edward Upward.

(iv) Roar Gloucestershire, do yourself proud... First printed in the *Modern Scot*, January 1932 ("Birthday ode"). Three stanzas beginning "These had stopped seeking..." first appeared in *Adelphi* ("Cautionary rhymes"), December 1931, and are reprinted in CP ("Like us") and CSP. Dedicated to John Warner.

(v) Though aware of our rank and alert to obey orders... First printed in *New signatures* (1932), and reprinted in SP, CP ("Which side am I supposed to be on"), CSP, and revised in PA ("Ode"), CSP2, and SelP. Dedicated "To my pupils."

(vi) Not, father, further do prolong... Reprinted in revised form in CP and CSP.

Epilogue: 'O where are you going' said reader to rider... Reprinted in SP, SoP, CP, CSP, PA ("The three companions"), CSP2, and SelP.

Notes: Published 19 May 1932 [*CCE* 26 May 1932] in an edition of 1,000 copies at 7/6d. The book was written while Auden was working at the Larchfield Academy, Helensburgh, and was published, he says, as soon as it was finished. In 1945 Auden described *The orators* as "a case of the fair notion fatally injured" (CP, p. [vii]).

John Hayward's copy, sold at Sotheby's on 12 July 1966, carried nine annotations and corrections by the author, not all of which were corrected in the second edition.

Reviews:
B. Dobrée. *Spectator*, CXLIX (20 August 1932), 239.
B. *Granta*, XLI (10 June 1932), 508.
J. G. Fletcher. *Poetry*, XLII (May 1933), 110–13.
D. Garman. *Scrutiny*, I (September 1932), 183–84.
G. Greene. *Oxford magazine*, LI (10 November 1932), 158–59.
G. E. G[rigson]. *Yorkshire post*, 15 August 1932, p. 6.
J. Hayward. *Criterion*, XII (October 1932), 131–34.
N. Mitchison. *Week-end review*, V (28 May 1932), 677–78.
H. B. Parkes. *Symposium*, IV (April 1933), 245–48.
W. Plomer. *Sunday referee*, 22 May 1932, p. 6.
Poetry review, XXIII (1932), 493.
A. Pryce-Jones. *London mercury*, XXVI (May 1932), 170–71.
M. Roberts. *Adelphi*, IV (August 1932), 793–96.
G. W. Stonier. *New statesman & nation*, n.s. III (28 May 1932), 710–11.
Times literary supplement, 6 June 1932, p. 424.
R. P. Warren. *American review*, III (May 1934), 224–27.
H. Wolfe. *Observer*, 26 June 1932, p. 5.

b) Second edition   1934

[The transcription of the title page is identical with that of the first edition.]

Collation: 8¾ x 5½ in. [A]–G⁸, pp. [1–6] 7–112.
[1]: 'THE ORATORS | AN ENGLISH STUDY'. [2]: 'BY THE SAME AUTHOR | [star] | POEMS'. [3]: title page. [4]: 'FIRST PUBLISHED IN MCMXXXII | BY FABER AND FABER LIMITED | 24 RUSSELL SQUARE

LONDON W.C.1 | SECOND EDITION SEPTEMBER MCMXXXIV | PRINTED IN GREAT BRITAIN BY | R. MACLEHOSE AND COMPANY LIMITED | [two lines]'. [5]: 'TO | STEPHEN SPENDER | [three lines]'. [6]: blank. 7–113: text, 8, 10, 38, 78, and 80 blank.

Binding: As the first edition. Light blue dust jacket printed in black. The third impression is lettered down the spine.

Paper: Cream unwatermarked wove paper.

Contents: As the first edition with some verbal corrections and the following excisions (the page references are to the first edition):

Book II   Journal of an airman
   Pages 49–50 lines 29–39 and 1–14 omitted.
   Page 62 lines 23–27 and p. 63 lines 1–3 omitted.
   Page 73 lines 16–22, all p. 74, and p. 75 lines 1–13 omitted.

Book III   Six odes
   (iii)   Stanza thirteen is omitted.

Notes: Published in September 1934 in an impression of 1,000 copies at 7/6d. Reprinted in September 1943 (500 copies) and April 1946 (1,000 copies). Out of print in 1959.

c)   Third edition   1966

THE ORATORS | AN ENGLISH STUDY | BY | W. H. AUDEN | FABER AND FABER | 24 Russell Square | London

Collation: 8½ x 5½ in. [A]–F⁸ G⁴, pp. [1–6] 7–102 [103–104].
   [1]: 'THE ORATORS | AN ENGLISH STUDY'. [2]: *'by the same author |* [star] | [twenty four lines]'. [3]: title page. [4]: *'First published in mcmxxxii | by Faber and Faber Limited | 24 Russell Square London W.C.1 | Second Edition mcmxxxiv | Reprinted mcmxliii | and mcmxlvi | Third Edition mcmlxvi | Printed in Great Britain by | R. MacLehose and Company Limited | The University Press Glasgow | [one line] | © This edition 1966 by W. H. Auden'.* [5]: 'TO | STEPHEN SPENDER | [three lines]'. [6]: blank: 7–8: foreword. 9–102: text; 10, 12, 40, and 76 blank. [103–104]: blank.

Binding: Bound in moderate blue (182) cloth lettered down the spine in gold: 'THE ORATORS W. H. AUDEN FABER'. All edges trimmed. Shiny white dust jacket printed in black, grey, and red.

Paper: White unwatermarked wove paper.

Contents: As the second edition with some corrections and the following excisions (the page references are to the second edition):

Book I   The initiates
   Pages 22–23 lines 25 and 1–3 omitted.

Book II   Journal of an airman
   Pages 42–43 lines 10–27 and 1–5 omitted.
   Pages 55–56 lines 10–28 and 1–3 omitted.
   Pages 62–65, all omitted except the last five lines on page 65.

Book III   Five odes
   Pages 85–88 [former Ode II] omitted.
   Page 97 lines 11–18 omitted.
   Pages 101–102 lines 20–27 and all page 102 omitted.
   Page 105 lines 4–13 omitted.
   Page 108 lines 12–27 omitted.

There are other verbal changes and revisions, and Auden's foreword is newly added.

Notes: Published 29 September 1966 in an edition of 3,000 copies at 21/–.
Reviews:
  A. Alvarez. *Observer*, 27 November 1966, p. 27.
  G. MacBeth, *Listener*, LXXVI (20 October 1966), 579.
  P. Oettlé. *Poetry Australia*, 19 (December 1967), 41–44.
  [J. Fuller.] *Times literary supplement*, 6 October 1966, p. 918.

d) First separate American edition   1967

W · H · AUDEN | THE ORATORS | AN ENGLISH STUDY | [device: a house] | RANDOM HOUSE NEW YORK

Collation: 8¼ x 5⅜ in. [1–6]⁸, pp. [*–**, i–vi] vii–viii, [1–2] 3–85 [86].
  [*]: blank. [**]: '*By W. H. Auden* | [thirty lines]'. [i]: 'THE ORATORS |
  AN ENGLISH STUDY'. [ii]: blank. [iii]: title page. [iv]: '*First American
  Edition, 1967* | [eleven lines] | *Manufactured in the United States of America* |
  by the Haddon Craftsmen, Scranton, Pennsylvania | *Designed by Betty Ander-
  son*'. [v] 'TO | Stephen Spender | [three lines]'. [vi]: blank. vii–viii: foreword.
  [1]–85: text; 2, 4, 6, 30, and 62 blank. [86]: about the author.
Binding: Quarter bound in rough white cloth lettered down the spine in gold:
  'W. H. AUDEN [device across the spine with the words 'Random | House'] THE
  ORATORS', with moderate purplish red (258) paper boards. All edges trimmed
  and the top edge only stained black. White dust jacket printed in pale yellow,
  purple, and black.
Paper: Cream unwatermarked wove paper.
Contents: As the third English edition, with some slight revisions.
Notes: Published 26 October 1967 in an edition of 2,500 copies at $4. The text of
  the first edition had previously been included in AP.
Reviews:
  W. J. Smith. *New York times*, 12 November 1967, section 7, p. 52.
  C. Walsh. *Book world*, I (19 November 1967), 1–2.

A 4   THE DANCE OF DEATH   1933

W. H. | AUDEN | [large red period] | THE | DANCE | OF | DEATH | [large red period] | FABER & | FABER

Collation: 8¾ x 5½ in. [A]–E⁴, pp. [1–6] 7–37 [38–40]. $1 signed 'A.D.D.', except A.
  [1]: 'THE DANCE OF DEATH'. [2]: 'By the same Author | [black period] |
  THE ORATORS | POEMS'. [3]: title page. [4]: 'FIRST PUBLISHED IN
  NOVEMBER MCMXXXIII | BY FABER AND FABER LIMITED | 24 RUS-
  SELL SQUARE LONDON W.C.1 | PRINTED IN GREAT BRITAIN BY |
  R. MACLEHOSE AND COMPANY LIMITED | [two lines]'. [5]: 'To |
  ROBERT MEDLEY | and | RUPERT DOONE'. [6]: blank. 7–[38]: text.
  [39–40]: blank.
Binding: Bound in brilliant yellowish green (130) paper-covered boards lettered
  down the spine in black: 'THE DANCE OF DEATH *by* W. H. AUDEN', and
  across the foot of the spine: 'F | & | F'. The front cover is lettered in black as the
  title page. Top and leading edges trimmed. Green dust jacket printed in black
  and red.

The second and subsequent impressions are bound in black cloth and lettered on the spine only in gold.

Paper: White unwatermarked wove paper.

Contents: The dance of death.

Notes: Published 9 November 1933 in a impression of 1,200 copies at 2/6d. (It should however be noted that the printer's records show 1,940 copies for this impression.) The book was reprinted in September 1935 (1,300 copies), November 1941 (1,000 copies), and December 1945 (1,155 copies). Out of print in August 1953.

Auden was introduced to the Group Theatre by Robert Medley, with whom he had been at Gresham's School, Holt; and Rupert Doone, the director, suggested that Auden should write a play on the theme of Orpheus and Eurydice. It was to be in modern dress and there was to be a part for dance or mime. In fulfilment of this brief Auden wrote *The dance of death*, which was first produced by the Group Theatre at the Westminster Theatre in two "club performances" on 25 February and 4 March 1934 on Sundays, with the mediaeval play *The deluge* forming the other part of the bill, and afterwards in the Group Theatre's season at the Westminster Theatre from 1 October 1935, with incidental music by Herbert Murrill. It is probable that Auden wrote the synopsis of *The dance of death* which appears on p. [6] of the programme for the 1934 performances, and in revised form on p. [4] of the programme used in 1935.

The text of the production was revised for performance and a copy is lodged in the Lord Chamberlain's office. The revisions are discussed by M. Jurak in *Acta neophilologica*, I (1968), 67–68, and there is an account of the genesis of the play by Rupert Doone in *Theatre newsletter*, VI (29 September 1951), 5. A copy of the printed text with some changes in Auden's hand, and a 2 fol. manuscript with additional material, are both in the Berg Collection at the New York Public Library.

The play was first produced in the United States by the Experimental Theatre at Vassar College under the title *Come out into the sun* on 2–3 August 1935, and later on 19 May 1936 with the original title by the Federal Theater Project of the W.P.A.

Reviews:

L. Bonnerot. *Revue anglo-américaine*, XII (December 1934), 156–57.

D. G. Bridson. *New English weekly*, IV (21 December 1933), 234–35.

F. C. *Granta*, XLIII (29 November 1933), 170.

G. Ewart. *New verse*, 7 (February 1934), 21–22.

Y. ffrench. *London mercury*, XXIX (January 1934), 258–59.

T. Greenidge. *Socialist review*, n.s. V (January 1934), 58–59.

J. A. H. *Cherwell*, XXXIX (18 November 1933), 143.

F. R. Leavis. *Scrutiny*, III (June 1934), 70–83.

J. Pudney. *Week-end review*, VIII (16 December 1933), 668, 670.

Times literary supplement, 15 March 1934, p. 190. *Ibid.*, 24 January 1935, p. 37.

C. H. Waddington. *Cambridge review*, LV (1 December 1933), 147–48.

Reviews of the performance:

A. Dukes. *Theatre arts monthly*, XIX (December 1935), 906–8.

M. Sayers. *New English weekly*, VII (10 October 1935), 435. Cf. letter by A. D. Hawkins, VIII (24 October 1935), 39–40.

D. Verschoyle. *Spectator*, CLV (11 October 1935), 547.

The "club performances" are reviewed in *New statesman & nation*, n.s. VII (3 March 1934), 303, and *New English weekly*, IV (12 April 1934), 617; the latter by A. D. Hawkins.

A review of the W.P.A. performance:

W. R. Benét. *Saturday review of literature*, XIV (6 June 1936), 18.

A 5   THE WITNESSES   1933

The Witnesses | [poem in four columns with wood engraving on left and right margins, across the bottom of the sheet, and in lower half of the two centre columns. Below right of the woodcut] *From* THE LISTENER, 12 *July* 1933

Collation: 8 x 13 in. Single sheet printed on one side only.
Binding: None.
Paper: Cream unwatermarked wove paper, similar to "cartridge" paper.
Contents: The witnesses: You dowagers with Roman noses... An offprint from
   Listener, 12 July 1933. The first and second parts of the poem are dropped, and
   the third section revised, in DBS, and this revision is reprinted in CP, CSP, and
   CSP2. The original is reprinted in *Living age,* October 1933.
Notes: It appears that about 20 copies of this broadside were printed on better paper
   than that used for *Listener;* some are signed by Auden and Gwen Raverat (who
   did the wood engraving), and some by Raverat alone. The Harvard copy is
   numbered "19/20" and signed by both; a copy belonging to John Whitehead is
   numbered "9/20" and signed by Raverat; while Bloomfield's copy is unnumbered
   and signed by Raverat. Both signatures and numbering are usually in pencil. The
   editor of the *Listener* poetry supplement from which this offprint was made was
   Janet Adam Smith, but she has no more exact recollection of the circumstances
   surrounding the production. Copies were made principally for the author and
   illustrator and were not distributed or sold.

A 6   POEM   1933

POEM | [star] | W. H. | AUDEN | 1933

Collation: 6½ x 4½ in. One unsigned gathering of six leaves.
   [1–4]: blank. [5]: title page. [6–7]: text. [8]: 'Of this poem, which first appeared in
   the "Criterion," | twenty-two copies were printed for the author: five copies | on
   Kelmscott, numbered 1–5; five on Fabriano, numbered | I–V; five on Navarre,
   numbered a–e; five on Japan vellum, | numbered A–E; and two on Imperial vellum,
   numbered | x and xx. | This is number [in black ink] III'. [9–12]: blank.
Binding: Stitched with a black cord, except 1–5 which have blue cords, with a paper
   wrapper folded round the last blank leaves. A paper label on the front cover is
   lettered: 'POEM | [star] | W. H. AUDEN', and a duplicate is stuck inside the last
   rear blank leaf. The variations of the bindings are as follows: 1–5: marbled peacock
   blue and green with a grey label; I–V: black with a gold label; a–e: marbled choco-
   late and cinnamon with a gold label; A–E: patterned red and green on Japanese
   silver with a white label; x and xx: patterned white on silver with a dull gold label.
     The trial copy on Arnold paper in the Lockwood Memorial Library at the State
   University of New York, Buffalo, has a green wrapper and cord, and a gold label
   while the copy in the Harris Collection at Brown University is described (in
   pencil) as "one of two copies on rice paper" and has an orange and gold wrapper
   with a yellow label.
Paper: As specified above.
Contents: Hearing of harvest rotting in the valley... Reprinted from *Criterion,*
   July 1933, and reprinted in LS, SP, CP ("Paysage moralisé"), CSP, and CSP2. The
   first-line reading was changed to 'harvests' in LS.

Notes: Printed and bound by Frederic Prokosch in Bryn Mawr, Pennsylvania, in November 1933. In John Hayward's copy there is a letter from Auden to Eliot which says: "An American fan printed 22 copies of a poem of mine as a Christmas present." This would seem to date the printing fairly accurately. There is a copy in the Berg Collection in New York Public Library. There may perhaps be other trial copies in existence.[5]

A 7   POEMS   1934

W · H · AUDEN | [in brown with fancy initial] *Poems* | [device: a house] | RANDOM HOUSE · NEW YORK

Collation: 8¾ x 5¾ in. [1–14]⁸, pp. [i–ii, 1–6] 7–218 [219–222].
   [i–ii]: blank. [1]: title page. [2]: 'COPYRIGHT 1934 · THE MODERN LI-BRARY · INC | PRINTED IN THE UNITED STATES OF AMERICA | BY THE SPIRAL PRESS · NEW YORK'. [3]: contents. [4]: blank. [5]–218: text; 6, 56, 86, 88, 90, 92, 114, 116, 154, 182, and 184 blank. [219–222]: blank.
Binding: Bound in dark reddish orange (38) cloth lettered up the spine in gold: 'W. H. AUDEN [diamond] POEMS', and across the front cover: '*Poems*'. All edges trimmed. Cream dust jacket printed in brown and black.
Paper: Cream unwatermarked wove paper.
Contents:
   All the poems in P2.
   The orators [first edition text].
   The dance of death.
Notes: Published 11 September 1934 [CCE 17 September 1934] in an impression of 1,575 copies at $2.50, and reprinted in January 1935 (1,000 copies), November 1937 (1,000 copies), and October 1941 (1,000 copies). Out of print in 1945.
Reviews:
   R. P. Blackmur. *Mosaic*, I (Spring 1935), 29–32.
   P. Burnham. *Commonweal*, XXI (28 December 1934), 255–57.
   M. Cowley. *New republic*, LXXX (26 September 1934), 189–90.
   B. Deutsch. *Virginia quarterly review*, XI (January 1935), 131–32.
   P. M. Jack. *New York times*, 23 September 1934, section 6, p. 2.
   R. Lechlitner. *New York herald tribune*, 23 September 1934, section 7, p. 8.
   D. McCord. *Yale review*, XXIV (December 1934), 391–93.
   S. Rodman. *Common sense*, III (November 1934), 25–26.
   A. J. M. Smith. *Poetry*. XLVII (October 1935), 43–46.
   G. Sylander. *Bozart-Westminster*, I (Spring–Summer 1935), 39–41.
   L. Untermeyer. *Saturday review of literature*, XI (10 November 1934), 274–75.

A 8   TWO POEMS   1934

TWO POEMS | [star] | W. H. AUDEN | [four stars vertically] | XMAS | 1934

Collation: 6½ x 4½ in. One unsigned gathering of six leaves.
   [1–4]: blank. [5]: title page. [6–7]: text. [8]: 'Twenty-two copies of these poems were printed [in sans serif] for the author: | five on Arnold, numbered 1–5; five on

---

[5] For a note on a similar case see Donald C. Gallup, *T. S. Eliot: a bibliography* (London: Faber, 1952), A28, p. 23.

Oland, numbered I–V; five on | Curfew, numbered a–e; five on Japan vellum, numbered A–E; and | two on Imperial vellum, numbered x and xx. | This is number [in black ink] 3'. [9–12]: blank.

Binding: Stitched with a cord with a paper wrapper folded round the last blank leaves, and a label lettered: 'TWO POEMS | [star] | W. H. AUDEN'. Variations of the binding are: 1–5: yellow with a gold label and bl. ck cord; I–V: marbled blue, green, and brown with a white label and brown cord; a–e: patterned green on gold Japan paper with a grey label and black cord; A–E: marbled pale blue and emerald with a silver label and blue cord; x and xx: patterned red and green on gold Japan paper with a gold label and brown cord. A duplicate label is stuck in.

Paper: As specified above.

Contents:

  I   Sleep on beside me though I wake for you . . .
  II The latest ferrule now has tapped the curb . . .
      Both poems first printed in *New verse*, October 1933.

Notes: Printed and bound by Frederic Prokosch in Bryn Mawr, Pennsylvania, in November 1934. There are two copies on Kelmscott which we have not located; another on orange vellum is in the Berg Collection in New York Public Library; another on blue vellum is in the University of Texas Library; and another on cherry vellum is in the Bodleian.

Some copies are described in the colophon in Prokosch's hand as "one of four preliminary [*in one copy* original] trial copies in Bodoni (which was then discarded in favor of sans-serif)." The trial copies are bound in marbled blue wrappers with a blue cord and a grey label. Of these "four" copies, six have been located: three in the University of Texas Library, one in the Berg Collection at the New York Public Library, one in the British Museum, and one in the possession of Perry Reed.

For a note on the separate editions of the two poems, see Appendix III.

A 9   THE DOG BENEATH THE SKIN   1935

a) First edition

THE DOG | BENEATH THE SKIN | *or* | WHERE IS FRANCIS? | *a play in three acts by* | W. H. Auden | *and* | Christopher Isherwood | *London* | Faber and Faber Limited | *24 Russell Square*

Collation: 8¾ x 5¾ in. [A]–K⁸L¹⁰, pp. [1–8] 9–180. L2 is signed.
   [1–2]: blank. [3]: half title. [4]: blank. [5]: title page. [6]: 'FIRST PUBLISHED IN MAY MCMXXXV | BY FABER AND FABER LIMITED | 24 RUSSELL SQUARE LONDON W.C.1 | PRINTED IN GREAT BRITAIN BY | R. MAC-LEHOSE AND COMPANY LIMITED | [two lines]'. [7]: 'To | ROBERT MOODY | [four lines]'. [8]: '*The first performance of this play will be given in the* | *autumn of this year by the Group Theatre under the* | *direction of Mr. Rupert Doone.*' 9: dramatis personae. [10]: blank. 11–180: text. The collation of the second impression is [A]–L⁸M⁴, with two final blank leaves.

Binding: Bound in deep red (13) cloth lettered down the spine in blue: 'THE DOG BENEATH THE SKIN FABER AND | BY W. H. AUDEN AND CHRISTO-PHER ISHERWOOD FABER'. Top edge only trimmed. Yellow dust jacket printed in blue and red.

Paper: White unwatermarked wove paper.

Contents: The dog beneath the skin.

The following pieces from the play also appeared separately:

Vicar's sermon. pp. 162–69. First printed in *Life and letters,* May 1934 ("Sermon by an armament manufacturer"), and reprinted in CP ("Depravity: a sermon").

Now through night's caressing grip . . . pp. 115–16. Set to music by Benjamin Britten, published by Boosey and Hawkes (1938), and reprinted in SP, SoP, CP, and CSP.

Seen when night is silent . . . p. 65. Reprinted with slight alterations in *Lysistrata,* May 1935, CP, CSP and, revised, in CSP2. The poem bears a strong resemblance to poem II in *New verse,* October 1933, p. 15.

Enter with him . . . pp. 26–28. First printed in *Twentieth century,* August 1933, and reprinted in *New republic,* 17 October 1934; reprinted with slight alterations in CP ("I shall be enchanted"), CSP ("Legend"), PA ("In legend"), CSP2 ("Legend"), and SelP.

The young men in Pressan tonight . . . pp. 13–16. The longest complete version of this poem is found first printed in *Listener,* 12 July 1933. The version in DBS drops the first and second parts of the poem and revises the text of the third part. The *Listener* version was printed as a broadside (A 5), and in *Living age,* October 1933; the DBS version in CP, CSP, and CSP2.

Love loath to enter . . . p. 179. First printed in *New Oxford outlook,* May 1934. This is a revised version which is reprinted in SP.

The Summer holds: upon its glittering lake . . . pp. 11–13. First published in *Left review,* May 1935, and reprinted in SP and SoP. Part of this chorus beginning "I see barns falling . . ." was reprinted in *Town and country planning,* December 1940.

You with shooting sticks and cases for field-glasses . . . pp. 54–56. Reprinted in SP.

Happy the hare at morning, for she cannot read . . . pp. 91–92. Reprinted in revised form in CP ("The cultural proposition") and CSP ("Culture").

You who return tonight to a narrow bed . . . pp. 140–41, 143–44. Reprinted in CSP ("Prothalamion").

Notes: Published 30 May 1935 in an impression of 2,000 copies at 7/6d. Reprinted in March 1936 (2,000 copies), November 1944 (573 copies), November 1946 (724 copies), February 1950 (1,000 copies), and April 1954 (1,500 copies). Out of print January 1966.

Isherwood says that early in 1935 Auden sent him the fully revised version of a play titled *The chase,* which was announced for publication by Faber and Faber on 21 March 1935. Isherwood suggested some revisions and improvements, and in this way they "drifted into a collaboration." When Auden visited Copenhagen, where Isherwood was staying, a final draft was evolved. Isherwood suggested that the collaboration arose because he was, at that time, still acting as censor to much of Auden's poetry.[6] Neither of them thought much of the play, but decided it was good enough to publish and submitted it to Faber and Faber. Meanwhile, Rupert Doone had got a copy, and by drastic cutting evolved a stage version; it was he who gave the play its present title. It was reasonably successful on the stage, and Faber and Faber agreed to publish this revised version but did not want to put Isherwood's name on the title page.[7] This was the occasion of disagreement, but the play was finally printed and credited to both authors. Isherwood says that most of the play is by Auden. (See M. Valgemae's account of the play's development in *Huntington library quarterly,* XXI [August 1968], 373–83.)

[6] Christopher Isherwood, *Lions and shadows* (London: Hogarth Press, 1938), p. 190.
[7] In April 1935 the play was still advertised as by Auden alone (see *New verse,* 14 [April 1935], [1].)

Auden confirmed Isherwood's story of the play's composition, but would not agree that most of it was, in fact, written by himself, maintaining that it was impossible to estimate each partner's contribution to a collaboration. He identified Act I, scene ii, with the exception of the song, about half of Act II, scene i, and the Destructive Desmond episode as being by Isherwood.

Faber and Faber can neither confirm nor deny Isherwood's account of the dispute about the crediting of the authorship of the play.

The play was produced by the Group Theatre for members on 30 January 1936 in its season at the Westminster Theatre, with incidental music by Herbert Murrill. In this production the executions of the workers and the Destructive Desmond episode were both omitted, a real woman was substituted for the dummy in Act II, scene iv, the sermon was left out from the final scene, and Sir Francis was shot to death by Mildred Luce.[8] The text of the stage version is available at the Lord Chamberlain's office, and is described by M. Jurak in *Acta neophilologica*, I (1968), 69–70. A prompt copy of the production text is in the Berg Collection at the New York Public Library, together with 33 pages of manuscript alterations by Auden. The text was again revised by Auden for a production at the Cherry Lane Theatre in New York on 22 July 1947, directed by Alexis Solomos. In this version Sir Francis is stabbed to death.[9] When Auden taught at Smith College in 1953 he sponsored a student competition to rewrite the end of the play along guide lines which he set.[10]

A radio adaptation was broadcast by the BBC Third programme on 29 October 1965.

Reviews:

T. R. Barnes. *Scrutiny*, IV (September 1935), 189–95.
L. Bonnerot. *Revue anglo-américaine*, [XIII] (April 1936), 361.
D. G. Bridson. *Time and tide*, XVI (17 August 1935), 1204.
J. Garrett. *Criterion*, XIV (July 1935), 687–90.
D. H. *Colosseum*, III (March 1936), 81–82.
D. Powell. *London mercury*, XXIX (January 1936), 397–98.
I. M. Parsons. *Spectator*, CLIV (28 June 1935), 1112, 1114.
Times literary supplement, 11 July 1935, p. 444.
Reviews of the performance:
K. A[llott]. *New verse*, 19 (February–March 1936), 15.
C. C[onnolly]. *New statesman & nation*, n.s. XI (12 February 1936), 188.
"Eric." *Punch*, CXC (12 February 1936), 189.
A. V. Cookman. *London mercury*, XXXIII (March 1936), 529.
M. Sayers. *New English weekly*, VIII (13 February 1936), 354–55.
D. Verschoyle. *Spectator*, CLVI (7 February 1936), 211.

b) First American edition   1935

The Dog Beneath The Skin | OR, WHERE IS FRANCIS? | [brown swelled rule] | A PLAY IN THREE ACTS BY | W. H. Auden | & | Christopher Isherwood | [device in brown: a house] | RANDOM HOUSE • NEW YORK | 1935

Collation: 8½ x 5½ in. [1]⁴[2–10]⁸, pp. [i–ii, 1–5] 7–161 [162–166].
  [i–ii]: blank. [1]: title page. [2]: 'COPYRIGHT, 1935, BY THE MODERN LIBRARY INC. | PRINTED IN THE UNITED STATES OF AMERICA'. [3]:

---

[8] *Ibid.*, 26–27 (November 1937), 20. See also *The times*, 1 February 1936, p. 10.
[9] *Masses and mainstream*, I (June 1948), 45.   [10] *Sophian*, I (28 April 1953), 1.

'TO ROBERT MOODY | [four lines]'. [4]: blank. [5]: dramatis personae. [6]: blank. 7–161: text. [162–166]: blank.

Binding: Bound in medium grey (265) cloth lettered down the spine in blue and red: '[in blue] THE DOG BENEATH THE SKIN | [in red] W. H. AUDEN & CHRISTOPHER ISHERWOOD'. On the front cover the publisher's device in blue. All edges trimmed. Grey dust jacket printed in dark blue and red.

Paper: White unwatermarked wove paper.

Contents: As the English edition.

Notes: Published 1 October 1935 in an edition of 1,400 copies at $1.50. Listed in the 1936 and 1937 Random House catalogues, but not in the 1938 issue, by which time it was presumably out of print.[11]

Reviews:

W. R. Benét. *Saturday review of literature*, XIII (30 November 1935), 16.
L. Bogan. *New republic*, LXXXV (27 November 1935), 79.
D. Davidson. *Southern review*, I (Spring 1936), 884–86.
R. Lechlitner. *New York herald tribune*, 1 December 1935, section 7, p. 38.
P. B. Rice. *Nation*, CXLI (27 November 1935), 626.
S. Rodman. *Common sense*, V (February 1936), 29.
G. Stone. *American review*, VI (November 1935), 126–28.

c) First American paperback edition   1958

Two Great Plays by | W. H. AUDEN AND | CHRISTOPHER ISHER-WOOD | [titles in fancy script] The | Dog | Beneath | the | Skin | The | Ascent | of F6 | [device: silhouette of a naked runner holding a torch, round the top 'MODERN LIBRARY' and underneath 'PAPERBACKS'] | PUBLISHED BY RANDOM HOUSE | NEW YORK

Collation: 7¼ x 4⅜ in. Ninety-six single leaves, pp. [i–iv, 1–5] 6–185 [186–188].
[i]: half title. [ii]: blank. [iii]: title page. [iv]: '[sixteen lines] | Manufactured in the United States of America by H. Wolff'. [1]: '[title in fancy script] The | Dog | Beneath | the | Skin | Or, Where Is Francis? | [paw print]'. [2]: dedication. [3]: dramatis personae. [4]: blank. [5]–112: text. [113]: '[title in fancy script] The | Ascent | of F6 | A Tragedy in Two Acts | [peak silhouette]'. [114]: dedication. [115]: characters. [116]: blank. [117]–185: text. [186]: blank. [187]: advertisement for *The American college dictionary*. [188]: blank.

Binding: A perfect binding glued in a white shiny card cover lettered down the spine: '[in black] W. H. AUDEN [red oblique stroke] CHRISTOPHER ISHER-WOOD [in pale blue fancy script] Two Great Plays [across the spine: device in black] | [in red] P48'. On the front cover: '[in red in the top right corner] 95° | [oblique black stroke across the corner] | [pale blue fancy script] Two Great Plays by | [authors' names in black] W. H. AUDEN | [pale blue short rule] | CHRISTOPHER ISHERWOOD | [red paw print and below, the black silhouette of a peak. On either side of these ornaments the titles in pale blue fancy script] The | Dog | Beneath | the | Skin | The | Ascent | of F6 | [red] A MODERN LI-BRARY PAPERBACK'. The rear cover is printed in red and black and contains a list of the Modern Library paperbacks. Top edge stained light brown.

Paper: Cream unwatermarked wove paper.

Contents:
The dog beneath the skin.
The ascent of F6 [American edition text].

---

[11] We are indebted to Professor Howard Winger of Chicago for help here.

Notes: Published 19 December 1958 in an edition of 15,000 copies at 95¢.
Review: S. Spender. *New republic*, CXLI (23 November 1959), 16–17.

d) First American paperback edition: second impression   1964

[Transcription identical with the first impression to the end of the play titles, then] | [device: a sun with a face] | VINTAGE BOOKS | A DIVISION OF RANDOM HOUSE | *New York*

Collation: 7¼ x 4¼ in., afterwards identical with the first impression.
    [i]: half title. [ii]: blank. [iii]: title page. [iv]: 'VINTAGE BOOKS | are published by ALFRED A. KNOPF, INC. | and RANDOM HOUSE, INC. | [sixteen lines] | Manufactured in the United States of America by H. Wolff'. [1]–185: identical with the first impression. [186–188]: list of Vintage Books.
Binding: A perfect binding glued in a matt white card cover lettered as the first impression down the spine except that the device and series number are replaced by: '[device: sun with face] Vintage [across the spine] V–158'. On the front cover the price is deleted from the top right corner and the last line is replaced by: 'A Vintage Book [device] V–158 $1.45'. The rear cover contains a descriptive note for the volume.
Paper: Cream unwatermarked wove paper.
Contents:
    The dog beneath the skin.
    The ascent of F6.
Notes: Issued 22 January 1964 in an impression of 2,000 copies, and reprinted in October 1965 (2,500 copies) and June 1967 (3,000 copies).
    Some copies of this issue were put out in a buckram-reinforced library binding on what seems to be better paper. The volume is sewn and collates: 7¼ x 4½ in. [1–5]^{16}, pp. [i–iv, 1–5] 6–185 [186–188], and is bound in moderate brown (58) buckram cloth, lettered across the spine in gold: '[device: sun with face] | [rule] | [on a dark green panel] TWO | GREAT | PLAYS | · | BY W. H. | Auden & | Christopher | Isherwood | [rule] | [on the spine] VINTAGE | [on a blind-stamped panel] BUCKRAM | REINFORCED | V–158'. The device is repeated on the front cover.

e) First English paperback impression   1968

[The transcription of the title page is identical with that of the first edition.]

Collation: 7½ x 5 in. Ninety single leaves, pp. [1–8] 9–180.
    [As the first edition with the following exceptions]: [6]: 'FIRST PUBLISHED IN MCMXXXV | BY FABER AND FABER LIMITED | 24 RUSSELL SQUARE, LONDON W.C.1 | FIRST PUBLISHED IN THIS EDITION MCMLXVIII | PRINTED IN GREAT BRITAIN BY | JOHN DICKENS & CO LTD, NORTHAMPTON | [eight lines]'. [8]: '*The first performance of this play was given in* | *January 1936 by the Group Theatre under the* | *direction of Mr. Rupert Doone.*' [This note was added in the second impression of the first edition.]
Binding: A perfect binding glued in a white card cover with the front and spine brilliant yellow (83), and lettered in black down the spine: 'AUDEN AND | ISHERWOOD [wide white rule continuing across the front cover] THE DOG BENEATH THE SKIN [in white on a deep orange (51) panel] FABER'. Across

the front cover: 'W. H. AUDEN & | C. ISHERWOOD | [wide white rule] | THE | DOG | BENEATH | THE | SKIN', and down the leading edge of the front cover in white on a deep orange panel: 'FABER paper covered EDITIONS'. The rear cover, inside and out, bears a list of other titles in the series, and the inside front cover carries comments on the play.

Paper: White unwatermarked wove paper.

Contents: As the first edition.

Notes: Published 6 May 1968 in an impression of 6,000 copies at 8/6d.

A 10   OUR HUNTING FATHERS   1935

OUR HUNTING | FATHERS | [star] | W. H. | AUDEN | 1935

Collation: 3 x 2¼ in. One unsigned gathering of six leaves.

[1–4]: blank. [5]: title page. [6–7]: text. [8]: 'Twenty-two copies of this poem were | printed for the author: five on Florentine, | numbered 1–5; five on Chinese rice, | numbered I–V; five on Normandie, num- | bered a–e; five on Incudine, numbered | A–E; and two on Halle, numbered X and | XX. | This is number [in black ink] E'. [9–12]: blank.

Binding: Stitched with a black cord, except A–E, with a paper wrapper folded round the last blank leaves, and a label lettered: 'OUR | HUNTING FATHERS | [star] | W. H. AUDEN'. Variations of the label are: 1–5: patterned red on Japan silver with a red label; I–V: black on white woodcut with a white label; a–e: patterned red and black circles with a white label; A–E: floral pattern green, red, black with a silver label and a blue cord; X and XX: patterned green and red on gold with a gold label. A duplicate label is inserted inside the rear wrapper.

Paper: As specified above.

Contents: Our hunting fathers told the story... First printed in the *Listener*, 30 May 1934, set to music by Britten and published by Boosey & Hawkes (1936), and reprinted in LS, SP, CP, CSP, and CSP2.

Notes: Printed in November 1935 by Cambridge University Press for Frederic Prokosch and bound by him. The University of Texas Library has a "number f. Special copy on Fabriano."

A 11   SONNET   1935

SONNET | [star] | W. H. | AUDEN | 1935

Collation: 3 x 2¼ in. One unsigned gathering of six leaves.

[1–2]: blank. [3]: title page. [4–5]: blank. [6–7]: text. [8–9]: blank. [10]: 'Twenty-two copies of this poem were | printed for the author: five on Normandie, | numbered 1–5; five on Brussels vellum | numbered I–V; five on Incudine, numbered | a–e; five on Japanese rice, numbered A–E; | and two on Rives, numbered X and XX. | This is number [in black ink] b'. [11–12]: blank.

Binding: Stitched with a blue cord, except I–V, X, and XX which have black cords, with a paper wrapper folded round the last blank leaves and a label lettered: 'SONNET | [star] | W. H. AUDEN'. Variations of the binding are: 1–5: marbled blood, chocolate, and emerald with a silver label; I–V: patterned moss-green woodcut on cream with a grey label; a–e: floral pattern, blue and white on black with a white label; A–E: patterned blue woodcut on beige with a white label; X and XX: orange on Japan gold with a gold label. A duplicate label is stuck in.

Paper: As specified above.
Contents: On the provincial lawn I watch you play . . .   First printed in *Rep*, October
   1934.
Notes: Printed in November 1935 by Cambridge University Press for Frederic
   Prokosch and bound by him. The University of Texas Library has a trial copy.
   The copy in the Lockwood Memorial Library carries this dedication in Auden's
   hand: "To John Betjeman | . . . with Xmas | greetings from | Wystan | 1935".

A 12   THE ASCENT OF F 6   1936

a) **First edition**

by W. H. Auden *and* | Christopher Isherwood | a tragedy in two acts |
THE ASCENT | OF F 6 | Faber & Faber Limited | 24 Russell Square |
London

Collation: 8¾ x 5½ in. [A]–H⁸, pp. [1–8] 9–123 [124–128].
   [1–2]: blank. [3]: 'THE ASCENT OF F 6'. [4]: *'by the same authors* | The Dog
   Beneath the Skin'. [5]: title page. [6]: *'First published in September Mcmxxxvi* |
   By Faber and Faber Limited | *24 Russell Square London W.C.1* | *Printed in Great*
   Britain by | *R. MacLehose and Company Limited* | *The University Press Glasgow*
   | [one line]'. [7]: 'To | JOHN BICKNELL AUDEN | [four lines of verse]'. [8]:
   blank. 9: characters. [10]: blank. [11]–123: text; 12, 56, 80, 102, and 106 blank. [124–
   128]: blank.
Binding: Bound in brilliant blue (177) cloth lettered down the spine in gold: '*The*
   Ascent of F..6—W. H. Auden and Christopher Isherwood'. Top and front edges
   trimmed. Cream dust jacket printed in blue and red.
Paper: Cream unwatermarked wove paper.
Contents: The ascent of F 6.
   The following pieces of verse from the play also appeared separately:
      Death like his is right and splendid . . . pp. 88–89.   Reprinted in SP.
      Acts of injustice done . . . pp. 117–18.   Reprinted in SoP.
      Stop all the clocks, cut off the telephone . . . p. 113.   Reprinted in revised form
         in AT, CP, CSP, and CSP2.
      At last the secret is out, as it always must come in the end . . . pp. 116–17. Re-
         printed in CP, CSP, and CSP2.
      Some have tennis elbow . . . p. 96.   About half this little piece of verse first ap-
         peared in *New verse*, April–May 1936 ("Foxtrot from a play").
Notes: Published 24 September 1936 in an edition of 2,000 copies at 6/–.
   Isherwood told the following story of the genesis of this play. Both he and Auden
   had now come to feel that they were now writing for a serious and creative dramatic group, and accordingly, they now sought a more definite plot than that of
   The dog beneath the skin. The play was written in Sintra when Auden was on a
   short visit to Isherwood. Isherwood sketched the plot line and says he regarded
   the play as a kind of opera with Auden's poetry taking the part of the music and
   he being the librettist. Thus the prose is Isherwood's and the poetry Auden's. The
   play was submitted to Faber and Faber and to Rupert Doone for the Group
   Theatre. Faber and Faber agreed to publish the play and Doone set about preparing
   a stage version.
   Meanwhile Auden had gone to Spain, but the stage revision still proceeded in the
   hands of Doone and Isherwood. Auden did not see the play until about a week
   after the opening when he returned. Faber and Faber had already set up the original
   draft they received and were loath to incorporate the late revisions; they therefore

published the original version. The revisions carried out by Doone and Isherwood were published in the second edition, and a comparison of the texts makes it seem likely that the American edition, which agrees substantially with the second edition, except in part of Act II, scene iii, is a revision of a slightly earlier date than the second edition. This is borne out by the respective publication dates.[12] (For a description of the production text, see M. Jurak, *Acta neophilologica*, I [1968], 71–75. An early typescript of the play, with corrections in Isherwood's hand, is in the Berg Collection at the New York Public Library; taking account of the corrections this text is identical with the first published edition.)

Both Auden and Doone confirm Isherwood's story of the writing of this play.

The play was produced by the Group Theatre at the Mercury Theatre on 26 February 1937, with incidental music by Benjamin Britten, and transferred to the Little Theatre on 30 April 1937. The play was also presented at the Arts Theatre, Cambridge, on Friday, 23 April 1937, "thanks to Mr Maynard Keynes" (C. Isherwood, "The Group Theatre," *Cambridge review*, LIX [19 November 1937], 104), apparently using the text of the American edition, since A. R. Humphreys wrote, "The Mercury Theatre performance, however, omitted the phantasmagoria and everything following his immolation before his mother's spirit.... The Arts Theatre performance admitted the 'political' conclusion and left the last words with Mr and Mrs A..." (*Cambridge review*, LVIII [30 April 1937], 354). Isherwood says much of the play's success was due to good casting. Doone was critical of the play's ending because, like all these authors' plays, it "ended in dream" and did not work to a dramatic climax. Both authors were conscious of this and Auden told Bloomfield that "we never did get that ending right," and they rewrote it for a production "in a living room" by the Drove Players in New York on 21–23 April 1939 which was directed by Forrest Thayr, Jr.; the text of this version has not been found, but it is perhaps similar to that used by the Group Theatre revival at the Old Vic, produced on 27 June 1939. Of this revival Doone told a reporter, "The authors, at our suggestion, have altered the final scene.... Previously Michael Ransom... had a long dream-interview with his mother at the summit. Now she is merely seen as a kind of apparition, and the play ends with a B.B.C. talk" (*Evening standard*, 19 June 1939, p. 9). A prompt copy of this version is in the Berg Collection at New York Public Library. Isherwood wrote to John Lehmann in May 1939 "F 6 is being done, quite grandly [in New York], some time in August. We have written a new ending..." (John Lehmann, *The whispering gallery* [London: Longmans, 1955], p. 330), but this production seems not to have taken place. Auden again revised the ending, as well as other brief passages, for a production at Swarthmore College on 19–21 April 1945. The text of this revision survives and there is a Xerox copy in the College library. The production was directed by Seyril Schochen Rubin and Auden played the cowled monk in Act II, scene i. (See E. F. von Erffa, "Auden at Swarthmore," *National Theatre Conference bulletin*, VII [November 1945], 27–32.)

A radio adaptation was broadcast by the BBC on its National programme on 4 December 1938, and is reviewed by G. W. Goldie in *Listener*, XX (15 December 1938), 1326; and an excerpt was televised by the BBC on 26 September 1938.

A mimeographed edition of the play was issued by the Universitetets Studentkontor in Oslo in 1942 during the German occupation. The title page reads approximately as the Faber edition with the addition of the following: 'UNIVERSITETETS STUDENTKONTOR | S.S.S.S.—TRYKK | Skrivemaskinstua—Oslo

---

[12] However Isherwood and Doone must have been working from some of Auden's drafts, for although most of the revisions are purely for increased dramatic effect, the American and second editions introduce "Michael, you shall be renowned," which is by Auden. See also "An interview with Christopher Isherwood," *Shenandoah*, XVI (Spring 1965), 39–41.

1942'. The edition collates: 11¼ x 7⅜ in. fols. [i–iv], 1–51 [55 single sheets]. Folio [ii] is a half title, and fols. [iii–iv] bear a review of the English edition of the play by L. Eckhoff, apparently reprinted from *Dagbladet* (Oslo), 28 November 1939.
Reviews:
G. Armitage. *English review*, LXIII (November 1936), 526–27.
J. Beevers. *New statesman & nation*, XII (10 October 1936), 531.
C. Day Lewis. *Poetry*, XLIX (January 1937), 225–28.
C. Dyment. *Time and tide*, XVII (17 October 1936), 1452.
G. Ewart. *University forward*, III (November 1936), 16.
E. M. Forster. *Listener*, XVI (supplement 31, 14 October 1936), vii.
F. R. Leavis. *Scrutiny*, V (December 1936), 323–27.
C. Powell. *Manchester guardian*, 6 November 1936, p. 6.
D. Powell. *London mercury*, XXXIV (October 1936), 561.
H. G. Porteus. *Twentieth century verse*, 1 (January 1937), [12–16].
J. A. Smith. *Criterion*, XVI (January 1937), 329–33.
S. Spender. *Left review*, II (November 1936), 779–82; abridged in *Living age*, CCCLI (January 1937), 450–52.
G.M.T. *Colosseum*, III (December 1936), 312–14.
Reviews of the performances:
A. V. Cookman. *London mercury*, XXXV (April 1937), 619.
A. Dukes. *Theatre arts monthly*, XXI (May 1937), 353, 355–56.
E. B. H. *Cambridge review*, LVIII (30 April 1937), 365.
G. J. Nathan. *Scribner's magazine*, CII (September 1937), 66, 68.
B. Nixon. *Left review*, III (May 1937), 254.
H. G. Porteus. *New English weekly*, X (11 March 1937), 432–33.
J. Symons. *Twentieth century verse*, 3 (April–May 1937), [19–20].
D. Verschoyle. *Spectator*, CLVIII (5 March 1937), 403.
D. W. *Punch*, CXCII (10 March 1937), 272.
Reviews of the revival:
G. W. Stonier. *New statesman & nation*, XVIII (1 July 1939), 13.
P. T[ravers]. *New English weekly*, XV (20 July 1939), 223–24.

b) First American edition   1937

THE ASCENT OF | [in red] F 6 | A TRAGEDY IN TWO ACTS | BY | W. H. AUDEN | & | CHRISTOPHER ISHERWOOD | [device in red: a house] | RANDOM HOUSE • NEW YORK

Collation: 8½ x 5½ in. [1–8]⁸, pp. [i–ii, 1–10] 11–123 [124–126].
[i–ii]: blank. [1]: 'THE ASCENT OF F 6'. [2]: blank. [3]: title page. [4]: 'COPYRIGHT, 1937, BY RANDOM HOUSE, INC. | PRINTED IN THE UNITED STATES OF AMERICA'. [5]: 'TO JOHN BICKNELL AUDEN | [four lines of verse]'. [6]: blank. [7]: characters. [8]: blank. [9]–123: text; 10 and 56 blank. [124–126]: blank.
Binding: Bound in pale yellow (89) cloth lettered down the spine in gold on a red panel within two gold rules: 'THE ASCENT OF F 6'. Across the foot of the spine in gold: 'R [device] H'. On the front cover a red, double gold-ruled, oval panel with a representation of a mountain and, in gold: 'THE ASCENT | OF F 6'. All edges trimmed. Grey dust jacket printed in red, black, pale blue, and bluish grey.
Paper: Cream unwatermarked wove paper.
Contents: The ascent of F 6. The ending and the text of Act II, scene i, are substantially revised.
The following piece of verse appears separately:

Michael, you shall be renowned . . . p. 54. Reprinted in SP.
Notes: Published 8 March 1937 in an edition of 1,500 copies at $1.50, and out of print in 1945.

Auden wrote to Bennett Cerf from Birmingham on 6 October 1936: "Isherwood and I are now altering it quite considerably. Faber published it early against our will and I shall be very glad if the American edition were to be the definitive one."
Reviews:

B. Belitt, *Nation*, CXLIV (17 April 1937), 439–40.

W. R. Benét. *Saturday review of literature*, XVI (8 May 1937), 20.

L. Bogan. *New Yorker*, XII (13 February 1937), 64–65 [New York edition, pp. 76–77].

M. M. Colum. *Forum*, XCVII (June 1937), 355.

H. Gregory. *New masses*, XXIII (20 April 1937), 25–27.

P. M. Jack. *New York times*, 30 May 1937, section 6, p. 3.

R. Lechlitner. *New York herald tribune*, 8 August 1937, section 10, p. 2.

K. Quinn. *Virginia quarterly review*, XIII (Autumn 1937), 616–20.

S. Rodman. *Common sense*, VI (June 1937), 27–28.

E. Wilson. *New republic*, XC (24 February 1937), 77–78.

c) Second English edition   1937

[The transcription of the title page is identical with that of the first edition.]

Collation: 8¾ x 5½ in. [A]–H⁸, pp. [1–8] 9–123 [124–128].
[1–2]: blank. [3]: 'THE ASCENT OF F 6'. [4]: '*by the same authors* | The Dog Beneath the Skin'. [5]: title page. [6]: '*First published in September Mcmxxxvi* | *By Faber and Faber Limited* | 24 *Russell Square London W.C.*1 | *Second Edition March Mcmxxxvii* | *Printed in Great Britain by* | *R. MacLehose and Company Limited* | *The University Press Glasgow* | [one line]'. [7]: 'To | JOHN BICKNELL AUDEN | [four lines]'. [8]: blank. 9: characters. [10]: blank. [11]–123: text; 12, 56, 58, 104, and 108 blank. [124–128]: blank.
Binding: As the first edition. Light grey dust jacket printed in red and blue.
Paper: Cream unwatermarked wove paper.
Contents: The ascent of F 6. This gives the substantive text of the play. Most of the revisions are to be found in Act II, scenes i and iii, and the last scene of the play.
Notes: Published in March 1937 in an impression of 1,500 copies at 6/– and reprinted in September 1937 (2,000 copies), January 1939 (2,000 copies), May 1944 (888 copies), July 1945 (2,000 copies), November 1946 (2,000 copies), November 1949 (2,150 copies), January 1953 (2,000 copies), and May 1957 (2,000 copies).

Later impressions add to the list of characters on p. [9] the names of the actors who played the parts in the first production and the details of the direction and date.

d) First paperback edition   1958

THE ASCENT OF F.6 | and | ON THE FRONTIER | *by* W. H. Auden *and* | Christopher Isherwood | Faber & Faber Limited | 24 Russell Square | London

Collation: 7¼ x 4¾ in. Ninety-six single leaves, [A]–M⁸, pp. [1–12] 13–191 [192]. $1 signed 'T.P.'.

[1]: half title. [2]: 'by the same authors | The Dog Beneath the Skin'. [3]: title page. [4]: 'First published in this edition mcmlviii | By Faber and Faber Limited | 24 Russell Square London W.C. 1 | Printed in Great Britain by | Wyman and Sons Ltd., | London, Reading and Fakenham | [one line]'. [5]–97: The ascent of F 6. [98]: blank. [99]–191: On the frontier. [192]: blank.

Binding: A perfect binding glued in a white card cover glassine-covered and printed in strong red (12) and lettered in black down the spine: '*Ascent of F 6* [vertical swelled rule] *On the Frontier* [in white on a black panel] FABER'. Across the front cover: 'by W. H. Auden and | Christopher Isherwood | [swelled rule] | [title in rising diagonal] *The Ascent | of F 6* | [half swelled rule] *AND* [half swelled rule] | *On the | Frontier* | [publishers' name in white on a black panel] FABER 5s. *net*', and down the leading edge of the front cover in white on a black panel: 'FABER paper covered EDITIONS'. The outside rear cover only bears a list of other titles in the series. All edges trimmed.

Paper: White unwatermarked wove paper.

Contents:

The ascent of F 6 [second English edition text].

On the frontier.

Notes: Published 15 August 1958 in an impression of 14,000 copies at 5/–, and reprinted in January 1962 (7,500 copies) and September 1965 (7,000 copies).

e) First American paperback edition 1958

For details of this edition see A 11c.

f) First American paperback edition: second impression 1964

For details of this impression see A 11d.

A 13 LOOK STRANGER! 1936

a) First edition

POEMS BY W. H. AUDEN | LOOK, | STRANGER! | FABER & FABER LIMITED | LONDON

Collation: 8¾ x 5½ in. [A]–C⁸D¹⁰, pp. [1–8] 9–68. D2 is signed.

[1–2]: blank. [3]: half title. [4]: 'by the same author | [star] | THE DANCE OF DEATH | THE ORATORS | POEMS'. [5]: title page. [6]: 'First published in October Mcmxxxvi | by Faber and Faber Limited | 24 Russell Square London W.C.1 | Printed in Great Britain by | R. MacLehose and Company Limited | The University Press Glasgow | [one line]'. [7]: 'To | ERIKA MANN | [four lines of verse]'. [8]: blank. 9–10: contents. 11–68: text.

Binding: Bound in light grey (264) cloth and lettered down the spine in gold: '*Look, stranger! by W. H. Auden Faber & Faber*'. Top edge only trimmed. Yellow dust jacket printed in pink and grey.

Paper: Cream unwatermarked wove paper.

Contents:

To Erika Mann: Since the external disorder, and extravagant lies . . .

    I Prologue: O love, the interest itself in thoughtless Heaven . . . First printed in *New statesman & nation*, 16 July 1932, and reprinted in *New country* (1933). It is here revised and reprinted in SP, SoP, CP ("Perhaps"), and CSP.

II   Out on the lawn I lie in bed... First printed in *Listener*, 7 March 1934 ("Summer night"); set to music by Benjamin Britten in "Spring Symphony", published by Boosey and Hawkes (1949); and reprinted in SP, SoP, and, in revised form, CP ("A summer night 1933"), CSP, and CSP2 ("A summer night"). Partly reprinted in *Badger*, Autumn 1965. Dedicated to Geoffrey Hoyland.

III   Our hunting fathers told the story... First printed in *Listener*, 30 May 1934 ("Poem"); set to music by Benjamin Britten, and published by Boosey and Hawkes (1936); reprinted as a pamphlet by Frederic Prokosch (1935) and in SP, CP ("In Father's footsteps"), CSP ("Our hunting fathers"), and CSP2.

IV   Song: Let the florid music praise... Set to music by Benjamin Britten, published by Boosey and Hawkes (1938), and reprinted in SoP, CP, CSP, and revised in CSP2.

V   Look, stranger, at this island now... First printed in *Listener*, 18 December 1935 ("Seaside"), and reprinted in *Living age*, June 1936; set to music by Benjamin Britten ("Seascape") and published by Boosey and Hawkes (1938); reprinted in SP, SoP, CP, CSP, PA ("Seascape"), and CSP2 ("On this island").

VI   O what is that sound which so thrills the ear... First printed in *New verse*, December 1934 ("Ballad"), and reprinted, in slightly revised form, in CP, CSP, PA ("The quarry"), CSP2 ("O what is that sound"), and SelP.

VII   Hearing of harvests rotting in the valleys... First printed in *Criterion*, July 1933; reprinted as a pamphlet by Frederic Prokosch (1933) and in SP, CP ("Paysage moralisé"), CSP, and CSP2.

VIII Now the leaves are falling fast... First printed in *New statesman & nation*, 14 March 1936; set to music by Benjamin Britten and published by Boosey and Hawkes (1938); reprinted in SP, SoP, CP, CSP, PA ("Autumn song"), CSP2, and revised in SelP.

IX   The earth turns over, our side feels the cold... First printed in *New verse*, February 1934; reprinted in SP, SoP, and, in a revised version, CP ("Through the looking glass"), CSP, and again revised in CSP2.

X   Now from my window-sill I watch the night... First printed as part II of "A happy new year" in *New country* (1933). This is the revised text, further revised and reprinted in CP ("Not all the candidates pass"), CSP, revised again in PA ("The watchers"), and CSP2. Originally dedicated to Gerald Heard.

XI   Just as his dream foretold, he met them all... First printed in *Bryanston saga*, Summer 1934, and reprinted in CP ("Nobody understands me"), CSP, and CSP2 ("A misunderstanding").

XII   As it is, plenty... Set to music by Benjamin Britten and published by Boosey and Hawkes (1938); reprinted and revised in CP ("His Excellency"), CSP, and CSP2.

XIII A shilling life will give you all the facts... First printed in *Rep*, April 1934, and reprinted in SP, SoP, CP ("Who's who"), CSP, and CSP2.

XIV   Brothers, who when the sirens roar... First printed in *Twentieth century*, September 1932, and *New country* (1933) and revised here.

XV   The chimneys are smoking, the crocus is out in the border... First printed in *New country* (1933); reprinted, in a revised form, in CSP ("Two worlds").

XVI   May with its light behaving... First printed in *Listener*, 15 May 1935, and reprinted in SP, SoP, CP, CSP, and CSP2 ("May").

XVII   Here on the cropped grass of the narrow ridge I stand... First printed in *New Oxford outlook*, November 1933 ("The Malverns"); reprinted in *Dynamo*, Summer 1934, SP, SoP, and, in revised form, CSP.

XVIII   The sun shines down on ships at sea... An earlier version of this poem is in *New Oxford outlook*, May 1933 ("To a young man on his 21st birthday").

XIX   To lie flat on the back with the knees flexed... Reprinted in CP ("What's the matter?") and CSP.

XX   Fleeing the short-haired mad executives... First printed in *New Oxford outlook*, November 1933, and reprinted in CP ("The climbers"), CSP, and revised in CSP2 ("Two climbs").

XXI   Easily, my dear, you move, easily your head... First printed in *Listener*, 20 February 1935 ("A bride in the '30s"). Here revised and reprinted in SP, SoP, and, in a revised form, CP, CSP, and CSP2.

XXII   Two songs: Night covers up the rigid land...
                Underneath the abject willow...
The second poem was set to music by Benjamin Britten and published by Boosey and Hawkes (1937); reprinted in SP and, in a revised form, CP, CSP, PA, and CSP2. Both poems are dedicated to Britten.

XXIII   To settle in this village of the heart... First printed in *New verse*, June 1934, and reprinted, in a revised form, in CP ("It's so dull here") and CSP.

XXIV   O for doors to be open and an invite with gilded edges... First printed in *Spectator*, 31 May 1935 ("In the square"); reprinted in SP, SoP, and, in a revised form, CP, CSP, CSP2, and SelP ("Song of the beggars").

XXV   Casino: Only the hands are living; to the wheel attracted... Reprinted in CP and CSP, and revised in CSP2.

XXVI   That night when joy began... First printed in *Twentieth century*, November 1933, and reprinted in CP, CSP, and CSP2.

XXVII   Fish in the unruffled lakes... First printed in *Listener*, 15 April 1936; set to music by Benjamin Britten and published by Boosey and Hawkes (1937); reprinted in SoP, CP, CSP, and CSP2.

XXVIII   Dear, though the night is gone... First printed in *New verse*, April–May 1936, and reprinted in CP, CSP, PA ("A dream"), and CSP2.

XXIX   Love had him fast, but though he fought for breath... First printed in *New verse*, October 1933, and, in a revised form, in CP ("Meiosis"), CSP, and CSP2.

XXX   August for the people and their favourite islands... First printed in *New verse*, October–November 1935 ("To a writer on his birthday"), reprinted in SP, SoP, and, in a revised form, CSP.

XXXI   Epilogue: Certainly our city—with the byres of poverty down to... First printed in *Time and tide*, 23 May 1936, and reprinted in SP and, in a revised form, CP ("As we like it"), and CSP ("Our city").

Notes: Published 22 October 1936 in an impression of 2,350 copies at 5/– and reprinted December 1936 (2,000 copies), November 1939 (1,500 copies), May 1945 (646 copies), and April 1946 (1,000 copies). Out of print in March 1956. Uncorrected proof copies are bound in purple wrappers, titled *Poems 1936*, and include "The fruit in which your parents hid you, boy..." in place of poem IV.

    Auden wrote to Bennett Cerf of Random House from Birmingham [October 1936?]: "As regards the latter [*Look, stranger!*], Faber invented a bloody title while I was away without telling me. It sounds like the work of a vegetarian lady novelist. Will you please call the American edition *On this island*." In the same letter Auden noted the following misprints in the Faber edition: IX, stanza 5, line 6, for 'dream' read 'room'; XVIII, stanza 6, line 3, for 'could only' read 'can only'. Auden was awarded the King's Gold Medal for poetry on the publication of this book.

Reviews:
C. Dyment. *Time and tide*, XVII (5 December 1936), 1726.
G. Ewart. *University forward*, III (November 1936), 16.
F. R. Leavis. *Scrutiny*, V (December 1936), 323–27.
C. Day Lewis. *Life and letters today*, XV (Winter 1936–37), 38–39.
C. Day Lewis. *Poetry*, XLIX (January 1937), 225–28.
[L. MacNeice.] *Listener*, XVI (30 December 1936), 1257.
E. Muir. *Spectator*, CLVII (4 December 1936), 1008.
H. G. Porteus. *Twentieth century verse*, 1 (January 1937), [12–16].
D. Powell. *London mercury*, XXXV (November 1936), 76–77.
J. A. Smith. *Criterion*, XVI (January 1937), 329–33.
G. W. Stonier. *New statesman & nation*, XII (14 November 1936), 776, 778.
Times literary supplement, 28 November 1936, p. 991.
D. A. T[raversi]. *Arena*, 1 (April 1937), 64–65.
L. Whistler. *Poetry review*, XXVIII (January–February 1937), 7–13.

b) First American edition   1937

W · H · AUDEN | [in red] *On this Island* | [device: a house] | RANDOM HOUSE · NEW YORK

Collation: 8¾ x 5¾ in. [1]⁴[2–5]⁸, p. [1–8] 9–68 [69–72].
[1–2]: blank. [3]: half-title. [4]: 'BY W. H. AUDEN | *Poems* | · | IN COLLABORATION WITH | CHRISTOPHER ISHERWOOD | *The Dog Beneath the Skin* | *The Ascent of F-6*'. [5]: title page [6]: 'FIRST EDITION | COPYRIGHT · 1937 · BY RANDOM HOUSE · INC. | PRINTED IN THE UNITED STATES OF AMERICA | BY THE SPIRAL PRESS · NEW YORK'. [7]: '[swelled rule] | TO ERIKA MANN | [four lines of verse] | [swelled rule]'. [8]: blank. 9–10: contents. 11–68: text. [69–72]: blank.

Binding: Bound in moderate brown (58) cloth and lettered up the spine in gold: 'ON THIS ISLAND BY W · H · AUDEN', and across the front cover: '*On this Island*'. All edges trimmed. Cream dust jacket printed in black and brown. Binding orders for the first impression were made in January 1937 (1,000 copies) and February 1937 (1,000 copies). Binding orders for the second impression were made in January 1938 (500 copies), March 1939 (100 copies), and February 1940 (100 copies). Some copies of the second impression are found with a rounded spine, unlike the flat spine of first impression bindings. Other copies have a flat spine lettered in black on grey cloth; these may be the remaining 300 copies of the second impression.

Paper: White wove paper watermarked 'AMERICAN EGGSHELL TEXT'.

Contents: As the English edition.

Notes: Published 2 February 1937 in an impression of 2,000 copies at $1.50, and reprinted in February 1938 (1,000 copies). Out of print in 1942. The copy used by Auden in revising those poems included in CP is in Swarthmore College Library.

Reviews:
W. R. Benét. *Saturday review of literature*, XV (13 February 1937), 16.
L. Bogan. *New Yorker*, XII (13 February 1937), 63–64 [New York edition, pp. 75–76].
R. C. B. Brown. *Voices*, 90 (Summer 1937), 42–45.

H. Gregory. *New masses*, XXIII (20 April 1937), 25–27.
R. Humphries. *New masses*, XXII (23 February 1937), 22–23.
F. O. Matthiessen. *Southern review*, II (Spring 1937), 827–30.
C. Poore. *New York times*, 7 February 1937, section 7, p. 3.
F. Prokosch. *New York herald tribune*, 7 February 1937, section 10, p. 4.
S. Rodman. *Common sense*, VI (April 1937), 28.
E. L. Walton. *Nation*, CXLIV (20 February 1937), 214.
E. Wilson. *New republic*, XC (24 February 1937), 77–78.

A 14   **SPAIN**   **1937**

a) First edition

W. H. AUDEN | SPAIN | FABER AND | FABER

Collation: 8¾ x 5½ in. One unsigned gathering of eight leaves, pp. [1–6] 7–12 [13–16].
[1]: half title. [2]: '*by the same author* | [star] | Look, Stranger! | Poems | The Orators | The Dance of Death | with *Christopher Isherwood* | [star] | The Dog Beneath the Skin | The Ascent of F 6'. [3]: title page. [4]: '*First published in May Mcmxxxvii* | *by Faber and Faber Limited* | *24 Russell Square London W.C.1* | *Printed in Great Britain by* | *R. MacLehose and Company Limited* | *The University Press Glasgow* | *[one line]*'. [5]: 'SPAIN'. [6]: blank. 7–12: text. [13–16]: blank.
Binding: Stapled with a white card cover round which is folded a strong red (12) wrapper. The wrapper is lettered in black as the title page. Inside front wrapper 'All the author's royalties | from the sale of this poem | go to *Medical Aid for Spain* | 1s. | net'.
Paper: Cream unwatermarked wove paper.
Contents: Spain: Yesterday all the past. The language of size... Also printed by Nancy Cunard at the Hours Press (1937), in the *Saturday review of literature*, 22 May 1937, and, in a revised form, in AT ("Spain 1937"), CP, and CSP.
Notes: Published 20 May 1937 in an impression of 2,913 copies at 1/– and reprinted in July 1937 (1,972 copies). Out of print in August 1942.
   Faber and Faber have no record of when the manuscript of Auden's poem was received, but the printer commenced setting on 1 April 1937, and sent back proofs on 6 April, which were returned for press on 24 April.
Reviews:
A. Clarke. *Dublin magazine*, XIII (April–June 1938), 77–78.
C. Connolly. *New statesman & nation*, XIII (5 June 1937), 926, 928.
E. V. Heming. *Poetry review*, XXVIII (September–October 1937), 414.
[C. Day Lewis.] *Listener*, XVII (26 May 1937), 1050, 1053.
London mercury, XXXVI (June 1937), 220.
E. Muir. *Criterion*, XVII (October 1937), 150–51.
Times literary supplement, 22 May 1937, p. 392.

b) Hours Press edition   **1937**

DEUX POÈMES: | W. H. AUDEN | RAUL GONZALEZ | TUNON | LES POÈTES DU MONDE DÉFENDENT | LE PEUPLE ESPAG- NOL | 5 | [eight lines] | *NUMÉRO CINQ–COMPOSÉ A LA MAIN*

PAR | NANCY CUNARD ET PABLO NERUDA | TOUT LE PRO-DUIT DE LA VENTE IRA AU | PEUPLE DE L'ESPAGNE RÉPU-BLICAINE | Déjà paru: Pablo Neruda, Nancy Cunard | [four lines]

Collation: 10¾ x 7¾ in. Two quarto sheets folded once and stapled together.
   [1]: title page. [2–3]: poem 'Madrid' by González Tuñón. [4–8]: 'Spain', dated April 1937.
Binding: None.
Paper: White laid paper watermarked 'LAPINA PARIS BFK RIVES'.
Contents: Spain.
Notes: In an undated letter to Faber, Auden wrote: "Nancy Cunard wants to print a special edition in Paris of 100 copies on pure gold paper or something. May she? I don't mind, and I fancy that it doesn't touch you." Faber agreed to this. Copies were apparently sold at 1/- each. Miss Cunard was then living at La Chapelle-Réanville, Eure, and the composition and proofing was carried out there, although the actual printing was done at Paris (*Those were the hours,* by N. Cunard [Carbondale: Southern Illinois University Press, 1969], pp. 196–97). The reviewer, Mr. A. R. A. Hobson, of the first edition of this bibliography in the *Times literary supplement* gives some further details which he gathered from Miss Cunard: "there was no time to consult Auden about the partial illegibility of his manuscript or to send him proofs; the doubtful words were interpreted, rightly or wrongly, with much use of magnifying glasses by Miss Cunard aided by Samuel Beckett, and the pamphlet hastily printed and sold for the benefit of the Spanish Republic. (Auden was indulgent about the misprints and said that 'it didn't matter'.)" (*Times literary supplement,* 1 July 1965, p. 568.) The manuscript from which Miss Cunard set and Auden's covering letter are both undated, so it appears the date at the end of the text, "April 1937," was added to the copy by the printers. Two presentation copies signed by Miss Cunard are both dated "July 1937" in manuscript.
   Auden in an undated letter to Miss Cunard from the Downs School, Colwall (where the summer term would have ended in late July) wrote sending back his answer to the questionnaire, dated June 1937, which was subsequently printed in *Authors take sides on the Spanish war.* In the course of the letter he remarked "Thank you so much for the books with the copies of Spain which looked lovely and doesn't contain the stupid mistake which was in the Faber copy." It would therefore appear on balance more likely that the Faber edition precedes the Hours Press edition.

A 15   LETTERS FROM ICELAND   1937

a) **First edition**

W. H. Auden | Louis MacNeice | [ornamental swelled rule] | LET-TERS | FROM ICELAND | [ornamental swelled rule] | Faber and Faber | 24 Russell Square | London

Collation: 8½ x 5¼ in. [A]–R⁸, pp. [1–8] 9–268 [269–272].
   [1–2]: blank. [3]: half title. [4]: blank. [frontispiece]. [5]: title page. [6]: *'First published in July Mcmxxxvii | by Faber and Faber Limited | 24 Russell Square London W.C.1 | Printed in Great Britain by | R. MacLehose and Company Limited | The University Press Glasgow | [one line]'.* [7]: 'To | GEORGE AUGUSTUS AUDEN'. [8]: blank. 9: preface signed by both authors. [10]: blank. 11: contents. [12]: blank. 13–15: illustrations. [16]: blank. 17–261: text; illustrations

face pages 26, 32, 38, 42, 64, 80, 96, 112, 144, 148, 156, 160, 214, 218, and 224. 262–268: appendix. [coloured folding map]. [269–272]: blank.

Binding: Bound in brilliant yellowish green (130) cloth lettered down the spine: '[in red] LETTERS FROM ICELAND | [in bluish grey] *W. H. Auden and Louis MacNeice'.* Across the foot of the spine in bluish grey: 'FABER'. All edges trimmed, and top edge stained light grey. White dust jacket with a halftone photograph and printed in red and black.

Paper: White unwatermarked wove paper.

Contents:

Letter to Lord Byron
    I   Excuse, my lord, the liberty I take...
    II I'm writing this in pencil on my knee...
    III My last remarks were sent you from a boat...
    IV A ship again; this time the *Dettifoss*...
    V Autumn is here. The beech leaves strew the lawn... Revised and reprinted in *Longer contemporary poems* (1966), and then in LFI2 and CLP.

Journey to Iceland; a letter to Christopher Isherwood, Esq.: And the traveller hopes: 'Let me be far from any... First printed in *Listener,* 7 October 1936; reprinted in *Poetry,* January and November 1937, and SP, SoP, and, in a revised form, CP, CSP, and, further revised, *Iceland review,* Autumn 1964, and CSP2.

For tourists.

W. H. A. to E. M. A.—No. 1 [prose letter]. Contains the following piece of verse: Detective story: For who is ever quite without his landscape... Reprinted in CSP2.

W. H. A. to E. M. A.—No. 2 [prose letter]. Contains the following piece of verse: O who can ever praise enough... First printed in *Poetry,* January 1937, and reprinted in CP, CSP, and, in a revised form, CSP2 ("The price").

Letter to Kristian Andreirsson, Esq. [prose letter]

Letter to William Coldstream, Esq. [prose introduction and verse letter:] 'But landscape,' cries the Literary Supplement... This poem contains within itself the lyric: O who can ever gaze his fill... First printed in the *New statesman & nation,* 16 January 1937; reprinted in SP and, in revised form, CP, CSP, PA ("The dead echo"), and CSP2 ("Death's echo").

Auden and MacNeice: their last will and testament: We, Wystan Hugh Auden and Louis MacNeice...

Notes: Originally intended to be published 8 July 1937, but actually published 6 August 1937 (*New verse,* 26–27 [November 1937], 36; *CCE;* and the *English catalogue*) in an edition of 10,240 copies at 9/-. Out of print in May 1949. The volume was a Book Society choice.

Alan C. Collins, of the New York Office of Curtis Brown, sent Bennett Cerf two proof copies of the Faber edition on 7 July 1937 and writes: "The copy bound in green [wrappers] is *not* setting copy. This is important as it contains libel which has been omitted from the sewn set of sheets, which is setting copy. Faber published July seventh." In a later letter dated 23 July 1937 Collins wrote that the Faber publication date had been postponed to 6 August 1937, and in another letter to Bennett Cerf, dated 18 August 1937, he reported that the Faber edition had an advance sale of over 8,000 copies.

The book was an indefinite commission, and contracts were signed and some advance royalties paid for expenses.[13] Auden told Bloomfield that only a few poems were written on the actual trip, most of the book being composed on his return. In a letter to *Time and tide* (XVIII [21 August 1937], 1118), Auden states that 81

[13] *Letters from Iceland,* p. 108.

of the total 240 pages were written by MacNeice, and the dust jacket states that Auden took the photographs which illustrate the book. The journey was made, and some of the material written, before the composition of *Spain*, which precedes this item in actual date of publication.[14]

Reviews:
B. de Sélincourt. *Manchester guardian*, 6 August 1937, p. 5.
E. V. Heming. *Poetry review*, XXVIII (September–October 1937), 415.
[C. Isherwood.] *Listener*, XVIII (11 August 1937), 311.
E. Muir. *Criterion*, XVII (October 1937), 154.
G. Rees. *Spectator*, CLIX (3 September 1937), 391.
M. Roberts. *London mercury*, XXXVI (September 1937), 483–84.
E. Sackville-West. *New statesman & nation*, XIV (7 August 1937), 226.
S. S[igurðsson]. *Eimreiðin*, XLIV (October–December 1938), 445–49.
Times literary supplement, 7 August 1937, p. 572.
G. Walton. *Scrutiny*, VII (June 1938), 93–95.

b) First American edition 1937

Letters | FROM ICELAND | BY W. H. AUDEN | AND LOUIS MAC-NEICE | RANDOM HOUSE • NEW YORK | [line drawing in blue, of a ship passing a rocky coast]

Collation: 8¾ x 5¾ in. [1–17]⁸, pp. [1–16] 17–269 [270–272].
[1]: half title. [2]: blank. [3]: title page. [4]: '[double rule] | COPYRIGHT, 1937, BY W. H. AUDEN | MANUFACTURED IN THE U.S.A.'. [5]: '[double rule] | *To* GEORGE AUGUSTUS AUDEN'. [6]: blank. [7]: preface. [8]: blank. [9]: contents. [10]: blank. [11–13]: illustrations. [14]: blank. [15]–269: text. [270–272]: blank.

Binding: Bound in rough light greyish yellowish brown (79) cloth lettered in blue on a white paper panel struck on the spine: 'LETTERS | FROM | ICELAND | AUDEN & | MACNEICE | Random House | [ship passing coast]'. A similar label on the front cover bears the title and drawing as the title page in blue. All edges trimmed, and top edge stained light blue. Buff dust jacket printed in light brown and blue.
The first 2,000 copies were bound as described in November 1937; copies bound in a second binding of smooth bluish grey (191) cloth, the top edges of which are not stained, are the remaindered 970 sheets which were ordered to be bound in February 1939.

Paper: White wove paper watermarked: 'WARREN'S OLDE STYLE'.

Contents: As the English edition.

Notes: Published 23 November 1937 in an edition of 3,000 copies at $3, and out of print in 1939. Printed by H. Wolff, Mount Vernon, New York. In this edition the map is transferred to the end papers.

Reviews:
L. Bogan. *Nation*, CXLV (11 December 1937), 658.
B. Deutsch. *New York herald tribune*, 12 December 1937, section 10, p. 28.
P. M. Jack. *New York times*, 16 January 1938, section 6, p. 10.
S. Rodman. *Common sense*, VII (January 1938), 28–29.
T. C. Wilson. *New masses*, XXVI (11 January 1938), 22.
——. *Poetry*, LII (April 1938), 39–42.

[14] *Ibid*, p. 123.

c) **Second English edition**   1967

[The transcription of the title page is identical with that of the first edition.]

Collation: 7⅞ x 5⅛ in. One hundred and twenty-eight single leaves, [A]–H¹⁶, pp. [1–6] 7–253 [254–256].
[1]: half title. [2]: blank. [3]: title page. [4]: '*First published in mcmxxxvii | by Faber and Faber Limited | 24 Russell Square London W.C.1 | First published in this edition mcmlxvii | Printed in Great Britain by | John Dickens & Co Ltd | [ten lines]*'. [5]: 'To | GEORGE AUGUSTUS AUDEN'. [6]: blank. 7–9: foreword. [10]: blank. 11: preface. [12]: blank. 13: contents. [14]: blank. 15–253: text. [254–255]: map. [256]: blank.
Binding: A perfect binding glued in a shiny white card cover lettered down the spine: '[in black] *LETTERS FROM ICELAND* [in white on a red panel] FABER | [in blue] *W. H. AUDEN & LOUIS MACNEICE*'. Across the front cover in alternate black and blue lines: '*LETTERS | FROM | ICELAND* | [red band] | *W. H. | Auden & | Louis | MacNeice*'. Down the leading edge of the front cover in white on a blue panel: 'FABER paper covered EDITIONS'. The rear cover carries a similar panel, and the inside and outside rear cover bears a list of other titles in the series.
Paper: White unwatermarked wove paper.
Contents: As the first edition with some cuts and revisions, particularly in the "Letter to Lord Byron." The foreword on pp. 7–9 is newly added.
Notes: Published 7 December 1967 in an impression of 8,000 copies at 10/6d.

d) **Second American edition**   1969

LETTERS | FROM | ICELAND | [ornamental swelled rule] | by | W. H. Auden | and Louis MacNeice | [ornamental swelled rule] | RANDOM HOUSE • NEW YORK [device: a house]

Collation: 8¼ x 5½ in. [A]–H¹⁶, pp. [1–6] 7–253 [254–256].
[1]: half title. [2]: '*by W. H. Auden* | [thirty-one lines]'. [3]: title page. [4]: 'First Printing | Copyright 1937, © 1969 by W. H. Auden | [seven lines] | Manufactured in the United States of America | by the Book Press, Brattleboro, Vermont'. [5]: 'To | GEORGE AUGUSTUS AUDEN'. [6]: blank. 7–9: foreword. [10]: blank. 11: preface. [12]: blank. 13: contents. [14]: blank. 15–253: text. [254–255]: map. [256]: biographical notes.
Binding: Quarter bound in black cloth with light blue (181) boards lettered down the spine in silver: 'LETTERS FROM | ICELAND | [device and publisher's name across the spine] [device] | RANDOM | HOUSE | [down the spine] W. H. AUDEN AND | LOUIS MACNEICE'. Top edge only trimmed and stained blue. White dust jacket printed in pale yellow, blue, and black.
Paper: Cream unwatermarked wove paper.
Contents: As the second English edition.
Notes: Published 14 April 1969 in an edition of 3,000 copies at $7.50.
Reviews:
D. Donoghue. *New York review of books,* XII (19 June 1969), 22–23.
L. Lönnroth. *Scandinavica,* IX (May 1970), 49–50.

A 16 NIGHT MAIL [1938?]

NIGHT MAIL | [thirty-four lines of text. The verso carries twenty lines of text, is signed 'W. H. AUDEN' and carries a GPO monogram.]

Collation: 9½ x 6½ in. Single sheet printed on both sides.
Binding: None.
Paper: Cream laid unwatermarked paper.
Contents: Night mail: This is the night mail crossing the border ... First printed in G[eneral] P[ost] O[ffice] *Film Library: notes and synopses,* 1936, and the issues for 1937 and 1938, and reprinted here and in *TPO: the centenary of the Travelling Post Office* (London: General Post Office, 1938), and CSP2. See also L2.
Notes: Printed in blue throughout. The particular monogram used on the verso was only employed by the Public Relations Department. This broadside was probably printed in 1938 at the press of the Savings Department of the Post Office which was situated in Blyth Road. Printing requisitions made to this department were only kept for three years and no record of the number of copies printed or issue date seems to survive in the Post Office records.

It is probable that the broadside was printed to accompany showings of the film which were frequently given at many exhibitions, shows, and schools often by means of Post Office's travelling cinema vans. The film was first shown on a commercial bill at the Carlton Theatre on 3 March 1936; later it was shown on 26 November 1936 at the King George V hall to the Postmaster General of the United States, and also shown at the Post Office exhibition in Charing Cross underground station from 25 May to 13 June 1936. The film was subsequently shown at the Ideal Home exhibitions in Spring 1937 and Spring 1938 and at the Empire exhibition at Glasgow which opened on 3 May 1938. It is therefore likely that this broadside is dated between May 1936 and May 1938. (We are indebted for his generous help to Mr. E. C. Baker, formerly archivist of the Post Office.) The text is identical with that of the 1937 issue of *GPO Film Library: notes and synopses.*

A 17 SELECTED POEMS 1938

SELECTED POEMS | by | W. H. AUDEN | FABER AND FABER | 24 Russell Square | London

Collation: 7 x 4½ in. [A]–H⁸, pp. [1–4] 5–128.
[1]: '*THE FABER LIBRARY—No.* 39 | [swelled rule] | SELECTED POEMS'. [2]: by the same author, etc. [3]: title page. [4]: '*First published in May Mcmxxx-viii | by Faber and Faber Limited | 24 Russell Square, London | Printed in Great Britain by | Western Printing Services Ltd., Bristol | [one line]*'. 5–6: contents. [7]–128: text.
Binding: Bound in strong red (12) cloth lettered across the spine in gold: '[ornament: foliage] | SELECTED | POEMS | [diamond] | W. H. | AUDEN | FABER | AND FABER | [ornament: foliage]'. Top and leading edges trimmed. Yellow dust jacket printed in black and bluish green. The publisher's name at the foot of the spine of a second binding of the first impression, and in the second impression reads: 'FABER | & FABER'.
Paper: Cream unwatermarked wove paper.
Contents:
from *Poems* (1930):

Paid on both sides.
Doom is dark and deeper than any sea-dingle . . .   Reprinted from P2.
Since you are going to begin to-day . . .
Watch any day his nonchalant pauses, see . . .
What's in your mind, my dove, my coney . . .   Reprinted from P2.
To ask the hard question is simple . . .   Reprinted from P2.
from *The orators:*
Prologue: By landscape reminded once of his mother's figure . . .
Ode: What siren zooming is sounding our coming . . .
Ode: Though aware of our rank and alert to obey orders . . .
Epilogue: 'O where are you going?' said reader to rider . . .
from *The dog beneath the skin:*
Chorus: The Summer holds: upon its glittering lake . . .
Chorus: You with shooting sticks and cases for field glasses . . .
Chorus: Now through night's caressing grip . . .
Semi-chorus: Love, loath to enter . . .
from *The ascent of F 6:*
Michael, you shall be renowned . . .
Death like his is right and splendid . . .
from *Look, stranger!:*
Prologue: O love, the interest itself in thoughtless Heaven . . .
Out on the lawn I lie in bed . . .
Our hunting fathers told the story . . .
Look, stranger, at this island now . . .
Hearing of harvests rotting in the valleys . . .
Now the leaves are falling fast . . .
The earth turns over, our side feels the cold . . .
A shilling life will give you all the facts . . .
May with its light behaving . . .
Here on the cropped grass of the narrow ridge I stand . . .
Easily, my dear, you move, easily your head . . .
Underneath the abject willow . . .
O for doors to be open and an invite with gilded edges . . .
August for the people and their favourite islands . . .
Epilogue: Certainly our city—with the byres of poverty down to . . .
from *Letters from Iceland:*
Journey to Iceland: And the traveller hopes: 'Let me be far from any . . .
'O who can ever gaze his fill . . .
Notes: Published 12 May 1938 in an impression of 4,080 copies at 3/– and reprinted in
October 1939 (2,000 copies). Out of print in January 1944.
   The dust jacket states, *pace* Auden as reported by Spears, that the selection was
made by Auden himself.
Reviews:
F. Prokosch. *Spectator*, CLX (3 June 1938), 1018.
J. Wahl. *Études anglaises*, III (January–March 1939), 64–65.

A 18   ON THE FRONTIER   1938

a) First edition

by W. H. Auden *and* | Christopher Isherwood | a melodrama in three acts |
ON THE FRONTIER | Faber & Faber Limited | 24 Russell Square | Lon-
don

Collation: 8¾ x 5½ in. [A]–H⁸, pp. [1–8] 9–123 [124–128]. $1 signed 'O.F.', except A. [1–2]: blank. [3]: 'ON THE FRONTIER'. [4]: *'by the same authors* | The Dog Beneath the Skin | The Ascent of F 6'. [5]: title page. [6]: '*First published in October Mcmxxxviii* | *By Faber and Faber Limited* | 24 *Russell Square London, W.C.1* | *Printed in Great Britain by* | *R. MacLehose and Company Limited* | *The University Press Glasgow* | [six lines] | *On the Frontier* is to be produced on | November 14th 1938 by Rupert Doone | for the GROUP THEATRE, with music by Benjamin Britten, scenery | and costumes by Robert Medley, at the | ARTS THEATRE, CAMBRIDGE'. [7]: 'To | BENJAMIN BRITTEN | [four lines of verse]'. [8]: blank. 9: dramatis personae. [10]: blank. 11–12: notes on the characters. 13: scenes. [14]: blank. [15]–123: text; 16, 54, 56, 76, 86, and 88 blank. [124–128]: blank.

Binding: Bound in vivid red (11) cloth lettered down the spine in gold: '*On the Frontier—W. H. Auden and Christopher Isherwood*'. Top edge trimmed. Cream dust jacket printed in red and black.

Paper: Cream unwatermarked wove paper.

Contents: On the frontier.

Notes: Published 27 October 1938 in an impression of 3,000 copies at 6/- and re-printed in January 1939 (2,000 copies). Out of print in November 1956.

This was the last of the three plays of the partnership, and Doone had little to do either with the writing or the revision. Auden says most of the play was written at Dover; Isherwood agrees, but adds that they also worked on the play on the voyage to China. Auden wrote to Bennett Cerf from Birmingham on 11 September 1937: "Isherwood and I have just finished a new play *On the Frontier.*"

The details of the first performance are given above, but the production subsequently moved to the Globe Theatre, London, on 12 February 1939. The Cambridge production was partly backed by J. M. Keynes. For use in the production Decca recorded the Ostnia and Westland songs as performed by the London Labour Choral Union, but this recording was apparently never released.

Reviews:

H. Adler. *London mercury*, XXXIX (January 1939), 368.

K. A[llott]. *New verse*, n.s. 1 (January 1939), 24–25.

T. R. Barnes. *Scrutiny*, VII (December 1938), 361–63.

L. C. Bonnerot. *Études anglaises*, IV (January–March 1940), 77–78.

A. H. N. Green-Armytage. *Colosseum*, V (January 1939), 66–68.

A. D. Hawkins. *Purpose*, XI (January–March 1939), 55–57.

[C. Day Lewis.] *Listener*, XX (24 November 1938), 1145.

J. G. MacLeod. *Townsman*, II (January 1939), 22–24.

J. A. Smith. *Criterion*, XVIII (January 1939), 322–23.

N. R. Smith. *Time and tide*, XVIII (19 November 1938), 1619–20.

J. Symons. *Twentieth century verse*, 15–16 (February 1939), 164.

Times literary supplement, 29 October 1938, p. 689.

Reviews of the performance:

Cambridge review, LX (25 November 1938), 134.

A. Dukes. *Theatre arts monthly*, XXIII (January 1939), 18–24.

L. MacNeice. *Spectator*, CLXI (18 November 1938), 858.

T. Paine. *New Statesman & nation*, XVI (19 November 1938), 826–27.

P. T[ravers]. *New English weekly*, XIV (23 February 1939), 302–3.

b) First American edition 1939

[large red fancy capital] On the Frontier | A MELODRAMA IN THREE ACTS | BY W. H. AUDEN *and* | CHRISTOPHER ISHERWOOD |

[short thick-thin double rule] | R [device: a house] H | RANDOM
HOUSE · NEW YORK | [short thick-thin double rule]

Collation: 9 x 5¾ in. [1–8]⁸, pp. [i–ii, 1–14] 15–120 [121–126].
  [i–ii]: blank. [1]: 'ON THE FRONTIER'. [2]: *'by the same authors* | The Dog
  Beneath the Skin | The Ascent of F 6'. [3]: title page. [4]: 'Copyright, 1938, by |
  Wystan Hugh Auden and | Christopher Isherwood | FIRST EDITION | [four
  lines] | Manufactured in the | United States of America'. [5]: 'To | BENJAMIN
  BRITTEN | [four lines of verse]'. [6]: blank. [7]: characters. [8]: blank. [9–10]:
  notes on the characters. [11]: scenes. [12]: blank. [13]–[121]: text. [122–126]:
  blank.
Binding: Bound in yellowish grey (93) cloth lettered down the spine in red: 'ON
  THE FRONTIER Auden & Isherwood RANDOM HOUSE'. On the front cover
  in red: '[black band down the left side] [large fancy capital] ON THE | FRON-
  TIER | R [device] H'. All edges trimmed. Light grey dust jacket printed in black
  and red.
    A binding order for 600 copies was made on 15 February 1939, and for another
  600 copies on 27 February 1939.
Contents: On the frontier. The stage directions differ slightly from those of the
  English edition, but the text is virtually identical.
Notes: Published 7 March 1939 in an edition of 1,275 copies at $1.75, and out of print
  in 1945.
Reviews:
  B. Deutsch. *New York herald tribune,* 26 March 1939, section 9, p. 19.
  P. M. Jack. *New York times,* 16 April 1939, section 6, p. 16.
  S. Rodman. *Common sense,* VIII (May 1939), 25–26.
  N. Rosten. *One act play magazine,* III (January 1940), 85–87.
  J. G. S[outhworth]. *Saturday review of literature,* XIX (18 March 1939), 20, 22.

c) First paperback edition   1958

For details of this edition see **A 12d.**

A 19   EDUCATION TODAY AND TOMORROW   1939

EDUCATION | TODAY–AND TOMORROW | W. H. AUDEN and
T. C. WORSLEY | [device: wolf's head] | THE HOGARTH PRESS |
52 TAVISTOCK SQUARE, | LONDON, W.C.1 | 1939

Collation: 7¼ x 5 in. [A]–B⁸C¹⁰, pp. [1–4] 5–51 [52]. C2 is signed 'C*'.
  [1]: half title. [2]: list of the series. [3]: title page. [4]: *'First pubished* 1939 | [two
  lines]'. 5–51: text. [52]: blank.
Binding: Glued in a strong reddish orange (35) wrapper lettered across the front
  cover in black: 'DAY TO DAY PAMPHLETS | No. 40 | EDUCATION | TO-
  DAY–AND TOMORROW | W. H. AUDEN and T. C. WORSLEY | [device] |
  THE HOGARTH PRESS | *One Shilling and Sixpence net',* and up the spine:
  'EDUCATION TODAY–AND TOMORROW W. H. AUDEN and T. C.
  WORSLEY'. All edges trimmed.
Paper: White unwatermarked wove paper.
Contents: Education today and tomorrow.
Notes: Published 2 March 1939 in an edition of 1,520 copies at 1/6d.
    Auden cannot remember the pamphlet or how it came to be written, but

Worsley, in a letter to Bloomfield, wrote: "The pamphlet was originally for the editions of *Fact*, a left-wing monthly which came out in the Thirties and devoted each number to one subject.... Wystan was asked to produce a number on education, and as was his practice on this sort of thing [?], took a collaborator—me. The result was—not unsurprisingly—far too little factual for FACT! And they turned it down flat. Then John Lehmann who was with the Hogarth... snapped it up for that series of theirs."

Reviews:
New verse, n.s. 2 (May 1939), 54–55.
Times literary supplement, 8 April 1939, p. 200.

A 20   JOURNEY TO A WAR   1939

a) First edition

by | W. H. AUDEN | and | CHRISTOPHER ISHERWOOD | [rule] | [title hollow] JOURNEY | TO A WAR | [rule] | FABER & FABER LIMITED | 24 Russell Square | London

Collation: 8¾ x 5¼ in. [A]–Q, *–**, [R]–T⁸, pp. [1–12] 13–253 [254–256] [32 un-numbered pages of plates] [257–258] 259–301 [302] [folding map] [303–304].
  [1–4]: blank. [5]: half title. [6–7]: blank. [8]: frontispiece by Yet Chian-yu in black and red titled 'Terror bequeathed'. [9]: title page. [10]: *First published in March Mcmxxxix | by Faber and Faber Limited | 24 Russell Square, London, W.C.1 | Printed in Great Britain by | Western Printing Services Ltd., Bristol | [one line]'.* [11]: 'To E. M. FORSTER | [sonnet]'. [12]: blank. 13–14: foreword. [15]–23: London to Hongkong, verse by Auden. [24]: blank. [25]–253: travel diary, prose by Isherwood. [254]: blank. [255]: picture commentary. [256]: blank. [32 pages of plates]. [257]–301: In time of war: a sonnet sequence with a verse commentary, by Auden. [302]: blank. [folding map of China]. [303–304]: blank.
Binding: Bound in black varnished cloth, giving a grey appearance, and lettered across the spine in yellow: '[red rule] | [title on a red panel] *Journey | to a | WAR* | [red rule] | *W. H. | Auden & | Christopher | Isherwood | Faber | and Faber'*.
  All edges trimmed and top edge stained yellow. Cream dust jacket printed in red and black, with a blue wrap around label printed in red: 'Recommended by the Book Society'.
Contents:
  To E. M. Forster: Here, though the bombs are real and dangerous... Reprinted in CP, CSP, and, revised, as the last of the "Sonnets from China" in CSP2.
  London to Hongkong [one poem and five sonnets]
    The voyage: Where does the journey look which the watcher upon the quay ... Reprinted in CP and CSP, and revised in CSP2 ("Whither").
    The sphinx: Did it once issue from the carver's hand healthy... Reprinted in SoP, CP, CSP, PA, and CSP2.
    The ship: The streets are brightly lit; our city is kept clean... First printed in *Listener*, 18 August 1938, and reprinted in *New republic*, 7 December 1939, CP, CSP, and revised in CSP2.
    The traveller: Holding the distance up before his face... First printed in *New statesman & nation*, 27 August 1938, and reprinted in CP and CSP.
    Macao: A weed from Catholic Europe, it took root... Reprinted in CP, CSP, PA, and CSP2.
    Hongkong: The leading characters are wise and witty... Reprinted with minor changes in CP, CSP, and CSP2.

In time of war: a sonnet sequence with a verse commentary
>   I   So from the years the gifts were showered; each...
>   II   They wondered why the fruit had been forbidden...
>   III   Only a smell had feelings to make known...
>   IV   He stayed: and was imprisoned in possession...
>   V   His generous bearing was a new invention...
>   VI   He watched the stars and noted birds in flight...
>   VII   He was their servant—some say he was blind... Reprinted in PA ("The bard")
>   VIII He turned his field into a meeting-place...
>   IX   They died and entered the closed life like nuns...
>   X   As a young child the wisest could adore him...
>   XI   He looked in all His wisdom from the throne... Reprinted in *Common sense*, April 1939 ("Ganymede"), SoP, and PA.
>   XII   And the age ended, and the last deliverer died... The original version of the poem was printed in *New verse*, June–July 1936; reprinted in SoP and PA ("A new age").
>   XIII Certainly praise: let the song mount again and again... Part of this poem is contained in "Press conference," *New republic*, 7 December 1938.
>   XIV   Yes, we are going to suffer, now; the sky... Part of this poem is contained in "Air raid," *New republic*, 7 December 1938.
>   XV   Engines bear them through the sky: they're free...
>   XVI   Here war is simple like a monument...
>   XVII They are and suffer; that is all they do... Reprinted in PA ("Surgical ward").
>   XVIII Far from the heart of culture he was used... The original version of the poem was first printed in *New statesman & nation*, 2 July 1938, and reprinted in *Living age*, September 1938, *China weekly review*, 29 October 1938, and *New republic*, 7 December 1938, and 25 December 1944. A manuscript facsimile appeared in *Ta kung pao* (Hankow), 22 April 1938.
>   XIX   But in the evening the oppression lifted... Revised and reprinted in PA ("Embassy").
>   XX   They carry terror with them like a purse...
>   XXI   The life of man is never quite completed... First printed in *New writing*, Autumn 1938 ("Exiles"), and reprinted in *New republic*, 7 December 1938, and *Penguin new writing*, April 1941. This is a revised version.
>   XXII Simple like all dream wishes, they employ...
>   XXIII When all the apparatus of report...
>   XXIV No, not their names. It was the others who built...
>   XXV   Nothing is given: we must find our law... Revised and reprinted in CSP2 ("A major port").
>   XXVI Always far from the centre of our names...
>   XXVII Wandering lost upon the mountains of our choice... The original version of this poem appeared in *Listener*, 3 November 1938 ("Sonnet") and 14 January 1954. In the CSP2 revision the first line reads "Chilled by the Present, its gloom and its noise...."

Commentary: Season inherits legally from dying season... The last part, beginning "Night falls on China...," is reprinted in SoP.

All the sonnets and the Commentary are reprinted in CP and CSP, but the Commentary is revised and omits lines 187–89 and 270–73. CSP2 drops sonnets 9, 10, 14, 15, 20, 25, 26, and the Commentary, and severely revises and rearranges those remaining ("Sonnets from China"). This text is reprinted in SelP. The CSP2 text first appeared, with some variants, in Auden's *Opere poetiche*, vol. 1 (Milan: Lerici, 1966), pp. 76–117.

Notes: Published 16 March 1939 in an edition of 2,060 copies at 12/6d. Out of print in August 1943.

"Early in the summer of 1937, we were commissioned by Messrs. Faber and Faber of London and by Random House of New York to write a travel book about the East. The choice of itinerary was left to our own discretion. The outbreak of the Sino-Japanese war in August decided us to go to China. We left England in January 1938, returning at the end of July" (Foreword, p. 13).

Isherwood told Bloomfield that Auden wrote most of the sonnets during the actual voyages which the journey entailed. The travel diary was made from their separate diaries, which Isherwood wrote into final form, crediting any particular just line or appreciation which he took from Auden's record.[15] Recommended by the Book Society.

Auden took most of the photographs for the book.

The running title (recto) of the travel diary is: 'HONGKONG-MACAO'.

Reviews:

J. Bertram. *Listener*, XXI, supplement 44 (16 March 1939), vii.
L. C. Bonnerot. *Études anglaises*, IV (January–March 1940), 75–77.
M. Collis. *Time and tide*, XX (22 April 1939), 510.
G. E. G[rigson]. *New verse*, n.s. 2 (May 1939), 47–49.
W. Plomer. *London mercury*, XXXIX (April 1939), 642–44.
G. W. Stonier. *New statesman & nation*, XVII (18 March 1939), 428, 430.
Times literary supplement, 18 March 1939, p. 158.
R. Todd. *Twentieth century verse*, 17 (April–May 1939), 20–21.
E. Waugh. *Spectator*, CLXII (24 March 1939), 496, 498.

b) First American edition 1939

[within a border of a red rule] JOURNEY | TO A | WAR | By | W. H. AUDEN | & | CHRISTOPHER ISHERWOOD | [in red] R [device: a house] H | RANDOM HOUSE • NEW YORK

Collation: 8¾ x 5½ in. [1–16] [2 unsigned gatherings of plates] [17–19]⁸, pp. [1–12] 13–253 [254–256] [plates] [257–258] 259–301 [302–304].

[1–4]: blank. [5]: half title. [6–7]: blank. [8]: frontispiece. [9]: title page. [10]: 'COPYRIGHT, 1939, | [two lines]'. [11]: 'To E. M. FORSTER | [sonnet]'. [12]: blank. 13–14: foreword. [15]–301: text. [302–304]: blank. For a more detailed listing of the book see the English edition.

Binding: Bound in rough light yellow (86) cloth lettered across the spine in olive green: '[on a brown panel within a rule] JOURNEY | TO A | WAR | AUDEN & | ISHERWOOD | [outside the panel on the cloth] RANDOM | HOUSE'. On the front cover: 'R [device] H'. All edges trimmed, and top edge stained dark grey. White dust jacket printed in dark blue, green, and red.

A binding order for 2,000 copies as described above was placed in May 1939. No binding order can be found for the remaining 1,000 copies which were apparently remaindered in a light reddish brown (42) cloth without the device on the front cover and with the top edge unstained.

Paper: Cream unwatermarked wove paper.

Contents: As the English edition.

---

[15] *Shenandoah*, XVI (Spring 1965), 42.

Notes: Published 11 August 1939 [*CCE* 1 August 1939] in an edition of 3,000 copies at $3. Out of print in 1941. Printed by the Reehl Litho Co., New York.

In this edition the folding map is transferred to the endpapers, and the running title (recto) of the travel diary is: 'HONGKONG-SHANGHAI'.

Reviews:

T. A. Bisson. *Saturday review of literature*, XX (5 August 1939), 6.

M. Boie. *Atlantic*, CLXIV (November 1939), [unpaged].

R. L. Duffus. *New York times*, 6 August 1939, section 6, p. 1.

L. Kirstein. *Nation*, CXLIX (5 August 1939), 151–52.

L. Kronenberger. *New Yorker*, XV (12 August 1939), 53.

R. Lechlitner. *New York herald tribune*, 6 August 1939, section 9, p. 3.

N. Peffer. *New republic*, C (27 September 1939), 221–22.

V. S. Pritchett. *Christian science monitor*, 29 April 1939, p. 10.

R. H. Rovere. *New masses*, XXXII (15 August 1939), 25–26.

A 21   EPITHALAMION   1939

[ornament] | [title in shaded type] EPITHALAMION | COMMEMO-RATING THE MARRIAGE OF | [shaded] GIUSEPPE ANTONIO BORGESE | AND | [shaded] ELISABETH MANN | AT | PRINCE-TON, NEW JERSEY | NOVEMBER 23, 1939 | [ornament]

Collation: 10 x 14¼ in., folding once to 10 x 7⅛ in. Single sheet printed on both sides, pp. [1–4].
[1]: title page. [2–3]: text in double columns. [4]: blank.
Binding: None.
Paper: White unwatermarked laid paper.
Contents: Epithalamion: While explosives blow to dust . . . Signed on p. [3]: 'W. H. AUDEN'. Reprinted in AT, CP, and CSP.
Notes: Auden told Bloomfield: "I went to some little printer in New York, but can't now remember their name," and it appears that probably about 100 copies were printed. Only two copies have been examined, one in a private English collection and the other in the Beinecke Library, Yale University; both are numbered on p. [1] by Auden, 40 and 16 respectively, and both have a correction whereby line 4 of stanza 5 is marked in ink to become line 7. Mrs. Borgese has no more exact recollection of the circumstances of production. There is a reference to the pamphlet, with a quotation, in *Poetry*, LV, 4 (January 1940), 224–25.

A 22   ANOTHER TIME   1940

a) First edition

ANOTHER TIME | Poems | BY W. H. AUDEN | [device: a house] | RANDOM HOUSE · NEW YORK

Collation: 8¾ x 5¾ in. [1–8]⁸, pp. [i–x, 1–2] 3–114 [115–118].
[i–ii]: blank. [iii]: half title. [iv]: blank. [v]: title page. [vi]: 'FIRST PRINT-ING | COPYRIGHT, 1940, BY W. H. AUDEN | PRINTED IN U.S.A. | CL'.
[vii]: 'TO CHESTER KALLMAN | [twelve lines of verse]'. [viii]: blank. [ix-x]: contents. [1]: 'PART ONE | PEOPLE AND PLACES'. [2]: blank: 3–51: text. [52]: blank [53]: 'PART TWO | LIGHTER POEMS'. [54]: blank. 55–86: text.

[87]: 'PART THREE | OCCASIONAL POEMS'. [88]: blank. 89–110: text. [111]: index of first lines. [112]: blank. 113–114: index. [115–118]: blank.

Binding: Bound in dark reddish orange (38) cloth lettered down the spine in gold: 'ANOTHER TIME · *Poems* · W. H. AUDEN'. The publisher's device is stamped in gold on the front cover. All edges trimmed. Cream dust jacket printed in black and reddish brown.

A binding order for 750 copies was made in January 1940, and the remaining 750 copies were ordered to be bound in February 1940.

Paper: Cream unwatermarked wove paper.

Contents:

To Chester Kallman: Every eye must weep alone . . .

Part I People and places

i Wrapped in a yielding air, beside . . . Revised from *New writing*, Autumn 1937, and reprinted in CP ("As he is"), CSP, PA ("Able at times to cry"), CSP2 ("As he is"), and SelP.

ii Law, say the gardeners, is the sun . . . Reprinted in CP ("Law like love"), CSP, PA, and CSP2.

iii The creatures: They are our past and our future: the poles between which our desire unceasingly is discharged . . . Set to music by Britten in a fuller version in the cycle *Our hunting fathers* (1936), and reprinted in CP and CSP.

iv Schoolchildren: Here are all the captivities; the cells are as real . . . First printed in *Listener*, 21 July 1937 ("Hegel and the schoolchildren"), and reprinted in CP, CSP, and CSP2.

v Oxford: Nature is so near: the rooks in the college garden . . . First printed in *Listener*, 9 February 1938, and reprinted in revised form in CP and CSP, and revised again in CSP2.

vi A. E. Housman: No one, not even Cambridge, was to blame . . . First printed in *New writing*, Spring 1939, and revised in CSP2.

vii Edward Lear: Left by his friend to breakfast alone on the white . . . First published in the *Times literary supplement*, 25 March 1939, and reprinted in CP, CSP, and CSP2.

viii It's farewell to the drawing-room's civilised cry . . . First printed in *Listener*, 17 February 1937 ("Song for the new year"); partly reprinted in the *Ballad of heroes*, by Britten (1939) ("Dance of death"), and, in a revised form, in CP ("Danse macabre") and CSP, and revised again in CSP2.

ix Perhaps I always knew what they were saying . . . First printed in *Spectator*, 25 August 1939 ("The prophets"), and reprinted in *Southern review*, Autumn 1939, *Life and letters today*, February 1940, CP, CSP, and revised in CSP2.

x Brussels in winter: Wandering the cold streets tangled like old string . . . First printed in *New writing*, Spring 1939, and reprinted, in revised form, in CP, CSP, and CSP2.

xi Rimbaud: The nights, the railway-arches, the bad sky . . . First printed in *New writing*, Spring 1939, and reprinted in CP, CSP, PA, and CSP2.

xii Hell is neither here nor there . . . First printed in *Harper's bazaar*, January 1940 ("Hell"), and reprinted in CP, CSP, PA, and CSP2.

xiii Herman Melville: Towards the end he sailed into an extraordinary mildness . . . First printed in *Southern review*, Autumn 1939. This is a revised version which is reprinted in CP and CSP, and revised again in CSP2. Dedicated to Lincoln Kirstein.

xiv The capital: Quarter of pleasures where the rich are always waiting . . .

First printed in *New writing*, Spring 1939. This is a slightly revised form and is reprinted in CP, CSP, PA, and CSP2.

xv   The hour-glass whispers to the lion's paw... Reprinted in CP ("Our bias"), CSP, and revised in PA and CSP2.

xvi   Pascal: O had his mother, near her time, been praying... First printed in *Southern review*, Autumn 1939, and reprinted in *Life and letters today*, January 1940, CP, and CSP.

xvii Voltaire at Ferney: Perfectly happy now, he looked at his estate... First printed in *Listener*, 9 March 1939; reprinted in *Poetry*, June 1939, and, in revised form, CP, CSP, and CSP2.

xviii Lay your sleeping head, my love... First printed in *New writing*, Spring 1937, and reprinted in *Penguin new writing*, February 1941, CP, CSP, PA ("Lullaby"), CSP2. and SelP.

xix   Orpheus: What does the song hope for? And the moved hands... First printed in *London mercury*, June 1937, and reprinted in CP, CSP, and CSP2.

xx   The novelist: Encased in talent like a uniform... First printed in *New writing*, Spring 1939; reprinted in *Penguin new writing*, November 1941, CP, CSP, and CSP2; also in *New York times*, 5 August 1966, section 7, p. 2, from CP.

xxi   Musée des beaux arts: About suffering they were never wrong... First printed in *New writing*, Spring 1939 ("Palais des beaux arts"), and reprinted in *Penguin new writing*, September 1942, *Choix*, 1944, CP, CSP, PA, *Icarus*, 1966, CSP2, *Studies in the twentieth century*, Spring 1968, and SelP.

xxii The composer: All the others translate: the painter sketches... First printed in *New writing*, Spring 1939, and reprinted in CP, CSP, and CSP2.

xxiii Not as that dream Napoleon, rumour's dread and centre... First printed in *Southern review*, Autumn 1939 ("Territory of the heart"), and reprinted in CP ("Please make yourself at home"), CSP ("Like a vocation"), and CSP2.

xxiv Where do They come from? Those whom we so much dread... First printed in *Atlantic*, September 1939 ("Crisis"), and reprinted in *Horizon*, January 1940, CP, and CSP. There is an analysis of the stages in the composition of this poem in *Reading poems*, by C. W. Thomas and S. G. Brown (New York: Oxford University Press, 1941).

xxv   Gare du Midi: A nondescript express in from the South... First printed in *New writing*, Spring 1939. This slightly revised form is reprinted in CP, CSP, PA, and CSP2.

xxvi As I walked out one evening... First printed in *New statesman & nation*, 15 January 1938, and reprinted in CP, CSP, PA ("One evening"), CSP2, and SelP.

xxvii Matthew Arnold: His gift knew what he was—a dark disordered city... First printed in *Listener*, 14 September 1939, and reprinted in *Nation*, 30 September 1939, CP, and CSP.

xxviii Dover: Steep roads, a tunnel through the downs are the approaches... First printed in *New verse*, November 1937. This is a slightly revised version which is reprinted in CP and CSP, and revised again in CSP2. The original version was also reprinted in *New verse: an anthology*, ed. by G. E. H. Grigson (1939).

xxix Song: Warm are the still and lucky miles... Reprinted in CP, CSP, PA, and CSP2.

xxx For us like any other fugitive... Reprinted in CP ("Another time"), CSP, PA, and CSP2.

xxxi Underneath the leaves of life... First printed in *New republic*, 26 July 1939 ("The leaves of life"), and reprinted in *New writing*, Christmas 1939, *Penguin new writing*, June 1941, CP, and CSP ("The riddle"), and revised in CSP2.

Part II Lighter poems

   i Sharp and silent in the... Reprinted, with revisions, in CP ("Heavy date"), CSP, and CSP2.

   ii Three ballads

1. Miss Gee: Let me tell you a little story... First printed in *New writing*, Autumn 1937. This revised version is reprinted in CP, CSP, PA, and CSP2.

2. James Honeyman: James Honeyman was a silent child... First printed in *Ploughshare*, November–December 1937.

3. Victor: Victor was a little baby... First printed in *New writing*, Autumn 1937, and reprinted in *Penguin new writing*, October–December 1944. This is a revised version which is reprinted in CP, CSP, PA, and CSP2.

   iii Four cabaret songs for Miss Hedli Anderson

1. Johnny: O the valley in the summer where I and my John... Reprinted in *Harper's bazaar*, April 1941, CP, CSP, PA, and CSP2.

2. O tell me the truth about love: Some say that Love's a little boy... Reprinted in *Harper's bazaar*, April 1940, and revised in CSP2.

3. Funeral blues: Stop all the clocks, cut off the telephone... This is a partial reprint of the lyric from *The ascent of F 6*, with the last half rewritten. Reprinted in CP, CSP, PA, and CSP2.

4. Calypso: Driver, drive faster and make a good run... Reprinted in *Harper's bazaar*, 15 September 1941, and CSP2.

These four poems were set to music by Britten in 1938; the music is unpublished.

   iv Madrigal: O lurcher-loving collier, black as night... First printed in *New verse*, Summer 1938, and reprinted in CP, CSP, PA, and CSP2. The poem is from Auden's script for the film *Coal face* (see L1).

   v Roman wall blues: Over the heather the wet wind blows... Reprinted in *Harper's bazaar*, February 1941, CP, CSP, PA, CSP2, and SelP. The poem is from the radio programme *Hadrian's wall*.

   vi Epitaph on a tyrant: Perfection, of a kind, was what he was after... First printed in *New statesman & nation*, 31 January 1939, and reprinted in CP, CSP, PA, and CSP2.

   vii The unknown citizen: He was found by the Bureau of Statistics to be... First printed in *Listener*, 3 August 1939, and reprinted in *New Yorker*, 6 January 1940. This revised version is reprinted in CP, CSP, and CSP2. A motion picture version of the poem was produced and directed by Marc Stone (Toronto: Halewyn Films, 1969 [Visual poetry]).

   viii Refugee blues: Say this city has ten million souls... First printed in *New Yorker*, 15 April 1939, and reprinted in *New writing*, Christmas 1939, *Penguin new writing*, April 1942, CP, CSP, and CSP2.

Part III

   i Spain 1937: Yesterday all the past. The language of size... First printed by Faber and Faber (1937) and by Nancy Cunard in pamphlet form.

II In memory of W. B. Yeats: He disappeared in the dead of winter... First printed in *New republic*, 8 March 1939, and reprinted in this slightly longer version in *London mercury*, April 1939, CP, CSP, and revised in PA, CSP2, and SelP.

III In memory of Ernst Toller: The shining neutral summer has no voice... First printed in *New Yorker*, 17 June 1939, and reprinted in *New writing*, Christmas 1939, *Penguin new writing*, September 1942, CP, CSP, and CSP2.

IV September 1, 1939: I sit in one of the dives... First printed in *New republic*, 18 October 1939; reprinted in *New republic*, 22 November 1954, and, in a revised form, in CP and CSP. Auden revised one word for *The new pocket anthology of American verse*, ed. by Oscar Williams (New York: Pocket Library; Cleveland: World, 1955).

V In memory of Sigmund Freud: When there are so many we shall have to mourn... First printed in *Kenyon review*, Winter 1940; reprinted in *Horizon*, March 1940, CP, CSP, *Griffin*, December 1962, PA, and CSP2.

VI Epithalamion: While explosives blow to dust... First printed as a separate pamphlet (1939), and reprinted in CP and CSP. Dedicated to Giuseppe Antonio Borgese and Elisabeth Mann.

Notes: Published 7 February 1940 in an edition of 1,500 copies at $2, and out of print in 1941. Printed by the Country Life Press, Garden City, New York. Microfilm and xerographic copies have been available since 1959 from University Microfilms.

Reviews:

J. P. Bishop. *Nation*, CL (6 April 1940), 452–54.
L. Bogan. *New Yorker*, XVI (24 February 1940), 76.
M. M. Colum. *Forum*, CIII (April 1940), 328.
D. Daiches. *Poetry*, LVI (April 1940), 40–43.
R. Eberhart. *Boston transcript*, 27 March 1940, p. 13.
P. M. Jack. *New York times*, 18 February 1940, section 6, p. 2.
A. Kreymborg. *Living age*, CCCLVIII (April 1940), 195–97.
R. Lechlitner. *New York herald tribune*, 3 March 1940, section 9, p. 21.
L. MacNeice. *Common sense*, IX (April 1940), 24–25.
I. Schneider. *New masses*, XXXIV (19 March 1940), 26–27.
A. Wanning. *Furioso*, I (Spring 1940), 36–41.

b) First English edition   1940

POEMS BY W. H. AUDEN | ANOTHER | TIME | FABER & FABER LIMITED | LONDON

Collation: 8½ x 5½ in. [A]–H⁸, pp. [1–8] 9–125 [126–128].
[1–2]: blank. [3]: half title. [4]: 'By the same author | [six lines]'. [5]: title page. [6]: '*First published in June Mcmxl | by Faber and Faber Limited | 24 Russell Square London W.C.1 | Printed in Great Britain by | R. MacLehose and Company Limited | The University Press Glasgow* | [one line]'. [7]: 'To | CHESTER KALLMAN | [twelve lines of verse]'. [8]: blank. 9–11: contents. [12]: blank. [13]–125: text; 14, 66, 100, and 102 blank. [126–128]: blank.

Binding: Bound in vivid red (11) cloth lettered down the spine in gold: '*Another Time by W. H. Auden Faber & Faber*'. Top edge only trimmed. Reddish orange dust jacket printed in black. The fourth impression is bound in green cloth.

Paper: White wove paper watermarked: '[crown] | Abbey Mills | Greenfield' in gothic.

Contents: As the American edition.
Notes: Published 20 June 1940 in an impression of 2,000 copies at 7/6d. and reprinted
   in November 1940 (1,370 copies), February 1944 (500 copies), October 1945 (500
   copies), and June 1946 (1,000 copies). Out of print in February 1954.
   Faber and Faber say that "if Random House publish Auden's work first we work
   from the American edition."
Reviews:
   Durham University journal, XXXIII (n.s. II) (December 1940), 72–73.
   F. R. L[eavis]. *Scrutiny,* IX (September 1940), 200.
   [R. Church.] *Listener,* XXIV (22 August 1940), 282–83.
   E. Muir. *Purpose,* XII (July–December 1940), 149–52.
   K. J. Raine. *Horizon,* III (January 1941), 63–68.
   M. Roberts. *Spectator,* CLXV (26 July 1940), 100.
   Times literary supplement, 6 July 1940, p. 328.
   M. Turnell. *Tablet,* CLXXVI (20 July 1940), 54.
   A. Wordsworth. *Time and tide,* XXI (20 July 1940), 764.
   T. C. Worsley. *New statesman & nation,* XX (27 July 1940), 92.

A 23   SOME POEMS   1940

SOME POEMS | by | W. H. AUDEN | Faber and Faber | 24 Russell
Square | London

Collation: 7½ x 4¾ in. [A.A]–A.D⁸E⁸, pp. [1–4] 5–80.
   [1]: half title. [2]: blank. [3]: title page. [4]: 'FIRST PUBLISHED IN MARCH
   MCMXL | BY FABER AND FABER LIMITED | 24 RUSSELL SQUARE,
   LONDON, W.C.1 | PRINTED IN GREAT BRITAIN BY | WESTERN
   PRINTING SERVICES LTD., BRISTOL | [one line]'. 5: select bibliography.
   [6]: blank. 7–8. contents. 9–80: text.
Binding: Bound in light yellowish pink (28) paper boards lettered down the spine in
   blue: 'SOME POEMS BY W. H. AUDEN FABER', and across the front cover:
   '*Some Poems* | [star] | *W. H. Auden*'. Top and leading edges trimmed. Light blue
   dust jacket printed in blue.
Paper: Cream unwatermarked wove paper.
Contents:
   from *Poems* (1930):
       1 Paid on both sides [a selection].
       2 Doom is dark and deeper than any sea-dingle...   Reprinted from P2.
       3 Watch any day his nonchalant pauses...
       4 It was Easter as I walked in the public gardens...
       5 Sir, no man's enemy, forgiving all...
   from *The orators:*
       6 'O where are you going?' said reader to rider...
   from *The dog beneath the skin:*
       7 The Summer holds: upon its glittering lake...
       8 Now through night's caressing grip...
   from *The ascent of F 6:*
       9 Chorus: Acts of injustice done...
   from *Look, stranger!:*
       10 O love the interest itself in thoughtless Heaven...
       11 Out on the lawn I lie in bed...
       12 Look, stranger, at this island now...
       13 Now the leaves are falling fast...

14 The earth turns over, our side feels the cold...
15 A shilling life will give you all the facts...
16 May with its light behaving...
17 Here on the cropped grass of the narrow ridge I stand...
18 Easily, my dear, you move, easily your head...
19 O for doors to be open and an invite with gilded edges...
20 Fish in the unruffled lakes...
21 August for the people and their favourite islands...
from *Letters from Iceland:*
22 Journey to Iceland: And the traveller hopes: 'Let me be far from any...
from *Journey to a war:*
23 Three sonnets. The sphinx: Did it once issue from the carver's hand...
He looked in all his wisdom from the throne... And the age ended, and
the last deliverer died...
24 Night falls on China; the great arc of travelling shadow...

Notes: Published 14 March 1940 in an impression of 3,550 copies at 2/6d. in the series
of Sesame books and reprinted in February 1941 (3,000 copies), May 1943 (2,000
copies), April 1944 (2,925 copies), April 1946 (2,000 copies), October 1947 (2,070
copies), and March 1952 (2,700 copies). Out of print in June 1968.

The selection was apparently not made by Auden.

A 24   THE DOUBLE MAN   1941

a) First edition

W·H·AUDEN | [title in red] *The Double Man* | "We are, I know not
how, double in ourselves, | so that what we believe we disbelieve, and |
cannot rid ourselves of what we condemn." | MONTAIGNE | [device in
red: a house with the letters R H] | RANDOM HOUSE · NEW YORK

Collation: 8¾ x 5½ in. [1–12]⁸, pp. [1–10] 11–189 [190–192].
[1]: half title. [2]: 'BY W. H. AUDEN | [eleven lines]'. [3]: title page. [4]:
'FIRST PRINTING | COPYRIGHT, 1941, BY W. H. AUDEN | MANUFAC-
TURED IN THE U.S.A. BY H. WOLFF, NEW YORK'. [5]: 'TO | ELIZA-
BETH MAYER'. [6]: blank. [7]: contents. [8]: blank. [9]: 'PROLOGUE'. [10]:
blank. 11–12: text. [13]: 'NEW YEAR LETTER | (*January 1, 1940*)'. [14]: blank.
15–71: text. [72]: blank. [73]: 'NOTES'. [74]: blank. 75–162: text. [163]: 'THE
QUEST'. [164]: blank. 165–184: text. [185]: 'EPILOGUE'. [186]: blank. 187–189:
text. [190–192]: blank.
Binding: Bound in strong reddish brown (40) cloth lettered down the spine in gold:
'W. H. AUDEN [diamond] THE DOUBLE MAN [device and initials R H
across the spine]', and across the front cover: '*The Double Man*'. All edges
trimmed, and top edge stained dark bluish grey. Cream dust jacket printed in black
and orange.
Paper: White unwatermarked wove paper.
Contents:
Prologue: O season of repetition and return... First printed in the Allied Relief
Ball Souvenir Program, May 10, 1940 ("Spring in wartime"), and reprinted in
Horizon, July 1940, and CP ("Spring 1940").
New Year letter: Under the familiar weight... First printed in *Atlantic,* January
and February 1941 ("Letter to Elizabeth Mayer"), and reprinted in CP and CLP.

There are minor variants in the English edition of DM; the CP text is based on the American edition, the CLP text on the English edition. The notes to the poem contain the following pieces of verse which appear separately:

Clocks cannot tell our time of day... Reprinted in *Furioso*, Summer 1941, CP ("We're late"), and CSP2 ("No time").

Motionless, deep in his mind, lies the past the poet's forgotten... Reprinted in CSP2.

How he survived them they could never understand... Reprinted in CP ("The diaspora"), and CSP2.

Nietzsche: O masterly debunker of our liberal fallacies, how... First printed in *Common sense*, August 1940 ("Elegiacs for Nietzsche").

His aging nature is the same... Reprinted in CP ("True enough") and CSP2.

The Hidden Law does not deny... Reprinted in CP ("Aera sub lege") and CSP2 ("The hidden law").

With conscience cocked to listen for the thunder... First printed in *Christian century*, October 1940 ("Luther"), and reprinted in CP and CSP2.

Outside his library window he could see... Reprinted in CP ("Montaigne") and CSP2.

In gorgeous robes befitting the occasion... Reprinted in CP ("For the last time") and CSP2 ("The council").

Anthropos apteros for days... First printed in *Vice versa*, November–December 1940, and reprinted in CP ("The labyrinth") and CSP2 ("The maze").

Round the three actors in any Blessed Event... First printed in *Harper's bazaar*, December 1939, and reprinted in CP ("Blessed event") and CSP2.

In addition, the following brief pieces from the notes are reprinted in CSP2 ("Shorts"):

Infants in their mothers' arms... Revised.

Do we want to return to the womb? Not at all...

Once for candy cook had stolen...

Base words are uttered only by the base...

Those public men who seem so to enjoy their dominion...

Hans-in-Kelder, Hans-in-Kelder...

Whether determined by God or their neural structure, still...

The Champion smiles—what personality...

Standing among the ruins the horror-struck conqueror exclaimed...

When statesmen gravely say "We must be realistic...

Don't you dream of a world, a society with no coercion...

To the man-in-the-street, who, I'm sorry to say...

"Hard cases make bad law," as the politician learns to his cost...

What will cure the nation's ill... Revised.

What was that? Why are the public buildings so high? O... Revised.

With what conviction the young man spoke...

The quest

The door: Out of its steps the future of the poor...

The preparations: All had been ordered weeks before the start...

The crossroads: The friends who met here and embraced are gone...

The traveler: No window in his suburb lights that bedroom where...

The city: In villages from which their childhoods came...

The first temptation: Ashamed to be the darling of his grief...

The second temptation: The library annoyed him with its look...

The third temptation: He watched with all his organs of concern... First printed in *Poetry*, October 1940.

The tower: This is an architecture for the odd...
The presumptuous: They noticed that virginity was needed...
The average: His peasant parents killed themselves with toil...
Vocation: Incredulous, he stared at the amused...
The useful: The over-logical fell for the witch...
The way: Fresh addenda are published every day...
The lucky: Suppose he'd listened to the erudite committee...
The hero: He carried every question that they hurled... 'Carried' here is a
    misprint for 'parried'. This is corrected in *New Year letter* (Faber, 1941).
Adventure: Others had swerved off to the left before...
The adventurers: Spinning upon their central thirst like tops...
The waters: Poet, oracle and wit...
The garden: Within these gates all opening begins...
    The sequence was first printed in *New republic*, 25 November 1940,
and reprinted in CP. The second, third (revised), tenth, twelfth, thirteenth,
fifteenth, and fourteenth poems are reprinted, in that order, under the title
"The quest" in PA, and the whole series, with the seventeenth poem also re-
vised, in CSP2 and SelP. The CSP2 text first appeared, with some variants, in
Auden's *Opere poetiche*, vol. 1 (Milan: Lerici, 1966), pp. 34–73. The separate
titles are dropped in CSP2 and SelP.
Epilogue: Returning each morning from a timeless world... First printed in
    Nation, 7 December 1940 ("Autumn 1940"), and reprinted in CP ("Autumn
    1940") and CSP2 ("The dark years").
Notes: Published 21 March 1941 in an edition of 2,000 copies at $2, and out of print
in 1943.
    "As to my return to the church, it was a gradual business without any abrupt
leaps. *The Double Man*, written Jan.–Oct. 1940 covers a period when I was beginning to think seriously about such things without committing myself. I started
going to church again just about October. It [*The Double Man*] is therefore full
of heretical remarks" (Auden to Kenneth Lewars, quoted in Lewars, "The quest
in Auden's poems and plays," M.A. thesis, Columbia University, 1947, p. 104).
    The publisher asked Auden for a synopsis of the book for the Spring 1941 an-
nouncement catalogue, and this synopsis was reprinted as the second paragraph of
the blurb on the front flap of the dust jacket itself.
    Fair copies of early versions of the notes to "New Year letter," and "The quest,"
are now in the Berg Collection at the New York Public Library.
Reviews:
S. Alexander. *Common sense*, X (June 1941), 185–86.
L. Bogan. *New Yorker*, XVII (12 April 1941), 84–85.
C. Brooks. *Kenyon review*, IV (Spring 1942), 244–47.
E. Bustin. *Christianity and society*, VII [for VI] (Fall 1941), 46–48.
M. M. Colum. *American mercury*, LII (June 1941), 767–68.
M. Cowley. *New republic*, CIV (7 April 1941), 473–74.
B. Deutsch. *Poetry*, LVIII (June 1941), 148–52.
D. Fitts. *Furioso*, I (Summer 1941), 58–61.
L. Frankenberg. *New York herald tribune*, 11 May 1941, section 9, p. 5.
W. T. Grace. *Commonweal*, XXXIV (11 July 1941), 279–81.
H. Gregory. *Sewanee review*, LII (Autumn 1944), 578–83.
R. Jarrell. *Nation*, CLII (12 April 1941), 440–41.
M. Moore. *Decision*, I (May 1940), 70–71.
A. Tate. *Accent*, II (Winter 1942), 118–19.
D. Thompson. *Vice versa*, I (January 1942), 62–64.
L. Untermeyer. *Saturday review of literature*, XXIV (17 May 1941), 18.

b) First English edition 1941

New Year Letter | [ornamental swelled rule] | *W. H. Auden* | *Faber and Faber*

Collation: 8½ x 5½ in. [A]–M⁸, pp. [1–8] 9–188 [189–192].
  [1–2]: blank. [3]: half title. [4]: blank. [5]: title page. [6]: '*First published in May Mcmxli* | *by Faber and Faber Limited* | *24 Russell Square London W.C.1* | *Printed in Great Britain by* | *R. MacLehose and Company Limited* | *The University Press Glasgow* | [one line]'. [7]: 'To | ELIZABETH MAYER | [quotation from Montaigne in five lines]'. [8]: blank. 9: contents. [10]: blank. [11]: 'PROLOGUE'. [12]: blank. 13–14: text. [15]: 'LETTER'. [16]: blank. 17–75: text. [76]: blank. [77]: 'NOTES TO LETTER'. [78]: blank. 79–160: text. [161]: 'THE QUEST'. [162]: blank. 163–182: text. [183]: 'EPILOGUE'. [184]: blank. 185–188: text. [189–192]: blank.
Binding: Bound in yellowish grey (93) cloth lettered down the spine in red: '*NEW YEAR LETTER* | *W. H. AUDEN* | [across the foot of the spine] FABER'. All edges trimmed. Orange dust jacket printed in black. The third impression and the so-called 'second impression' (actually the fourth) were both bound in strong red (12) cloth and lettered in gold, the dust jacket of the fourth impression being white printed in black, light blue, and bluish green.
Paper: Cream unwatermarked wove paper. The fourth impression is on white unwatermarked wove paper.
Contents: As the American edition, except that the "Modern sources" section is omitted from the notes, and the notes themselves have numerous changes, the English edition often being fuller.
Notes: Published 29 May 1941 in an impression of 2,000 copies at 10/6d. and reprinted in December 1942 (1,000 copies), and October 1946 (1,000 copies). A fourth impression, described as a second impression, was issued on 20 May 1965 (2,000 copies) at 18/–.
Reviews:
  G. Every. *Theology,* XLIII (October 1941), 217–19.
  [M. Roberts.] *Listener,* XXVI (24 July 1941), 136, 139.
  E. Muir. *Horizon,* IV (August 1941), 139–43.
  H. Palmer. *Poetry review,* XXXII (July–August 1941), 227–32.
  H. Read. *Spectator,* CLXVI (6 June 1941), 613–14.
  G. W. Stonier. *New statesman & nation,* XXII (5 July 1941), 16.
  Times literary supplement, 21 June 1941, p. 302 (cf. *ibid.,* "Poets and society," p. 299).
  M. Turnell. *Tablet,* CLXXVII (28 June 1941), 502.
  C. Williams. *Dublin review,* CCIX (July 1941), 99–101.
  R. O. C. Winkler. *Scrutiny,* X (October 1941), 206–11.

A 25   THREE SONGS FOR ST. CECILIA'S DAY   1941

Three Songs | *for* | *St. Cecilia's Day* | BY | W. H. AUDEN | *PRIVATELY PRINTED* | 1941

Collation: 7 x 4½ in. One unsigned gathering of eight leaves.
  [1–2]: blank. [3]: title page. [4]: 'THIS EDITION IS | LIMITED TO | TWO HUNDRED AND FIFTY | COPIES'. [5]: '[five lines] | *By good fortune I was*

the guest of | W. H. Auden when the following poems | appeared in Harper's
Bazaar. I persuaded | Mr. Auden to let me reproduce them... | [five lines] | With
Christmas wishes | CAROLINE NEWTON | [one line] | New York City'. [6]:
blank. [7]: 'Three Songs | for | St. Cecilia's Day'. [8]: blank. [9]: first song.
[10]: blank. [11]: second song. [12–13]: third song. [14–16]: blank.
Binding: Stitched in a moderate purplish blue (200) wrapper with a blue cord and
lettered in black across the front wrapper: 'Three Songs | for | St. Cecilia's Day |
BY | W. H. AUDEN'.
Paper: White unwatermarked wove paper.
Contents:
Three songs for St. Cecilia's day
    I   In a garden shady this holy lady...
    II I cannot grow...
    III O ear whose creatures cannot wish to fall...
    All first printed in *Harper's bazaar*, December 1941, and reprinted in CP
    ("Song for St. Cecilia's day), CSP, and CSP2 ("Anthem for St. Cecilia's
    day").
Notes: The circumstances of the production of this pamphlet are outlined above.

A 26   FOR THE TIME BEING   1947

a) First edition

[on a yellow title page] For the Time Being | by W. H. AUDEN | Ran-
dom House • New York [device: a house]

Collation: 8 x 5¼ in [1]⁴[2–9]⁸, pp. [i–iv, 1–2] 3–132.
    [i]: half title. [ii]: 'BOOKS BY W. H. AUDEN | [fifteen lines]'. [iii]: title page.
[iv]: 'FIRST PRINTING | THIS IS A WARTIME BOOK | [three lines] |
[device superimposed over an open book forming the letter V] | Copyright, 1944,
by W. H. Auden | Published simultaneously in Canada by | Random House of
Canada Limited | Manufactured in the United States of America | by H. Wolff,
New York | Designed by Stefan Salter'. [1]: 'THE SEA AND THE MIRROR |
A Commentary on Shakespeare's The Tempest | TO JAMES AND TANIA
STERN | [six-line quotation from Emily Brontë]'. [2]: blank. 3–59: text. [60]:
blank. [61]: 'FOR THE TIME BEING | A Christmas Oratorio | IN MEMO-
RIAM | CONSTANCE ROSALIE AUDEN | 1870–1941 | [three-line quotation
from Romans, chap. 6]'. [62]: blank. 63–132: text.
Binding: Quarter bound in white cloth with dark purplish blue (201) paper boards
lettered on the spine in gold: '[across] Auden | [down] FOR THE TIME BEING
| [across] [device] Random | House'. All edges trimmed, and top edge stained
dark blue. Grey dust jacket printed in black and reddish orange. The second im-
pression is bound in moderate brown (58) cloth lettered in gold.
Paper: White laid paper watermarked 'R [a house] H'.
Contents:
The sea and the mirror. Reprinted in CP and CLP. The following pieces appear
    separately as stated:
        Preface: The aged catch their breath... First printed in *Atlantic*, August
        1944.
        Sing, Ariel, sing... Reprinted in PA ("Invocation to Ariel"), CSP2, and
        SelP.
        Dear son, when the warm multitudes cry... First printed in *Partisan re-
        view*, September–October 1943 ("Alonso to Ferdinand"). "Stephano's song,"

"Trinculo's song," "Alonso to Ferdinand," "Song of the master and the boatswain," "Miranda's song," and "Caliban to the audience" are reprinted in PA, and the entire second section of the poem is reprinted in SelP.

For the time being. Reprinted and revised in CP and CLP. The following pieces appear separately as stated:

O shut your bright eyes that mine must endanger... First printed in *Commonweal*, 25 December 1942 ("At the manger").

Because I am bewildered, because I must decide... First printed in *Harper's magazine*, December 1943 ("Herod considers the massacre of the innocents").

When the Sex War ended with the slaughter of the Grandmothers... Reprinted in PA ("Song of the old soldier") and CSP2.

Well, so that is that. Now we must dismantle the tree... First printed in *Harper's magazine*, January 1944 ("After Christmas").

Notes: Published 6 September 1944 in an impression of 1,700 copies at $2 and reprinted in October 1944 (500 copies). Out of print in 1945. "For the time being" was written in 1941–42; most of the manuscript drafts are now to be found in the Berg Collection at the New York Public Library. "The sea and the mirror" was written between 1942 and 1944 and the manuscript drafts are now in the Berg Collection at the New York Public Library and the Lockwood Memorial Library. On 18 September [1944] Auden wrote to Random House to correct an error in the first impression: on p. 128, line 3, for 'looked' read 'locked'.

Reviews:

L. Bogan. *New Yorker*, XX (23 September 1944), 77–78.

R. C. B. Brown. *Voices*, 120 (Winter 1945), 41–44.

M. Cowley. *Poetry*, LXV (January 1945), 202–9 (see also March 1945, p. 345).

D. Daiches. *Virginia quarterly review*, XXI (Winter 1945), 145–46.

F. W. Dupee. *Nation*, CLIX (28 October 1944), 537–38.

A. Fremantle. *Commonweal*, XLI (8 December 1944), 194–98.

H. Gregory. *Saturday review of literature*, XXVII (2 December 1944), 48.

R. Lechlitner. *New York herald tribune*, 1 October 1944, section 6, p. 4.

H. Levin. *New republic*, CXI (18 September 1944), 347–48.

A. Mizener. *Accent*, V (Winter 1945), 117–20.

M. Schorer. *New York times*, 17 September 1944, section 7, p. 4.

L. Untermeyer. *Yale review*, XXXIV (December 1944), 345–46.

T. Weiss. *Quarterly review of literature*, II (1945), 158–60.

b) First English edition   1945

FOR | THE TIME BEING | [swelled rule] | BY | W. H. AUDEN | FABER AND FABER

Collation: 8¾ x 5½ in. [A]–G⁸H⁶, pp. [1–4] 5–124.

[1]: half title. [2]: 'by the same author | [fifteen lines]'. [3]: title page. [4]: '*First published in Mcmxlv | by Faber and Faber Limited | 24 Russell Square London W.C.1 | Printed in Great Britain by | R. MacLehose and Company Limited | The University Press Glasgow | [one line]*'. 5: contents. [6]: blank. 7–60: The sea and the mirror. 61–124: For the time being.

Binding: Bound in deep reddish orange (36) cloth lettered down the spine in gold: 'FOR THE TIME BEING   W. H. AUDEN   FABER'. Top edge only trimmed. Cream dust jacket printed in black and red.

Paper: Cream unwatermarked wove paper.

Contents: As the American edition; except that lines 4–6 from last page of the American edition are omitted, presumably in error since they appeared in an earlier periodical text and are restored in CP and CLP.

Notes: Published 2 March 1945 in an impression of 4,000 copies at 8/6d. and re-printed in July 1945 (2,000 copies), March 1946 (1,500 copies), November 1953 (1,000 copies), November 1958 (1,500 copies), and October 1966 (1,500 copies).

"The sea and the mirror" was performed at Oxford on 7–11 May 1968 with cuts in Caliban's speech which were approved by Auden.

Reviews:

G. Every. *New English weekly*, XXVII (26 April 1945), 18–19.
G. S. Fraser. *Poetry* (London), 11 (September–October 1947), 52–59.
H. Kingsmill. *New English review*, XI (May 1945), 79–81.
R. G. Lienhardt. *Scrutiny*, XIII (September 1945), 138–42.
[G. Grigson.] *Listener*, XXXIII (12 April 1945), 413–14.
W. P. M. *Dublin magazine*, XXI (April–June 1946), 52–53.
D. MacCarthy. *Sunday Times*, 11 March 1945, p. 3.
H. Reed. *New writing & daylight*, VI (1945), 131–35.
S. Shannon. *Spectator*, CLXXIV (11 May 1945), 433.
S. Spender. *Poetry quarterly*, VII (Spring 1945), 22–26.
——. *Time and tide*, XXVI (25 August 1945), 711–12.
G. W. Stonier. *New statesman & nation*, XXIX (17 March 1945), 175–76.
J. Symons. *Focus*, 2 (1946), 127–37.
Times literary supplement, 24 March 1945, p. 140.

A 27   **THE COLLECTED POETRY**   **1945**

[all within a green rule border] THE | COLLECTED | POETRY OF | W. H. AUDEN | [large device in green: a house] | *RANDOM HOUSE · NEW YORK*

Collation: 8¼ x 5½ in. [1–15]¹⁶, pp. [i–viii] ix–xiv, [1–2] 3–466.
[i]: half title. [ii]: '*Books by W. H. Auden* | [nineteen lines]'. [iii]: title page. [iv]: '*Copyright, 1945, by W. H. Auden* | [four lines] | FIRST PRINTING | [five lines] | *Manufactured in the United States of America* | *by Kingsport Press, Inc. Kingsport, Tennessee*'. [v]: 'TO | CHRISTOPHER ISHERWOOD | AND | CHESTER KALLMAN | [four lines]'. [vi]: blank. [vii]: preface. [viii]: blank. ix–xiv: contents. [1]: '*Part I* | POEMS'. [2]: blank. 3–188: text. [189]: '*Part II* | LETTER TO A WOUND'. [190]: blank. 191–193: text. [194]: blank. [195]: '*Part III* | SONGS AND OTHER MUSICAL PIECES'. [196]: blank. 197–239: text. [240]: blank. [241]: '*Part IV* | DEPRAVITY | *A Sermon*'. [242]: '*Note* | [four-teen lines]'. 243–247: text. [248]: blank. [249]: '*Part V* | THE QUEST | *A Sonnet Sequence*'. [250]: blank. 251–262: text. [263]: '*Part VI* | NEW YEAR LETTER | (*January 1, 1940*) | TO ELIZABETH MAYER'. [264]: blank. 265–316: text. [317]: '*Part VII* | IN TIME OF WAR | *A Sonnet Sequence* | *with a verse com-mentary*'. [318]: blank. 319–334: sonnet sequence. [335]: 'COMMENTARY'. [336]: blank. 337–347: text. [348]: blank. [349]: '*Part VIII* | THE SEA AND THE MIRROR | *A Commentary on Shakespeare's* The Tempest | TO JAMES AND TANIA STERN | [six lines]'. [350]: blank. 351–404: text. [405]: '*Part IX* | FOR THE TIME BEING | *A Christmas Oratorio* | IN MEMORIAM | CON-STANCE ROSALIE AUDEN | 1870–1941 | [three lines]'. [406]: blank. 407–466: text.

Binding: Bound in dark bluish green (165) cloth lettered across the spine in gold on a brown panel not covering the full width of the spine: '[wavy rule] | *THE* | *COLLECTED* | POETRY OF | W. H. AUDEN | [wavy rule] | *RANDOM*

HOUSE | [wavy rule]'. All edges trimmed, and the top edge stained dark green. Pink dust jacket printed in black and brown.

The title pages of the second through ninth impressions are printed in grey and black, rather than the green and black of the first impression; the title pages of the tenth through twenty-first impressions are printed entirely in black. The top edges of the second through twenty-first impressions are stained black or various shades of grey, with the exception of the fourth impression, which is stained reddish brown. These later impressions are bound in various coloured cloths, as follows: 2nd–3rd: light grey; 4th: dark green; 5th: light grey; 6th: brown; 7th: red; 8th: brown; 9th–13th: red; 14th: brown; 15th–17th: grey; 18th: light blue; 19th: some light blue, some red; 20th–21st: red. After the first impression, spine panels are printed in black, instead of the brown of the first, and generally run to the full width of the spine. The second and third impressions are approximately ½″ smaller in height and width; the fourth impression approximately 1″ smaller.

Paper: White unwatermarked wove paper.

Contents: [Note: The asterisks, taken from the text of CP, which are found against the titles of some poems indicate first publication in a collected volume by Auden; see also the notes below.]

To Christopher Isherwood and Chester Kallman: Whether conditioned by God or the neural structure, still . . . Reprinted in CSP and CSP2.

Part I   Poems

Musée des beaux arts: About suffering they were never wrong . . . Reprinted from AT.

In war time*: Abruptly mounting her ramshackle wheel . . . First printed in *Title*, May 1944, and reprinted in CSP. Dedicated to Caroline Newton.

Two's company: Again in conversations . . . Reprinted from P.

The composer: All the others translate: the painter sketches . . . Reprinted from AT.

Voltaire at Ferney: Almost happy now, he looked at his estate . . . Reprinted from AT.

Journey to Iceland: And the traveller hopes: "Let me be far from any . . . Reprinted from LFI.

Gare du Midi: A nondescript express in from the South . . . Reprinted from AT.

The labyrinth: Anthropos apteros for days . . . Reprinted from DM.

Kairos and Logos*: Around them boomed the rhetoric of time . . . First printed in *Southern review*, Spring 1941, and reprinted in CSP.

Who's who: A shilling life will give you all the facts . . . Reprinted from LS.

His excellency: As it is, plenty . . . Reprinted from LS.

Macao: A weed from Catholic Europe, it took root . . . Reprinted from JTW.

This one: Before this loved one . . . Reprinted from P.

Atlantis*: Being set on the idea . . . Reprinted in CSP, PA, CSP2, and SelP.

Make up your mind: Between attention and attention . . . Reprinted from P2.

Adolescence: By landscape reminded once of his mother's figure . . . Reprinted from O.

Always in trouble: Can speak of trouble, pressure on men . . . Reprinted from "Paid on both sides" in P.

As we like it: Certainly our city with its byres of poverty down to . . . Reprinted from LS.

We're late: Clocks cannot tell our time of day . . . Reprinted from DM.

Consider: Consider this and in our time . . . Reprinted from P.

The secret agent: Control of the passes was, he saw, the key . . . Reprinted from P (1928).

In sickness and in health*: Dear, all benevolence of fingering lips . . . Reprinted in *Mint*, 1946, CSP, and CSP2. Dedicated to Maurice and Gwen Mandelbaum.

The sphinx: Did it once issue from the carver's hand... Reprinted from JTW.

Something is bound to happen: Doom is dark and deeper than any sea-dingle... Reprinted from P2.

Are you there*: Each lover has some theory of his own... First printed in *Harper's bazaar*, 15 March 1941, and reprinted in CSP ("Alone") and CSP2.

A bride in the 30's: Easily, my dear, you move, easily your head... Reprinted from LS.

The novelist: Encased in talent like a uniform... Reprinted from AT.

I shall be enchanted: Enter with him... Reprinted from DBS.

The climbers: Fleeing the short-haired mad executives... Reprinted from LS.

Another time: For us like any other fugitive... Reprinted from AT.

To you simply*: For what as easy... First printed in *New signatures* (1932) and revised here; reprinted in CSP and CSP2.

Missing: From scars where kestrels hover... Reprinted from P.

The love letter: From the very first coming down... Reprinted from P (1928).

The model*: Generally, reading palms or handwriting or faces... First printed in *Dodo* (Swarthmore College), February 1943 ("To the model"), and reprinted in *Harper's bazaar*, April 1945, CSP, PA, and CSP2.

The cultural presupposition: Happy the hare at morning, for she cannot read... Reprinted from DBS.

Paysage moralisé: Hearing of harvests rotting in the valleys... Reprinted from LS.

In memory of W. B. Yeats: He disappeared in the dead of winter... Reprinted from AT.

Hell: Hell is neither here nor there... Reprinted from AT.

Schoolchildren: Here are all the captivities; the cells are as real... Reprinted from AT.

To E. M. Forster: Here, though the bombs are real and dangerous... Reprinted from JTW.

True enough: His aging nature is the same... Reprinted from DM.

Matthew Arnold: His gift knew what he was—a dark disordered city... Reprinted from AT.

The traveller: Holding the distance up before his face... Reprinted from JTW.

The diaspora: How he survived them they could never understand... Reprinted from DM.

For the last time: In gorgeous robes befitting the occasion... Reprinted from DM.

September 1, 1939: I sit in one of the dives... Reprinted from AT.

Danse macabre: It's farewell to the drawing-room's civilised cry... Reprinted from AT.

Hongkong 1938: Its leading characters are wise and witty... Reprinted from JTW.

1929: It was Easter as I walked in the public gardens... Reprinted from P.

Many happy returns*: Johnny, since today is... Reprinted in CSP. Dedicated to John Rettger.

Nobody understands me: Just as his dream foretold, he met them all... Reprinted from LS.

Mundus et infans*: Kicking his mother until she let go of his soul... First printed in *Commonweal*, 30 October 1942, and reprinted in CSP, PA, and CSP2. Dedicated to Arthur and Angelyn Stevens.

Law like love: Law, say the gardeners, is the sun ... Reprinted from AT.

Edward Lear: Left by his friend to breakfast alone on the white ... Reprinted from AT.

The bonfires: Look there! The sunk road winding ... Reprinted from P2.

Too dear, too vague: Love by ambition ... Reprinted from P.

Meiosis: Love had him fast but though he fought for breath ... Reprinted from LS.

Oxford: Nature is so near: the rooks in the college garden ... Reprinted from AT.

Please make yourself at home: Not as that dream Napoleon, rumour's dread and centre ... Reprinted from AT.

All over again: Not from this life, not from this life is any ... Reprinted from "Paid on both sides" in P.

Not all the candidates pass: Now from my window-sill I watch the night ... Reprinted from LS.

Pascal: O had his mother, near her time, been praying ... Reprinted from AT.

Perhaps: O Love, the interest itself in thoughtless Heaven ... Reprinted from LS.

Casino: Only the hands are living; to the wheel attracted ... Reprinted from LS.

Such nice people: On Sunday walks ... Reprinted from P.

Spring 1940: O season of repetition and return ... Reprinted from DM.

In Father's footsteps: Our hunting fathers told the story ... Reprinted from LS.

A summer night 1933: Out on the lawn I lie in bed ... Reprinted from LS.

Montaigne: Outside his library window he could see ... Reprinted from DM.

Epitaph on a tyrant: Perfection, of a kind, was what he was after ... Reprinted from AT.

The prophets: Perhaps I always knew what they were saying ... Reprinted from AT.

The capital: Quarter of pleasures where the rich are always waiting ... Reprinted from AT.

Autumn 1940: Returning each morning from a timeless world ... Reprinted from DM.

Shut your eyes and open your mouth: Sentries against inner and outer ... Reprinted from P.

Heavy date: Sharp and silent in the ... Reprinted from AT.

Venus will now say a few words: Since you are going to begin today ... Reprinted from P.

Petition: Sir, no man's enemy, forgiving all ... Reprinted from P.

Dover 1937: Steep roads, a tunnel through the downs are the approaches ... Reprinted from AT.

As well as can be expected: Taller today, we remember similar evenings ... Reprinted from P.

Through the looking-glass: The earth turns over; our side feels the cold ... Reprinted from LS.

The lesson*: The first time that I dreamed, we were in flight ... Reprinted in CSP, PA, and CSP2.

Aera sub lege: The hidden law does not deny ... Reprinted from DM.

Our bias: The hour-glass whispers to the lion's paw ... Reprinted from AT.

Christmas 1940*: The journals give the quantities of wrong... First printed
  in *Decision*, February 1941, and reprinted in *Horizon*, April 1941, and CSP.
Rimbaud: The nights, the railway-arches, the bad sky... Reprinted from
  AT.
The decoys: There are some birds in these valleys... Reprinted from O.
Like us: These had stopped seeking... Reprinted from O.
Leap before you look*: The sense of danger must not disappear... First
  printed in *Decision*, April 1941; revised and reprinted in CSP and CSP2.
In memory of Ernst Toller: The shining neutral summer has no voice...
  Reprinted from AT.
Happy ending: The silly fool, the silly fool... Reprinted from P.
At the grave of Henry James*: The snow, less intransigeant than their mar-
  ble... First printed in *Horizon*, June 1941; reprinted in the *Partisan re-
  view*, July–August 1941, and in this revised form in CSP. Revised again in
  CSP2.
It's too much: The spring unsettles sleeping partnerships... Reprinted from
  "Paid on both sides" in P.
The ship: The streets are brightly lit; our city is kept clean... Reprinted
  from JTW.
Family ghosts: The string's excitement, the applauding drum... Reprinted
  from P.
The creatures: They are our past and our future; the poles between which our
  desire unceasingly is discharged... Reprinted from AT.
A healthy spot*: They're nice—one would never dream of going over...
  Reprinted in CSP and CSP2.
Pur: This lunar beauty... Reprinted from P.
But I can't*: Time will say nothing but I told you so... First printed in
  Vice versa, January–February 1941, and reprinted in CSP, PA ("If I could
  tell you"), CSP2, and SelP.
Which side am I supposed to be on?: Though aware of our rank and alert to
  obey orders... Reprinted from O.
Year after year: Though he believe it, no man is strong... Reprinted from
  "Paid on both sides" in P.
What do *you* think?: To ask the hard question is simple... Reprinted from
  P2.
The unknown citizen: He was found by the Bureau of Statistics to be...
  Reprinted from AT.
What's the matter?: To lie flat on the back with the knees flexed... Re-
  printed from LS.
Remember: Tonight the many come to mind... Reprinted from "Paid on
  both sides" in P.
It's so dull here: To settle in this village of the heart... Reprinted from LS.
The walking tour: To throw away the key and walk away... Reprinted
  from "Paid on both sides" in P.
Herman Melville: Towards the end he sailed into an extraordinary mildness...
  Reprinted from AT.
When the devil drives: Under boughs between our tentative endearments how
  should we hear... Reprinted from P.
The riddle: Underneath the leaves of life... Reprinted from AT.
Do be careful: Upon this line between adventure... Reprinted from P.
Brussels in winter: Wandering the cold streets tangled like old string... Re-
  printed from AT.
We all make mistakes: Watch any day his nonchalant pauses, see... Re-
  printed from P.

January 1, 1931: Watching in three planes from a room overlooking the court-yard... Reprinted from O.

Have a good time: "We have brought you," they said, "a map of the country... Reprinted from O.

Let history be my judge: We made all possible preparations... Reprinted from P.

Orpheus: What does the song hope for? And the moved hands... Reprinted from AT.

The exiles: What siren zooming is sounding our coming... Reprinted from O.

Few and simple*: Whenever you are thought, the mind... Reprinted in CSP.

Canzone*: When shall we learn, what should be clear as day... First printed in *Partisan review*, September–October 1943 and in the *Bulletin of the New York Public Library*, November 1943; reprinted in CSP.

In memory of Sigmund Freud: When there are so many we shall have to mourn... Reprinted from AT.

The voyage: Where does the journey look which the watcher upon the quay... Reprinted from JTW.

Crisis: Where do They come from? Those whom we so much dread... Reprinted from AT.

Epithalamion: While explosives blow to dust... Reprinted from AT.

The watershed: Who stands, the crux left of the watershed... Reprinted from P (1928).

Better not: Who will endure... Reprinted from P2.

The questioner who sits so sly: Will you turn a deaf ear... Reprinted from P.

Luther: With conscience cocked to listen for the thunder... Reprinted from DM.

As he is: Wrapped in a yielding air, beside... Reprinted from AT.

Spain 1937: Yesterday all the past. The language of size... Reprinted from the pamphlet (1937).

The witnesses: Young men late in the night... Reprinted from DBS.

Part II Letter to a wound. Reprinted from O.

Part III Songs and other musical pieces

    I As I walked out one evening... Reprinted from AT.

    II At last the secret is out, as it always must come in the end... Reprinted from AF6.

    III *Carry her over the water... From the libretto *Paul Bunyan;* reprinted in CSP and CSP2.

    IV Dear, though the night is gone... Reprinted from LS.

    V *Eyes look into the well... Reprinted in CSP and CSP2.

    VI Fish in the unruffled lakes... Reprinted from LS.

    VII *"Gold in the North," came the blizzard to say... From the libretto *Paul Bunyan;* reprinted in CSP.

    VIII *Song for St. Cecilia's day: In a garden shady this holy lady... Reprinted from the pamphlet (1941).

    IX *Jumbled in the common box... First printed in *Nation*, 29 March 1941, and reprinted in *Mint*, 1946, CSP, PA ("Doomsday song"), CSP2, and revised in SelP ("Domesday song").

    X *Lady, weeping at the crossroads... From the radio script *The dark valley;* reprinted in CSP, PA, and CSP2.

    XI Lay your sleeping head, my love... Reprinted from AT.

    XII Let me tell you a little story... Reprinted from AT.

XIII Let the florid music praise... Reprinted from LS.
XIV Look, stranger, on this island now... Reprinted from LS.
XV May with its light behaving... Reprinted from LS.
XVI *My second thoughts condemn... Reprinted in CSP and CSP2.
XVII Not, Father, further do prolong... Reprinted from O.
XVIII Now the leaves are falling fast... Reprinted from LS.
XIX Now through night's caressing grip... Reprinted from DBS.
XX "O for doors to be open and an invite with gilded edges... Reprinted from LS.
XXI O lurcher-loving collier, black as night... Reprinted from AT.
XXII O the valley in the summer where I and my John... Reprinted from AT.
XXIII Over the heather the wet wind blows... Reprinted from AT.
XXIV O what is that sound which so thrills the ear... Reprinted from AT.
XXV "O where are you going?" said reader to rider... Reprinted from O.
XXVI "O who can ever gaze his fill"... Reprinted from LFI.
XXVII O who can ever praise enough... Reprinted from LFI.
XXVIII Say this city has ten million souls... Reprinted from AT.
XXIX Seen when night is silent... Reprinted from DBS.
XXX Stop all clocks, cut off the telephone... Reprinted from AF6 originally, and this version from AT.
XXXI That night when joy began... Reprinted from LS.
XXXII *The single creature leads a partial life... From the libretto *Paul Bunyan;* reprinted in *Harper's bazaar*, April 1945, CSP, and CSP2.
XXXIII The summer quickens all... Reprinted from "Paid on both sides" in P.
XXXIV *Though determined Nature can... Reprinted in CSP and CSP2.
XXXV Underneath the abject willow... Reprinted from LS.
XXXVI Victor was a little baby... Reprinted from AT.
XXXVII Warm are the still and lucky miles... Reprinted from AT.
XXXVIII What's in your mind, my dove, my coney... Reprinted from P2.
Part IV Depravity: A sermon. Reprinted from DBS.
Part V The quest: A sonnet sequence. Reprinted from DM.
Part VI New Year letter. Reprinted from DM.
Part VII In time of war: A sonnet sequence with a verse commentary. Reprinted from JTW.
Part VIII The sea and the mirror: A commentary on Shakespeare's *The tempest*. Reprinted from FTB.
Part IX For the time being: A Christmas oratorio. Reprinted from FTB.

Notes: Published 5 April 1945 in an impression of 4,800 copies at $3.75, and reprinted in April 1945 (3,800 copies), June 1945 (2,250 copies), July 1945 (3,800 copies), April 1946 (5,500 copies), December 1948 (2,000 copies), November 1949 (1,500 copies), February 1951 (2,500 copies), December 1952 (1,950 copies), April 1954 (1,400 copies), August 1955 (1,400 copies), February 1956 (1,400 copies), March 1957 (1,000 copies), January 1958 (2,400 copies), May 1959 (1,500 copies), August 1960 (2,000 copies), December 1961 (2,050 copies), July 1963 (2,500 copies), September 1964 (3,000 copies), April 1966 (3,000 copies), and June 1967 (3,000 copies).

The proposal for the book first came from Auden in a letter to Bennett Cerf dated 8 January 1942 from Ann Arbor. The publisher was not enthusiastic, and Auden wrote several letters before Random House agreed to publish. The book was first planned for a publication date in April 1944, before FTB, but this was delayed. The manuscript was delivered to the publisher on 13 December 1943. Auden added further poems in a letter dated 18 September [1944], from Swarthmore; another letter dated 20 September [1944] refers to *"Poems 1928–1942* (or 43)" as "the definitive collection of all I wish to preserve." On 7 November [1944] Auden asked that this sentence be used as the dust jacket copy for the book: "This volume contains all that Mr Auden wishes to preserve of the poetry he has written so far." On 20 January 1945 Auden wrote: "As to the title, I want *Poems 1928–1945*. The word Collected suggests finality which I *hope*, anyway, is incorrect," but Auden's editor resisted this, saying that readers would lose interest if the book were so dated. The decision to include FTB was made very late, for in a number of letters Auden asked for a postscript to his preface explaining why CP has been delayed until after the publication of FTB. On 23 March [1945] Auden asked that the epigraph be corrected in the second impression (for 'the neural' read 'their neural'), and that asterisks be added to the titles of the poems "Atlantis" and "But I can't"; these and some other corrections were made.

Later John Lehmann wrote, "Indeed, I was disarmed myself when he told me at parting, with a pleasure that found an immediate response in me, that the American Navy had ordered 1,100 copies of his collected poems" (J. Lehmann, *I am my brother* [London: Longmans, 1960], pp. 290–91).

Reviews:

K. Bache. *Yale poetry review*, I (Autumn 1945), 30–34.

L. Bogan. *New Yorker*, XXI (14 April 1945), 78, 81 [New York edition, pp. 86, 89].

B. Deutsch. *New York herald tribune*, 8 July 1945, section 6, p. 2.

F. W. Dupee. *Nation*, CLX (26 May 1945), 605.

F. C. Flint. *New York times*, 8 April 1945, section 7, pp. 1, 28–29.

A. Fremantle. *Commonweal*, XLII (25 May 1945), 141–43.

R. Lechlitner. *Poetry*, LXVI (July 1945), 204–15.

G. A. McCanliff. *Spirit*, XII (September 1945), 122–24.

D. S. Norton. *Virginia quarterly review*, XXI (Summer 1945), 434–41.

R. Richman. *Accent*, V (Summer 1945), 249–53.

T. Spencer. *Atlantic*, CLXXV (June 1945), 127.

D. A. Stauffer. *Yale review*, XXXIV (June 1945), 733–34.

L. Untermeyer. *Saturday review of literature*, XXVIII (28 April 1945), 10.

U.S. quarterly book list, I (September 1945), 11–12.

J. van Druten. *Kenyon review*, VII (Summer 1945), 507–11.

O. Williams. *Tomorrow*, IV (June 1945), 74.

A 28   LITANY AND ANTHEM FOR   1946 S. MATTHEW'S DAY

[in brown] [a kneeling angel with scroll bearing 'S • MATTHEW • +'] | LITANY AND | ANTHEM FOR | S. MATTHEW'S | DAY | [in black] BY W. H. | AUDEN | WRITTEN FOR THE CHURCH OF | S. MATTHEW, NORTHAMPTON, FOR | THE DEDICATION AND PATRONAL | FESTIVAL, 21 SEPTEMBER 1946

Collation: 8 x 16 in. folding twice to 8 x 5⅗₀ in. Single sheet printed on both sides.
Binding: None.
Paper: Cream unwatermarked wove paper.
Contents:
    Litany for S. Matthew's day.

Anthem for S. Matthew's day
> Praise ye the lord: Let the whole creation give out another sweetness...
> Bless ye the lord: We elude Him, lie to Him, yet His love observes...   Revised in AA. A substantial excerpt is quoted in *Time*, L (21 July 1947), 57.

Notes: Stanton and Son, the printers, of Northampton say that they printed 500 copies of this piece.

This piece was specially written for the Festival of holy music and poetry at S. Matthew's Church and was performed on 21 September 1946 at 3 p.m. Britten and Valentine Dyall also took part.

There are copies in the British Museum Library, Harvard College Library, and the Lockwood Memorial Library.

A 29   THE AGE OF ANXIETY   1947

a) **First edition**

THE | AGE OF ANXIETY | *A BAROQUE ECLOGUE* | [double rule] | W. H. AUDEN | *Lacrimosa dies illa* | *Qua resurget ex favilla* | *Iudicandus homo reus* | Thomas a Celano (?) | *Dies Irae* | [rule] | RANDOM HOUSE · NEW YORK

Collation: 7 x 4¾ in. [1–3]¹⁶ [4]⁸ [5]¹⁶, pp. [i–vi, 1–2] 3–138.
[i]: half title. [ii]: blank. [iii]: title page. [iv]: 'COPYRIGHT, 1946, 1947, BY W. H. AUDEN | FIRST PRINTING | [five lines] | ...PUBLISHED IN NEW YORK BY RANDOM | HOUSE, INC., AND SIMULTANEOUSLY IN TORONTO, CANADA, BY | RANDOM HOUSE OF CANADA, LIMITED, 1947. | MANUFACTURED IN THE UNITED STATES OF AMERICA | BY KINGSPORT PRESS, INC., KINGSPORT, TENN. | A.B.' [v]: 'To | JOHN BETJEMAN'. [vi]: blank. [1]–138: text; 2, 26, 28, 58, 60, 108, 128, and 130 blank.
Binding: Bound in dark bluish green (165) cloth lettered across the spine in gold: '[double rule and floral ornament] | [author and title on a brown panel between two brown gold-bordered bands] | [gold rule] | THE | AGE | OF | ANX- | IETY | *W. H.* | *Auden* | [gold rule] | [on the cloth] RANDOM | HOUSE | [double rule]'. All edges trimmed, and top edge stained reddish brown. Cream dust jacket printed in black and red.
The fourth and fifth impressions are bound in brown cloth.
Paper: White unwatermarked wove paper.
Contents: The age of anxiety.
The following pieces also appeared separately:
> How still it is; the horses...p. 62. First printed in *Silo*, Spring 1946 ("Noon"), and reprinted, with two other short pieces (Lights are moving...p. 63, Bending forward...p. 64), in PA ("Three dreams") and CSP2.
> These ancient harbours are hailed by the morning...pp. 71–72. First printed in *Inventario*, Autumn–Winter 1946–47 ("Landfall").
> The scene has all the signs of a facetious culture...pp. 75–77. First printed in *Commonweal*, 20 December 1946 ("Metropolis").
> Opera glasses on the ormolu table...pp. 80–81. First printed in *New Yorker*, 28 September 1946 ("Spinster's song").
> How tempting to trespass in these Italian gardens...pp. 87–88. First published in *Changing world*, Summer 1947 ("Baroque").
> Sob, heavy world...pp. 104–6. Reprinted in *Horizon*, March 1948 ("Lament for a lawgiver").

To elude Him, lie to Him, yet His love observes ... pp. 137–38. First printed
in *Litany and anthem for S. Matthew's day* (1946) and revised here.
The whole piece is reprinted with slight revisions in CLP.

Notes: Published 11 July 1947 in an impression of 3,500 copies at $2.50, and re-
printed in August 1947 (3,000 copies), October 1947 (1,500 copies), June 1948
(1,000 copies), August 1949 (1,000 copies), September 1951 (726 copies), May 1953
(1,000 copies), November 1956 (1,000 copies), May 1960 (1,000 copies), October
1962 (1,050 copies), October 1966 (1,000 copies), and December 1967 (1,500
copies).

The second impression extensively revises and corrects the text and drops,
unintentionally, line 25 on p. 18. A copy of the first impression at Harvard College
Library is dated by Auden on p. 138 "July '44–Nov. '46", and includes in manuscript the corrections made in the second impression, together with some others.
A draft manuscript of the poem is in the University of Texas Library.

The first stage version of the poem appears to have been that presented at the
Living Theatre Studio in New York opening on 18 March 1954, directed by
Judith Malina and Julian Beck. Music was by Jackson MacLow, and James Agee
was a member of the cast. The printed programme gives no indication that Auden
took any part. The poem was staged again at Princeton University by the "Theatre
Intime," in a version by Graham Ferguson and John Becker, 28 April–7 May 1960.
The music was by Norm Symonds, and had been broadcast by the CBC in Febru-
ary 1958. For this production Auden, Sean O'Faolain, Jimmy Durante, and Fanny
Hurst recorded the narration, which was played back through a television set on
stage.[16] (Auden is listed in the printed programme as "Communicator.") A further
revised version, by Becker alone, was to have been produced at the Sheridan
Square Playhouse in New York in late 1961 or 1962, with a filmed insert of Auden
reading the narration, but this production seems never to have reached the stage.
A typescript of a version by Ferguson (1962?) is in Brown University Library.

The work became the basis of Leonard Bernstein's *Symphony, no. 2* in 1948,
which in turn was used in Jerome Robbins's ballet *The age of anxiety* in 1950.

Auden was awarded a Pulitzer Prize for 1948 for this piece.

Reviews:

J. Barzun. *Harper's magazine*, CXCV (September 1947), [back matter, pp. i–ii].

L. Bogan. *New Yorker*, XXIII (26 July 1947), 57–59 [New York edition, pp. 64–66].

W. Elder. *Atlantic*, CLXXX (September 1947), 126–27.

W. Elton. *Poetry*, LXXI (November 1947), 90–94.

J. Ingalls. *Saturday review of literature*, XXX (19 July 1947), 18.

R. Jarrell. *Nation*, CLXV (18 October 1947), 424.

L. Martz. *Yale review*, XXXVII (December 1947), 333–35.

G. Mayberry. *New republic*, CXVII (14 July 1947), 28–29.

M. Moore. *New York times*, 27 July 1947, section 7, p. 5.

C. G. Paulding. *Commonweal*, XLVI (29 August 1947), 485–86.

M. L. Rosenthal. *New York herald tribune*, 20 July 1947, section 6, p. 3.

D. Schwartz. *Partisan review*, XIV (September–October 1947), 528–30.

U.S. quarterly book list, IV (March 1948), 23.

b) First English edition   1948

THE | AGE OF ANXIETY | [double rule] | *A BAROQUE EC-
LOGUE* | by | W. H. AUDEN | *Lacrimosa dies illa* | *Qua resurget ex*

---

[16] Two excerpts from this adaptation were published in *University: a Princeton magazine*,
5 (Summer 1960), 21, 23, 25.

favilla | *Iudicandus homo reus* | Thomas a Celano (?) | Dies Irae | FABER AND FABER LIMITED | 24 Russell Square | London

Collation: 8½ x 5½ in. [A]–H⁸, pp. [1–10] 11–126 [127–128].
  [1–2]: blank. [3]: half title. [4]: blank. [5]: title page. [6]: '*First published in Mcmxlviii* | *by Faber and Faber Limited* | *24 Russell Square London W.C.1* | *Printed in Breat Britain by* | *Western Printing Services Ltd., Bristol* | [one line]'. [7]: 'To | JOHN BETJEMAN'. [8]: blank. [9]–126: text; 10, 30, 32, 56, 58, 94, 96, 100, 102, 118, and 120 blank. [127–128]: blank.
Binding: Bound in brilliant greenish yellow (98) cloth lettered down the spine in gold: 'THE AGE OF ANXIETY   W. H. AUDEN   FABER'. All edges trimmed. Light blue dust jacket printed in brown.
Paper: Cream unwatermarked wove paper.
Contents: As the American edition.
Notes: Published 17 September 1948 in an impression of 3,000 copies at 8/6d. and reprinted in January 1949 (1,500 copies) and March 1956 (1,516 copies). Out of print in June 1966.
Reviews:
  H. A. L. Craig. *Spectator*, CLXXXI (10 December 1948), 774, 776.
  P. Dickinson. *Horizon*, XIX (May 1949), 377–78.
  W. Gardiner. *Poetry quarterly*, X (Summer 1948), 107–10.
  H. A. Mason. *Scrutiny*, XV (Spring 1948), 155–60.
  N. Moore. *Poetry* (London), 15 (May 1949), 21–23.
  G. D. Painter. *Listener*, XL (7 October 1948), 537–38.
  H. Peschmann. *New English weekly*, XXIV (3 February 1949), 200–201.
  S. Rafferty. *Time and tide*, XXIX (6 November 1948), 1130.
  G. Romilly. *New statesman & nation*, XXXVI (30 October 1948), 376.
  Times literary supplement, 23 October 1948, p. 596 (see also subsequent correspondence, 13 November 1948, p. 639).

A 30   COLLECTED SHORTER POEMS, 1930–1944   1950

COLLECTED | SHORTER POEMS | 1930–1944 | by | W. H. AUDEN | FABER AND FABER LTD | 24 Russell Square | London

Collation: 8 x 5¼ in. [A]–T⁸, pp. [1–8] 9–303 [304].
  [1–2]: blank. [3]: half title. [4]: 'by W. H. Auden | [twenty lines]'. [5]: title page. [6]: '*First published in mcml* | *by Faber and Faber Limited* | *24 Russell Square London W.C.1* | *Printed in Great Britain by* | *Latimer Trend & Co. Ltd. Plymouth* | [one line]'. [7]: 'To | Christopher Isherwood | and | Chester Kallman'. [8]: quatrain. 9: preface. [10]: blank. 11–15: contents. [16]: blank. [17]: 'PART ONE | [star] | *Poems*'. [18]: blank. 19–196: text: [197]: 'PART TWO | [star] | *Paid on Both Sides*'. [198]: blank. 199–223: text. [224]: blank. [225]: 'PART THREE | [star] | *Songs and Other Musical Pieces*'. [226]: blank. 227–268: text. [269]: 'PART FOUR | [star] | *In Time of War* | *A Sonnet Sequence* | *with a verse commentary*'. [270]: blank. 271–296: text. 297–303: index of first lines. [304]: blank.
Binding: Bound in brilliant blue (177) cloth lettered across the spine in gold: 'Collected | Shorter | Poems | 1930–1944 | [star] | W. H. | AUDEN | Faber'. All edges trimmed. Yellow dust jacket printed in black and red.
Paper: Cream unwatermarked wove paper.
Contents:
  Whether conditioned by God or their neural structure, still ... Reprinted from CP.

Part I Poems. Most of the poems in this section are identical with those in the comparable section in CP, but the following changes should be noted:

"The labyrinth," "Always in trouble," "We're late," "True enough," "The diaspora," "For the last time," "All over again," "Spring 1940," "Montaigne," "Autumn 1940," "Blessed event," "It's too much," "Year after year," "Remember," "Aera sub lege," "The walking tour," and "Luther" are omitted. These poems were all originally published as parts of longer works.

The following poems change title:

American title	English title
Two's company	Never stronger
Make up your mind	Easy knowledge
As we like it	Our city
Something is bound to happen	The wanderer
Are you there?	Alone
I shall be enchanted	Legend
The cultural presupposition	Culture
Nobody understands me	Nobody understands
Please make yourself at home	Like a vocation
In father's footsteps	Our hunting fathers
As well as can be expected	Taller today
Pur	Like a dream
But I can't	If I could tell you
What do you think?	The hard question
Do be careful	Between adventure
We all make mistakes	A free one

The following poems are added:

Birthday poem (to Christopher Isherwood): August for the people and their favourite islands... Reprinted from LS.

The Malverns: Here on the cropped grass of the narrow ridge I stand... Reprinted from LS.

Two worlds: The chimneys are smoking, the crocus is out in the border... Reprinted from LS.

Prothalamion: You who return tonight to a narrow bed... Reprinted from DBS.

Part II Paid on both sides. Reprinted from P.

Part III Songs and other musical pieces. This section is identical with that in CP except that XXXIII, which is taken from "Paid on both sides," is omitted.

Part IV In time of war. This section is identical with that in CP.

Notes: Published 9 March 1950 in an impression of 5,280 copies at 15/–, and reprinted in August 1953 (2,000 copies), March 1956 (2,000 copies), January 1959 (3,000 copies), and November 1962 (3,000 copies).

Most of the book was probably set up from a corrected copy of CP, since on p. [4] the Faber edition copies the CP list of Auden's books which gives P as including O and DD, which, of course, is not so in the English editions.

Reviews:

R. Abercrombie. *Spectator*, CLXXXIV (14 April 1950), 510, 512.

R. Campbell. *Nine*, II (Autumn 1950), 344–46.

E. Gillett. *National and English review*, CXXXV (July 1950), 136–40.

G. Grigson. *World review*, n.s. 21 (November 1950), 30–31.

G. D. Painter. *Listener*, XLIII (20 April 1950), 705–6.

S. Spender. *New statesman & nation*, XXXIX (18 March 1950), 306, 308.

——. *Times literary supplement*, 6 August 1954, p. vi (see also subsequent correspondence, 10 September 1954, p. 573).

Wind and the rain, VII (1951), 192–97.

A 31   THE ENCHAFÈD FLOOD   1950

a) First edition

The Enchafèd Flood | OR *The Romantic Iconography of the Sea* | W. H.
AUDEN | [wavy rule] | [rule] | [wavy rule] | RANDOM HOUSE ·
NEW YORK | [device: a house]

Collation: 7½ x 5 in. [1–3]¹⁶[4]²⁰[5]¹⁶ pp. [i–x, 1] 2–154 [155–158].
   [i]: half title. [ii]: 'These lectures were delivered at | the University of Virginia
under | the Page-Barbour Foundation on | March 22, 23, 24, 1949.' [iii]: title page.
[iv]: '[two lines] | First Printing | [etc.]'. [v]: 'FOR | ALAN ANSEN | [double
rule] | [three-line quotation from Baudelaire]'. [vi]: blank. [vii]: acknowledge-
ment. [viii]: blank. [ix]: contents. [x]: blank. [1]–154: text; 2, 40, 42, and 92 blank.
[155–158]: blank.
Binding: Bound in very dark green (147) cloth lettered down the spine in white:
'[in a rectangle superimposed on another rectangle] The Enchafèd Flood · *W. H.
AUDEN* | [across the foot of the spine] [device] | *RANDOM* | *HOUSE*', and
on the front cover: 'The Enchafèd Flood | [ornament]'. All edges trimmed, and
the top edge stained green. Grey dust jacket printed in black and red.
Paper: White unwatermarked wove paper.
Contents:
   The enchafèd flood
      I   The sea and the desert.
      II   The stone and the shell.
      III   Ishmael—Don Quixote.
Notes: Published 17 March 1950 [*CCE* 23 February 1950] in an edition of 2,500
copies at $2.50. Out of print in 1952.
Reviews:
   J. Barzun. *Yale review*, XXXIX (June 1950), 730–33.
   R. C. B. Brown. *Voices*, 143 (Autumn 1950), 41–45.
   D. Bush. *Virginia quarterly review*, XXVI (Summer 1950), 472–76.
   R. Chase. *Kenyon review*, XII (Autumn 1950), 717–21.
   D. Daiches. *New republic*, CXXII (17 April 1950), 27.
   B. Deutsch. *New York herald tribune*, 26 March 1950, section 6, p. 10.
   D. Fitts. *New York times*, 10 September 1950, section 7, p. 35.
   J. Gray. *Saturday review of literature*, XXXIII (15 April 1950), 40–42.
   M. Greenberg. *Nation*, CLXX (29 April 1950), 407–8.
   G. Grigson. *World review*, n.s. 21 (November 1950), 30–31.
   J. Randall. *Hopkins review*, III (Summer 1950), 39–42.
   M. K. Spears. *Poetry*, LXXVI (August 1950), 291–94.
   U.S. quarterly book list, VI (June 1950), 149.
   E. Wilson. *New Yorker*, XXVI (15 April 1950), 106, 109 [New York edition, pp.
   129–30].

b) First English edition   1951

THE | ENCHAFÈD FLOOD | *or* | *The Romantic Iconography* | *of the*
Sea | by | W. H. AUDEN | [ornament: a shell] | FABER AND FABER
LIMITED | 24 Russell Square | London

Collation: 8½ x 5½ in. [A]–H⁸, pp. [1–8] 9–126 [127–128].
[1–2]: blank. [3]: half title. [4]: 'by the same author | [eleven lines]'. [5]: title
page. [6]: '*First published in Mcmli | by Faber and Faber Limited | 24 Russell
Square London W. C. 1 | Printed in Great Britain by | Latimer Trend & Co. Ltd.
Plymouth |* [one line]'. [7]: 'For | ALAN ANSEL [sic] | [ornament and three-
line quotation]'. [8]: blank. 9: acknowledgement. [10]: blank. 11: contents. [12]:
blank. [13]–126: text; 14, 44, 80, and 82 blank. [127–128]: blank.
Binding: Bound in brilliant blue (177) cloth lettered across the spine in gold:
'[triple wavy rule] | *The | Enchafèd | Flood |* [triple wavy rule] | *W. H. |
AUDEN | Faber*'. All edges trimmed. White dust jacket printed in red, blue, and
pale green.
Paper: Cream unwatermarked wove paper.
Contents: As the American edition.
Notes: Published 26 January 1951 in an edition of 3,430 copies at 10/6d. and out of
print in November 1960.
Reviews:
R. G. Cox. *Scrutiny*, XVIII (Autumn 1951), 158–59.
C. Davy. *Time and tide*, XXXII (17 March 1951), 240–41.
E. M. Forster. *Listener*, XLV (26 April 1951), 673.
E. Muir. *Observer*, 18 March 1951, p. 7.
D. Newton. *Poetry* (London), 23 (Winter 1951), 30.
K. Raine. *New statesman & nation*, XLI (3 March 1951), 252–53.
S. Spender. *Spectator*, CLXXXVI (9 February 1951), 183.
Times literary supplement, 23 February 1951, p. 114.

c) First paperback impression   1967

THE | ENCHAFÈD | FLOOD | *or* | *The Romantic Iconography* | *of the
Sea* | W. H. AUDEN | [device: sun with a face] | VINTAGE BOOKS |
A DIVISION OF RANDOM HOUSE | NEW YORK

Collation: 7¼ x 4¼ in. Eighty single leaves, pp. [i–viii, 1–2] 3–151 [152].
[i]: half title. [ii]: note on the lectures. [iii]: title page. [iv]: 'FIRST VINTAGE
BOOKS EDITION, September, 1967 | [twelve lines]'. [v]: dedication [vi]: ac-
knowledgement. [vii]: contents. [viii]: blank. [1]–151: text; 88 blank. [152]:
biographical note on Auden.
Binding: A perfect binding glued in a stiff white card cover printed with a brilliant
blue (177) spine and front cover and lettered down the spine: '[in red] *W. H.
AUDEN* [in white] *THE ENCHAFÈD FLOOD* | [across the spine] [device] |
Vintage | V–398', and on the front cover: '[on a white panel in red] *W. H.
AUDEN* | [title in white on black] *The | Enchafèd | Flood* [subtitle in blue on
black] *Three critical essays | on the romantic spirit* | [in white on blue] *V–398*
[in white on red] *A Vintage Book* [in white on blue] [device] *$1.65*'. The rear
cover carries extracts from reviews of the original publication. Cover design by
George Salter. All edges trimmed.
Paper: White unwatermarked wove paper.
Contents: As the first edition.
Notes: Published 23 October 1967 in an impression of 7,184 copies at $1.65. (Some
copies of this impression were hardbound and issued by Peter Smith, Magnolia,
Mass., in 1968 at $3.75.) Reprinted January 1969 (3,051 copies).

A 32   NONES   1951

a) **First edition**

NONES | [rule] | *W. H. AUDEN* | [device: a house] | RANDOM
HOUSE · NEW YORK

Collation: 9 x 5¾ in. [1–5]⁸, pp. [3–10] 11–81 [82].
    [pp. 1 and 2 are the front flyleaf]. [3]: half title. [4]: blank. [5]: title page. [6]:
'*First Printing* | [six lines] | COPYRIGHT, . . . 1951, BY W. H. AUDEN |
[etc.]'. [7]: 'To Reinhold and Ursula Niebuhr | [twenty-eight lines of verse]'.
[8]: blank. [9–10]: contents. 11–81: text. [82]: blank.
Binding: Quarter bound in dark blue (183) cloth with yellowish grey paper boards,
    and lettered down the spine in gold: '*W. H. AUDEN* [grey rule] NONES [grey
rule] RANDOM HOUSE'. The rules are continued on the front cover to form
a rectangle within which are the dates: '1947–1950', and the publisher's device is
within a similar rectangle on the rear cover. All edges trimmed, and the top edge
stained dark blue. Pale grey dust jacket printed in grey and red. The fourth and
fifth impressions are lettered in silver.
Paper: White unwatermarked wove paper.
Contents:

    To Reinhold and Ursula Niebuhr: We, too, had known golden hours . . . Re-
    printed in CSP2.
    Prime: Simultaneously, as soundlessly . . . The "first" publication of this poem
    is on the recording *Pleasure dome* (1949). This poem was also distributed by
Auden as a 3 fol. mimeographed leaflet to the audience at a lecture he gave at
Swarthmore College on 9 March 1950, titled "Nature, history, and poetry";
this leaflet includes extensive quotations from early manuscript readings. The
poem is reprinted in SA, PA, CSP2, and SelP.
    In praise of limestone: If it form the one landscape that we the inconstant ones . . .
    First printed in *Horizon*, July 1948, and revised in PA, CSP2, and SelP.
    One circumlocution: Sometimes we see astonishingly clearly . . . First printed in
    Third hour, 1951, and reprinted in PA and CSP2.
    Their lonely betters: As I listened from a beach-chair in the shade . . . Reprinted
    in PA and CSP2.
    Serenade: On and on and on . . . First printed in *Atlantic*, November 1947, and
    reprinted in *Phoenix quarterly*, 1948, and CSP2.
    Song: Deftly, admiral, cast your fly . . . First printed in *Horizon*, November 1948,
    and reprinted in *Voices*, Spring 1949, revised here and reprinted in PA and
CSP2. Also reprinted in *New York herald tribune*, 24 April 1949, section 2, p. 6.
    The love feast: In an upper room at midnight . . . Reprinted in CSP2.
    Air port: Let out where two fears intersect, a point selected . . . Reprinted in
    CSP2 ("In transit").
    Ischia: There is a time to admit how much the sword decides . . . First printed
    in *Botteghe oscure*, 2 (1948), and reprinted in *Nation*, 22 April 1950, PA, and
CSP2. Dedicated to Brian Howard.
    Pleasure island: What there is as a surround to our figures . . . First printed in
    Commentary, May 1949, and reprinted in CSP2.
    In Schrafft's: Having finished the Blue-plate Special . . . First printed in *New
    Yorker*, 12 February 1949, and reprinted in CSP2.
    The fall of Rome: The piers are pummelled by the waves . . . First printed in
    Horizon, April 1947, and reprinted in *Nation*, 14 June 1947, PA, CSP2, SelP,
and *I and thou*, January–February 1969. Dedicated to Cyril Connolly.

Music ho: The Emperor's favourite concubine... Reprinted in CSP2.

Nursery rhyme: Their learned kings bent down to chat with frogs... First printed in *Mademoiselle*, October 1947, and reprinted in CSP2.

The managers: In the bad old days it was not so bad... First printed in *Horizon*, November 1948, and reprinted in *Reporter*, 10 May 1949, PA, and CSP2.

Memorial for the city: The eyes of the crow and the eye of the camera open... First printed in *Horizon*, November 1949, and reprinted in CSP2 where it is dedicated to Charles Williams. Part III is reprinted in PA ("Barbed wire").

Under Sirius: Yes, these are the dog-days, Fortunatus... First printed in *Horizon*, October 1949, and reprinted in PA and CSP2.

Not in Baedeker: There were lead-mines here before the Romans... Reprinted in CSP2.

Cattivo tempo: Sirocco brings the minor devils... First printed in *Horizon*, October 1949, and reprinted in CSP2.

The chimeras: Absence of heart—as in public buildings... Reprinted in *Times literary supplement*, 9 March 1951, and CSP2.

Secrets: That we are always glad... First printed in *Ladies' home journal*, August 1950, and reprinted in CSP2.

Numbers and faces: The Kingdom of Number is all boundaries... Reprinted in PA and CSP2.

Nones: What we know to be not possible... Reprinted in SA, PA, CSP2, and SelP.

A household: When, to disarm suspicious minds at lunch... Reprinted in PA and CSP2.

The duet: All winter long the huge sad lady... First printed in *Kenyon review*, Autumn 1947, and reprinted in *Changing world*, May–July 1948, and *Listener*, 24 November 1949, and CSP2.

Footnotes to Dr. Sheldon: Behold the manly mesomorph... Give me a doctor partridge-plump... Reprinted in CSP2.

Under which lyre, a reactionary tract for the times: Ares at last has quit the field... First printed in *Harvard alumni bulletin*, 15 June 1946, and reprinted in *Harper's magazine*, June 1947, and CSP2. Phi Beta Kappa poem, Harvard 1946.

To T. S. Eliot on his sixtieth birthday: When things began to happen to our favourite spot... First printed in *T. S. Eliot: a symposium*, comp. by R. March and M. J. Tambimuttu (1948), and reprinted in CSP2.

Music is international: Orchestras have so long been speaking... First printed in *American scholar*, Autumn 1947, and reprinted in *Horizon*, October 1947, and CSP2. Phi Beta Kappa poem, Columbia 1947.

Precious five: Be patient, solemn nose... First printed in *Harper's magazine*, October 1950, and here revised. Reprinted in PA and CSP2.

A walk after dark: A cloudless night like this... First printed in *Commonweal*, 11 March 1949, and reprinted in CSP2 and revised in SelP.

Notes: Published 21 February 1951 [*CCE* 7 February 1951] in an impression of 4,000 copies at $2.50, and reprinted in August 1951 (1,000 copies), February 1953 (1,000 copies), March 1960 (500 copies), and September 1966 (1,011 copies). The second impression is corrected.

Reviews:

L. Bogan. *New York times*, 25 February 1951, section 7, p. 10.

—. *New Yorker*, XXVII (9 June 1951), 94, 97 [New York edition, pp. 110, 113].

H. Carruth. *Nation*, CLXXII (2 June 1951), 524–25.

J. P. Clancy. *Thought*, XXVII (Winter 1952–53), 590–92.

D. Daiches. *Yale review*, XLI (September 1951), 155–56.

D. Fitts. *Saturday review of literature*, XXXIV (21 July 1951), 23, 26.

R. Fitzgerald. *Hudson review,* IV (Summer 1951), 309–12.
H. Norse. *Voices,* 146 (September–December 1951), 37–43.
S. Rodman. *New York herald tribune,* 18 March 1951, section 6, p. 4.
M. L. Rosenthal. *New republic,* CXXV (1 October 1951), 19–20.
S. Spender. *Poetry,* LXXVIII (September 1951), 352–56.
U.S. quarterly book list. VII (June 1951), 145–46.
P. Viereck. *Atlantic,* CLXXXIX (January 1952), 81.
N. Weiss. *Freeman,* I (21 May 1951), 539–40.
R. Wilbur. *Hopkins review,* V (Fall 1951), 63–65.

b) First English edition   1952

W. H. AUDEN | [rule] | NONES | FABER AND FABER | 24 Russell
Square | London

Collation: 8½ x 5½ in. [A]–D⁸ E⁴, pp. [1–6] 7–72. $1 signed 'A.N.', except A.
   [1]: half title. [2]: 'by the same author | [ten lines]'. [3]: title page. [4]: *'First
   published in mcmlii | by Faber and Faber Limited | 24 Russell Square London
   W.C.1 | Printed in Great Britain by | R. MacLehose and Company Limited | The
   University Press Glasgow | [one line]'.* [5]: 'To Reinhold and Ursula Niebuhr |
   [twenty-eight lines of verse]'. [6]: acknowledgement. 7: contents. [8]: blank.
   9–72: text.
Binding: Bound in brilliant blue (177) cloth lettered across the spine in gold: '[rule
   crossed by two diagonal rules] | N | O | N | E | S | [crossed rules] | A | U | D |
   E | N | [crossed rules] | F | & | F'. All edges trimmed. Orange dust jacket printed
   in black and blue.
Paper: Cream unwatermarked wove paper.
Contents: As the American edition.
Notes: Published 22 February 1952 in an impression of 3,000 copies at 10/6d., and
   reprinted in April 1953 (1,600 copies). Out of print in May 1958.
Reviews:
   G. S. Fraser. *New statesman & nation,* XLIII (1 March 1952), 249.
   J. Heath-Stubbs. *Poetry and poverty,* 2 ([Autumn 1952]), 36–38.
   R. Mayhead. *Scrutiny,* XVIII (June 1952), 315–19.
   S. Spender. *Spectator,* CLXXXVIII (29 February 1952), 267.
   F. G. Steiner. *Departure,* I, 1 ([1952]), 17–19.
   G. Taylor. *Time and tide,* XXXIII (8 March 1952), 231–32.
   Times literary supplement, 4 July 1952, p. 432.

A 33   THE RAKE'S PROGRESS   1951

a) Libretto: first edition

THE RAKE'S PROGRESS | OPERA IN THREE ACTS | *Music by* |
IGOR STRAWINSKY | *Libretto* | *by* | W. H. AUDEN and CHESTER
KALLMAN | *Price 2/6 Net* | (1951) | BOOSEY AND HAWKES
LTD. | *London . New York . Toronto . Sydney . Capetown . Buenos
Aires . Paris . Bonn*

Collation: 8 x 5 in. One unsigned gathering of thirty leaves. p. [1–2] 3–60.
   [1]: title page. [2]: 'Copyright 1951 by Boosey & Hawkes Inc., New York | [four
   lines] | PRINTED IN ENGLAND | FREDK. W. KAHN LTD., LONDON,
   E.C.1.' 3: characters. 4: scenes. 5–60: text.

Binding: Stapled twice in a light greenish yellow (101) card wrapper lettered across
the front in black: 'W. H. AUDEN and CHESTER KALLMAN | THE |
RAKE'S PROGRESS | *Music by* | IGOR STRAWINSKY | BOOSEY &
HAWKES'. All edges trimmed.

Paper: White unwatermarked wove paper.

Contents: The rake's progress.

The following piece appears separately:
> Gently, little boat... pp. 56–57. Reprinted in SA ("Barcarolle").

Notes: Published 17 August 1951 in an impression of 3,000 copies at 2/6d., and reprinted in January 1959 (500 copies), July 1962 (500 copies), and March 1964
(500 copies). Copies of the first impression had the price raised later to 3/6d. by
overstamping the title page. Some copies were sold in United States at 75¢. The
type of the first impression was distributed in March 1957. Impressions after the
first omit the bracketed date from the title page and were printed at Boosey &
Hawkes's Edgeware factory. The second and later impressions incorporate corrections which first appear in the American impression described below.

Auden says that Stravinsky approached him, through his agent, with the idea
of writing this libretto, after he, Stravinsky, had been inspired by Hogarth's
pictures. For fuller accounts of the genesis of the libretto see *Memories and commentaries,* by Igor Stravinsky and Robert Craft (Garden City, N.Y.: Doubleday,
1960, pp. 144–54; London: Faber, 1960, pp. 154–66), which also contains on pp.
155–67 (Faber, pp. 167–76) Auden and Stravinsky's first scenario for the libretto.
See also *Stravinsky: the composer and his works,* by Eric W. White (London:
Faber, 1966, pp. 412–28); and "New Stravinsky opera...," by Chester Kallman
(*New York herald tribune,* 8 February 1953, section 4, p. 6). For an account of a
lecture by Auden and Kallman on the libretto, see "Notes on the Rake," *Opera
news,* XVII (9 March 1953), 24.

Alan Ansen, Auden's secretary at that time, attributes to Auden the first half of
scene 1 and all of scene 2 in Act I; the second half of scene 1 and all of scene 3 in
Act II; and the beginning and end of scene 2 and all of scene 3 in Act III (*Hudson
review,* IX [1956], 319–20).

The work was first performed in Venice at La Fenice Theatre on 11 September
1951, at the XIV International Festival of Contemporary Music.

While American sales of the libretto were for some time satisfied by importing
copies from England, a new impression was called for when the work was added
to the repertory of the Metropolitan Opera in New York, where the first performance was on 14 February 1953. This impression was produced photolithographically from a corrected copy of the first English impression, and collates as
follows:

[all within two rule borders, the outer thin, the inner thick] IGOR STRA-
WINSKY | [title hollow] THE | RAKE'S PROGRESS | OPERA IN
THREE ACTS | *Libretto by* | W. H. AUDEN AND CHESTER KALL-
MAN | BOOSEY *and* HAWKES

Collation: 8½ x 5½ in. One unsigned gathering of thirty-two leaves, pp. [1] 2–62
[63–64].
> [1]: title page. 2: characters; '... | PRINTED IN U.S.A.'. 3–5: story of the opera.
> 6: summary of acts and scenes. 7–62: text. [63]: blank. [64]: advertisement.

Binding: Stapled twice in a light olive grey (112) card cover lettered across the
front in black: 'PRICE 75 CENTS | METROPOLITAN OPERA ASSOCI-
ATION, INCORPORATED | METROPOLITAN | OPERA | LIBRETTO |
[ornament] | THE RAKE'S PROGRESS | [ornament] | FRED RULLMAN,
Inc. | *17 East 42 Street, New York 17, N.Y.* | THE ONLY CORRECT AND

AUTHORIZED EDITION | KNABE PIANO USED EXCLUSIVELY | Printed in U.S.A.' Some copies appear to have been sold without the card cover.
Paper: White unwatermarked wove paper.
Contents: The rake's progress.
Notes: Published in February 1953 at 75¢. The Metropolitan Opera Association estimates that 3,500 copies were ordered from the American branch of Boosey & Hawkes; this is presumably the size of the impression. The work was dropped from the repertory after the 1952–53 season and the libretto was not reissued in this form.

Boosey & Hawkes in New York did however issue three further American-printed impressions, all of which derive photolithographically from a copy of the second English impression. The first was printed in August 1962 (2,000 copies), the second in September 1966 (1,000 copies), and the third in March 1967 (1,000 copies). The first and second measure 8 x 5 in., the third 10½ x 6⅞ in. The first has a card cover similar to that on the English edition; the second and third were issued without a cover.

An edition of the libretto was included with the first recording of the opera, issued in America as Columbia SL-125 [1953], in England as Philips ABL 3055–57 [1954], and elsewhere in Europe as Philips A 01 181–83 L. Another edition of the libretto with a note by Kallman on its composition titled "Looking and thinking back" (pp. 33–34) was issued to accompany the second recording, issued in America as Columbia M3L 310/M3S 710 [1964] and in England as CBS BRG 77278–80/SBRG 77278–80 [1965]. These texts apparently have no authority.

b) Libretto: second English edition   1966

THE RAKE'S PROGRESS | OPERA IN THREE ACTS | *Music by* | IGOR STRAVINSKY | *Libretto* | *by* | W. H. AUDEN and CHESTER KALLMAN | Boosey & Hawkes | Music Publishers Limited | *London* • *Paris* • *Bonn* • *Johannesburg* • *Sydney* • *Toronto* • *New York*

Collation: 8 x 5 in. One unsigned gathering of thirty leaves, pp. [1–2] 3–60.
   [1]: title page. [2]: 'Copyright 1951 by Boosey & Hawkes Inc., New York | [four lines] | PRINTED IN ENGLAND'. 3: characters. 4: scenes. 5–60: text; at foot of p. 60 'Dec./Jan. 64/65'.
Binding: Stapled twice in a brilliant yellow (83) card cover lettered across the front cover in black: 'W. H. AUDEN and CHESTER KALLMAN | THE | RAKE'S PROGRESS | *Music by* | IGOR STRAVINSKY | BOOSEY & HAWKES'. All edges trimmed.
Paper: White unwatermarked wove paper.
Contents: The rake's progress [corrected and reset].
Notes: Published May 1966 in an impression of 1,000 copies at 5/–, and printed by Herbert Fitch and Co.
   Many of the textual changes in the first American impression were incorporated in this second edition.

c) Full score: three volume edition   1951

IGOR STRAWINSKY | THE RAKE'S PROGRESS | (Der Wüstling) | *an Opera in 3 Acts* | *Oper in 3 Akten* | a Fable by eine Fabel von | W. H. AUDEN AND CHESTER KALLMAN | *Deutsche Übersetzung* | *von*

Fritz Schröder | Full Score | Partitur | BOOSEY & HAWKES | *London New York Paris Bonn Sydney Cape Town Toronto*

Collation: 12¼ x 9¼ in. [vol. 1] [π]²[1–7]⁸[8]¹⁰, pp. [i–iv, 1] 2–130 [131–132]; [vol. 2] [1–5]⁸[6–7]¹⁰, pp. 1–119 [120]; [vol. 3] [1–9]⁸[10]¹⁰, pp. 1–164. Plate mark: 'B. & H. 17853'.
[vol. 1] [i]: title page. [ii]: characters. [iii]: personen. [iv]: orchestration. [1]–130: score. [131–132]: advertisements, plate marks 531 and 537. At the foot of p. [1]: 'Copyright 1951 by Boosey & Hawkes Inc. New York. Printed in England | [one line]'. Stave three on p. 25 is cancelled by a paste-over slip. [vol. 2] 1–119: score. [120]: advertisement, plate marked 530. [vol. 3] 1–164: score. The first three staves on p. 102 are cancelled by a paste-over slip.
Binding: Glued in a light yellowish brown (76) wrapper lettered across the front cover in black: 'ACT [act number] | IGOR STRAWINSKY | [swelled rule] | THE RAKE'S PROGRESS | [swelled rule] | *Full Score | Partitur |* BOOSEY & HAWKES'. All edges trimmed.
Paper: Cream unwatermarked wove paper.
Contents: The rake's progress.
Notes: Not published. A first impression of 48 copies was printed on 17 August 1951 at Boosey & Hawkes's printing house in Berners Street, and reprinted at the same place in November 1951 (32 copies). These copies were made principally for the performance and hire libraries. Some few copies in typewritten wrappers were produced for copyright entry.

d) Full score: miniature score   1962

Igor Stravinsky | The Rake's Progress | An Opera in Three Acts | by W. H. Auden and Chester Kallman | HPS 739 | [rule] | BOOSEY & HAWKES | LONDON

Collation: 10½ x 7¼ in. [1–25]⁸[26]¹⁰, pp. [i–vi, 1] 2–414. Plate mark: 'B. & H. 17853'.
[i]: title page. [ii]: copyright statements. [iii]: characters. [iv]: orchestration. [v]: details of the first performance. [vi]: blank. [1]–414: text and score.
Binding: Glued in a greyish yellow green (122) card cover lettered across the spine in black: 'STRAVINSKY | [rule] | THE RAKE'S PROGRESS' and across the front cover: '[in black] *Igor Stravinsky* | [title in white] *The Rake's | Progress* | [in black] Boosey & Hawkes'. All edges trimmed.
  The second impression was issued in dark purplish blue (201) buckram lettered across the spine in gold as above, and with a monogram 'IS' across the front cover.
Paper: White unwatermarked wove paper.
Contents: The rake's progress.
Notes: Published May 1962 in an impression of 500 copies at 90/–, and reprinted December 1963 (500 copies), and November 1969 (500 copies). A reduced photographic reproduction of the first impression of the full score with some corrections and new preliminaries.

e) Full score: published edition   1962

Igor Stravinsky | The Rake's Progress | An Opera in Three Acts | by W. H. Auden and Chester Kallman | *Full Score* | Boosey & Hawkes | Music Publishers Limited | [place names in one line]

Collation: 12¼ x 9¼ in. [1–25]⁸[26]¹⁰, pp. [i–vi, 1] 2–414. Plate mark: 'B. & H. 17853'.
Collation identical with that of the preceding miniature score.
Binding: Glued in a yellowish grey (93) card cover lettered across the front cover in red as the title page except for the imprint: 'BOOSEY & HAWKES'. All edges trimmed. Some copies were later issued hardbound.
Paper: White unwatermarked wove paper.
Contents: The rake's progress.
Notes: Published in August 1962 in an edition of 250 copies at £ 15 15s. od.

f) Vocal score   1951

[The transcription of the title page is as that of the full score except for the substitution of the following for '*Full Score | Partitur*': '*Vocal Score by Klavierauszug von | Leopold Spinner*', and the cities in the imprint are in roman upper case.]

Collation: 12 x 9 in. [π]²1–15⁸, pp. [i–iv], 1–240. Plate mark: 'B. & H. 17088'.
    [i]: title page. [ii]: characters. [iii]: personen. [iv]: orchestration. 1–240: score; colophon: 'Stich und Druck der Universitätsdruckerei H. Stürtz A. G., Wurzburg.'
Binding: Glued in a moderate yellow green (120) card cover lettered across the front in red: 'IGOR STRAWINSKY | [swelled rule] | THE RAKE'S PROGRESS | [swelled rule] | *Vocal Score | Klavierauszug* | BOOSEY & HAWKES'. All edges trimmed.
Paper: White unwatermarked wove paper.
Contents: The rake's progress.
Notes: Published 4 September 1951 in an impression of 100 copies at 55/–, and reprinted in November 1952 (282 copies), July 1953 (200 copies), July 1956 (500 copies), February 1961 (490 copies), October 1962 (500 copies), March 1964 (500 copies), October 1966 (500 copies), and April 1968 (500 copies). The first three impressions were printed by Stürtz, and those following by Lowe and Brydone.
    Some early copies of the vocal score were issued in light yellowish brown (76) wrappers lettered in black in two volumes, the division being made following p. 139. The words 'Der Wüstling' are also missing from the transcription of the title page of these copies. It is not known how many copies were so issued; they are presumably early copies issued for rehearsals of the first performance, but the publishers have been unable to trace any details of the printing.
    Later impressions conflate pp. ii and iii, and substitute on p. iii the details of the first performance.

A 34   MOUNTAINS   1954

[A lithographed title page depicting a pinnacle surmounted by a rock, round which are a river and trees] [on the rock] MOUNTAINS | [on the pinnacle] *BY* | W. H. AUDEN | FABER & FABER | 24 Russell Square | LONDON | [in the lower right corner] E B

Collation: 8½ x 5½ in. One unsigned gathering of four leaves.
    [1]: front wrapper. [2]: blank. [3]: title page. [4]: coloured lithograph of an easel and mountain. [5–7]: text followed by lithograph of vampire flying over railway track which vanishes into the mountain and colophon: 'First published in mcmliv

by Faber & Faber Limited, 24 Russell Square, London, WC1 | Printed in Great Britain by Jesse Broad & Co. Ltd., Manchester. All rights reserved'. [8]: list of the titles in the series.

Binding: The outside of the end leaves is coloured light greenish yellow (101) and lettered across the front in black: 'Ariel Poem | [ornamental rule] | MOUNTAINS | *by* | W. H. AUDEN | *illustrated by* | EDWARD BAWDEN | [ornamental rule] | FABER AND FABER'. The pamphlet is issued stitched, and in a strong pink (2) envelope lettered in black: '*An Ariel Poem—Mountains* | *by* W. H. AUDEN, *illustrated by* EDWARD BAWDEN | [within a rectangle] *Price* | *2/–* | *net* | [outside the rectangle] *Published by Faber and Faber Limited, 24 Russell Square, London, W.C.1*'.

Paper: White unwatermarked wove paper.

Contents: Mountains: I know a retired dentist who only paints mountains... Reprinted in SA, PA, CSP2, and SelP.

Notes: Published 26 October 1954 in an edition of 10,000 copies at 2/–. A remainder of 4,400 copies was sold to W. Heffer & Sons in June 1971.

Reviews:

L. Bonnerot. *Études anglaises*, VIII (October–December 1955), 357–58.

Times literary supplement, 10 December 1954, p. 801.

A 35   THE SHIELD OF ACHILLES   1955

a) First edition

THE | SHIELD | OF | ACHILLES | *W. H. AUDEN* | [device: a house] | RANDOM HOUSE · NEW YORK

Collation: 9 x 5¾ in. [1]¹⁶[2]¹²[3]¹⁶, pp. [1–10] 11–84 [85–88].
    [1]: half title. [2]: blank. [3]: title page. [4]: 'First Printing | COPYRIGHT, 1951, 1952, 1953, 1954, 1955 BY W. H. AUDEN | [four lines] | PUBLISHED IN NEW YORK BY RANDOM HOUSE, INC., AND | SIMULTANEOUSLY IN TORONTO, CANADA, BY RANDOM HOUSE | OF CANADA, LIMITED. | [one line] | MANUFACTURED IN THE UNITED STATES OF AMERICA'. [5]: 'For Lincoln and Fidelma Kirstein | [four lines of verse]'. [6]: note. [7]: contents. [8]: blank. [9]: 'I | BUCOLICS | [three lines]'. [10]: blank. 11–31: text. [32]: blank. [33]: 'II | IN SUNSHINE AND IN SHADE | [four lines]'. [34]: blank. 35–59: text. [60]: blank. [61]: III | HORAE CANONICAE | [one line]'. [62]: blank. 63–84: text. [85–88]: blank.

Binding: Quarter bound in moderate orange (53) cloth with black paper boards lettered down the spine in grey: 'W. H. AUDEN [gold rule] THE SHIELD OF ACHILLES [gold rule] RANDOM HOUSE'. All edges trimmed, and the top edge stained orange. Grey endpapers. Cream dust jacket printed in black and orange.

Paper: White unwatermarked wove paper.

Contents:

For Lincoln and Fidelma Kirstein: From bad lands where eggs are small and dear... Reprinted in PA and CSP2.

I Bucolics
        Fair is Middle-Earth nor changes, though to Age... Reprinted in CSP2.
        Winds: Deep below our violences... First printed in *London magazine*, November 1954. Dedicated to Alexis Leger.
    II Woods: Sylvan meant savage in those primal woods... First printed in *Listener*, 11 December 1952, and reprinted in the anthology *New poems*

> *by American poets*, ed. by R. Humphries (1953). Dedicated to Nicholas Nabokov.
>
> III   Mountains: I know a retired dentist who only paints mountains... Reprinted from the pamphlet (1954) and here dedicated to Hedwig Petzold.
>
> IV   Lakes: A lake allows an average father, walking slowly... First printed in the anthology *New poems by American poets*, ed. by R. Humphries (1953). Dedicated to Isaiah Berlin.
>
> V   Islands: Old saints on millstones float with cats... Dedicated to Giocondo Sacchetti; changed to Giovanni Maresca in CSP2.
>
> VI   Plains: I can imagine quite easily ending up... First printed in *London magazine*, April 1954, and reprinted in *Atlantic*, November 1954. Dedicated to Wendell Johnson. Revised in the English edition.
>
> VII   Streams: Dear water, clear water, playful in all your streams... First printed in *Encounter*, June 1954. Dedicated to Elizabeth Drew.
>
> All the "Bucolics" were reprinted in PA, CSP2, and SelP.

II   In sunshine and in shade

Guard, Civility, with guns... Reprinted in CSP2.

The shield of Achilles: She looked over his shoulder... First printed in *Poetry*, October 1952, and awarded the 40th Anniversary Prize. Reprinted in PA, CSP2, and SelP.

Fleet visit: The sailors come ashore... First printed in *Listener*, 3 January 1952, and reprinted in PA, CSP2, and SelP.

Hunting season: A shot: from crag to crag... First printed in *Third hour*, 1954, and reprinted in CSP2.

The willow-wren and the stare: A starling and a willow-wren... First printed in *Encounter*, November 1953, and reprinted in PA and CSP2.

The proof: "When rites and melodies begin... First printed in *Times literary supplement*, 17 September 1954 ("The trial"), and reprinted in *Harper's bazaar*, December 1954. This text is revised and reprinted in PA and CSP2.

"The truest poetry is the most feigning": By all means sing of love but, if you do... First printed in *New Yorker*, 13 November 1954, and reprinted in CSP2. Dedicated to Edgar Wind.

A sanguine thought: O where would those choleric boys... Reprinted in CSP2.

A permanent way: Self-drivers may curse their luck... Reprinted in PA and CSP2.

Barcarolle: Gently, little boat... Reprinted from *The rake's progress*.

Nocturne I: Appearing unannounced, the moon... First printed in *Botteghe oscure*, 1951 ("A face in the moon"), and reprinted in *Third hour*, 1954 ("The moon like X"), and CSP2. Also reprinted in *New York times*, 6 March 1955, section 7, p. 2.

Nocturne II: Make this night lovable... Reprinted in PA and CSP2. Also reprinted in *New York times*, 6 March 1955, section 7, p. 2.

In memoriam L. K-A.: At peace under this mandarin, sleep, Lucina... Reprinted in *Semi-colon*, [1955], PA, and CSP2.

Epitaph for the unknown soldier: To save your world you asked this man to die... Reprinted in CSP2.

Ode to Gaea: From this new culture of the air we finally see... First printed in *Listener*, 15 December 1954, and reprinted in CSP2.

III   Horae canonicae

> I   Prime: Simultaneously, as soundlessly... Reprinted from N.
>
> II   Terce: After shaking paws with his dog... First printed in *Catholic worker*, January 1954.
>
> III   Sext: You need not see what someone is doing...

IV   Nones: What we know to be not possible... Reprinted from N.

V   Vespers: If the hill overlooking our city has always been known as Adam's... First printed in *Encounter*, February 1955. Revised in the English edition.

VI   Compline: Now, as desire and the things desired...
Lauds: Among the leaves the small birds sing... A revised version of the final part of "Delia" published in *Botteghe oscure*, 1953.

All the "Horae canonicae" are reprinted in PA, CSP2, and SelP.

Notes: Published 21 February 1955 [*CCE* 24 February 1955] in an impression of 4,000 copies at $3, and reprinted in January 1956 (2,000 copies), August 1961 (900 copies), and June 1967 (1,000 copies). Printed by the H. Wolff Mfg. Co., New York. The second impression is corrected.

On 7 February 1956 Auden received the National Book Award for this volume of poems.

Reviews:

E. Ayer. *Voices*, 158 (September–December 1955), 42–48.

L. Bogan. *New Yorker*, XXXI (30 April 1955), 123–24.

H. Carruth. *Poetry*, LXXXVI (June 1955), 169–70.

J. Ciardi. *Nation*, CLXXX (30 April 1955), 378–79.

J. P. Clancy. *Thought*, XXX (Winter 1955), 455–57.

D. Davie. *Shenandoah*, VII (Autumn 1955), 93–95.

B. Deutsch. *Accent*, XV (Spring 1955), 149–52.

F. C. Flint. *Virginia quarterly review*, XXXI (Autumn 1955), 655–56.

H. Gregory. *New York herald tribune*, 26 February 1955, section 6, p. 4.

R. Jarrell. *Yale review*, XLIV (June 1955), 603–8.

A. Lombardo. *Spettatore italiano*, VIII (August 1955), 326–28.

H. Nemerov. *Kenyon review*, XVII (Summer 1955), 482–84.

D. Rainer. *American scholar*, XXIV (Summer 1955), 375–76.

K. Shapiro. *New York times*, 20 February 1955, section 7, p. 6.

L. Untermeyer. *Saturday review*, XXXVIII (12 March 1955), 15–16.

U.S. quarterly book list, XI (September 1955), 354.

R. Whittemore. *Sewanee review*, LXIII (Autumn 1955), 650–54.

b) First English edition   1955

W. H. AUDEN | *The Shield of Achilles* | FABER AND FABER | 24 Russell Square | London

Collation: 8½ x 5¼ in. [A]–E⁸, pp. [1–8] 9–80.
[1–2]: blank. [3]: half title. [4]: 'Other books by W. H. Auden | [fifteen lines]'. [5]: title page. [6]: 'First published in mcmlv | by Faber and Faber Limited | 24 Russell Square, London, W.C.1 | Printed in Great Britain by | Western Printing Services Limited | [one line]'. [7]: 'For | LINCOLN & FIDELMA KIRSTEIN | [four lines of verse]'. [8]: blank. 9–10: contents. 11: note. [12]: blank. [13]: 'I | BUCOLICS | [three lines]'. [14]: blank. 15–32: text. [33]: 'II | IN SUNSHINE AND IN SHADE | [four lines]'. [34]: blank. 35–58: text. [59]: 'III | HORAE CANONICAE | [one line]'. [60]: blank. 61–80: text.

Binding: Bound in dark purplish red (259) cloth lettered down the spine in gold: 'W. H. Auden [double rule] The Shield of Achilles Faber'. All edges trimmed. Yellow dust jacket printed in black and red. Some copies are bound in very deep purplish red (257) and are very slightly smaller.

Paper: White unwatermarked wove paper.

Contents: As the American edition, except that the first poem, "Winds," is numbered 1 in its section, "Bucolics"; and the last poem, "Lauds," is numbered 7 in its section, "Horae canonicae."

Notes: Published 11 November 1955 in an edition of 4,000 copies at 10/6d., and out of print in September 1965.

Reviews:

H. Corke, *Listener*, LIV (1 December 1955), 958, 961.

Dublin magazine, XXXI (April–June 1956), 42–43.

K. Foster. *Blackfriars*, XXXVII (April 1956), 189–90.

G. S. Fraser. *New statesman & nation*, L (26 November 1955), 712, 714.

P. Larkin. *Listen*, II (Summer 1956), 22–26.

L. D. Lerner. *London magazine*, III (March 1956), 71–74.

K. Nott. *Observer*, 1 January 1956, p. 7.

Times, 12 January 1956, p. 11.

Times literary supplement, 20 January 1956, p. 38.

A 36   THE OLD MAN'S ROAD   1956

a) **Limited signed edition**

W. H. AUDEN | [rule] | *THE* | *OLD* | *MAN'S* | *ROAD* | *VOYAGES* | [short rule] | *NEW YORK 1956*

Collation: 9 x 5¾ in. One unsigned gathering of twelve leaves, pp. [1–24].
[1–2]: blank. [3]: title page. [4]: 'First Edition | Copyright 1956 by *Voyages*. | VOYAGES | 35 West 75th Street | New York 23, N.Y.'. [5]: 'THE OLD MAN'S ROAD'. [6]: blank. [7–21]: text. [22]: 'This edition of *The Old Man's Road* by W. H. Auden is | limited to seven hundred and fifty copies, of which fifty, | on Ticonderoga laid text, have been numbered and signed | by the author. | This is copy [copy number in ink followed by Auden's signature]'. [23–24]: blank.

Binding: Stapled twice in a cream card cover round which is folded a light grey (264) wrapper lettered across the front cover in black as the title page but omitting the date.

Paper: White unwatermarked laid paper.

Contents:

The old man's road: Across the Great Schism, through our whole landscape... First printed in *Perspectives*, Winter 1956, and reprinted in *Listen*, Summer–Autumn 1957, HTC, CSP2, and SelP.

The epigoni: No use invoking Apollo in a case like theirs... First printed in *Poetry London–New York*, March–April 1956, and reprinted in *Nimbus*, Summer 1956, HTC, and CSP2.

Makers of history: Serious historians study coins and weapons... First printed in *London magazine*, September 1955, and reprinted in HTC and CSP2.

The history of science: All fables of adventure stress... First printed in *New statesman*, 9 June 1956, and reprinted in HTC and CSP2.

Merax & Mullin: There is one devil in the lexicon... First printed in *Semi-colon*, [1956], and reprinted in HTC and CSP2.

C. 500 A.D.: *Hail, future friend whose present I*... Reprinted in HTC ("Bathtub thoughts") and CSP2.

Homage to Clio: Our hill has made its submission and the green... First printed in *Encounter*, November 1955, and reprinted in HTC and CSP2.

Notes: Mrs. M. Cohn told Mendelson that Clark Mills, of the Voyages Press, delivered copies of the limited signed edition to the House of Books Ltd., on 6 June 1956, and these were priced at $3.50.

b) **Regular edition** 1956

W. H. AUDEN | [rule] | *THE | OLD | MAN'S | ROAD* | [device: galleon in sail] VOYAGES PRESS, NEW YORK 1956

Collation: 8⅛ x 5¼ in. One unsigned gathering of sixteen leaves, pp. [1–32].
   [1–4]: blank. [5]: half title. [6]: blank. [7]: title page. [8]: 'First Edition | Copyright 1956 by *Voyages.* | 35 West 75th Street, New York 23, N.Y.'. [9]: 'THE OLD MAN'S ROAD'. [10]: blank. [11–25]: text. [26]: blank. [27]: 'This edition of *The Old Man's Road* by W. H. Auden is limited | to seven hundred and fifty copies, of which fifty have been | numbered and signed by the author. | Designed and printed by Igal Roodenko, *printer*, New York.'. [28–32]: blank.
Binding: Stapled twice in a plain white card cover round which is a rough pale yellow (89) paper wrapper lettered across the front cover in black: 'W. H. AUDEN | [rule] | *THE | OLD | MAN'S | ROAD* | [device] | [running up the cover] PRESS | [under the device] VOYAGES'.
Paper: White wove paper watermarked: '*Ticonderoga | Text*'.
Contents: As the limited signed edition.
Notes: Mrs. M. Cohn told Mendelson that Clark Mills, of the Voyages Press, delivered copies of the regular edition to the House of Books Ltd., on 1 August 1956, and these were priced at $1.50. A different setting of type from the limited signed edition.
Reviews:
   K. Koch. *Poetry*, XC (April 1957), 47–52.
   M. Rosenthal. *Nation*, CLXXXIV (23 March 1957), 260–61.

A 37   **THE MAGIC FLUTE**   1956

a) **First edition**

THE MAGIC FLUTE | *An Opera in two acts | Music by* W. A. MOZART | *English version after the Libretto | of Schikaneder and Giesecke | by* W. H. AUDEN | *and* CHESTER KALLMAN | [device: a house] | *Random House   New York*

Collation: 9 x 5⅞ in. [1–4]¹⁶, pp. [i–vii] viii–xv [xvi–xx, 1–3] 4–108.
   [i]: half title. [ii]: illustration. [iii]: title page. [iv]: 'FIRST PRINTING | [eighteen lines] | Manufactured in the United States of America by H. Wolff, New York | Illustrations by Rouben Ter-Arutunian | DESIGN: Marshall Lee'. [v]: '*To* ANNE *and* IRVING WEISS | [four lines of verse]'. [vi]: blank. [vii]–xv: preface. [xvi]: dramatis personae. [xvii–xviii]: '*The Magic Flute* was commissioned by the National Broadcasting | Company and produced on television by the NBC Opera Theatre on | Sunday, January 15, 1956, with the following cast and production | staff: | [list follows]'. [xix–xx]: proem. [1]–100: text; 2, 36, and 44 blank. [101]–102: postscript. [103]–108: notes.
Binding: Quarter bound in black cloth with pink and grey striped paper boards lettered down the spine: '[in violet] THE [in blue] MAGIC [in orange] FLUTE [in silver] *W. H. Auden : Chester Kallman* | RANDOM HOUSE [device]', and on the front board an orange sun and a violet new moon. All edges trimmed, and the top edge stained black. Yellow endpapers. White dust jacket printed in black, blue, and pink.

Paper: White unwatermarked wove paper.
Contents: The magic flute.
   The following pieces appear separately as follows:
      Metalogue: Relax, Maestro, put your baton down... First published in
         Harper's bazaar, January 1956, and reprinted in *Listener*, 26 January 1956,
         HTC, and CSP2.
      Act 2 appeared first in *The score and I.M.A. magazine*, March 1956.
      The translation of the aria "O Isis and Osiris" is reprinted in *Favorite arias
         from the great operas*, edited by M. J. Cross (New York: Doubleday, 1958,
         pp. 131–33.)
Notes: Published 16 July 1956 [*CCE* 14 June 1956] in an edition of 4,000 copies at
   $3.50. The copyright entry for the unpublished typescript is dated 6 October 1955.
   The plates were scrapped by the publisher in June 1966.
   Kallman says the "Proem" and "Metalogue" are by Auden; the "Postscript" by
   Auden and Kallman in collaboration.
Reviews:
   J. Kerman. *Hudson review*, X (Summer 1957), 309–16.
   W. Meredith. *Poetry*, LXXXIX (January 1957), 255–57.
   J. Slater. *Saturday review*, XXXIX (15 December 1956), 35–36.

b) First English edition   1957

THE MAGIC FLUTE | *An opera in two acts* | *Music by* | W. A. MO-
ZART | *English version after the libretto* | *of Schikaneder and Giesecke* |
by | W. H. AUDEN | *and* | CHESTER KALLMAN | FABER AND
FABER | 24 Russell Square | London

Collation: 8½ x 5⅜ in. [A]–G⁸H⁴, pp. [1–8] 9–120.
   [1–2]: blank. [3]: half title. [4]: books by W. H. Auden. [5]: title page. [6]: '*First
   published in England in mcmlvii* | *by Faber and Faber Limited* | *24 Russell Square,
   London, W.C.1* | *Printed in Great Britain* | *by Western Printing Services Ltd.
   Bristol* | [one line]'. [7]: 'To | ANNE and IRVING WEISS | [four lines of verse]'.
   [8]: blank. [9–16]: preface. 17: dramatis personae. 18–19: note on the original
   production and staff. [20]: blank. 21–22: proem. [23]–114: text; 20, 24, 56, 62, and
   64 blank. 115–116: postscript. 117–120: notes.
Binding: Bound in light greyish olive (109) cloth lettered down the spine in gold:
   '[authors and title on a red panel bordered by an ornamental gold rule, title in
   fancy] THE MAGIC FLUTE—*Auden and Kallman* [across the foot of the spine]
   Faber'. All edges trimmed, and top edge stained yellow. White dust jacket printed
   in black and green.
Paper: White unwatermarked wove paper.
Contents: As the American edition.
Notes: Published 30 August 1957 in an edition of 2,090 copies at 15/–.
Reviews:
   J. Cross. *Tempo*, 45 (Autumn 1957), 6–8.
   [E. M. Forster]. *Listener*, LVIII (21 November 1957), 850, 853.
   D. Shawe-Taylor. *New statesman*, LIV (21 September 1957), 355–56.
   Times literary supplement, 27 September 1957, p. 572.

A 38   MAKING, KNOWING AND JUDGING   1956

MAKING, KNOWING | AND JUDGING | BY | W. H. AUDEN,
M.A. | PROFESSOR OF POETRY | *An Inaugural Lecture* | DELIV-

ERED BEFORE | THE UNIVERSITY OF OXFORD | ON 11 JUNE
1956 | OXFORD | AT THE CLARENDON PRESS | 1956

Collation: 8½ x 5½ in. One gathering of eighteen leaves, pp. [1–3] 4–33 [34–36].
Second leaf signed '5973 A 2', and sixth leaf '5973 A 3'.
[1]: title page. [2]: '[addresses of Oxford University Press in four lines] | [short
swelled rule] | PRINTED IN GREAT BRITAIN'. [3]–33: text. [34]: 'PRINTED
IN | GREAT BRITAIN | AT THE | UNIVERSITY PRESS | OXFORD | BY |
CHARLES BATEY | PRINTER | TO THE | UNIVERSITY'. [35–36]: blank.

Binding: Stitched in a greenish white (153) wrapper lettered across the front wrapper
in brown: 'MAKING | KNOWING | AND | JUDGING | [swelled rule] | *An*
Inaugural Lecture | *delivered before* | *the University of Oxford* | *on 11 June 1956*
| [swelled rule] | W. H. AUDEN'. Top edge trimmed.

Paper: Cream unwatermarked laid paper.

Contents: Making, knowing and judging. A selection from the lecture was first
printed in *Sunday times*, 17 June 1956, and further selections were reprinted in
Periodical, Winter 1956–57, and *Atlantic*, January 1957. The entire lecture was reprinted in DH.

Notes: Published 24 August 1956 in an impression of 3,000 copies at 2/6d., and reprinted in October 1956 (1,000 copies), May 1957 (1,000 copies), October 1957
(1,000 copies), and March 1960 (1,000 copies). The press sent copies to the United
States where they were published on 17 January 1957 at 75¢.

Reviews:
C. Brooks. *Sewanee review*, LXV (Summer 1957), 488–89.
E. Morgan. *Review of English studies*, IX (February 1959), 123.
P. Quennell. *Spectator*, CLXXXXVIII (11 January 1957), 53 (see subsequent cor-
respondence, 1 February 1957, p. 144).
W. W. Robson. *Twentieth century*, CLXI (March 1957), 255–63.
D. Stanford. *Norseman*, XIV (November–December 1956), 429–30.

A 39   REFLECTIONS IN A FOREST   1957

Reflections in a Forest | [poem in forty lines] | W. H. Auden | AMERI-
CAN ARTS FESTIVAL POEM | DEPAUW UNIVERSITY | COPY-
RIGHT 1957, W. H. AUDEN

Collation: 6½ x 13 in. Single sheet printed on one side only.
Binding: None.
Paper: White unwatermarked wove paper, with deckle edge at the foot of the sheet.
Contents: Reflections in a forest: Beneath the silence of the trees... Reprinted in
DePauw alumnus, December 1957; revised in *Listener*, 23 July 1959, and HTC.
Notes: Printed in an edition of 500 copies by the University and distributed on 14
November 1957 when Auden lectured and read the poem.

A 40   W. H. AUDEN: A SELECTION BY THE AUTHOR   1958

a) First edition

W. H. AUDEN | [double rule] | A SELECTION BY THE AUTHOR |
From bad lands, where eggs are small and dear, | *Climbing to worse by a*
stonier | *Track, when all are spent, we hear it–the right song* | *For the*
wrong time of year. | PENGUIN BOOKS | IN ASSOCIATION WITH
| FABER AND FABER

Collation: 7⅛ x 4⅜ in. [A]–E¹⁶ F²⁰, pp. [1–8] 9–200. F3 signed as 'F2'.
[1]: half title. [2]: 'The Works of W. H. Auden | [twelve lines; "Nones" mis-printed as "Notes"]'. [3]: title page. [4]: '[four lines] | First published 1958 | [two lines] | Made and Printed in Great Britain | by Spottiswoode, Ballantyne & Co Ltd | London and Colchester'. [5–7]: contents. [8]: blank. 9–194: text. 195–196: index of titles. 197–200: index of first lines.

Binding: Glued in a stiff white card cover printed in a repeat pattern of black lines and moderate olive green (125) and deep orange (51), lettered across the spine in black on a white panel: '[three olive green rules] | D 41 | [olive green rule] | [down the spine] W. H. Auden | [olive green rule] | D 41 | [three olive green rules]', and on the front cover on a white panel within a border of three olive green rules: '*W. H. Auden* | [olive green star] | SELECTED | BY THE AUTHOR | [device: a penguin in olive green] | THE PENGUIN | POETS | *3/6*'. On the rear cover: 'NOT FOR SALE IN THE U.S.A. OR CANADA'.
        On the cover of the second impression the price is raised to 4/6d.
        The cover of the third impression is redesigned and is printed in a new repeat pattern in black, deep reddish purple (238), and strong brown (55). The spine lettering is identical with the first impression except that all the rules are brown; the panel on the front cover is smaller and reads: '[all within three brown rules] *W. H. Auden* | SELECTED BY THE | AUTHOR | [device: a penguin in brown] | THE PENGUIN POETS | *4/6*'; and the rear cover reads in white on a black panel '*For copyright reasons this edition is not for sale | in the U.S.A. or Canada*'. The fourth impression removes the device from the half title and puts it on the title page; it is perfect bound, as are all later impressions. The cover of the fifth impression is again redesigned, using the repeat pattern of the third impression on a shiny card. On the spine in black on a white panel: '[down] W. H. Auden | [across] D 41'; on a white panel across the top of the front cover: '[device: a penguin] W. H. Auden | [brown rule] | 4/6 [in purple] The Penguin Poets | Selected by the author'; and on a similar white panel at the top of the rear cover: 'W. H. Auden [device] | [brown rule] | [in purple] Cover design by Stephen Russ | For copyright reasons this edition is | not for sale in the U.S.A. or Canada'.

Paper: White unwatermarked wove paper.

Contents:
From bad lands where eggs are small and dear . . . [on title page] Reprinted from SA.
The letter: From the very first coming down . . . Reprinted from P (1928).
Taller to-day: Taller to-day, we remember similar evenings . . . Reprinted from P (1928).
The journey: To throw away the key and walk away . . . Reprinted from P (1928).
No change of place: Who will endure . . . Reprinted from P2.
The question: To ask the hard question is simple . . . Reprinted from P2.
This lunar beauty . . . Reprinted from P.
This one: Before this loved one . . . Reprinted from P.
Chorus: Doom is dark and deeper than any sea-dingle . . . Reprinted from P2.
The watchers: Now from my window-sill I watch the night . . . Reprinted from LS.
Ode: Though aware of our rank and alert to obey orders . . . Reprinted from O.
The decoys: There are some birds in these valleys . . . Reprinted from O.
The three companions: 'O where are you going?' said reader to rider . . . Reprinted from O.
In legend: Enter with him . . . Reprinted from DBS.
The quarry: O what is that sound which so thrills the ear . . . Reprinted from LS.
Seascape: Look, stranger, on this island now . . . Reprinted from LS.

A dream: Dear, though the night is gone... Reprinted from LS.

Song: 'O for doors to be open and an invite with gilded edges... Reprinted from LS.

Autumn song: Now the leaves are falling fast... Reprinted from LS.

One evening: As I walked out one evening... Reprinted from AT.

Lullaby: Lay your sleeping head, my love... Reprinted from AT.

Underneath the abject willow... Reprinted from LS.

Madrigal: O lurcher-loving collier, black as night... Reprinted from AT.

Able at times to cry: Wrapped in a yielding air beside... Reprinted from AT.

Two songs for Hedli Anderson: Stop all the clocks, cut off the telephone... O the valley in the summer where I and my John... Reprinted from AT.

Miss Gee, a ballad: Let me tell you a little story... Reprinted from AT.

Roman wall blues: Over the heather the wet wind blows... Reprinted from AT.

Victor, a ballad: Victor was a little baby... Reprinted from AT.

The dead echo: 'O who can ever gaze his fill'... Reprinted from LFI.

Ganymede: He looked in all his wisdom from the throne... Reprinted from JTW.

A new age: So an age ended, and its last deliverer died... Reprinted from JTW.

Surgical ward: They are and suffer; that is all they do... Reprinted from JTW.

Embassy: As evening fell the day's oppression lifted... Reprinted from JTW.

The sphinx: Did it once issue from the carver's hand... Reprinted from JTW.

Macao: A weed from Catholic Europe, it took root... Reprinted from JTW.

The bard: He was their servant—some say he was blind... Reprinted from JTW.

Musée des beaux arts: About suffering they were never wrong... Reprinted from AT.

Gare du midi: A nondescript express in from the South... Reprinted from AT.

Rimbaud: The nights, the railway arches, the bad sky... Reprinted from AT.

The capital: Quarter of pleasures where the rich are always waiting... Reprinted from AT.

Epitaph on a tyrant: Perfection, of a kind, was what he was after... Reprinted from AT.

In memory of W. B. Yeats: He disappeared in the dead of winter... Reprinted from AT.

In memory of Sigmund Freud: When there are so many we shall have to mourn... Reprinted from AT.

The quest [seven poems]. All reprinted from DM.

    All had been ordered weeks before the start...

    Two friends who met here and embraced are gone...

    They noticed that virginity was needed...

    Incredulous, he stared at the amused...

    The over-logical fell for the witch...

    Suppose he'd listened to the erudite committee...

    Fresh addenda are published every day...

Law like love: Law, say the gardeners, is the sun... Reprinted from AT.

Another time: For us like any other fugitive... Reprinted from AT.

Our bias: The hour-glass whispers to the lion's roar... Reprinted from AT.

Hell: Hell is neither here nor there... Reprinted from AT.

Song: Warm are the still and lucky miles... Reprinted from AT.

Lady, weeping at the crossroads... Reprinted from CP.

If I could tell you: Time will say nothing but I told you so... Reprinted from CP.

The model: Generally, reading palms or handwriting or faces... Reprinted from CP.

Atlantis: Being set on the idea... Reprinted from CP.

Doomsday song: Jumbled in the common box... Reprinted from CP.

Song of the old soldier: When the Sex War ended with the slaughter of the grand-mothers... Reprinted from FTB.
Mundus et infans: Kicking his mother until she let go of his soul... Reprinted from CP.
The lesson: The first time that I dreamed, we were in flight... Reprinted from CP.
Invocation to Ariel: Sing, Ariel, sing...
Stephano's song: Embrace me, belly, like a bride...
Trinculo's song: Mechanic, merchant, king...
Alonso to Ferdinand: Dear son, when the warm multitudes cry...
Song of the master and boatswain: At Dirty Dick's and Sloppy Joe's...
Miranda's song: My Dear One is mine as mirrors are lonely...
Caliban to the audience.
    The seven preceding poems are reprinted from "The sea and the mirror" in FTB.
Three dreams: How still it is; our horses... Lights are moving... Bending forward... Reprinted from AA.
In praise of limestone: If it form the one landscape that we the inconstant ones... Reprinted from N.
One circumlocution: Sometimes we see astonishingly clearly... Reprinted from N.
Their lonely betters: As I listened from a beach-chair in the shade... Reprinted from N.
Song: Deftly, admiral, cast your fly... Reprinted from N.
Pleasure island: What there is as a surround to our figures... Reprinted from N.
The fall of Rome: The piers are pummelled by the waves... Reprinted from N.
The managers: In the bad old days it was not so bad... Reprinted from N.
Barbed wire: Across the square... Reprinted from "Memorial for the city" in N.
Under Sirius: Yes, these are the dog-days, Fortunatus... Reprinted from N.
Numbers and faces: The Kingdom of Number is all boundaries... Reprinted from N.
A household: When to disarm suspicious minds at lunch... Reprinted from N.
Precious five: Be patient, solemn nose... Reprinted from N.
The shield of Achilles: She looked over his shoulder... Reprinted from SA.
Fleet visit: The sailors come ashore... Reprinted from SA.
The willow-wren and the stare: A starling and a willow-wren... Reprinted from SA.
The proof: 'When rites and melodies begin... Reprinted from SA.
A permanent way: Self-drivers may curse their luck... Reprinted from SA.
Nocturne: Make this night loveable... Reprinted from SA.
In memoriam L. K-A. 1950–1952: At peace under this mandarin sleep, Lucina... Reprinted from SA.
Bucolics [seven poems]. Reprinted from SA.
Horae canonicae [seven poems]. Reprinted from SA, except "Prime" and "Nones" which had previously appeared in N.
Notes: Published 28 August 1958 in an impression of 30,000 copies at 3/6d., and re-printed in March 1962 (12,500 copies), June 1964 (15,000 copies), February 1966 (15,000 copies), December 1966 (18,000 copies), and November 1967 (20,000 copies).
"The poems in this volume are arranged more or less in the chronological order of their writing: the first dates from 1927, the last from 1954. Some of them I have revised in the interests of euphony or sense or both. W.H.A." (p. [7]).
    Although this is a substantive collection and revision of Auden's poetry, we have not been able to trace any reviews either of the English or the American edition.

b) First American edition 1959

SELECTED POETRY OF | W. H. AUDEN | *Chosen for this edition by the author* | [four lines of verse] | [device: running figure with torch] | THE MODERN LIBRARY · NEW YORK

Collation: 7 x 4¾ in. [1–6]¹⁶, pp. [i–viii, 1–2] 3–180 [181–184].
   [i]: half title. [ii]: blank. [iii]: title page. [iv]: 'FIRST MODERN LIBRARY EDITION, 1959 | [six lines] | *Random House* IS THE PUBLISHER OF *The Modern Library* | BENNETT CERF · DONALD S. KLOPFER | Manufactured in the United States of America by H. Wolff'. [v–viii]: contents. [1]–173: text. [174]: blank. 175–176: index of poems. 177–180: index of first lines. [181–183]: advertisements. [184]: blank.
Binding: Bound in deep purplish blue (197) cloth lettered across the spine in gold: '[device] | [all on a black panel within a gold-rule border] Selected | Poetry | of | W. H. | Auden | [point] | MODERN | LIBRARY', and across the front cover: '[within a gold-ruled rectangle: device in the lower right corner, and a central black panel with a gold-rule border lettered] Selected | Poetry | of | W. H. Auden'. All edges trimmed, and the top edge stained dark blue. Grey endpapers bearing a repeat pattern of the letters 'ml' and the device in the centre of each endpaper. White shiny dust jacket printed in black, yellow, and light blue, and carrying on the verso the list of other titles in the series.
   All later impressions have slightly different bindings.
Paper: White unwatermarked wove paper.
Contents: As the English edition.
Notes: Published 16 February 1959 in an edition of 7,500 copies at $1.65, and reprinted in November 1959 (5,000 copies), May 1961 (5,000 copies), June 1962 (5,000 copies), May 1963 (5,525 copies), February 1965 (5,000 copies), October 1965 (6,000 copies), January 1967 (6,000 copies), August 1967 (7,775 copies), and February 1969 (7,800 copies). No. 160 in the series.

A 41   GOOD-BYE TO THE MEZZOGIORNO   1958

W. H. AUDEN | [title in red] GOOD-BYE | TO THE MEZZO-GIORNO | *poesia inedita* | *e versione italiana* | *di Carlo Izzo* | [device: fish within a circle with the letters G S] | ALL'INSEGNA DEL PESCE D'ORO | MILANO · MCMLVIII

Collation: 7⅛ x 5 in. [1–4]², pp. [1–4] 5–15 [16].
   [1]: half title. [2]: blank. [3]: title page. [4]: '© *1958 by W. H. Auden* | PRINTED IN ITALY'. [5]: occasione; signed 'C.I.' 6–11: text; English on verso, and Italian on recto. [12]: blank. 13: note. [14]: blank. 15: notizia. [16]: 'QUESTO VOLUMETTO A CURA DI VANNI SCHEIWILLER | È STATO IMPRESSO DALLA TIPOGRAFIA U. ALLEGRETTI | DI CAMPI A MILANO IN MILLE COPIE NUMERATE | DA 1 a 1000 | IL 31 DECEMBRE 1958 | COPIA N. [copy number printed]'.
Binding: Glued within a white card cover round which is folded a pale orange yellow (73) paper wrapper lettered across the front as the title page. A white band bearing the title in Italian printed in red is usually tucked round the wrapper.
Paper: White unwatermarked wove paper.
Contents: Good-bye to the Mezzogiorno: Out of a gothic North, the pallid chil-

dren... First printed in *Encounter*, November 1958, and reprinted and revised in HTC and CSP2. Dedicated to Carlo Izzo.

Notes: Details of the printing are given above. The volume was published at 400 lire, and listed in the publisher's catalogue as "Fascicoli di poesia, 5." Izzo states in the preface that he received the original manuscript from Auden on 23 September 1958; however, in the considerably more detailed account he gives in *Shenandoah* (XVIII [Winter 1967], 80–82) he states he received a corrected typescript of the poem, and goes on to say that most of the copies were "sent by Mr. Scheiwiller mostly to friends, as a New Year gift."

A 42   HOMAGE TO CLIO   1960

a) First edition

HOMAGE TO CLIO | By | W. H. AUDEN | [device: a house] | Random House | NEW YORK

Collation: 9 x 5⅞ in. [1–3]⁸[4]⁴[5–7]⁸, pp. [i–viii, 1–2] 3–91 [92–96].
[i]: half title. [ii]: 'By W. H. Auden | [twenty-one lines]'. [iii]: title page. [iv]: 'First Printing | [ten lines] | Manufactured in the United States of America | by the Haddon Craftsmen, Inc., Scranton, Pa.'. [v]: 'For E. R. and A. E. Dodds | [four lines of verse]'. [vi]: blank. [vii–viii]: contents. [1]–91: text; 2, 32, 34, 50, 52, and 84 blank. [92]: blank. [93]: about the author. [94–96]: blank.

Binding: Quarter bound in black cloth with pale orange yellow (73) paper boards lettered down the spine in gold: 'W. H. AUDEN Homage to Clio RANDOM HOUSE', and across the cloth of the front cover: 'Homage to Clio | W. H. AUDEN'. All edges trimmed, and the top edge stained red. Cream dust jacket printed in black and red.

Paper: White unwatermarked wove paper.

Contents:

For E. R. and A. E. Dodds: Bullroarers cannot keep up the annual rain... Reprinted in CSP2.

Part I

Between those happenings that prefigure it...

Homage to Clio: Our hill has made its submission and the green... Reprinted from OMR.

Reflections in a forest: Within a shadowland of trees... Revised and reprinted from the broadside (1957).

Hands: We don't need a face in a picture to know...

The sabbath: Waking on the Seventh Day of Creation... First printed in *Observer*, 6 September 1969, and reprinted in *Poetry London–New York*, Summer 1960, and SelP.

Merax & Mullin: There is one devil in the lexicon... Reprinted from OMR.

On installing an American kitchen in lower Austria: Should the shade of Plato... First printed in *New Yorker*, 7 March 1959, and reprinted in ATH ("Grub first, then ethics") and SelP. Dedicated to Margaret Gardiner.

Objects: All that which lies outside our sort of why... First printed in *Encounter*, January 1957, and reprinted in CSP2.

Words: A sentence uttered makes a world appear... Reprinted in CSP2.

The song: So large a morning so itself to lean... First printed in *Truth*, 12 October 1956, and reprinted in CSP2.

Makers of history: Serious historians care for coins and weapons... Reprinted from OMR.

T the great: Begot like other children, he . . . Reprinted in CSP2.

Secondary epic: No, Virgil, no . . . First printed in *Mid-century*, December 1959, and reprinted in CSP2.

The epigoni: No use invoking Apollo in a case like theirs . . . Reprinted from OMR.

Parable: The watch upon my wrist . . .

The more loving one: Looking up at the stars, I know quite well . . . First printed in *Esquire*, April 1958, and reprinted in *New York times*, 21 August 1960, and CSP2.

Interlude

Dichtung und Wahrheit (an unwritten poem). Reprinted in *Proceedings of the American Academy of Arts and Letters* . . . (1961).

Part II

Although you be, as I am, one of those . . . Reprinted in CSP2.

Dame Kind: Steatopygous, sow-dugged . . . Reprinted in *Encounter*, May 1960.

First things first: Woken, I lay in the arms of my own warmth and listened . . . First printed in *New Yorker*, 9 March 1957, and reprinted in CSP2, and revised in SelP.

An island cemetery: This graveyard with its umbrella pines . . . First printed in *Gemini*, Autumn 1957, and reprinted in *Inventario*, January–December 1959, and CSP2.

Bathtub thoughts: *Hail, future friend, whose present I* . . . Reprinted from OMR.

The old man's road: Across the Great Schism, through our whole landscape . . . Reprinted from OMR.

Walks: I choose the road from here to there . . .

The history of truth: In that ago when being was believing . . . First printed in *Observer*, 29 March 1959 ("In that ago"), and reprinted in CSP2.

The history of science: All fables of adventure stress . . . Reprinted from OMR.

History of the boudoir: A Young Person came out of the mists . . . Reprinted in CSP2.

Metalogue to *The Magic Flute:* Relax, Maestro, put your baton down . . . Reprinted from *The magic flute* (1956).

The aesthetic point of view: As the poets have mournfully sung . . . Reprinted in CSP2.

Limbo culture: The tribes of Limbo, travelers report . . . First printed in *Atlantic*, November 1957, and reprinted in CSP2.

There will be no peace: Though mild clear weather . . . First printed in *Time and tide*, 1 December 1956, and reprinted in CSP2.

Friday's child: He told us we were free to choose . . . First printed in *Listener*, 25 December 1958, and reprinted in SelP. In memory of Dietrich Bonhoeffer.

Good-bye to the Mezzogiorno: Out of a gothic North, the pallid children . . . Reprinted from the pamphlet (1958). Dedicated to Carlo Izzo.

Academic graffiti. A few of these pieces were first printed in *New Yorker*, 4 April 1953 ("People").

Lines addressed to Dr. Claude Jenkins: Let both our Common Rooms combine to cheer . . . Reprinted in CSP2.

Notes: Published 29 April 1960 [CCE 22 April 1960] in an impression of 5,000 copies at $3.50, and reprinted in August 1960 (1,500 copies), and January 1967 (1,000 copies).

Reviews:
  L. Bogan. *New Yorker*, XXXVI (8 October 1960), 197–99.
  J. P. Clancy. *Commonweal*, LXXII (16 September 1960), 500–501.
  F. W. Dupee. *New York times*, 15 May 1960, section 7, p. 4.
  T. Gunn. *Yale review*, L (September 1960), 133–35.
  J. Holmes. *Voices*, 175 (May–August 1961), 36–38.
  J. Levine. *Prairie schooner*, XXXIV (Fall 1960), 193–94.
  E. Sandeen. *Poetry*, XCIII (March 1961), 380–86.

b) First English edition   1960

HOMAGE TO CLIO | *by* | W. H. AUDEN | FABER AND FABER |
24 Russell Square | London

Collation: 8½ x 5½ in. [A]–F⁸, pp. [1–8] 9–91 [92–96].
  [1–2]: blank. [3]: half title. [4]: by the same author. [5]: title page. [6]: *'First
  published in mcmlx | by Faber and Faber Limited | 24 Russell Square London
  W.C. 1 | Printed in Great Britain | at the Bowering Press Plymouth | [two lines]'*.
  [7]: 'For | E. R. and A. E. DODDS | [four lines of verse]'. [8]: blank. 9–10: con-
  tents. 11: acknowledgements. [12]: blank. [13]–91: text; 14, 40, 52, 54, and 84 blank.
Binding: Bound in very deep purplish red (257) cloth lettered down the spine in
  gold with the author and title between thick gold rules: '[treble gold rules] W. H.
  AUDEN [treble gold rules] HOMAGE TO CLIO [treble gold rules] FABER'.
  All edges trimmed. Pale green dust jacket printed in black and red.
Paper: White unwatermarked wove paper.
Contents: As the American edition.
Notes: Published 8 July 1960 in an edition of 4,000 copies at 12/6d.
Reviews:
  A Alvarez. *Observer*, 10 July 1960, p. 27 (see reply by M. Cox, 14 August 1960,
    p. 14).
  K. W. Gransden. *Twentieth century*, CLXVIII (September 1960), 274–76.
  D. Hall. *New statesman*, LX (9 July 1960), 61–62.
  R. Hoggart. *Guardian*, 8 July 1960, p. 4.
  G. Hough. *Listener*, LXIV (28 July 1960), 159–60.
  P. Larkin. *Spectator*, CCV (15 July 1960), 104–5.
  D. Moraes. *Time and tide*, XLI (9 July 1960), 803.
  Times literary supplement, 19 August 1960, p. 530.

A 43   ELEGY FOR YOUNG LOVERS   1961

a) Libretto

Elegy for Young Lovers | Opera in three acts by | W. H. Auden and Ches-
ter Kallman | Music by | Hans Werner Henze | B. SCHOTT'S SÖHNE •
MAINZ | Schott & Co. Ltd., London • B. Schott's Söhne (Editions Max
Eschig), Paris | Schott Music Corp. (Associated Music Publishers Inc.),
New York

Collation: 7¾ x 5¼ in. [1–4]⁸, pp. [1–7] 8–63 [64].
  [1]: title page. [2]: 'All rights including that of translation reserved. | © by
  B. Schott's Söhne 1961. — Printed in Germany. | Published by B. Schott's Söhne,
  Mainz.' [3]: dedication to Hofmannsthal. [5]: blank. [6]: dramatis personae.

[7]: blank. 8–59: text. [60]: blank. 61–63: genesis of a libretto, by Auden and Kallman. [64]: blank.

Binding: Glued in a yellowish white (92) card cover lettered across the front cover, title in green, and the remainder in black: '*Elegy | for Young Lovers* | Opera in three acts | *Textbook* | [swelled rule] | B. SCHOTT'S SÖHNE · MAINZ'. All edges trimmed.

Paper: White unwatermarked wove paper.

Contents:

Elegy for young lovers.

Genesis of a libretto. Reprinted in the programme book of the *Glyndebourne festival opera*, 1961.

Notes: Published 5 June 1961 [*CCE* 20 May 1961] in an impression of 1,000 copies at DM 2, and reprinted in July 1961 (2,000 copies).

The second impression adds the code 'BSS 40 553' to the imprint on the verso of the title page, and reads 'W, H. Auden' on the dedication page.

Henze wrote: "In the late Autumn of 1958, I first asked my friends Auden and Kallman to write a libretto for me. We corresponded between Naples and New York, and met at last in the summer of 1959 in Auden's country house in Lower Austria. There followed lay-outs and rough sketches, and in December the libretto was ready. Only small changes and revisions have later been necessary" (*Glyndebourne festival opera* [programme book], 1961, p. 40; this programme also reprints "Genesis of a libretto," pp. 37-39). The opera was first performed in German at the Schwetzingen Festspiele, Stuttgart, on 20 May 1961, and the world première in the original language was at Glyndebourne on 13 July 1961.

Parts for singers and the conductor, which were not published, were printed on 21 November 1960.

Selections from the opera were recorded on DGG LPM 18 876/ SLPM 138 876 [1964].

The German translation of the libretto, in which the authors collaborated, was published 15 May 1961 [*CCE* 20 May 1961] in an impression of 3,000 copies, and reprinted in January 1963 (2,000 copies). See T97.

b) Miniature score   1961

[left-hand title] Elegy for Young Lovers | Opera in three acts by | Wystan H. Auden and Chester Kallman | Music by | Hans Werner Henze | Miniature Score | Edition Schott 5040 | B. SCHOTT'S SÖHNE · MAINZ | [addresses in two lines]

[right-hand title] Elegie für junge Liebende | Oper in drei Akten von | Wystan H. Auden und Chester Kallman | Musik von | Hans Werner | Henze | Deutsche Fassung von Ludwig Landgraf | unter Mitarbeit von Werner Schachteli und dem Komponisten | Studien-Partitur | Edition Schott 5040 | [three lines]

Collation: 10¾ x 7½ in. [1–34]⁸, pp. [i–xii, 1] 2–532. Plate marked on p. 532 '40461a'. [i]: blank. [ii–iii]: title pages. [iv]: blank. [v]: '[dedication to Hofmannsthal in five lines] | The opera was commissioned by the Suddeutscher Rundfunk, Stuttgart | [one line]'. [vi–vii]: dramatis personae. [viii–ix]: index. [x–xi]: orchestra. [xii]: blank. [1]–532: score and text.

Binding: Glued in a light grey (264) card cover lettered up the spine in black: 'HENZE · ELEGY FOR YOUNG LOVERS' and across the front cover: 'HANS

WERNER HENZE | ELEGY FOR YOUNG LOVERS | ELEGIE FÜR
JUNGE LIEBENDE | Opera in three acts | [device in orange] | Studien-Partitur
| EDITION SCHOTT | 5040'. All edges trimmed.
Paper: White unwatermarked wove paper.
Contents: Elegy for young lovers.
Notes: Printed 18 May 1961 [*CCE* 20 June 1961] in an edition of 800 copies at DM 48.

c) **Piano score**   1961

[left-hand title] Elegy for Young Lovers | Opera in three acts by | Wys-
tan H. Auden and Chester Kallman | Music by | Hans Werner Henze |
Piano Score by Markus Lehmann | Edition Schott 5100 | B. SCHOTT'S
SÖHNE · MAINZ | [addresses in two lines]

[right-hand title] Elegie für junge Liebende | Oper in drei Akten von |
Wystan H. Auden und Chester Kallman | Musik von | Hans Werner Henze
| Deutsche Fassung von Ludwig Landgraf | unter Mitarbeit von Werner
Schachteli und den Komponisten | Klavier—Auszug von Markus Lehmann
| Edition Schott 5100 | B. SCHOTT'S SÖHNE · MAINZ | [addresses
in two lines]

Collation: 11¾ x 9 in. [1–28]⁸[29]⁴, pp. [i–xii, 1] 2–443 [444]. Plate marked on p. 443
   '40463'.
   [i]: blank. [ii–iii]: title pages. [iv]: 'Cover designed by Werner Schachteli · Ein-
   bandentwurf von Werner Schachteli'. [v]: dedication. [vi–vii]: orchestra. [viii–
   ix]: index. [x–xi]: dramatis personae. [xii]: details of the first performance. [1]–
   443: text. [444]: blank.
Binding: Quarter bound in light grey (264) linen with shiny card covers, the front
   cover bearing a green and blue abstract design, lettered across the front cover:
   '[in light blue] HANS | WERNER | HENZE | [in fancy outline letters] ELEGY
   | FOR | YOUNG | LOVERS | ELEGIE | FÜR | JUNGE | LIEBENDE | [in
   light blue] SCHOTT'. The rear cover is blank.
Paper: White unwatermarked wove paper.
Contents: Elegy for young lovers.
Notes: Printed 10 July 1961 [*CCE* 20 June 1961] in an impression of 800 copies at
   DM 45, and reprinted in April 1967 (500 copies).

A 44   **W. H. AUDEN: A SELECTION**   1961

[name in shaded type] W. H. AUDEN | *A Selection* | [swelled rule] |
With notes and a critical essay by | RICHARD HOGGART | [device: a
bull within an oval] | HUTCHINSON EDUCATIONAL

Collation: 7¼ x 4¾ in. [A]–G¹⁶, pp. [1–6] 7–223 [224].
   [1]: half title. [2]: 'HUTCHINSON ENGLISH TEXTS | [eight lines]'. [3]:
   title page. [4]: '[six lines] | *First published 1961* | © the poems W. H. Auden |
   © this edition Richard Hoggart 1961 | *This book has been set in Spectrum type
   face. It has* | *been printed in Great Britain by The Anchor Press,* | *Ltd., in Tiptree,
   Essex, on Smooth Wove paper and* | *bound by Taylor Garnett Evans & Co., Ltd.,
   in* | *Watford, Herts.*' [5]: acknowledgements. [6]: blank. 7: preface. [8]: blank.
   [9–12]: contents. 13–41: introduction. [42]: blank. [43]–195: text. [196]: blank.
   [197–224]: notes. 200: blank.

Binding: Bound in brilliant bluish green (159) imitation cloth-grained paper boards lettered on the spine in silver: '[across] Edited by | RICHARD | HOGGART | [ornamental rule] | [down] W. H. Auden: A Selection | [across] [ornamental rule] | [device within an oval] | [fancy type within an oval] H E T'. All edges trimmed.

Paper: White unwatermarked wove paper.

Contents: The texts of this selection have no authority and are all reprinted without revision; they are therefore not listed here.

Notes: Published 31 July 1961 in an impression of 4,000 copies at 6/-, and reprinted in September 1963 (2,500 copies), March 1964 (4,000 copies), August 1965 (5,000 copies), and March 1969 (5,000 copies).

A 45 THE DYER'S HAND 1962

a) First edition

[swelled rule] | W. H. AUDEN | [short swelled rule] | THE | DYER'S | HAND | *and other essays* | [ornament] | [device: a house] | Random House • New York

Collation: 8¼ x 5½ in. [1–17]¹⁶, pp. [i–xi] xii [xiii–xvi, 1–3] 4–527 [528].
[i]: half title. [ii]: '*By W. H. Auden* | [other titles in twenty-four lines]'. [iii]: title page. [iv]: 'FIRST PRINTING | [five lines] | *Manufactured in the United States of America* | *by The Haddon Craftsmen, Inc., Scranton, Pa.* | [one line] | Designed by Ruth Smerechniak | [seven lines]'. [v–vi]: acknowledgements. [vii]: '*For* | *NEVILL COGHILL* | [four lines]'. [viii]: blank. [ix]: epigraph from Nietzsche. [x]: blank. [xi]–xii: foreword. [xiii–xv]: contents. [xvi]: blank. [1]: 'PART ONE | Prologue'. [2]: blank. [3]–27: text. [28]: blank. [29]: 'PART TWO | The Dyer's Hand'. [30]: blank. [31]–89: text. [90]: blank. [91]: 'PART THREE | The Well of Narcissus'. [92]: blank. [92]–167: text. [168]: blank. [169]: 'PART FOUR | The Shakespearian | City'. [170]: blank. [171]–274: text. [275]: 'PART FIVE | Two Bestiaries'. [276]: blank. [277]–305: text. [306]: blank. [307]: 'PART SIX | Americana'. [308]: blank. [309]–368: text. [369]: 'PART SEVEN | The Shield of Perseus'. [370]: blank. [371]–461: text. [462]: blank. [463]: 'PART EIGHT | Homage to | Igor Stravinsky'. [464]: blank. [465]–527: text. [528]: about the author.

Binding: Bound in light bluish green (163) cloth lettered across the spine in gold on a black panel not running to the full width of the spine: '[wavy rule] | *THE* | *DYER'S HAND* | *by* | W. H. AUDEN | [wavy rule] | RANDOM HOUSE | [wavy rule]'. The device is blind-stamped on the front cover. All edges trimmed, and the top edge stained dark grey. Grey dust jacket printed in orange and brown.

Paper: White unwatermarked wove paper.

Contents: [Note: Many sections for which no previous source is listed are partially compiled from earlier reviews, lectures, etc.]
Part I Prologue
  Reading. Reprinted in SE.
  Writing. Reprinted in SE.
Part II The dyer's hand
  Making, knowing and judging. Reprinted from the pamphlet (1956).
  The virgin and the dynamo.
  The poet and the city. First printed in *Massachusetts review*, Spring 1962.
    Both these pieces bear relationship to the three following previously printed pieces: "Squares and oblongs" from *Poets at work* (1948); "Nature, his-

tory, and poetry," *Thought*, September 1950; and "The dyer's hand," *Listener*, June 1955.

Part III   The well of Narcissus
   Hic et ille.   Reprinted from *Encounter*, April 1956, and *Vogue*, December 1962 ("Mirror").
   Balaam and his ass.   Reprinted from *Thought*, Summer 1954.
   The guilty vicarage.   Reprinted from *Harper's magazine*, May 1948.
   The I without a self.   Reprinted from *Mid-century*, Fall 1960 ("K").

Part IV   The Shakespearian city
   The Globe.
   The Prince's dog.   Reprinted from *Encounter*, November 1959 ("The fallen City"), and reprinted in SE.
   Interlude: the wish game.   Reprinted from *New Yorker*, 16 March 1957.
   Brothers and others.   Reprinted in SE.
   Interlude: West's disease.   Reprinted from *Griffin*, May 1957.
   The joker in the pack.   Reprinted from *Encounter*, August 1961 ("The alienated city"), and reprinted in SE.
   Postscript: infernal science.

Part V   Two bestiaries
   D. H. Lawrence.
   Marianne Moore.

Part VI   Americana
   The American scene.   Reprinted from the edition published by Scribners (1946).
   Postscript: Rome v. Monticello.
   Red ribbon on a white horse.   Reprinted from the book by A. Yezierska (1950).
   Postscript: the Almighty dollar.
   Robert Frost.
   American poetry.   Reprinted from *The Faber book of modern American verse* (1956).

Part VII   The shield of Perseus
   Notes on the comic.   Reprinted from *Thought*, Spring 1952.
   Don Juan.
   Dingley Dell and the Fleet.   Reprinted in SE.
   Postscript: the frivolous and the earnest.
   Genius and apostle.   Partly reprinted from the introduction to *Brand* (1960), and reprinted in SE.
   Postscript: Christianity and art.   Reprinted in SE.

Part VIII   Homage to Igor Stravinsky
   Notes on music and opera.   Reprinted and revised from *Tempo*, Summer 1951.
   Cav & Pag.   Reprinted from the libretto booklet accompanying records of *Cavelleria rusticana* and *I Pagliacci*, RCA Victor WDM 6106 (1953).
   Translating opera libretti [with Chester Kallman].
   Music in Shakespeare.   Reprinted from *Encounter*, December 1957.

Notes: Published 27 November 1962 [*CCE* 21 November 1962] in an edition of 7,500 copies at $7.50.

   Much of the book apparently consists of revised versions of the lectures delivered by Auden as Professor of Poetry at Oxford. The titles and dates of these lectures, as announced in *Oxford University gazette*, are as follows:
   Making, knowing, and judging. [Inaugural lecture.] 11 June 1956.
   Robert Frost. 6 May 1957.
   D. H. Lawrence. 13 May 1957.

The dramatic use of music in Shakespeare's plays. 20 May 1957.
Byron's Don Juan. 12 May 1958.
The quest hero. 19 May 1958.
Dingley Dell and the Fleet: reflections on *Pickwick papers*. 26 May 1958.
Marianne Moore. 4 May 1959.
Translating opera libretti. 11 May 1959.
The fallen city: some reflections on Shakespeare's Henry IV. 25 May 1959.
   [*Cf.* "The prince's dog" in DH.]
The hero in modern poetry. 2 May 1960.
The alienated city, I: reflections on *The merchant of Venice*. 9 May 1960. [*Cf.*
   "Brothers and others" in DH.]
The alienated city, II: reflections on *Othello*. 16 May 1960. [*Cf.* "The joker
   in the pack" in DH.]
The genius and the apostle: a problem of poetic presentation. 24 October 1960.
Mainly valedictory. 31 October 1960.

Reviews:

J. Berryman. *New York review of books*, [I (February 1963)], 19.
J. M. Brinnin. *Saturday review*, XLV (1 December 1962), 48.
E. Callan. *Critic*, XXI (February–March 1963), 77–78.
——. *Christian scholar*, XLVI (Summer 1963), 168–73.
P. Cruttwell. *Hudson review*, XVI (Summer 1963), 316–20.
B. Deutsch. *Prairie schooner*, XXXVII (Summer 1963), 175–76.
J. Epstein. *Partisan review*, XXX (Summer 1963), 281–85.
R. Hecht & C. Hallett. *Sewanee review*, LXXXII (Summer 1963), 536–40.
S. E. Hyman. *New leader*, XLV (26 November 1962), 22–23.
S. Hynes. *Ramparts*, II (Autumn 1963), 86–89.
A. Kazin. *Reporter*, XXVIII (31 January 1963), 53–54.
D. Malcolm. *New Yorker*, XXXIX (4 May 1963), 185–90.
W. Meredith. *Poetry*, CVII (November 1965), 118–20.
A. Rosen. *Kenyon review*, XXV (Autumn 1963), 739–43.
R. P. Rushmore. *Shenandoah*, XIV (Spring 1963), 52–57.
L. Simpson. *American scholar*, XXXII (Spring 1963), 314–16.
G. Steiner. *New York times*, 7 April 1963, section 7, p. 54.
H. Tracy. *New republic*, CXLVIII (16 March 1963), 22–23.
H. Zinnes. *Books abroad*, XXXVIII (Winter 1964), 77–78.

b) First English edition   1963

W. H. AUDEN | [swelled rule] | THE | DYER'S | HAND | *and other
essays* | [ornament] | FABER AND FABER | 24 Russell Square | London

Collation: 8½ x 5¼ in. [1–34]⁸, pp. [i–xi] xii [xiii–xvi, 1–3] 4–527 [528].
   [i]: half title. [ii]: '*also by W. H. Auden* | [other titles and collaborators in eigh-
   teen lines]'. [iii]: title page. [iv]: '*First published in England in mcmlxiii* | *by
   Faber & Faber Limited* | *24 Russell Square London W.C.1* | *Printed in Great Britain
   by* | *Latimer Trend & Co Ltd Whitstable* | [three lines]'. The remainder of the
   collation is identical with the American edition, only the Random House device
   being removed from the final page.
Binding: Bound in moderate bluish green (164) cloth lettered across the spine in
   gold: '[double rule] | THE | DYER'S | HAND | [star] | W. H. | AUDEN |
   [double rule] | FABER AND | FABER'. All edges trimmed, and top edge stained
   yellow. Light green dust jacket printed in black and red.
Paper: White unwatermarked wove paper.

Contents: As the American edition.
Notes: Published 19 April 1963 in an impression of 3,000 copies at 42/–, and reprinted
   in April 1964 (1,940 copies). A lithographic reprint of the American edition with
   some corrections; the second impression has further corrections.
Reviews:
   J. Bayley. *Encounter,* XXI (August 1963), 74–76, 78–81.
   B. Bergonzi. *Spectator,* CCX (17 May 1963), 640.
   W. Empson. *New statesman,* LXV (19 April 1963), 592, 594–95.
   A. J. Farmer. *Études anglaises,* XVII (April–June 1963), 206–7.
   R. Hoggart. *Listener,* LXIX (25 April 1963), 720.
   G. LeBreton. *Mercure de France,* CCCLII (September 1964), 150–56.
   L. Lerner. *London magazine,* n.s. III (November 1963), 85–88.
   R. P. Laidlaw. *Poetry Australia,* 19 (December 1967), 45–47.
   H. Peschmann. *English,* XIV (Autumn 1963), 240.
   Times literary supplement, 7 June 1963, p. 404.
   R. Williams. *Review of English studies,* XV (August 1964), 337–39.

c) First paperback impression   1968

[left-hand title] VINTAGE BOOKS | A Division of Random House |
New York | [device: sun with a face]

[right-hand title] W. H. AUDEN | [swelled rule] | THE | DYER'S |
HAND | *and other essays* | [ornament]

Collation: 7¼ x 4¼ in. Two hundred and seventy-two single leaves, pp. [i–xi] xii
   [xiii–xvi, 1–3] 4–527 [528].
   The collation is identical with that of the first edition except for p. [ii] which is
   described above as the left-hand title page and that the biographical note on p.
   [528] is revised and reset.
Binding: A perfect binding glued in a white card cover printed in black on the spine
   and front cover and in moderate reddish purple (241) on the rear cover. Lettered
   down the spine in blue: 'THE DYER'S HAND [across the spine] [purple rule] |
   [in white] W. H. | AUDEN | [device in purple] | [in white] VINTAGE |
   V–418'. Across the front cover: '[blue rule] | [in purple] THE | DYER'S | HAND
   | [in white] AND OTHER ESSAYS | [in blue] W. H. AUDEN | [in purple:
   four-line quotation from a review by Alfred Kazin] | [in white] A Vintage Book
   [device] V–418 $2.45'. The rear cover carries extracts from other reviews of the
   first edition. All edges trimmed.
Paper: White wove unwatermarked paper.
Contents: As the first edition. There are some slight corrections.
Notes: Published in March 1968 in an impression of 7,500 copies at $2.45.

A 46   LOUIS MACNEICE   1963

LOUIS MACNEICE | *a memorial address* | *by* | W. H. AUDEN | deliv-
ered at | All Souls, Langham Place | on 17 October, 1963 | [illustration of
All Souls church] | Privately printed for | FABER AND FABER, LON-
DON

Collation: 8½ x 5½ in. One unsigned gathering of eight leaves, pp. [1–6] 7–14
   [15–16].
   [1–2]: blank. [3]: half title. [4]: blank. [5]: title page. [6]: '*Printed in Great Britain*

| *by R. MacLehose & Co. Ltd Glasgow* | [one line] | © *1963 by W. H. Auden*'. 7–14: text. At the foot of p. 14: 'Part of this address has already been published in *The Listener*.' [15–16]: blank.

Binding: Stitched in a light greyish purplish red (261) wrapper folded round the end leaves and lettered in black across the front wrapper as the title page. All edges trimmed.

Paper: Cream laid paper watermarked '[crown] | Abbey Mills | Greenfield' in gothic.

Contents: Louis MacNeice: a memorial address. First partially printed in *Listener*, 24 October 1963.

Notes: Printed for private distribution by Faber & Faber in an edition of 250 copies in November 1963. Not distributed at the memorial service, but sent out afterwards to a number of personal friends whose names were mainly suggested by Mrs. Mac-Neice.

A 47   SELECTED ESSAYS   1964

SELECTED ESSAYS | by | W. H. AUDEN | FABER AND FABER | 24 Russell Square | London

Collation: 7¼ x 4¾ in. One hundred and twelve single leaves, [A]–G¹⁶, pp. [1–6] 7–224.
    [1–2]: blank. [3]: half title. [4]: '*by the same author* | [names of collaborators and titles in nineteen lines]'. [5]: title page. [6]: '*First published in this edition mcmlxiv | by Faber and Faber Limited | 24 Russell Square London W.C.1 | Printed in Great Britain by | R. MacLehose and Company Limited | The University Press Glasgow | [seven lines]*'. 7: contents. [8]: blank. 9–224: text.

Binding: A perfect binding glued in a shiny white card cover lettered down the spine: '[purple rule] [in black] W. H. AUDEN   Selected Essays [in white on a purple panel] FABER', and across the front cover: '[purple rule] | [author and title in black] W. H. | [purple rule] | AUDEN | [purple rule] | Selected | [purple rule] | Essays | [purple rule] | [in white on a black panel] FABER', and down the leading edge on a similar panel: 'FABER paper covered EDITIONS'; this panel is repeated on the rear cover which carries, inside and out, a list of other titles in the series. All edges trimmed.

Paper: White unwatermarked wove paper.

Contents:
Reading.
Writing.
The Prince's dog.
Brothers and others.
The joker in the pack.
D. H. Lawrence.
Robert Frost.
Dingley Dell and the Fleet.
Genius and apostle.
Postscript: Christianity and art.
    All reprinted from DH.

Notes: Published 8 May 1964 in an edition of 12,000 copies at 7/6d. "This selection has been specially made by Mr. Auden for inclusion in Faber Paper Covered Editions. All the Essays in it appeared originally in *The Dyer's Hand*, his collection of critical pieces which was first published in this country in 1963 ..." (inside front wrapper). There are some slight corrections to the text.
    The three essays titled "Reading," "Writing," and "Postscript: Christianity and

art" were published in English in a Japanese edition with Japanese notes, which
may be briefly described as follows: [title page] 'Nan'un-do's Contemporary Li-
brary | [rule] | READING | AND WRITING | W. H. AUDEN | *EDITED
WITH NOTES | BY* | Koichi Yashima | [rule] | Tokyo | NAN'UN-DO | [de-
vice] | C-A6'. The book collates 7⅛ x 5 in. [1–6]⁸[7]², pp. [*–**] i–iii [iv–vi],
1–90 [91–92], and was published 20 February 1966 in an impression of 3,000 copies
at Yen 260, and reprinted in February 1967 (1,500 copies). On the verso of the
title page it is stated that the essays are taken from SE. This is no. 6 in Nan'un-do's
Contemporary Library.

A 48   THE COMMON LIFE   1964

W. H. AUDEN | The Common Life | *Deutsch von Dieter Leisegang* |
J. G. BLÄSCHKE VERLAG DARMSTADT

Collation: 8 x 5 in. One unsigned gathering of twelve leaves, pp. [1–24].
   [1–2]: blank. [3]: '*Das Neueste Gedicht* [device: an hourglass] *Band 5* | *Heraus-
gegeben von* | *Horst Heiderhoff und Dieter Leisegang*'. [4]: abstract illustration in
black and white. [5]: title page. [6–19]: text; English on versos, German on rectos.
[20]: '*Einige Gedanken zur vorliegenden Übertragung* | [thirty-seven lines, signed]
D. L.'. [21–22]: notes on Auden and his work. [23–24]: blank.
Binding: A perfect binding glued in a white card cover round which is a medium
grey (265) wrapper lettered across the front cover in black: 'W. H. Auden | The
Common Life | *Englisch—Deutsch* | [device]'. All edges trimmed.
   A second issue is bound in light yellowish pink (28) wrappers and omits '*En-
glisch—Deutsch*' from the cover.
Paper: White unwatermarked wove paper.
Contents:
   Ascension day 1964: From leaf to leaf in silence... First printed in *London maga-
zine*, August 1964, and reprinted in ATH.
   The common life: A living-room, the catholic area you... First printed in *New
York review of books*, 26 December 1963, and reprinted in *London magazine*,
January 1964, and ATH.
Notes: Published in September 1964 in an edition of 1,500 copies at DM 2.20. "Mr
Auden sent us these four poems [i.e., these two and those subsequently published
in *The cave of making*] himself in summer 1964" (Dieter Leisegang in a letter to
Bloomfield).
   'Auflage 1500 Exemplare | Copyright 1964 by Horst Heiderhoff und Dieter
Leisegang, Frankfurt am Main | Textur Seite 4 von Jolei | Schrift Caslon-Antiqua
mit kursiv, D. Stempel AG, Frankfurt am Main | Printed in Germany' (p. [22]).
   The second issue in light yellowish pink wrappers seems to have been issued in
late 1968 or early 1969. The new colour was used because the original paper, which
came from France, could no longer be obtained.

A 49   ABOUT THE HOUSE   1965

a) First edition

[left-hand title] [device: a house] | RANDOM HOUSE | NEW YORK

[right-hand title] ABOUT | THE HOUSE | [rule] | W. H. AUDEN

Collation: 8¼ x 5½ in. [1–6]⁸, pp. [i–x, 1–2] 3–84 [85–86].
   [i]: blank. [ii]: '*By W. H. Auden* | [titles and collaborators in twenty-four lines]'.

[iii]: half title. [iv–v]: title pages. [vi]: '*First Printing* | [copyright statements and acknowledgements in seventeen lines] | *Manufactured in the United States of America* | *by The Haddon Craftsmen, Scranton, Pennsylvania* | *Designed by Betty Anderson*'. [vii]: 'FOR | Edmund AND Elena | Wilson | [four lines of verse]'. [viii]: blank. [ix–x]: contents. [1]–84: text; 2 and 40 blank. [85]: about the author. [86]: blank.

Binding: Quarter bound in black cloth with greyish brown (61) paper-covered boards, and lettered down the spine in gold: 'W. H. AUDEN [device and publisher's name across the spine] [device] | Random | House | ABOUT THE HOUSE'. Top and leading edges trimmed, and the top edge stained light blue. White dust jacket printed in pale yellow, black, and light blue.

Paper: Cream unwatermarked wove paper.

Contents:

For Edmund and Elena Wilson: A moon profaned by . . .

Thanksgiving for a habitat

    I   Prologue. The birth of architecture: From gallery-grave and the hunt of a wren-king . . . Dedicated to John Bayley.

   II Thanksgiving for a habitat: Nobody I know would like to be buried . . . First printed in *New Yorker*, 17 August 1963. Dedicated to Geoffrey Gorer.

  III The cave of making: For this and all enclosures like it the archetype . . . First printed in *Listener*, 1 October 1964, and reprinted in *Observer* [colour magazine], 9 January 1966, and as a pamphlet (1965). In memoriam Louis MacNeice.

  IV Down there: A cellar underneath the house, though not lived in . . . First printed in *John Crowe Ransom, a tribute* (1964). Dedicated to Irving Weiss.

   V Up there: Men would never have come to need an attic . . . First printed in *John Crowe Ransom, a tribute* (1964). Dedicated to Anne Weiss.

  VI The geography of the house: Seated after breakfast . . . Dedicated to Christopher Isherwood.

 VII Encomium balnei: it is odd that the English . . . First printed in *Encounter*, August 1962. Dedicated to Neil Little.

VIII Grub first, then ethics (Brecht): Should the shade of Plato . . . Reprinted from HTC.

  IX For friends only: Ours yet not ours, being set apart . . . Dedicated to John and Teckla Clark.

   X Tonight at seven-thirty: The life of plants . . . Dedicated to M. F. K. Fisher.

  XI The cave of nakedness: Don Juan needs no bed, being far too impatient to undress . . . First printed in *Encounter*, December 1963. Dedicated to Louis and Emmie Kronenberger.

 XII The common life: A living room, the catholic area you . . . First printed in *New York review of books*, 26 December 1963, and reprinted in *London magazine*, January 1964, and in a pamphlet (1964). Dedicated to Chester Kallman.

The entire sequence, without the "postscripts" to poems I, III, and XI, is reprinted in SelP.

In and out

    We've covered ground since that awkward day . . .

    A change of air: Corns, heartburn, sinus headaches, such minor ailments . . . First printed in *Encounter*, January 1962, and reprinted (together with Auden's reply to his critics in a symposium on the poem) in *Kenyon review*, Winter 1964, and in a pamphlet *The cave of making* (1965).

You: Really, must you... First printed in *Badger*, Autumn 1960, and reprinted in *Saturday evening post*, 3 March 1962.

Et in Arcadia ego: Who, now, seeing Her so... First printed in *New York
review of books*, 3 June 1965.

Hammerfest: For over forty years I'd paid it atlas homage... First printed
in *London magazine*, March 1962.

Iceland revisited: Unwashed, unshat... First printed in *Lesbók morgunblaðsins*, 31 May 1964, and reprinted in *Encounter*, July 1964, and *Iceland
review*, [Autumn] 1964. Dedicated to Basil and Susan Boothby.

On the circuit: Among Pelagian travelers... First printed in *New Yorker*,
4 July 1964.

Four occasional poems

    A toast: What on earth does one say at a Gaudy...

    A short ode to a philologist: Necessity knows no Speech. Not even...
    First printed in *English and mediaeval studies presented to J. R. R.
    Tolkien* (1962).

    Elegy for J. F. K.: Why *then*, why *there*... Printed in *Sunday times*, 22
    November 1964, *Evening standard*, 23 November 1964, in a musical
    setting by Stravinsky (1964), and (in a facsimile of the poet's manu-
    script) in *Adam*, 300 (1963–65).

    Lines for Elizabeth Mayer: Withdrawn from the Object-World...

Symmetries and asymmetries.

Four transliterations

    I   The romantic [by Adam Mickiewicz]: "Silly girl, listen!"... First
       printed in *Wiadomości*, 19 February 1956, and reprinted in *Selected
       poems of Adam Mickiewicz* (1956).

    II Volcanoes [by Bella Akhmadulina]: Extinct volcanoes are silent...

    III The complaint book [by Evgeni Vinokurov]: Every railroad station
       keeps a book for complaints...

    IV Parabolic ballad [by Andrei Voznesensky]: Along a parabola like a
       rocket flies...

    II, III, and IV were first printed in *Encounter*, April 1963, and were re-
    printed in *Half-way to the moon*, ed. by Patricia Blake and Max Hayward
    (1964). IV was also reprinted in *Antiworlds*, by Andrei Voznesensky
    (1966).

The maker: Unmarried, nearsighted, rather deaf... First printed in *Poetry
in crystal* (1963), reprinted in *New York times*, 28 April 1963 in an advertisement, and in *Of books and humankind* (1964).

At the party: Unrhymed, unrhythmical, the chatter goes...

Lost: Lost on a fogbound spit of sand...

Bestiaries are out: A sweet tooth taught us to admire...

After reading a child's guide to modern physics: If all a top physicist knows
... First printed in *New Yorker*, 17 November 1962.

Ascension day, 1964: From leaf to leaf in silence... First printed in *London
magazine*, August 1964, and reprinted in a pamphlet *The common life*
(1964).

Whitsunday in Kirchstetten: *Komm Schöpfer Geist* I bellow as Herr Beer...
First printed in *Reporter*, 6 December 1962, and reprinted in *Wort und
Wahrheit*, May 1963, and *Listener*, 7 November 1963. Dedicated to H. A.
Reinhold.

Notes: Published 13 July 1965 [*CCE* 21 June 1965] in an impression of 2,000 copies
at $3 and reprinted in June 1965 (1,200 copies), August 1965 (1,500 copies), Sep-
tember 1965 (2,000 copies), and December 1965 (2,450 copies). 5,300 copies were
either sold or subscribed on publication day.

The second impression transposes the last two lines on p. 66, but these are re-stored in the third, which also contains further corrections. The fifth impression carries no statement on the verso of the right-hand title page as to which impression it is; its paper-covered boards are sometimes found in moderate brown (58).

Reviews:
H. Carruth. *Poetry*, CVIII (May 1966), 119–21.
D. Donoghue. *Hudson review*, XVIII (Winter 1965–66), 602–3.
I. Ehrenpreis. *Virginia quarterly review*, XLII (Winter 1966), 163–65.
G. P. Elliott. *Book week*, II (18 July 1965), 2, 11.
G. S. Fraser. *New York times*, 18 July 1965, section 7, p. 5.
H. Kramer. *New leader*, XLVIII (16 August 1965), 12–13.
R. Mazzocco. *New York review of books*, V (5 August 1965), 5–7.
A. Pryce-Jones. *New York times*, 4 August 1965, p. 19.
W. J. Smith. *Harper's magazine*, CCXXI (August 1965), 108.
R. D. Spector. *Saturday review*, XLVIII (7 August 1965), 29.
J. Updike. *Motive*, XXVI (November 1965), 50–52.
F. J. Warnke. *New republic*, CLIV (15 January 1966), 28, 30.
K. Weatherhead. *Northwest review*, VIII (Spring 1967), 86–87.

b) First English edition   1966

About the House | by | W. H. AUDEN | FABER AND FABER | 24 Russell Square | London

Collation: 8½ x 5⅜ in. [A]–F⁸, pp. [1–8] 9–94 [95–96].
  [1]: half title. [2]: '*by the same author* | [names of collaborators and titles in twenty-three lines]'. [3]: title page. [4]: '*First published in England in mcmlxvi* | *by Faber and Faber Limited* | *24 Russell Square London WC1* | *Printed in Great Britain* | *by the Bowering Press Plymouth* | [two lines]'. [5]: 'FOR | EDMUND AND ELENA | WILSON | [four lines of verse]'. [6]: blank. [7]: acknowledgements. [8]: blank. 9–10: contents. [11]–94: text, 12 and 50 blank. [95–96]: blank.
Binding: Bound in light purplish blue (199) cloth lettered down the spine in gold: 'ABOUT THE HOUSE · W. H. AUDEN FABER'. All edges trimmed. White dust jacket printed in black, olive green, and purple.
Paper: White unwatermarked wove paper.
Contents: As the American edition.
Notes: Published 27 January 1966 in an edition of 4,000 copies at 15/–, and reprinted in March 1966 (4,000 copies). In the first impression an erratum slip is tipped in facing p. [8] correcting the spelling of 'Iclandic' (p. 59) and 'Tolkein' (p. 61); these, and some other corrections, are made in the second impression.
Reviews:
C. B. Cox. *Spectator*, CCXVI (4 February 1966), 141–42.
C. Falck. *Encounter*, XXVII (August 1966), 77–80.
J. Fuller. *London magazine*, n.s. VI (April 1966), 116–20.
F. Kermode. *Guardian*, 28 January 1966, p. 9; reprinted in *Manchester guardian weekly*, XCIV (3 February 1966), 11.
G. Martin. *Listener*, LXXV (3 February 1966), 179.
P. Oettlé. *Poetry Australia*, IV (December 1967), 41–44.
J. Press. *Punch*, CCL (23 March 1966), 431.
C. Ricks. *New statesman*, LXXI (4 February 1966), 166.
H. Sergeant. *English*, XVI (Autumn 1966), 113.
Times literary supplement, 17 March 1966, p. 224.

P. Toynbee. *Observer*, 30 January 1966, p. 26; a French translation appeared in *Table ronde*, 220 (May 1966), 143–46.

A 50   THE CAVE OF MAKING   1965

W. H. AUDEN | The Cave of Making | *Deutsch von Dieter Leisegang* | J. G. BLÄSCHKE VERLAG DARMSTADT

Collation: 8 x 5 in. One unsigned gathering of twelve leaves, pp. [1–24].
   [1–2]: blank. [3]: '*Das Neueste Gedicht* [device: an hourglass] *Band 15* | *Heraus-gegeben von* | *Horst Heiderhoff und Dieter Leisegang*'. [4]: abstract illustration in black and white. [5]: title page. [6–21]: text; English on versos, German on rectos. [22–23]: notes on Auden and his work. [24]: blank. A thin sheet of pink tissue is inserted facing the frontispiece.
Binding: A perfect binding glued in a white card cover round which is a pale yellow (89) wrapper lettered across the front cover in black: 'W. H. Auden | The Cave of Making | *Englisch—Deutsch* | [device]'. All edges trimmed.
Paper: White unwatermarked wove paper.
Contents:
   The cave of making: For this and for all enclosures like it the archetype ...   First printed in *Listener*, 1 October 1964, and reprinted in *Observer*, 9 January 1966, and ATH. In memoriam Louis MacNeice.
   A change of air: Corns, heartburn, sinus headaches, such minor ailments ...   First printed in *Encounter*, January 1962, and reprinted in *Kenyon review* (with Auden's reply to his critics in a symposium on the poem), Winter 1964, and ATH.
Notes: Published in October 1965 in an edition of 1,500 copies at DM 2.20.
   'Auflage 1500 Exemplare | © 1965 Horst Heiderhoff und Dieter Leisegang, Frankfurt am Main | Textur Seite 4 von Jolei | Schrift: Caslon-Antiqua mit Kursiv der D. Stempel AG, Frankfurt am Main | Druck: J. G. Bläschke Presse Darmstadt | Printed in Germany' (p. [23]). See also the notes to A48.

A 51   HALF-WAY   1965

[drawing by Laurence Scott in blue] | [signed by Scott in pencil] | *Half-Way* | [text in two columns of thirteen lines] | (*Revised from an old note-book, c. 1931.*) | W. H. AUDEN | [Auden's signature in ink] | This poem is here published for the first time in an edition limited to seventy-five copies, of which this is No. [number in ink]. It is set in | 14-point Caslon Roman type, and was printed on a hand-press in Harvard Yard, by *The Lowell-Adams House Printers,* | November, 1965. Drawing by Laurence Scott.

Collation: 18 x 11½ in. Single sheet printed on one side only.
Binding: None.
Paper: White wove paper watermarked 'WARREN'S | OLDE STYLE'.
Contents: Half-way: Having abdicated with comparative ease ...   An earlier version appeared in *Cambridge left*, Summer 1933 ("Interview"), and was reprinted in *Bozart-Westminster*, Spring–Summer 1935. This revised version is reprinted in CSP2.
Notes: Details of the printing are given above. The productions of this press are not

normally for sale, and copies were presumably distributed by the printer. However, some copies were apparently sold at $65. Described from the copy at Harvard College Library; other copies are at Brown University, Columbia University, Yale University, and the New York Public Library.

A 52   BUT I CAN'T   1966

[Illustration by Laurence Scott signed "Scott" on the plate in blue "2 iii 66"; this copy signed in pencil and inscribed "For Mac Hammond"] | BUT I CAN'T | [text in nineteen lines] | W. H. AUDEN | [Auden's signature in ink] | Printed for SVATAVA PIRKOVA JAKOBSON by Laurence Scott with the author's permission, this broadside | edition consists of ten numbered copies. March, 1966, at Cambridge, Massachusetts. NUMBER [number in blue ink]

Collation: 27 x 15 in. Single sheet printed on one side only.
Binding: None.
Paper: White laid paper, deckle edge left, blind stamped in the lower left corner: 'VERITABLE PAPIER D'ARCHES | FIN'.
Contents: But I can't: Time will say nothing but I told you so . . . Reprinted from CP.
Notes: The circumstances of the printing are given above; however, some copies were apparently sold at $400. Described from the copy in the Lockwood Memorial Library.

A 53   PORTRAITS   1966

[ornamental treble rule] | PORTRAITS | [ornamental treble rule] | POEMS by W. H. AUDEN | WOOD ENGRAVINGS by M. W. BROWAR | APIARY PRESS 1966

Collation: 7½ x 7½ in. One unsigned gathering of ten leaves, pp. [1–20].
[1–2]: blank. [3]: title page. [4]: blank. [5]: wood engraving of Auden. [6]: wood engraving of E. M. Forster. [7–8]: text. [9]: wood engraving of Matthew Arnold. [10]: wood engraving of Herman Melville and text. [11–12]: text. [13]: wood engraving of Edward Lear and text. [14]: text. [15–16]: blank. [17]: 'Twenty copies of this book | have been printed at The Apiary | Press, Northampton, Massachusetts. | The text is hand-set in Bembo types | and printed on Franklin Cream. | The wood engravings are by | Margaret Browar. This is | copy number [number in ink] | [device: a bee]'. [18–20]: blank.
Binding: Stitched in a moderate yellowish brown (77) wrapper lettered across the front cover in black: '[ornamental treble rule] | PORTRAITS | [ornamental treble rule]'.
Paper: Cream laid paper watermarked with a P interlaced with a Z. Deckle at the foot of each leaf.
Contents:
  E. M. Forster: Here though the bombs are real and dangerous . . . Reprinted from JTW.
  Matthew Arnold: His gift knew what he was—a dark disordered city . . . Reprinted from AT.

Herman Melville: Towards the end he sailed into an extraordinary mildness...
Reprinted from AT.

Edward Lear: Left by his friends to breakfast alone on the white... Reprinted
from AT.

Notes: Apart from the details given above Miss Browar sent Bloomfield the following
information: "I printed the book in twenty copies as my final project at Smith
College...under the tutelage of Mr Leonard Baskin. Each copy was hand-set,
hand-printed, and hand-bound and the wood engravings are my own work."
Probably finished in April or May 1966.

A 54   **THE BASSARIDS**   **1966**

a) Vocal score

DIE BASSARIDEN | Opera seria mit Intermezzo | in einem Akt | nach
den ,,Bacchanten" des Euripides | von W. H. Auden und Chester Kall-
man | Musik von | HANS WERNER HENZE | Klavierauszug | Edition
Schott 5490 | B. SCHOTT'S SÖHNE • MAINZ | Schott & Co. Ltd., Lon-
don • B. Schott's Söhne (Editions Max Eschig), Paris | Schott Music Corp.
(Associated Music Publishers Inc.), New York | Printed in Germany

Collation: 11⅞ x 9 in. [1]¹⁰[2–39]⁸[40]¹⁰, pp. [i–xx, 1] 2–629 [630]. On p. 629
'Verlag B. Schott' [*sic*] Söhne, Mainz 41 447'.
[i–ii]: blank. [iii]: half title. [iv]: blank. [v]: title page. [vi]: 'Einrichtung von
Helmut Reinold | Ins Deutsche übersetzt von Maria Bosse-Sporleder | [star]
Klavierauszug von Carlos Berner | [star] | Umschlagentwurf: Günter Hädeler |
[star] | Die Oper wurde im Auftrag | der Salzburger Festspiele komponiert | und
am 6. August 1966 | im Grossen Festspielhaus uraufgeführt. | Musikalische Leitung:
Christoph von Dohnányi; | Regie: Gustav Rudolf Sellner; | Ausstattung: Filippo
Sanjust; | Choreographie: Derryk Mendel | Chor der Wiener Staatsoper | (Ein-
studierung: Walter Hagen-Groll); | Die Wiener Philharmoniker'. [vii]: '*Die
Mythe log* ... | Gottfried Benn'. [viii–ix]: characters in the opera. [x]: index. [xi]:
instruments of the orchestra. [xii–xv]: Genealogical tree, mythological background,
religious attitudes of the characters, synopsis of the action; English on versos,
German on rectos, signed by Auden and Kallman. [xx]: blank. [1]–629: score
and text. [630]: blank.
Binding: Quarter bound in rough yellowish white (92) cloth with shiny deep red
(13) paper-covered boards lettered across the front cover in white: 'HANS
WERNER HENZE | THE BASSARIDS | SCHOTT'. All edges trimmed. Some
copies were issued bound in stiff card covers instead of boards.
Paper: White unwatermarked wove paper.
Contents: The Bassarids [text in English and German].
Notes: Published 26 July 1966 in an impression of 300 copies at DM 56, and reprinted
in September 1966 (500 copies).
     "Auden suggested *The Bacchae* of Euripides as the subject.... Auden handed
the libretto over to me in the Summer of 1963.... I asked Auden and Kallman to
mould the opera to the form of a symphony, and the libretto is designed to make
it a symphony in four movements" (Henze in an interview with Alan Blyth,
Opera, XVII [August 1966], 609). The libretto was written between May and
August 1963 (H. Geitel, *Hans Werner Henze* [Berlin: Rembrandt Verlag, 1968],
p. 114), and the copyright entry for the typescript of the libretto at the Library
of Congress is dated 13 January 1964. The details of the first performance are
given above.

For a production at Santa Fe, New Mexico, on 7 August 1968, the intermezzo was dropped and a new prologue was added, spoken and sung by Dionysus. This was not written by Auden or Kallman.

b) Libretto 1966

The Bassarids | Opera Seria with Intermezzo | in One Act | based on "The Bacchae" of Euripides | by W. H. Auden and Chester Kallman | Music by | HANS WERNER HENZE | B. SCHOTT'S SÖHNE · MAINZ | [other addresses in two lines]

Collation: 7¾ x 5 in. One unsigned gathering of thirty-four leaves, pp. [1–5] 6–67 [68].
[1]: title page. [2]: '© by B. Schott's Söhne, Mainz, 1966 · BSS 41 450 | Production: Mainzer Verlagsanstalt und Druckerei, Will und Rothe KG, Mainz. | Printed in Germany'. [3]: characters in the opera. [4]: epigraph. [5]–67: text. [68]: blank.
Binding: Stapled twice in a yellowish white (92) card cover lettered across the front cover, title in blue, the rest in black: 'HANS WERNER HENZE | The Bassarids | Opera Seria with Intermezzo in One Act | based on "The Bacchae" of Euripides | by W. H. Auden and Chester Kallman | *Text* | [swelled rule] | B. SCHOTT'S SÖHNE · MAINZ'. An ornament in black is on the rear cover. All edges trimmed.
Paper: White unwatermarked wove paper.
Contents: The Bassarids.
Notes: Published 3 August 1966 [*CCE* 1 August 1966] in an edition of 2,000 copies at DM 3.

A 55   MARGINALIA   1966

MARGINALIA *by* W. H. AUDEN

Collation: 6⅞ x 7¾ in. One unsigned gathering of twelve leaves, pp. [1–24].
[1–3]: blank. [4]: illustration in bluish grey. [5]: title page. [6]: 'Copyright © 1966 by W. H. Auden'. [7–18]: text, and illustrations in bluish grey. [19–20]: blank. [21]: '[on the left as ibex head in bluish grey] THIS IS NUMBER [number in red ink] OF AN EDITION LIMITED TO ONE | HUNDRED & FIFTY COPIES (OF WHICH FORTY-FIVE ARE | HORS COMMERCE), PRINTED AT CAMBRIDGE, MASSACHU- | SETTS, APRIL, 1966, BY THE IBEX PRESS, WITH ENGRAV- | INGS BY LAURENCE SCOTT. | [manuscript signature of Auden and Scott]'. [22–24]: blank.
Binding: Stitched in a white card cover round which is folded a blackish blue (188) marbled paper wrapper. A white label is stuck on the front cover and lettered across in black: 'MARGINALIA *by* W. H. AUDEN'. All edges untrimmed.
Paper: White laid paper watermarked with a hand, Veronica's handkerchief and the date 1399, and the letters FJH in cursive.
Contents: Marginalia. First printed, in different form, in *New York review of books*, 3 February 1966, and reprinted, again in a different form, in CWW.
Notes: Printing details are given above. The pamphlet was not actually published until October 1966, and copies were sold at $37.50. There are also some lettered copies of which some have a variant label with the lettering measuring 5¾ x ¾ in. instead of the usual 4¼ x ⅜ in.

A 56   COLLECTED SHORTER POEMS   1966
1927–1957

a) First edition

W. H. AUDEN | [ornamental swelled rule] | *Collected Shorter Poems* | *1927–1957* | FABER AND FABER LIMITED | 24 Russell Square | London

Collation: 8½ x 5⅜ in. [A]–Y⁸, pp. [1–8] 9–351 [352]. $1 signed 'A.C.S.P.'
[1–2]: blank. [3]: half title. [4]: 'by the same author | [names of collaborators and titles in twenty-three lines]'. [5]: title page. [6]: *'First published in mcmlxvi | by Faber and Faber Limited | 24 Russell Square London W.C.1 | Printed in Great Britain by | R. MacLehose and Company Limited | The University Press Glasgow | [three lines]'*. [7]: 'For | CHRISTOPHER ISHERWOOD | and | CHESTER KALLMAN | [four lines of verse]'. [8]: blank. 9–14: contents. 15–16: foreword. [17]: 'Part I | [swelled rule] | *1927–1932*'. [18]: blank. 19–66: text. [67]: 'Part II | [swelled rule] | *1933–1938*'. [68]: blank. 69–138: text, [139]: 'Part III | [swelled rule] | *1939–1947*'. [140]: blank. 141–233: text. [234]: blank. [235]: 'Part IV | [swelled rule] | *1948–1957*'. [236]: blank. 237–341: text. [342]: blank. 343–351: index of first lines. [352]: blank.
Binding: Bound in deep blue (179) cloth lettered across the spine in gold: 'W. H. AUDEN | [ornamental swelled rule] | *Collected | Shorter | Poems | 1927–1957* | FABER'. All edges trimmed. White dust jacket printed in black, yellow, and olive brown.
Paper: White unwatermarked wove paper.
Contents:
  For Christopher Isherwood and Chester Kallman: Although you be, as I am, one
    of those... Reprinted from HTC.
  Part I: 1927–1932
        The letter: From the very first coming down... Reprinted from P (1928).
        Taller to-day: Taller to-day, we remember similar evenings... Reprinted
          from P (1928).
        Missing: From scars where kestrels hover... Reprinted from P.
        The secret agent: Control of the passes was, he saw, the key... Reprinted
          from P (1928).
        The watershed: Who stands, the crux left of the watershed... Reprinted
          from P (1928).
        No change of place: Who will endure... Reprinted from P2.
        Let history be my judge: We made all possible preparations... Reprinted
          from P.
        Never stronger: Again in conversations... Reprinted from P.
        This loved one: Before this loved one... Reprinted from P.
        Easy knowledge: Between attention and attention... Reprinted from P2.
        Too dear, too vague: Love by ambition... Reprinted from P.
        Between adventure: Upon this line between adventure... Reprinted from P.
        A free one: Watch any day his nonchalant pauses, see... Reprinted from P.
        Family ghosts: The strings' excitement, the applauding drum... Reprinted
          from P.
        The questioner who sits so sly: Will you turn a deaf ear... Reprinted from
          P.
        Venus will now say a few words: Since you are going to begin to-day...
          Reprinted from P.
        1929: It was Easter as I walked in the public gardens... Reprinted from P.

The bonfires: Look there! The sunk road winding... Reprinted from P2.

On Sunday walks: On Sunday walks... Reprinted from P.

Shorts: Pick a quarrel, go to war... The friends of the born nurse... When he is well... You're a long way off becoming a saint... I'm afraid there's many a spectacled sod... I'm beginning to lose patience... Those who will not reason... All first printed here. Let us honour if we can... Reprinted from P. These had stopped seeking... Reprinted from O. Private faces in public places... Reprinted from O.

Happy ending: The silly fool, the silly fool... Reprinted from P.

This lunar beauty: This lunar beauty... Reprinted from P.

The question: To ask the hard question is simple... Reprinted from P2.

Five songs

   I   What's in your mind, my dove, my coney... Reprinted from P2.
   II   That night when joy began... Reprinted from LS.
   III For what as easy... Reprinted from CP.
   IV   Seen when nights are silent... Reprinted from DBS.
   V   'O where are you going?' said reader to rider... Reprinted from O.

Uncle Henry: When the Flyin' Scot...

Consider: Consider this and in our time... Reprinted from P.

The wanderer: Doom is dark and deeper than any sea-dingle... Reprinted from P2.

The watchers: Now from my window-sill I watch the night... Reprinted from LS.

Adolescence: By landscape reminded once of his mother's figure... Reprinted from O.

The exiles: What siren zooming is sounding our coming... Reprinted from O.

The decoys: There are some birds in these valleys... Reprinted from O.

Have a good time: 'We have brought you', they said, 'a map of the country... Reprinted from O.

Half way: Having abdicated with comparative ease... An early version was printed in *Cambridge left*, Summer 1933 ("Interview"), and reprinted in *Bozart-Westminster*, Spring–Summer 1935; revised and printed as a broadside (1965).

Ode: Though aware of our rank and alert to obey orders... Reprinted from O.

Legend: Enter with him... Reprinted from DBS.

The witnesses: Young men late in the night... Reprinted from DBS.

Part II: 1933–1938

A summer night: Out on the lawn I lie in bed... Reprinted from LS.

Paysage moralisé: Hearing of harvests rotting in the valleys... Reprinted from LS.

O what is that sound: O what is that sound which so thrills the ear... Reprinted from LS.

Our hunting fathers: Our hunting fathers told the story... Reprinted from LS.

Through the looking-glass: Earth has turned over; our side feels the cold... Reprinted from LS.

Two climbs: Fleeing the short-haired mad executives... Reprinted from LS.

Meiosis: Love had him fast but though he fought for breath... Reprinted from LS.

A misunderstanding: Just as his dream foretold, he met them all... Reprinted from LS.

Who's who: A shilling life will give you all the facts... Reprinted from LS.

Schoolchildren: Here are all the captivities, the cells are as real ...   Reprinted from AT.

May: May with its light behaving ...   Reprinted from LS.

A bride in the '30s: Easily you move, easily your head ...   Reprinted from LS.

On this island: Look, stranger, on this island now ...   Reprinted from LS.

Night mail: This is the Night Mail crossing the Border ...   First printed in *GPO Film Library: notes and synopses*, 1936, and reprinted in the issues for 1937 and 1938, and a pamphlet *TPO: centenary of the Travelling Post Office* (1938), and as a separate broadside (1938?).

As I walked out one evening ...   Reprinted from AT.

Twelve songs

    I   'O for doors to be open and an invite with gilded edges ...   Reprinted from LS.

    II   O lurcher-loving collier, black as night ...   Reprinted from AT.

    III Let a florid music praise ...   Reprinted from LS.

    IV Dear, though the night is gone ...   Reprinted from LS.

    V   Fish in the unruffled lakes ...   Reprinted from LS.

    VI Now the leaves are falling fast ...   Reprinted from LS.

    VII Underneath an abject willow ...   Reprinted from LS.

    VIII At last the secret is out, as it always must come in the end ...   Reprinted from AF6.

    IX Stop all the clocks, cut off the telephone ...   Reprinted from AF6.

    X   O the valley in the summer where I and my John ...   Reprinted from AT.

    XI Over the heather the wet wind blows ...   Reprinted from AT.

    XII Some say that love's a little boy ...   Reprinted from AT.

His excellency: As it is, plenty ...   Reprinted from LS.

Casino: Only their hands are living, to the wheel attracted ...   Reprinted from LS.

Oxford: Nature invades: old rooks in each college garden ...   Reprinted from AT.

Dover: Steep roads, a tunnel through chalk downs, are the approaches ...   Reprinted from AT.

Journey to Iceland: Each traveller prays *Let me be far from any* ...   Reprinted from LFI.

Detective story: Who is ever quite without his landscape ...   Reprinted from LFI.

Death's echo: 'O who can ever gaze his fill ...   Reprinted from LFI.

The price: Who can ever praise enough ...   Reprinted from LFI.

Danse macabre: It's farewell to the drawing-room's mannerly cry ...   Reprinted from AT.

Lullaby: Lay your sleeping head, my love ...   Reprinted from AT.

Orpheus: What does the song hope for? And his moved hands ...   Reprinted from AT.

Miss Gee: Let me tell you a little story ...   Reprinted from AT.

Victor: Victor was a little baby ...   Reprinted from AT.

As he is: Wrapped in a yielding air, beside ...   Reprinted from AT.

A voyage. All reprinted from JTW.

    I   Whither?: Where does this journey look which the watcher upon the quay ...

    II   The ship: All streets are brightly lit; our city is kept clean ...

    III The sphinx: Did it once issue from the carver's hand ...

    IV Hong Kong: Its leading characters are wise and witty ...

The prophets: Perhaps I always knew what they were saying... **Reprinted from AT.**
Like a vocation: Not as that dream Napoleon, rumour's dread and **centre**... Reprinted from AT.
The riddle: Underneath the leaves of life... Reprinted from AT.
Heavy date: Sharp and silent in the... Reprinted from AT.
Law like love: Law, say the gardeners, is the sun... Reprinted from AT.
The hidden law: The Hidden Law does not deny... Reprinted from DM.
Twelve songs
    I   Say this city has ten million souls... Reprinted from AT.
    II (Calypso): Driver, drive faster and make a good **run**... Reprinted from AT.
    III Warm are the still and lucky miles... Reprinted from AT.
    IV Carry her over the water... Reprinted from CP.
    V The single creature leads a partial life... Reprinted from CP.
    VI Eyes look into the well... Reprinted from CP.
    VII Jumbled in one common box... Reprinted from CP.
    VIII Though determined Nature can... Reprinted from CP.
    IX My second thoughts condemn... Reprinted from CP.
    X On and on and on... Reprinted from N.
    XI Sing, Ariel, sing... Reprinted from FTB.
    XII When the Sex War ended with the slaughter of the Grandmothers... Reprinted from FTB.
In memory of Sigmund Freud: When there are so many we shall have to mourn... Reprinted from AT.
Another time: For us like any other fugitive... Reprinted from AT.
Our bias: The hour-glass whispers to the lion's roar... Reprinted from AT.
Hell: Hell is neither here nor there... Reprinted from AT.
Lady weeping at the crossroads: Lady, weeping at the crossroads... Reprinted from CP.
Anthem for St. Cecilia's day. Reprinted from the pamphlet (1941).
    I In a garden shady this holy lady...
    II I cannot grow...
    III O ear whose creatures cannot wish to fall...
The dark years: Returning each morning from a timeless world... Reprinted from DM.
The quest. All reprinted from DM.
    I Out of it steps our future, through this door...
    II All had been ordered weeks before the start...
    III Two friends who met here and embraced are gone...
    IV No window in his suburb lights that bedroom where...
    V In villages from which their childhoods came...
    VI Ashamed to be the darling of his grief...
    VII His library annoyed him with its look...
    VIII He watched with all his organs of concern...
    IX This is an architecture for the odd...
    X They noticed that virginity was needed...
    XI His peasant parents killed themselves with toil...
    XII Incredulous, he stared at the amused...
    XIII The over-logical fell for the witch...
    XIV Fresh addenda are published every day...
    XV Suppose he'd listened to the erudite committee...
    XVI He parried every question that they hurled...
    XVII Others had found it prudent to withdraw...

XVIII Spinning upon their central thirst like tops...
XIX Poet, oracle, and wit...
XX Within these gates all opening begins...
Shorts. All reprinted from DM.
Motionless, deep in his mind, lies the past the poet's forgotten... Whether determined by God or their neural structure, still... His ageing nature is the same... Babies in their mothers' arms... Do we want to return to the womb? Not at all... Once for candy Cook had stolen... With what conviction the young man spoke... To the man-in-the-street who, I'm sorry to say... Base words are uttered only by the base... These public men who seem so to enjoy their dominion... The Champion smiles— What Personality... When Statesmen gravely say 'We must be realistic'... Who will cure the nation's ill?... Standing among the ruins, the horror-struck conqueror exclaimed... Why are the public buildings so high? How come you don't know... 'Hard cases make bad law', as the politician learns to his cost... Don't you dream of a world, a society, with no coercion?... Hans-in-Kelder, Hans-in-Kelder...
No time: Clocks cannot tell our time of day... Reprinted from DM.
Diaspora: How he survived them they could never understand... Reprinted from DM.
Luther: With conscience cocked to listen for the thunder... Reprinted from DM.
Montaigne: Outside his library window he could see... Reprinted from DM.
The council: In gorgeous robes befitting the occasion... Reprinted from DM.
At the grave of Henry James: The snow, less intransigeant than their marble... Reprinted from CP.
Alone: Each lover has a theory of his own... Reprinted from CP.
Leap before you look: The sense of danger must not disappear... Reprinted from CP.
If I could tell you: Time will say nothing but I told you so... Reprinted from CP.
Atlantis: Being set on the idea... Reprinted from CP.
In sickness and in health: Dear, all benevolence of fingering lips... Reprinted from CP.
Many happy returns: Johnny, since to-day is... Reprinted from CP.
Mundus et infans: Kicking his mother until she let go of his soul... Reprinted from CP.
Few and simple: Whenever you are thought, the mind... Reprinted from CP.
The lesson: The first time that I dreamed, we were in flight... Reprinted from CP.
A healthy spot: They're nice—one would never dream of going over... Reprinted from CP.
The model: Generally, reading palms or handwriting or faces... Reprinted from CP.
Three dreams. All reprinted from AA.
I How still it is; our horses...
II Lights are moving...
III Bending forward...
The fall of Rome: The piers are pummelled by the waves... Reprinted from N.
Nursery rhyme: Their learned kings bent down to chat with frogs... Reprinted from N.

In Schrafft's: Having finished the Blue-plate special... Reprinted from N.

Under which lyre, a reactionary tract for the times: Ares at last has quit the field... Reprinted from N.

Music is international: Orchestras have so long been speaking... Reprinted from N.

The duet: All winter long the huge sad lady... Reprinted from N.

Pleasure island: What there is as a surround to our figures... Reprinted from N.

A walk after dark: A cloudless night like this... Reprinted from N.

Part IV: 1948–1957

In transit: Let out where two fears intersect, a point selected... Reprinted from N.

In praise of limestone: If it form the one landscape that we, the inconstant ones... Reprinted from N.

Ischia: There is a time to admit how much the sword decides... Reprinted from N.

Under Sirius: Yes, these are the dog-days, Fortunatus... Reprinted from N.

Cattivo tempo: Sirocco brings the minor devils... Reprinted from N.

Hunting season: A shot: from crag to crag... Reprinted from SA.

Fleet visit: The sailors come ashore... Reprinted from SA.

An island cemetery: This graveyard with its umbrella pines... Reprinted from HTC.

Not in Baedeker: There were lead-mines here before the Romans... Reprinted from N.

Ode to Gaea: From this new culture of the air we finally see... Reprinted from SA.

Bucolics. All reprinted from SA.

   1 Winds: Deep, deep below our violences...

   2 Woods: Sylvan meant savage in those primal woods...

   3 Mountains: I know a retired dentist who only paints mountains...

   4 Lakes: A lake allows an average father, walking slowly...

   5 Islands: Old saints on millstones float with cats...

   6 Plains: I can imagine quite easily ending up...

   7 Streams: Dear water, clear water, playful in all your streams...

Shorts

In memoriam L K-A. 1950–1952: At peace under this mandarin, sleep, Lucina... Reprinted from SA.

Epitaph for the unknown soldier: To save your world, you asked this man to die... Reprinted from SA.

O where would those choleric boys... Reprinted from SA.

Behold the manly mesomorph... Reprinted from N.

Give me a doctor, partridge plump... Reprinted from N.

Fair is Middle-Earth nor changes, though to Age... Reprinted from SA.

A Young Person came out of the mists... Reprinted from HTC.

As the poets have mournfully sung... Reprinted from HTC.

Guard, Civility, with guns... Reprinted from SA.

Bull-roarers cannot keep up the annual rain... Reprinted from HTC.

From bad lands where eggs are small and dear... Reprinted from SA.

Five songs

   I Deftly, admiral, cast your fly... Reprinted from N.

   II The Emperor's favourite concubine... Reprinted from N.

   III A starling and a willow-wren... Reprinted from SA.

   IV 'When rites and melodies begin... Reprinted from SA.

   V Make this night loveable... Reprinted from SA.

Three occasional poems

    I   To T. S. Eliot on his sixtieth birthday. (1948): When things began to happen to our favourite spot... Reprinted from N.

   II Metalogue to the Magic Flute: Relax, Maestro, put your baton down... Reprinted from *The magic flute* (1956) and HTC.

  III Lines addressed to Dr. Claude Jenkins: Let both our Common Rooms combine to cheer... Reprinted from HTC.

Their lonely betters: As I listened from a beach-chair in the shade... Reprinted from N.

First things first: Woken, I lay in the arms of my own warmth and listened... Reprinted from HTC.

The more loving one: Looking up at the stars, I know quite well... Reprinted from HTC.

A permanent way: Self-drivers may curse their luck... Reprinted from SA.

Nocturne: Appearing unannounced, the moon... Reprinted from SA.

Precious five: Be patient, solemn nose... Reprinted from N.

Memorial for the city: The eyes of the crow and the eye of the camera open... Reprinted from N; but here dedicated to Charles Williams.

The shield of Achilles: She looked over his shoulder... Reprinted from SA.

Secondary epic: No, Virgil, no... Reprinted from HTC.

Makers of history: Serious historians care for coins and weapons... Reprinted from OMR.

T the great: Begot like other children, he... Reprinted from HTC.

The managers: In the bad old days it was not so bad... Reprinted from N.

The epigoni: No use invoking Apollo in a case like theirs... Reprinted from OMR.

Bathtub thoughts: *Hail, future friend, whose present I*... Reprinted from OMR.

The old man's road: Across the Great Schism, through our whole landscape... Reprinted from OMR.

The history of science: All fables of adventure stress... Reprinted from OMR.

The history of truth: In that ago when being was believing... Reprinted from HTC.

Homage to Clio: Our hill has made its submission and the green... Reprinted from HTC.

The love feast: In an upper room at midnight... Reprinted from N.

The chimeras: Absence of heart—as in public buildings... Reprinted from N.

Merax & Mullin: There is one devil in the lexicon... Reprinted from OMR.

Limbo culture: The tribes of Limbo, travellers report... Reprinted from HTC.

There will be no peace: Though mild clear weather... Reprinted from HTC.

A household: When to disarm suspicious minds at lunch... Reprinted from N.

'The truest poetry is the most feigning': By all means sing of love but, if you do... Reprinted from SA.

We too had known golden hours... Reprinted from N.

Secrets: That we are always glad... Reprinted from N.

Numbers and faces: The Kingdom of Number is all boundaries... Reprinted from N.

Objects: All that which lies outside our sort of why... Reprinted from HTC.

Words: A sentence uttered makes a world appear... Reprinted from HTC.

The song: So large a morning so itself to lean... Reprinted from HTC.

One circumlocution: Sometimes we see astonishingly clearly... Reprinted
from N.

Horae canonicae. "Prime" and "Nones" reprinted from N; all the others
from SA

1 Prime: Simultaneously, as soundlessly...
2 Terce: After shaking paws with his dog...
3 Sext: You need not see what someone is doing...
4 Nones: What we know to be not possible...
5 Vespers: If the hill overlooking our city...
6 Compline: Now, as desire and the things desired...
7 Lauds: Among the leaves the small birds sing...

Good-bye to the mezzogiorno: Out of a gothic North, the pallid children...
Reprinted from the pamphlet (1958), and HTC.

Notes: Published 24 November 1966 in an edition of 7,310 copies at 42/–.

Reviews:

A. Alvarez. *Observer*, 27 November 1966, p. 27.
F. Berry. *Tablet*, CCXX (31 December 1966), 1473–74.
J. Carey. *New statesman*, LXXII (23 December 1966), 941.
C. Connolly. *Sunday times*, 27 November 1966, p. 24.
K. W. Gransden. *Tracks*, 1 (Summer 1967), 28–32.
G. Hough. *Critical quarterly*, IX (Spring 1967), 9–17.
M. Kelly. *Month*, n.s. XXXVII (March 1967), 188–89.
R. P. Laidlaw. *Poetry Australia*, 19 (December 1967), 45–47.
G. Martin. *Listener*, LXXVII (23 February 1967), 267–68.
D. Parker. *Poetry review*, LVIII (Summer 1967), 157–59.
J. Whitehead. *Essays in criticism*, XVIII (October 1967), 487–95.

b) First American edition   1967

W. H. Auden *Collected* | *Shorter* | *Poems* | *1927–1957* | Random House,
NEW YORK [device: a house]

Collation: 8¼ x 5½ in. [1–11]¹⁶, pp. [3–8] 9–351 [352–354].
Signatures from the first edition are present, but do not correspond to the make-up
of the book.
[pp. 1 and 2 are the front flyleaf]. [3]: half title. [4]: '*By* W. H. Auden | [col-
laborators and titles in thirty lines]'. [5]: title page. [6]: 'FIRST PRINTING |
[fourteen lines] | Manufactured in the United States of America'. [The rest of the
collation is identical with the first edition until] [353]: biographical note on Auden.
[354]: blank.

Binding: Quarter bound in vivid orange yellow (66) cloth with vivid green (139)
cloth covers lettered down the spine in shiny green: '[title in two lines, Auden's
name following and centred between them] COLLECTED SHORTER | POEMS
1927–1957 | · W.H.AUDEN | [across the spine] [device] | RANDOM |
HOUSE', and across the front in gold: '1927–1957'. Top and leading edges
trimmed, and the top edge stained green. White dust jacket printed in black, pale
yellow, and green.

Paper: White unwatermarked wove paper.

Contents: As the English edition, with corrections.

Notes: Published 26 October 1967 in an impression of 6,500 copies at $7.50, and re-
printed in August 1968 (2,500 copies).
   Basically a lithographic reprint of the English edition with the preliminary pages
and section titles reset, and the addition of the biographical notes about the author.
There are some corrections.

Reviews:
L. Bogan. *New Yorker*, XLIV (20 March 1968), 137.
H. Carruth. *Southern review*, n.s. VI (Winter 1970), 245–49.
S. Hampshire. *New York review of books*, X (15 February 1968), 3–4.
A. Hecht. *Hudson review*, XXI (Spring 1968), 207–11.
H. Kenner. *National review*, XIX (26 December 1967), 1432–33.
M. Maddocks. *Christian science monitor*, 7 December 1967, p. 3.
J. Unterecker. *Massachusetts review*, X (Winter 1969), 200–204.
C. Walsh. *Book world*, I (19 November 1967), 1–2.

c) First paperback impression 1969

[The transcription of the title page is identical with that of the first English impression.]

Collation: 7⅞ x 5¾ in. [A]–L¹⁶, pp. [1–8] 9–351 [352].
[1–2]: blank. [3]: half title [4]: 'by W. H. Auden | [star] | [names of collaborators and titles in twenty-seven lines]'. [5]: title page. [6]: *'First published in 1966 | by Faber and Faber Limited | 24 Russell Square London W.C.1 | First published in this edition 1969 | Printed in Great Britain by | R. MacLehose and Company Limited | The University Press Glasgow | [three lines] | S.B.N. 571 06878 2 (Hard-bound Edition) | S.B.N. 571 08735 3 (Faber Paper Covered Edition) | [six lines]'*. [7]: dedication. [8]: blank. 9–14: contents. 15–16: foreword. [17]–341: text; 18 and 236 blank. [342]: blank. 343–351: index of first lines. [352]: blank.
Binding: Glued in a white card cover printed in strong yellowish pink (26), vivid orange (48), brilliant yellow (83), and lettered in black, down the spine: '[on pink] auden [orange band] [on yellow, first two words in two lines, the next word centred and following] collected | shorter | poems [in white on a black panel] FABER', and across the front cover: '[on pink] W H | AUDEN | [orange band] | [on yellow] collected | shorter | POEMS | [orange band] | [on pink] 1927–1957'. Along the leading edge in white on a black panel: 'FABER paper covered EDITIONS', and this panel is repeated on the rear cover. The front inner wrapper carries a description of the book, and the inner and outer rear cover carry a list of titles in the series. All edges trimmed.
Paper: White unwatermarked wove paper.
Contents: As the first impression. The corrections made in the American edition are incorporated.
Notes: Published 21 April 1969 in an edition of 10,000 copies at 15/–.

A 57 RIVER PROFILE 1967

[left-hand side: illustration in green, signed and dated in pencil] 18/50 Scott | iv/67

[right-hand side] RIVER PROFILE | *Our body is a moulded river* | —Novalis | [text in forty-eight lines] | —W. H. AUDEN | [Auden's signature in ink]

[centred at the foot of the sheet] TEXT PRINTED BY LAURENCE SCOTT IN CAMBRIDGE, MASS., APRIL, 1967 | LITHOGRAPH PRINTED AT IMPRESSIONS WORKSHOP, BOSTON | COPYRIGHT, 1967, BY W. H. AUDEN

Collation: 28¼ x 22½ in. Single sheet printed on one side only.
Binding: None.
Paper: White unwatermarked laid paper; but see notes below.
Contents: River profile: Out of a bellicose fore-time, thundering... First printed
   in *New York review of books*, 22 September 1966, and revised and reprinted in
   Poems by W. H. Auden [and others] (1966), and CWW.
Notes: The copy described is that in the Bodleian Library. "The large-format broadside edition that I have done of it [River profile] is limited to fifty numbered
   copies, and each has been signed by both the author and the illustrator-printer.
   The illustration (printed in deep olive green) is a lithograph done especially for
   the edition. The text was hand-set in 24 and 36 pt. Goudy 'Deepdene' type is
   printed in black on hand-made French Rives 'BFK' white paper. Dimensions: 22 x
   28 inches. Price per copy: $150" (quoted from a letter from Scott addressed to The
   Johns Hopkins University Library dated 15 May 1967 inviting purchase. Similar
   letters were sent to many large libraries, usually including a photograph of the
   broadside.). Another copy in Harvard College Library lacks a copy number, has
   an inscription below the pencilled date, and the word "Proof" in pencil above the
   colophon.

A 58   TWO SONGS   1968

Two Songs | W. H. Auden | THE PHOENIX BOOK SHOP | New York
| 1968

Collation: 5 x 7 in. One unsigned gathering of ten leaves, pp. [1–20].
   [1–2]: blank. [3]: title page. [4]: 'Copyright 1968 by W. H. Auden'. [5]: '*I: Song
   of the Ogres*'. [6]: blank. [7–8]: text. [9]: '*II: Song of the Devil*'. [10]: blank.
   [11–17]: text. [18]: blank. [19]: '*This first edition of* Two Songs | *is limited to
   twenty-six copies lettered A to Z,* | *not for sale, and one hundred copies,* | *num-
   bered and signed by the author.* | *This is copy No.* [number in red ink] | [Auden's
   signature in ink]'. [20]: '*Printed at the Ferguson Press* | *Cambridge, Mass.*'
Binding: Stitched with black thread in a light olive grey (112) paper wrapper im-
   pregnated with silk thread folded to wrap completely round a cream card cover.
   A white label on the front cover is lettered in red: '*Two Songs* | W. H. Auden'.
   Issued in a plain brown envelope.
Paper: White wove paper watermarked 'FABRIANO'.
Contents:
   I   Song of the ogres: Little fellow, you're amusing... Reprinted in *New states-
      man*, 1 August 1969, and CWW.
   II Song of the devil: Ever since observation taught me temptation... First
      printed in *Isis*, 25 October 1967; revised here and reprinted in CWW.
Notes: Published 24 March 1968 in an edition of 100 copies numbered and for sale
   at $12.50, and twenty-six copies lettered A–Z not for sale. The publisher later listed
   this as No. 2 in "The Oblong Octavo Series."

A 59   SELECTED POEMS   1968

SELECTED POEMS | by | W. H. AUDEN | FABER AND FABER |
24 Russell Square | London

Collation: 7¼ x 4¾ in. Seventy-two single leaves, [A]–D¹⁶E⁸, pp. [1–4] 5–144.
   $1 signed 'A.S.P.', except A.

[1]: half title. [2]: '*by W. H. Auden* | [star] | [names of collaborators and titles in twenty-six lines]'. [3]: title page. [4]: '*First published in this edition mcmlxviii* | *by Faber and Faber Limited* | *24 Russell Square London WC1* | *Printed in Great Britain by* | *R. MacLehose and Company Limited* | *The University Press Glasgow* | [one line] | © *this selection W. H. Auden* | 1968 | [six lines]'. 5–6: contents. 7–143: text. 144: index of titles.

Binding: A perfect binding glued in a white card cover printed in very light greenish blue (171), light brown (57), moderate reddish orange (37), and lettered in black, down the spine: '[on orange] Selected POEMS [brown band] [on blue] W. H. AUDEN | [in white on black] FABER', across the front cover: '[on orange] W. H. | AUDEN | [brown band] | [on blue] Selected | POEMS | [brown band] | [orange panel]'. Along the leading edge in white on a black panel: 'FABER paper covered EDITIONS', and this is repeated on the rear cover. The front inner cover carries a note on the book, and the inner and outer rear cover carry a list of titles in the series.

Paper: White unwatermarked wove paper.

Contents:

The secret agent: Control of the passes was, he saw, the key . . . Reprinted from P (1928).

The watershed: Who stands, the crux left of the watershed . . . Reprinted from P (1928).

O where are you going: 'O where are you going?' said reader to rider . . . Reprinted from O.

The wanderer: Doom is dark and deeper than any sea-dingle . . . Reprinted from P2.

Ode: Though aware of our rank and alert to obey orders . . . Reprinted from O.

Legend: Enter with him . . . Reprinted from DBS.

O what is that sound: O what is that sound which so thrills the ear . . . Reprinted from LS.

As I walked out one evening: As I walked out one evening . . . Reprinted from AT.

Song of the beggars: —'O for doors to be open and an invite with gilded edges . . . Reprinted from LS.

Autumn song: Now the leaves are falling fast . . . Reprinted from LS.

Roman wall blues: Over the heather the wet wind blows . . . Reprinted from AT.

Lullaby: Lay your sleeping head, my love . . . Reprinted from AT.

As he is: Wrapped in a yielding air, beside . . . Reprinted from AT.

Musée des beaux arts: About suffering they were never wrong . . . Reprinted from AT.

Sonnets from China [twenty-one sonnets]. Reprinted from JTW, in the revision printed in CSP2.

In memory of W. B. Yeats: He disappeared in the dead of winter . . . Reprinted from AT.

Domesday song: Jumbled in one common box . . . Reprinted from CP.

If I could tell you: Time will say nothing but I told you so . . . Reprinted from CP.

Atlantis: Being set on the idea . . . Reprinted from CP.

The fall of Rome: The piers are pummelled by the waves . . . Reprinted from N.

A walk after dark: A cloudless night like this . . . Reprinted from N.

The quest [twenty sonnets]. Reprinted from DM.

From *The sea and the mirror:* II. The supporting cast, sotto voce. Reprinted from FTB.

In praise of limestone: If it form the one landscape that we, the inconstant ones . . . Reprinted from N.

Fleet visit: The sailors come ashore ... Reprinted from SA.
The shield of Achilles: She looked over his shoulder ... Reprinted from SA.
The sabbath: Waking on the Seventh Day of Creation ... Reprinted from HTC.
First things first: Woken, I lay in the arms of my own warmth and listened ...
     Reprinted from HTC.
The old man's road: Across the Great Schism, through our whole landscape ...
     Reprinted from OMR.
Friday's child: He told us we were free to choose ... Reprinted from HTC.
Bucolics [seven poems]. Reprinted from SA.
Horae canonicae [seven poems]. "Prime" and "Nones" reprinted from N, the
     rest from SA.
Thanksgiving for a habitat. Reprinted, with the omission of the various "post-
     scripts," from ATH.
Notes: Published 17 June 1968 in an edition of 10,000 copies at 7/6d.

A 60   WORTE UND NOTEN   1968

WYSTAN HUGH AUDEN | WORTE UND NOTEN | REDE ZUR
ERÖFFNUNG | DER SALZBURGER FESTSPIELE 1968 | FEST-
UNGSVERLAG SALZBURG

Collation: 8⅛ x 5¾ in. [1–2]⁸[3]⁶[4]⁸, pp. [i–ii, 1–6] 7–57 [58].
     [i–ii]: blank. [1]: half title. [2]: blank. [3]: title page. [4]: 'HERAUSGEGEBEN
VON MAX KAINDL-HÖNIG | (FRANZÖSISCHE ÜBERSETZUNG VON
MARTHA EISSLER) | DIE DRUCKLEGUNG FÖRDERTEN DAS BUN-
DESMINISTERIUM | FUR UNTERRICHT UND LAND UND STADT
SALZBURG | © 1968 FESTUNGSVERLAG SALZBURG | EINBAND: KAY
KRASNITZKY | DRUCK: ERNST MÜLLER, SALZBURG'. [5]: prefatory
note. [6]: blank. 7–22: German text. 23: biographical note in German. [24]: blank.
25–37: English text. 38: biographical note in English. 39–54: text in French. 55:
biographical note in French. [56]: blank. 57: contents. [58]: blank.
Binding: Glued in a cream card cover around which is folded a white wrapper lettered up the spine in black: 'SALZBURGER FESTREDEN V 1968', and across
the front wrapper in black: 'WYSTAN HUGH AUDEN | WORTE UND
NOTEN | FESTUNGSVERLAG SALZBURG'. Over this cover is wrapped a
translucent wrapper printed in brownish orange (54) with a repeat pattern sym-
bolising the tiers of an opera house and with four armorial bearings on the rear
wrapper, one of them being the publisher's device. All edges trimmed.
Paper: White unwatermarked wove paper.
Contents: Words and notes.
Notes: Published 25 July 1968 in an edition of 2,000 copies at 56 Austrian schillings.

A 61   COLLECTED LONGER POEMS   1968

a) First edition

COLLECTED | LONGER POEMS | by | W. H. AUDEN | FABER
AND FABER | 24 Russell Square | London

Collation: 8½ x 5½ in. [1–21]⁸[22]¹⁰, pp. [1–6] 7–356.
     [1–2]: blank. [3]: half title. [4]: 'by the same author | [star] | [collaborators and
titles in twenty-eight lines]'. [5]: title page. [6]: '*First published in 1968 | by Faber*

and Faber Limited | *24 Russell Square London WC1* | *Printed in Great Britain by* | *Western Printing Services Limited* | *Bristol* | [one line] | SBN 571 08388 9 | [two lines]'. 7: contents. [8]: blank. [9]: 'Paid on Both Sides | A Charade | TO CECIL DAY-LEWIS'. [10]: blank. [11]: characters. 12–34: text. [35]: 'Letter to Lord Byron'. [36]: blank. 37–76: text. [77]: 'New Year Letter | (January 1, 1940) | TO ELIZABETH MAYER'. [78]: blank. 79–130: text. [131]: 'For the Time Being | *A Christmas Oratorio* | IN MEMORIAM | CONSTANCE ROSALIE AUDEN | 1870–1941 | [three lines]'. [132]: blank. 133–197: text. [198]: blank. [199]: 'The Sea and the Mirror | *A Commentary on Shakespeare's* The Tempest | TO JAMES AND TANIA STERN | [six lines]'. [200]: blank. 201–252: text. [253]: 'The Age of Anxiety | *A BAROQUE ECLOGUE* | TO JOHN BETJEMAN | [five lines]'. [254]: blank. 255–353: text. 354–356: a note on the text.

Binding: Bound in moderate blue (182) cloth lettered across the spine in gold: 'W. H. AUDEN | [swelled ornamental rule] | *Collected* | *Longer* | *Poems* | FABER'. All edges trimmed. White dust jacket printed in black, bluish grey, and orange.

Paper: White unwatermarked wove paper.

Contents:
Paid on both sides.   Reprinted from P.
Letter to Lord Byron.   Reprinted from LFI.
New Year letter.   Reprinted from DM.
For the time being.   Reprinted from FTB.
The sea and the mirror.   Reprinted from FTB.
The age of anxiety.   Reprinted from the previous edition (1947).

Notes: Published 14 October 1968 in an edition of 7,000 copies at 45/–.

Reviews:
C. Connolly. *Sunday times*, 20 October 1968, p. 61.
B. Hardy. *Daily telegraph*, 31 October 1968, p. 8.
P. J. Kavanagh. *Guardian*, 18 October 1968, p. 7.
R. Mayne. *New statesman*, LXXVI (13 December 1968), 838.
J. Robson. *Encounter*, XXXIV (January 1970), 73–74.
P. Toynbee. *Observer*, 13 October 1968, p. 29.
J. Symons. *Punch*, CCLV (13 November 1968), 707.

b) First American edition   1969

W. H. Auden | [star] | Collected | Longer Poems | [device: a house] | RANDOM HOUSE | New York

Collation: 8¼ x 5½ in. [1–9]¹⁶[10]²⁰[11]¹⁶, pp. [1–11] 12–356 [357–60].
  [1–2]: blank. [3]: half title. [4]: 'By W. H. Auden | [star] | [collaborators and titles in thirty-two lines]'. [5]: title page. [6]: 'FIRST PRINTING | [ten lines] | *Manufactured in the United States of America* | by The Book Press, Brattleboro, Vt.'. [7]: contents. [8]: blank. [9]–353: text. 354–356: note on the text. [357]: biographical note. [358–360]: blank. For a more detailed listing see the first edition.

Binding: Quarter bound in vivid orange yellow (66) cloth with vivid green (139) cloth covers, lettered down the spine in gold: 'COLLECTED LONGER POEMS | [star] W. H. AUDEN | [across the foot of the spine in shiny purple] [device] | RANDOM | HOUSE', and across the front in gold: 'A'. Top and leading edges trimmed, and the top edge stained red. White dust jacket printed in black, pale yellow, and reddish orange.

Paper: Cream unwatermarked wove paper.

Contents: As the English edition.

Notes: Published 14 April 1969 in an edition of 6,500 copies at $7.50.

Reviews:
P. Adams. *Atlantic*, CCXXIII (May 1969), 113.
D. Donoghue. *New York review of books*, XII (19 June 1969), 19, 22–24.
M. K. Spears. *Yale review*, LX (Autumn 1970), 98.

A 62   **SECONDARY WORLDS**   **1969**

a) First edition

SECONDARY WORLDS | by | W. H. AUDEN | THE T. S. ELIOT
MEMORIAL LECTURES | *Delivered at Eliot College in the University
of Kent | at Canterbury, October, 1967* | FABER AND FABER | 24 Russell Square | London

Collation: 8½ x 5½ in. [A]–I⁸, pp. [1–8] 9–144.
   [1–2]: blank. [3]: half title. [4]: *'by W. H. Auden* | [star] | [collaborators and
titles in twenty-seven lines]'. [5]: title page. [6]: *'First published in 1968 | by Faber
and Faber Limited | 24 Russell Square London WC1 | Printed in Great Britain by |
Latimer Trend & Co Ltd Plymouth* | [one line] | *S.B.N. 571 08389 7* | [one line]'.
[7]: 'For | VALERIE ELIOT'. [8]: blank. 9: contents. [10]: blank. 11–12: fore-
word. [13]: 'I | THE MARTYR AS DRAMATIC | HERO'. [14]: blank. 15–45:
text. [46]: blank. [47]: 'II | THE WORLD OF THE SAGAS'. [48]: blank. 49–84:
text. [85]: 'III | THE WORLD OF OPERA'. [86]: blank. 87–116: text. [117]:
'IV | WORDS AND THE WORD'. [118]: blank. 119–144: text.
Binding: Bound in moderate red (15) cloth lettered on the spine in gold: '[across]
W. H. | AUDEN | [down within a rectangular rule border] SECONDARY
WORLDS | [across] FABER'. All edges trimmed. Shiny white dust jacket printed
in yellowish white, red, and blue.
Paper: White unwatermarked wove paper.
Contents:
   Secondary worlds
          I The martyr as dramatic hero.   First printed, in part, in *Holiday*, October
             1967, and in *Listener*, 4 January 1968.
         II The world of the sagas.
        III The world of opera.   First printed, in part, in *Times literary supplement*,
             2 November 1967.
         IV Words and the word.   Parts of this lecture were first printed, under
             different titles, in *Listener*, 17 March 1966, and in Auden's acceptance
             speech for the National Medal for Literature, 1967.
Notes: Published 25 November 1968 in an edition of 3,000 copies at 30/–. The first
series of Eliot lectures.
Reviews:
   G. S. Fraser. *Frontier*, XII (February 1969), 74–75.
   P. N. Furbank. *Listener*, LXXXI (9 January 1969), 55.
   P. Levi. *Month*, n.s. LXI (January 1969), 51–52.
   R. Mayne. *New statesman*, LXXVI (13 December 1968), 838.
   Times literary supplement, 23 January 1969, p. 81.
   A. Weatherhead. *New blackfriars*, LI (January 1970), 54–55.
   J. P. White. *Tablet*, CCXXII (7 December 1968), 1218–19.

b) First American edition   1969

SECONDARY | WORLDS | [rule] | ESSAYS BY | W. H. AUDEN |
RANDOM HOUSE [device: a house] *NEW YORK*

Collation: 8⅛ x 5½ in. [1–3]¹⁶[4]⁸[5]¹⁶, pp. [3–8] 9–144 [145–146].
    [3]: half title. [4]: 'BY W. H. AUDEN | [collaborators and titles in twenty-three lines]'. [5]: title page. [6]: 'First American Edition. Copyright © 1968 by W. H. Auden . . . | [six lines]'. [7]: 'For | VALERIE ELIOT'. [8]: blank. 9: contents. [10]: blank. 11–144: text. [145]: biographical note. [146]: blank. For a more detailed listing see the first edition.
Binding: Quarter bound in greyish yellow (90) cloth with a flat back and pale orange yellow (73) paper boards. Lettered down the spine in gold: 'SECONDARY WORLDS · W. H. AUDEN [device across the spine] RANDOM HOUSE'; and across the front: 'W · H · A'. All edges trimmed, and the top edge stained reddish purple. White dust jacket printed in pale yellow, black, and violet.
    On Bloomfield's copy there is a band of shiny tape across part of the lower half of the spine, and the last part of Auden's name, the device, and the first syllable of the publisher's name are printed on this strip.
Paper: White unwatermarked wove paper.
Contents: As the English edition.
Notes: Published 31 January 1969 in an edition of 5,051 copies at $4.95. A lithographic reprint of the English edition with new preliminary pages and the addition of the biographical notice.
Reviews:
    H. Bloom. *New republic,* CLX (5 April 1969), 25–28.
    R. Bloom. *Virginia quarterly review,* XLV (Spring 1969), 365–68.
    H. Carruth. *New York times,* 5 October 1969, section 7, p. 4.
    D. Donoghue. *New York review of books,* XII (19 June 1969), 19, 22–24.
    V. Howes. *Christian science monitor,* 6 May 1969, p. 9.
    M. K. Spears. *Yale review,* LX (Autumn 1970), 96–98.

A 63   CITY WITHOUT WALLS   1969

a) First edition

City without Walls | and other poems | by | W. H. AUDEN | FABER AND FABER | London

Collation: 8½ x 5⅜ in. [A]–H⁸, pp. [1–8] 9–124 [125–128].
    [1]: half title. [2]: 'by the same author | [star] | [collaborators and titles in twenty-nine lines]'. [3]: title page. [4]: '*First published in 1969* | *by Faber and Faber Limited* | *24 Russell Square London WC1* | *Printed in Great Britain by* | *The Bowering Press Plymouth* | [one line] | SBN 571 09150 4 | [one line]'. [5]: acknowledgement. [6]: blank. [7]: 'For | PETER HEYWORTH | [two lines of verse]'. [8]: blank. 9–10: contents. 11–124: text; 16, 32, 46, 52, 54, 72, 74, 86, 100, 102, and 120 blank. [125–128]: blank. The last leaf is laid down as an endpaper.
Binding: Bound in black cloth lettered across the spine in gold: 'City | without | Walls | W. H. | AUDEN | Faber'. All edges trimmed. Cream dust jacket printed in black and reddish brown.
Paper: Cream unwatermarked wove paper.
Contents:
    For Peter Heyworth: At Twenty we find our friends for ourselves, but it takes Heaven . . .
    City without walls: . . ."Those fantastic forms, fang-sharp . . . First printed in *New Yorker,* 27 April 1968.
    Five occasional poems
        Joseph Weinheber (1892–1945): Reaching my gate, a narrow . . . First printed in *London magazine,* July 1965.

Epithalamium (for Peter Mumford and Rita Auden, May 15th, 1965): All folk-tales mean by ending... First printed in *New Yorker*, 31 July 1965, and reprinted in *Holy door*, Winter 1965.

Eulogy (for Professor Nevill Coghill on the occasion of his retirement in 1966): In our beginning... First printed in *To Nevill Coghill from friends* (1966) ("To Professor Nevill Coghill upon his retirement in A.D. 1966").

Elegy. In memoriam Emma Eiermann (ob. Nov. 4th, 1967): *Liebe Frau Emma*... First printed in *London magazine*, August 1968 ("In memoriam Emma Eiermann").

Mosaic for Marianne Moore: The concluded gardens of personal liking... First printed in *New York review of books*, 9 November 1967, and reprinted in *Wilson library bulletin*, March 1969.

The Horatians: Into what fictive realms can imagination... First printed in *New Yorker*, 24 May 1969.

Profile: He thanks God daily... A longer version was first printed in *Quest*, Winter 1965–66 ("Precious me").

Since: On a mid-December day... First printed in *Encounter*, May 1965.

Amor loci: I could draw its map by heart... First printed in *New measure*, Autumn 1965, and reprinted in *Quest*, Spring 1966.

Metaphor: Nose, I am free... First printed in *Quest*, Spring 1967.

Bird language: Trying to understand the words...

Two songs. Both reprinted from *Two songs* (1968).
  I Song of the ogres: Little fellow, you're amusing...
  II Song of the devil: Ever since observation taught me temptation...

Forty years on: Except where blast-furnaces and generating-stations... First printed in *New York review of books*, 26 September 1968.

Marginalia: Fate succumbs... This sequence of short poems is compiled from poems previously printed in *Quest*, Winter 1965–66 ("Precious me"), *New York review of books*, 3 February 1966 ("Marginalia"), *New York review of books*, 12 May 1966 ("Filler"), *Harvard advocate*, Fall 1966 ("Dear diary"), and in *Marginalia* (1966).

Eight songs from Mother Courage. First printed in *Delos*, 1 (1968) ("Songs from *Mutter Courage*").

In due season: Spring-time, Summer and Fall: days to behold a world... First printed in *Confrontation*, Spring 1969.

Rois fainéants: On High Feast-Days they were given a public airing...

Partition: Unbiased at least he was when he arrived on his mission... First printed in *Atlantic*, December 1966.

August, 1968: The Ogre does what ogres can... First printed in *Observer*, 8 September 1968.

Fairground: Thumping old tunes give a voice to its whereabouts... First printed in *New Yorker*, 20 August 1966.

River profile: Out of a bellicose fore-time, thundering... First printed in *New York review of books*, 22 September 1966, and reprinted in a slightly revised version in *Poems by W. H. Auden* [and others] (1966), ed. by E. W. White, and, with the original text, as a broadside (1967).

Insignificant elephants: Talented creatures, on the defensive because... First printed in *Encounter*, September 1966.

Ode to Terminus: The High Priests of telescopes and cyclotrons... First printed in *New York review of books*, 11 July 1968.

Four commissioned texts
  Runner. First printed in the mimeographed transcript of the film (1962).
  The twelve. First printed in the musical score by Sir William Walton (1965), and reprinted in the programme of the performance at Westminster Abbey, 2 January 1966.

Moralities. First printed in *London magazine,* February 1968, and reprinted in a different form in the program book of the Forty-seventh May Festival at Cincinnati, 17–25 May 1968, with the recording issued in 1968 (DGG 139 374), and in the musical score by Hans Werner Henze (1969).

A reminder. First printed in the Christ Church son et lumière souvenir programme [27 June–28 September 1968].

Prologue at sixty: Dark-green upon distant heights... First printed in *New York review of books,* 18 May 1967.

Notes: Published 15 September 1969 in an edition of 5,000 copies at 20/–.

Uncorrected proof copies were bound in cream wrappers; these copies include neither "August, 1968" nor "A reminder," and the section in which the latter would appear is therefore headed "Three commissioned texts."

Reviews:

J. Bayley. *Listener,* LXXII (25 September 1969), 413–14.
J. Fletcher. *Spectator,* CCXXIII (13 December 1969), 827–28.
R. Fuller. *New statesman,* LXXVIII (26 September 1969), 421–22.
D. Grant. *Critical quarterly,* XI (Autumn 1969), 195, 197–98.
J. Gross. *Observer,* 14 September 1969, p. 29.
R. Heppenstall, *Sunday times,* 14 September 1969, p. 61.
P. Porter. *London magazine,* n.s. IX (October 1969), 81–84.

A 64   A NEW YEAR GREETING   1969

[deep yellow (85) cover-title, lettered in strong reddish brown (40), with the title on a moderate olive green (125) disc which has a pattern of fancy lower-case letters in deep yellow] [fancy] a | new | year | greeting | [outside the disc] W. H. AUDEN

Collation: 6 x 6 in. One unsigned gathering of eight leaves, pp. [1–16].

[1]: 'The following verses were composed after | the writer had read the article "Life on the | Human Skin," by Mary J. Marples, in the | January 1969 issue of SCIENTIFIC AMERICAN. | The poem first appeared in the December | 1969 issue of SCIENTIFIC AMERICAN. It is re- | printed here with the permission of the author.' [2–14, versos only]: illustrations. [3–15, rectos only]: text. [16]: 'Illustrations by Thomas Prentiss'. The text is printed in dark green, the illustrations in dark green, pink, and red. The illustrations are reprinted from the article by M. J. Marples.

Binding: Stapled twice in a deep yellow paper cover-title, lettered as above. Across the inside front cover in reddish brown: 'Copyright © 1969 by SCIENTIFIC AMERICAN, Inc.' Enclosed, with another pamphlet of similar format, *The dance of the solids,* by John Updike, in a white card sleeve lettered across the front in red: 'season's greetings | from | SCIENTIFIC | AMERICAN' (some copies omit the periodical title). This sleeve is in turn enclosed in a printed white card mailing carton.

Paper: Yellowish green unwatermarked wove paper.

Contents: A New Year greeting: On this day tradition allots... First printed in *Scientific American,* December 1969, and reprinted in *Poetry review,* Winter 1969–70.

Notes: Printed December 1969 in an edition of 6,200 copies for use as a Christmas card by the editors of *Scientific American* in New York.

B

WORKS EDITED, TRANSLATED, OR HAVING CONTRIBUTIONS BY W. H. AUDEN

B 1   **PUBLIC SCHOOL VERSE**   1924

PUBLIC SCHOOL VERSE | AN ANTHOLOGY | Volume IV | 1923–1924 | [device: a windmill on a hill with the letters W. H all within a rule border] | LONDON | WILLIAM HEINEMANN LTD.

Collation: 7¼ x 4¾ in. a–f⁴, pp. [i–iv] v–viii, 1–37 [38–40].
Binding: Quarter bound in light olive grey (112) ridged cloth with grey paper boards and a white label on the spine lettered across in black: 'PUBLIC | SCHOOLS | VERSE | 1923 | 1924 | Heinemann'.
Contents: Woods in rain: It is a lovely sight and good . . . (p. 18)
Notes: Published in September 1924 in an edition of 500 copies. The author's name was misspelt as 'W. H. Arden'. Included in this volume is a poem titled "Night mail," by A. Henderson, which affords an interesting comparison with Auden's more celebrated poem of the same name. See also *The world, the flesh, and myself,* by Michael Davidson (London: Arthur Barker, 1962), pp. 126–30.

B 2   **OXFORD POETRY**   1926

OXFORD POETRY | 1926 | EDITED BY | CHARLES PLUMB & W. H. AUDEN | OXFORD: BASIL BLACKWELL | MCMXXVI

Collation: 7¼ x 4¾ in. [a]⁴b–c⁸d¹⁰, pp. [i–iv] vi–vii [viii], 1–51 [52].
Binding: Quarter bound in white parchment paper with dark purplish blue (201) paper boards. A label in the top left corner of the front cover reads: '[all within a rule border] Oxford | Poetry | 1926 | Oxford | Basil Blackwell'. Some copies were issued in paper wrappers with a similar label. The bound copies also have a label on the spine lettered across in black: '[rule] | O | X | F | O | R | D | P | O | E | T | R | Y | [rule]'.
Contents:
Preface. (p. v)
Thomas epilogises (for C.I.): Inexorable Rembrandt rays, which stab . . . (pp. 1–3)
The letter: He reads and finds the meaning plain . . . (pp. 4–5)
Cinders: Four walls are drawn tight round the crew of us . . . (pp. 6–7)   First printed in the *Oxford University review,* 3 June 1926.
Notes: Published in November 1926 in an edition of 1,000 copies. Some copies were issued in the United States in Spring 1927 (listed in *Publishers' weekly,* 11 June 1927) with title page reading: 'OXFORD POETRY | 1926 | EDITED BY | CHARLES PLUMB & W. H. AUDEN | [device] | D. APPLETON AND COMPANY | NEW YORK MDCCCCXXVII' and bound as the English edition except

that the label on the front cover reads: '[all within a rule border] Oxford | Poetry | 1926 | D Appleton & Co | New York'.

B 3   **OXFORD POETRY**   **1927**

OXFORD POETRY | 1927 | EDITED BY | W. H. AUDEN & C. DAY-LEWIS | OXFORD: BASIL BLACKWELL | MCMXXVII

Collation: 7¼ x 4¾ in. [a]–d⁸, pp. [*–**, i–iv] v–ix [x], 1–48 [49–52]. The last leaf is laid down as an endpaper.
Binding: As **B 2**, with the substitution of the date, and the lettering on the spine is not on a label.
Contents:
Preface. (pp. v–vii)
Extract (for J. B. A.): Consider if you will how lovers stand ... (p. 1)   Reprinted in P (1928).
Notes: Published in November 1927 in an edition of 760 copies. See C. Day Lewis, *The buried day* (London: Chatto, 1960), pp. 178–79, on the authorship of the preface. Some copies were issued in the United States early in 1928 (listed in *Publishers' weekly*, 3 March 1928) with title page reading 'OXFORD POETRY | 1927 | EDITED BY | W. H. AUDEN & C. DAY-LEWIS | [device] | D APPLETON AND COMPANY | NEW YORK MCMXXVIII', and the label on the front cover reads: '[all within a rule border] Oxford | Poetry | 1927 | New York | D. Appleton & Co.'
    A letter signed by both editors asking for contributions appears in *Isis*, 731 (15 June 1927), 4, and a similar but not identical letter appears in *Cherwell*, XX, n.s. 7 (18 June 1927), 204.

B 4   **OXFORD POETRY**   **1928**

OXFORD POETRY | 1928 | Edited | With a Plea for Better Criticism | by CLERE PARSONS and B. B. | BASIL BLACKWELL | OXFORD | 1928

Collation: 7¼ x 4¾ in. [a]–d⁸e⁴, pp. [i–iv] v–xi [xii], 1–59 [60].
Binding: As **B 3**, with the substitution of the date, and the lettering in blue.
Contents: In due season: In Spring we waited. Princes felt ... (p. 2)   First printed in *Oxford outlook*, December 1926.
Notes: Published 9 November 1928 in an edition of 750 copies. Some copies were issued in the United States in Spring 1929 (listed in *Publishers' weekly*, 23 March 1929) with a cancel title page with the last three lines reading: '[device] | D. APPLETON AND COMPANY | NEW YORK MCMXXIX', and the label on the front cover reading in blue: '[all within a blue rule] Oxford | Poetry | 1928 | New York | Appleton'.

B 5   **NEW SIGNATURES**   **1932**

NEW SIGNATURES | POEMS BY SEVERAL HANDS | COLLECTED BY | MICHAEL ROBERTS | [device: wolf's head] | *Published by Leonard & Virginia Woolf at The* | *Hogarth Press, 52 Tavistock Square, London, W.C.1* | 1932

Collation: 7¼ x 4¾ in. [1]–6⁸7⁴, pp. [1–4] 5–102 [103–104].

Binding: Bound in strong greenish blue (169) paper boards lettered in gold up the spine: 'HOGARTH LIVING POETS. No. 24. NEW SIGNATURES'. On the front cover: '[within a double rule border] HOGARTH LIVING POETS | No. 24 | NEW SIGNATURES | [device: wolf's head] | THE HOGARTH PRESS'.

Contents:

Ode (To my pupils): Though aware of our rank and alert to obey orders... (pp. 23–29) Reprinted in O.

Chorus from a play: Doom is dark and deeper than any sea-dingle... (pp. 30–31) Reprinted in P2.

Poem: For what as easy... (p. 32) Reprinted in CP, CSP, and CSP2.

Notes: Published 25 February 1932 in an impression of 600 copies. Reprinted in March 1932 (750 copies) and, photolithographically, in September 1934 (1,025 sheets) and 1935 (1,025 sheets). This information has been obtained from the printers since the publishers say their records give no guidance for this period.

"He [Roberts] was reading new poets: Auden, Empson, Spender, Day Lewis. Meeting John Lehmann one day in the office of the Hogarth Press, he proposed the publication of a collection of work by these poets, with a critical introduction by himself. This volume, *New Signatures,* appeared in 1932" (*A portrait of Michael Roberts,* ed. by T. W. Eason and R. Hamilton [Chelsea: College of S. Mark and S. John, 1949], p. 6).

B 6   AN OUTLINE FOR BOYS AND   1932
                 GIRLS AND THEIR PARENTS

[left-hand title] ILLUSTRATED BY WM. KERMODE & ISTA BROUNCKER | AN OUTLINE FOR | BOYS & GIRLS | AND THEIR PARENTS | SCIENCE | [three illustrations: vacuum tube, geometrical diagram, comet] | PHYSICS MATHEMATICS ASTRONOMY | [two illustrations: heart, flame] | PHYSIOLOGY PSYCHOLOGY | [two illustrations: cell in mitosis, lines of spectrum] | BIOLOGY CHEMISTRY | [three illustrations: artist's materials, sculpting tools, architectural instruments] | PAINTING SCULPTURE ARCHITECTURE | VICTOR GOLLANCZ LTD | 14 HENRIETTA STREET W.C.2 | 1932

[right-hand title] EDITED BY NAOMI MITCHISON | [title in three lines as above] | CIVILISATION | [three illustrations: sword, explosion, question mark] | PAST PRESENT FUTURE | [two illustrations: mother, child and nurse, two globes] | THE FAMILY THE WORLD | [two illustrations: cogs, currency symbols] | GOVERNMENT ECONOMICS | [three illustrations: dancer, handwriting, musical notation] | DANCING WRITING MUSIC | [imprint in three lines as above]

Collation: 8½ x 5¼ in. [AG]⁶BG–EEG¹⁶FFG¹⁰, pp. [i–iv] vi–ix [x–xii, 1–3] 4–916. FFG2 is signed.

Binding: Bound in black cloth lettered across the spine in gold: 'AN OUTLINE | FOR BOYS | AND GIRLS | AND THEIR | PARENTS | GOLLANCZ'.

Contents: Writing: or the pattern between people. (pp. 849–68)

Notes: Published 26 September 1932 and not reprinted. *Left book news* (1 [May

1936], p. 11) says, "Since 1932 nearly 25,000 copies of the Outline have been sold." A "cheap edition" was issued on 25 May 1936 bound in light-blue cloth and lettered in black. According to the publisher total sales were approximately 36,000 copies.

B 7　　　　　　　　**NEW COUNTRY**　　　　　　　　**1933**

NEW COUNTRY | Prose and Poetry by the authors of | *New Signatures* | Edited by | MICHAEL ROBERTS | [device: wolf's head] | PUBLISHED BY LEONARD AND VIRGINIA WOOLF | AT THE HOGARTH PRESS, 52 TAVISTOCK SQUARE | LONDON W.C. | 1933

Collation: 8½ x 5½ in. [A]–Q⁸, pp. [1–6] 7–256.
Binding: Bound in moderate yellowish green (136) cloth lettered across the spine in gold: 'NEW | COUNTRY | · | *By the authors of* | NEW SIGNATURES | · | *Edited by* | MICHAEL ROBERTS | THE | HOGARTH | PRESS'.
Contents:
　Prologue: O love, the interest itself in thoughtless heaven... (pp. 193–94)　Reprinted in LS.
　A happy New Year, to Gerald Heard: The third week in December the frost came at last... (pp. 195–208)　Partly reprinted in LS.
　A communist to others: Comrades, who when the sirens roar... (pp. 209–13)　Reprinted in LS.
　Poem: Me, March, you do with your movements master and rock... (pp. 214–16)　Reprinted in LS, with the first line "The chimneys are smoking, the crocus is out in the border."
Notes: Published 21 March 1933 in an edition of 1,200 copies. (We owe this printing figure to Mr. Alan Clodd who obtained it from Leonard Woolf for use in a projected bibliography of Christopher Isherwood.)

B 8　　　　**OXFORD AND THE GROUPS**　　　　**1934**

OXFORD | AND THE | GROUPS | *The Influence of the Groups* | *considered by* | [names of contributors in eleven lines] | Edited by R. H. S. CROSSMAN | Preface by Dr. W. B. SELBIE | BASIL BLACKWELL · OXFORD | MCMXXXIV

Collation: 7¼ x 4¾ in. [A]–O⁸, pp. [*–**, i–iv] v–xiv, 1–208.
Binding: Bound in bluish black (193) cloth lettered across the spine in gold: 'OXFORD | AND THE | GROUPS | BLACKWELL'.
Contents: The group movement and the middle classes. (pp. 89–101)
Notes: Published 23 January 1934 in an impression of 3,000 copies and reprinted in March 1934 (1,000 copies).

B 9　　　　　　**THE OLD SCHOOL**　　　　　　**1934**

The | OLD SCHOOL | Essays | by Divers Hands | Edited by | GRAHAM GREENE | [device: vase of flowers and letters JC] | Jonathan Cape | Thirty Bedford Square | London

Collation: 7¾ x 5¼ in. [A]–Q⁸, pp. [1–4] 5–256.
Binding: Bound in black cloth lettered across the spine in pale blue: 'THE OLD |
SCHOOL | [three short rules] | GRAHAM | GREENE | JONATHAN | CAPE'.
On the front cover: 'THE OLD SCHOOL'. The binding of the second impres-
sion substitutes the publisher's device for his name at the foot of the spine.
Contents: Honour. (pp. 9–20)
Notes: Published 23 July 1934 in an impression of 1,517 copies and reprinted in Au-
gust 1934 (1,003 copies). The second impression was described on sale as the
"First cheap edition."

B 10   **THE GREAT TUDORS**   1935

THE | GREAT TUDORS | EDITED BY | KATHARINE GARVIN |
1935 | IVOR NICHOLSON & WATSON | LIMITED LONDON

Collation: 8½ x 5½ in. *a*, 1–2¹⁶3–4¹²5–6¹⁶ 7–8¹² 9–10¹⁶ 11–12¹² 13–14¹⁶ 15–16¹² 17–18¹⁶
19–20¹² 21¹⁶ 22–23¹² 24¹⁰, pp. [i–iv] v–xxxi [xxxii, 1–2] 3–658 [659–660]. \$5 signed,
except 24 (24₂ signed) and gatherings in duodecimo.
Binding: Bound in moderate red (15) cloth lettered across the spine in gold: 'THE |
GREAT | TUDORS | [rose] | IVOR NICHOLSON | & WATSON'.
Contents: John Skelton. (pp. 55–67)
Notes: Published in March 1935. It has been impossible to get any estimate of the
number of copies published either from the publisher or the printer. In the United
States 520 copies were issued on 11 September 1935 by Dutton with a cancel title
page, with the last three lines reading: 'NEW YORK | E. P. DUTTON AND
CO. INC. | 1935', and bound in dark reddish orange (38) cloth lettered across the
spine in gold: '*The* | GREAT | TUDORS | *Edited by* | *KATHARINE GARVIN*
| DUTTON' and a device across the front cover.
    The title was reprinted by Eyre and Spottiswoode in 1956, but Auden's essay
was not included in this reprint.

B 11   **THE POET'S TONGUE**   1935

a) First edition

THE | POET'S TONGUE | An Anthology | chosen | by | W. H. AU-
DEN | and | JOHN GARRETT | FIRST [SECOND] PART | LON-
DON | G. BELL & SONS LTD | 1935

Collation: [volume 1] 7¼ x 4¾ in. [*a*]⁸*b*⁴1–13⁸, pp. [i–iv] v–xxii [xxiii–xxiv], 1–207
[208]. Gatherings 1–12 are signed 'I'. [volume 2] 7¼ x 4¾ in. [*a*]⁸*b*⁶1–14⁸, pp.
[i–iv] v–xxvii [xxviii], 1–222 [223–224]. Gatherings 1–14 are signed 'II'.
Binding: Volume I is bound in moderate bluish green (164) cloth, and volume II in
dark purplish blue (201) cloth. Both volumes are lettered across the spine in white:
'THE | POET'S | TONGUE | I [II] | AUDEN | & | GARRETT | BELL'. On
the front cover: 'THE POET'S TONGUE | [star] | W. H. AUDEN & JOHN
GARRETT | I [II]'.
Contents:
    [Volume I] Introduction. (pp. v–xi)
    [Volume II] Introduction. (pp. v–xi)

Notes: Published 20 June 1935, and reprinted in September 1935, December 1935, July 1937, June 1938, April 1940, September 1941, April 1943, February 1945, April 1946, July 1947, July 1948, November 1949, May 1951, November 1953, October 1955, September 1957, November 1961, and September 1966. This was the school edition, and the publisher prefers not to give the number of copies in each impression.

b) One-volume trade issue 1935

[The title-page transcription is identical with that of the school edition with the omission of the volume statement.]

Collation: 7¼ x 4¾ in. [*a*]–*b*⁸ *c*² 1–13⁸ [II]¹1–14⁸, pp. [i–iv] v–xxxiv [xxxv–xxxvi], 1–207 [208] [*–**] 1–222 [223–224]. The extra volume signatures are retained.
Binding: Bound in dark purplish blue (201) cloth lettered across the spine in gold: 'THE | POET'S | TONGUE | [star] | W. H. AUDEN | & | J. GARRETT | BELL'. On the front cover: 'THE POET'S TONGUE | [star] | W. H. AUDEN & JOHN GARRETT'. Top edge gilt.
Contents: Introduction. (pp. v–x) This omits four paragraphs on schools and poetry which are found in the two-volume school edition.
Notes: This trade edition was published on 8 August 1935, and reprinted as above. The publisher prefers not to disclose the number of copies in each impression.

B 12   THE ARTS TODAY   1935

THE ARTS | TO-DAY | Edited, with an Introduction, by | GEOFFREY GRIGSON | [swelled rule] | PSYCHOLOGY AND ART | W. H. Auden | [other titles and authors in fourteen lines] | [swelled rule] | LONDON | JOHN LANE   THE BODLEY HEAD

Collation: 8½ x 5¼ in. [A]–U⁸, pp. [i–x] xi–xiv [xv–xvi], 1–301 [302–304].
Binding: Bound in deep yellowish pink (27) cloth lettered across the spine in black: 'THE | ARTS | TO-DAY | [rule] | W. H. Auden | [the names of other contributors in seven lines] | [device: head of Bodley in oval ornamented frame and the letters JL] | THE BODLEY HEAD'. Top edge stained red.
Contents: Psychology and art to-day. (pp. xv–xvi, 1–21)
Notes: Published 6 September 1935 in an impression of 1,980 copies and apparently reprinted at least once. A "cheap edition" was issued on 9 September 1938 consisting of some copies of both impressions, bound in cream cloth and lettered in green with no device, with the publisher's name in three lines. Copies of the second impression do not have '*First published in 1935*' on p. [vi].

B 13   CHRISTIANITY AND THE SOCIAL REVOLUTION   1935

CHRISTIANITY | AND THE | SOCIAL REVOLUTION | [triple short rule] | *Edited by* | JOHN LEWIS | KARL POLANYI | DONALD K. KITCHIN | [ten lines describing the editorial board] | London | VICTOR GOLLANCZ LTD | 1935

Collation: 7¼ x 4¾ in. [AR]–QR¹⁶RR⁸, pp. [1–5] 6–526 [527–528].
Binding: Bound in strong red (12) cloth lettered across the spine in black: "CHRIS-TIANITY | AND THE | SOCIAL | REVOLUTION | GOLLANCZ'.

The Left Book Club impression is bound in vivid reddish orange (34) limp cloth lettered across the spine in black: 'CHRISTIANITY | AND THE | SOCIAL | REVOLUTION | GOLLANCZ', and across the front cover: 'CHRISTIANITY | AND THE | SOCIAL REVOLUTION | LEFT BOOK CLUB EDITION | NOT FOR SALE TO THE PUBLIC'.
Contents: The good life. (pp. 31–50)
Notes: Published 28 October 1935. There were two impressions, the second of which was for the Left Book Club and includes a "Special preface to the [May] 1937 Left Book Club edition" by John Lewis. This is contained in a new gathering π¹², and the volume pages [i–v] vi–xxv, [2–5] 6–526 [527–528]. The total sales of both impressions amounted to 10,500 copies. Some copies were issued in the United States in February 1936 with a title page on which the imprint reads: 'New York | CHARLES SCRIBNER'S SONS | 1936'. The sheets were printed in England and since the fore-edge is untrimmed copies measure 7¼ x 5 in. and are bound in deep red (13) cloth lettered across the spine in gold: '[rule] | CHRISTIANITY | AND THE | SOCIAL | REVOLUTION | SCRIBNERS | [rule]'.

B 14   OUR HUNTING FATHERS   1936

a) First edition

Written especially for the Norfolk & Norwich Triennial Musical Festival (Sept. 1936) | BENJAMIN BRITTEN | (Opus 8) | [ornament: hunts-man blowing horn with riding and running figures under tree] | OUR HUNTING FATHERS | SYMPHONIC CYCLE | *for* | SOPRANO SOLO & ORCHESTRA | *Devised by* | W. H. AUDEN | PIANO–VO-CAL SCORE | PRICE 5/– NET | (Orchestral parts may be hired) | WINTHROP ROGERS EDITION [device: standing figure against globe with legs passing through the O of the name Rogers] | [four addresses of Boosey and Hawkes in three lines]

Collation: 12 x 9¼ in. One gathering of 26 leaves, pp. [1–2] 3–49 [50–52]. Plate-marked 'H. 14556'.
Binding: Stitched in a deep red (13) paper wrapper lettered across the front cover in black: 'BENJAMIN BRITTEN | (Opus 8) | [ornament] | OUR HUNTING FATHERS | [short rule] | *Devised by* | W. H. AUDEN | WINTHROP ROG-ERS EDITION [device as title page]'. A larger version of the device is repeated on the rear cover.
Contents:
Prologue: They are our past and our future...(pp. 3–5)   Revised and reprinted in LS.
Rats away!: Rats. I command all the rats that are here about...(Modernized words by Auden. pp. 7–15)
Epilogue and funeral march: Our hunting fathers told the story...(pp. 41–46) Reprinted in LS.
Notes: Published 22 September 1936, and reprinted in January 1949 and May 1968. The publishers prefer not to give the number of copies in each impression. Some copies of the first impression have a sheet tipped in facing p. [3] which carries the text of the songs. This text is printed on p. [2] of the later impressions.

b) Full score 1964

Written for the 1936 Norfolk and Norwich Triennial Festival | Benjamin Britten | Our Hunting | Fathers | *Symphonic cycle for* | *high voice and orchestra* | Op. 8 | Devised by W. H. Auden | *Full Score* | Boosey & Hawkes | Music Publishers Limited | *London • Paris • Bonn • Johannesburg • Sydney • Toronto • New York*

Collation: 13¾ x 10½ in. [1–5]⁸ [6]⁷, pp. [i–vi], 1–88. Plate marked 'B. & H. 19079'.
Binding: Glued in light grey (264) wrappers lettered across the front in black: 'Benjamin Britten | Our Hunting Fathers | *Full Score* | Boosey & Hawkes'. The rear cover carries an advertisement for other works by Britten styled 'No.2' and dated '1.59'.
Contents: [Texts.] (p. v)
Notes: Published 26 May 1964. The publisher prefers not to reveal the number of copies printed.

c) Miniature score 1964

HAWKES POCKET SCORES | *Written for the 1936 Norfolk and Norwich Triennial Festival* | BENJAMIN BRITTEN | OUR HUNTING FATHERS | Op. 8 | *Symphonic cycle for* | *high voice and orchestra* | Devised by W. H. Auden | BOOSEY & HAWKES | MUSIC PUBLISHERS LIMITED | [one line of place names] | MADE IN ENGLAND

Collation: 7¼ x 5¼ in. [1–6]⁸, pp. [i–vi], 1–88 [89–90]. Plate marked 'B. & H. 19079'.
Binding: Glued in a dark greyish yellow (91) card cover lettered across the front in dark green: 'HAWKES POCKET SCORES | [in natural colour on a dark green panel] BENJAMIN BRITTEN | OUR HUNTING | FATHERS | Op. 8 | [on the cover in green] BOOSEY & HAWKES | H. P. S. 755'. The rear cover carries an advertisement for more titles in the series numbered 'No. 16' and dated '1/61'.
Contents: [Texts.] (pp. iv–v)
Notes: Published 26 May 1964. The publisher prefers not to reveal the number of copies printed. A reduced facsimile of the full score with the preliminaries reset.

B 15   SELECTED POEMS BY ROBERT FROST   1936

SELECTED POEMS | *by* | ROBERT FROST | *Chosen by the Author* | With | *Introductory Essays* | *by* | W. H. Auden | [other names in four lines] | [device: vase of flowers and the letters JC] | JONATHAN CAPE | THIRTY BEDFORD SQUARE | LONDON

Collation: 8 x 5¼ in. [A]–O⁸, pp. [1–4] 5–221 [222–224]
Binding: Bound in moderate blue (182) cloth lettered across the spine in gold: 'SELECTED | POEMS | ROBERT | FROST | [device]'. Top edge stained dark blue.
Contents: [Introductory essay.] (pp. 11–17) This essay was reprinted in *Recognition of Robert Frost*, ed. by R. Thornton (New York: Holt, 1937), and partially

reprinted under the title "Nature poetry" in *The English critic from Chaucer to Auden*, ed. by N. L. Clay (London: Heinemann, 1939).
Notes: Published 13 November 1936 in an edition of 1,509 copies.

B 16   NO MORE PEACE! BY ERNST TOLLER   1937

a) First edition

[double rule, one of which has a moulded edge] | NO MORE PEACE! | a thoughtful comedy by | ERNST TOLLER | translated by Edward Crankshaw | lyrics translated and adapted by W. H. Auden | music by Herbert Murrill | FARRAR & RINEHART, INC. | NEW YORK   TORONTO | [double rule as above]

Collation: 7¾ x 5¼ in. [1–10]⁸[11]⁴[12]⁸, pp. [i–xii, 1–2] 3–166 [167–172].
Binding: Bound in vivid red (11) cloth lettered down the spine in gold: 'NO MORE PEACE! ERNST TOLLER [across, within a rule border] fr'. Top edge stained black.
Contents: [Lyrics.] (pp. 24–25, 41–44, 44–46, 50–51, 97–99, 104–7, 118–21, 134–36, 155–57) "Noah's song" was first published in *New statesman & nation*, 13 June 1936, and three more of the lyrics first appeared in *London mercury*, October 1936.
Notes: Published 6 April 1937 in an impression of 1,550 copies. Another impression was published in New York in 1939 by the Dramatists Play Service.
    First produced in America at the Vassar Experimental Theatre, 26 February 1937.
    A monologue by Toller and Auden entitled "The demagogue" was performed as part of the revue *Pepper mill*, produced by Erika Mann, at the Chanin Auditorium in New York on 5 January 1937. This was "The dictator's song" from *No more peace!*

b) First English edition   1937

NO MORE PEACE! | a thoughtful comedy by | ERNST TOLLER | translated by Edward Crankshaw | lyrics adapted by W. H. Auden | music by Herbert Murrill | JOHN LANE THE BODLEY HEAD | LONDON

Collation: 7½ x 4¾ in. [A]–G⁸H⁴, pp. [i–viii] ix–xi [xii], 1–103 [104–108].
Binding: Bound in black cloth lettered across the spine in gold: 'NO | MORE | PEACE | ERNST | TOLLER | The | Bodley | Head'. Top edge stained dark blue.
Contents: [Lyrics.] (pp. 14–15, 23–26, 27–28, 30–31, 59–60, 63–65, 72–75, 83–84, 95–97) The text and stage directions differ slightly from the American edition.
Notes: Published 14 September 1937 in an edition of 1,000 copies, of which 414 copies were destroyed by enemy action in 1941. The play was first produced at the Gate Theatre in London on 11 June 1936.

B 17   FROM ANNE TO VICTORIA   1937

[ornament: a vase of flowers flanked by two cornucopias] | *FROM* | *ANNE TO VICTORIA* | *Essays by various hands* | *Edited by* | *Bonamy*

Dobrée | [device: kneeling huntress with bow] | CASSELL | *and Company Limited* | *London, Toronto, Melbourne* | *and Sydney*

Collation: 8¼ x 5½ in. [1]–40⁸, pp. [i–iv] v–x, 1–630.

Binding: Bound in dark red (16) cloth lettered across the spine in gold: '[ornament: a helmet with leaves] | [within a double rule border] FROM | ANNE | TO | VICTORIA | [star] | DOBRÉE | [outside the border] [pendent decoration] | CASSELL'. Top edge stained dark grey.

Contents: Pope, 1688–1744. (pp. 89–107) Reprinted in *Essays in criticism*, July 1951.

Notes: Published 18 February 1937 in an edition of 5,000 copies. Some 970 copies of the original edition were exported, jacketed and bound, and issued in the United States in September 1937 by Scribners with a cancel title page with the imprint reading: 'NEW YORK | CHARLES SCRIBNER'S SONS | 1937.' and 'SCRIBNERS' substituted for 'CASSELL' on the binding. The title was reprinted photolithographically in the United States in 1967 by Books for Libraries Press.

B 18 AUTHORS TAKE SIDES ON THE SPANISH WAR 1937

AUTHORS TAKE SIDES | ON THE SPANISH WAR | LEFT REVIEW | 2 Parton Street | London | W.C.1

Collation: 9¾ x 6 in. One unsigned gathering of 16 leaves, pp. [1–32].

Binding: Stapled twice in a light greenish yellow (101) card wrapper lettered across in red: '[star] | Authors | take | sides | *on the* | *Spanish* | *War* | 148 CONTRIBUTIONS | 10,000 WORDS | [down the right side of the cover the names of forty authors] | *and over 100 others* | [rule] | PRICE SIXPENCE'. On the rear wrapper is an advertisement for *New writing*, no. 4.

Contents:

[Questionnaire signed, amongst others, by Auden.] (p. 3)

[Auden's declaration.] (p. 6)

Notes: Published in December 1937 in an edition of 5,000 copies. The printers say, "Although we quoted for a further quantity a few months after, it does not appear that we did a second printing."

B 19 LIONS AND SHADOWS, BY 1938
CHRISTOPHER ISHERWOOD

LIONS AND SHADOWS | AN EDUCATION IN THE TWENTIES | CHRISTOPHER ISHERWOOD | [device: wolf's head] | PUBLISHED BY LEONARD & VIRGINIA WOOLF AT THE | HOGARTH PRESS, 52 TAVISTOCK SQUARE, LONDON, W.C. 1 | 1938

Collation: 7¾ x 4¾ in. [A]–U⁸, pp. [1–8] 9–312 [313–314]. The first and last leaves are laid down as endpapers.

Binding: Bound in strong blue (178) cloth lettered across the spine in black: 'LIONS | AND | SHADOWS | CHRISTOPHER | ISHERWOOD | THE | HOGARTH | PRESS'.

Contents:

The traction engine: Its days are over now; no farmyard airs...

The engine house: It was quiet in there after the crushing...

Rain: This peace can last no longer than the storm . . .   Reprinted from P (1928).
The rookery: When we were half asleep it seemed . . . (pp. 186–88)
Notes: Published 17 March 1938 in an edition of 3,580 copies, of which 2,039 copies
were sold up to 31 March 1939. (We owe this information to Mr. Alan Clodd.)

Because Auden's contribution to this volume was involuntary, later editions are
not described, but the title was reprinted by the Hogarth Press (1943), New Directions (1947), Methuen (1953), and other publishers.

B 20   OXFORD BOOK OF LIGHT VERSE   1938

The | Oxford Book | Of Light Verse | Chosen by | W. H. Auden | Ox-
ford | At the Clarendon Press | 1938

Collation: 7¼ x 4¾ in. [A]¹²V–S¹⁶T⁶, pp. [i–vi] vii–xxiv, 1–553 [554–556]. $1 signed
'4484' except [A]. T2 is signed.
Binding: Bound in deep purplish blue (197) cloth with the spine and front cover
bordered in gold, and the back cover with a blind-stamped border. Lettered across
the spine in gold: 'The Oxford | Book of | Light Verse | [scroll and arms of the
university]'; on the front cover: 'THE | OXFORD BOOK | OF | LIGHT
VERSE'. Top edge gilt.

The American issue of the first impression has a binding lettered on the spine:
'The Oxford | Book of | Light | Verse | [scroll and arms of the university]', and
the gilt border on the front cover only runs along the head and foot. The edges
are trimmed closer, and the volume stands almost ¼ in. shorter.
Contents:
Introduction. (pp. vii–xx)
Editorial note and acknowledgements. (pp. xxi–xxiv)
Notes: Published in October 1938, reprinted in a corrected and slightly altered impression in December 1938, and subsequently photolithographically in 1941, 1942,
1945, 1949, 1952, and 1962 from sheets of the second impression. The press prefers
not to disclose the numbers of copies printed for these impressions. The American
issue was published 1 December 1938.

The second impression revises the Contents list and acknowledgements, replaces
poem 12 by another, and adds three stanzas to poem 13.

B 21   POET VENTURERS   1938

POET VENTURERS | *A COLLECTION OF POEMS* | WRITTEN
BY | BRISTOL SCHOOL BOYS AND GIRLS | WITH A FORE-
WORD BY | W. H. AUDEN | *The Proceeds from the Sale of these
Poems will go to the Fund for* | *CHINESE MEDICAL AID*

Collation: 8½ x 5⅜ in. One unsigned gathering of 16 leaves, pp. [1–2] 3–31 [32]. The
fifth leaf is signed 'B'.
Binding: Stapled twice in a light green (144) paper wrapper lettered across the front
cover in black: 'POET | VENTURERS | [block of a Chinese peasant planting
rice with sword and ploughshare superimposed; signed MS] | "Swords into Plough-
shares" '.
Contents: Foreword. (p. 3)
Notes: The printer has no record of the number of copies printed or for whom, and
no more details have been found. Auden's foreword is dated 29 October 1938. The
copy described here is in the Bristol Collection in Bristol Public Reference Library,
but several copies have recently been sold by booksellers.

B 22 POEMS OF FREEDOM 1938

POEMS OF FREEDOM | Edited by | JOHN MULGAN | With an Introduction by | W. H. AUDEN | LONDON | VICTOR GOLLANCZ LTD | 1938

Collation: 7¼ x 4¾ in. [AF]–MF⁸, pp. [1–6] 7–192.

Binding: Bound in light blue (181) cloth lettered across the spine in black: 'POEMS | OF | FREEDOM | Edited by | JOHN | MULGAN | GOLLANCZ'.

The Left Book Club issue is bound in strong red (12) paper boards and lettered across the spine in black: ' [editor's name and title within a single-rule border] POEMS | OF | FREEDOM | Edited by | JOHN | MULGAN | GOLLANCZ', and across the front cover: 'POEMS OF FREEDOM | Edited by | JOHN MULGAN | [device: the letters LBC within a single-rule border] | LEFT BOOK CLUB EDITION | NOT FOR SALE TO THE PUBLIC'.

Contents: Introduction. (pp. 7–9). The volume also contains selections from the poem "Brothers, who when the sirens roar..." by Auden, reprinted from *New country* (1933).

Notes: Published 12 December 1938. There were two bindings issued simultaneously, one for the trade, the other for the Left Book Club. The publisher says total sales amounted to 5,500 copies. The Left Book Club issue, an alternative, not a regular choice, was still in print in March 1939 according to a leaflet inserted in the file of *Left book news* held in the British Library of Political and Economic Science.

B 23 I BELIEVE 1939

a) First edition

[all within a double red rule border] I BELIEVE | *The Personal Philosophies* | *of Certain Eminent* | *Men and Women* | *of Our Time* | [red rule] | Edited, with an Introduction | and Biographical Notes, by | CLIFTON FADIMAN | 19 [device in red: a sower] 39 | [red rule] | SIMON AND SCHUSTER · NEW YORK

Collation: 9¼ x 6 in. [1–28]⁸, pp. [i–iv] v–xiv, [1–2] 3–429 [430–434].

Binding: Bound in dark blue (183) buckram lettered across the spine in gold: '[on a red panel within a gold-rule border] *I* | *Believe* | [gold rule] | A SERIES OF | INTIMATE | CREDOS | [gold rule] | *Edited by* | *Clifton Fadiman* | [on the cloth] SIMON AND SCHUSTER'. Top edge stained reddish purple.

Contents: W. H. Auden. (pp. 1–16)

Notes: Published 15 August 1939; a total of 15,700 copies were issued in at least five impressions, and the book was out of print in 1962.

Auden's essay is a revised version of his contribution to *Nation*, 24 December 1938, and the book was conceived as a revision of a similar title issued by the same publisher in 1931.

b) First English edition 1940

I Believe | W. H. Auden. Pearl Buck. Stuart Chase | [eleven lines containing the names of other contributors] | London: George Allen & Unwin Ltd

Collation: 8⅜ x 5½ in. [A]–M¹⁶N⁸, pp. [1–10] 11–390 [391–400]. $5 signed, except A and N.

Binding: Bound in dark red (16) cloth lettered in gold across the spine: '[double gold rule] | [title on a black panel] I Believe | THE PERSONAL | PHILOSOPHIES | OF | TWENTY-THREE | EMINENT | MEN AND WOMEN | OF OUR TIME | [double gold rule] | [at the foot of the spine] GEORGE ALLEN | AND UNWIN'. Top edge stained red.

Contents: W. H. Auden. (pp. 15–31)

Notes: Published in May 1940 in an impression of 2,000 copies, and reprinted in 1941 (2,000 copies), 1942 (2,000 copies), 1943 (3,000 copies), 1945 (2,000 copies), 1947 (2,670 copies), 1948 (5,000 copies), and 1952 (3,290 copies).

The complete text was reprinted photolithographically by the Humanities Press in New York in 1962.

A paperback selection from this volume entitled *I believe: nineteen personal philosophies* was published by Allen and Unwin 25 October 1962 (Unwin books, no. 34) in an impression of 10,250 copies, and reprinted in June 1965 (5,100 copies), and October 1969 (5,000 copies). Auden's contribution is on pp. 7–17.

B 24   **THE LYRIC PSALTER**   **1940**

[all within a double-rule border with ornamental corners, title in gothic] The | Lyric Psalter | THE MODERN READER'S | BOOK OF PSALMS | *Edited by* | HARRY H. MAYER | [device] | LIVERIGHT PUBLISH-ING CORPORATION | NEW YORK

Collation: 9¼ x 6 in. [1–24]⁸, pp. [i–vi] vii–ix [x, 1–2] 3–370 [371–374].

Binding: Bound in strong purplish blue (196) cloth lettered across the spine in gold: '[single and double rules] | [title and editor on a dark blue panel] *The* | LYRIC PSALTER | [short rule] | THE MODERN READERS | BOOK OF PSALMS | [ornament] | MAYER | [double rule] | [seven vertical rules] | [double rule] | [on a dark blue panel] LIVERIGHT | [double and single rules]'. On the front cover on a dark blue panel, title in gothic: 'The | Lyric Psalter | THE MODERN READER'S | BOOK OF PSALMS'. Top edge stained brown.

Contents: After reading psalm 27: Lord in the day of inundation . . . (pp. 49–50)

Notes: Published 25 May 1940. A revised impression titled *The modern reader's book of psalms* was issued in July 1944 [*CCE* 8 September 1944] consisting of 3,000 copies. Auden's contribution is not revised.

B 25   **BEST BROADCASTS OF 1939–40**   **1940**

Best Broadcasts | of 1939–40 | *Selected and Edited by* | MAX WYLIE | Director of Scripts and Continuity, | Columbia Broadcasting System; Lecturer, New York University | Radio Workshop | [curlicue rule] | *New York* WHITTLESEY HOUSE *London* | McGRAW-HILL BOOK COMPANY, INC.

Collation: 9 x 6 in. [1–24]⁸, pp. [i–iv] v–xiv, [1–2] 3–368 [369–70].

Binding: Bound in cloth with the top half of the covers yellowish grey (93) and the bottom half dark purplish blue (201). Lettered across the spine in deep blue: 'MAX WYLIE | [lightning flash] | BEST | BROADCASTS | OF | 1939–40 | [lightning flash] | WHITTLESEY | HOUSE'. On the top half of the front cover in blue is a representation of a microphone.

Contents: The dark valley. (pp. 30–43)
   Contains the following pieces of verse which appear separately:
      Eyes look into the well... Reprinted in CP, CSP, and CSP2.
      Lady weeping at the crossroads... Reprinted in *Mint*, 1946, CP, CSP, PA, and CSP2

Notes: Published 2 December 1940 and reprinted in October 1942. "In the spring of 1940, the Columbia Workshop invited the young English poet W. H. Auden to write an original piece for American radio.... The original title of the Auden piece... read something like this... 'The Psychological Experiences and Sensations of the Woman who Killed the Goose That Laid the Golden Egg.'... The Columbia Workshop changed the title to 'The Dark Valley.' It was heard on the evening of June 2, 1940" (pp. 30–31). Dame May Whitty played the sole part, and the incidental music was by Britten. The piece is based on the sketch "Alfred" first published in *New writing*, Autumn 1936, and reprinted in *New letters in America*, 1937.

B 26   FIFTEEN POETS   1941

FIFTEEN POETS | [names of the poets in five lines] | [device] | OXFORD | AT THE CLARENDON PRESS | 1941

Collation: 7 x 4¾ in. [A]–Ii⁸Kk⁴, pp. [*–**, i–vii] viii–xiv, 1–503 [504]. $1 signed '4560', except A.

Binding: Bound in dark purplish blue (201) cloth lettered across the spine in gold: '[triple rule] | FIFTEEN | POETS | [diamond] | FROM CHAUCER | TO ARNOLD | [triple rule] | OXFORD'.
   The American issue of the first impression is bound in dark blue (179) cloth and lettered across the spine in gold: 'FIFTEEN | POETS | [ornament: a bird] | *From Chaucer | to Arnold* | [ornament] | OXFORD', and across the front cover: '[ornament] | FIFTEEN POETS | [ornament]'. The page size is slightly taller (7¼ in.).

Contents: George Gordon Byron. (pp. 293–96)

Notes: Published 9 January 1941 in an impression of 5,000 copies and reprinted in May 1941 (5,000 copies), October 1942 (10,000 copies), July 1945 (10,000 copies), November 1949 (10,000 copies), November 1954 (20,000 copies), and March 1960 (20,000 copies).
   In a letter the press states, "The book however has a somewhat complicated history, as part of it appears as *Eight poets* (which includes Byron), and though it has been reprinted regularly since publication it would require rather elaborate research to know whether the whole or part of the book was being reprinted at any particular time."

B 27   THE INTENT OF THE CRITIC   1941

THE INTENT | OF THE CRITIC | BY | Edmund Wilson | Norman Foerster | John Crowe Ransom | W. H. Auden | EDITED, WITH AN INTRODUCTION, BY | Donald A. Stauffer | [swelled rule] | PRINCETON | PRINCETON UNIVERSITY PRESS

Collation: 8½ x 5½ in. [1–10]⁸, pp. [i–vi, 1–2] 3–147 [148–154].

Binding: Bound in moderate yellowish pink (29) cloth with a repeat pattern of seven silver bars across the spine, and lettered in white on a dark grey paper panel on the spine: 'THE | INTENT | OF THE | CRITIC'.

Contents: Criticism in a mass society. (pp. 125–47)   Reprinted in *Mint*, 1948.

Notes: Published 16 September 1941 in an edition of 1,250 copies. Copies sold in England were published by Oxford University Press on 12 February 1942. The title was reprinted photolithographically in the United States by Peter Smith in 1963, and was published in a reset paperback Matrix edition (SM 1051) published by Bantam Books in November 1966.

B 28   A SELECTION FROM THE POEMS OF ALFRED,   1944 LORD TENNYSON

a) First edition

A SELECTION FROM THE | [fancy] *POEMS* | OF ALFRED, | [fancy] *Lord Tennyson* | SELECTED AND WITH AN INTRODUC-TION BY | [fancy] *W. H. Auden* | [device and ornament: dolphin with anchor, and foliage on either side] | DOUBLEDAY, DORAN AND CO., INC. GARDEN CITY N.Y. 1944

Collation: 7⅜ x 4½ in. [1–9]¹⁶, pp. [i–iv] v–xx, 1–268.

Binding: Bound in bluish grey (191) cloth lettered across the spine in gold: '[all within a single-rule border] | [ornament: foliage] | [rule] | *Auden* | [rule] | A | SELECTION | FROM THE | *POEMS* | OF | ALFRED | *Lord* | *Tennyson* | [rule] | DOUBLEDAY | DORAN | [rule] | [ornament: foliage]'. Top edge stained grey.

Contents: Introduction. (pp. ix–xx)

Notes: Published 1 September 1944 [*CCE* 2 November 1944] in an impression of 4,000 copies and reprinted in October 1947 (750 copies). Out of print in October 1949.

b) First English edition   1946

Tennyson | AN INTRODUCTION AND A SELECTION BY | W. H. Auden | [device: flying phoenix] | PHOENIX HOUSE LIMITED | LONDON | 1946

Collation: 7¼ x 4¾ in. [A]–I¹⁶, pp. [i–iv] v–xx, 1–266 [267–68]. $5 signed, except A.

Binding: Bound in vivid purplish blue (194) cloth lettered down the spine in gold: 'TENNYSON [oblique stroke] AUDEN [across the foot of the spine] Phoenix'.

Contents: Introduction. (pp. ix–xx)

Notes: Published 13 December 1946 in an edition of 4,500 copies.

B 29   THE FLOWER OF GRASS, BY   1945 E. CAMMAERTS

[all within a wavy double-rule border] *The Flower* | *of Grass* | [orna-ment] | EMILE CAMMAERTS | *"For all flesh is as grass and all glory of* | *man as the flower of grass"* (1 PETER, 1:24) | [device: hand grasping torch and the letters HB] | HARPER & BROTHERS PUBLISHERS | NEW YORK and LONDON

Collation: 7½ x 4½ in. [1]⁴[2–7]¹⁶, pp. [i–vi] vii–xx [xxi–xxii], 1–176 [177–78].
Binding: Bound in moderate bluish green (164) cloth lettered down the spine in black: 'The Flower of Grass [ornament] *Cammaerts* [across the spine] HARPER'. Device in black on the lower right front cover.
Contents: Foreword. (pp. ix–xvii)
Notes: Published 13 June 1945 and out of print in September 1950. The publisher prefers not to disclose the number of copies printed.

B 30   **THE AMERICAN SCENE,**   1946
                  BY H. JAMES

THE AMERICAN SCENE | TOGETHER WITH THREE ESSAYS | FROM | "PORTRAITS OF PLACES" | BY | HENRY JAMES | *Edited with an Introduction by* | W. H. Auden | [device: lamp on a laurel circle] | NEW YORK | CHARLES SCRIBNER'S SONS | 1946

Collation: 8¼ x 5¼ in. [1–16]¹⁶[17]¹²[18]¹ [gathering of plates]⁸, pp. [I–V] VI–XXX [XXXI–XXXII, 1] 2–501 [502–504]. $1 and 9 signed, except 17 and 18.
Binding: Bound in very dark yellowish green (138) cloth lettered across the spine in gold: '[within a double thick-thin rule border] THE | AMERICAN | SCENE | [star] | HENRY | JAMES | [outside the border] SCRIBNERS'. On the front cover: [within a double thick-thin rule border] THE AMERICAN | SCENE | [star] | HENRY JAMES'. Top edge stained pink.
Contents: Introduction. (pp. v–xxiii)
Notes: Published 6 September 1946 [*CCE* 9 September 1946] and out of print in June 1952. There were at least two impressions, the later lacking the final letter 'A' after the copyright statement on p. [iv] and bound in a lighter deep yellowish green (118) cloth. Sales amounted to 4,165 copies.

B 31   **THE KAFKA PROBLEM**   1946

edited by angel flores | the k [fancy initial] *afka* | problem | *new directions*

Collation: 8¼ x 5½ in. [1]⁸[2–15]¹⁶[16]⁸, pp. [i–vi] vii–xii, 1–468.
Binding: Bound in light grey (264) cloth lettered down the spine in black: 'the kafka problem'. Top edge stained dark grey.
Contents: K's quest. (pp. 47–52)
Notes: Published 2 November 1946. The book went out of print in 1958, and the total number of copies printed and bound was 2,726. Copies sold in England were published by the Falcon Press in June 1947 and subsequently sold by Grey Walls Press.

Octagon Books issued a photolithographic reprint in 1963 which contained a revised bibliography, but no change in Auden's essay.

B 32   **POEMS, BY J. MURRAY**   1947

[all within a chequered border] POEMS | BY JOAN MURRAY | 1917–1942 | EDITED BY GRANT CODE | WITH A FOREWORD BY |

W. H. AUDEN | NEW HAVEN | YALE UNIVERSITY PRESS |
LONDON · GEOFFREY CUMBERLEGE · OXFORD UNIVERSITY
PRESS | 1947

Collation: 7¾ x 5¼ in. [1–7]⁸[8]¹⁰[9]⁸, pp. [i–ii, 1–4] 5–145 [146].
Binding: Bound in light greenish grey (154) paper boards and lettered down the
   spine in black: 'MURRAY POEMS *YALE*'. In grey on a black panel on the front
   cover: '*The Yale Series of Younger Poets* | [rule] | POEMS BY JOAN MURRAY
   | 1917–1942'.
Contents: Foreword. (pp. 5–6)
Notes: Published 20 May 1947 in an edition of 1,020 copies. Auden became editor of
   the series with this volume, no. 45.

B 33   SLICK BUT NOT STREAMLINED,   1947
                         BY J. BETJEMAN

SLICK | BUT NOT | *Streamlined* | [ornament: girl on bicycle] | POEMS
& SHORT PIECES BY | *John Betjeman* | [ornament: three leaves] | SE-
LECTED, & WITH AN | INTRODUCTION BY | *W. H. AUDEN* |
GARDEN CITY, N.Y. 1947 | DOUBLEDAY & COMPANY, INC.

Collation: 7½ x 5 in. [1–12]⁸, pp. [i–ii, 1–6] 7–185 [186–90].
Binding: Bound in black cloth lettered down the spine in gold: 'JOHN BETJEMAN
   Slick but not Streamlined DOUBLEDAY'. On the front cover: '[a dripping tap
   within a single-rule square]'.
Contents: Introduction. (pp. 9–16)   Reprinted from *Town and country*, July 1947.
Notes: Published 24 July 1947 in an impression of 1,750 copies and reprinted in Sep-
   tember 1947 (1,000 copies).

B 34   INTIMATE JOURNALS, BY C. BAUDELAIRE   1947

a) First edition with Auden's introduction

[within a border of two double rules] *Charles Baudelaire* | INTIMATE
JOURNALS | TRANSLATED BY | Christopher Isherwood | INTRO-
DUCTION BY | W. H. Auden | MARCEL RODD · HOLLYWOOD |
1947

Collation: 9 x 6 in. [1–8]⁸, pp. [1–4] 5–128.
Binding: Bound in moderate brown (58) cloth lettered down the spine in gold:
   '*Baudelaire* [ornament] INTIMATE JOURNALS [ornament] *Marcel Rodd*'. On
   the front cover a facsimile signature: 'Charles Baudelaire'. There is another later
   binding lettered in red on dark purplish blue (201) smooth cloth with no facsimile
   signature on the front cover, issued when the publisher moved to New York.
Contents: Introduction. (pp. 13–28)
Notes: Published 15 September 1947 in an edition of 1,000 copies.

b) First English edition with Auden's introduction   1949

CHARLES BAUDELAIRE | [ornamental swelled rule] | [title in red]
INTIMATE JOURNALS | TRANSLATED BY | CHRISTOPHER

ISHERWOOD | INTRODUCTION BY | W. H. AUDEN | WITH
SIX COLLOTYPE PLATES AND | ONE LINE DRAWING | *LON-
DON* | [rule] | METHUEN & CO. LTD | *1949*

Collation: 8½ x 5¼ in. [1–12]⁴, pp. [i–iv] v–xxiv, [1–2] 3–71 [72].
Binding: Bound in moderate blue (182) cloth lettered across the spine in gold: '[or-
nament] | *Intimate* | *Journals* | *of* | *Charles* | *Baudelaire* | [ornament] | ME-
THUEN'. Top edge gilt.
Contents: Introduction. (pp. xiii–xxiv)
Notes: "This translation was originally published in a limited edition by the Blacka-
more Press in 1930. First published in an edition limited to 750 copies, by Methuen
& Co. Ltd in [17 November] 1949" (p. iv). The book went out of print in 1953.
A paperback impression was published in the United States by the Beacon Press
on 4 September 1957 (10,000 copies) and a reset paperback edition by Panther
Books in England in March 1969. Microfilm and xerographic copies have been
available from University Microfilms since 1965.

In August 1958 Gaberbocchus Press issued an ephemeron titled *Roast poet*, by
W. H. Auden (Gaberbocchus loose leaf, no. 5) in an edition of 1,000 copies. This
is not by Auden and is in fact a quotation from the translation by Isherwood of
part of Squib XVII.

B 35   **POETS AT WORK**   1948

Poets at Work | ESSAYS BASED ON THE MODERN POETRY |
COLLECTION AT THE LOCKWOOD MEMORIAL | LIBRARY,
UNIVERSITY OF BUFFALO, *by* | RUDOLF ARNHEIM | W. H.
AUDEN | KARL SHAPIRO | DONALD A. STAUFFER | *Introduc-
tion by* CHARLES D. ABBOTT | *New York* | HARCOURT, BRACE
AND COMPANY

Collation: 8 x 5¼ in. [1–4]¹⁶[5]¹⁸[6]¹⁶, pp. [i–vi], vii–ix [x, 1–2] 3–186.
Binding: Bound in very deep red (14) cloth lettered across the spine in gold: 'ARN-
HEIM | AUDEN | SHAPIRO | STAUFFER | [on a black panel] *Poets* | *at* |
Work | [on the cloth] Harcourt, Brace | and Company'.
Contents: Squares and oblongs. (pp. 163–81)
Notes: Published 22 January 1948 in an impression of 2,500 copies and reprinted in
February 1948 (1,500 copies).

B 36   **A BEGINNING, BY R. HORAN**   1948

A Beginning | BY | Robert Horan | *With a Foreword by* | W. H. Auden |
NEW HAVEN | Yale University Press | [one line] | 1948

Collation: 7¾ x 5¼ in. [1–4]⁸[5]⁴[6]⁸, pp. [1–6] 7–87 [88].
Binding: Bound in light greenish grey (154) paper boards lettered down the spine
in black: 'HORAN: A BEGINNING *YALE*'. On a black panel on the front
cover: '*The Yale Series of Younger Poets* | [rule] | A BEGINNING | [rule] |
HORAN'.
Contents: Foreword. (pp. 7–10)
Notes: Published 11 April 1948 [*CCE* 11 May 1948] in an edition of 1,014 copies; no.
46 in the series.

B 37   **THE PORTABLE GREEK READER**   1948

THE PORTABLE | GREEK | READER | EDITED, AND WITH AN
INTRODUCTION, BY | W. H. AUDEN | MCMXLVIII | NEW
YORK • THE VIKING PRESS

Collation: 6½ x 4¼ in. [1–23]¹⁶, pp. [i–iv] v–x, 1–726.
Binding: Bound in greyish reddish orange (39) cloth lettered across the spine in
black: '[double rule] | [star] | [double rule] | GREEK | READER | [double
rule] | [star] | [double rule] | THE | VIKING | PORTABLE | LIBRARY |
[double rule] | EDITED | BY | W. H. | Auden | [double rule] | THE | VIKING
| PRESS | [double rule]. On the front cover: '[within a decorated border panel]
THE PORTABLE | GREEK | READER'. All edges stained dark blue.
Contents: Editor's introduction. (pp. 1–38)
Notes: Published 1 September 1948 in an impression of 10,000 copies and reprinted
in October 1950 (5,000 copies). A corrected paperback impression was issued 10
March 1955 (15,000 copies) and reprinted in October 1955 (10,000 copies), July
1958 (5,000 copies), April 1959 (5,000 copies), March 1960 (5,000 copies), Octo-
ber 1960 (5,000 copies), December 1961 (5,000 copies), August 1963 (5,000 copies),
July 1964 (5,000 copies), August 1965 (5,000 copies), May 1966 (5,000 copies),
August 1967 (6,000 copies), and August 1968 (6,000 copies). Some copies of these
impressions are also issued bound in cloth. Some copies were printed for a book
club as *The indispensable Greek reader*, with the imprint: New York: The Book
Society, 1951.

B 38   **T. S. ELIOT**   1948

T. S. ELIOT | A symposium from Conrad Aiken, Luciano Anceschi, |
[names of other contributors in seventeen lines] | Compiled by Richard
March and Tambimuttu | [fancy] PL | Editions Poetry London | 1948

Collation: 8½ x 5¼ in. [1]¹⁰[2–8]¹⁶[9]⁸, pp. [1–4] 5–259 [260].
Binding: Bound in yellowish grey (93) cloth lettered across the spine in gold: '[on a
brown panel] [curved bow] | T. S. | ELIOT | [curved bow] | A Symposium |
compiled by | Richard | March | and | Tambimuttu | [at the foot of the spine on a
brown panel; fancy] PL'. Top edge stained dark purple.
    The American impression is bound in smooth moderate orange yellow (71)
cloth and is lettered on the spine in blue: ' [across] [rule] | [wavy rule] | [down
the spine] T. S. Eliot: *Symposium* [star] | [across the spine] [rule] | [wavy rule] |
REGNERY | [rule]'.
Contents: For T. S. Eliot: When things began to happen to our favourite spot...
    (p. 43)   Reprinted in N and CSP2.
Notes: Published 27 September 1948 in an impression of 2,500 copies and reprinted
in December 1948 (1,500 copies). Both these impressions were printed by Henry
Ling of Dorchester.
    An impression perhaps of 1,000 copies was printed by the Garden City Press,
Letchworth, for the American issue, published 16 November 1949, which substi-
tutes the following imprint on the title page: '[ornament: an Italianate house] |
Henry Regnery Company | Chicago, Illinois' for the original.
    The title was reissued in a photolithographic reprint by Frank Cass & Co. in
1965 in England, and in the United States by Tambimuttu and Mass. It was again
reprinted photolithographically by the Books for Libraries Press in 1968.

B 39 THE GRASSHOPPER'S MAN, BY R. MOORE 1949

The | Grasshopper's Man | AND OTHER POEMS | BY | ROSALIE MOORE | *With a Foreword by* | W. H. Auden | NEW HAVEN | Yale University Press | [one line] | 1949

Collation: 7¾ x 5¼ in. [1–2]⁸[3]¹⁰[4]⁸, pp. [i–ii, 1–6] 7–66.
Binding: Bound in light greenish grey (154) paper boards lettered down the spine in black: 'MOORE: THE GRASSHOPPER'S MAN *YALE*'. On a black panel on the front cover: '*The Yale Series of Younger Poets* | *EDITED BY W. H. AUDEN* | [rule] | THE GRASSHOPPER'S MAN | [rule] | *ROSALIE MOORE*'.
Contents: Foreword. (pp. 7–10)
Notes: Published 18 May 1949 in an edition of 728 copies; no. 47 in the series.

B 40 RED RIBBON ON A WHITE HORSE, 1950
BY A. YEZIERSKA

Red Ribbon | *on a* | *White Horse* | BY | ANZIA YEZIERSKA | WITH AN | INTRODUCTION BY | W. H. AUDEN | NEW YORK | CHARLES SCRIBNER'S SONS | 1950

Collation: 8 x 5¼ in. [1–7]¹⁶, pp. [1–8] 9–220 [221–224].
Binding: Quarter bound in black cloth with deep red (13) paper boards, lettered across the spine in white: 'RED | RIBBON | ON A | WHITE | HORSE | [ornament] | YEZIERSKA | SCRIBNERS'. On the front cover: '[ornament: a leaping horse]'.
Contents: Introduction. (pp. 11–19) Reprinted in DH.
Notes: Published 11 September 1950 in an edition of 5,000 copies.

B 41 POETS OF THE ENGLISH LANGUAGE 1950

a) First edition

[general title page] [within a decorated floral border] *The Viking Portable Library* | POETS OF THE | ENGLISH LANGUAGE | *Edited by* | W. H. AUDEN | *and* | NORMAN HOLMES PEARSON | VOLUME I: LANGLAND TO SPENSER | VOLUME II: MARLOWE TO MARVELL | VOLUME III: MILTON TO GOLDSMITH | VOLUME IV: BLAKE TO POE | VOLUME V: TENNYSON TO YEATS

[volume I] [within a decorated floral border] POETS | OF THE | ENGLISH | LANGUAGE | I | *Langland to Spenser* | *With emendations of texts, and glosses, by* | E. TALBOT DONALDSON | NEW YORK | *The Viking Press* | 1950

The transcription of the title pages of the other individual volumes is similar to that of volume I, with the substitution of the relevant numbers and titles and the omission of the note crediting the authorship of the emendations and glosses.

Collation: 6½ x 4 in. [vol. I] [1–21]¹⁶, pp. [i–iv] v–xlv [xlvi–xlviii], 1–619 [620–624];
[vol. II] [1–19]¹⁶, pp. [i–iv] v–xlv [xlvi–xlviii], 1–556 [557–560]; [vol. III]
[1–21]¹⁶, pp. [i–iv] v–xliv [xlv–xlvi], 1–622 [623–626]; [vol. IV] [1–18]¹⁶, pp.
[i–iv] v–xxxviii [xxxix–xl], 1–535 [536]; [vol. V] [1–21]¹⁶, pp. [i–vi] vii–xlvii
[xlviii], 1–624.

Binding: Quarter bound in pale yellow (89) cloth with dark red (16) cloth covers
lettered across the spine in red: '[double rule] | [star] | [rule] | [general and
volume titles in gold on a red panel] POETS | OF THE | ENGLISH | LAN-
GUAGE | I. LANGLAND | TO SPENSER | [rule] | [star] | [double rule] |
THE | VIKING | PORTABLE | LIBRARY | [double rule] | EDITED | BY |
W. H. Auden | and | Norman Holmes | Pearson | [double rule] | THE | VIKING
| PRESS | [double rule]'. The series title and device, a galley in sail, are blind-
stamped on the front cover. Top edge stained yellow.

Contents: The introductions to all volumes are unsigned, but are by Auden.

    [Vol. I]   Introduction. (pp. xxxi–xxxvii)
                   General principles. (pp. v–vii)
    [Vol. II]   Introduction. (pp. xv–xxxii)
                   General principles. (pp. xxxiii–xxxv)
    [Vol. III] Introduction. (pp. xiii–xxvi)
                   General principles. (pp. xxvi–xxix)
    [Vol. IV] Introduction. (pp. xiii–xxvii)
    [Vol. V]   Introduction. (pp. xvii–xxvii)

Notes: Published 29 September 1950 [*CCE* 21 September 1950] in an impression of
14,000 copies and reprinted in January 1954 (5,000 copies). Copies of the second
impression are dated December 1953. The third impression dated December 1957
was the first paperback issue, published 3 January 1958, and for this impression the
volume titles on the right-hand title pages were changed as follows: vol. I: Mediaeval and renaissance poets; vol. II: Elizabethan and Jacobean poets; vol. III:
Restoration and Augustan poets; vol. IV: Romantic poets; vol. V: Victorian and
Edwardian poets. Beginning with the third impression, the various volumes were
then reprinted as follows, and some copies of some printings were issued hardbound as well as in paperback.

Vol. I: December 1957 (9,056 copies), March 1961 (4,510 copies), November 1962
    (4,507 copies), November 1964 (4,966 copies), January 1968 (3,027 copies), and
    February 1969 (2,965 copies).

Vol. II: December 1957 (9,992 copies), November 1960 (4,490 copies), June 1961
    (4,616 copies), November 1962 (4,577 copies), November 1964 (5,010 copies),
    March 1967 (2,741 copies), March 1968 (3,085 copies), and February 1969 (3,044
    copies).

Vol. III: December 1957 (9,047 copies), November 1960 (4,639 copies), Septem-
    ber 1961 (4,556 copies), June 1963 (4,979 copies), March 1965 (5,016 copies),
    February 1967 (3,006 copies), March 1968 (3,051 copies), and February 1969
    (2,965 copies).

Vol. IV: December 1957 (9,679 copies), May 1960 (4,970 copies), May 1961 (5,554
    copies), October 1961 (5,007 copies), November 1962 (5,115 copies), August
    1963 (5,026 copies), June 1965 (5,082 copies), June 1966 (3,902 copies), June
    1967 (4,864 copies), and September 1968 (3,029 copies).

Vol. V: December 1957 (10,775 copies), May 1960 (4,926 copies), June 1962 (4,600
    copies), June 1963 (4,490 copies), January 1965 (4,961 copies), April 1966 (5,038
    copies), and July 1968 (5,059 copies).

Some copies of the first impression were on superior paper, and were published
20 October 1950 as a boxed "deluxe edition." These copies are quarter bound in
dark blue (183) cloth with gold cloth covers lettered across the spine in gold:
'[double rule] | [star] | [double rule] | POETS | [four lines as the trade edition] |

[double rule] | [star] | [continuing as the trade edition]'. On the front cover is blind-stamped the series device, a winged horse, but no title. The top edge is gilt, end papers are dark blue, and each volume has a dark blue ribbon. A later issue, not indicated as such in the copyright statement, has greyish-red end papers, blue top edges, and no ribbon.

While the introductions are by Auden, a pamphlet by Norman Holmes Pearson containing bibliographical notes for the anthology was published separately on 9 November 1950, collating: 6½ x 4 in., one unsigned gathering of thirty-two leaves, pp. [1–6] 7–62 [63–64]. These notes are incorporated in the third and later impressions of the anthology in the appropriate volumes.

b) First English edition   1952

[The transcription of the general title page is identical with that of the American edition with the omission of the American series title. The transcription of the individual volume title pages is also the same as that of the American edition with the substitution of: ' LONDON | *Eyre & Spottiswoode* | 1952' for the American imprint.]

Collation: 7 x 4½ in. [vol. I] [1]–20^{16}, pp. [i–iv] v–xlv [xlvi–xlviii], 1–619 [620]; [vol. II] [1]–18^{16}19^{14}, pp. [i–iv] v–xlv [xlvi–xlviii], 1–556; [vol. III] [1]–20^{16}21^{14}, pp. [i–iv] v–xliv [xlv–xlvi], 1–622; [vol. IV] [1]–18^{16}, pp. [i–iv] v–xxxviii [xxxix–xl], 1–535 [536]; [vol. V] [1]–21^{16}, pp. [i–vi] vii–xlvii [xlviii], 1–624. \$1 signed 'PEL [volume number]'.

Binding: Quarter bound in white cloth with deep red (13) cloth covers lettered across the spine in gold: '[double rule] | POETS | *of the* | ENGLISH | LANGUAGE | [double rule] | [volume number] | [double rule] | [volume title] | [three double rules] | EYRE & | SPOTTISWOODE | [double rule]'. All the lettering, with the exception of the volume numbers, is on red panels on the white cloth. Top edge stained reddish purple.

Contents: As the American edition.

Notes: Published 29 August 1952 in an edition of 4,840 copies. The work was reissued by Heron Books, a subscription book agency, late in 1969 as a reduced premium offer to attract subscribers for the series "Women who made history." This issue was also advertised under the title *The treasury of immortal poems.*

B 42   SELECTED PROSE & POETRY   1950
OF E. A. POE

Edgar Allan Poe | [curved rule] | SELECTED PROSE AND POETRY | *Edited with an Introduction by W. H. Auden* | New York *Rinehart & Co., Inc.* Toronto

Collation: 7¼ x 4¾ in. [1–8]^{16}[9–10]^{12}[11–18]^{16}, pp. [i–iv] v–xxvi [xxvii–xxviii], 1–528 [529–532].

Binding: Glued in dark pink (6) paper covers lettered down the spine in black: 'POE · *Selected Prose and Poetry* [across the foot of the spine] 42 | [fancy] *RE*'. On the front cover: '*Rinehart Editions* | [white rule] | EDGAR ALLEN [*sic*] POE | SELECTED PROSE | AND POETRY | INTRODUCTION BY W. H. AUDEN | [publisher's name in white] RINEHART & COMPANY · INCORPORATED | [black rule] | *42* | [white fancy] *RE*'.

Contents: Introduction. (pp. v–xvii)
Notes: Published 6 December 1950 [*CCE* 14 December 1950] in an impression of
15,000 copies and reprinted in June 1954 (5,000 copies). A revised edition was published 27 January 1956 in an impression of 5,000 copies. This has the words 'RE-
VISED EDITION' after the title on the title page, and the collation runs: 7¼ x
4¾ in. [1–16]¹⁶, pp. [i–iv] v–xxvi [xxvii–xxviii], 1–482 [483–484]. Auden's introduction is revised. This revised edition was reprinted in July 1956 (5,000
copies), July 1957 (5,000 copies), December 1959 (5,000 copies), April 1960 (5,000
copies), 1961 (7,500 copies), 1962 (6,000 copies), 1963 (6,000 copies), June 1964
(7,500 copies), September 1965 (7,500 copies), August 1966 (5,000 copies), 1967
(7,500 copies), and 1968 (7,500 copies).

B 43   A CHANGE OF WORLD, BY A. C. RICH   1951

A CHANGE OF WORLD | BY ADRIENNE CECILE RICH | with a
foreword by W. H. Auden | New Haven: Yale University Press: 1951 |
[one line]

Collation: 7½ x 4¾ in. [1–6]⁸, pp. [i–iv, 1–6] 7–85 [86–92].
Binding: Bound in dark yellowish pink (30) paper boards lettered across the front
cover in brown: '[ornament: leaf] A CHANGE OF WORLD | YALE SERIES
OF YOUNGER POETS'.
Contents: Foreword. (pp. 7–11)
Notes: Published 18 April 1951 in an impression of 551 copies and reprinted in De-
cember 1951 (503 copies). No. 48 in the series.

B 44   INDIAN CONGRESS FOR CULTURAL   1951
FREEDOM

[vertical rule down three-quarters of the title page; to the right] INDIAN
| CONGRESS | FOR | CULTURAL | FREEDOM | [below the rule]
MARCH 28 TO 31, 1951

Collation: 8⅜ x 5¼ in. [1]⁴2–19⁸20⁴[21]², pp. [i–viii,1] 2–299 [300].
Binding: Bound in shiny dark green (146) paper-covered boards lettered across the
spine in copperish gold: 'INDIAN | CONGRESS | FOR | CULTURAL | FREE-
DOM | 1951'.
Contents: Address. (pp. 76–81)
Notes: Published in Bombay in August 1951 in an edition of 2,000 copies.

B 45   A MASK FOR JANUS, BY W. S. MERWIN   1952

A MASK FOR JANUS | by W. S. MERWIN | with a Foreword by
W. H. Auden | New Haven: Yale University Press: 1952 | [one line]

Collation: 8 x 4¾ in. [1–4]⁸[5]⁴[6]⁸, pp. [*–**, i–vi] vii–xiii [xiv], 1–67 [68–72].
Binding: Bound in dark greyish blue (187) paper boards lettered down the spine in
white: 'MERWIN [oblique stroke] A MASK FOR JANUS YALE'. On the
front cover: '[line drawing of a two-faced head] | YALE SERIES OF YOUNGER
POETS'.
Contents: Foreword. (pp. vii–xi)

Notes: Published 21 May 1952 in an impression of 511 copies and reprinted in May 1953. Of the 550 sheets of this second impression 250 were bound and the other 300 were scrapped. The book was out of print in February 1960. No. 49 in the series.

B 46   THE LIVING THOUGHTS OF KIERKEGAARD   1952

a) First edition

THE LIVING THOUGHTS OF | KIERKEGAARD | *PRESENTED BY* | W. H. AUDEN| THE LIVING THOUGHTS LIBRARY | EDITED BY ALFRED O. MENDEL | DAVID McKAY COMPANY, INC. | NEW YORK

Collation: 7¼ x 4¾ in. [1–15]⁸, pp. [i–x, 1–2] 3–225 [226–230].
Binding: Bound in vivid red (11) cloth lettered across the spine in gold: '[rule] | [series device: LT [spiral] L within a circle] | [two double rules] | KIERKE-GAARD | *PRESENTED* | *BY* | W. H. AUDEN | [double rule] | [rule] | *McKay* | [rule] | [rule]'.
Contents: Presenting Kierkegaard. (pp. 3–22)
Notes: Published 17 October 1952 [*CCE* 8 October 1952] in an edition of 4,000 copies. Reissued by Indiana University Press as a Midland book (MB 47) in a paperback impression on 15 April 1963, and reprinted in 1966.

b) First English edition   1955

KIERKEGAARD | Selected and Introduced by | W. H. AUDEN | [device: kneeling huntress] | CASSELL AND COMPANY LTD | LONDON

Collation: 7¾ x 5 in. [1]–12⁸, pp. [i–vi] vii–viii, 1–184.
Binding: Bound in black cloth lettered across the spine in gold: '[double rule] | Kierkegaard | Selected and | introduced by | W. H. AUDEN | [double rule] | CASSELL'.
Contents: Introduction. (pp. 1–17)
Notes: Published 19 May 1955 in an edition of 2,015 copies.

B 47   TALES OF GRIMM AND ANDERSEN   1952

TALES OF GRIMM | AND | ANDERSEN | [ornament: six spokes] | SELECTED BY FREDERICK JACOBI, JR. | INTRODUCTION BY W. H. AUDEN | [series device: leaping figure with torch in upstretched arm] | [ornamental rule] | THE MODERN LIBRARY · NEW YORK

Collation: 8 x 5¼ in. [1–24]¹⁶, pp. [i–iv] v–xxi [xxii, 1–2] 3–746.
Binding: Bound in moderate purplish blue (200) cloth lettered across the spine in gold: '[on a red panel] [two rules] | TALES | OF | GRIMM | AND | ANDERSEN | *Modern Library* | [two rules] | [device on a gold-bordered oval red panel]'. The device is repeated on the front cover. Top edge stained red.
Contents: Introduction. (pp. xiii–xxi).   Reprinted in *New world writing*, November 1952.

Notes: Published 3 November 1952 by Random House in an impression of 7,500
copies and reprinted in September 1953 (5,000 copies), September 1955 (5,000
copies), August 1957 (5,000 copies), February 1960 (5,000 copies), April 1962
(5,000 copies), March 1965 (4,500 copies), December 1965 (4,000 copies), and
October 1969 (2,000 copies).

**B 48   THE DESIRE & PURSUIT OF THE WHOLE,   1953
BY F. ROLFE**

a) **First edition with Auden's foreword**

THE | DESIRE | AND | PURSUIT | OF THE | WHOLE | *A Romance
of Modern Venice* | BY | FREDERICK ROLFE | BARON CORVO |
[one line] | With an Introduction by | A. J. A. SYMONS | and | Fore-
word by | W. H. AUDEN | [device: kneeling huntress] | CASSELL |
and Company, Limited | London, Toronto, Melbourne | and Sydney

Collation: 8½ x 5½ in. [A]–U⁸, pp. [*–**, i–iv] v–xvi, 1–299 [300–302].
Binding: Bound in very dark green (147) cloth lettered across the spine in gold:
    'THE | DESIRE | AND | PURSUIT | OF THE | WHOLE | BARON | CORVO
    | CASSELL'.
Contents: Foreword. (pp. v–ix)
Notes: Published 30 April 1953 in an impression of 3,168 copies, and reprinted in
    October 1961 (1,000 copies). The book was originally published in 1934, but that
    edition did not contain Auden's foreword.

b) **First American edition**   1953

THE | DESIRE | AND | PURSUIT | OF THE | WHOLE | *A Romance
of Modern Venice* | BY | FREDERICK ROLFE | BARON CORVO |
[one line] | With an Introduction by | A. J. A. SYMONS | and | Foreword
by | W. H. AUDEN | A NEW DIRECTIONS BOOK

Collation: 8 x 4⅞ in. [1–10]¹⁶, pp. [*–**, i–iv] v–xvi [xvii–xviii], 1–299 [300].
Binding: Bound in light bluish green (163) cloth lettered down the spine in imitation
    script in silver: 'Corvo the desire and pursuit of the whole'. Some later copies are
    bound in light green cloth and lettered in black.
Contents: Foreword. (pp. v–ix)
Notes: Published 15 July 1953 in an edition of 2,650 copies.

B 49   VARIOUS JANGLING KEYS, BY E. BOGARDUS   1953

[left-hand title page] EDGAR BOGARDUS: | WITH A FOREWORD
BY W. H. AUDEN

[right-hand title page] *Various Jangling Keys* | New Haven: | *Yale Uni-
versity Press* | [three lines] | 1953

Collation: 8 x 5 in [1]¹⁰[2–3]⁸, pp. [i–ii, 1–6] 7–49 [50].
Binding: Bound in greyish blue (186) paper boards with a decorative repeat pattern

in pale grey and lettered down the spine in white: 'BOGARDUS: VARIOUS JANGLING KEYS [across the spine] YALE'. On the front cover: 'VARIOUS JANGLING KEYS | YALE SERIES OF YOUNGER POETS'.
Contents: Foreword. (pp. 7–12)
Notes: Published 20 May 1953 in an edition of 801 copies; no. 50 in the series.

B 50   **RUDOLF KASSNER**   1953

RUDOLF KASSNER | *zum* | *achtzigsten Geburtstag* | GEDENKBUCH | Herausgegeben | von | A. CL. KENSIK UND D. BODMER | IM EUGEN RENTSCH VERLAG

Collation: 8⅝ x 5⅝ in. [1–15]⁸[16]⁶, pp. [1–6] 7–250 [251–252].
Binding: Bound in plain white card covers with a yellowish white (92) paper wrapper lettered up the spine in black: 'RUDOLF KASSNER [light brown dot] GED-ENKBUCH'. Across the front wrapper: *'Rudolf Kassner* | [in light brown] *zum achtzigsten Geburtstag* | [light brown swelled rule] | GEDENKBUCH'.
Contents: Zahl und Gesicht. (p. 58, English text)
Notes: Published in Erlenbach–Zürich on 9 September 1953 in an edition of 1,000 copies, and out of print in 1963.

B 51   **NEW POEMS BY AMERICAN POETS**   1953

NEW | POEMS | *By American Poets* | [rule] | Edited by ROLFE HUM-PHRIES | BALLANTINE BOOKS • NEW YORK • 1953

Collation: 7¾ x 5 in. [1–5]¹⁶[6]⁴[7]¹⁶, pp. [i–xx], 1–179 [180].
Binding: Bound in light bluish green (163) imitation cloth-weave paper boards lettered down the spine in yellow: 'NEW POEMS [oblique stroke] by American Poets [across the spine: device]'. On the front cover: 'NEW POEMS | [rule] | By American Poets'.
    The simultaneous paperback impression measures 7⅛ x 4¼ in., pp. [i–xx], 1–179 [180–188], and is in a yellow and light blue paper cover lettered in white and black with all edges stained yellow.
Contents:
Lakes: A lake allows an average father, walking slowly . . . (pp. 6–7)
Woods: Sylvan men at [*sic*] savage in those primal woods . . . (pp. 8–9)
    Both reprinted in SA.
Notes: Published 21 September 1953 in a hardbound impression of 3,000 copies and a paperback impression of 100,180 copies. Out of print in 1968.

B 52   **AN ARMADA OF THIRTY WHALES,**   1954
                    BY D. G. HOFFMAN

[left-hand title page] [all within a bracket on the right side] *New Haven:* | *Yale University Press* | [three lines] | 1954

[right-hand title page] AN | A[large initial]RMADA | OF THIRTY WHALES | *by* DANIEL G. HOFFMAN | WITH A FOREWORD BY W. H. AUDEN

Collation: 8 x 4¾ in. [1–2]⁸[3]¹⁰[4]⁸, pp. [i–xvi, 1–2] 3–48 [49–50].
Binding: Bound in light yellow (86) paper boards with a pattern of black lines and
  lettered down the spine in black: 'AN ARMADA OF THIRTY WHALES:
  HOFFMAN YALE'. On the front cover: 'THE YALE SERIES OF YOUNGER
  POETS'.
Contents: Foreword. (pp. vii–xii)
Notes: Published 21 April 1954 in an edition of 789 copies and out of print in May
  1957. No. 51 in the Yale series of younger poets. Microfilm or xerographic copies
  are available from University Microfilms.

B 53   **THE VISIONARY NOVELS OF**   1954
                        GEORGE MACDONALD

[left-hand title page] NEW YORK | THE VISIONARY NOVELS |
EDITED BY ANNE FREMANTLE–WITH | AN INTRODUC-
TION BY W. H. AUDEN

[right-hand title page] THE NOONDAY PRESS [device: three fish] |
of GEORGE MACDONALD | *Lilith Phantastes*

Collation: 8¼ x 5½ in. [1–14]¹⁶, pp. [i–xii, 1–2] 3–434 [435–436].
Binding: Quarter bound in dark purplish blue (201) cloth with moderate bluish
  green (164) paper boards lettered across the spine in shiny green (general title,
  rules, and publisher's name) and silver (individual titles and author's name): 'The |
  Visionary | Novels | of | GEORGE | MACDONALD | [rule] | Lilith | [rule] |
  Phantastes | [rule] | NOONDAY'. The device is repeated in silver on the front
  cover. Top edge stained dark blue.
Contents: Introduction. (pp. v–x)
Notes: Published 11 October 1954 in an edition of 3,000 copies and out of print in
  1960. We have seen a copy with a review slip giving the publication date as 15
  November 1954.

B 54   **HERMIT SONGS, BY S. BARBER**   1954

SAMUEL BARBER | Op. 29 | HERMIT SONGS | to poems translated
from anonymous Irish | texts of the eighth to thirteenth centuries | G.
SCHIRMER, Inc. | NEW YORK

Collation: 12 x 8⅞ in. One gathering of sixteen leaves. Plate marked '43275', pp.
  [i–iv, 1–2] 3–28. The fourth leaf is signed '43275 C'.
Binding: Stapled twice in a light grey (264) card wrapper lettered across the front
  cover in black: 'SAMUEL BARBER | HERMIT SONGS | [illustration] | [ar-
  row] HIGH LOW | $2.50 | (In U.S.A.) | G. SCHIRMER | NEW YORK'. The
  rear cover carries a single column of advertisements for Barber's other work, and
  the number 'A-1034'.
Contents:
  The monk and his cat, translated by W. H. Auden. (pp. 19–22)
  The praises of God, translated by W. H. Auden. (pp. 23–24)
Notes: "The *Hermit Songs*, commissioned by the Elizabeth Sprague Coolidge Foundation, were first performed by Leontyne Price, soprano, with the composer at the
  piano, at the Library of Congress, Washington, D.C. on October 30, 1953 . . .

where existing translations seemed inadequate, [others] were especially made by W. H. Auden" (p. [iv]).

Published 18 October 1954. There had been six impressions of the high-voice issue by 1969 for a total of 3,967 copies, and four impressions of the low-voice issue totalling 2,734 copies. Later impressions insert 'Ed. 2176' on the title page between the title and the imprint, carry two columns of advertising on the rear cover, and bear a later number on the lower left corner. A recording of the songs was issued as Columbia ML 4988 [1955] and reissued as Odyssey 32 16 0230 [1968]; one of the songs, "The monk and his cat" was also recorded on Decca LXT 6336/SXL 6336 [1968].

B 55   AN ELIZABETHAN SONG BOOK   1955

a) First edition

AN | ELIZABETHAN | SONG BOOK | *Lute songs* | *Madrigals* | *and Rounds* | MUSIC EDITED BY | NOAH GREENBERG | TEXT EDITED BY | W. H. AUDEN | AND | CHESTER KALLMAN | DOUBLEDAY ANCHOR BOOKS | DOUBLEDAY & COMPANY, INC., GARDEN CITY, N.Y. | 1955

Collation: 7 x 4¼ in. One hundred and forty single leaves, pp. [i–iv] v–xxix [xxx, 1] 2–243 [244–250].

Binding: A perfect binding glued in an illustrated card cover lettered in black down the spine: 'AN ELIZABETHAN SONG BOOK | *Noah Greenberg, W. H. Auden & Chester Kallman* | [across the foot of the spine] *Anchor* | *A 56*'. On the front cover: '[an illustration in green, black, blue, and yellow showing a bank with a tree, a lute, and music with two figures by a riverbank] *$1.25* | *In Canada $1.45* | *Anchor A 56* | A [fancy] n | ELIZABETHAN | SONG BOOK | LUTE SONGS: Madrigals & Rounds | Music edited by NOAH GREENBERG | Text edited by W. H. AUDEN | and CHESTER KALLMAN | *A Doubleday Anchor Original* [device: dolphin and anchor]'. The rear covers bears a descriptive note on the book.

Contents: Introduction: The poems, [signed] W. H. Auden [and] Chester Kallman. (pp. xi–xxiv)

Notes: Published 20 October 1955 in an impression of 25,000 copies, and reprinted in May 1956 (12,500 copies), May 1960 (10,000 copies), and March 1964 (10,000 copies). Out of print in August 1968.

b) First clothbound edition   1956

AN ELIZABETHAN | SONG BOOK | *Lute Songs, Madrigals and Rounds* | [ornament: mermaid on the sea playing a lyre] | Music edited by Noah Greenberg | Text edited by W. H. Auden and | Chester Kallman | DOUBLEDAY & CO., INC., GARDEN CITY, NEW YORK, 1956

Collation: 11 x 8¼ in. [1–16]⁸, pp. [i–iv] v–xv [xvi, 1] 2–240.

Binding: Bound in yellowish grey (93) cloth lettered across the spine in gold: 'GREENBERG | AUDEN & | KALLMAN | [down] AN ELIZABETHAN SONG BOOK | [across] DOUBLEDAY'. On the front cover: 'AN ELIZABETHAN SONG BOOK | [ornament]'.

Contents: Introduction: The poems, [signed] Chester Kallman [and] W. H. Auden.
(pp. vii–xiii)
Notes: Published 20 September 1956 in an edition of 3,000 copies, and out of print in
January 1959. Reprinted photolithographically in New York by Hillary House in
1968.

c) First English edition   1957

[The transcription of the title page is identical with that of the American
clothbound edition with the substitution of the following for the original
imprint: 'FABER AND FABER LIMITED | 24 RUSSELL SQUARE
LONDON'.]

Collation: 11 x 8 in. [1–16]⁸, pp. [i–iv] v–xv [xvi, 1] 2–240.
Binding: Bound in moderate red (15) cloth lettered across the spine in gold: '[double
curved rule] | [title on light grey panel] *An* | *Eliza=* | *bethan* | *Song* | *Book* |
Edited by | *Auden,* | *Greenberg* | *and* | *Kallman* | *Faber &* | *Faber'*. On front cover
an ornament in gold: lute, flute, and foliage. Top edge stained yellow.
Contents: As the first clothbound edition.
Notes: Published 24 May 1957 in an edition of 3,000 copies. Out of print in 1969. A
paperback impression was published 11 November 1968.

B 56   SOME TREES, BY J. ASHBERY   1956

Some Trees | [illustration of trees] | *by John Ashbery* | WITH A FORE-
WORD BY W. H. AUDEN | NEW HAVEN | YALE UNIVERSITY
PRESS 1956 | [two lines]

Collation: 8 x 4¾ in. [1]⁸[2]⁴[3–6]⁸, pp. [1–10] 11–87 [88].
Binding: Bound in shiny black cloth lettered down the spine in gold: 'SOME TREES
[ornament across the spine: two leaves] ASHBERY [across] *Yale'*.
Contents: Foreword. (pp. 11–16)
Notes: Published 28 March 1956 in an edition of 817 copies and out of print in 1964.
No. 52 in the Yale series of younger poets.

B 57   MODERN CANTERBURY PILGRIMS   1956

a) First edition

MODERN | CANTERBURY PILGRIMS | *And Why They Chose* | *the*
Episcopal Church | [names of the twenty-two contributors in two columns,
eleven lines] | *Edited, with an essay, by* | JAMES A. PIKE | MORE-
HOUSE-GORHAM CO. | New York 1956

Collation: 8 x 5¼ in. [1–10]¹⁶, pp. [1–6] 7–317 [318–320].
Binding: Bound in smooth moderate blue (182) cloth lettered down the spine in
silver: '*Pike: Modern Canterbury Pilgrims* | [across] M-G'.
Contents: W. H. Auden. (pp. 32–43)
Notes: Published 21 May 1956 [CCE 23 April 1956] in an impression of 6,000 copies,
and reprinted in September 1956 (2,327 copies), October 1956 (2,581 copies), and

April 1957 (2,500 copies). Out of print in April 1960. An abridged paperback edition, without Auden's essay, was published 31 July 1959.

The publisher states that the third impression was a replacement for the second, a number of copies having been spoiled at the printers.

b) First English edition 1956

MODERN | CANTERBURY PILGRIMS | *The Story of Twenty-three Converts | and why they chose the Anglican Communion | Edited by |* THE DEAN OF NEW YORK | *With an Introduction by* | BISHOP STEPHEN NEILL | [device] | LONDON | A. R. MOWBRAY & Co. LIMITED

Collation: 7¼ x 4¾ in. 1–10¹⁶, pp. [*–**, 1–2] 3–317 [318].
Binding: Bound in strong blue (178) imitation weave-grained paper boards lettered across the spine in silver: '*MODERN | CANTERBURY | PILGRIMS | MOW-BRAYS*'.
Contents: W. H. Auden. (p. 32–43)
Notes: Published 26 October 1956 in an impression of 2,500 copies. Reprinted in September 1957 (1,500 copies), and out of print in December 1960.

B 58   SELECTED POEMS OF ADAM MICKIEWICZ   1956

[left-hand title page] ADAM | 1798–1855 | Edited by Clark Mills | [device: three fishes]

[right-hand title page] MICKIEWICZ | SELECTED POEMS | With a Critical Appreciation by Jan Lechoń | *New York* THE NOONDAY PRESS

Collation: 8¼ x 5½ in. [1–8]⁸, pp. [i–ii, 1–11] 12–124 [125–126].
Binding: Quarter bound in black cloth with moderate brown (58) paper boards lettered down the spine in silver: 'ADAM MICKIEWICZ [device in orange] | [across] *Noonday*', and down the front cloth hinge: 'SELECTED POEMS'.
Contents: The romantic, translated by W. H. Auden. (pp. 67–69) First printed in *Wiadamośći*, 19 February 1956, and reprinted in ATH.
Notes: Published 29 June 1956, and out of print in December 1960. The number of copies printed is not known.

B 59   THE DESCENT OF THE DOVE,   1956
BY C. WILLIAMS

THE | DESCENT | OF | THE | DOVE | *A History of the Holy Spirit in the Church | by* CHARLES WILLIAMS | *Introduction by* W. H. AUDEN | LIVING AGE BOOKS | *published by* MERIDIAN BOOKS *New York* 1956

Collation: 7⅛ x 4¼ in. [1–8]¹⁶, pp. [i–iv] v–xv [xvi], 1–240.
Binding: Glued in a card cover the upper half of which is moderate blue (182) and the lower half of which is moderate olive (107) lettered on the spine in white: '[across] LA 5 | [down, upper case in olive] The Descent of the Dove [in blue]

CHARLES WILLIAMS [in red] *Living Age'*, and on the front cover: '[in white]
The Descent of the Dove | [in olive] THE HISTORY OF THE HOLY SPIRIT
IN THE CHURCH | [in white] *by CHARLES WILLIAMS* | *with an introduc-
tion by* | *W. H. AUDEN* | [illustration in red, olive, and white] | [in red] *Living
Age* | *Books* | [two lines]'. The rear cover carries the title and details of Williams's
writings.
Contents: Introduction. (pp. v–xii)   A longer version appeared in *Christian century,*
2 May 1956.
Notes: Published 20 August 1956 in an impression of 6,000 copies, and reprinted in
1957 (5,000 copies), and 1959 (4,000 copies). Out of print in 1961.

B 60   THE FABER BOOK OF MODERN   1956
                       AMERICAN VERSE

a) First edition

The Faber Book | *of* | *Modern American Verse* | edited by | W. H. AU-
DEN | FABER AND FABER LIMITED | 24 Russell Square | London

Collation: 8 x 5 in. [π]⁴A–X⁸, pp. [i–viii], 1–336.
Binding: Bound in brilliant blue (177) cloth lettered across the spine in gold:
   '[swelled rule] | THE | FABER | BOOK | OF | Modern | American | Verse |
   [swelled rule] | *Edited by* | W. H. |AUDEN | [swelled rule] | FABER'.
Contents: Introduction. (pp. 9–21)   First printed in *Anchor review*, 1955, and re-
printed in DH.
Notes: Published 3 September 1956 in an edition of 5,300 copies, and out of print in
March 1965.

b) First American edition   1956

The *Criterion Book* | of *Modern* | *American Verse* | Edited with an intro-
duction by | *W. H. Auden* | CRITERION BOOKS   NEW YORK

Collation: 8¼ x 5½ [1–11]¹⁶, pp. [i–viii], 1–336 [337–344].
Binding: Quarter bound in black cloth with light grey (264) paper boards with
   alternate green and black vertical wavy lines, lettered across the spine in silver:
   'The | *Criterion Book* | of | *Modern* | *American* | *Verse* | *W. H. Auden* | Criterion'.
Contents: Introduction. (pp. 9–21)   The last two paragraphs from the first edition
are omitted.
Notes: Published 15 November 1956 [*CCE* 11 November 1956]. No information is
available from the publisher for this title, but according to Auden's agent sales
were 4,288 copies.
   A lithographic reprint of the Faber edition with the half title, title page, and
acknowledgements reset (pp. i, iii, 319–27).

B 61   SELECTED WRITINGS OF SYDNEY SMITH   1956

a) First edition

SELECTED WRITINGS OF | Sydney Smith | [swelled rule] | ED-
ITED AND WITH AN INTRODUCTION BY | W. H. Auden |
FARRAR, STRAUS AND CUDAHY | NEW YORK

Collation: 8¼ x 5½ in. [1–13]¹⁶, pp. [i–iv] v–xx, [1–2] 3–396.
Binding: Bound in greyish reddish orange (39) cloth lettered across the spine in gold: '[treble rule] | SELECTED | WRITINGS | OF | Sydney | Smith | [treble rule] | Auden | FARRAR, STRAUS | AND | CUDAHY'.
Contents: Introduction. (pp. vii–xx) An earlier version of the introduction was published in *English miscellany*, 1952.
Notes: Published 19 November 1956 in an edition of 5,200 copies, and out of print in December 1962. Some copies of this edition were remaindered in England.

b) First English edition 1957

[The transcription of the title page is identical with that of the first edition with the substitution of the following for the original imprint: 'FABER AND FABER LIMITED | 24 Russell Square | London'.]

Collation: 8½ x 5¼ in. [1]–26⁸, pp. [i–iv] v–xx, [1–2] 3–396.
Binding: Bound in brilliant blue (177) cloth lettered across the spine in gold: 'Selected | Writings | of | SYDNEY | SMITH | edited | by | W. H. Auden | Faber & | Faber'. Top edge stained yellow.
Contents: Introduction. (pp. vii–xx)
Notes: Published 11 October 1957 in an edition of 2,000 copies.

B 62   THE GREEN WALL, BY J. WRIGHT 1957

[left-hand title page] JAMES WRIGHT: [large hollow shaded upper case] THE

[right-hand title page] *With a Foreword by W. H. AUDEN* | [large hollow shaded upper case] GREEN WALL | *New Haven: YALE UNIVERSITY PRESS, 1957* | [one line]

Collation: 8 x 4¾ in. [1]⁴[2–8]⁸, pp. [*–**, i–viii] ix–xix [xx, 1–2] 3–93 [94–98].
Binding: Bound in smooth paper patterned boards basically yellowish white (92) with wavy vertical lines and lettered down the spine in gold: '[ornament: leaf] [within a gold-rule border on a deep red panel] WRIGHT [rule] THE GREEN WALL [rule] YALE [outside the panel and rule] [ornament: leaf]'.
Contents: Foreword. (pp. ix–xvi)
Notes: Published 17 April 1957 in an impression of 772 copies and reprinted in March 1958 (779 copies). Out of print in 1967. No. 53 in the Yale series of younger poets.

B 63   NEW POEMS BY AMERICAN POETS, 2 1957

NEW | POEMS | BY AMERICAN POETS | No. 2 | *edited by Rolfe Humphries* | Ballantine Books • New York • 1957 | [rule]

Collation: 8 x 5¼ in. [1–6]¹⁶, pp. [i–xii], 1–179 [180].
Binding: Bound in yellowish grey (93) cloth lettered down the spine in red: 'HUMPHRIES NEW POEMS BALLANTINE'. The simultaneously published paperback impression measures 7⅛ x 4¼ in., pp. [i–xii], 1–180, and is perfect bound in a white card cover printed in blue, red, and black, with all edges stained yellow.

Contents:

There will be no peace: Though mild clear weather . . . (p. 6)   Reprinted in HTC
and CSP2.

First things first: Woken, I lay in the arms of my own warmth and listened . . .
(pp. 6–7)   Reprinted in HTC and CSP2.

Objects: All that which lies outside our sort of why . . . (pp. 7–8)   Reprinted in
HTC and CSP2.

The island cemetery: This graveyard with its umbrella pines . . . (p. 8)   Reprinted
in HTC and CSP2.

Song: So large a morning, so itself, to lean . . . (p. 9)   Reprinted in HTC and
CSP2.

Notes: Published 16 September 1957 [*CCE* 15 August 1957], in a hardbound impression of 3,136 copies and a paperback impression of 63,220 copies. The book is out
of print.

B 64   LANGUAGE   1957

[left-hand title page] *SCIENCE OF CULTURE SERIES* | Volume VIII |
Planned and Edited by | RUTH NANDA ANSHEN

[right-hand title page] LANGUAGE: | AN ENQUIRY INTO ITS |
MEANING AND FUNCTION | [device: a torch] *HARPER &*
BROTHERS, PUBLISHERS | *NEW YORK*

Collation: 9¼ x 6 in. [1–12]¹⁶, pp. [i–viii] ix–xviii, [1–2] 3–366.
Binding: Bound in brownish orange (54) cloth lettered on the spine in silver: '[across]
Anshen | [down] LANGUAGE: | An Enquiry into Its Meaning and Function |
[across] *Harper*', and on the front cover: 'HB' and a torch all within a double
circle. The "College" issue is lettered in black.
Contents: Squares and oblongs. (pp. 174–78)   Not the same essay as that included in
B 35.
Notes: Published 2 October 1957 in trade and "college" issues, and out of print in
July 1964. The publisher prefers not to reveal the number of copies printed.

B 65   LANDMARKS AND VOYAGES   1957

[title in hollow shaded upper case] LANDMARKS | AND | VOYAGES |
Poetry Supplement | *edited by* | *VERNON WATKINS* | *for the Poetry*
Book Society | *Christmas* 1957 | POETRY BOOK SOCIETY LTD |
4 ST JAMES'S SQUARE | LONDON SW1

Collation: 7¾ x 5¼ in. One unsigned gathering of six leaves, pp. [1–12].
Binding: None. Stapled twice.
Contents: The more loving one: Looking up at the stars, I know quite well . . . (p. 8)
Reprinted in HTC and CSP2.
Notes: Published in December 1957 in an edition of 1,200 copies.

B 66   ROMEO AND JULIET, BY   1958
                         W. SHAKESPEARE

The Laurel Shakespeare | *Francis Fergusson, General Editor* | Romeo and
Juliet | *by William Shakespeare* | *Text edited by Charles Jasper Sisson* |
Commentary by W. H. Auden

Collation: 6⅜ x 4⅛ in. One hundred and twelve single leaves, pp. [1–7] 8–223 [224].
Binding: A perfect binding glued in a white card cover lettered down the spine:
'[on an olive triangle] LB 114 [in olive] Romeo and Juliet [laurel leaves] [across in
black] DELL'. On the front cover: 'DELL | LB 114 [laurel leaves] | 35¢ *THE
LAUREL SHAKESPEARE* | Romeo | And Juliet | *Francis Fergusson, General
Editor* | *With a Modern Commentary by* | *W. H. AUDEN* | [silhouette of re-
clining female torso and head]'. The publisher's name and the price are on olive
panels, and the title and laurel leaves are in olive. The rear cover carries other
titles in the series and a quotation from Auden's commentary.
Contents: Commentary on the poetry and tragedy of "Romeo and Juliet". (pp. 21–
39)
Notes: Published April 1958 [*CCE* 29 April 1958] in an impression of 76,000 copies,
and reprinted in November 1958 (26,000 copies), November 1960 (26,000 copies),
March 1962 (26,000 copies), April 1963 (26,000 copies), January 1964 (24,000
copies), September 1964 (25,000 copies), April 1965 (24,000 copies), August
1966 (25,000 copies), and January 1968 (25,000 copies).

B 67   A CRACKLING OF THORNS, BY   1958
J. HOLLANDER

[printed in black over a light grey representation of thorn twigs] A
Crackling of Thorns | by John Hollander | Foreword by W. H. Auden |
New Haven: Yale University Press, 1958

Collation: 9¾ x 6¼ in. [1–6]⁸, pp. [*–**, i–vi] vii–xvi [xvii–xx], 1–71 [72–74].
Binding: Bound in shiny black cloth lettered down the spine in gold: 'Hollander: A
Crackling of Thorns Yale', with three small gold dots in a line on the front cover.
Contents: Foreword. (pp. vii–xiv)
Notes: Published 21 May 1958 in an edition of 1,564 copies. No. 54 in the Yale series
of younger poets.

B 68   JEAN SANS TERRE, BY YVAN GOLL   1958

[left-hand title page] *JEAN SANS TERRE* | by YVAN GOLL | preface
by W. H. AUDEN | drawings by EUGENE BERMAN | MARC
CHAGALL |SALVADOR DALI | [ornament: a house] | *New York •*
THOMAS YOSELOFF • *London*

[right-hand title page] critical notes by LOUISE BOGAN | CLARK
MILLS | JULES ROMAINS | ALLEN TATE | translations of the
Poems by | [names of the translators in seven lines, upper case]

Collation: 8¼ x 4¾ in. [1–6]¹⁶, pp. [1–4] 5–190 [191–192].
Binding: Bound in greyish brown (61) cloth lettered down the spine in silver:
'YVAN GOLL [title in shiny blue fancy] Jean Sans Terre THOMAS YOSE-
LOFF'.
Contents: Preface. (pp. 5–8)
Notes: Published 14 November 1958 in an edition of 3,000 copies.

B 69   OF THE FESTIVITY, BY W. DICKEY   1959

William Dickey | [title on a red eleven-pointed star] *Of the* | *Festivity* |
Foreword by W. H. Auden | *New Haven: Yale University Press, 1959*

Collation: 9¾ x 6 in. [1–4]⁸, pp. [i–vi] vii–xii [xiii–xiv, 1–2] 3–47 [48–50].
Binding: Bound in vivid red (11) cloth lettered down the spine in gold: 'William
   Dickey [rule] Of the Festivity [across] YALE', and on the front cover: '[outlines
   of two eight-pointed stars superimposed on each other, the bottom one in dotted
   line]'.
Contents: Foreword. (pp. vii–xii)
Notes: Published 20 May 1959 in an edition of 951 copies and out of print in 1963.
   No. 55 in the Yale series of younger poets. With this volume Auden gave up the
   editorship of the series.

B 70   **THE PLAY OF DANIEL**   1959

A THIRTEENTH-CENTURY MUSICAL DRAMA | [title in fancy]
The Play of Daniel | EDITED FOR MODERN PERFORMANCE | BY
NOAH GREENBERG | *Based on the transcription from* | BRITISH
MUSEUM EGERTON 2615 | *by* REV. REMBERT WEAKLAND,
O.S.B. | *Narration by* W. H. AUDEN | [device] | NEW YORK ·
OXFORD UNIVERSITY PRESS · MCMLIX

Collation: 10¾ x 7¾ in. [1–4]¹⁶, pp. [i–iv] v–x, [1] 2–118.
Binding: Bound in pale yellow (89) weave-grained paper boards lettered down the
   spine: '[in red] THE PLAY OF DANIEL [in bluish grey] OXFORD'. On the
   front cover in bluish grey: '[fancy] The Play of Daniel | A THIRTEENTH-
   CENTURY MUSICAL DRAMA | [illustration from mediaeval manuscript] |
   EDITED BY NOAH GREENBERG | OXFORD UNIVERSITY PRESS'. Some
   copies were issued in similar paper covers.
Contents: Narration. (pp. 3, 20, 28, 44, 60, 68, 79, 86, 89, 94)   First published in *Jubilee*, January 1958, and reprinted in a booklet bound into the sleeve of the recording
   The play of Daniel, Decca DL 9402 [1958], reissued in 1962 as Decca DCM 3200.
Notes: Published 12 November 1959 in an impression of 6,000 copies of which 2,800
   were bound in paper covers, and reprinted in March 1963 [dated 1964] (3,579
   copies). The second impression is corrected and adds one line to the Narrator's
   speech on p. 20. All copies in the second impression were issued in paper covers.
      First performed by Pro Musica Antiqua at The Cloisters, New York, 2 January
   1958; recorded and issued as above.

B 71   **BRAND, BY H. IBSEN**   1960

BRAND | [rule] | Henrik Ibsen | NEWLY TRANSLATED FROM |
THE NORWEGIAN BY | MICHAEL MEYER | FOREWORD BY
W. H. AUDEN | Anchor Books | Doubleday & Company, Inc. | Garden
City, New York | 1960

Collation: 7 x 4 in. Eighty separate leaves, pp. [1–11] 12–157 [158–160].
Binding: A perfect binding glued in a white card cover lettered down the spine in
   black: 'HENRIK IBSEN BRAND [across] ANCHOR | A215a'. On the front
   cover: 'A215a $1.10 IN CANADA 95¢ | BRAND | HENRIK IBSEN | [illustra-
   tion] | *Newly translated from the Norwegian* | *by Michael Meyer* | *Introduction by*
   W. H. AUDEN | [device] A DOUBLEDAY ANCHOR BOOK'. The rear cover
   carries a descriptive note on the book.
Contents: Foreword. (pp. 23–40)   Partly reprinted in DH.

Notes: Published 8 July 1960 in an impression of 20,000 copies, and reprinted in August 1965 (10,000 copies), and April 1967 (10,000 copies).

B 72   TIMES THREE, BY P. MCGINLEY   1960

a) First edition

PHYLLIS McGINLEY | Times Three | SELECTED VERSE FROM THREE DECADES | WITH SEVENTY NEW POEMS | [ornamental initials of the author and stars] | FOREWORD BY W. H. AUDEN | NEW YORK THE VIKING PRESS 1960

Collation: 8⅜ x 5½ in. [1–10]¹⁶, pp. [i–viii] ix–xvi, [1–2] 3–304.
Binding: Bound in moderate greenish blue (173) cloth lettered across the spine in silver: 'Times | Three | PHYLLIS | McGINLEY | [rule] | [blind-stamped ornamental initials of the author] | [rule] | [blind-stamped initials] | [rule] | [blind-stamped initials] | [rule] | VIKING'. Blind-stamped device on the lower right front cover. Top edge stained yellow.
Contents: Foreword. (pp. ix–xvi)
Notes: Published 23 September 1960 in an impression of 17,829 copies, and reprinted in April 1961 (3,886 copies), September 1961 (2,808 copies), November 1961 (twice: 3,572 and 4,120 copies), June 1962 (4,093 copies), and January 1967 (6,066 copies). The top edge of the second impression is stained green. Reissued as a Compass paperback on 8 May 1968 (5,041 copies), and reprinted in September 1968 (3,089 copies).

b) First English edition   1961

[The transcription of the title page is identical with that of the first edition with the substitution of the following for the original imprint: 'LONDON SECKER & WARBURG   1961'.]

Collation: 8½ x 5½ in. [1–10]¹⁶, pp. [i–viii] ix–xvi, [1–2] 3–304.
Binding: Bound in moderate reddish orange (37) imitation weave-grained paper boards lettered across the spine in silver: 'Times | Three | [rule] | PHYLLIS | McGINLEY | SECKER & | WARBURG'.
Contents: Foreword. (pp. ix– xvi)
Notes: Published 16 October 1961 in an edition of 2,000 copies of which 1,024 were bound.

B 73   PLAYS, BY B. BRECHT   1960
             VOLUME ONE

BERTOLT BRECHT | PLAYS   VOLUME I | [double thick-thin rule] | THE CAUCASIAN CHALK | CIRCLE | THE THREEPENNY OPERA | THE TRIAL OF LUCULLUS | THE LIFE OF GALILEO | LONDON | METHUEN & CO LTD | 36 ESSEX STREET · W C 2

Collation: 8 x 5 in. [A]–X⁸Y¹⁰, pp. [i–iv] v–ix [x, 1–2] 3–345 [346]. Y2 signed 'Y1'.
Binding: Bound in moderate reddish orange (37) cloth lettered across the spine in

gold: '[inverted brevet rule, one-half solid and one-half double] | Bertolt | Brecht | [brevet rule, one-half double and one-half solid] | PLAYS | Volume 1 | Methuen'.

Contents: The Caucasian chalk circle, translated by James and Tania Stern with W. H. Auden. (pp. 3–96)   Act V first published in *Kenyon review*, Spring 1946.

Notes: Published 24 November 1960 in an impression of 4,000 copies; reprinted with minor corrections in August 1961 (3,000 copies), and again in May 1963 (3,000 copies) and February 1966 (1,500 copies). A paperback edition of the single play *The Caucasian chalk circle* was published 6 June 1963 (7,500 copies) and reprinted in April 1965 (10,000 copies), September 1966 (12,500 copies), May 1968 (12,500 copies), and August 1969 (15,000 copies).

B 74   DON GIOVANNI   1961

a) First edition

G. SCHIRMER'S | COLLECTION OF | OPERA LIBRETTOS | [rule] | DON GIOVANNI | Opera in Two Acts | *Music by* | W. A. Mozart | Libretto by | LORENZO DA PONTE | After the play by | TIRSO DE MOLINA | English Version by | W. H. AUDEN | and | CHESTER KALLMAN | Ed. 2408 | G. SCHIRMER, INC. | New York

Collation: 10⅜ x 6⅞ in. One unsigned gathering of forty-two leaves, pp. [I] II–V, 1 1–39 39, [one blank page]. Italian and English texts on facing pages in double pagination.

Binding: Stapled three times in a bluish white (189) card wrapper lettered in black as the title page with the omission of the rule and the edition number, and all within an ornamental border. The rear cover carries a list of Schirmer's clothbound vocal scores of standard operas and the number 'A1116'.

Later impressions are stapled in a light greyish yellowish brown (79) card cover and substitute a calligraphic flourish for the rule, and a later number on the rear cover.

Contents: Don Giovanni. (pp. 1–39 *bis*)

Notes: Published 3 January 1961. By 1969 there had been six impressions totalling 5,583 copies. A separate issue of this libertto (Ed. 2533) was first printed for the Metropolitan Opera in October 1963, and there were three further impressions by 1969 for a total of 14,083 copies.

This translation was first performed by the National Broadcasting Company Opera Theatre in New York on 10 April 1960. The translation was reprinted in *The great operas of Mozart* published by Schirmer and Grosset & Dunlap on 24 August 1962 and issued in a paperback edition by W. W. Norton in its Norton library (N 256) on 26 October 1964. The translation of the aria "Il mio tesoro" was first printed in *Favorite arias from the great operas*, edited by M. J. Cross (Garden City, N.Y.: Doubleday, 1958, pp. 113–16). The translation was copyrighted as an unpublished text on 19 November 1957.

b) Vocal score   1961

DON GIOVANNI | Opera in Two Acts | *Music by* | *W. A. Mozart* | Libretto by | LORENZO DA PONTE | After the play by | TIRSO DE MOLINA | English Version by | W. H. AUDEN | and | CHESTER KALLMAN | Ed. 2424 | G. SCHIRMER, INC. | New York

Collation: 10¾ x 7¼ in. [1–9]¹⁶ [10]¹², pp. [i] ii–xii, 1–300. Plate mark: '44917'.
Binding: Bound in dark green (146) cloth lettered down the spine in gold: 'DON GIOVANNI MOZART' and across the front cover 'MOZART | DON GIO-VANNI | Vocal Score | G. SCHIRMER'.
Contents: Don Giovanni. (pp. 8–300)
Notes: Published 14 December 1961; there were three impressions between 1961 and 1969 totalling 8,527 copies.

B 75   THE COMPLETE POEMS OF CAVAFY   1961

a) First edition

[ornament] | THE COMPLETE POEMS OF | [author's name in large fancy upper case] CAVAFY TRANSLATED | BY RAE DALVEN · WITH AN | INTRODUCTION BY W. H. AUDEN | HARCOURT, BRACE & WORLD, INC. NEW YORK

Collation: 8¼ x 5½ in. [1–8]¹⁶, pp. [i–v] vi–xxii, [1–2] 3–234.
Binding: Bound in rough yellowish grey (93) cloth lettered down the spine in gold: 'THE COMPLETE POEMS OF CAVAFY | TRANSLATED BY RAE DAL-VEN · HARCOURT, BRACE & WORLD'. The title page ornament is blind-stamped on the upper front cover.
Contents: Introduction. (pp. vii–xv)   First printed in *Atlantic*, April 1961.
Notes: Published 12 April 1961 in an impression of 4,000 copies of which 3,000 were bound and 1,000 sheets were for the Hogarth Press issue. Reprinted in October 1961 (3,275 copies; 750 sheets for the Hogarth Press), January 1963 (750 sheets for the Hogarth Press), and February 1966 (1,000 copies). A paperback impression was published as Harvest book 108 on 19 October 1966 in an impression of 6,000 copies, and reprinted in April 1968 (2,500 copies); some copies of each impression were clothbound.

b) English issue   1961

[The transcription of the title page is identical with that of the first issue with the substitution of the following for the original imprint: 'THE HOGARTH PRESS LTD. · LONDON'.]

Collation: 8¼ x 5⅝ in. [1–8]¹⁶, pp. [i–v], vi–xxii, [1–2] 3–234.
Binding: Bound in light purplish blue (199) cloth lettered across the spine in gold: 'The | Complete | Poems of | CAVAFY | [star] | *Translated by* | RAE | DALVEN | [star] | *With an* | *Introduction by* | W. H. AUDEN | THE | HOGARTH | PRESS'.
Contents: As the first edition.
Notes: Published 10 August 1961 in an issue of 1,000 sheets imported in February 1961 from Harcourt Brace, and reissued in February 1962 (836 sheets imported), and November 1963 (750 sheets imported). Reprinted photolithographically in England in May 1964 (1,000 copies), and August 1966 (4,000 copies); 2,000 copies of this last impression were issued as a paperback in December 1968 (CWP 27), by Chatto and Windus.

B 76   VAN GOGH: A SELF PORTRAIT   1961

a) First edition, first issue

VAN GOGH | A Self-Portrait | Letters revealing his life | as a painter,
selected by | W. H. AUDEN | [device] | New York Graphic Society |
Greenwich, Connecticut

Collation: 8¾ x 6¼ in. [1]⁸[gathering of plates]⁸[2–24]⁸, pp. [1–5] 6–16 [17–32
    plates] 33–398 [399–400].
Binding: Bound in moderate yellow (87) cloth lettered down the spine: '[in red]
    VAN GOGH | [in black] *a self-portrait: letters selected by W. H. Auden* |
    [across in red] NEW YORK | GRAPHIC | SOCIETY'. On the front cover in
    red a facsimile signature: 'Vincent'. Top edge stained red.
Contents: Foreword. (p. 5)
Notes: Published 5 September 1961 in an impression of 15,000 copies, of which 8,000
    were for a book club, and 3,000 for the English publisher. A paperback impression
    of 7,800 copies was published by Dutton (D 116) on 29 March 1963.

b) First English issue   1961

VAN GOGH | *a self-portrait* | Letters revealing his life as a painter |
selected by W. H. AUDEN | [device: dolphin and letters 'T & H'] |
THAMES AND HUDSON · LONDON

Collation: As the first issue.
Binding: As the first issue with the substitution of 'THAMES | [device] | HUDSON'
    for the original name of the publisher on the spine.
Contents: As the first issue.
Notes: Published 18 September 1961 in an issue of 3,000 copies and out of print in
    June 1965.

B 77   ON POETRY, BY ST.-JOHN PERSE   1961

ST.-JOHN PERSE | On Poetry | *SPEECH OF ACCEPTANCE UPON
THE AWARD OF* | *THE NOBEL PRIZE FOR LITERATURE* |
DELIVERED IN STOCKHOLM | *DECEMBER 10, 1960* | TRANS-
LATED BY | W. H. AUDEN | WITH THE FRENCH TEXT |
[device] | *BOLLINGEN SERIES*

Collation: 8 x 4¾ in. [1–4]⁴, pp. [i–iv, 1–6] 8–21 [22–28].
Binding: First and last leaves glued in a white card cover within a greyish yellow
    green (122) wrapper lettered across the front cover in green: '*St.-John Perse* |
    ON POETRY | [device]'.
Contents: [Translation]. (pp. 7–12)
Notes: Published 20 October 1961 in an edition of 2,500 copies and not for sale. The
    translation was reissued in *Two addresses,* by St.-John Perse (pp. 9–14) which was
    issued by the Pantheon Press for the Bollingen Foundation on 12 October 1966 in
    an edition of 2,000 copies as Bollingen series LXXXVI.

B 78 THE SEVEN DEADLY SINS 1962

a) First issue

[left-hand title page] *The Seven* | *Angus Wilson* | *Edith Sitwell* | *Cyril Connolly* | *Patrick Leigh Fermor* | *Evelyn Waugh* | *Christopher Sykes* | *W. H. Auden* | Introduction by RAYMOND MORTIMER | SUNDAY TIMES PUBLICATIONS LTD

[right-hand title page] *Deadly Sins* | [illustration]

Collation: 8½ x 5½ in. [1]⁶[2]⁴[3–7]⁸, pp. [i–ix] x–xii, [1] 2–87 [88].
Binding: Bound in smooth vivid red (11) cloth lettered up the spine in gold: '*The Seven Deadly Sins* [across the foot of the spine] SUNDAY | TIMES'.
Contents: Anger. (pp. 79–87) First printed in *Sunday times*, 21 January 1962.
Notes: Published 29 October 1962 in an issue of 6,500 copies. There is a later binding which is lettered in black, and copies of this binding were reduced in price for the National Book Sale, 1965. The book was out of print in 1969.

b) First American issue 1962

[The transcription of the title pages is identical with that of the first issue except for the insertion of 'Special Foreword by IAN FLEMING' after Auden's name and the substitution of 'WILLIAM MORROW AND COMPANY | NEW YORK' for the original imprint.]

Collation: 8½ x 5⅜ in. [1]⁸[2]⁴[3–7]⁸, pp. [i–vii] viii–xvi, [1] 2–87 [88].
Binding: Bound in smooth vivid red (11) cloth lettered up the spine in gold: '*The Seven Deadly Sins* | [across the foot of the spine] MORROW'.
Contents: Anger. (pp. 79–87)
Notes: Published 20 November 1962 in an issue of 7,500 copies. Reset and published in a paperback edition by Morrow (Apollo editions A-146) in May 1967 (5,000 copies) with Auden's contribution on pp. 67–75.

B 79 ITALIAN JOURNEY, BY J. W. VON GOETHE 1962

J. W. GOETHE | [title in red] ITALIAN JOURNEY | <1786–1788> | COLLINS | ST. JAMES'S PLACE · LONDON | 1962

Collation: 10¾ x 7 in. [1]⁶[2–37]⁸[38]², pp. [*–**, I–IV] V–XXIV [XXV–XXVI, 1–4] 5–43 [44] 45–80 [2] 81–108 [2] 109–116 [2] 117–122 [2] 123–130 [2] 131–138 [2] 139–144 [2] 145–148 [2] 149–154 [2] 155–160 [2] 161–164 [2] 165–172 [2] 173–178 [2] 179–184 [2] 185–190 [2] 191–194 [2] 195–198 [2] 199–204 [2] 205–210 [2] 211–240 [2] 241–250 [2] 251–254 [2] 255–262 [2] 263–268 [2] 269–290 [2] 291–296 [2] 297–306 [2] 307–310 [2] 311–314 [2] 315–320 [2] 321–326 [2] 327–330 [2] 331–342 [2] 343–350 [2] 351–362 [2] 363–384 [2] 385–396 [2] 397–414 [2] 415–450 [2] 451–458 [2] 459–466 [2] 467–478 [2] 479–508 [509–512].
Binding: Bound in rough natural colour cloth patterned with light green and light brown leaves and lettered across the spine in gold on a light brown panel: '[all within a border of a double gold rule] GOETHE | [star] | ITALIAN | JOUR-NEY'. Top edge stained yellow.

Contents: Introduction, [signed] W. H. Auden [and] Elizabeth Mayer. (pp. XIII–XXV). First printed in *Encounter*, November 1962 ("On Goethe").

Notes: Published 12 November 1962 in an issue of 2,500 copies and out of print in 1969. Some copies were sold at a reduced price in the National Book Sale, 1968.

"This edition of the 'Italian journey', on Fabriano paper, was printed for Wm. Collins, Sons & Co., Ltd., London, by Giovanni Mardersteig at the Stamperia Valdonega, Verona, July MCMLXII [device]" (p. 510).

The American issue substitutes the imprint 'PANTHEON BOOKS' for that described above, adds a copyright statement to p. [IV], and the statement on p. 510 reads: "This edition of the 'Italian journey' is limited to 2,500 copies, of which 2,450 copies are for sale. It was printed for Pantheon Books, New York, on Fabriano paper, by Giovanni Mardersteig, at the Stamperia Valdonega, Verona, July MCMLXII [device]." It was announced for publication 21 November 1962.

The American issue was reissued by Schocken Books in paperback and clothbound bindings on 15 November 1968. *A letter of December 25th 1787 from the Italienische Reise of Johann Wolfgang von Goethe* was extracted from this translation and published in an edition of 50 copies by the Pandora Press, Leicester, in December 1966.

B 80   **THE VIKING BOOK OF APHORISMS**   1962

a) First edition

[ornamental scroll] | [double rule] | THE | VIKING BOOK OF | APHORISMS | [rule] | *A Personal Selection* | BY | W. H. AUDEN | AND | LOUIS KRONENBERGER | [rule] | *New York • The Viking Press • Publishers* | [double rule]

Collation: 8½ x 5¼ in. [1–13]¹⁶, pp. [i–iv] v–viii, [1–2] 3–405 [406–408].

Binding: Quarter bound in dark purplish blue (201) cloth with moderate greenish blue (173) cloth covers, and lettered across the spine in gold: '[ornamental scroll] | [double rule] | THE VIKING | BOOK OF | APHORISMS | [rule] | W. H. AUDEN | AND | LOUIS | KRONENBERGER | [rule] | VIKING | [double rule] | [ornamental scroll]'. On the front cover: '[ornamental scroll] | [double rule] | THE VIKING | BOOK OF | APHORISMS | [rule] | AUDEN AND | KRONENBERGER | [double rule] | [ornamental scroll]'. Top edge stained dark blue; there is a purple ribbon.

Contents: Foreword, [signed] W. H. A. [and] L. K. (pp. v–vi)

Notes: Published 26 November 1962 in an impression of 5,000 copies, and reprinted in February 1963 (6,000 copies, of which 3,000 copies were for the Readers' Subscription book club). A paperback Compass edition was published 7 January 1966 (5,000 copies), and reprinted in June 1966 (5,000 copies) and March 1967 (6,000 copies); this includes a new catchword index compiled by Edwin Kennebeck. Some copies of the third impression of this edition were issued bound in light blue cloth lettered down the spine in black: '*The Viking Book of APHORISMS* | AUDEN AND KRONENBERGER [across the foot of the spine] [ornament] | VIKING'.

b) First English edition   1965

[The transcription of the title page is identical with that of the first printing except for 'VIKING' read 'FABER' in the title, and with the substitution of the following for the original imprint: 'FABER AND FABER LIM-ITED | 24 Russell Square, London']

Collation: 7⅞ x 5⅛ in. [1–26]⁸, pp. [i–iv] v–x, [1–2] 3–405 [406]
Binding: Bound in moderate bluish green (164) cloth lettered across the spine in gold: '[curlicue] | *The | Faber | Book | of | Aphorisms* | [curlicue] | W. H. Auden | and | Louis | Kronenberger | *Faber*'.
Contents: Foreword, [signed] W. H. A. [and] L. K. (pp. vii–viii)
Notes: Published 18 October 1964 in an impression of 5,250 copies, and reprinted in January 1965 (3,500 copies), and March 1965 (3,000 copies). Apart from small changes, a photolithographic reprint of the first edition.

B 81   ENGLISH AND MEDIAEVAL STUDIES   1962

ENGLISH AND | MEDIAEVAL STUDIES | *Presented to J. R. R. TOLKIEN | on the Occasion of | his Seventieth Birthday* | EDITED BY | NORMAN DAVIS AND C. L. WRENN | *London* | GEORGE ALLEN & UNWIN LTD | RUSKIN HOUSE MUSEUM STREET

Collation: 8½ x 5¼ in. [A]–K¹⁶L¹⁰, pp. [1–7] 8–339 [340]
L2 is signed 'L*'. Frontispiece and plates facing pp. 93 and 324.
Binding: Bound in moderate blue (182) weave-grained imitation-cloth paper boards lettered across the spine in gold: 'ENGLISH | AND | MEDIEVAL | STUDIES | *Presented to* | J. R. R. TOLKIEN | *on the | Occasion | of his | Seventieth | Birthday* | [hollow swelled rule] | EDITED BY | NORMAN | DAVIS | AND | C. L. | WRENN | GEORGE | ALLEN | AND | UNWIN' with a facsimile signature on the front cover in gold: 'J. R. R. Tolkien'. Top edge stained blue.
Contents: A short ode to a philologist: Necessity knows no speech, not even... Reprinted in ATH.
Notes: Published 6 December 1962 in an edition of 2,250 copies. Distributed in the United States by Humanities Press, 11 October 1963.

B 82   POETRY IN CRYSTAL   1963

[left-hand title page in red] Interpretations in crystal of | thirty-one new poems | by contemporary American poets

[right-hand title page] [snowflake in red] | [title in black] POETRY IN CRYSTAL | [in red] BY STEUBEN GLASS | [snowflake in black]

Collation: 10½ x 7 in. [1]⁶[2–9]⁴[10]⁶, pp. [1–6] 7–86 [87–88]. (Between 12 and 73 rectos only are paged.)
Binding: Bound in smooth dark red (16) cloth lettered down the spine in gold: 'POETRY IN CRYSTAL', and across the front cover: 'Poetry | in | Crystal'.
Contents: The maker: Unmarried, near-sighted, rather deaf... (p. 16) Reprinted in an advertisement for this book in *New York times*, 28 April 1963, in ATH, and also, by permission of Steuben Glass, in the *National sculpture review*, Spring 1963, *Literary cavalcade*, March 1964, and the *Chicago daily news*, 27 April 1964. These last three appearances have no textual authority and are not listed in section C or elsewhere in the bibliography.
Notes: Published 18 April 1963 in an impression of 10,000 copies. There was a limited

issue of 250 copies quarter bound in deep red fabrikoid with greyish yellow cloth covers lettered as the ordinary issue, and the verso of the title page carries a statement of limitation and the copy number. The ordinary issue was reprinted in March 1964 (5,000 copies) and March 1965 (3,000 copies).

The book was published simultaneously with the opening of the exhibition of the same name. "In 1961 Steuben Glass and The Poetry Society of America undertook a joint experiment—the inspiration of design from poetry.... Thirty-one poets, selected by the Poetry Society as representative of American poetry, were commissioned by Steuben to write poems of their own choosing. The manuscripts were circulated among Steuben's artists and designers—their mission being to capture the theme or spirit of each poem in crystal" (from a brochure describing the exhibition).

B 83   A CHOICE OF DE LA MARE'S VERSE   1963

A CHOICE OF | DE LA MARE'S VERSE | *Selected* | *with an intro-duction* | *by* | W. H. AUDEN | FABER AND FABER | 24 Russell Square | London

Collation: 7¼ x 4¾ in. [A]–G¹⁶, one hundred and twelve single leaves, pp. [1–6] 7–223 [224].

Binding: A perfect binding glued in a card cover lettered down the spine in black: 'A Choice of DE LA MARE'S VERSE [in white on a black panel] FABER'. Across the front cover: 'A Choice | of | de la Mare's | Verse | [rule] | Selected | with an introduction | by W. H. AUDEN | [in white on a black panel] FABER', and down the leading edge of the front cover in white on black: 'FABER paper covered EDITIONS'. The rear cover carries a similar panel and a list of other titles in the series. The cover is mainly strong yellowish green (131) but the front cover is diagonally divided from left to right into green and light greenish blue (172).

Contents: Introduction. (pp. 13–25)

Notes: Published 17 May 1963 in an edition of 15,880 copies.

B 84   THE PLOUGH AND THE PEN   1963

The Plough and the Pen | [rule] | WRITINGS FROM HUNGARY | 1930–1956 | EDITED BY | ILONA DUCZYŃSKA | AND KARL POLANYI | *With a Foreword by W. H. Auden* | [device] | PETER OWEN · LONDON

Collation: 8½ x 5⅜ in. [A]–F¹⁶G⁴H¹⁶, pp. [1–4] 5–231 [232].

Binding: Bound in dark olive green (126) imitation weave-grained paper boards lettered across the spine in copperish gold: 'THE | PLOUGH | AND | THE PEN | [device] | PETER | OWEN'.

Contents: Foreword. (pp. 9–11)

Notes: Published 31 May 1963 in an impression of 2,000 copies. There was a Canadian issue of 1,265 copies which was published 22 June 1963 and went out of print in May 1966. This issue substitutes 'McClelland and Stewart Limited' for the original device and imprint on the title page, and 'McClelland | and | Stewart' for the original publisher's name on the spine.

B 85   THE PIED PIPER, BY J. JACOBS   1963

[a coloured illustration of a mouse standing on a piece of cheese] | [title in red fancy] *The Pied Piper* | [in black] AND OTHER FAIRY TALES OF Joseph Jacobs | WITH COMMENTARY BY W. H. Auden | IL-LUSTRATED BY James Hill | [red rule] | *The Macmillan Company, New York* [oblique stroke] *Collier-Macmillan Ltd., London* | [date in red] *1963*

Collation: 13 x 9½ in. [1–3]⁸, pp. [i–viii], 1–40.
Binding: Bound in white shiny paper boards lettered down the spine: '[in red] JACOBS [in black] THE PIED PIPER AND OTHER FAIRY TALES [in red] MACMILLAN'. Across the front cover: '[title in red fancy] *The Pied Piper* | [in black] AND OTHER FAIRY TALES OF JOSEPH JACOBS | WITH COMMENTARY BY W. H. AUDEN | *ILLUSTRATED BY JAMES HILL* | [coloured picture of the Pied Piper]'. The rear cover carries advertising for similar titles in red and black.
     "Reinforced library edition" copies are bound in deep reddish orange (36) cloth lettered down the spine: '[in blue] JACOBS [in white] THE PIED PIPER [in blue] AND OTHER FAIRY TALES   MACMILLAN'. Across the front cover: '[title in white fancy] *The Pied Piper* | [in blue] AND OTHER FAIRY TALES OF | [in white] Joseph Jacobs | [drawing in blue]'. Across the rear cover: '[in blue] MACMILLAN | MASTER LIBRARY | EDITION | [in white] 74755'.
Contents:
     Telling tales: an introduction. (pp. iv–vi)
     More about these tales. (pp. 37–40)
Notes: The *English catalogue* lists the publication date as 23 September 1963, and *Library journal* announced the American publication date as 14 October 1963, while the publisher gives the date as December 1963. The first impression was of 30,000 copies of which 5,000 were "reinforced library editions," and the second printing of 7,500 copies was entirely bound as "reinforced library editions."

B 86   THE ART OF EATING, BY M. F. K. FISHER   1963

[all within an ornamental border] *THE* | *ART OF* | *EATING* | M • F • K • FISHER | WITH AN INTRODUCTION BY | W. H. AUDEN | FABER AND FABER | 24 Russell Square, London

Collation: 7¾ x 5 in. [1–16]¹⁶, [17]¹²[18–19]¹⁶, pp. [i–iv] v–xvii [xviii, 1–4] 5–578 [579–582].
Binding: Bound in dark red (16) cloth lettered across the spine in gold: '[title within a gold rule border and on a black panel] THE ART | OF | EATING | M. F. K. | FISHER | FABER'.
Contents: Introduction. (pp. v–xi)   Revised from *Griffin*, June 1958.
Notes: Published 25 October 1963 in an edition of 2,700 copies.

B 87   JOHN CROWE RANSOM   1964

John Crowe Ransom | Gentleman, Teacher, Poet, Editor | Founder of The Kenyon Review | A Tribute from the | Community of Letters |

Edited by | D. David Long and Michael R. Burr | [fancy] *The Kenyon* [gothic] Collegian | A Supplement to Vol. LXXXX, No. 7 | Gambier, Ohio | 1964

Collation: 11 x 8½ in. One unsigned gathering of twenty-eight leaves, pp. [1–5] 6–56.
Binding: Stapled twice in a white card cover lettered across the front in gold: '[all within a gold rule border] John Crowe Ransom | Gentleman, Teacher, Poet, Editor | Founder of The Kenyon Review | A Tribute from the | Community of Letters'.
Contents:
    Two poems. (pp. 38–39)   Both reprinted in ATH.
        Down there: A cellar underneath the house, though not lived in . . .
        Up there: Men would never have come to need an attic . . .
Notes: Published 24 January 1964 [*CCE* 7 February 1964] in an impression of 800 copies, and reprinted in 1964 (2,000 copies), and 1965 (2,000 copies).

B 88   **OF BOOKS AND HUMANKIND**   **1964**

OF BOOKS AND | HUMANKIND | [rule] | Essays and Poems | Presented to | Bonamy Dobrée | [rule] | EDITED BY JOHN BUTT | *Assisted by J. M. Cameron | D. W. Jefferson and Robin Skelton* | [device] | Routledge and Kegan Paul | LONDON

Collation: 8½ x 5¼ in. [A]–O⁸P¹⁰, pp. [i–iv] v–x, [1–2] 3–232. P2 signed 'P*'. Frontispiece.
Binding: Bound in dark purplish red (259) cloth lettered up the spine in gold: 'Of Books and Humankind BUTT | [across the foot of the spine] Routledge | and | Kegan Paul'.
Contents: The maker: Unmarried, near-sighted, rather deaf . . . (p. 167) First printed in *Poetry in crystal* (New York: Steuben Glass, 1963) and reprinted in ATH.
Notes: Published 30 January 1964. The publisher prefers not to disclose the number of copies printed.

B 89   **THE PROTESTANT MYSTICS**   **1964**

a) First edition

THE | Protestant | Mystics | [three ornamental crosses] | *selected and edited by* | ANNE FREMANTLE | *with an introduction by* | W. H. AUDEN | [device] | LITTLE, BROWN AND COMPANY · BOS-TON · TORONTO

Collation: 8¼ x 5⅜ in. [1–13]¹⁶, pp. [*–**, i–iv] v–xi [xii–xiv, 1–3] 4–396 [397–402].
Binding: Bound in rough moderate blue (182) cloth lettered across the spine in gold: 'FREMANTLE | [eight ornamental crosses] | *The* | Protes- | tant | Mystics | LITTLE, | BROWN'. Device blind-stamped on the front cover and top edge stained light brown.
Contents: Introduction. (pp. 3–37)
Notes: Published 5 May 1964 [*CCE* 16 May 1964] in an edition of 6,000 copies. The New American Library published a paperback Mentor edition (MQ 628) in May 1965 (52,458 copies).

b) **First English issue** 1964

[The transcription of the title page is identical with that of the first edition with the substitution of the following for the original imprint: '*WEIDEN-FELD AND NICOLSON* | 20 NEW BOND STREET LONDON W 1'.]

Collation: 8¼ x 5⅜ in. [1–13]¹⁶, pp. [*–**, i–iv] v–xi [xii–xiv, 1–3] 4–396 [397–402].
Binding: Bound in dark purplish blue (201) cloth lettered across the spine in gold: 'THE | PROTESTANT | MYSTICS | [double rule] | Anne Fremantle | and | W. H. Auden | WEIDENFELD | & NICOLSON'. Top edge stained orange.
Contents: As the first edition.
Notes: Published 28 August 1964 in an edition of 1,500 copies, and out of print in July 1968.

B 90 THE INFERNAL MACHINE AND OTHER PLAYS, 1964 BY J. COCTEAU

THE INFERNAL | MACHINE AND | OTHER PLAYS BY | JEAN COCTEAU | A NEW DIRECTIONS BOOK

Collation: 8 x 5¼ in. [1–13]¹⁶, pp. [i–vi, 1–4] 5–409 [410].
Binding: Bound in deep blue (179) cloth lettered across the spine in gold: 'The | Infernal | Machine | & | Other | Plays | by | Jean | Cocteau | New | Directions', with the device of a kneeling man in gold on the lower right front cover.
Contents: The knights of the Round Table, translated by W. H. Auden. (pp. 188–291)
Notes: Published 27 April 1964 in an impression of approximately 4,000 copies. A paperback issue (NDP 235) was published 16 October 1967 in an impression of approximately 6,000 copies.

Auden translated the play at the request of Rupert Doone for the Group Theatre and a production was planned for the Edinburgh Festival in 1952. The text Auden supplied included alternate passages for stage and radio versions, and the first performance was in fact an adaptation by Peter Watts produced for the BBC Third programme, broadcast on 22 May 1951, and subsequently rebroadcast. The Edinburgh Festival production never took place, but the Group Theatre later produced the play at the Playhouse Theatre, Salisbury, on 3 May 1954, directed by Richard Scott (see *Times*, 4 May 1954, p. 10).

Microfilm copies of a 90 fol. agency typescript containing passages for stage and radio use are in Columbia University Library and the Library of the University of California, Berkeley. The Berg Collection at New York Public Library possesses five typescript copies of the stage version, all 115 fol., but with numerous variations.

B 91 MARKINGS, BY D. HAMMARSKJÖLD 1964

a) **First American edition**

[floral ornament] | [short rule] | *Dag Hammarskjöld* | MARKINGS | [short rule] | [floral ornament] | TRANSLATED FROM THE SWED-

ISH BY | Leif Sjöberg & W · H · Auden | WITH A FOREWORD BY |
W · H · AUDEN | [device: running borzoi] | *New York: Alfred · A ·
Knopf* | 1964

Collation: 8¼ x 5½ in. [1–8]¹⁶, pp. [*–**, i–vi] vii–xxiii [xxiv–xxvi, 1–4] 5–221
    [222–228].
Binding: Bound in strong greenish blue (169) rough cloth lettered on the spine in
    gold: '[across] [ornament and block of five rules] [down] Markings [diamond]
    Dag Hammarskjöld [across][block of five rules] | KNOPF | [block of five rules
    and ornament]'. The initials 'DH' are blind-stamped within a circle on the front
    cover, and the publisher's device is blind-stamped on the lower right rear cover.
    Top edge only cut and stained yellow.
Contents:
    Foreword. (pp. vii–xxiv)
    Footnotes signed by Auden appear throughout the text.
        Excerpts from the translation appeared in an article by O. Clausen in the
        New York times, 28 June 1964; and in *Harper's*, September 1964; *Vogue*,
        1 October 1964; and *Reader's digest*, March 1965.
Notes: Published 15 October 1964 in an impression of 12,000 copies, and reprinted in
    October 1964 (7,500 copies), November 1964 (five times: 7,500; 15,000; 10,000;
    15,000; and 20,000 copies), December 1964 (three times: 20,000; 20,000; and 15,000
    copies), February 1965 (20,000 copies), March 1965 (20,000 copies), June 1965
    (30,000 copies), July 1965 (30, 000 copies), October 1965 (20,000 copies), Novem-
    ber 1965 (20,000 copies), January 1966 (25,000 copies), April 1966 (25,000 copies),
    December 1966 (20,000 copies), November 1967 (10,000 copies), February 1968
    (19,200 copies), January 1969 (14,550 copies), October 1969 (10,000 copies), and
    December 1969 (10,000 copies). The impression dated November 1967 adds a
    postscript to Auden's Foreword which was first printed in the reset de luxe
    edition. This collates 10 x 6½ in., [1–8]¹⁶, pp. [*–**, i–vi] vii–xxvii [xxviii–xxx,
    1–4] 5–216 [217–224], and was published 18 October 1966 in an impression of
    12,500 copies, and reprinted in March 1968 (3,600 copies).
        The Literary Guild, a book club, offered the book to its members from Decem-
    ber 1964; these copies lack an impression statement and carry the words "Book
    Club Edition" on the front flap of the dust jacket.

b) First English edition   1964

MARKINGS | by | Dag Hammarskjöld | *translated by* | LEIF SJÖBERG
& W. H. AUDEN | *with a foreword by* | W. H. AUDEN | FABER AND
FABER | 24 Russell Square | London

Collation: 8½ x 5⅜ in. [A]–M⁸, pp. [1–6] 7–186 [187–190]. $1 signed 'H.M.', except
    A. Last leaf laid down as an endpaper.
Binding: Bound in strong blue (178) cloth lettered down the spine in gold: '[title
    on a black panel within a gold border] MARKINGS DAG HAMMARSKJÖLD |
    [across] Faber'.
Contents: Foreword. (pp. 9–26)
Notes: Published 15 October 1964 in an impression of 3,000 copies, and reprinted in
    November 1964 (2,000 copies), December 1964 (2,000 copies), January 1965 (2,000
    copies), February 1965 (2,864 copies), March 1965 (3,000 copies), June 1965
    (3,000 copies), September 1965 (4,000 copies), and December 1965 (3,000 copies).
    A paperback impression was issued in March 1966 (30,000 copies), and reprinted
    in March 1966 (20,000 copies), and June 1966 (25,000 copies).

B 92   THE SONNETS, BY W. SHAKESPEARE   1964

William Shakespeare | *THE SONNETS* | INTRODUCTION BY W. H. AUDEN | EDITED BY WILLIAM BURTO | THE SIGNET CLASSIC SHAKESPEARE | GENERAL EDITOR: SYLVAN BARNET | [device] | PUBLISHED BY THE NEW AMERICAN LIBRARY, NEW YORK | AND | THE NEW ENGLISH LIBRARY LIMITED, LONDON

Collation: 7 x 4¼ in. One hundred and twenty single leaves, pp. [i-vi] vii–xxxviii [39–40] 41–240.
Binding: A perfect binding glued in a white card cover lettered in black down the spine: '[across] [device in white on black] | CD | 257 | [down] THE SONNETS *William Shakespeare*'. The front cover has a thick and thin black rule border and is lettered: 'CD 257 [device] 50¢ [vertical rule] *The Signet Classic* | Shakespeare | [rule to the full measure] | The Sonnets | [illustration of man and woman in 17th-century dress with highlights in colour, signed *'Milton Glaser'*]'.
Contents:
Introduction. (pp. xvii–xxxviii)   First published in *Listener*, 2 and 9 July 1964.
Footnotes on pp. 168, 175, and 183 are signed 'W. H. A.'
Notes: Published October 1964 [*CCE* 15 October 1964] in an impression of 76,808 copies. There was a further printing for Canada in March 1965 of 3,295 copies.

B 93   SELECTED POEMS, BY LOUIS MACNEICE   1964

LOUIS MACNEICE | *Selected Poems* | *Selected* | *and introduced by* | W. H. AUDEN | FABER AND FABER | 24 Russell Square | London

Collation: 7¼ x 4¾ in. Eighty single leaves, [A]–E¹⁶, pp. [1–4] 5–160.
Binding: A perfect binding glued in a white card cover lettered down the spine in black: '[olive green spot] Selected Poems of Louis MacNeice [olive green spot] [in white on a light blue panel] FABER'. Across the front cover: 'Selected | Poems of | Louis | MacNeice | [olive green panel] | [in light blue] edited by | W. H. Auden', and down the leading edge of the front cover in white on light blue: 'FABER paper covered EDITIONS'. The rear cover carries a similar panel and lists other titles in the series.
Contents: Introduction. (pp. 9–10)
Notes: Published 10 December 1964 in an edition of 12,000 copies.

B 94   ELEGY FOR J. F. K.   1964
BY I. STRAVINSKY

IGOR STRAVINSKY | ELEGY FOR J. F. K. | *Baritone Solo* [or *'Mezzo Soprano Solo'*] | BOOSEY & HAWKES | MUSIC PUBLISHERS LIMITED

Collation: 12¼ x 9¼ in. Two conjugate leaves, pp. [1] 2–4. Plate mark: 'B. & H. 19267' for baritone and 'B. & H. 19266' for mezzo soprano.

Binding: Stapled twice in a yellowish grey (93) card cover lettered across the front
as the title page.
Contents: Elegy for J. F. K.: When a just man dies ... (pp. 2–4)
Notes: Published December 1964 [*CCE* 17 December 1964] in separate impressions
for baritone and mezzo soprano. The mezzo soprano version was reprinted in June
1967; the rear wrapper of this impression bears an advertisement. The publisher
prefers not to reveal the number of copies printed. Separate clarinet parts also
include the text and are plate marked 'B. & H. 19270'. Recorded on Columbia ML
6454/MS 7054 [1967]. First performed in Los Angeles at the Monday Evening
concerts on 6 April 1964.

For Stravinsky's account of the composition of the work, see the interview,
"J. F. K., ultimate sacrilege, and Stravinsky," *New York times*, 6 December 1964,
section 2, p. 15; reprinted in: Igor Stravinsky and Robert Craft, *Themes and episodes* (New York: Knopf, 1966), pp. 56–59. Stravinsky here quotes Auden's in-
structions (in a letter?) to alter a word in the text.

B 95   **W. H. AUDEN: A BIBLIOGRAPHY**   **1964**

W. H. AUDEN | *A BIBLIOGRAPHY* | The Early Years through 1955 |
[swelled rule] | BY | *B. C. Bloomfield* | WITH A FOREWORD BY |
W. H. Auden | PUBLISHED FOR THE BIBLIOGRAPHICAL SO-
CIETY | OF THE UNIVERSITY OF VIRGINIA | *The University
Press of Virginia* | CHARLOTTESVILLE

Collation: 8⅞ x 5⅞ in. [1–2]¹⁶[3]¹⁸[4–6]¹⁶, pp. [i–vi] vii–xix [xx–xxii], 1–171 [172–
174].
Binding: Bound in dark blue (183) cloth lettered down the spine in gold: '*Bloom-
field*   W. H. Auden—*A Bibliography* [across the foot of the spine] *Virginia*'. On
the front cover: 'W. H. AUDEN | *A Bibliography*'.
Contents: Foreword. (pp. vii–ix)
Notes: Published 31 December 1964 in an edition of 1,020 copies and out of print in
February 1966.

B 96   **THE TREE AND THE MASTER,**   **1965**
                   BY SISTER MARY IMMACULATE

[all within a single-rule border] [rule] THE TREE AND | THE Master
[leaf ornament] | AN ANTHOLOGY OF | LITERATURE ON | THE
CROSS OF Christ | [rule] | EDITED BY | *Sister Mary Immaculate* |
OF THE CONGREGATION OF THE SISTERS OF THE HOLY
CROSS | [rule] | *Preface by W. H. Auden* | New York   Random House
[device] | [rule]

Collation: 9¼ x 6¼ in. [1–9]¹⁶, pp. [*–**, i–v] vi–xxviii, [1–2] 3–254 [255–258].
Binding: Bound in very deep red (14) cloth lettered down the spine in gold: '[leaf
ornament] *The TREE and the MASTER* [leaf ornament. Then across the spine]
Sister | *Mary* | *Immaculate,* | *C.S.C.* | [device] | RANDOM HOUSE'. Top edge
stained yellow.
Contents: Preface. (pp. xiii–xvi)
Notes: Published 30 April 1965 [*CCE* 2 April 1965] in an edition of 5,325 copies.

B 97 THE TWELVE, BY SIR W. WALTON 1966

William Walton | THE TWELVE | *Words by* W. H. AUDEN | [rule] | ORCHESTRATION | [seven lines] | This work was given its first performance (with organ) | on 16 May 1965 by the choir of Christ Church, Oxford, | directed by Sydney Watson. | [rule] | OXFORD UNIVER-SITY PRESS | MUSIC DEPARTMENT 44 CONDUIT STREET LONDON W.1

Collation: 10 x 7 in. One unsigned gathering of sixteen leaves, pp. [i–ii, 1] 2–30.
Binding: Stapled twice in a light greenish yellow (101) card cover printed in moderate yellowish brown (77). On the front cover in yellow on a brown ground: 'William Walton | THE TWELVE | AN ANTHEM | FOR THE FEAST OF ANY APOSTLE | *Words by* W. H. AUDEN | *For Mixed Voices and Organ (or Orchestra)* | [treble rule] | OXFORD UNIVERSITY PRESS | 6s. net'. The rear cover carries a list of Walton's orchestral works.
Contents: The twelve. (p. ii) Reprinted in CWW.
Notes: Published 20 January 1966 in an edition of 3,000 copies.

B 98 NINETEENTH CENTURY BRITISH 1966
MINOR POETS

a) First edition

19th Century | *British* | *Minor Poets* | Edited, with an introduction, by | W. H. AUDEN | Notes by George R. Creeger | [device: 'd p' on a black roundel] | *Delacorte Press* | *New York*

Collation: 8¼ x 5½ in. [1–12]¹⁶, pp. [1–14] 15–383 [384].
Binding: Bound in moderate blue (182) cloth lettered across the spine in silver: '*19th Century* | *British* | *Minor Poets* | W. H. Auden | [device] | DELACORTE PRESS'.
Contents: Introduction. (pp. 15–23)
Notes: Published 15 March 1966 [CCE 24 February 1966], in an edition of 5,000 copies. A paperback impression was published in August 1966, although announced for 16 September 1966, by the Dell Publishing Co. in its Laurel poetry series (6429) in an impression of 75,024 copies.

b) First English edition 1967

NINETEENTH | CENTURY | MINOR POETS | edited by W. H. Auden | [ornament] | *Notes by George R. Creeger* | FABER & FABER | 24 Russell Square London

Collation: 8½ x 5⅜ in. [1–24]⁸[25]⁴[26]⁸, pp. [1–6] 7–408.
Binding: Bound in moderate red (15) cloth lettered across the spine in gold: '[double thick-thin rule] [title on a black panel] 19th | Century | Minor | Poets | [rule] | *edited by* | W. H. | AUDEN | [double thick-thin rule] | FABER'.
Contents: Introduction. (pp. 17–23)
Notes: Published 29 June 1967 in an edition of 2,950 copies.

B 99   **LONGER CONTEMPORARY POEMS**   **1966**

LONGER | CONTEMPORARY | POEMS | *Introduced and edited by* | *David Wright* | [device] | PENGUIN BOOKS

Collation: 7⅛ x 4¼ in. One hundred and twenty single leaves, pp. [1–8] 9–234 [235–240].

Binding: A perfect binding glued in a black card cover printed in white, orange, and light brown, lettered down the spine in white: '[device across] Longer Contemporary Poems [across] D87'. On the front cover in white: '[left-hand side] Longer | Contemporary | Poems | 6/– [right-hand side] [device] | [names of the authors and their poems in orange and light brown in twenty-one lines]'. On the rear cover: '[left-hand side] Edited with an | introduction by David Wright [right-hand side] [device] | Cover design by Brian Mayers | [two lines] | [names of the authors and their poems in twenty-one lines]'.

Contents: Letter to Lord Byron. (pp. 15–53) "The present version has been revised by the author, and a number of stanzas omitted at his request" (p. 11). This revised text is reprinted in LFI2 and CLP.

Notes: Published 26 May 1966 in an impression of 25,000 copies.

B 100   **ANTIWORLDS, BY A. VOZNESENSKY**   **1966**

[left-hand title page] *Translated by* | W. H. AUDEN | Poetry by | JEAN GARRIGUE | MAX HAYWARD | STANLEY KUNITZ | STANLEY MOSS | WILLIAM JAY SMITH | RICHARD WILBUR

[right-hand title page] ANTIWORLDS | ANDREI VOZNESENSKY | *Edited by* PATRICIA BLAKE *and* MAX HAYWARD | *With a Foreword by* W. H. AUDEN | BASIC BOOKS, INC., *Publishers* New York

Collation: 8¾ x 6 in. [1–9]⁸, pp. [i–iv] v–xxii, [1–2] 3–120 [121–122].

Binding: Bound in rough black cloth lettered down the spine in shiny light green: 'ANTIWORLDS [author's name in shiny blue] ANDREI VOZNESENSKY [across the spine in green] BASIC | BOOKS'. The initials 'A V' are blind-stamped on the front cover. Top edge stained light green.

Contents:

Foreword. (pp. v–vii)

The following poems are translated by Auden:

My Achilles heart. (p. 4)   Reprinted in *Newsweek*, 11 July 1966.

Hunting a hare. (pp. 7–9)   Reprinted in *Listener*, 8 June 1967.

The cashier. (pp. 14–15)

Autumn in Sigulda. (pp. 19–21)   First published in *Saturday review*, 21 May 1966.

The party. (p. 26)   First published in *New republic*, 16 April 1966, and reprinted in *Observer*, 18 June 1967.

Parabolic ballad. (pp. 49–50)   First published in *Encounter*, April 1963, and reprinted in *Half-way to the moon* (1964), and ATH.

The nose. (pp. 78–79)   Reprinted in *Critical quarterly*, Spring 1967.

The Foreword, "My Achilles heart," and "The cashier" were first printed in *New York review of books*, 14 April 1966.

Notes: Published 17 June 1966 in an impression of 3,000 copies, and reprinted in

December 1966 (2,000 copies), and June 1967 (1,000 copies). A reset bilingual edition entitled *Antiworlds and 'The fifth ace'* was published by Doubleday as a paperback Anchor book (A 595) on 18 August 1967 in an edition of 10,000 copies, and this was also issued in a hardbound edition by Basic Books on 5 October 1967 (2,000 copies); both contain Auden's translations and foreword. A paperback reprint of the original Basic Books edition was published in England by Oxford University Press in June 1967 (6,000 copies) in its Oxford Paperbacks series (no. 115), and a reprint of the Doubleday edition of *Antiworlds and 'The fifth ace'* was also published by Oxford University Press on 31 October 1968 (2,000 copies).

B 101   TO NEVILL COGHILL FROM FRIENDS   1966

To | Nevill Coghill | *from Friends* | [rule with star in the middle] | Collected by | JOHN LAWLOR | and | W. H. AUDEN | FABER AND FABER LTD | 24 Russell Square | London

Collation: 8½ x 5½ in. [A]–K⁸, pp. [1–8] 9–156 [157–160]. $1 signed 'N.C.' except A. Frontispiece and one plate facing p. 104.
Binding: Bound in moderate red (15) cloth lettered down the spine in gold: '*To* [name on a black gold-bordered panel] Nevill Coghill *from Friends* [across] *Faber*'. Top edge stained yellow.
Contents:
[Prefatory note, signed] J. L. [and] W. H. A. (p. 7)
To Professor Nevill Coghill on his retirement in A.D. 1966: In our beginning... (pp. 151–56) Reprinted in CWW ("Eulogy").
Notes: Published 29 September 1966 in an edition of 2,000 copies.

B 102   POEMS, EDITED BY E. W. WHITE   1966

POEMS *by* | W. H. Auden • George Barker | [other names in six lines] | *Edited for the* POETRY BOOK | SOCIETY *by* Eric W. White | *Christmas 1966*

Collation: 8½ x 5 in. One unsigned gathering of eight leaves, pp. [1–16].
Binding: None. Stapled twice.
Contents: River profile: Out of a bellicose fore-time, thundering... (pp. 3–4) Reprinted in CWW.
Notes: Published in December 1966 in an edition of 1,200 copies.

B 103   TRADITION AND INNOVATION IN   1966   CONTEMPORARY LITERATURE

TRADITION AND | INNOVATION IN | CONTEMPORARY | LITERATURE | TRADITION ET | MODERNITÉ DANS | LA LITTÉRATURE | DE NOTRE TEMPS | P.E.N. | HUNGARY | HONGRIE

Collation: 7⅞ x 4½ in. [1–10]⁸[9]⁴[10]⁸, pp. [1–4] 5–183 [184].
Binding: Glued in a glazed deep blue (179) card cover lettered up the spine in fancy

cursive with all English lettering in white and French in yellow: '[all within a black rule border] P.E.N. round table Budapest P.E.N. table ronde Budapest'. Across the front cover: '[all within a black rule border] Tradition and | Innovation | in Contemporary | Literature | Tradition et | modernité dans | la littérature de | notre temps | [feather in black] | P.E.N. round table Budapest | P.E.N. table ronde Budapest'. The rear cover carries a black rule border.

Contents: A short defense of poetry. (pp. 29–32) For an earlier version of this see "Aus der Budapester PEN—Diskussion über Tradition und Moderne: W. H. Auden" in *Sinn und Form*, XVII, 5 (1965), 785–86.

Notes: Published by the Corvina Press in Budapest in the last days of December 1966 in an edition of 3,200 copies.

B 104   SELECTED POETRY AND PROSE OF BYRON   1966

George Gordon, Lord Byron | *SELECTED POETRY* | *AND PROSE* | Edited by W. H. Auden | *The Signet Classic Poetry Series* | GENERAL EDITOR: JOHN HOLLANDER | [device] | PUBLISHED BY | THE NEW AMERICAN LIBRARY, NEW YORK AND TORONTO | THE NEW ENGLISH LIBRARY LIMITED, LONDON

Collation: 7 x 4⅛ in. One hundred and sixty single leaves, pp. [i–iv] v–xxxiv, 35–320.

Binding: A perfect binding glued in a white card cover lettered on the spine in black: '[across] [device in white on black] | CQ | 346 | [down the spine] SELECTED POETRY AND PROSE [rule] GEORGE GORDON, LORD BYRON'. On the front cover within a rule border: 'CQ 346 [device] 95c. [or '7s.6d.'] | THE SELECTED POETRY AND PROSE OF | BYRON | INTRODUCTION BY W. H. AUDEN | [rule] | [illustration of stone lion's head in dark green and pale blue]'. The rear cover carries a note on this title and the series.

Contents:

Introduction. (pp. vii–xxiv) First printed in *New York review of books*, 18 August 1966 ("Byron: the making of a comic poet").

A note on this edition. (p. xxx)

Notes: Published December 1966 [*CCE* 28 December 1966] in an edition of 72,353 copies. There was a Canadian issue at the same time of 2,291 copies; copies sold in England were published by the New English Library in April 1967.

B 105   NO MAN'S TIME, BY V. S. YANOVSKY   1967

a) First edition

No Man's Time | A NOVEL BY | V. S. YANOVSKY | *Translated from the Russian by Isabella Levitin* | *and Roger Nyle Parris* | WITH A FOREWORD BY | W. H. AUDEN | 1967 | CHATTO & WINDUS | LONDON

Collation: 7¾ x 5 in. [A]–O⁸, pp. [1–7] 8–224.

Binding: Bound in deep yellow green (118) weave-grained imitation-cloth paper boards lettered across the spine in gold: 'NO MAN'S | TIME | [star] | V. S. | Yanovsky | CHATTO | & WINDUS'.

Contents: Foreword. (pp. 7–13)
Notes: Published 13 April 1967 in an edition of 2,500 copies.

b) First American edition   1967

[The transcription of the title page is identical with that of the first edition with the substitution of the following for the original imprint 'WEY-BRIGHT AND TALLEY | *New York*']

Collation: 8 x 5¼ in. [1–7]¹⁶, pp. [1–7] 8–224.
Binding: Bound in black cloth lettered down the spine: '[in silver] NO MAN'S TIME [three concentric squares in green] [in green] *V. S. Yanovsky* | [across] WEYBRIGHT | AND TALLEY'.
Contents: Foreword. (pp. 7–13)
Notes: Published 11 September 1967 in an edition of 3,000 copies. A photolithographic reprint of the English edition with the title page and verso revised.

B 106   HISTORY IN ENGLISH WORDS,   1967
BY O. BARFIELD

HISTORY IN | ENGLISH WORDS | by | OWEN BARFIELD | William B. Eerdmans Publishing Company | Grand Rapids, Michigan

Collation: 8 x 5 in. [1–6]¹⁶[7]¹²[8]¹⁶, pp. [1–4] 5–246 [247–248].
Binding: Glued in a strong green (141) card cover lettered down the spine in white: 'HISTORY IN ENGLISH WORDS Barfield EERDMANS', and across the front cover: 'HISTORY | IN | ENGLISH | WORDS | Owen Barfield', on a repeat pattern of words in light olive green and pale blue. The rear cover carries the publisher's name and address and previous reviews of the book all printed in light blue.
Contents: Foreword. (pp. 5–10)
Notes: Published 24 April 1967 [*CCE* 19 April 1967] in an impression of 5,129 copies. Basically a lithographic reprint of the Faber edition with corrections, and the addition of Auden's Foreword.

B 107   THE GOLDEN KEY, BY G. MACDONALD   1967

THE GOLDEN KEY | [rule] | *by* | GEORGE MACDONALD | *With pictures by* | MAURICE SENDAK | *Afterword by W. H. Auden* | [ornament] | *An Ariel Book* | FARRAR, STRAUS AND GIROUX | *New York*

Collation: 7¼ x 4¾ in. [1–6]⁸, pp. [i–viii], 1–85 [86–88].
Binding: Bound in dark blue (183) cloth lettered down the spine in gold: 'THE GOLDEN KEY [ornament] MACDONALD · SENDAK [across] F S G'. The front cover is heavily ornamented in gold.
Contents: Afterword. (pp. 81–86) First published in *Horn book*, April 1967.
Notes: Published 29 June 1967 and reprinted in 1968. The publishers prefer not to reveal the number of copies printed.

B 108   AUTHORS TAKE SIDES ON VIETNAM   1967

a) First edition

[short vertical rule to the left of the title] AUTHORS | TAKE SIDES
ON VIETNAM | Two questions on the war in Vietnam | answered by
the authors of several nations | EDITED BY | CECIL WOOLF AND
JOHN BAGGULEY | [device] | PETER OWEN · LONDON

Collation: 8½ x 5¼ in. [A]–F¹⁶G⁸H¹⁶, pp. [*–****, i–vi] vii–xii, 13–232 [233–236].
   First and last leaves laid down as endpapers.
Binding: Bound in black weave-grained imitation-cloth paper boards lettered down
   the spine in silver: 'authors take sides on Vietnam [across the spine] [device] |
   Peter | Owen'.
      Three hundred copies were bound in dark purplish blue (201) cloth lettered
   down the spine in gold: 'Authors Take Sides on Vietnam | Edited by Cecil Woolf
   and John Bagguley [across] PETER OWEN'; top edge stained dark blue. These
   copies were for presentation.
Contents: W. H. Auden. (pp. 59–60)   Reprinted in *Envoy*, September 1967, in the
   course of an article about the book in *New York times*, 18 September 1967, p. 2,
   and in *The age* (Melbourne), 30 December 1967, p. 19.
Notes: Published 18 September 1967 in an edition of 2,300 copies.

b) First American edition   1967

AUTHORS | TAKE | SIDES | ON VIETNAM | Two Questions | on
the War in Vietnam | Answered by the Authors | of Several Nations |
Edited by | CECIL WOOLF and | JOHN BAGGULEY | [device: a
sower in a rectangle] SIMON AND SCHUSTER, NEW YORK

Collation: 11 x 8½ in. [1–3]¹⁶, pp. [1–13] 14–92 [93–96].
Binding: Glued in a black card cover lettered in red, but with the title always in white,
   down the spine: 'Authors take Sides on Vietnam edited by Cecil Woolf and John
   Bagguley Simon and Schuster. On the front cover: '[left-hand side] [up the
   inner edge in white] $1.95 [across] edited by | Cecil Woolf and | John Bagguley |
   two questions | "Are you for, | or against, | the intervention | of the | United
   States | in Vietnam?" | "How, | in your opinion | should | the conflict | in Vietnam
   | be resolved?" | answered by | [names of the respondents in twenty-seven lines] |
   [right-hand side of the front cover continues the names of the respondents in
   forty-seven lines]'. Names are continued on the back cover. In the middle of the
   front cover: 'Authors | Take | Sides | on | Vietnam'.
Contents: W. H. Auden. (p. 18)
Notes: Published 31 October 1967 in an impression of 10,000 copies, and reprinted
   in April 1968 (3,500 copies).

B 109   H. A. R.: THE AUTOBIOGRAPHY OF   1968
                    FATHER REINHOLD

H. A. R. | The Autobiography | of Father Reinhold | HERDER AND
HERDER

Collation: 8 x 5¼ in. [1–5]¹⁶, pp. [i–vi] vii–x, [1–4] 5–150.
Binding: Bound in strong red (12) cloth lettered down the spine in black: 'H. A. R. The Autobiography of Father Reinhold [device across the foot of the spine: two h's suggesting a cross]'.
Contents: Foreword. (pp. vii–x)
Notes: Published 1 February 1968 in an edition of 5,000 copies. Copies sold in England were published by Burns and Oates on 14 March 1968.

B 110   VÖLUSPÁ: THE SONG OF THE SYBIL   1968

Translated by Paul B. Taylor and W. H. Auden | VÖLUSPÁ [ornament and colon in blue] THE SONG OF THE SYBIL | with the Icelandic text edited by Peter H. Salus | and Paul B. Taylor | The Windhover Press: The University of Iowa | Iowa City 1968

Collation: 9⅞ x 6½ in. [A–F]⁴, with a fold-out leaf tipped in between [E] and [F], pp. [1–46]. First and last leaves laid down as endpapers.
Binding: Bound in greenish grey (155) paper boards lettered across the front in gold: 'VÖLUSPÁ: THE SONG OF THE SYBIL | [blind-stamped ornament: a hammer]'.
Contents: Völuspá: the song of the sybil, translated by Paul B. Taylor and W. H. Auden. (C1r–D3r, rectos only)   Reprinted in *The elder edda* (1969).
Notes: "Four hundred fifty copies have been set in Bembo type and printed on Rives Heavy paper by T. Hunter Wilson, James Brooks, and K. K. Merker..." (D4r) and published 15 October 1968. Ten copies were issued in paper wrappers with a white label printed in black; these were intended as review copies. The first book from this private press.

B 111   C. DAY-LEWIS, THE POET LAUREATE: 1968
A BIBLIOGRAPHY, BY G. HANDLEY-TAYLOR
AND T. D'ARCH SMITH

[name in hollow upper case] C. DAY-LEWIS | The Poet Laureate | A BIBLIOGRAPHY | compiled by | GEOFFREY HANDLEY-TAYLOR | and | TIMOTHY D'ARCH SMITH | with a Letter of Introduction | by | W. H. AUDEN | ST. JAMES PRESS | Chicago and London | 1968

Collation: 8⅞ x 6¼ in. [1–2]⁸[unsigned gathering of plates]⁶ [4]⁸[5]⁶, pp. [*–****, i–iv] v–xii, [1–2] 3–16 [plates] 17–42 [43–44].
Binding: Bound in vivid purplish blue (194) imitation leather cloth lettered down the spine in gold: '[rule] C. DAY-LEWIS · A BIBLIOGRAPHY [rule] HANDLEY-TAYLOR · D'ARCH SMITH [rule]'. Across the front cover: 'C. *Day-Lewis*'.
Contents: A letter of introduction. (pp. v–vi)
Notes: Published 19 November 1968 in an edition of 5,000 copies of which 2,000 were bound, and 3,000 left as sheets. The entire first gathering was cancelled before binding, as Day-Lewis wished to change a word in the poem printed there. No bound copy of this state exists.
   About a week after the first publication date, one hundred additional copies were issued, signed and numbered by Day-Lewis. On these copies the following statement appears at the foot of the half title: '[signature of Day-Lewis] | *Of the one hundred numbered copies, specially issued,* | *and signed by The Poet Laureate, this is number* [numbered in ink by Day-Lewis]'. Numbers 50–60 were temporarily

mislaid and replacements were prepared, signed by Day-Lewis, but numbered by the binders. However the originals were later discovered, and the replacements were not put on sale. Except for the statement of limitation, the signed copies are identical with the first issue.

B 112   MORALITIES, BY H. W. HENZE   1969

[left-hand title page] HANS WERNER HENZE | Moralities | Three scenic plays by W. H. Auden from fables by Esop | Version for 2 pianos | or for Harpsichord and 2 pianos | Edition Schott 6033 | B. SCHOTT'S SÖHNE • MAINZ | [two lines]

[right-hand title page] HANS WERNER HENZE | Moralitäten | Drei szenische Spiele von W. H. Auden nach Fabeln des Äsop | Deutsche Übersetzung von | Maria Bosse-Sporleder | Fassung für 2 Klaviere | oder für Cembalo und 2 Klaviere | Edition Scott 6033 | B. SCHOTT'S SÖHNE • MAINZ | [two lines]

Collation: 12 x 9 in. [1–11]⁸[12]¹⁰, pp. [i–iv, 1] 2–119 [120].
Binding: Stitched in a pale orange yellow (73) card cover, lettered across the front in black: 'HANS WERNER HENZE | Moralities Moralitäten | Version for 2 pianos   Fassung für 2 Klaviere | or for harpsichord and 2 pianos   oder für Cembalo und 2 Klaviere | [device in brown] | EDITION SCHOTT | 6033'.
Contents: Moralities.   Reprinted in CWW.
Notes: Published 1 April 1969 in an edition of 600 copies. The work was commissioned by the Cincinnati Musical Festival Association, and first performed on 18 May 1969. Recorded on DGG SLPM 139 374 [1968], and also issued as a tape cassette DGG C 923 094; the disc is accompanied by a printed text.

B 113   THE PENDULUM, BY A. ROSSITER   1969

THE PENDULUM | A ROUND TRIP TO REVELATION | by | ANTHONY ROSSITER | [device: stylized helix] | HELIX PRESS [oblique stroke] *Garrett Publications* [oblique stroke] NEW YORK

Collation: 8¼ x 5½ in. [1–3]¹⁶[4–5]⁴[6–8]¹⁶, pp. [i–viii] ix–xiii [xiv–xviii], 13–199 [200–202]. An unsigned gathering of plates is inserted between [4] and [5].
Binding: Bound in brilliant bluish green (159) cloth lettered across the spine in black: 'Rossiter | T | H | E | P | E | N | D | U | L | U | M | HELIX | [device] | GARRETT'.
Contents: Foreword to the American edition. (pp. ix–xiii)
Notes: Published 15 September 1969 in an edition of 1,000 copies. The book was originally scheduled for publication on 22 April 1969, the copyright date, but the dust jackets were lost in the publisher's warehouse and had to be replaced. The English edition (London: Gollancz, 1966) does not contain Auden's foreword.

B 114   PERSONS FROM PORLOCK, BY L. MACNEICE   1969

Louis MacNeice | Persons from Porlock | AND OTHER PLAYS FOR RADIO | WITH AN INTRODUCTION | BY W. H. AUDEN | British Broadcasting Corporation

Collation: 9½ x 6 in. [A]–D¹⁶E⁸, pp. [1–6] 7–144. $5 signed, except E.

Binding: Bound in dark green (146) cloth lettered down the spine in gold: '[between two long rules] LOUIS MacNEICE PERSONS FROM PORLOCK BBC'.

Contents: Foreword. (pp. 7–9)

Notes: Published 25 September 1969 in an edition of 2,500 copies. 250 copies were supplied to the New York branch of the Oxford University Press for American distribution.

B 115   THE ELDER EDDA: A SELECTION   1969

The Elder Edda | *A Selection* | [star] | TRANSLATED FROM THE ICELANDIC BY | PAUL B. TAYLOR AND W. H. AUDEN | IN- TRODUCTION BY | PETER H. SALUS & PAUL B. TAYLOR | NOTES BY | PETER H. SALUS | FABER AND FABER | London

Collation: 8½ x 5⅜ in. [A]–L⁸, pp. [1–8] 9–173 [174–176]. $1 signed 'T.E.E.', ex- cept A.

Binding: Bound in black cloth lettered down the spine in gold: 'THE ELDER EDDA | Paul B. Taylor, W. H. Auden, Peter H. Salus | [across the foot of the spine] Faber'.

Contents:

The elder edda: a selection

The words of the high one.

The lay of Grimnir. First printed in *New York review of books*, 27 February 1969.

The lay of Vafthrudnir.

The words of the all-wise.

The lay of Thrym. First printed in *New York review of books*, 28 September 1967 ("The lay of Hrym").

The lay of Hymir.

The lay of Erik.

The treachery of Asmund.

The waking of Angantyr. First printed in *Atlantic*, September 1968.

The lay of Völund. First printed in *New York review of books*, 26 January 1967.

Brunhild's Hel-ride. First printed in *New York review of books*, 28 Septem- ber 1967.

Baldur's dreams.

Skirnir's ride. First printed in *Massachusetts review*, Spring 1968.

The lay of Harbard.

Loki's flyting. First printed in *Quest*, Spring 1968.

Song of the sybil. First printed in a separate edition as *Völuspá* (1968).

Notes: Published 8 December 1969 in an edition of 3,000 copies.

C

CONTRIBUTIONS BY W. H. AUDEN TO PERIODICALS

IN JANUARY 1937 Auden and Michael Roberts edited the special "English" number of *Poetry*, and Auden was active in 1940–1941 on the editorial board of the magazine *Decision*. Together with Jacques Barzun and Lionel Trilling he served on the editorial board of The Readers' Subscription (1951–1959) and The Mid-Century Book Club (1959–1962), and the three of them wrote most of the clubs' magazines, *Griffin* and *Mid-century* respectively. Auden was also listed as a member of the advisory board of *Contemporary poetry* (Baltimore) from 1946 through 1965, although he seems not to have been an active member, and in 1968 he was one of the founder members of the editorial board of *Delos*, the journal of translation.

Previously published poems entirely reprinted in the course of critical articles are not listed. Two such items were listed in the first edition: "It was Easter as I walked in the public gardens . . ." in *Scholastic*, 11 January 1936, and "Sonnet XXVIII" in *Pacific spectator*, Spring 1949. A third item listed in the first edition of the bibliography has also been deleted as it contains nothing by Auden; this is "Alfred, lord Tennyson, 1809–1892 versus W. H. Auden, 1907– " in *Scholastic*, 15 January 1945. All three were originally included on the basis of misleading entries from general indexes to periodicals.

1926

C1 Lead's the best: The fells sweep upward to drag down the sun . . . *Oxford outlook*, VIII, 38 (May 1926), 119–20.

C2 At parting: Though Time now tears apart . . . Portrait: The lips so apt for deeds of passion . . . *Cherwell*, XVII, n.s. 4 (22 May 1926), 130.

C3 Amor vincit omnia: Six feet from One to One . . . *Oxford outlook*, VIII, 39 (June 1926), 180.

C4 Chloe to Daphnis in Hyde Park: Stop fingering your tie; walk slower . . . *Oxford outlook*, VIII, 39 (June 1926), 209–10.

C5 Cinders: Four walls are drawn tight round the crew of us . . . *Oxford University review*, I, 8 (3 June 1926), 284.

C6 The sunken lane: Fine evenings always bring their thoughts of her . . . *Oxford magazine*, Commemoration number, 19 June 1926, p. 8.

C 7   Bank holiday: The princes rush downward on to the shore ...   *Oxford outlook*, VIII, 40 (November 1926), 242–44.

C 8   Consequences: She said, "How tiring the lights are!" ...   *Oxford University review*, II, 5 (18 November 1926), 177.

C 9   In due season: In Spring we waited. Princes felt ...   *Oxford outlook*, VIII, 41 (December 1926), 298.

1928

C 10   Thomas prologizes: They are all gone upstairs into the world ...
Oxford magazine, XLVI, 17 (3 May 1928), 467–68.
Unsigned.

1930

C 11   Paid on both sides: a charade (for Cecil Day-Lewis).   *Criterion,* IX, 35 (January 1930), 268–90.

C 12   [A review of] *Instinct and intuition*, by G. B. Dibblee.   *Criterion,* IX, 36 (April 1930), 567–69.

1931

C 13   Get there if you can and see the land you once were proud to own ...   *Twentieth century* (Promethean Society), I, 1 (March 1931), 10–11.

C 14   Case-histories: The Mother had wanted ...   When I remarked at table ...   *Adelphi*, n.s. II, 3 (June 1931), 198.

C 15   Speech for a prize-day.   *Criterion*, XI, 42 (October 1931), 60–64.

C 16   Cautionary rhymes: These ordered light ...   Why all this fuss ...
New life needs freedom first ...   *Adelphi*, n.s. III, 3 (December 1931), 181.

1932

C 17   Poem: Watching in three planes from a room overlooking the court-yard ...   *Dope*, 1 (New Year 1932), 4.

C 18   Birthday ode: Roar, Gloucestershire, do yourself proud ...   *Modern Scot*, II, 4 (Winter number, January 1932), 277–84.

C 19   [A review of] *The complete poems* of John Skelton.   *Criterion*, XI, 43 (January 1932), 316–19.

C 20   [A review of] *Edda and saga*, by B. Phillpotts.   *Criterion*, XI, 43 (January 1932), 368.
Signed "W. H. A."

C 21 [A review of] *The prisoner's soul and our own,* by E. Berggrav. *Criterion,* XI, 45 (July 1932), 752.
Signed "W. H. A."

C 22 Poem: O love, the interest itself in thoughtless Heaven... *New statesman & nation,* IV, n.s. 73 (16 July 1932), 69.

C 23 A communist to others: Comrades who when the sirens roar... *Twentieth century* (Promethean Society), IV, 19 (September 1932), 7–8.

C 24 Private pleasure. *Scrutiny,* I, 2 (September 1932), 191–94.
A review of the *Yearbook of education, The triumph of the Dalton plan,* by C. W. Kimmins and B. Rennie, and *Reminiscences of a public schoolboy,* by W. N. Marcy.

C 25 Problems of education. *New statesman & nation,* IV, [86] (Autumn book supplement, 15 October 1932), viii, x.
A review of *Education and the social order,* by B. Russell.

1933

C 26 [A review of] *The evolution of sex,* by G. Maranon, and *The biological tragedy of women,* by A. Nemilov. *Criterion,* XII, 47 (January 1933), 287–89.

C 27 Song: I have a handsome profile... *New verse,* 1 (January 1933), 3–5.

C 28 Look there! the sunk road winding... *Twentieth century* (Promethean Society), IV, 24 (February 1933), 16–17.

C 29 Gentleman versus player. *Scrutiny,* I, 4 (March 1933), 410–13.
A review of *Thoughts and adventures,* by W. Churchill.

C 30 [A review of] *Dark places in education,* by H. Schohaus. *Criterion,* XII, 48 (April 1933), 537–38.
Signed "W. H. A."

C 31 A poet tells us how to be masters of the machine. *Daily herald,* 28 April 1933, p. 17.

C 32 [What is a highbrow?] *Twentieth century* (Promethean Society), V, 27 (May 1933), 188–90.
A review of *Culture and environment,* by F. R. Leavis and D. Thompson, *How to teach reading,* by F. R. Leavis, and *How many children had Lady Macbeth?,* by L. C. Knights. Title of the article taken from the magazine wrapper.

C 33 To a young man on his twenty-first birthday: The sun shines down on the ships at sea... *New Oxford outlook,* I, 1 (May 1933), 73–74.

C 34 Interview: Having abdicated with comparative ease... *Cambridge left,* I, 1 (Summer 1933), 5.

C 35 Poem: The fruit in which your parents hid you, boy... *New verse,* 4 (July 1933), 8.

C 36 [A review of] *The poems of William Dunbar,* ed. by W. M. Mackenzie. *Criterion,* XII, 49 (July 1933), 676–78.

C 37 Two poems: To ask the hard question is simple... Hearing of harvest rotting in the valley... *Criterion*, XII, 49 (July 1933), 605–7.

C 38 Song: I have a handsome profile... *New republic*, LXXV, 971 (12 July 1933), 227.

C 39 The witnesses: You dowagers with Roman noses... *Listener*, X, [235] (poetry supplement, 12 July 1933), ii–iii.

C 40 Enter with him these legends, love: Enter with him... *Twentieth century* (Promethean Society), V, 30 (August 1933), 357.

C 41 [A review of] *The book of Talbot*, by V. Clifton. *Criterion*, XIII, 50 (October 1933), 167–68.

C 42 Five poems: Sleep on beside me though I wake for you... I see it often since you've been away... At the far end of the enormous room... The latest ferrule now has tapped the curb... Love had him fast: but though he caught his breath... *New verse*, 5 (October 1933), 14–17.

C 43 The witnesses: You dowagers with Roman noses... *Living age*, CCCXLV, 4405 (October 1933), 164–68.
Reprinted from C 39.

C 44 The Malverns: Here on the cropped grass of the narrow ridge I stand... *New Oxford outlook*, I, 2 (November 1933), 148–52.

C 45 Poem: Fleeing the short-haired mad executives... *New Oxford outlook*, I, 2 (November 1933), 153.

C 46 Two poems: What's in your mind, my dove, my coney... The night when joy began... *Twentieth century* (Promethean Society), VI, 32 (November 1933), 71.

C 47 The first Lord Melchett. *Scrutiny*, II, 3 (December 1933), 307–10.
A review of *Alfred Mond*, by H. Bolitho.

1934

C 48 Poem: The earth turns over, our side feels the cold... *New verse*, 7 (February 1934), 6–7.

C 49 "T. E. Lawrence" [by B. H. L. Hart] reviewed by W. H. Auden. *Now and then*, 47 (Spring 1934), 30, 33.
Reprinted in *Then and now: a selection... 1921–1935* (London: Cape, 1935).

C 50 Life's old boy. *Scrutiny*, II, 4 (March 1934), 405–9.
A review of *Lessons from the varsity of life*, by R. S. S. Baden-Powell.

C 51 Summer night: Out on the lawn I lie in bed... *Listener*, XI, 269 (7 March 1934), 421.

C 52 Poem: A shilling life will give you all the facts... *Rep* (magazine of the Croydon Repertory Theatre), I, 3 (April 1934), 5.

C 53 [A review of] *Gerard Manley Hopkins*, by E. E. Phare. *Criterion*, XIII, 52 (April 1934), 497–500.

C 54   Poem: Love, loath to enter . . .   *New Oxford outlook*, II, 1 (May 1934), 82–84.

C 55   Sermon by an armament manufacturer.   *Life and letters*, X, 53 (May 1934), 164–67.

C 56   Poem: Our hunting fathers told the story . . .   *Listener*, XI, 281 (30 May 1934), 911.

C 57   Poem: Just as his dream foretold, he met them all . . .   *Bryanston saga*, 11 (Summer 1934), 40.

C 58   The Malverns: Here on the cropped grass of the narrow ridge I stand . . .   *Dynamo*, I, 3 (Summer 1934), 7–10.

C 59   Poem: To settle in this village of the heart . . .   *New verse*, 9 (June 1934), 12.

C 60   [A review of] *English poetry for children*, by R. L. Mégroz. *Criterion*, XIII, 53 (July 1934), 704–5.
Signed "W. H. A."

C 61   In search of Dracula [I].   *Badger* (Downs School magazine), II, 4 (Autumn 1934), 21–24.
Signed "W. H. A."

C 62   Poem: On the provincial lawn I watch you play . . .   *Rep* (magazine of the Croydon Repertory Theatre), I, 6 (October 1934), 8.

C 63   Poem: Enter with him . . .   *New republic*, LXXX, 1037 (17 October 1934), 267.

C 64   To unravel happiness.   *Listener*, XII, [307] (late Autumn book supplement, 28 November 1934), viii, xi.
A review of *A life of one's own*, by J. Field.

C 65   Lowes Dickinson.   *Scrutiny*, III, 3 (December 1934), 303–6.
A review of *Goldsworthy Lowes Dickinson*, by E. M. Forster.

C 66   Ballad: O what is that sound which so thrills the ear . . .   *New verse*, 12 (December 1934), 4–5.

1935

C 67   Speech from a play: . . . you too are patients . . .   *New verse*, 13 (February 1935), 10–11.
From the otherwise unpublished play *The chase*.

C 68   A bride in the '30s (for Madame Mougeot [*sic*]): Easily, my dear, you move, easily your head . . .   *Listener*, XIII, 319 (20 February 1935), 317.

C 69   In search of Dracula [II].   *Badger* (Downs School magazine), III, 5 (Spring 1935), 16–18.
Signed "W. H. A."

C 70   Everyman's freedom.   *New statesman & nation*, IX, n.s. 213 (23 March 1935), 422–23.

A review of *Plain ordinary man*, by A. Radford, and *Education and the citizen*, by A. E. Loftus.

C 71   Interview: Having abdicated with comparative ease... *Bozart-Westminster*, [I, 1] (Spring-Summer 1935), 9.
Also numbered and described as *Bozart*, IX, 1, and *Westminster magazine* (Oglethorpe University), XXIV, 1, this is the first issue of the amalgamated journal.

C 72   The dog beneath the skin, opening chorus: The summer holds: upon its glittering lake... *Left review*, I, 8 (May 1935), [289]-90.

C 73   Song: Seen when night was silent... *Lysistrata*, II, 1 (May 1935), 51.

C 74   Poem: May with its light behaving... *Listener*, XIII, 331 (15 May 1935), 834.

C 75   In the square: O for doors to be open and an invite with gilded edges... *Spectator*, CLIV, 5579 (31 May 1935), 917.

C 76   Epilogue: Now is the time when all our spirits mount... *Badger* (Downs School magazine), III, 6 (Autumn 1935), 46-47.

C 77   The bond and the free. *Scrutiny*, IV, 2 (September 1935), 200-202.
A review of *Growing opinions*, ed. by A. C. Johnson, *I was a prisoner*, by W. Holt, *Means test man*, by W. Brierley, and *Caliban shrieks*, by J. Hilton.

C 78   To a writer on his birthday: August for the people and their favourite islands... *New verse*, 17 (October-November 1935), 7-9.

C 79   Seaside: Look, stranger, at this island now... *Listener*, XIV, 362 (18 December 1935), 1110.

1936

C 80   Poem: Now the leaves are falling fast... *New statesman & nation*, XI, n.s. 264 (14 March 1936), 392.

C 81   The dream: Dear, though the night is gone... *New verse*, 20 (April-May 1936), 12.

C 82   Foxtrot from a play: The soldier loves his rifle... *New verse*, 20 (April-May 1936), 12-13.

C 83   Psychology and criticism. *New verse*, 20 (April-May 1936), 22-24.
A review of *In defence of Shelley*, by H. Read.

C 84   Poem: Fish in the unruffled lakes... *Listener*, XV, 379 (15 April 1936), 732.

C 85   Poetry and film. *Janus*, May 1936, pp. 11-12.
An authorized report, in the third person, of a lecture to the North London Film Society.

C 86   Europe 1936: Certainly our city: with the byres of poverty down to... *Time and tide*, XVII, 21 (23 May 1936), 754.

C 87   Seaside; Look, stranger, at this island now . . .   *Living age*, CCCL, 4437 (June 1936), 339.
Reprinted from C 79.

C 88   Selling the Group Theatre.   *Group Theatre paper*, 1 (June 1936), [3].
Signed "W.H.A."

C 89   The economic man: And the age ended, and the last deliverer died . . .   *New verse*, 21 (June–July 1936), 8.

C 90   Honest doubt [some questions on surrealism].   *New verse*, 21 (June–July 1936), 14–16.
Signed "J. B." Attributed to Auden on the evidence of the *New verse* checklist and of the manuscript at the University of Texas.

C 91   Noah's song, by E. Toller, adapted by W. H. Auden.   *New statesman & nation*, XI, n.s. 277 (13 June 1936), 931.

C 92   Alfred (a cabaret sketch for Therese Giehse).   *New writing*, 2 (Autumn 1936), 201–3.

C 93   Raynes Park [County Grammar] School Song: Time will make its utter changes . . .   *Spur* (school magazine), I, 1 (October 1936), [1].

C 94   Three poems [Socrates' song; Rachel's song; Duet] by E. Toller, adapted by W. H. Auden.   *London mercury*, XXIV, 204 (October 1936), 484–85.

C 95   Journey to Iceland: And the traveller hopes: 'Let me be far from any . . .   *Listener*, XVI, 404 (7 October 1936), 670.

C 96   The "Agamemnon" of Aeschylus.   Mr. W. H. Auden on the use of masks.   *Times*, 27 October 1936, p. 12.
Only included in the four- and five-star editions. Partial reprint of C 97.

C 97   A modern use of masks: an apologia.   *Group Theatre paper*, 5 (November 1936), 3–4.
Unsigned.

C 98   The average man.   *New statesman & nation*, XII, n.s. 298 (7 November 1936), 740, 742.
A review of *Portrait of an unknown Victorian*, by R. H. Mottram.

C 99   Poetry, poets, and taste.   *Highway* (Workers' Educational Association), XXIX (December 1936), 43–44.

C 100   Adventures in the air.   *Listener*, XVI, [412] (Supplement 32, 2 December 1936), xvi.
A review of *High failure*, by J. Grierson.

1937

C 101   Night mail [commentary]: This is the night mail crossing the border . . .   *G*[eneral] *P*[ost] *O*[ffice] *Film Library: notes and synopses* . . ., 1937, pp. 26–28.

C 102 Alfred (a cabaret sketch for Therese Giehse). *New letters in America*, [1], (1937), 71–73.
Reprinted from C 92.

C 103 Journey to Iceland: And the traveller hopes: let me be far from any ... *Poetry*, XLIX, 4 (January 1937), 179–81.

C 104 Poem: O who can ever praise enough ... *Poetry*, XLIX, 4 (January 1937), 182.
This whole number was an "English number" edited by Auden and Michael Roberts.

C 105 A novelist's poems. *Poetry*, XLIX, 4 (January 1937), 223–24.
A review of *Visiting the caves*, by W. Plomer.

C 106 Song: "O who can ever look his fill" ... *New statesman & nation*, XIII, n.s. 308 (16 January 1937), 81.

C 107 Impressions of Valencia. *New statesman & nation*, XIII, n.s. 310 (30 January 1937), 159.

C 108 Song for the New Year: It's farewell to the drawing-room's civilized cry ... *Listener*, XVII, 423 (17 February 1937), 304.

C 109 Poem: Lay your sleeping head, my love ... *New writing*, 3 (Spring 1937), 122–23.

C 110 Royal poets. *Listener*, XVII, [433] (supplement 34, 28 April 1937), xii.
A review of *The muse of monarchy*, by E. Grant.

C 111 Blues (for Hedli Anderson): Ladies and gentlemen, sitting here ... *New verse*, 25 (May 1937), 4.

C 112 [A review of] *Illusion and reality*, by C. Caudwell. *New verse*, 25 (May 1937), 20–22.

C 113 Spain: Yesterday all the past. The language of size ... *Saturday review of literature*, XVI, 4 (22 May 1937), 10.

C 114 Orpheus: What does the song hope for? And the moved hands ... *London mercury*, XXXVI, 212 (June 1937), 118.

C 115 Christopher Sprigg memorial. *Left book news*, 15 (July 1937), [452].
Letter signed by Auden and eight others.

C 116 Hegel and the schoolchildren: Here are all the captivities; the cells are as real ... *Listener*, XVIII, 445 (21 July 1937), 130.

C 117 [Letter on MacNeice's contribution to *Letters from Iceland*.] *Time and tide*, XVIII, 34 (21 August 1937), 1118.

C 118 Poem: Under the fronds of life, beside ... *New writing*, 4 (Autumn 1937), 170–71.

C 119 Two ballads. Miss Gee: Let me tell you a little story ... Victor: Victor was a little baby ... *New writing*, 4 (Autumn 1937), 161–69.

C 120 Preface [to the catalogue of the exhibition of oil paintings by past and present members of the Downs School, Colwall, 19–31 July 1937]. *Badger* (Downs School magazine), V, 10 (Autumn 1937), 37.

C 121   The carter's funeral: Sixty odd years of poaching and drink...
Allendale: The smelting mill-stack is crumbling, no smoke is alive there...
New verse, 26–27 (November 1937), 4–5.
Quoted by Isherwood in the course of his article "Some notes on Auden's early
poetry."

C 122   Consider if you will how lovers stand... *New verse*, 26–27 (November 1937), 6–7.
See note to C 121.

C 123   Dover: Steep roads, a tunnel through the downs, are the approaches... *New verse*, 26–27 (November 1937), 2–3.

C 124   The fruit in which your parents hid you, boy... *New verse*,
26–27 (November 1937), 31.
A facsimile of the original manuscript first printed as C 35.

C 125   Journey to Iceland: And the traveller hopes: let me be far from
any... *Poetry*, LI, 2 (November 1937), 93–94.
Reprinted from C 103, since the poem was awarded the magazine's Guarantor's Prize
for 1937.

C 126   James Honeyman: James Honeyman was a silent child; he didn't
laugh or cry... *Ploughshare*, 20 (November–December 1937), 10–11.

C 127   A good scout. *Listener*, XVIII, [465] (supplement 38, 8 December 1937), xx, xxiii.
A review of *Bare knee days*, by F. H. Dimmock.

C 128   In defence of gossip. *Listener*, XVIII, 467 (22 December 1937),
1371–72.

1938

C 129   Night mail [commentary]: This is the night mail crossing the
border... *G[eneral] P[ost] O[ffice] Film Library: notes and synopses...*, 1938, pp. 22–24.

C 130   Jehovah Housman and Satan Housman. *New verse*, 28 (January
1938), 16–17.
A review of *A. E. H.: a memoir*, by L. Housman.

C 131   Song: As I walked out one evening... *New statesman & nation*,
XV, n.s. 360 (15 January 1938), 81–82.

C 132   In defence of gossip. *Living age*, CCCLIII, 4457 (February
1938), 534–38.
Reprinted from C 128.

C 133   Oxford: Nature is so near. The rooks in the college garden...
Listener, XIX, 474 (9 February 1938), 323.

C 134   From the film "Coal-face": O lurcher-loving collier black as
night... *New verse*, 30 (Summer 1938), 5.

C 135   Chinese diary, by W. H. Auden and Christopher Isherwood.
New republic, LXXXXV, 1226 (1 June 1938), 94–97.

C 136   Chinese soldier: Far from the heart of culture he was used...
New statesman & nation, XVI, n.s. 384 (2 July 1938), 14.

C 137   Meeting the Japanese. Two English writers report. [By] W. H.
Auden & Christopher Isherwood. *New masses*, XXVIII, 8 (16 August
1938), 10.

C 138   The ship: The streets are brightly lit; our city is kept clean...
Listener, XX, 501 (18 August 1938), 343.

C 139   The traveller: Holding the distance up before his face... *New
statesman & nation*, XVI, n.s. 392 (27 August 1938), 314.

C 140   The sportsmen: a parable. *New verse*, 31–32 (Autumn 1938),
2–4.

C 141   Exiles: The course of man is never quite completed... *New
writing*, n.s. 1 (Autumn 1938), 4.

C 142   Chinese soldier: Far from the heart of culture he was used...
Living age, CCCLV, 4464 (September 1938), 24.
Reprinted from C 136.

C 143   Escales, by W. H. Auden and Christopher Isherwood. *Harper's
bazaar*, LXXII, 12 (October 1938), 78–79, 126–27.

C 144   Men of thought and action. *Town crier* (Birmingham), n.s. 993
(14 October 1938), 2.
A review of *The coming victory of democracy*, by T. Mann, and *Days of hope*, by
A. Malraux.

C 145   Ironworks and university. *Town crier* (Birmingham), n.s. 994
(21 October 1938), 2.
A review of *Living*, by H. Green, *Goldsworthy Lowes Dickinson*, by E. M. Forster,
and *The culture of cities*, by L. Mumford.

C 146   Nonsense poetry. *Town crier* (Birmingham), n.s. 995 (28 October 1938), 2.
A review of the *Collected verse of Lewis Carroll* and *The Lear omnibus*.

C 147   Chinese soldier: Far from the heart of culture he was used...
China weekly review, LXXXVI, 9 (29 October 1938), 302.
Reprinted from C 136.

C 148   Sonnet: Wandering lost upon the mountains of our choice...
Listener, XX, 512 (3 November 1938), 943.

C 149   The noble savage. *Town crier* (Birmingham), n.s. 996 (4 November 1938), 2.
A review of *Patterns of culture*, by R. Benedict.

C 150   A new short story writer. *Town crier* (Birmingham), n.s. 998
(18 November 1938), 2.
A review of *Something wrong*, by J. Stern.

C 151   The teaching of English. *Town crier* (Birmingham), n.s. 999 (25
November 1938), 2.

C 152   Five sonnets from China. The ship: The streets are brightly lit;
our city is kept clean... Press conference: Officials are always glad to

give you information... Exiles: Man does not die and never is completed... Air raid: Our rays investigate the throbbing sky... Chinese soldier: Far from the heart of culture he was used... *New republic,* LXXXXVII, 1253 (7 December 1938), 130.

C 153   Morality in an age of change [no. 7 in a series, "Living philosophies"]. *Nation,* CXLVII, 26 (24 December 1938), 688–91.
Expanded and reprinted in *I believe.*

1939

C 154   Democracy's reply to the challenge of dictators. *New era in home and school,* XX, 1 (January 1939), 5–8.
"This version of Mr. Auden's speech has had to be published without his consent and —more serious—without his corrections..." (Editorial note).

C 155   Epitaph on a tyrant: Perfection, of a kind, was what he was after... *New statesman & nation,* XVII, n.s. 413 (31 January 1939), 81.

C 156   What the Chinese war is like. *Listener,* XXI, 525 (2 February 1939), 247–48.
A radio talk.

C 157   Eight poems. The capital: Quarter of pleasures where the rich are always waiting... Brussels in winter: Wandering the cold streets tangled like old string... Gare du Midi: A nondescript express in from the south... Palais des Beaux Arts: About suffering they were never wrong... Rimbaud: The nights, the railway arches, the bad sky... A. E. Housman: No one, not even Cambridge, was to blame... The novelist: Encased in talent like a uniform... The composer: All the others translate: the painter sketches... *New writing,* n.s. 2 (Spring 1939), 1–5.

C 158   The public v. the late Mr. William Butler Yeats. *Partisan review,* VI, 3 (Spring 1939), 46–51.

C 159   In memory of W. B. Yeats: He disappeared in the dead of winter... *New republic,* LXXXXVIII, 1266 (8 March 1939), 123.

C 160   Voltaire at Ferney: Perfectly happy now, he looked at his estate... *Listener,* XXI, 530 (9 March 1939), 531.

C 161   A great democrat. *Nation,* CXXXXVIII, 13 (25 March 1939), 352–53.
A review of *The spirit of Voltaire,* by N. L. Torrey, and *Voltaire,* by A. Noyes.

C 162   Edward Lear: Left by his friend to breakfast alone on the white... *Times literary supplement,* 38th year, 1338 (Spring book section, 25 March 1939), i.

C 163   Whitman and Arnold. *Common sense,* VII, 4 (April 1939), 23–24.
A review of *Matthew Arnold,* by L. Trilling.

C 164 Ganymede: He watched in all his wisdom from the throne... *Common sense*, VII, 4 (April 1939), 25.

C 165 In memory of W. B. Yeats: He disappeared in the dead of winter... *London mercury*, XXXIX, 234 (April 1939), 578–80.

C 166 Song: Say this city has ten million souls... *New Yorker*, XV, 9 (15 April 1939), 21.

C 167 How not to be a genius. *New republic*, LXXXXVIII, 1273 (26 April 1939), 348, 350.
A review of *Enemies of promise*, by C. Connolly.

C 168 Effective democracy. *Booksellers quarterly*, I, 3 (May 1939), 5–8.
Text of an address to the Foreign Correspondents' Dinner Forum, New York, 16 March 1939.

C 169 Love letter: The movies and the magazines are all of them liars... *Hika* (Kenyon College), VI [*sic*, for V], 8 (June 1939), 9.

C 170 Ode: The vacation at last is approaching... *Vindex* (St. Mark's School, Southborough, Mass.), LXIII, 6 (June 1939), 174–75.
Signed "The Feather Merchant." This poem together with one by Richard Eberhart is printed on better paper than the rest of the magazine and stapled in the centre. It may also have been circulated separately as an offprint.

C 171 Voltaire at Ferney: Perfectly happy now, he looked at his estate... *Poetry*, LIV, 3 (June 1939), 119–21.

C 172 In memoriam: Ernst Toller: The shining neutral summer has no voice... *New Yorker*, XV, 18 (17 June 1939), 80 [New York edition, p. 92].

C 173 The outlook for "poetic drama." *France-Grande Bretagne*, XXII, 188 (July–August 1939), 226–34.

C 174 The leaves of life: Underneath the leaves of life... *New republic*, LXXXXIX, 1286 (26 July 1939), 331.

C 175 The unknown citizen: He was found by the Bureau of Statistics to be... *Listener*, XXII, 551 (3 August 1939), 215.

C 176 The prophets: Perhaps I always knew what they were saying... *Spectator*, CLXIII, 5800 (25 August 1939), 285.

C 177 Four poems. The territory of the heart: Not as that dream Napoleon, rumor's dread and center... Herman Melville: Towards the end he sailed into an extraordinary mildness... The prophets: Perhaps I always knew what they were saying... Pascal: O had his mother near her time been praying... *Southern review*, V, 2 (Autumn 1939), 366–73.

C 178 Crisis: Where do they come from? Those whom we so much dread... *Atlantic*, CLXIV, 3 (September 1939), 358–59.

C 179 Rilke in English. *New republic*, C, 1292 (6 September 1939), 135–36.
A review of the *Duino elegies*, tr. by J. B. Leishman and S. Spender.

C 180   Christian on the left. *Nation*, CXLIX, 11 (9 September 1939), [273].
A review of *The clue to history*, by J. MacMurray.

C 181   Matthew Arnold: His gift knew what he was—a dark disordered city . . . *Listener*, XXII, 557 (14 September 1939), 508.

C 182   Matthew Arnold: His gift knew what he was—a dark disordered city . . . *Nation*, CXLIX, 14 (30 September 1939), 350.

C 183   Democracy is hard. *Nation*, CXLIX, 15 (7 October 1939), 386, 388.
A review of *Of human freedom*, by J. Barzun.

C 184   September: 1939: I sit in one of the dives . . . *New republic*, LXXXXX, 1298 (18 October 1939), 297.

C 185   The dyer's hand. *Nation*, CXLIX, 17 (21 October 1939), 444–45.
A review of *Shakespeare*, by M. van Doren.

C 186   Heretics. *New republic*, C, 1300 (1 November 1939), 373–74.
A review of *Rimbaud*, by E. Starkie, and *D. H. Lawrence and Susan his cow*, by W. Y. Tindall.

C 187   Nativity: About the three actors in any blessed event . . . *Harper's bazaar*, LXXIII, 14 (December 1939), 110.

C 188   Louis MacNeice. *We moderns: Gotham Book Mart 1920–1940*, catalogue 42 ([December 1939]), p. 48.

C 189   Inside China. *New republic*, CI, 1305 (6 December 1939), 208–9.
A review of *Moment in Peking*, by Lin Yutang.

C 190   Three poems. Song: Say this city has ten million souls . . . In memoriam Ernst Toller: The shining neutral summer has no voice . . . The leaves of life: Underneath the leaves of life . . . *New writing*, n.s. 3 (Christmas 1939), 37–40.

C 191   Jacob and the angel. *New republic*, CI, 1308 (27 December 1939), 292–93.
A review of *Behold this dreamer*, by W. de la Mare.

1940

C 192   For Sigmund Freud: When there are so many we shall have to mourn . . . *Kenyon review*, II, 1 (Winter 1940), 30–34.

C 193   Crisis: Where do They come from, those whom we so much dread . . . *Horizon*, I, 1 (January 1940), 10–11.

C 194   Hell: Hell is neither here nor there . . . *Harper's bazaar*, LXXIV, 1 (January 1940), 118.

C 195   Pascal: Oh had his mother near her time been praying . . . *Life and letters today*, XXIV, 29 (January 1940), 64–67.

C 196   Poet and politician. *Common sense*, IX, 1 (January 1940), 23–24.
A review of *Men in battle*, by A. Bessie.

C 197   The unknown citizen: He was found by the Bureau of Statistics to be . . .   *New Yorker*, XV, 47 (6 January 1940), 19.

C 198   The icon and the portrait. *Nation*, CL, 2 (13 January 1940), 48.
A review of *The last flower*, by J. Thurber, and *About people*, by W. Steig.

C 199   Tradition and value. *New republic*, CII, 1311 (15 January 1940), 90–91.
A review of *The novel and the modern world*, by D. Daiches.

C 200   The prophets: Perhaps I always knew what they were saying . . .
Life and letters today, XXIV, 30 (February 1940), 177.

C 201   Against romanticism. *New republic*, CII, 1314 (5 February 1940), 187.
A review of *Modern poetry and the tradition*, by C. Brooks.

C 202   In memory of Sigmund Freud: When there are so many we shall have to mourn . . .   *Horizon*, I, 3 (March 1940), 151–54.

C 203   The double focus: Sandburg's Lincoln. *Common sense*, IX, 3 (March 1940), 25–26.
A review of *Abraham Lincoln: the war years*, by C. Sandburg.

C 204   O tell me the truth about love: Some say that love's a little boy . . .
Harper's bazaar, LXXIV, 5 (April 1940) 75.

C 205   Empirics for the million. *Common sense*, IX, 5 (May 1940), 24–25.
A review of *Dangerous thoughts*, by L. Hogben.

C 206   A literary transference. *Southern review*, VI, 1 (Summer 1940), 78–86.

C 207   Yeats: master of diction. *Saturday review of literature*, XXII, 7 (8 June 1940), 14.
A review of *Last poems and plays*, by W. B. Yeats.

C 208   A literary transference. *Purpose*, XII, 3 & 4 (July–December 1940), 127–35.

C 209   Spring in wartime: O season of repetition and return . . .   *Horizon*, I, 7 (July 1940), 529–30.

C 210   What is culture? *Nation*, CLI, 1 (6 July 1940), 18.
A review of *Historian and scientist*, by G. Salvemini.

C 211   Poet in wartime. *New republic*, CIII, 1336 (8 July 1940), 59–60.
A review of *The wartime letters*, by R. M. Rilke, and *Fifty selected poems*, by R. M. Rilke.

C 212   Romantic or free? The commencement address, June 17, 1940.
Smith alumnae quarterly, XXXI, 4 (August 1940), 353–58.

C 213   Open letter to Knut Hamsun. *Common sense*, IX, 8 (August 1940), 22–23.

C 214   Elegiacs for Nietzsche: O masterly debunker of our liberal fallacies, how . . .   *Common sense*, IX, 8 (August 1940), 23.

C 215   The glamour boys and girls have grievances too: You've no idea how dull it is . . .   *New Yorker*, XVI, 28 (24 August 1940), 20.
From the libretto *Paul Bunyan*.

C 216   Poem: He watched with all his organs of concern... *Poetry*, LVII, 1 (October 1940), 9.

C 217   Who shall plan the planners? *Common sense*, IX, 11 (November 1940), 22–23.
A review of *To the Finland station*, by E. Wilson.

C 218   The maze: Anthropos apteros for days... *Vice versa*, I, 1 (November–December 1940), 6–7.

C 219   The quest [a series of twenty sonnets, numbered 1–20]. *New republic*, CIII, 1356 (25 November 1940), 716–19.
Includes a note never reprinted by Auden.

C 220   I see barns falling: I see barns falling, fences broken... *Town and country planning*, VIII, 32 (December 1940), 69.
Part of the opening chorus from DBS reprinted from SoP.

C 221   Autumn 1940: Returning each morning from a timeless world... *Nation*, CLI, 23 (7 December 1940), 563.

1941

C 222   Mimesis and allegory. *English Institute annual 1940* (New York: Columbia University Press, 1941), pp. 1–19.

C 223   Symposium [the role of intellectuals in political affairs]. Wystan H. Auden. *Decision*, I, 1 (January 1941), 44–45.

C 224   Where are we now? *Decision*, I, 1 (January 1941), 49–52.
A review of *Where do we go from here?*, by H. Laski.

C 225   Villanelle: Time can say nothing but I told you so... *Vice versa*, I, 2 (January–February 1941), 19.

C 226   Letter to Elizabeth Mayer (January 1, 1940): Under the familiar weight... *Atlantic*, CLXVII, 1 (January 1941), 56–63, *and* 2 (February 1941), 185–93.

C 227   Tract for the times. *Nation*, CLII, 1 (4 January 1941), 24–25.
A review of *Christianity and power politics*, by R. Niebuhr.

C 228   Poem: The journals give the quantities of wrong... *Decision*, I, 2 (February 1941), 19–20.

C 229   Two poems, by C. P. Cavafy, tr. by M. Yourcenar and W. H. Auden. *Decision*, I, 2 (February 1941), 42–43.

C 230   Lay your sleeping head: Lay your sleeping head, my love... *Penguin new writing*, 3 (February 1941), 26–27.

C 231   Roman wall blues: Over the heather the wet wind blows... *Harper's bazaar*, LXXV, 2 (February 1941), 117.

C 232   A note on order. *Nation*, CLII, 5 (1 February 1941), 131–33.

C 233   The wandering Jew. *New republic*, CIV, 1367 (10 February 1941), 185–86.
A review of three books by F. Kafka.

C 234 Kairos and Logos: Around them boomed the rhetoric of time . . . *Southern review*, VI, 4 (Spring 1941), 729–34.

C 235 James Joyce and Richard Wagner. *Common sense*, X, 3 (March 1941), 89–90.

C 236 Excerpts from speech of W. H. Auden. *Yale daily news*, LXIV, 126 (6 March 1941), 3, 5, 7.
Parts of this text are not present in **C 239**.

C 237 [A review of] *Open house*, by T. Roethke. *Browse* (State College, Pa.), 7 (8 March 1941), 1–2.

C 238 Each lover has some theory of his own . . . *Harper's bazaar*, LXXV, 4 (15 March 1941), 80.

C 239 W. H. Auden's News banquet address . . . *Yale alumni magazine*, IV, 15 (21 March 1941), 13–14.
Partially reprinted in an article in *Education*, February 1942. This excerpt then appeared in *Hispania*, October 1943.

C 240 Song: Jumbled in the common box . . . *Nation*, CLII, 13 (29 March 1941), 382.

C 241 Note [to Joan Murray, "Orpheus: three eclogues"]. *Decision*, I, 4 (April 1941), 53.

C 242 Exiles: The course of man is never quite completed . . . *Penguin new writing*, 5 (April 1941), 79.

C 243 Johnny: O the valley in the summer where I and my John . . . *Harper's bazaar*, LXXV, 5 (April 1941), 138.

C 244 Poem: The journals give the quantities of wrong . . . *Horizon*, III, 15 (April 1941), 239–41.

C 245 Poem: The sense of danger must not disappear . . . *Decision*, I, 4 (April 1941), 43.

C 246 [A review of] *Open house*, by T. Roethke. *Saturday review of literature*, XXIII, 24 (5 April 1941), 30–31.
Reprint of **C 237**.

C 247 The masses defined. *Decision*, I, 5 (May 1941), 63–65.
A review of *Towards a philosophy of history*, by J. Ortega y Gasset.

C 248 Opera on an American legend. Problem of putting the story of Paul Bunyan on the stage. *New York times*, 4 May 1941, section 9, p. 7.

C 249 Poem: Clocks cannot tell our time of day . . . *Furioso*, I, 4 (Summer 1941), 12.

C 250 A mother goes out [*and*] The belly speaks to his owner, by B. Viertel, tr. by W. H. Auden. *Decision*, I, 6 (June 1941), 61–62.

C 251 At the grave of Henry James: The snow, less intransigeant than their marble . . . *Horizon*, III, 18 (June 1941), 379–83.

C 252 The leaves of life: Underneath the leaves of life . . . *Penguin new writing*, 7 (June 1941), 80–82.

C 253   The means of grace. *New republic*, CIV, 1383 (2 June 1941), 765–66.
An article dealing mainly with *The nature and destiny of man*, by R. Niebuhr.

C 254   Ambiguous answers. *New republic*, CIV, 1386 (23 June 1941), 861–62.
A review of *Darwin, Marx and Wagner*, by J. Barzun.

C 255   Eros and Agape. *Nation*, CLII, 26 (28 June 1941), 756–58.
A review of *Love in the western world*, by D. de Rougemont.

C 256   A grammar of assent. *New republic*, CV, 1389 (14 July 1941), 59.
A review of *The philosophy of literary form*, by K. Burke.

C 257   At the grave of Henry James: The snow, less intransigeant than their marble ... *Partisan review*, VIII, 4 (July–August 1941), 266–70.

C 258   Calypso: Driver, drive faster and make a good run ... *Harper's bazaar*, LXXV, 11 (15 September 1941), 94.

C 259   Last words. *Harper's bazaar*, LXXV, 12 (October 1941), 83, 118–19.

C 260   The novelist: Encased in talent like a uniform ... *Penguin new writing*, 10 (November 1941), 119.

C 261   Three songs for St. Cecilia's day: In a garden shady this holy lady ... I cannot grow ... O ear whose creatures cannot wish to fall ... *Harper's bazaar*, LXXV, 14 (December 1941), 63.

1942

C 262   Song: Say this city has ten million souls ... *Penguin new writing*, 12 (April 1942), 129–30.

C 263   The rewards of patience. *Partisan review*, IX, 4 (July–August 1942), 336–40.
A review of *Poems and new poems*, by L. Bogan.

C 264   Two poems. Palais des Beaux Arts: About suffering they were never wrong ... In memoriam Ernst Toller: The shining neutral summer has no voice ... *Penguin new writing*, 14 (September 1942), 70–71.

C 265   The Fabian Figaro. *Commonweal*, XXXVII, 1 (23 October 1942), 12–13.
A review of *G. B. S.: a full length portrait*, by H. Pearson.

C 266   Mundus et infans: Kicking his mother until she let go of his soul ... *Commonweal*, XXXVII, 2 (30 October 1942), 37.

C 267   At the manger, extract from a Christmas oratorio: O shut your bright eyes that mine must endanger ... *Commonweal*, XXXVII, 10 (25 December 1942), 246–47.

1943

C 268 To the model: Generally, reading palms or handwriting or faces . . . *Dodo* (Swarthmore College), [IV, 2] (February 1943), 2.

C 269 Auden calls "Night" fun but not art. *Phoenix* (Swarthmore College), LXII, 20 (13 April 1943), 6.
A review of a production of *Night must fall*, by E. Williams.

C 270 Purely subjective. *Chimera*, II, 1 (Summer 1943), 3–22.

C 271 Two poems. Alonzo to Ferdinand: Dear son, when the warm multitudes cry . . . Canzone: When shall we learn what should be clear as day . . . *Partisan review*, X, 5 (September–October 1943), 386–90.

C 272 The poet of the encirclement. *New republic*, CIX, 1508 (24 October 1943), 579–81.
A review of *A choice of Kipling's verse*, made by T. S. Eliot. There is an ensuing correspondence with W. R. Benét in CX, 1519 (10 January 1944), 55–56.

C 273 Canzone: When shall we learn what should be clear as day . . . *Bulletin of the New York Public Library*, XLVII, 11 (November 1943), 812–13.
Reprinted from C 271. The collection of poems in this issue of the *Bulletin* was issued as an offprinted pamphlet by the library in November 1943 under the title *The poets speak*.

C 274 Herod considers the massacre of the innocents: Because I am bewildered, because I must decide . . . *Harper's magazine*, CLXXXVIII, 1123 (December 1943), 64–67.

1944

C 275 Palais des Beaux Arts: About suffering they were never wrong . . . *Choix*, I, 1 ([1944]), 67.

C 276 Victor: Victor was a little baby . . . *Penguin new writing*, 19 (1944), 116–21.

C 277 After Christmas, a passage from a Christmas oratorio: Well, so that is that. Now we must dismantle the tree . . . *Harper's magazine*, CLXXXVIII, 1124 (January 1944), 154–55.

C 278 Student government – or bombs? *Phoenix* (Swarthmore College), LXIV, 2 (21 March 1944), 1–2.

C 279 In war time: Abruptly mounting her ramshackle wheel . . . *Title* (Bryn Mawr College), May 1944, p. 3.

C 280 A preface to Kierkegaard. *New republic*, CX, 1537 (15 May 1944), 683–84, 686.
A review of *Either/or*, tr. by D. F. and L. M. Swenson and W. Lowrie, with comments on other translations.

C 281   Preface. The stage manager to the critics: The aged catch their breath ...   *Atlantic*, CLXXIV, 2 (August 1944), 78.

C 282   A knight of the infinite.   *New republic*, CXI, 1551 (21 August 1944), 223–24.
A review of *Gerard Manley Hopkins: a life*, by E. Ruggles.

C 283   In poor shape.   *Sewanee review*, LII, 4 (Autumn 1944), 593–97.
A review of *The condition of man*, by L. Mumford.

C 284   Children of Abraham.   *Nation*, CLIX, 13 (23 September 1944), 355–56.
A review of *The Jew in our day*, by W. Frank.

C 285   Augustus to Augustine.   *New republic*, CXI, 1556 (25 September 1944), 373–74, 376.
A review of *Christianity and classical culture*, by C. N. Cochrane.

C 286   William Shakespeare, in a wartime format.   *New York times*, 1 October 1944, section 7, pp. 7, 24.
A review of *The portable Shakespeare*.

C 287   New poems.   *New York times*, 15 October 1944, section 7, pp. 7, 20.
A review of *Nevertheless*, by M. Moore.

C 288   The giving of thanks.   *Mademoiselle*, XX, 1 (November 1944), 123, 188–89.

C 289   In praise of the brothers Grimm.   *New York times*, 12 November 1944, section 7, pp. 1, 28.
A review of *Fairy tales*, by J. L. K. and W. K. Grimm, ed. by J. Stern.

C 290   Agee on films [letter].   *Nation*, CLIX, 21 (18 November 1944), 628.
Reprinted in C 554 and *Agee on film* ([New York]: McDowell-Obolensky, [1958]).

C 291   Henry James and the dedicated.   *New York times*, 17 December 1944, section 7, p. 3.
A review of *Stories of writers and artists*, by H. James.

C 292   Foghorn bellow, sly bitchery spark Shakespeare's worst play.   *Phoenix* (Swarthmore College), LXV, 7 (19 December 1944), 3.
A review of a student production of *The taming of the shrew*.

C 293   On a Chinese soldier: Far from the heart of culture he was used ...   *New republic*, CXI, 26 (25 December 1944), 865.
Reprinted from JTW.

1945

C 294   Mr. Welch.   *New York times*, 18 March 1945, section 7, p. 4.
A review of *Maiden voyage*, by D. Welch.

C 295   The model: Generally, reading palms or handwriting or faces ...   *Harper's bazaar*, LXXIX, 4 (April 1945), 134.

C 296   Poem: The single creature leads a partial life ...   *Harper's bazaar*, LXXIX, 4 (April 1945), 150.

C 297 A toast [for Thomas Mann]. *Die neue Rundschau*, Sonderheft (6 June 1945), [39].

C 298 Concerning the village of Gschaid and its mountain. *New York times*, 18 November 1945, section 7, p. 6.
A review of *Rock crystal*, by A. Stifter.

C 299 The day-by-day jottings of Piotr Tchaikovsky. *New York times*, 2 December 1945, section 7, p. 4.
A review of the *Diaries*, tr. by W. Lakond.

C 300 The Christian tragic hero. *New York times*, 16 December 1945, section 7, pp. 1, 21.
On *Moby Dick*, and Greek tragedy.

1946

C 301 Four poems. In sickness and in health: Dear, all benevolence of fingering lips... Jumbled in the common box... Lady, weeping at the crossroads... Canzone: When shall we learn what should be clear as day... *Mint*, 1 (1946), 15–23.

C 302 As hateful Ares bids. *Commonweal*, XLIII, 14 (18 January 1946), 355–57.
A review of *War and the poet*, ed. by R. Eberhart and S. Rodman.

C 303 The Caucasian circle of chalk, by B. Brecht, tr. from the German by James Stern and W. H. Auden. *Kenyon review*, VIII, 2 (Spring 1946), 188–202.
A translation only of Act V.

C 304 Noon: How still it is: the horses... *Silo* (Bennington College), VII, 2 (Spring 1946), 17.

C 305 Mozart and the middlebrow. *Harper's bazaar*, LXXX, 3 (March 1946), 153, 252.

C 306 Red lizards and white stallions. *Saturday review of literature*, XXIX, 15 (13 April 1946), 22–23.
A review of *The great divorce*, by C. S. Lewis.

C 307 Henry James and the American scene. *Town and country*, C, 4285 (June 1946), 49–51, 101–3.

C 308 Under which lyre, a reactionary tract for the times: Ares at last has quit the field... *Harvard alumni bulletin*, XLVIII, 17 (15 June 1946), 707.
The Phi Beta Kappa poem, Harvard University, 1946. There are two states of this number: the first 7,000 copies are uncorrected, but the last 4,000 are corrected so that stanza 1 reads 'fractured' for 'ruined', stanza 18 'Homers' for 'Hermes', and stanza 19 'spousal' for 'sponsal'.

C 309 Spinster's song: Opera glasses on the ormolu table... *New Yorker*, XXII, 33 (28 September 1946), 34.

C 310 Landfall: These ancient harbours are hailed by the morning... *Inventario* (Milan), I, 3–4 (Autumn–Winter 1946–47), 29.

C 311   Metropolis: The scene has all the signs of a facetious culture ...
Commonweal, XLV, 10 (20 December 1946), 246.

1947

C 312   Address on Henry James.   *Gazette of the Grolier club*, II, 7 (January 1947), 211–25.
C 313   Henry James's "The American scene."   *Horizon*, XV, 86 (February 1947), 77–90.
First printed in the edition published by Scribner's in 1946.
C 314   Old formulae in a new light.   *New York times*, 30 March 1947, section 7, pp. 34–35.
A review of *Productive thinking*, by M. Wertheimer.
C 315   The fall of Rome (to C. C.): The piers are pummelled by the waves ...   *Horizon*, XV, 87 (April 1947), 155.
C 316   Some notes on D. H. Lawrence.   *Nation*, CLXIV, 17 (26 April 1947), 482–84.
A review of *The portable D. H. Lawrence*, ed. by D. Trilling.
C 317   Baroque: How tempting to trespass in these Italian gardens ...
Changing world, 1 (Summer 1947), 52.
C 318   Under which lyre, a reactionary tract for the times: Ares at last has quit the field ...   *Harper's magazine*, CXCIV, 1165 (June 1947), 508–9.
C 319   The fall of Rome: The piers are pummelled by the waves ...   *Nation*, CLXIV, 24 (14 June 1947), 716.
A reprint of C 314.
C 320   The essence of Dante.   *New York times*, 29 June 1947, section 7, pp. 4, 23.
A review of *The portable Dante*, ed. by P. Milano.
C 321   The practiced topophile [John Betjeman].   *Town and country*, CI, 4298 (July 1947), 64, 101.
C 322   The duet: All winter long the huge sad lady ...   *Kenyon review*, IX, 4 (Autumn 1947), 563–64.
C 323   Music is international: Orchestras have so long been speaking ...
American scholar, XVI, 4 (Autumn 1947), 404–6.
The Phi Beta Kappa poem, Columbia University, 1947.
C 324   Music is international: Orchestras have so long been speaking ...
Horizon, XVI, 93–94 (October 1947), 46–47.
C 325   The mythical sex.   *Harper's bazaar*, LXXXI, 10 (October 1947), 181–82, 314–16.
C 326   Nursery rhyme: Their learned kings bent down to chat with frogs ...   *Mademoiselle*, XXVI, 6 (October 1947), 176.
C 327   Serenade: On and on and on ...   *Atlantic*, CLXXX, 5 (November 1947), 62.
C 328   I like it cold.   *House and garden*, XCII, 6 (December 1947), 110, 189–90.

C 329   Mystic—and prophet. *New York times*, 14 December 1947, section 7, pp. 4, 27.
A review of *A man without a mask*, by J. Bronowski.

1948

C 330   Criticism in a mass society. *Mint*, 2 (1948), 1–13.
Reprinted from *The intent of the critic*, ed. by D. A. Stauffer (Princeton, N.J.: Princeton University Press, 1941).

C 331   Philosophy with courage and imagination. *Quarterly review of literature*, IV, 1 ([1948]), 99–102.
A review of *Nature and man*, by P. Weiss.

C 332   Yeats as an example. *Kenyon review*, X, 2 (Spring 1948), 187–95.

C 333   Lament for a lawgiver: Sob, heavy world . . . *Horizon*, XVII, 99 (March 1948), 161–63.

C 334   The duet: All winter long the huge sad lady . . . *Changing world*, 4 (May–July 1948), 43–44.

C 335   The guilty vicarage: notes on the detective story, by an addict. *Harper's magazine*, CXCVI, 1176 (May 1948), 406–12.

C 336   The poet's life—and his work. *New York times*, 2 May 1948, section 7, p. 6.
A review of *Art and faith:* letters between J. Maritain and J. Cocteau.

C 337   Henry James and the artist in America. *Harper's magazine*, CXCVII, 1178 (July 1948), 36–40.

C 338   In praise of limestone: If it form the one landscape that we the inconstant ones . . . *Horizon*, XVIII, 103 (July 1948), 1–3.

C 339   Opera addict. *Vogue*, CXI, 11 (July 1948), 65, 101.
Reprinted in the English edition in March 1949.

C 340   Ischia (for Brian Howard): There is a time to admit how much the sword decides . . . *Botteghe oscure*, 2 ([Autumn] 1948), 243–45.

C 341   Serenade: On and on and on . . . *Phoenix quarterly*, I, 3 ([Autumn] 1948), 21.

C 342   The managers: In the bad old days it was not so bad . . . Song: Deftly, admiral, cast your fly . . . *Horizon*, XVIII, 107 (November 1948), 300–302.

C 343   My favorite records. *Saturday review of literature*, XXXI, 48 (27 November 1948), 48.
A list with no annotation.

1949

C 344   The ironic hero: some reflections on Don Quixote. *Third hour*, IV (1949), 43–50.

C 345   In Schrafft's: Having finished the Blue-Plate Special ...   *New Yorker*, XXIV, 51 (12 February 1949), 32.

C 346   The heresy of our time.   *Renascence*, I, 2 (Spring 1949), 23–24.
From an NBC broadcast on *The ministry of fear*, by G. Greene.

C 347   Song: Deftly, admiral, cast your fly ...   *Voices: a quarterly of poetry*, 137 (Spring 1949), 22.

C 348   A walk after dark: A cloudless night like this ...   *Commonweal*, XLIX, 22 (11 March 1949), 540.

C 349   Port and nuts with the Eliots.   *New Yorker*, XXV, 9 (23 April 1949), 92–94, 97.
A review of *Notes towards the definition of culture*, by T. S. Eliot.

C 350   Pleasure island: What there is as a surround to our figures ...   *Commentary*, VII, 5 (May 1949), 437–38.

C 351   The question of the Pound award. W. H. Auden.   *Partisan review*, XVI, 5 (May 1949), 512–13.

C 352   The managers: In the bad old days it was not so bad ...   *Reporter*, I, 2 (10 May 1949), 18.

C 353   A note on Graham Greene.   *Wind and the rain*, VI, 1 (Summer 1949), 53–54.
The same text as C 346.

C 354   More on Pound.   *Saturday review of literature*, XXXII, 31 (30 July 1949), 22.
Letter signed by Auden and eleven others.

C 355   The ironic hero: some reflections on Don Quixote.   *Horizon*, XX, 116 (August 1949), 86–94.

C 356   Conversation on Cornelia street: dialogue with W. H. Auden, by H. Griffin.   *Accent*, X, 1 (Autumn 1949), 51–58.

C 357   Under Sirius: Yes, these are the dog-days, Fortunatus ...   Cattivo tempo: Sirocco brings the minor devils ...   *Horizon*, XX, 118 (October 1949), 209–12.

C 358   Sixty-six sestets.   *New York times*, 9 October 1949, section 7, pp. 7, 30.
A review of *An acre in the seed*, by T. Spencer.

C 359   Notebooks of Somerset Maugham.   *New York times*, 23 October 1949, section 7, pp. 1, 22.
A review of *A writer's notebook*, by W. S. Maugham.

C 360   Memorial for the city: The eyes of the crow and the eye of the camera open ...   *Horizon*, XX, 119 (November 1949), 287–91.

C 361   Firbank revisited.   *New York times*, 20 November 1949, section 7, p. 5.
A review of *Five novels*, by R. Firbank.

C 362   The duet: All the winter long the huge sad lady ...   *Listener*, XLII, 1087 (24 November 1949), 894.

1950

C 363   Religion and the intellectuals [a symposium]. W. H. Auden. *Partisan review*, XVII, 2 (February 1950), 120–28.
All contributions to the symposium were reprinted in a pamphlet *Religion and the intellectuals* (PR series, no. 3; New York: Partisan Review, 1950) in which Auden's statement is to be found on pp. 22–31.

C 364   Jean Cocteau. *Flair*, I, 1 (February 1950), 101–2.

C 365   Then and now: 1935–1950. *Mademoiselle*, XXX, 4 (February 1950), 96, 160–62.

C 366   A playboy of the western world: St. Oscar, the homintern martyr. *Partisan review*, XVII, 4 (April 1950), 390–94.
A review of *The paradox of Oscar Wilde,* by G. Woodcock.

C 367   Of poetry in troubled Greece. *New York times,* 2 April 1950, section 7, p. 5.
A review of *Modern Greek poetry,* ed. by R. Dalven.

C 368   A guidebook for all good counter-revolutionaries. *Nation,* CLXX, 14 (8 April 1950), 327–28.
A review of *Recollections,* by A. de Tocqueville.

C 369   Ischia (for Brian Howard): There is a time to admit how much the sword decides ... *Nation,* CLXX, 16 (22 April 1950), 374–75.

C 370   The score and scale of Berlioz. *New York times,* 14 May 1950, section 7, pp. 1, 18.
A review of *Berlioz and the romantic century,* by J. Barzun.

C 371   Secrets: That we are always glad ... *Ladies' home journal,* LXVII, 8 (August 1950), 63.

C 372   Nature, history and poetry. *Thought,* XXV, 98 (September 1950), 412–22.

C 373   Precious five: Be patient, solemn nose ... *Harper's magazine,* CCI, 1205 (October 1950), 58–59.

C 374   The things which are Caesar's. *Theology,* LIII, 365 (November 1950), 410–17, *and* 366 (December 1950), 449–55.

C 375   Young Boswell. *New Yorker,* XXVI, 40 (25 November 1950), 134–36 [New York edition, pp. 146–48].
A review of Boswell's *London journal, 1762–1763,* ed. by F. A. Pottle.

1951

C 376   One circumlocution: Sometimes we see astonishingly clearly ... *Third hour,* V (1951), 77.

C 377   In an age like ours, the artist works in a state of siege. *New York times,* 4 February 1951, section 7, p. 3.
A review of *Old friends and new music,* by N. Nabokov.

C 378   Culture: Happy the hare at morning, for she cannot read ...   *Oasis* (Queen's College, Cambridge), 1 ([March 1951]), [4].
Reprinted from CSP.

C 379   The chimeras: Absence of heart—as in public buildings ...   *Times literary supplement*, 50th year, 2562 (9 March 1951), 143.

C 380   "Aeneid" for our time.   *Nation*, CLXXII, 10 (10 March 1951), 231–32.
A review of the *Aeneid of Virgil*, translated by R. Humphries.

C 381   Aid for a poet [a letter signed by Auden, Eliot, MacLeish, and Wilder appealing for aid for Kenneth Patchen].   *Nation*, CLXXII, 13 (31 March 1951), 308.
A longer undated version of this letter headed "The Kenneth Patchen Fund" and bearing the facsimile signatures of the authors was also distributed as a single sheet.

C 382   Some reflections on opera as a medium.   *Tempo*, 20 (Summer 1951), 6–10.
See also C 395.

C 383   The philosophy of a lunatic.   *Observer*, 8349 (10 June 1951), 7.
A review of *Wisdom, madness and folly*, by J. Custance.

C 384   Alexander Pope.   *Essays in criticism*, I, 3 (July 1951), 208–24.
Reprinted from *From Anne to Victoria*, ed. by B. Dobrée (London: Cassell, 1937).

C 385   A face in the moon: Appearing unannounced, the moon ...   *Botteghe oscure*, VIII ([Autumn] 1951), 222–23.

C 386   Reflections on opera.   *Observer*, 8363 (16 September 1951), 6.
"This article appears in the current issue of the quarterly 'Tempo.'"

C 387   Com'è nato il libretto dell'opera "The rake's progress."   *Biennale di Venezia*, 6 (October 1951), 11, 16.

C 388   Eliot on Eliot.   *Observer*, 8369 (28 October 1951), 7.
A review of *Poetry and drama*, by T. S. Eliot.

C 389   Keats in his letters.   *Partisan review*, XVIII, 6 (November–December 1951), 701–6.
A review of *Selected letters of John Keats*, ed. by L. Trilling.

C 390   A dialogue with W. H. Auden, by H. Griffin.   *Hudson review*, III, 4 (Winter 1951), 575–91.
On war and *Macbeth*.

C 391   [A review of] *Short novels of Colette*.   *Griffin*, I, 2 ([December] 1951), 1–3.

C 392   The world that books have made.   *New York times*, 2 December 1951, section 7, pp. 1, 55.

1952

C 393   Portrait of a whig [Sydney Smith].   *English miscellany*, III (1952), 141–58.

C 394   Some reflections on music and opera.   *Partisan review*, XIX, 1 (January–February 1952), 10–18.

C 395   Auden replies [to Ronald Duncan on C 382]. *Opera*, III, 1
January 1952), 34–35, 60.
Duncan's "An answer to Auden" appeared in II, 11 (November 1951), 630–32.

C 396   Fleet visit: The sailors come ashore ... *Listener*, XLVII, 1192 (3
January 1952), 23.

C 397   The adult voice of America. *Observer*, 8379 (6 January 1952), 7.
A review of *The New Yorker 25th anniversary album.*

C 398   While the oboes came up, the bagpipes went down. *New York
times*, 24 February 1952, section 7, p. 5.
A review of *A composer's world*, by P. Hindemith.

C 399   Notes on the comic. *Thought*, XXVII, 104 (Spring 1952), 57–71.

C 400   Our Italy. *Griffin*, I, 5 ([April] 1952), 1–4.
A review of *Rome and a villa*, by E. Clark.

C 401   De droite et de gauche. *Preuves*, II, 15 (May 1952), 17–24.
"Traduit de l'anglais par Christine Lalou." For a note on this item see *ibid.*, 14 (April
1952), [65]. Unpublished in English; some of this material was later incorporated into
"Hic et ille."

C 402   Keeping the oriflamme burning. *New Yorker*, XXVIII, 21 (12
July 1952), 78, 81–84.
A review of *Henry Irving*, by L. Irving.

C 403   The shield of Achilles: She looked over his shoulder ... *Poetry*,
LXXXI, 1 (October 1952), 3–5.

C 404   Sigmund Freud. *New republic*, CXXVII, 1975 (6 October 1952),
16–17, 31.

C 405   Some notes on Grimm and Andersen. *New world writing*, 2
(November 1952), 266–75.

C 406   Conversation on Cornelia street, IV: a dialogue with W. H. Auden,
by H. Griffin. *Accent*, XII, 1 (Winter 1952), 49–61.

C 407   Woods: Sylvan meant savage in those primal woods ... *Listener*,
XLVIII, 1241 (11 December 1952), 974.

1953

C 408   Snobbery and sainthood: a dialogue with W. H. Auden, by H.
Griffin. *Avon book of modern writing*, [1] (1953), 135–43.

C 409   A dialogue with W. H. Auden, by H. Griffin. *Partisan review*,
XX, 1 (January–February 1953), 74–85.
On acting and personal relationships.

C 410   The rake's progress. *Harper's bazaar*, LXXXVII, 2 (February
1953), 165.

C 411   Opera as a medium. *Opera news*, XVII, 15 (9 February 1953),
9–11.

C 412   [A review of] *Short novels of Colette. Perspectives USA*, 3
(Spring 1953), 133–36.

Reprinted from C 391. In Great Britain this magazine was called *Perspectives;* translated editions were called in France *Profils,* in Italy *Prospetti,* and in Germany *Perspektiven.*

C 413 T. S. Eliot so far. *Griffin,* II, 3 ([March] 1953), 1–3.
A review of *Complete poems and plays,* by T. S. Eliot.

C 414 Two sides to a thorny problem. Exploring below surface of Shakespeare's "Merchant." *New York times,* 1 March 1953, section 2, pp. 1, 3.

C 415 People: Fulke Greville... *New Yorker,* XXIX, 7 (4 April 1953), 36.
All but two of these short poems are reprinted in HTC ("Academic graffiti").

C 416 Through the collarbone of a hare. *New Yorker,* XXIX, 11 (2 May 1953), 112, 114, 117–20 [New York edition, pp. 120, 122, 125–28].
A review of *My host the world,* by G. Santayana.

C 417 Verga's place. *Griffin,* II, 6 (July 1953), 3–6.
A review of *The house by the medlar tree.*

C 418 Delia: or a masque of night (libretto for a one-act opera), by W. H. Auden and Chester Kallman. *Botteghe oscure,* XII ([Autumn] 1953), 164–210.
Auden says that the printers omitted a page of the manuscript when setting this libretto. The U.S. copyright entry of the unpublished work is dated 18 April 1952. Some offprints were issued wrappered.

C 419 [A review of] *Selected essays of T. S. Eliot.* *Griffin,* II, 9 (October 1953), 4–7.

C 420 Huck and Oliver. *Listener,* L, 1283 (1 October 1953), 540–41.

C 421 The greatness of Freud. *Listener,* L, 1284 (8 October 1953), 593, 595.
A review of the first volume of *The life and work of Sigmund Freud,* by E. Jones.

C 422 Conversation on Cornelia street: a dialog with W. H. Auden, by H. Griffin. *Poetry,* LXXXIII, 2 (November 1953), 96–106.
On *Antony and Cleopatra.*

C 423 The willow wren and the stare: A starling and a willow wren... *Encounter,* I, 2 (November 1953), 13–14.

C 424 Dylan Thomas fund [letter signed by Auden and six others]. *Nation,* CLXXVII, 22 (28 November 1953), [cover ii].
A fuller version of this letter was distributed as a single sheet, dated 10 November 1953, and published in *Partisan review,* XXI, 1 (January–February 1954), 128. A shortened version was published in *Saturday review,* XXXVI, 49 (5 December 1953), 30.

C 425 Conversation on Cornelia street, V: a dialogue with W. H. Auden, by H. Griffin. *Accent,* XIII, 1 (Winter 1953), 42–47.
On Dante.

C 426 In memory of Sigmund Freud. *Griffin,* II, 11 (December 1953), 11–14.
Reprinted from CP.

C 427 Translation and tradition. *Encounter,* I, 3 (December 1953), 75–76, 78.
A review of *The translations* of Ezra Pound.

C 428 Transplanted Englishman views U.S. *St. Louis post-dispatch*, 13 December 1953, 75th anniversary supplement, p. 21.
A longer version of C 420.

C 429 Speaking of books. *New York times*, 20 December 1953, section 7, p. 2.

1954

C 430 Two poems. Hunting season: A shot: from crag to crag ... The moon like X: Appearing unannounced, the moon ... *Third hour*, VI (1954), 3–4.

C 431 Terce: After shaking paws with his dog ... *Catholic worker*, XX, 6 (January 1954), 2.

C 432 Words and music. *Encounter*, II, 1 (January 1954), 44–48.
A review article on *Rhythm and tempo,* by C. Sachs.

C 433 Sonnet: Wandering lost upon the mountains of our choice ... *Listener*, LI, 1298 (14 January 1954), 103.
Reprinted from C 148.

C 434 Ballet's present Eden: example of The Nutcracker. *Center* (New York City Center magazine), I, 1 (February 1954), 2–4.
This article was reprinted in the souvenir program book of the City Center production of the Nutcracker ballet [2 February 1954, pp. 13–14] and reprinted in an illustrated booklet included with the 1957 Westminster recording of the Nutcracker suite (OPW 1205).

C 435 A contemporary epic. *Encounter*, II, 2 (February 1954), 67–71.
A review of *Anathemata,* by D. Jones.

C 436 The man who wrote "Alice." *New York times*, 28 February 1954, section 7, p. 4.
A review of *The diaries of Lewis Carroll,* ed. by R. L. Green.

C 437 Handbook to antiquity. *Griffin*, III, 3 (March 1954), 4–7.
A review of *Ancilla to classical reading,* by M. Hadas.

C 438 A consciousness of reality. *New Yorker*, XXX, 3 (6 March 1954), 99–104 [New York edition, pp. 111–16].
A review of *A writer's diary,* by V. Woolf.

C 439 A European view of peace. *Griffin*, III, 4 (April 1954), 4–8.
A review of *The century of total war,* by R. Aron.

C 440 Plains (for Wendell Johnson): I can imagine quite easily ending up ... *London magazine*, I, 3 (April 1954), 13–15.

C 441 The word and the machine. *Encounter*, II, 4 (April 1954), 3–4.

C 442 England: six unexpected days. *Vogue*, CXXIII, 9 (15 May 1954), 62–63.

C 443 Balaam and the ass: the master-servant relationship in literature. *Thought*, XXIX, 113 (Summer 1954), 237–70.

C 444 The Freud-Fleiss letters. *Griffin*, III, 6 (June 1954), 4–10.
A review of *Sigmund Freud's letters: the origins of psychoanalysis,* by S. Freud.

C 445   Streams (for Elizabeth Drew): Dear water, clear water, playful in all your streams ... *Encounter*, II, 6 (June 1954), 30–31.

C 446   Balaam and the ass: on the literary use of the master-servant relationship. *Encounter*, III, 1 (July 1954), 35–53.

C 447   How cruel is April? *Times literary supplement*, 53rd year, 2746 (American writing today [special supplement], 17 September 1954), i.
This whole issue was reprinted as *American writing today*, ed. by A. Angoff (New York: New York University Press, 1957). Auden's contribution is on pp. 8–11.

C 448   The trial: "When rites and melodies begin ... *Times literary supplement*, 53rd year, 2746 (American writing today [special supplement], 17 September 1954), vi.
See note to C 447.

C 449   Holding the mirror up to history. *New Yorker*, XXX, 32 (25 September 1954), 116–18, 121–22 [New York edition, pp. 131–34, 137–38].
A review of *The hedgehog and the fox*, by I. Berlin.

C 450   The hero is a hobbit. *New York times*, 31 October 1954, section 7, p. 37.
A review of *The fellowship of the ring*, by J. R. R. Tolkien.

C 451   Plains: I can imagine quite easily ending up ... *Atlantic*, CXCIV, 5 (November 1954), 49–50.

C 452   The private diaries of Stendhal (1801–1814). *Griffin*, III, 11 (November 1954), 4–9.
A review of the *Private diaries*, ed. by R. Sage.

C 453   A world imaginary, but real. *Encounter*, III, 5 (November 1954), 59–60, 62.
A review of *The fellowship of the ring*, by J. R. R. Tolkien.

C 454   Winds (for Alexis Leger): Deep below our violences ... *London magazine*, I, 10 (November 1954), 15–16.

C 455   The truest poetry is the most feigning, or, Ars Poetica for hard times: By all means sing of love, but if you do ... *New Yorker*, XXX, 39 (13 November 1954), 44.

C 456   September–1939: I sit in one of the dives ... *New republic*, CXXXI, 2087 (22 November 1954), 55.
Reprinted from C 184.

C 457   Fog in the Mediterranean. *Christian scholar*, XXVII, 4 (December 1954), 531–34.
A review of *The rebel*, by A. Camus.

C 458   The proof: "When rites and melodies begin ... *Harper's bazaar*, LXXXVIII, 12 (December 1954), 100.

C 459   Ode to Gaea: From this new culture of the air we finally see ... *Listener*, LII, 1346 (16 December 1954), 1066.

C 460   The pool of Narcissus. *New Yorker*, XXX, 44 (18 December 1954), 127–30 [New York edition, pp. 142–46].
A review of *The private diaries of Stendhal*, ed. by R. Sage.

1955

C 461   Some notes on Andersen. *Adam*, 22nd year, 248–49 (1955), 9-13.

C 462   The Anglo-American difference: two views [D. Daiches and W. H. Auden]. *Anchor review*, 1 (1955), 205–19.

C 463   Qui e l'uom' felice: or Everyman in his Eden. *Grasshopper* (Gresham's School, Holt), 1955, pp. 35–37.

C 464   In memoriam L K-A: At peace under this mandarin, sleep, Lucina... *Semi-colon*, I, 2 ([1955]), 2.

C 465   Conversation: a dialog between W. H. Auden and H. Griffin. *Semi-colon*, I, 4 ([1955]), [1]–2.

C 466   Vespers: If the hill overlooking our city... *Encounter*, IV, 2 (February 1955), 10–11.

C 467   Authority in America. *Griffin*, IV, 3 (March 1955), 5–11.
A review of *An end to innocence*, by L. Fiedler.

C 468   [A review of] *The fellowship of the ring*, by J. R. R. Tolkien. *Griffin*, IV, 3 (March 1955), 19–20.
Reprint of C 450.

C 469   Le salut de trois grands poètes. New-York: W. H. Auden. *Figaro littéraire*, X, 463 (5 March 1955), [1].
Tribute to Claudel in French.

C 470   "I am of Ireland." *New Yorker*, XXXI, 5 (19 March 1955), 130–34, 137–38 [New York edition, pp. 142–46, 149–50].
A review of *The letters of W. B. Yeats*.

C 471   Am I that I am? *Encounter*, IV, 4 (April 1955), 66, 68–70, 72.
A review of *Cards of identity*, by N. Dennis.

C 472   Man before myth. *Griffin*, IV, 4 (April 1955), 4–8.
A review of *Young Sam Boswell*, by J. L. Clifford.

C 473   Streams: Dear water, clear water, playful in all your streams... *Atlantic*, CXCV, 5 (May 1955), 43–44.

C 474   Speaking of books. *New York times*, 15 May 1955, section 7, p. 2.

C 475   Expecting the barbarians, by C. Kavafis, tr. by M. Yourcenar and W. H. Auden. *Atlantic*, CLXXXXV, 6 (June 1955), 126.

C 476   The dyer's hand. *Listener*, LIII, 1372 (16 June 1955), 1063–66.

C 477   The poetic process [The dyer's hand, part II]. *Listener*, LIII, 1373 (23 June 1955), 1109–12.

C 478   On writing poetry today [The dyer's hand, part III]. *Listener*, LIII, 1374 (30 June 1955), 1151–54.

C 479   Makers of history: Serious historians study coins and weapons... *London magazine*, II, 9 (September 1955), 15–16.

C 480   The history of an historian. *Griffin*, IV, 11 (November 1955), 4–10.

A review of the second volume of *The life and work of Sigmund Freud*, by E. Jones.

C 481   Homage to Clio: Our hill has made its submission and the green . . . *Encounter*, V, 5 (November 1955), 30–31.

C 482   Am I that I am? *and* A self-policing people.   *Griffin*, IV, 12 (December 1955), 4–13.

A review of *Cards of identity*, by N. Dennis, and *Exploring English character*, by G. Gorer. The first item is a reprint of C 471.

C 483   Reflections on the "Magic flute."   *Center* (New York City Center magazine), II, 6 (December 1955), 3–7.

1956

C 484   Merax and mullin: There is one devil in the lexicon . . .   *Semicolon*, I, 6 ([1956]), 3.

C 485   Three poems. The old man's road: Across the great schism, through our whole landscape . . .   Hunting season: A shot: from crag to crag . . . Streams (for Elizabeth Drew): Dear water, clear water, playful in all your streams . . .   *Perspectives USA*, 14 (Winter 1956), 20–25.

C 486   Jameschoice for January [signed] W. H. A., J. B.[arzun], L. T.[rilling].   *Griffin*, V, 1 (January 1956), 4–6.

A note on *Finnegans wake*, by J. Joyce.

C 487   Metalogue to the Magic flute: Relax, Maestro, put your baton down . . .   *Harper's bazaar*, XC, 1 (January 1956), 96–97.

C 488   Putting it in English [on translating *The magic flute*].   *New York times*, 8 January 1956, section 2, p. 9.

C 489   Metalogue to "The magic flute": Relax, Maestro, put your baton down . . .   *Listener*, LV, 1404 (26 January 1956), 137–38.

C 490   At the end of the quest, victory.   *New York times*, 22 January 1956, section 7, p. 5.

A review of *The return of the King*, by J. R. R. Tolkien.

C 491   The romantic, by A. Mickiewicz, translated by W. H. Auden. *Wiadomości* (London), XI, 8 (19 February 1956), 1.

C 492   An appreciation of the lyric verse of Walter de la Mare.   *New York times*, 26 February 1956, section 7, p. 3.

A review of *O lovely England*, by W. de la Mare.

C 493   Stimulating scholarship.   *Griffin*, V, 3 (March 1956), 5–9.

A review of *English literature in the sixteenth century*, by C. S. Lewis.

C 494   The magic flute: act II.   *Score and I.M.A. magazine*, 15 (March 1956), 63–81.

From the translation by Auden and Kallman.

C 495   The epigoni: No use invoking Apollo in a case like theirs . . . *Poetry London–New York*, I, 1 (March–April 1956), 7–8.

C 496   Hic et ille.   *Encounter*, VI, 4 (April 1956), 33–39.

C 497 Wisdom, wit, music. *Griffin*, V, 5 (May 1956), 4–8.
A review of *Evenings with the orchestra*, by H. Berlioz.

C 498 Charles Williams. *Christian century*, LXXIII, 18 (2 May 1956), 552–54.
Partially reprinted as the introduction to *The descent of the dove* (1956).

C 499 The epigoni: No use invoking Apollo in a case like theirs... Merax and Mullin: There is one devil in the lexicon... *Nimbus*, III, 3 (Summer 1956), 3–4.

C 500 The history of science: All fables of adventure stress... *New statesman*, LI, n.s. 1317 (9 June 1956), 658.

C 501 The making of a poet. *Sunday times*, 6944 (17 June 1956), 6–7.
An extract from *Making, knowing and judging*.

C 502 Walter de la Mare. *Observer*, 8608 (24 June 1956), 10.

C 503 An eye for mystery. *Harper's bazaar*, XC, 7 (July 1956), 33–34, 103.

C 504 [A review of] *The great captains* [by H. Treece]. *Encounter*, VII, 3 (September 1956), 79–81.

C 505 D. H. Lawrence as a critic. *Griffin*, V, 9 (September 1956), 4–10.
A review of the *Selected criticism* of D. H. Lawrence.

C 506 Sydney Smith. *Griffin*, V, 10 (October 1956), 4–14.
A reprint of Auden's introduction to the *Selected writings of Sydney Smith*.

C 507 The song: So large a morning, so itself, to lean... *Truth*, CLVI, 4177 (12 October 1956), 1179.

C 508 Dostoevsky in Siberia. *Griffin*, V, 12 (November 1956), 13–17.
A review of *The house of the dead*, by F. Dostoevsky.

C 509 Concrete and fastidious. *New statesman*, LII, 1338 (3 November 1956), 551–52.
A review of *Njal's saga*, tr. by C. Bayerschmidt and L. Hollander.

C 510 There will be no peace: Though mild clear weather... *Time and tide*, XXXVII, 48 (1 December 1956), 1460.

C 511 My first master. *Periodical*, XXXI, 255 (Winter 1956–1957), 300–302.
An extract from *Making, knowing and judging*.

1957

C 512 The dyer's hand. *Anchor review*, 2 (1957), 255–301.

C 513 Making and judging poetry. *Atlantic*, CIC, 1 (January 1957), 44–52.
An abbreviated version of *Making, knowing and judging*.

C 514 Objects: All that which moves outside our sort of why... *Encounter*, VIII, 1 (January 1957), 67.

C 515   The Voltaire of music. *Time and tide*, XXXVIII, 6 (9 February 1957), 156, 158.
A review of *Life of Rossini*, by Stendhal.

C 516   A great hater. *Observer*, 8642 (17 February 1957), 14.
A review of *The diary of a writer*, by F. Dostoevsky.

C 517   A grecian eye. *Encounter*, VIII, 3 (March 1957), 77–79.
A review of *The stones of Troy*, by C. A. Trypanis.

C 518   First things first: Woken, I lay in the arms of my own warmth and listened . . . *New Yorker*, XXXIII, 3 (9 March 1957), 38.

C 519   The wish game. *New Yorker*, XXXIII, 4 (16 March 1957), 131–32, 134, 136–39 [New York edition, pp. 139–40, 142, 144–47].
A review of *The Borzoi book of French fairy tales*, ed. by P. Delarue.

C 520   Just how I feel. *Griffin*, VI, 3 (April 1957), 4–10.
A review of *Chaucer and the fifteenth century*, by H. S. Bennett, and *English literature at the close of the Middle Ages*, by E. K. Chambers.

C 521   Sydney Smith: the kind-hearted wit. *Sunday times*, 6988 (21 April 1957), 8.

C 522   West's disease. *Griffin*, VI, 4 (May 1957), 4–11.
A review of the *Complete works* of N. West.

C 523   Straw without bricks. *New statesman*, LIII, n.s. 1366 (18 May 1957), 643–44.
A review of *A. E. Housman: a divided life*, by G. L. Watson.

C 524   Seventh heavens. *Observer*, 8656 (26 May 1957), 16.
A review of *Mysticism sacred and profane*, by R. C. Zaehner.

C 525   The old man's road: Across the Great Schism, through our whole landscape . . . *Listen*, II, 3 (Summer-Autumn 1957), 8–9.

C 526   Crying spoils the appearance. *New Yorker*, XXXIII, 29 (7 September 1957), 130–34 [New York edition, pp. 142–46].
A review of *My dear Dorothea*, by G. B. Shaw.

C 527   Island cemetery: This graveyard with its umbrella pines . . . *Gemini*, I, 3 (Autumn 1957), 73–74.

C 528   The great divide. *Griffin*, VI, 9 (October 1957), 4–8.
A review of *The disinherited mind*, by E. Heller.

C 529   Limbo culture: The tribes of Limbo, travellers report . . . *Atlantic*, CC, 5 (November 1957), 132.

C 530   A mental prince [William Blake]. *Observer*, 8681 (17 November 1957), 12.

C 531   Talent, genius, and unhappiness. *New Yorker*, XXXIII, 41 (30 November 1957), 205–6, 208, 210, 213, 216–21 [New York edition, pp. 221–22, 224, 226, 229, 232–37].
A review of *Sainte-Beuve*, by H. Nicolson, and *Gogol: a life*, by D. Magarshack.

C 532   Music in Shakespeare: its dramatic use in his plays. *Encounter*, IX, 6 (December 1957), 31–44.
Cf. later letter by P. Seng in *Encounter*, X, 3 (March 1958), 67–68.

C 533   Reflections in a forest: Beneath the silence of the trees ... *De-Pauw alumnus*, XXII, 3 (December 1957), 4.

1958

C 534   Daniel: Welcome, good people, watch and listen ... *Jubilee*, V, 9 (January 1958), 30–36.
Some offprints were issued.

C 535   A jolly magpie. *New Yorker*, XXXIII, 52 (15 February 1958), 117–18, 121–22, 124–27 [New York edition, pp. 129–30, 133–34, 136–39].
A review of *Brief lives*, by J. Aubrey, ed. by O. L. Dick.

C 536   The magic flute: Auden-Kallman v. Cross. *Tempo*, 47 (Spring 1958), 82.

C 537   Reflections upon reading Werner Jaeger's *Paideia*. *Griffin*, VII, 3 (March 1958), 4–13.

C 538   The more loving one: Looking up at the stars, I know quite well ... *Esquire*, XLIX, 4 (April 1958), 82.

C 539   The life of a that-there poet. *New Yorker*, XXXIV, 10 (26 April 1958), 126–28, 131–38, 141–42 [New York edition, pp. 133–36, 139–46, 149–50].
A review of *Byron: a biography*, by L. Marchand.

C 540   The kitchen of life. *Griffin*, VII, 6 (June 1958), 4–11.
A review of *The art of eating*, by M. F. K. Fisher.

C 541   The sacred cold. *New statesman*, LVI, n.s. 1427 (19 July 1958), 88–89.
A review of *From the ends of the earth: an anthology of polar writings* ..., by A. Courtauld.

C 542   A song of life's power to renew. *New York times*, 27 July 1958, section 7, pp. 1, 12.
A review of *Seamarks*, by St.-John Perse.

C 543   Thinking what we are doing. *Griffin*, VII, 10 (October 1958), 4–12.
A review of *The human condition*, by H. Arendt.

C 544   [A note on Schopenhauer, signed by Auden, Barzun, and Trilling.] *Griffin*, VII, 11 (October 1958), 4–5.

C 545   Goodbye to the Mezzogiorno: Out of a gothic North, the pallid children ... *Encounter*, XI, 5 (November 1958), 6–8.

C 546   Friday's child: He told us we were free to choose ... *Listener*, LX, 1552 (25 December 1958), 1065.

1959

C 547   Island cemetery: This graveyard with its umbrella pines ... *Inventario* (Milan), XIV, 1–6 (January–December 1959), 185–86.

C 548   The Greek self.   *Griffin*, VIII, 2 (February 1959), 4–14.
A review of *The discovery of the mind*, by B. Snell and *Ancilla to the pre-Socratic philosophers*, by K. Freeman.

C 549   On installing an American kitchen in lower Austria: Should the shade of Plato . . .   *New Yorker*, XXXV, 3 (7 March 1959), 34.

C 550   In that ago: In that ago when being was believing . . .   *Observer*, 8752, (29 March 1959), 15.

C 551   Calm even in the catastrophe.   *Encounter*, XII, 4 (April 1959), 37–40.
A review of *The complete letters* of Vincent van Gogh.

C 552   Thinking what we are doing.   *Encounter*, XII, 6 (June 1959), 72–74, 76.
A review of *The human condition*, by H. Arendt. Reprint of **C 543**.

C 553   John Betjeman's poetic universe.   *Mid-century*, 1 (July 1959), 12–19.

C 554   Agee on the movies.   *Mid-century*, 1 (July 1959), 24–25.
Reprint of **C 290**.

C 555   Reflections in a forest: Within a shadowland of trees . . .   *Listener*, LXII, 1582 (23 July 1959), 135.

C 556   The creation of music and poetry.   *Mid-century*, 2 (August 1959), 18–27.

C 557   A personal interview with W. H. Auden, by G. Stillman.   *Trace*, 33 (August–September 1959), 18–20.

C 558   The sabbath: Waking on the seventh day of creation . . .   *Observer*, 8775 (6 September 1959), 24.

C 559   Calm even in the catastrophe.   *Mid-century*, 3 (September 1959), 22–27.
A review of *The complete letters* of Vincent van Gogh. Reprint of **C 551**, abridged.

C 560   The private life of a public man.   *Mid-century*, 4 (October 1959), 8–15.
A review of *Mythologies*, by W. B. Yeats.

C 561   Miss Marianne Moore, bless her!   *Mid-century*, 5 (Fall 1959), 4–9.
A review of *O to be a dragon*, by M. Moore.

C 562   The fallen city: some reflections on Shakespeare's "Henry IV."
Encounter, XIII, 5 (November 1959), 21–31.

C 563   Secondary epic: No, Vergil, no . . .   *Mid-century*, 7 (December 1959), 17–18.

1960

C 564   The magician from Mississippi.   *Mid-century*, 8 (January 1960), 3–9.
A review of *The mansion*, by W. Faulkner.

C 565 A children's anthology. *Mid-century*, 8 (January 1960), 18–19.
A review of *A treasure chest of tales: a collection of great stories for children.*

C 566 [A review of] *Apologies to the Iroquois* [by E. Wilson]. *Mid-century*, 9 (February 1960), 2–11.

C 567 An unclassical classic. *Mid-century*, 10 (March 1960), 15–24.
A review of *The anger of Achilles* [a tr. of *The Iliad*], by R. Graves.

C 568 Calm even in the catastrophe. *Mid-century*, 12 (May 1960), 19–24.
A review of *The complete letters* of Vincent van Gogh. Reprint of C 559.

C 569 Dame Kind: Steatopygous, sow-dugged . . . *Encounter*, XIV, 5 (May 1960), 17–18.

C 570 The Queen is never bored. *New Yorker*, XXXVI, 14 (21 May 1960), 146, 148–50, 153–66.
A review of *Queen Mary*, by J. Pope-Hennessy.

C 571 Statement by W. H. Auden on cultural freedom written on occasion of Congress anniversary. *Congress for cultural freedom news*, June 1960, p. 11.
Reprinted in a leaflet entitled *A word about the Congress* ([London, 1964]).

C 572 Greatness finding itself. *Mid-century*, 13 (June 1960), 9–18.
A review of *Young man Luther*, by E. Erikson.

C 573 The sabbath: Waking on the Seventh Day of Creation . . . *Poetry London–New York*, I, 4 (Summer 1960), 14–15.

C 574 The more loving one: Looking up at the stars, I know quite well . . . *New York times*, 21 August 1960, section 7, p. 2.

C 575 K. *Mid-century*, 17 (Fall 1960), 3–11.
A review of *The great wall of China*, by F. Kafka, and *Franz Kafka*, by M. Brod.

C 576 Two ways of poetry. *Mid-century*, 18 (October 1960), 11–16.
A review of *The less deceived*, by P. Larkin, and *For the unfallen*, by G. Hill.

C 577 The problem of nowness. *Mid-century*, 19 (November 1960), 14–20.
A review of *From roccoco to cubism in art and literature*, by W. Sypher.

1961

C 578 Dichtung und Wahrheit. *Proceedings of the American Academy of Arts and Letters and the National Institute of Arts and Letters*, 2nd ser., 11 (1961), 45–60.
Read by Auden on 2 February 1960, and here reprinted from HTC.

C 579 Three memoranda on the new Arden Shakespeare. From W. H. Auden. *Mid-century*, 21 (January 1961), 3–5.

C 580 A public art. *Opera*, XII, 1 (January 1961), 12–15.

C 581 Il faut payer. *Mid-century*, 22 (February 1961), 3–10.
A review of *Parade's end*, by F. M. Ford.

C 582 The poet as professor. *Observer*, 8849 (5 February 1961), 21.

C 583   The poems of C. P. Cavafy. *Atlantic,* CCVII, 4 (April 1961), 80–84.

C 584   Two cultural monuments. *Mid-century,* 24 (April 1961), 10–15.
A review of *Phaedra and Figaro,* tr. by R. Lowell and J. Barzun.

C 585   The case is curious. *Mid-century,* 26 (June 1961), 4–6.
A review of *The delights of detection,* by J. Barzun.

C 586   Ronald Firbank and an amateur world. *Listener,* LXV, 1680 (8 June 1961), 1004–5, 1008.

C 587   A poet of honor. *Mid-century,* 28 (July 1961), 3–9.
A review of *Collected poems,* by R. Graves.

C 588   The alienated city: reflections on "Othello." *Encounter,* XVII, 2 (August 1961), 3–14.

C 589   [A note on the New Arden edition of Shakespeare.] *Mid-century,* 29 (August 1961), 3–4.
A shortened reprint of C 579.

C 590   The seven deadly sins of the lower middle class, by B. Brecht, English version by W. H. Auden and Chester Kallman. *Tulane drama review,* VI, 1 (September 1961), 123–29.

C 591   Dag Hammarskjöld. *Encounter,* XVII, 5 (November 1961), 3–4.

C 592   The untruth about Beethoven. *Spectator,* CCVII, 6959 (10 November 1961), 672.
A review of *The letters of Beethoven,* tr. by E. Anderson.

C 593   A marriage of true minds. *Times literary supplement,* 60th year, 3115 (10 November 1961), 797–98.
Unsigned. A review of *The correspondence between Richard Strauss and Hugo von Hofmannsthal,* tr. by H. Hammelmann and E. Osers.

C 594   The quest hero. *Texas quarterly,* IV, 4 (Winter 1961), 81–93.

C 595   A universal eccentric. *Mid-century,* 33 (Christmas 1961), 2–7.
A review of *The genius of Leonardo da Vinci.*

C 596   The conscience of an artist. *Mid-century,* 34 (December 1961), 11–16.
A review of *The burning brand,* by C. Pavese.

C 597   Books of the year ... from W. H. Auden. *Sunday times,* 7232 (24 December 1961), 33.

1962

C 598   A change of air: Corns, heartburn, sinus headaches, such minor ailments ... *Encounter,* XVIII, 1 (January 1962), 93.

C 599   The chemical life. *Mid-century,* 35 (January 1962), 3–7.
A review of *The drug experience,* ed. by D. Ebin.

C 600   Anger [no. 7 in a series, "The seven deadly sins"]. *Sunday times,* 7236 (21 January 1962), 26.

C 601 [A review of] *A Marianne Moore reader*. *Mid-century*, 36 (February 1962), 2–7.

C 602 The poet and the city. *Massachusetts review*, III, 3 (Spring 1962), 449–74.

C 603 Hammerfest: For over forty years I'd paid it atlas-homage . . . *London magazine*, n.s. I, 12 (March 1962), 5–6.

C 604 A marriage of true minds. *Mid-century*, 37 (March 1962), 2–8.
A review of *A working friendship* [correspondence between Richard Strauss and Hugo von Hofmannsthal]. See also **C 593**.

C 605 You: Really, must you . . . *Saturday evening post*, CCXXXV, 9 (3 March 1962), 61.

C 606 Today's poet. *Mademoiselle*, LIV, 6 (April 1962), 187.

C 607 A disturbing novelist. *Mid-century*, 39 (May 1962), 5–8.
A review of *A Muriel Spark trio*.

C 608 "The geste says this and the man who was on the field . . ." *Mid-century*, 39 (May 1962), 9–14.
A review of *In parenthesis*, by D. Jones.

C 609 Today's "wonder-world" needs Alice. *New York times*, 1 July 1962, section 6, pp. 5, 14–15, 17, 19.

C 610 Encomium balnei: It is odd that the English . . . *Encounter*, XIX, 2 (August 1962), 53–55.

C 611 The justice of Dame Kind. *Mid-century*, 42 (Midsummer 1962), 5–8.
A review of *The senses of animals and men*, by L. J. and M. J. G. Milne.

C 612 Strachey's cry. *Encounter*, XIX, 4 (October 1962), 84–88.
A review of *The strangled cry*, by J. Strachey.

C 613 Shepherd's carol: O lift your little pinkie . . . *Musical times*, CIII, 1436 (October 1962), [musical supplement] 1–4.
Music by Britten; written and composed in 1944 for a BBC feature programme, "Poet's Christmas." Also sold separately by Novello; the text was reprinted to accompany the recording on Argo RG 424/ZRG 5424 [1964].

C 614 On Goethe: for a new translation. *Encounter*, XIX, 5 (November 1962), 61–67.
The introduction to the translation of the *Italian journey* by Auden and Elizabeth Mayer.

C 615 After reading a child's guide to modern physics: If all a top physicist knows . . . *New Yorker*, XXXVIII, 39 (17 November 1962), 48.

C 616 A poet of honor. *Shenandoah*, XIII, 2 (Winter 1962), 5–11.
Reprint of **C 587**.

C 617 Do you know too much? *Esquire*, LVIII, 6 (December 1962), 163, 269–70.

C 618 Sind die Engländer Europäer?: die Insel und der Kontinent [tr. by P. Stadelmayer]. *Wort und Wahrheit*, XVII, 12 (December 1962), 768–75.
A translation of a broadcast on the Bayerischer Rundfunk. Original untraced, but partially reprinted as **C 622**.

C 619   Mirror: a set of notes.   *Vogue*, CXL, 10 (December 1962), 116–17, 180–82.

C 620   Whitsunday in Kirchstetten (for H. A. Reinhold): *Komm Schopfer Geist* I bellow as Herr Bayer ... *Reporter*, XXVII, 10 (6 December 1962), 40–41.

1963

C 621   Homage to Marianne Moore on her 75th birthday. W. H. Auden. *Proceedings of the American Academy of Arts and Letters and the National Institute of Arts and Letters*, 2nd ser., 13 (1963), 278.

C 622   Going into Europe [a symposium]. W. H. Auden. *Encounter*, XX, 1 (January 1963), 53–54.

C 623   Adam as a Welshman.   *New York review of books*, special issue [I, 1 (February 1963)], 12.
A review of *Anathemata*, by D. Jones.

C 624   Beyond politics.   *Reporter*, XXVIII, 5 (28 February 1963), 52–54, 56.
A review of *One day in the life of Ivan Denisovich*, by A. Solzhenitsyn.

C 625   An improbable life.   *New Yorker*, XXIX, 3 (9 March 1963), 155–62, 165–66, 168, 170–77.
A review of *The letters of Oscar Wilde*, ed. by R. Hart-Davis. Reprinted as an introduction to *De profundis* (New York: Avon Books, 1964).

C 626   Parabolic ballad, by A. Voznesensky; Volcanoes, by B. Akhmadulina; Every railway station keeps a book for complaints ..., by E. Vinokurov; tr. by W. H. Auden.   *Encounter*, XX, 4 (April 1963), 52–53.
Reprinted in *Half-way to the moon*, ed. by P. Blake and M. Hayward (London: Weidenfeld and Nicolson, 1964).

C 627   The maker: Unmarried, near-sighted, rather deaf ...   *New York times*, 28 April 1963, section 6, p. 7.
Printed in an advertisement for the Steuben Glass exhibition, "Poetry in crystal."

C 628   Whitsunday in Kirchstetten: *Komm Schöpfer Geist* I bellow as Herr Bayer ...   *Wort und Wahrheit*, XVIII, 5 (May 1963), 336–38.
English and German texts.

C 629   Thanksgiving for a habitat (for Geoffrey Gorer): Nobody I know would like to be buried ...   *New Yorker*, XXXIX, 26 (17 August 1963), 30.

C 630   What we wish we'd learned in school, by A. Henley.   *Pageant*, XIX, 3 (September 1963), [W. H. Auden] 97–98.

C 631   Louis MacNeice: 1907–1963.   *Listener*, LXX, 1804 (24 October 1963), 646.
From Auden's memorial address.

C 632   Louis MacNeice.   *Encounter*, XXI, 5 (November 1963), 48–49.

C 633 Whitsunday in Kirchstetten: *Komm Schöpfer Geist* I bellow as Herr Beer... *Listener*, LXX, 1806 (7 November 1963), 731.

C 634 The cave of nakedness (for Louis and Emmie Kronenberger): Don Juan needs no bed, being far too impatient to undress... *Encounter*, XXI, 6 (December 1963), 32–33.

C 635 The common life (for Chester Kallman): A living room, the catholic area you... *New York review of books*, I, 9 (26 December 1963), 13.

1964

C 636 The common life (for Chester Kallman): A living room, the catholic area you... *London magazine*, n.s. III, 10 (January 1964), 31–33.

C 637 Iceland revisited: Unwashed, unshat... *Lesbók morgunblaðsins* (supplement to *Morgunblaðið*, Reykjavik), XXXIX, 20 (31 May 1964), 3.

C 638 Iceland revisited (for Basil and Susan Boothby): Unwashed, unshat... *Encounter*, XXIII, 1 (July 1964), 28.

C 639 Shakespeare's sonnets [I]. *Listener*, LXXII, 1840 (2 July 1964), 7–9.

C 640 On the circuit: Among pelagian travellers... *New Yorker*, XL, 20 (4 July 1964), 36.

C 641 Shakespeare's sonnets–II. *Listener*, LXXII, 1841 (9 July 1964), 45–47.

C 642 Ascension day 1964: From leaf to leaf in silence... *London magazine*, n.s. IV, 5 (August 1964), 5–6.

C 643 Luther: greatness finding itself. *Drama critique*, VII, 3 (Fall 1964), 172–75.
Reprint of C 572.

C 644 Journey to Iceland: And each traveller hopes: "Let me be far from any... Iceland revisited (for Basil and Susan Boothby): Unwashed, unshat... *Iceland review*, II, 3 ([Autumn] 1964), 21–22.

C 645 Poems from "Markings", by D. Hammarskjöld, tr. by L. Sjöberg and W. H. Auden. *Harper's*, CCXXIX, 1372 (September 1964), 104.

C 646 The cave of making (in memoriam Louis MacNeice): For this and all enclosures like it the archetype... *Listener*, LXXII, 1857 (1 October 1964), 525.

C 647 [Excerpts from] *Markings*, by D. Hammarskjöld [tr. by L. Sjöberg and W. H. Auden]. *Vogue*, CXLIV, 6 (1 October 1964), 192–93.

C 648 Speaking of books. *New York times*, 18 October 1964, section 7, p. 2.
On *Elective affinities*, by Goethe.

C 649   Private poet. *New York review of books*, III, 7 (5 November 1964), 8–10.
A review of *Rhymes of a Pfc*, by L. Kirstein.

C 650   Elegy for J. F. K.: Why *then?* why *there? ... Sunday times*, 7384 (22 November 1964), 47.

C 651   Elegy for J. F. K.: Why *then?* why *there? ... Evening standard*, 23 November 1964, p. 9.
Reprinted from *Of poetry and power*, ed. by E. A. Glikes and P. Schwaber (New York: Basic Books, 1964)

C 652   A change of air: Corns, heartburn, sinus headaches, such minor ailments... [and Auden's] Reply [to a symposium]. *Kenyon review*, XXVI, 1 (Winter 1964), 190–91, 204–8.
Reprinted in *The contemporary poet as artist and critic*, ed. by A. Ostroff (Boston: Little, Brown, 1964).

C 653   [Reply to a questionnaire on classics.] *Arion*, III, 4 (Winter 1964), 8–10.

1965

C 654   T. S. Eliot, O.M.: a tribute. *Listener*, LXXIII, 1857 (7 January 1965), 5.

C 655   Presidents [*sic*] address. *Lit* (Lambda Iota Tau, Fort Hays Kansas State College), 6 (Spring 1965), 1–3.

C 656   *Markings:* excerpts from the diary of Dag Hammarskjöld [tr. by L. Sjöberg and W. H. Auden]. *Reader's digest*, LXXXVI, 515 (March 1965), 84–86.

C 657   As it seemed to us. *New Yorker*, XLI, 7 (3 April 1965), 159–92.
A review of *A little learning*, by E. Waugh, and *Beginning again*, by L. Woolf.

C 658   Since: On a mid-December day... *Encounter*, XXIV, 5 (May 1965), 37.

C 659   Space visits, by N. Šop, tr. by B. Brusar and W. H. Auden. *Encounter*, XXIV, 5 (May 1965), 47–51.

C 660   Et in Arcadia ego: Who, now, seeing Her so... *New York review of books*, IV, 9 (3 June 1965), 5.

C 661   Joseph Weinheber (1892–1945): Reaching my gate a narrow... *London magazine*, n.s. V, 4 (July 1965), 21–24.

C 662   An epithalamium for Peter Mumford and Rita Auden: All folk tales mean by ending... *New Yorker*, XLI, 24 (31 July 1965), 34.

C 663   The corruption of innocent neutrons. *New York times*, 1 August 1965, section 6, pp. 18–19.

C 664   Mozart in the stacks. *New York review of books*, V, 1 (5 August 1965), 12.
A review of *Mozart: a documentary biography*, by O. E. Deutsch.

C 665 Amor loci: I could draw its map by heart... *New measure,* 1 (Autumn 1965), 5–6.

C 666 Out on the lawn (to Geoffrey Hoyland): Out on the lawn I lie in bed... *Badger* (Downs School, Colwall), 38 (Autumn 1965), 25.
Six stanzas only "reproduced by kind permission of the author."

C 667 One of the family. *New Yorker,* XLI, 36 (23 October 1965), 227–28, 231–38, 241–44.
A review of *Max,* by D. Cecil.

C 668 Of man and the atom. *Readers' digest,* LXXXVII, 523 (November 1965), 219–20, 222.
Abridged from C 663.

C 669 Epithalamium for Peter Mumford & Rita Auden: All folk-tales mean by ending... *Holy door,* 2 (Winter 1965), 1–2.

C 670 Precious me: On waking he thinks... *Quest,* I, 1 (Winter 1965–66), 3–4.

C 671 Elegy for J. F. K.: Why *then?* Why *there?*... *Adam,* 300 (1963–65 [*i.e.,* Winter 1965]), 62.
A facsimile of Auden's manuscript. Also issued as a hard-bound volume (London: Adams Books, Curwen Press, 1966).

C 672 Books of the year. A personal choice: W. H. Auden. *Observer,* 9103 (19 December 1965), 22.

1966

C 673 Musée des Beaux Arts: About suffering they were never wrong... *Icarus* (Trinity College, Dublin), 48 ([1966]), [28].
Reprinted from CSP.

C 674 Soviet writers under arrest [letter signed by Auden and others]. *New republic,* CLIV, 1 (1 January 1966), 36, 38.

C 675 The cave of making: For this and for all enclosures like it the archetype... *Observer,* 9105 (9 January 1966), colour magazine, pp. 22–23.

C 676 Marginalia. *New York review of books,* VI, 1 (3 February 1966), 8.

C 677 Noah Greenberg (1919–1966). *New York review of books,* VI, 1 (3 February 1966), 26.

C 678 Heresies. *New York review of books,* VI, 2 (17 February 1966), 5–6.
A review of *Pagan and christian in an age of anxiety,* by E. R. Dodds.

C 679 Amor loci: I could draw its map by heart... *Quest,* I, 2 (Spring 1966), 3–4.

C 680 Interview with W. H. Auden. *Island* (Cambridge, Mass.), 2 (Spring 1966), 2–7.

C 681   Our changing society: nowness and permanence [no. 8 in a series, "Tradition and the new"]. *Listener*, LXXV, 1929 (17 March 1966), 377–78.

C 682   The poetry of Voznesensky [with translations]. *New York review of books*, VI, 6 (14 April 1966), 3–4, 6.

C 683   The party, by A. Voznesensky, tr. by W. H. Auden. *New republic*, CLIV, 16 (16 April 1966), 28.

C 684   Filler: The Marquis de Sade and Genet... *New York review of books*, VI, 8 (12 May 1966), 8.

C 685   Autumn in Sigulda, by A. Voznesensky, tr. by W. H. Auden. *Saturday review*, XLIX, 21 (21 May 1966), 17.

C 686   My achilles heart, by A. Voznesensky, tr. by W. H. Auden. *Newsweek*, LXVIII, 2 (11 July 1966), 93.
For Voznesensky's own version see *Life*, LX, 13 (1 April 1966), 72.

C 687   Euripides wieder aktuell, by W. H. Auden and C. Kallman. *Österreichische Musikzeitschrift*, XXI, 8 (August 1966), 374–77.

C 688   W. H. Auden reflects on culture and leisure. *Unesco features*, 487 (August [II] 1966), 6–9.
Part of Auden's lecture which was one of five sponsored by the U.S. National Commission for UNESCO to celebrate the anniversary of the founding of the organisation. Reprinted in *Continuous learning*, V, 5 (September–October 1966), 231–34, and *Australian teacher*, XLIII, 2 (January 1968), 16–18. A more extensive excerpt is printed in *Ekistics* (Athens), XXIV, 144 (November 1967), 418–20. For the full version see **K 13**.

C 689   Auden on poetry: a conversation with Stanley Kunitz. *Atlantic*, CCXVIII, 2 (August 1966), 94–102.

C 690   Byron: the making of a comic poet. *New York review of books*, VII, 2 (18 August 1966), 14–18.

C 691   Fairground: Thumping old tunes give a voice to its whereabouts... *New Yorker*, XLII, 26 (20 August 1966), 32.

C 692   Dear diary: How odd it now seems... *Harvard advocate*, C, 3–4 (Fall 1966), 8.

C 693   Work and labour [an edited dialogue], by W. H. Auden and D. Munby. *Frontier*, IX, 3 (Autumn 1966), 173–77.

C 694   Insignificant elephants: Talented creatures, on the defensive because... *Encounter*, XXVII, 3 (September 1966), 9–10.

C 695   River profile: Out of a bellicose fore-time thundering... *New York review of books*, VII, 4 (22 September 1966), 4.

C 696   The twelve, anthem for the feast-day of any apostle (for Cuthbert Simpson): Without arms or charms of culture... *Christian century*, LXXXIII, 41 (12 October 1966), 1235.

C 697   Partition: Unbiased at least he was when he arrived on his mission... *Atlantic*, CCXVIII, 6 (December 1966), 94.

C 698 Books of the year: some personal choices. W. H. Auden. *Observer*, 9154 (18 December 1966), 23.

1967

C 699 Good and evil in *The lord of the rings*. *Tolkien journal*, III, 1 (1967), 5–8.

C 700 The lay of Völund, tr. by W. H. Auden and P. Taylor; notes by P. H. Salus. *New York review of books*, VIII, 1 (26 January 1967), 3–4.

C 701 Mr. G. *New York review of books*, VIII, 2 (9 February 1967), 10–12.
A review of *Goethe: conversations and encounters*, ed. by D. Luke and R. Pick.

C 702 The nose, by A. Voznesensky, tr. by W. H. Auden. *Critical quarterly*, IX, 1 (Spring 1967), 6–7.

C 703 Two poems, by G. Ekelöf, tr. by L. Sjöberg and W. H. Auden. *Quest*, II, 1 (Spring 1967), 3–5.

C 704 Metaphor: Nose, I am free … *Quest*, II, 1 (Spring 1967), 6.

C 705 Afterword: for a new edition of George MacDonald's *The golden key*. *Horn book*, XLIII, 2 (April 1967), 176–77.

C 706 Prologue at sixty: Dark-green upon distant heights … *New York review of books*, VIII, 9 (18 May 1967), 3.

C 707 A dialogue with his audience. *Barat review*, II, 2 (June 1967), 80–82.

C 708 A civilized man. *New York review of books*, VIII, 10 (1 June 1967), 16–18.
A review of *Selected essays*, by T. Spencer.

C 709 Hunting a hare, by A. Voznesensky, tr. by W. H. Auden. *Listener*, LXVII, 1993 (8 June 1967), 764.

C 710 The party, by A. Voznesensky, tr. by W. H. Auden. *Observer*, 9179 (18 June 1967), 22.

C 711 By the grace of God and Henry Tudor, archbishop. *Holiday*, XLII, 2 (August 1967), 99–100, 102.
On *Thomas Cranmer of Canterbury*, a play by C. Williams.

C 712 A poem, by G. Ekelöf [A blind man able to feel happy …], tr. by L. Sjöberg and W. H. Auden. *Nordstjernan-Svea* (New York), 17 August 1967, p. 4.

C 713 [On the Vietnam war.] *Envoy*, I, 4 (September 1967), 11.

C 714 The lay of Hrym, *and* Brunhild's Hel-ride, tr. by W. H. Auden and P. Taylor, notes by P. H. Salus. *New York review of books*, IX, 5 (28 September 1967), 16–17.

C 715 In my dreams I heard a voice … [by G. Ekelöf, tr. by L. Sjöberg and W. H. Auden]. *Östersunds-posten*, 29 September 1967, p. 2.

C 716   Song of the devil: Ever since observation taught me temptation . . .
Isis (Oxford), 25 October 1967, p. [12].

C 717   A don in the world.   *New York review of books*, IX, 7 (26 October 1967), 12, 14, 16.
A review of *Memories*, by Sir C. M. Bowra.

C 718   The mythical world of opera.   *Times literary supplement*, 66th year, 3427 (2 November 1967), 1037–39.
A shortened version of Auden's third Eliot lecture.

C 719   A mosaic for Marianne Moore: The concluded gardens of personal liking . . .   *New York review of books*, IX, 8 (9 November 1967), 3.

C 720   The true word twisted by misuse and magic.   *Washington post*, 3 December 1967, section B, p. 2.
The complete text of Auden's acceptance speech (see K 14), also printed as "W. H. Auden 'Citizen of the republic of letters' awarded National Medal for Literature," *Library journal*, XCII, 22 (15 December 1967), 4508–9, and as "The idle word, the black word," *ALA bulletin*, LXII, 4 (April 1968), 403–6. Extensive excerpts appeared as "The real world," *New republic*, CLVII, 24 (9 December 1967), 25–27; "To keep the human spirit breathing," *Book world* (*Washington post*), I, 16 (24 December 1967), 8; and "I speak in the name of all my fellow citizens of the Republic of Letters," *Chicago daily news*, 6 January 1968, *Panorama*, p. 6; other brief excerpts were widely reproduced.

1968

C 722   Songs from *Mutter Courage*, by B. Brecht, tr. by W. H. Auden. *Delos*, 1 (1968), 25–31.

C 723   The state of translation [reply to a questionnaire].   *Delos*, 2 (1968), 29–30.

C 724   The martyr as dramatic hero.   *Listener*, LXXIX, 2023 (4 January 1968), 1–6.
The first of Auden's Eliot lectures.

C 725   Solidarity [one of a group of statements on the arrest of Russian writers].   *Listener*, LXXIX, 2026 (25 January 1968), 99.

C 726   Moralities, text after Aesop, for music by Hans Werner Henze. *London magazine*, n.s. VII, 11 (February 1968), 34–40.

C 727   [Letter to the editor on an article by G. Kennan.]   *New York times*, 4 February 1968, section 6, pp. 19, 21.
Reprinted in *Democracy and the student left*, by G. Kennan (Boston: Atlantic-Little, Brown, [1968]).

C 728   A very inquisitive old party.   *New Yorker*, XLIV, 1 (24 February 1968), 121–24, 128–30, 133.
A review of *London labour and the London poor*, by H. Mayhew.

C 729   Skirnir's ride, tr. by W. H. Auden and P. Taylor; notes by P. Salus. *Massachusetts review*, IX, 2 (Spring 1968), 241–46.

C 730   Loki's flyting, tr. by P. Taylor and W. H. Auden; notes by P. Salus. *Quest*, II, 4 (Spring 1968), 273–82.

C 731   The tale of Fatumeh, by G. Ekelöf, tr. by W. H. Auden and L. Sjöberg. *Quest*, II, 4 (Spring 1968), 294–96.

C 732   Musée des Beaux Arts: About suffering they were never wrong... *Studies in the twentieth century*, 1 (Spring 1968), 5.
Reprinted from CP.

C 733   Good and evil in *The lord of the rings*. *Critical quarterly*, X, 1 & 2 (Spring & Summer 1968), 138–42.
Reprint of C 699. This whole issue of the journal was published in volume form under the title *Word in the desert* (London: Oxford University Press, 1968).

C 734   Domestic turmoil [letter to the editor]. *New York times*, 12 March 1968, p. 42.

C 735   City without walls: "Those fantastic forms, fang-sharp... *New Yorker*, XLIV, 10 (27 April 1968), 43.

C 736   On gossip. *Mademoiselle*, LXVII, 1 (May 1968), 78, 80, 82.
Reprint of C 128.

C 737   A knight of doleful countenance. *New Yorker*, XLIV, 14 (25 May 1968), 141–42, 146–48, 151–54, 157–58.
A review of *Journals and papers*, by S. Kierkegaard.

C 738   Ode to terminus: The High Priests of telescopes and cyclotrons... *New York review of books*, XI, 1 (11 July 1968), 6.

C 739   In memoriam Emma Eiermann: *Lieber Frau Emma*... *London magazine*, n.s. VIII, 5 (August 1968), 53–55.

C 740   The waking of Angantyr, tr. by P. Taylor and W. H. Auden; notes by P. Salus. *Atlantic*, CCII, 3 (September 1968), 80–83.

C 741   August 1968: The ogre does what ogres can... *Observer*, 9244 (8 September 1968), 26.

C 742   Forty years on: Except where blast-furnaces and generating stations... *New York review of books*, XI, 5 (26 September 1968), 5.

1969

C 743   Mr. Auden's acceptance. *Proceedings of the American Academy of Arts and Letters and the National Institute of Arts and Letters*, 2nd ser., 19 (1969), 54–60.
An acceptance speech, for the Gold Medal for Poetry awarded by the National Institute of Arts and Letters.

C 744   The fall of Rome (for Cyril Connolly): The piers are pummeled by the waves... *I and thou*, III, 1 (January–February 1969), 62.
Reprinted from CSP2.

C 745   The greatest of the monsters. *New Yorker*, XLIV, 46 (4 January 1969), 72, 75–78, 81–82.
A review of *Richard Wagner: the man, his mind, and his music*, by R. Gutman.

C 746   A civilized voice. *New Yorker*, XLV, 1 (22 February 1969), 128, 130, 133–40.
A review of *Alexander Pope: the education of a genius, 1688–1728*, by P. Quennell.

C 747   The lay of Grimnir, translated by P. B. Taylor and W. H. Auden, notes by P. H. Salus. *New York review of books*, XII, 4 (27 February 1969), 12–13.

C 748   To Stephen Spender on his 60th birthday: greetings from Auden. *Guardian*, 28 February 1969 [two-star edition only], p. 8.

C 749   In due season: Spring-time, Summer and Fall: days to behold a world... *Confrontation* (Long Island University), 2 (Spring 1969), 31.

C 750   A mosaic for Marianne Moore: The concluded gardens of personal liking... *Wilson library bulletin*, XLIII, 7 (March 1969), 624–25.
Reprinted from C 719.

C 751   Papa was a wise old sly-boots. *New York review of books*, XII, 6 (27 March 1969), 3–4.
A review of *My father and myself*, by J. R. Ackerley.

C 752   A piece of pure fiction in the Firbank mode. *New York times*, 4 May 1969, section 7, pt. 1, pp. 5, 20.
A review of *A nest of ninnies*, by J. Ashbery and J. Schuyler.

C 753   The Horatians: Into what fictive worlds can imagination... *New Yorker*, XLV, 14 (24 May 1969), 44.

C 754   Epistle to a godson: *DEAR PHILIP.* "Thank God for boozy godfathers"... *New York review of books*, XII, 11 (5 June 1969), 4.

C 755   Song of the ogres: Little fellow, you're amusing... *New statesman*, LXXVIII, 2003 (1 August 1969), 150.

C 756   Valéry: l'homme d'esprit. *Hudson review*, XXII, 3 (Autumn 1969), 425–32.

C 757   Circe: Her Telepathic Station transmits thoughtwaves... *London magazine*, n.s. IX, 6 (September 1969), 37–38.

C 758   Moon landing: It's natural the Boys should whoop it up for... *New Yorker*, XLV, 29 (6 September 1969), 38.

C 759   The art of healing (in memoriam David Protetch, M.D. 1923–1969): Most patients assume... *New Yorker*, XLV, 32 (27 September 1969), 38.

C 760   Natural linguistics (for Peter Salus): Every created thing has ways of pronouncing its ownhood... *Harper's*, CCXXXIX, 1433 (October 1969), 86.

C 761   Cottages in space, by N. Šop, tr. by B. Brusar and W. H. Auden. *Encounter*, XXXIII, 5 (November 1969), 3–7.

C 762   Moon landing: It's natural the Boys should whoop it up for... *Wort and Wahrheit*, XXIV, 6 (November–December 1969), 506–7.

C 763   Poems by Gunnar Ekelöf, tr. by W. H. Auden and L. Sjöberg. *New York review of books*, XIII, 9 (20 November 1969), 34–35.

C 764 In defense of the tall story. *New Yorker*, XLV, 41 (29 November 1969), 205–6, 208–10.

A review of *The artist as critic: critical writings of Oscar Wilde*, ed. by R. Ellmann.

C 765 A New Year greeting (for Vassily Yanowsky): On this day tradition allots... *Poetry review*, LX, 4 (Winter 1969–70), 223–24.

C 766 Overhead... [*and*] In summer suffering from thirst..., by G. Ekelöf, tr. by W. H. Auden and L. Sjöberg. *Bennington review*, III, 4 (Winter 1969), 47–48.

C 767 Doggerel by a senior citizen (for Robert Lederer): Our earth in 1969... *Poetry*, CXV, 3 (December 1969), 185–86.

C 768 A New Year greeting (for Vassily Yanowsky): On this day tradition allots... *Scientific American*, CCXXI, 6 (December 1969), 134.

"The following verses were written after the poet had read 'Life on the human skin,' by Mary J. Marples (*Scientific American*, January, 1969)..." (editorial note).

C 769 The ballad of Barnaby: Listen, good people, and you shall hear... *New York review of books*, XIII, 11 (18 December 1969), 1.

The first performance of this libretto was given at the Wykeham Rise School, Washington, Connecticut, 23–24 May 1969. The music was composed by the school's pupils. A newspaper article about the performance includes two paragraphs by Auden concerning the libertto (Harry Gilroy, "Auden writes opera narrative for a girls' school," *New York times*, 7 May 1969, p. 36).

Addenda

[A review of] *The grasshoppers come*, by D. Garnett. *Echanges*, 5 (December 1931), 169–70.

Verse commentary to "Night mail": This is the night mail crossing the border... G[eneral] P[ost] O[ffice] *film library: notes and synopses...*, 1936, pp. 11–12.

[A review of] *Documentary film*, by P. Rotha. *Listener*, XV, 371 (19 February 1936), 368–69.

Unsigned. Attributed to Auden in *World film news*, I (April 1936), 13.

[A review of] *Questions of our day*, by H. Ellis. *Listener*, XV, 380 (22 April 1936), 790.

Unsigned.

[A review of] *The book of Margery Kempe, a modern version*, by W. Butler-Bowdon. *Listener*, XVI, 407 (28 October 1936), 829–30.

Unsigned.

A school song: Time will make its utter changes... *Badger* (Downs School magazine), V, 10 (Autumn 1937), 73–74.

Signed "Very anon."

Sympathetic messages from British cultural leaders. W. H. Auden and Christopher Isherwood. *Far eastern magazine*, II, 8 (April 1939), 397–98.

"These messages were brought back to China by Professor Shelley Wang... who returned from London... in February 1939." (Editor's note.)

All about Ida. Simplified by W. H. Auden. *Saturday review of literature*, XXIII, 18 (22 February 1941), 8.
A review of *Ida*, by G. Stein.

Atlantis: Being set on the idea ... *Christianity and society*, VI, 3 (Summer 1941), 18.

In memoriam [letter to the editor]. *New York times*, 6 February 1949, section 7, p. 14.
On the death of Theodore Spencer.

The co-inherence. *National review*, VI, 18 (31 January 1959), 496–97.
A review of *The image of the city and other essays*, by C. Williams.

Plays at Princeton. Auden's Age of anxiety, stage version by Graham Ferguson and John Becker. *University: a Princeton magazine*, 5 (Summer 1960), 21, 23, 25.
Excerpts from the opening and closing scenes of the production.

The poet as "guilty conscience of his time," by Saint-John Perse, tr. by W. H. Auden. *Washington post*, 22 January 1961, section E, p. 1.
Reprinted as *On poetry* (1961).

Elegy for JFK: Why *then?* Why *there?* ... *Washington post*, 22 November 1964, section E, p. 1.

The cave of making: For this and all enclosures like it the archetype ... *Harper's bazaar*, 98th year, 3039 (February 1965), 118–19.
Includes the "Postscript" reprinted in ATH.

[Letter to the editors.] *Scientific American*, CCXIV, 5 (May 1966) 8, 10.
A reply to an article on the physiological effects of travel by air.

Literary myths as bearers of religious meaning. A conversation. *ARC directions*, [3] ([Spring 1967]), 1–2, 6.
Excerpts taken, "with a minimum of editing," from a discussion by Auden and others at a meeting in New York of Fellows of the Foundation for the Arts, Religion and Culture.

In due season: Spring-time, Summer and Fall: days to behold a world ... *Ver sacrum*, [1] (1969), 8.

Smelt and tasted: The nose and palate never doubt ... Heard and seen: Events recorded by the ear ... *Poet* (Madras), X, 6 (June 1969), 2–3.

D

CONTRIBUTIONS TO THEATRE
AND OTHER PROGRAMMES

APART from the items listed below two prospectuses of the Group Theatre contain policy statements that were partially written by Auden. The first, titled *The Group Theatre, 9 Great Newport Street, London, W.C.2* (4 pp.), was issued about April 1933; p. [3] contains "7 points about the Group Theatre." The second prospectus, titled *The Group Theatre, 9 Great Newport Street, London, W.C.2* (14 pp.), is dated January 1934 and contains on p. 3 an untitled policy statement, and on p. 4 "7 points about the Group Theatre," which is substantially identical with the statement in the first prospectus. All these statements are unsigned, but a manuscript note by Robert Medley in a copy of the second prospectus now in the Berg Collection, New York Public Library, asserts that "the wording of the policy statements, etc. was pulled into shape by Auden." This is confirmed by Ormerod Greenwood: " 'The Group Theatre is a co-operative [the opening words of the "7 points..."] ...' began the manifesto which W. H. Auden was bullied into writing for us" (*Ark*, 15 [1955], p. 36). "8 points about the Group Theatre," similar to the "7 points..." above, appear on the front page of the programme, *Croydon Repertory Theatre presents the Group Theatre in songs, dances and a play*, 24 July 1933.

For details of Auden's contribution to the programme of *Arcifanfano* see **K 6**.

D 1 I want the theatre to be . . . [Group Theatre programme of] *Sweeney Agonistes* and *The dance of death*, Westminster Theatre, 1 October 1935, p. [7].
Reprinted in an article by Ashley Dukes, "The English scene," *Theatre arts monthly*, XIX (December 1935), 907–8, and in an article by W. A. Darlington in *Discovery*, XVI (December 1935), 349. The synopsis of *The dance of death* on p. [4] may well be by Auden, and a slightly longer version of this synopsis first appeared in the programme of *The Group Theatre in The Deluge* [and] *The Dance of death*, Westminster Theatre, February 25 & March 4, 1934, p. [6].

D 2 Are you dissatisfied with this performance? [Group Theatre programme of] *The Agamemnon* of Aeschylus, Westminster Theatre, 1 and 8 November 1936, p. [4].

D 3 Spring in wartime: O season of repetition and return... *Allied*

Relief Ball Souvenir Program, Hotel Astor, New York, May 10, 1940, pp. [3–4].
Reprinted in DM.

D 4 Ferdinand: Flesh, fair, unique, and you, warm secret that my kiss . . .
McGregor room seminars in contemporary prose and poetry [program],
University of Virginia, 16 May 1947, p. [5].
Reprinted from CP.

D 5 From *New Year letter:* A weary Asia out of sight . . . *McGregor
room seminars in contemporary prose and poetry* [program], University
of Virginia, 16 May 1947, p. [5].
Auden's address entitled "Poetry and freedom" was afterwards circulated as a 9-page
mimeographed leaflet.

D 6 The Met at work: writing a libretto, by W. H. Auden and Chester
Kallman. *Metropolitan Opera* [program], 14 February 1953, p. 18.
The first American performance of *The rake's progress.*

D 7 A message. *Homage to Dylan Thomas.* [Souvenir programme],
Globe Theatre, 24 January 1954, p. [2].

D 8 Geburt eines Libretto, [by] W. H. Auden and Chester Kallman.
Schloss Schwetzingen 1961 [Schwetzingen Festspiele programme, Stutt-
gart], pp. 14–21.
This programme also contains "Ein persönlicher Kommentar," by Kallman, pp. 21–24.

D 9 Genesis of a libretto *and* Elegy for young lovers—synopsis, [by]
W. H. Auden and Chester Kallman. [Programme book, 10th edition, of
the] *Glyndebourne Festival Opera*, 24 May—20 August 1961, pp. 37–39,
53, 56.

D 10 A tribute. *Homage to T. S. Eliot.* [Souvenir programme], Globe
Theatre, 13 June 1965, p. [8].
Reprinted from *Listener*, 7 January 1965.

D 11 A word from W. H. Auden. *Poets in public.* [Edinburgh Festival
programme], Freemasons' Hall, 24–27 August 1965, p. [2].
Title taken from the Contents page. The programme also contains "Miranda's Song,"
which Auden read, on p. 27.

D 12 The twelve. [Programme of the] *B.B.C. Music programme . . .
Concert in celebration of the 900th anniversary of the founding of Westminster Abbey,* 2 January 1966, p. [2].
Admission was by programme, and all programmes were numbered. Reprinted in the
score and CWW.

D 13 Mythological background *and* Religious attitudes of the characters
and Synopsis of the action [by W. H. Auden and Chester Kallman].
[Programme of the] *Salzburger Festspiele 1966: Die Bassariden*, 6 August
1966, pp. [13–20].
Unsigned. Together with French and German versions. Reprinted in the vocal score
and there signed.

D 14 Moralities. *Forty-seventh May Festival at Cincinnati* [program
book], 17–25 May 1968, pp. 45–50.

The text differs slightly from that printed in the *London magazine*. Reprinted in CWW.

D 15   A reminder. *Christ Church son et lumière*. [Souvenir programme, 27 June—28 September 1968], p. 3.
Reprinted in CWW.

E

RECORD SLEEVES AND SIMILAR MATERIAL

E 1 Cav and Pag. [Libretto booklet to accompany] *Cavalleria rusticana* and *I Pagliacci*, RCA Victor WDM 6106 [1953], pp. 10–17.
Reprinted as "Verismo opera" in libretto booklets to accompany separate recordings of *Cavalleria rusticana*, RCA WDM 6046 [1956], and *I Pagliacci*, RCA LM 6045 [1956] and RCA LM 6084 [1960].

E 2 *W. H. Auden reading* [sleeve note]. Caedmon TC-1019 [1954].

E 3 *An evening of Elizabethan verse and its music* [sleeve note]. Columbia ML 5051 [1955], reissued as Odyssey 32 16 0171 [1968].
Auden also read the verse on this recording.

E 4 *Poems and songs of Middle Earth*, by J. R. R. Tolkien and Donald Swann [sleeve note]. Caedmon TC 1231 [1967].

Note: Auden and Kallman's libretto for *The rake's progress* was issued with the two recordings, Columbia SL 125 [1953], released in England as Philips ABL 3055–57 [1954], and Columbia M3L 310 / M3S 710 [1964], released in England as CBS BRG 72503 / SBRG 72071 [1965]; Auden's contributions to Samuel Barber's *Hermit songs* were printed on the sleeve of the recording Columbia ML 4988 [1955], reissued as Odyssey 32 16 0230 [1968]; "Ballet's present Eden" was reprinted in an illustrated booklet issued with the Westminster recording of the Nutcracker suite OPW 1205 [1957]; the narration to *The play of Daniel* was issued as "Daniel: a sermon" with Decca DL 9402 / DL 79402 [1958] and reissued as DCM 3240 [1962]; extracts from the text of *Elegy for young lovers* with French and German versions were issued with DGG LPM 18876 / SLPM 138876 [1964]; the texts of "Chorale" and "A shepherd's carol" with *Part songs* by Benjamin Britten, Argo RG 424 / ZRG 5424 [1964]; a brief excerpt from "The poetry of Andrei Voznesensky" was printed on the sleeve of the recording of *Antiworlds*, Columbia OL 6590 [1966], and CBS LP 70026 [1967]; the text of *Moralities* by Hans Werner Henze was issued with French and German versions with DGG 139374 [1968]; and that of Brecht's *Seven deadly sins* with the American issue of DGG 139 308 [1968].

G

ODDS AND ENDS

THIS omnium-gatherum heading signifies an attempt by the compilers to collect up fragments, sentences, facsimiles, and other stray pieces of Auden's work or speech that have found their way into print and that are not listed or referred to elsewhere in the bibliography, and to list books with which his connection has been tenuous. However quotations from columns like "Sayings of the week" in *Observer* (17 May 1964, p. 11; 19 June 1960, p. 4; 23 October 1966, p. 11), "Sayings of the year" in *Observer* (18 December 1966, p. 9), "People and words" in *Sunday times* (19 June 1960, p. 11), and ana like the detective story *Poetic justice,* by Amanda Cross (New York: Knopf; London: Gollancz, 1970) are not included.

G 1   Abbott, Anthony. *Prose pieces and poems.* London: Gollancz, 1929.
The verso of the title page carries a note: "Grateful thanks are due to Mr. D. A. Sington and Mr. W. H. Auden, for their kind help in the arrangement of these Verses and Essays."

G 2   Day Lewis, C. *Transitional poem.* London: Hogarth Press, 1929. (Hogarth living poets, No. 9.)
Four lines of verse used as an epigraph, beginning "The hatches are let down...," p. 55.

G 3   *New verse,* 26–27 (November 1937), 31.
Manuscript facsimile of "The fruit in which your parents hid you, boy...."

G 4   Elton, [*Sir*] Arthur, and Robert Fairthorne. *Why aeroplanes fly.* London: Longmans Green, [1936].
The first volume in *The march of time series,* edited by Sir Arthur Elton and W. H. Auden. Auden's part-editorship extended no further than this volume.

G 5   Redfern Gallery. *Oil paintings by past and present members of the Downs School, Colwall* [catalogue of an exhibition, London, July 19th—July 31st 1937].
Preface, p. [2], reprinted in *Badger,* Autumn 1937.

G 6   Riding, Laura. *Collected poems.* London: Cassell, 1938; New York: Random House, [1938].
On p. xxii in her note "To the reader" Miss Riding quotes a comment by Auden on her work. This may be taken from the comment prepared by Auden for use in the Random House announcement catalogue for Fall 1937 [not seen].

G 7   Poetry and culture [list of lectures]. *Curriculum* [of the] New School for Social Research, Spring 1940, p. 45.

G 8 Williams, Oscar. *The man coming towards you.* New York: Oxford University Press, 1940.
An extract from Auden's reader's report is on the front cover of the dust jacket; a slightly different extract is printed on an advertising postcard and order form distributed before publication; and an additional sentence was later published, at Williams's request, in *Poetry*, LVI, 4 (July 1940), 230.

G 9 Newton, Caroline. Goethe's "Reich" [letter]. *Saturday review of literature*, XXII, 21 (14 September 1940), 9.
Contains a brief translation from Goethe; reprinted by H. T. Lowe-Porter in *Symposium*, IX, 2 (Fall 1955), 267, and by John C. Thirlwell in his *In another language* (New York: Knopf, 1967), pp. 54 and 198.

G 10 The language and technique of poetry [syllabus note]. *Curriculum* [of the] New School for Social Research, 1940–1941, p. 68.

G 11 Thomas, Wright, and Stuart Gerry Brown. *Reading poems: an introduction to critical study.* New York: Oxford University Press, 1941.
Transcript of a working manuscript of "Where do they come from, those whom we so much dread...," pp. 630–33.

G 12 Armi, Anna Maria [*i.e.* Mrs. Maria Ascoli]. *Poems.* New York: Random House, [1941].
Auden's comment on Mrs. Ascoli's translations from Petrarch is paraphrased on the dust jacket of the book.

G 13 *Paul Bunyan* [programme]. Brander Matthews Hall, Columbia University, week of 5 May 1941.
A brief quotation, probably from a statement written for the production director, Dr. Milton Smith, p. [2].

G 14 Lewars, Kenneth. The quest in Auden's poems and plays. M.A., Columbia University, 1947.
Manuscript facsimile, with transcript, of a chart prepared at Swarthmore College in 1943, p. 136. Published by Lewars in *Connecticut review*, I, 2 (April 1968) 44, 48–49.

G 15 *Poets at work.* New York, Harcourt Brace, [1948].
Manuscript facsimile of part of the first page of "Where do they come from, they whom we so much dread...," p. 124.

G 16 Hoffman, Dan[iel] G. Paul Bunyan: last of the frontier demigods. M.A., Columbia University, 1949.
Extracts from *Paul Bunyan*, pp. 181–87, 206. Published in Hoffman's book of the same title (Philadelphia: University of Pennsylvania Press for Temple University publications, 1952), pp. 147–51, 188.

G 17 Esar, Evan, ed. *The dictionary of humorous quotations.* Garden City, N.Y.: Doubleday, 1949.
One sentence by Auden from an unidentified interview, p. 20.

G 18 Burnett, Whit, ed. *105 living authors present the world's best.* New York: Dial, 1950.
Auden's selection of a representative piece, "The massacre of the innocents" from FTB, with a brief comment, p. 479.

G 19 Bartlett, Phyllis. *Poems in process.* New York: Oxford University Press, 1951.
Brief extract from the working manuscript of "Miranda's song," p. 97.

G 20   *Riverside poetry 1953,* selected by W. H. Auden, Marianne Moore, Karl Shapiro. New York: Association Press, [1953].
Auden's association with the volume is no more than that described on the title page.

G 21   Hamilton, Gerald. The importance of not being Norris. *Punch,* CCXXVII, 5958 (17 November 1954), 639.
One stanza from a poem written for a New Year's eve party (probably 31 December 1938), beginning "Uncle Gerald, your charm is a mystery...." Reprinted in Hamilton's *Mr Norris and I* (London: Allan Wingate, 1956), p. 131, and the same author's *Desert drums* (2nd ed., Washington: Guild Press, 1966), p. 85, and *The way it was with me* (London: Leslie Frewin, [1969]), p. 56.

G 22   Williams, Oscar, ed. *The new pocket anthology of American verse.* New York: Pocket Library; Cleveland: World, [1955].
"September 1, 1939" is slightly revised at Auden's request, pp. 45–46. (See *Master poems,* ed. by O. Williams [New York: Trident Press, 1966], p. 1025.)

G 23   Bentley, Eric, ed. *The modern theatre,* vol. 2. Garden City, N.Y.: Doubleday, Anchor books, 1955.
In the acknowledgements Bentley notes that "W. H. Auden suggested a number of lines for the songs [in Bentley's translation of *Mother Courage*] that would fit Dessau's music better" (p. [vii]).

G 24   *Ezra Pound at 70.* [Norfolk, Conn.: New Directions, 1956.]
Brief extract from Auden's broadcast on WYBC on 5 December 1955, p. 4. There is a mimeographed transcript of the entire broadcast in the Beinecke Library at Yale University with Auden's contribution on pp. 14–15.

G 25   *Oratio Creweiana MCMLVI.* [Oxford: Oxford University Press, 1956.]
The Latin and English texts of the oration delivered by Auden at Encaenia, 20 June 1956, and printed by the University Press for free distribution in the Sheldonian Theatre.

Among the duties of the Professor of Poetry was the delivery in Latin, every second year, of the Creweian Oration, "in commemoration of Benefactors to the University, according to the intention of the Right Honourable Nathaniel Lord Crewe, Bishop of Durham." The Latin text was prepared by Mr. John G. Griffith, Dean and Tutor in Classics from Jesus College, and is printed on the numbered versos facing Auden's English text on the rectos. This English text often differs considerably in tone and substance from the Latin.

The pamphlet for the 1956 oration is titled on the first page 'ORATIO CREWE-IANA | MCMLVI', measures 8½ x 5½ in., and consists of one unsigned gathering of ten leaves stapled twice, pp. [1] 2–19 [20], printed on white wove unwatermarked paper. The last page carries the imprint *'University Press | Oxford'.* Auden's name does not appear. No copies were sold, and 1,500 copies were printed. The Latin text is reprinted in *Oxford University gazette,* LXXXVI, 2898 (21 June 1956), 1094–97.

G 26   *Oratio Creweiana MCMLVIII.* [Oxford: Oxford University Press, 1958.]
Similar to G 25. The pamphlet is titled on the first page 'ORATIO CREWEIANA | MCMLVIII', measures 8½ x 5½ in., and consists of one unsigned gathering of twelve leaves stapled twice, pp. [1] 2–23 [24]. The last page carries the imprint 'PRINTED IN | GREAT BRITAIN | AT THE | UNIVERSITY PRESS | OXFORD | BY | CHARLES BATEY | PRINTER | TO THE | UNIVERSITY'. The layout of the pamphlet is similar to that described in G 25, except that the English text is headed *'Paraphrase'* on p. 3. Printed in an edition of 1,500 copies for free distribution on 25

June 1958. The Latin text is reprinted in *Oxford University gazette*, LXXXVIII, 2973 (27 June 1958), 1228–31.

G 27 *Oratio Creweiana MDCCCCLX.* [Oxford: Oxford University Press, 1960.]
Similar to **G 25**. The pamphlet is titled on the first page 'ORATIO CREWEIANA | MDCCCCLX', measures 8½ x 5½ in., and consists of one unsigned gathering of eight leaves stapled twice, pp. [1] 2–15 [16]. The last page carries the imprint 'PRINTED IN GREAT BRITAIN | AT THE UNIVERSITY PRESS, OXFORD | BY VIVIAN RIDLER | PRINTER TO THE UNIVERSITY'. The layout is similar to that described in **G 25**, except that the English text is headed '*Abstract*' on p. 3. Printed in an edition of 1,500 copies for distribution on 22 June 1960. The Latin text is reprinted in *Oxford University gazette*, XC, 3049 (24 June 1960), 1430–32.

G 28 *Poetry pilot* [Academy of American Poets], 1 March 1959.
Auden selected the following poems for publication in this number: "Eve"; "Faire is my love," by Bartholomew Griffin; "Reflections," by Walter de la Mare; "Sonnet," by Herbert of Cherbury; "La Bella Bona Roba," by Richard Lovelace; "The silken tent," by Robert Frost. Contains nothing by Auden.

G 29 Stravinsky, Igor, and Robert Craft. *Memories and commentaries.* Garden City, N.Y.: Doubleday, 1960; London: Faber, [1960].
Stravinsky and Auden's first scenario for *The rake's progress*, pp. 156–67 (Faber, pp. 167–76).

G 30 *A catalogue of the books and manuscripts to be sold at private auction on November 19, 1960 for the benefit of the Modern Poetry Association following a dinner in honor of Mr. W. H. Auden.* Chicago: [Modern Poetry Association, 1960].
Manuscript facsimile of one stanza from "The shield of Achilles" beginning "The mass and majesty of this world, all...," p. [1].

G 31 Todd, Ruthven. *Garland for the winter solstice.* London: Dent, [1961]; Boston: Little, Brown, [1962].
A comment by Auden appears on the rear flap of the dust jacket of the Dent edition, and on the rear cover of the jacket of the Little, Brown edition.

G 32 Cater, Douglass. The Kennedy look in the arts. *Horizon*, IV, 1 (September 1961), 5.
Auden's brief inscription in the notebook presented by artists and scientists to John F. Kennedy at his inauguration.

G 33 [Statement on William Carlos Williams.] *Encounter* XVIII, 1 (January 1962), [125].
An advertisement for Williams's American publisher.

G 34 Spears, Monroe K. *The poetry of W. H. Auden.* New York: Oxford University Press, 1963.
A diagram from the notebook used for *The sea and the mirror*, and an extract from an early version of Caliban's speech beginning "Ladies and gentlemen, please keep your seats...," pp. 247, 249. This notebook is described by Edward Callan in *University of Toronto quarterly*, XXXV, 2 (January 1966), 140–41.

G 35 Simon, John. *Acid test.* New York: Stein and Day, [1963].
One sentence by Auden appears on the front flap of the dust jacket.

G 36 *The review*, 11–12 ([1965]), 82.
Manuscript facsimile of "Some say that handsome raider, still at large...," from the original owned by Gavin Ewart.

G 37 Skelton, Robin, ed. *Poetry of the thirties*. [Harmondsworth]: Penguin, [1964].
Auden's brief comment rejecting five early poems, p. 41.

G 38 MacNeice, Louis. *The dark tower*. London: Faber, 1964.
One sentence by Auden is on the inside front cover, and was taken from an early draft of Auden's introduction to MacNeice's *Selected poems*.

G 39 Sabljak, Tomislav. Portret pjesnika W. H. Audena. *Republika* (Zagreb), XX, 11 (November 1964), 478.
The article is illustrated by a facsimile manuscript of "Elegy for J. F. K.," which is not the same as that printed in *Adam 300*.

G 40 Whitehead, John. Auden: an early poetical notebook. *London magazine*, n.s. V, 2 (May 1965), 85–91, 93 [and plate facing p. 74].
Extensive extracts from a notebook used during 1927–1936 and now in the British Museum. A few words from this notebook are also quoted in Sotheby's sale catalogue, 11 May 1964, p. 32.

G 41 Auden, W. H. *Opere poetiche*. Milan, Rome: Lerici, [1966–1969].
Vol. 1 contains a manuscript facsimile of "The door," in the version beginning "Out of it steps our future, through this door...," p. 426; and vol. 2 a manuscript facsimile of "Autumn song," p. 178.

G 42 White, Eric Walter. *Stravinsky: the composer and his works*. London: Faber; Berkeley: University of California Press, [1966].
Manuscript facsimile of a page from a notebook used in writing *The rake's progress*, p. 415.

G 43 Sotheby and Co. *Catalogue of nineteenth century and modern first editions*. 12–13 July 1966.
Manuscript facsimile of the dedication page in John Hayward's copy of *Poems* (1928), p. 5.

G 44 *Poetry in the making: catalogue of an exhibition of poetry manuscripts in the British Museum, April–June 1967*, by Jenny Lewis. [London]: Turret Books, [1967].
Extracts from the manuscript of "Having abdicated with comparative ease...," pp. 40–41. Plate IV is a manuscript facsimile of an early draft of "Down there."

G 45 Rodway, Allan, ed. *Poetry of the 1930's*. [London]: Longmans, [1967].
Five poems appear in texts revised by Auden, pp. 21–22, 24, 33–37, 40–42.

G 46 *Proposal for an independent review*. [London: the signatories, Summer 1967.]
Single sheet signed by W. H. Auden, Isaiah Berlin, John Gross, Stuart Hampshire, Frank Kermode, Karl Miller, Stephen Spender. Issued after it was revealed that the C.I.A. had been partly responsible for backing the magazine *Encounter*. Auden withdrew poems in proof with the magazine at that time.

G 47 Dodds, E. R. Background to a poet: memories of Birmingham, 1924–36. *Shenandoah*, XVIII, 2 (Winter 1967), 8–10.
Brief transcripts from schoolboy poems.

G 48 Izzo, Carlo. "Goodbye to the Mezzogiorno." *Shenandoah*, XVIII, 2 (Winter 1967), 82.
Early readings from this poem.

G 49   Sotheby and Co. *Catalogue of nineteenth century and modern first editions*. 8–9 July 1968.
Manuscript facsimile of a page from a notebook used during 1934–35, plate facing p. 128.

G 50   Esar, Evan. *20,000 quips and quotes*. Garden City, N.Y.: Doubleday, [1968].
One sentence by Auden quoted from an unidentified interview, p. 87.

G 51   Mendelson, Edward. Auden's landscape. Ph.D., Johns Hopkins University, 1969.
Four lines from the 1945 revision of *The Ascent of F 6* performed at Swarthmore College, p. 123.

G 52   *Gerard Malanga is available*. New York: Andy Warhol Films, [1969].
A publicity flyer with one sentence by Auden.

G 53   [Statement in an advertisement for *The public life*, a periodical.] *New York review of books*, XII, 1 (16 January 1969), 20.

H

INTERVIEWS

This list, which is undoubtedly incomplete, includes those interviews in which Auden discusses his work in particular or poetry in general. Brief comments to the press on other matters are excluded. Some more formal interviews will be found in section C. Extensive quotations from Auden's conversation may also be found in Isherwood's *Lion and shadows*, Spender's *World within world*, and Stravinsky and Craft's *Dialogues and a diary*, *Themes and episodes*, and *Retrospectives and conclusions*.

H 1   Marriott, R. B.   W. H. Auden: "Dramatists should go to the music-hall." *Era*, 5 February 1936, p. 20.

H 2   "Quis." Mr Auden og fyrirætlanir hans. *Sunnudagsblað vísis* (Supplement to *Vísir*, Reykjavik), XXVI, 175 (28 June 1936), 5.

H 3   Appel, Benjamin. The exiled writers. *Saturday review of literature*, XXIII, 26 (19 October 1940), 5.

H 4   Zeiger, Arthur. Wystan Hugh Auden. M.A., Columbia University, 1941.
Quoted on pp. 60, 62, 67, 72.

H 5   Lyman, Dick. Rumors, awe surround Auden's arrival here. *Phoenix* (Swarthmore College), LXII, 2 (20 October 1942), 1.

H 6   Oursler, April. Purpose of poetry explained by Auden. *College news* (Bryn Mawr College), 14 October 1943, pp. 1, 4.

H 7   Seabury, Paul. Auden, would-be mine operator favors ungodly but intelligent. *Phoenix* (Swarthmore College), LXIII, 3 (14 December 1943), 3.

H 8   Cranston, Maurice. Poet's retreat. *John o'London's weekly*, LVII, 1329 (6 February 1948), [49]–50.

H 9   D[olbier], M[aurice]. Interviewing a poet at the breakfast table. *Providence journal*, 20 January 1952, section 6, p. 8.

H 10   Cézan, Claude. Le poète W. H. Auden nous présente l'oeuvre du XXᵉ siècle. *Nouvelles littéraires*, 1285 (17 April 1952), 1.

H 11   Beckley, Paul V. Librettists' reading to herald Stravinsky's "Rake's progress." *New York herald tribune*, 26 January 1953, p. 17.

H 12   Hewes, Henry. Broadway postscript: "Rake's progress." *Saturday review*, XXXVI, 7 (14 February 1953), 43.

H 13   Poets do better, one of them says. *Los Angeles times*, 16 March 1954, pp. 1, 3.

H 14   Spania, N. O poiētēs W. H. Auden. *Kypriaka grammata*, XIX, 233 (November 1954), 420–22.

H 15   Settanni, Ettore. Intervista ad Ischia con il poeta Auden. *Il giornale* (Naples), 10 October 1955, p. 9. [Not seen.]

H 16   Fields, Sidney. Only human. *New York mirror*, 29 January 1956, p. 35.

H 17   Mangini, Cecilia. Poesia senza oscurità. *Il punto* (Rome), 2 November 1957, p. 16. [Not seen].

H 18   Handler, M. S. Austria restful, W. H. Auden finds. *New York times*, 2 November 1958, section 1, p. 133.

H 19   Schmied, Wieland. Ein Ort für Dichter: Besuch bei W. H. Auden in Kirchstetten. *Die Presse* (Vienna), 5 July 1959, p. 17.

H 20   Koprowsky, Jan. Z Audenem o Polsce, Austrii i literaturze. *Odgłosy* (Łódź), II, 43 (25 October 1959), 8.

H 21   [Interview with] Alberico Sala. *Inventario*, XIV, 1–6 (January–December 1959), 344–346.

H 22   Koprowsky, Jan. Spotkanie z W. H. Audenem. *Życie literackie*, X, 12 (20 March 1960), 10.
A revised and expanded version appears in Koprowsky's book, Z *południa i północy* (Katowice: Śląsk, 1963), pp. 143–48.

H 23   "Difficult poetry" [partial transcript of an interview with P. H. Burton.] *Listener*, LXIII, 1623 (5 May 1960), 787–88.

H 24   Allsop, Kenneth. W. H. Auden on the economics of poetry. *Daily mail*, 15 June 1960, p. 8.

H 25   Aronson, S. M. L. It must be the poet. *Yale daily news*, 11 December 1963, p. 3.

H 26   Skáldið Auden í Íslandsvikíng í annað sinn. *Vísir*, 13 April 1964, pp. 1, 5.

H 27   Spjall við Auden. *Morgunblaðið* (Reykjavik), 14 April 1964, p. 12, 17.
Signed "M."

H 28   Ohlsson, Joel. Möte med Auden. *Lundagård*, XLV, 9 (1964), 5.

H 29   Sabljak, Tomislav. Susret s W. H. Audenem: zapravo, davno smo se već sreli. *Telegram* (Zagreb), V, 225 (14 August 1964), 3, 8.

H 30   Gustafsson, Lars. Frukost med mr Auden. *Expressen* (Stockholm), 26 November 1964, p. 4.

H 31   Jacobsen, Cornelia. Ein Halbes Jahr zu Gast in Berlin. *Die Zeit*, XX, 17 (23 April 1965), 22.

H 32   S., C. The poet who preaches love. *Glasgow herald,* 28 August 1965, p. 6.

H 33   Burstall, Christopher. Portrait gallery. *Sunday times magazine,* 21 November 1965, pp. 22–24.

H 34   Park, Lea Gibbs. Poet of perspectives. Ph.D., Northwestern University, 1966.
Quoted on pp. 206, 229, 363.

H 35   The elvish mode. *New Yorker,* XLI, 48 (15 January 1966), 24.

H 36   Stadlen, Peter. Beyond the reach of words. *Daily telegraph,* 29 October 1966, p. 11.

H 37   Campbell, Jeremy. In the house where Trotsky lived, W. H. Auden re-writes the Ring. *Evening standard,* 14 December 1966, p. 7.
Auden in fact has no plans to translate the Ring cycle.

H 38   Platt, Polly. W. H. Auden. *American scholar,* XXXVI, 2 (Spring 1967), 266–70.

H 39   Hodson, Phillip. W. H. Auden interviewed on the occasion of his poetry reading at the Union. *Isis,* 1544 (8 November 1967), 14.

H 40   Sokolov, Raymond A. Auden at sixty. *Newsweek,* LXXI, 5 (29 January 1968), 77–78.

H 41   Pryce-Jones, David. The rebel who got away. *Daily telegraph magazine,* 201 (9 August 1968), 20–22.
Reprinted in an abbreviated form in *Holiday,* XLV, 6 (June 1969), 56, 66–67.

H 42   Campbell, Jean. Moon madness and the poet. *Evening standard,* 1 January 1969, p. 11.

H 43   Honan, William H. Le mot juste for the moon. *Esquire,* LXXII, 1 (July 1969), 140–41.
Includes Auden's suggestion for the first words to be spoken on the moon.

H 44   Rogers, Byron. Poet's lament for bored youth. *Times,* 11 July 1969, p. 2.

H 45   Barnes, Susan. This island now: Britain through the eyes of its most famous living poet. *Sun* (London), 12 July 1969, p. 3.

H 46   "Pendennis." Are we going to survive? *Observer,* 21 September 1969, p. 44.
Includes an account of Auden's address to a conference at Stockholm.

H 47   Campbell, Jean. Lonely Auden: will Oxford give him refuge? *Evening standard,* 10 December 1969, p. 19.

I

PUBLISHED LETTERS

LETTERS written for publication are listed in other sections of the bibliography.

I 1 [Early 1930's]. John Pudney. *Home and away*. London: Michael Joseph, [1960].
On group-life and sexual attitudes, p. 206.

I 2 4 May 1932. Peter Stansky and William Abrahams. *Journey to the frontier*. London: Constable; Boston: Atlantic-Little, Brown [1966].
To John Cornford; complete letter on writing, pp. 173–74.

I 3 [Late 1933?]. B. C. Bloomfield. *W. H. Auden: a bibliography*. Charlottesville: University Press of Virginia, [1964].
To T. S. Eliot; briefly quoted on the printing of *Poem* (1933), p. 11.

I 4 28 January 1934. Frank Hollings bookshop. *First editions ... catalogue no. 289*. London, 1957.
Brief quotation from a letter to Geoffrey Grigson, p. 1.

I 5 4 December 1934. House of Books, Ltd. [*Catalogue*.] New York, [January 1960?].
Briefly quoted on school books, p. 3.

I 6 1935, 1935, and 1966. Alan Hancox, [bookseller]. *Catalogue no. 114*. Cheltenham, 1969, items 10, 11, 13.
Briefly quoted from three letters; to Geoffrey Grigson (on a contribution to *New verse*, and on a review of *The poet's tongue*) and to an enquirer (on the origin of the name Wystan). A longer extract from the third of these letters, dated 20 March [1966], appears in Paul C. Richards Autographs, *Catalogue no. 47* [Brookline, Mass., 1970], p. 6.

I 7 [Summer 1935?]. *The Beacon bulletin*, 14 (Paul C. Richards's catalogue 23, Brookline, Mass., [1967]), p. 5.
Briefly quoted on joining the G.P.O. film unit.

I 8 [Late 1936?]. Erika and Klaus Mann. *Escape to life*. Boston: Houghton Mifflin, 1939.
Three sentences on Auden's plans to go to Spain, p. 163.

I 9 [1938?]. John Lehmann. *The whispering gallery*. London: Longmans; New York: Harcourt Brace, [1955].
Briefly quoted on the influence of Hopkins, p. 329. Also printed in Lehmann's *In my own time* (Boston: Little, Brown, 1969), p. 221.

I 10   [March 1939?]. Frank MacShane. *The life and work of Ford Madox Ford.* London: Routledge & Kegan Paul; New York: Horizon Press, [1965].
To Ford; quoted on Auden's wish to meet him, p. 257.

I 11   21 March 1940 and [1946?]. Parke-Bernet Galleries. *Catalogue of sale 2254.* New York, 11 February 1964.
Brief quotations from two social notes, p. 5.

I 12   12 November 1941. Margaret Church. For this is Orpheus: or, Rilke, Auden and Spender. M.A., Columbia University, 1942.
Complete letter on Auden's German influences, p. iii.

I 13   [February 1945?]. Malcolm Cowley. Auden's versification. *Poetry,* LXV, 6 (March 1945), 345.
Indirectly quoted on verse forms in *The sea and the mirror.*

I 14   17 February 1947. *A creative century.* [Austin: Humanities Research Center], University of Texas, 1964.
To Lee Hollander; on Skaldic poetry and *The age of anxiety,* pp. 7, 9.

I 15   17 February 1947. Cecil E. Hinkel. A production study and text of the Auden and Isherwood *The ascent of F6* as presented at Catholic University. M.F.A., Catholic University, 1947.
Complete letter on productions of *The ascent of F6,* p. 36 of the appendix.

I 16   17 September 1947. Kenneth Lewars. The quest in Auden's poems and plays. M.A., Columbia University, 1947.
On the quest theme, and on his conversion, pp. 3, 19, 104.

I 17   12 October 1947—9 June 1951 (12 letters). Igor Stravinsky and Robert Craft. *Memories and commentaries.* Garden City, N.Y.: Doubleday, 1960; London: Faber, [1960].
Complete letters and telegrams on *The rake's progress,* pp. 145-54 and pp. 155-66 in the respective editions. This book was reprinted as part of *Stravinsky in conversation with Robert Craft* ([Harmondsworth]: Penguin, [1962]).

I 18   [1948?]. [Marie-Jacqueline Lancaster, ed.] *Brian Howard: portrait of a failure.* [London]: Blond, [1968].
To Brian Howard; on poetry, p. 493. A later [1967?] reminiscence is on p. ix.

I 19   [3 June 1948?]. Howard S. Mott [bookseller]. *Catalogue 189.* Sheffield, Mass., [1969].
Briefly quoted on students, p. 3.

I 20   17 January 1949. Dan[iel] G. Hoffman. Paul Bunyan: last of the frontier demigods. M.A., Columbia University, 1949.
Briefly quoted on *Paul Bunyan,* p. 178. Published in Hoffman's book of the same title (Philadelphia: University of Pennsylvania Press for Temple University Publications, 1952), p. 144.

I 21   22 August 1950, 1952, 8 July 1958. Carlo Izzo. "Goodbye to the Mezzogiorno." *Shenandoah,* XVIII, 2 (Winter 1967), 80-81.
Briefly quoted on Izzo's translations.

I 22   10 January 1951 and 9 April 1952. *Poesie di W. H. Auden,* introduzione, versione e note di Carlo Izzo. [Parma]: Guanda, [1952].
Briefly quoted, in Italian, on details in the poems, pp. xxiv, 218-19, 221-26, 228-29.

I 23 9 April 1952. Una lettera di W. H. Auden. *Studi Americani*, 5 (1959), 383.
To Carlo Izzo; complete letter on *The scarlet letter* as an opera.

I 24 [1958]. [Letter to the editor from D. P. M. Michael.] *Times literary supplement*, 65th year, 3337 (10 February 1966), 103.
On "A shilling life will give you all the facts"; gives Auden's letter to Michael.

I 25 [1958?] John Willett. *The theatre of Bertolt Brecht*. London: Methuen; [Norfolk, Conn.]: New Directions, [1959].
Two words on Brecht's influence, p. 220.

I 26 19 March 1962—11 May 1963 (5 letters). Monroe K. Spears. *The poetry of W. H. Auden*. New York: Oxford University Press, 1963.
Briefly quoted on influences and on details of composition of some poems, pp. 20, 157, 246, 271, 340, 341; indirect quotations on pp. 153, 230, and 241.

I 27 29 November 1962. Hugh D. Ford. *A poets' war: British poets and the Spanish civil war*. Philadelphia: University of Pennsylvania Press, 1965.
Briefly quoted on his visit to Spain, p. 288.

I 28 26 January 1963. William C. West. Concepts of reality in the poetic drama of W. B. Yeats, W. H. Auden and T. S. Eliot. Ph.D., Stanford University, 1964.
Briefly quoted on his visits to Berlin, pp. 91, 108.

I 29 30 March 1964. W. H. Auden. *Poezija*. Zagreb: Mladost, 1964 [for 1965].
To Tomislav Sabljak; briefly quoted on details of the poems, pp. 100–101.

I 30 18 March 1965. William J. Bruehl. The Auden/Isherwood plays. Ph.D., University of Pennsylvania, 1965.
On the composition of the plays, pp. 20, 29, 67, 105, 106; indirect quotations on pp. 54, 153, 232.

I 31 [Spring 1965?]. Breon Mitchell. W. H. Auden and Christopher Isherwood: the 'German influence.' *Oxford German studies*, 1 (1966), 165–166, 169–170.
Briefly quoted on the plays.

I 32 [September 1965]. *Opere poetiche di W. H. Auden*, vol. 1. Milan: Lerici, [1966].
To Aurora Ciliberti; in Italian, on revisions, p. 9.

I 33 [January 1966]. Interview with W. H. Auden. *Island* (Cambridge, Mass.), 2 (Spring 1966), 7.
To John Plotz; on revisions for CSP2.

I 34 3 March 1966. John M. Muste. *Say that we saw Spain die*. Seattle: University of Washington Press, [1966].
Briefly quoted on "Spain," p. 56.

I 35 20 April 1967. Richard Ellmann. *Eminent domain*. New York: Oxford University Press, 1967.
Briefly quoted on magic, p. 111.

J

MANUSCRIPTS BY W. H. AUDEN

THIS section cannot pretend to be complete; it merely records manuscripts that have come to light during the compilation of the bibliography. It is arranged in four divisions: first, collections and notebooks; second, manuscripts of published poems; third, manuscripts of published prose work; and fourth, manuscripts of unpublished work. The first three divisions are arranged roughly in chronological order of publication, while the fourth division is arranged by title. There are two points that ought to be noted with regard to Auden's manuscripts. First, it is generally his habit to work in notebooks when writing verse; and second, he has made a practice of making fair copies of his poems to give to his friends. The surviving typescripts of the two plays *The enemies of a bishop* and *The chase*, written in collaboration with Isherwood, are briefly described in section **K** and are not listed here.

The mansucripts of the poems listed as the Pudney Collection in the first edition of this bibliography have been dispersed, and some are now recorded in this section of the bibliography as held by other libraries. However, it has not proved possible to trace the present location of the following poems: "Hodge looks toward London," "In due season," "Consequences," "Aware," "Narcissus," "Easter Monday," "Tea-time in November," "Before," and "Quique amavit."

Collections and notebooks

J 1   Fisher collection. [1923–1928?]
The Rev. A. S. T. Fisher was friendly with Auden during the early period of his stay at Oxford. As is known, Auden was then often reluctant to commit his poetry to paper, but Mr. Fisher took some of the poems down at Auden's dictation, salvaged some of the early manuscripts, and obtained typed transcripts of some poems that Auden had written at school. The poems fall into three groups. The first consists of six typed manuscripts of early poems:
 The pumping engine, Cashwell: It is fifty years now...
 The mail-train, Crewe: Under the hundred lamps whose flare...
 Elegy: Why was it that you gave us no warning...
 So I must go my way...
 Whenever I see for the first time...
 He revisits the spot: Yes, this is the place...

The second consists of typed transcripts of somewhat later poems. These poems are numbered, and seem to be part of a collection.

3   The old colliery: The iron wheel hangs...

8   Stone walls: One almost takes a hedge for granted...   [With corrections *not* in Auden's hand]

9   The rookery: When we were half asleep we thought it seemed...   [With corrections *not* in Auden's hand]

10 Dawn: On the foaming waterfalls the flush of dawn gleams bright...   [With corrections *not* in Auden's hand]

11 Early morning: Perched on a nettled stump he stands...   [With corrections in Auden's hand]

13 Like other men, when I go past...   [A first draft MS is also present.]

14 The old lead-mine: This is the place where man has laid his hand...   [With title in Auden's hand]

21 The traction engine: Its days are over now, no farmyard airs...

25 Farglow: The room in the soft lamp glow...

26 In a train: The carriages slow...

30 Buzzards: Quite suddenly they flew...   [With title in Auden's hand]

33 After the burial: Words have been said, well-polished by use...

39 Now from far eastern wolds, the bay...

One manuscript poem is on the verso of poem 13, above:

The dew streams off the thatches...

The third group of poems is probably unrelated, consisting of transcripts made by A. S. T. Fisher and miscellaneous manuscripts:

The gypsy girl: A penny for a poor lass with a child...   [MS]

The road's your place: The stream I think persuaded me at first...   [MS, a fragment of seven lines; a transcript by A. S. T. F. of the entire poem is also present]

A wagtail splutters in the stream...   [MS; a variant of the first stanza is also present] This poem was apparently written in May 1925.

Cinders: Four walls are drawn tight round the crew of us...   [MS, dated May 28th 1927]

In a country churchyard...   [MS]

The carter's funeral: Sixty odd years of poaching and drink...   [MS]

Christmas eve: The afternoon sets red and cold...   [MS]

The canal Froghall: There runs no road except the towpath through the valley ...   [MS]

To Edward Thomas: Those thick walls never shake beneath the rumbling wheel...   [Transcribed by A. S. T. F.]

Chloe to Daphnis in Hyde Park: Stop fingering your tie; walk slower...   [Transcribed by A. S. T. F.]

Dethroned: Man finds himself no more omnipotent...   [Transcribed by A. S. T. F.]

Thomas prologizes: They are all gone upstairs into a world...   [Transcribed by A. S. T. F.]

Richard Jefferies: What of this man? No striding Amos sent...   [Transcribed by A. S. T. F.]

California (Birmingham): The twinkling lamps streamed up the hill...   [Transcribed by A. S. T. F.] This poem was transcribed from dictation by Auden's mother, who asserted that he wrote it at about the age of sixteen.

J 2   *Poems*. 1928

Corrected typescripts of 10 poems, together with some other poems and letters, formerly in the possession of Miss Caroline Newton, and now in the Berg Collection, New York Public Library.

J 3 *Manuscript notebook.* [1928–1930?]
Now in the British Museum (Add. MS 52430), formerly in the possession of Dr. T. O. Garland and given to him by Auden about 1934. Garland was the captain of Auden's house at Gresham's School and is referred to in the essay "Honour," which Auden contributed to *The old school* (1934), under the name of "Wreath." There are many excisions from this book, perhaps to be accounted for by the extraction of material for printing. The surviving material in this book which has been printed appeared in O and CSP2. There is a detailed description of the notebook by John Whitehead in the *London magazine*, May 1965.

J 4 *Manuscript notebook.* [192?–1929?]
In the possession of Alan Ansen, and containing, *inter alia*, first drafts for some of the choruses in "Paid on both sides."

J 5 *Manuscript notebook.* [August 1930—August 1932]
In Harvard College Library, where it was deposited by Ruthven Todd. The notebook contains unpublished poems and work which appears in O and LS.

J 6 *Manuscript notebook.* [September 1932–1934]
Now in Swarthmore College Library and given by Auden. The notebook contains a long unpublished poem in two cantos and other work principally published in LS. Described briefly in *Swarthmore College bulletin*, LXIV, 5 (March 1967), 24–25, with a photograph of part of one page.

J 7 *Manuscript notebook.* [1933–1934]
Containing drafts for DBS, here called *Where is Francis?*, and originally in the possesion of Frederic Prokosch to whom it was given by Auden. Sold at Sotheby's on 9 July 1968, and now in the University of Texas Library.

J 8 *Manuscript notebook.* [1937–1939]
In the possession of Christopher Isherwood. The notebook contains drafts for OTF, "Victor," "James Honeyman," and other poems.

J 9 *Manuscript notebooks.* [1940–1942]
12 notebooks containing sections of the notes to "New year letter, "The quest," "The sea and the mirror," FTB, and other poems and reviews, formerly in the possession of Miss Caroline Newton, and now in the Berg Collection, New York Public Library.

J 10 *New year letter.* 1940
Manuscript notebook containing the conclusion of Part II and Part III in the University of Texas Library.

J 11 *Manuscript notebook.* [1942–1943]
In the Lockwood Memorial Library, State University of New York at Buffalo. The book contains some sections of "The sea and the mirror."

J 12 *The age of anxiety.* 1947
Manuscript notebook containing this, and other material, now in the University of Texas Library (see *Times literary supplement*, 15 April 1965, p. 300).

The library also possesses one sheet more from another notebook which contained more of the poem. This sheet has the part beginning "Ingenious George reaches his journey's end...."

J 13 *Manuscript notebook.* [1947 and 1960–1964?]
In the British Museum (Add. MS 53772). The book contains early drafts of *The rake's progress*, of some prose essays, and of poems later printed in ATH.

J 14   *Manuscript notebook.* [1953–1954]
In the University of Texas Library containing most of the poems in SA.

J 15   *Homage to Clio.* 1960
The incomplete typescript of this book of poems is now in the University of Texas Library.

Manuscripts of individual poems

J 16   Bank holiday: The queen's hand on the King's cold shoulder falling . . .
3 pp. Manuscript in the possession of D. G. O. Ayerst.

J 17   The seekers: Consider if you will, how lovers lie . . .
1 p. Manuscript in the possession of the College of S. Mark and S. John.

J 18   The crowing of the cock . . .
3 pp. Manuscript in the University of Texas Library.

J 19   The four sat on the bare room . . .
1 p. Manuscript in Harvard College Library.

J 20   1) On the frontier at dawn getting down . . . [Zagreb, July]; 2) No trenchant parting this . . . [Dubrovnik, August]; 3) Truly our fathers had the gout . . . [Split, August]; 4) We, knowing the family history . . . [Harborne, August]; 5) Who stands the crux left of the watershed . . . [Harborne, August]; 6) Suppose they met the inevitable procedure . . . [Dalbuich, September].
7 pp. Manuscript with letter in the University of Texas Library. Poems 3 and 4 are unpublished.

J 21   This lunar beauty . . .
1 p. Typescript with MS corrections in the possession of W. D. Quesenbery, Jr.

J 22   This lunar beauty . . .
1 p. Manuscript in the possession of the University of Southern California and given by Christopher Isherwood.

J 23   Watch any day his nonchalant pauses see . . .
1 p. Manuscript in the Lockwood Memorial Library.

J 24   To return to the interest you were discussing . . .
2 pp. Typescript in Harvard College Library.

J 25   I have a handsome profile . . .
2 pp. Typescript with MS corrections in the Lockwood Memorial Library.

J 26   [Five poems.] I. Sleep on beside me though I wake for you . . .   II. I see it often since you've been away . . .   III. At the far end of the enormous room . . .   IV. The latest ferrule now has tapped the kerb . . .   V. Love had him fast: but though he caught his breath . . .
5 pp. Manuscript in the possession of D. G. O. Ayerst.

J 27   The fruit in which your parents hid you boy . . .
1 p. Manuscript with corrections in the Lockwood Memorial Library.

J 28   A bride in the '30s: Easily, my dear, you move, easily your head . . .
3 pp. Manuscript with corrections sold at Sotheby's on 19 June 1962 and now in the University of Texas Library.

J 29 Enter with him these legends love . . .
2 pp. Manuscript in the Newberry Library, Chicago.

J 30 Raynes Park [County Grammar] School song.
Manuscript [by Auden?] in the possession of the school.

J 31 The earth turns over, our side feels the cold . . .
2 fols. Manuscript in red ink with corrections in the University of Texas Library.

J 32 A shilling life will give you all the facts . . .
1 p. Manuscript in the possession of D. G. O. Ayerst.

J 33 To a writer on his birthday: August for the people and their favourite islands . . .
5 pp. Manuscript with corrections in the Lockwood Memorial Library.

J 34 The witnesses: You dowagers with Roman noses . . .
3 pp. Manuscript with corrections sold at Sotheby's on 19 June 1962 and now in the University of Texas Library.

J 35 [Fragment beginning:] Into town on the coal measures, crowded and dark . . .
1 p. Manuscript with corrections in the Lockwood Memorial Library. Part of "Speech from a play" published in *New verse*, February 1935.

J 36 Fox-trot from a play: The soldier loves his rifle . . .
2 pp. Manuscript with corrections in the Lockwood Memorial Library.

J 37 Ballad: O what is that sound which so thrills the ear . . .
2 pp. Manuscript with corrections in the Lockwood Memorial Library.

J 38 Dream: Dear though the night is gone . . .
1 p. Manuscript with corrections in the Lockwood Memorial Library.

J 39 Lay your sleeping head my love . . .
1 p. Manuscript with pencil emendations in the University of Texas Library.

J 40 Lay your sleeping head my love . . .
Manuscript written inside the front cover of the first copy of *Our hunting fathers* in the possession of Benjamin Britten.

J 41 Our hunting fathers told the story . . .
1 p. Manuscript in red ink with correction sold at Sotheby's on 19 June 1962 and now in a private English collection.

J 42 To settle in this village of the heart . . .
1 p. Manuscript with corrections in the Lockwood Memorial Library.

J 43 Poem: O who can ever praise enough . . .
1 p. Manuscript fair copy in the Lockwood Memorial Library.

J 44 Miss Gee: Let me tell you a little story . . .
4 fols. Manuscript in the University of Texas Library.

J 45 Victor: Victor was a little baby . . .
8 fols. Manuscript with emendations in the University of Texas Library.

J 46 Poem: Under the fronds of life, beside . . .
3 fols. Manuscript in the University of Texas Library.

J 47 Roman wall blues: Over the heather the wet wind blows . . .
1 p. Typescript with MS corrections in the possession of W. D. Quesenbery, Jr.

J 48 Blues: Ladies and gentlemen sitting here . . .
1 p. Manuscript with corrections in the Lockwood Memorial Library.

J 49   Calypso: Driver, drive faster and make a good run ...
1 p. Typescript with MS additions in the University of Texas Library.

J 50   Musée des beaux arts: About suffering they were never wrong ...
1 p. Manuscript in the Library of Congress.

J 51   Herman Melville: Towards the end he sailed into an extraordinary mildness ...
2 pp. Manuscript in Harvard College Library.

J 52   The prophets: Perhaps I always knew what they were saying ...
1 p. Manuscript in the possession of Alan Clodd.

J 53   The territory of the heart: Not as that dream Napoleon, rumour's dread and centre ...
1 p. Typescript in the University of Texas Library.

J 54   Crisis: Where do they come from ...
3 fols. Manuscript with corrections in the Lockwood Memorial Library.

J 55   The unknown citizen: He was found by the Bureau of Statistics to be ...
1 p. Manuscript in the Library of Congress. See its *Information bulletin*, XX (22 May 1961), [1].

J 56   In memoriam Ernst Toller: The shining neutral summer has no voice ...
1 p. Typescript with MS corrections in the University of Texas Library.

J 57   In memory of W. B. Yeats: He disappeared in the dead of winter ...
3 pp. Manuscript in the University of Texas Library. The library also possesses a typescript of the same poem.

J 58   Letter: The movies and the magazines are all of them liars ...
1 p. Typescript in the University of Texas Library.

J 59   The hero: He parried every question that they hurled ...
1 p. Typescript in the University of Texas Library.

J 60   Many happy returns: Johnny, since to-day is ...
Manuscript in the possession of John Rettger, to whom the poem is dedicated.

J 61   Mundus et infans: Kicking his mother until she let go of his soul ...
Manuscript in the possession of Albert and Angelyn Stevens, to whom the poem is dedicated.

J 62   Edward Lear: Left by his friend to breakfast alone on the white ...
1 p. Manuscript with a covering letter to the *Times literary supplement*, in the possession of Donald C. Gallup.

J 63   The journals give the quantities of wrong ...
2 fols. Typescript in the files of the magazine *Decision* in Yale University Library.

J 64   Poem: The sense of danger must not disappear ...
1 fol. Typescript in the files of the magazine *Decision* in Yale University Library.

J 65   An anthem for S. Matthew's day.
1 p. Manuscript in the possession of Benjamin Britten.

J 66   When creation shall give out another fragrance ...
1 p. Typescript in the possession of Alan Ansen. Originally conceived as the conclusion to Malin's last thought in the last section of AA, but revised and used in the *Litany and anthem for S. Matthew's day.*

J 67   Under which Lyre: Ares at last has quit the field . . .
8 pp. Manuscript in Harvard College Library.

J 68   Precious five: Be patient, solemn nose . . .
5 pp. Manuscript and typescript with MS corrections in the possession of the American Academy of Arts and Letters.

J 69   Serenade: On and on and on . . .
1 p. Manuscript with corrections in the University of Texas Library.

J 70   [Delia: or] A masque of night.
26 pp. Typescript, with a few MS corrections, marked up as printer's copy for *Botteghe oscure,* in the University of Texas Library.

J 71   The fall of Rome: The piers are pummelled by the waves . . .
1 p. Manuscript in the University of Texas Library.

J 72   [Music is international, lines 32–65:] The proud flesh founded on the self-made wound . . .
1 p. Manuscript with corrections in the Lockwood Memorial Library.

J 73   The shield of Achilles: She looked over his shoulder . . .
3 pp. Manuscript in the Library of Congress.

J 74   [To Professor Nevill Coghill:] In our beginning . . .
4 pp. Manuscript in the possession of Phillip Hodson.

J 75   Song of the devil: Ever since observation taught me temptation . . .
1 p. Manuscript with corrections in the possession of Phillip Hodson.

J 76   Two poems. Down there: A cellar underneath the house, though not lived in . . .   Up there: Men would never have come to need an attic . . .
2 pp. Typescript in Kenyon College Library.

Manuscripts of works in prose

J 77   Sermon by an armament manufacturer.
Typescript with MS corrections in the possession of John Johnson.

J 78   Honour.
Manuscript in the possession of John Johnson.

J 79   The nature of the artist.
15 pp. Manuscript with corrections in the Lockwood Memorial Library. The piece was published under the title "Psychology and art" in *The arts today* (1935).

J 80   [I want the theatre to be . . .]
1 p. Manuscript in the Berg Collection, New York Public Library.

J 81   Psychology and criticism [a review of] *In defence of Shelley* by Herbert Read.
2 pp. Manuscript with corrections in the Lockwood Memorial Library.

J 82   Selling the Group Theatre.
Typescript with MS corrections in the possession of John Johnson.

J 83   [Essay on] Robert Frost.
Manuscript in a private English collection.

J 84   [Review of] *Illusion and reality* by C. Caudwell.
3 pp. Manuscript with corrections in the Lockwood Memorial Library.

J 85 Jehovah Housman and Satan Housman [a review of] *A. E. H.: A memoir* by Laurence Housman.
3 pp. Typescript with corrections in the Lockwood Memorial Library.

J 86 Honest doubt.
2 fols. Manuscript in the University of Texas Library, with covering letter to Geoffrey Grigson. Marked as printer's copy.

J 87 Alfred: a cabaret sketch (For Therese Giehse).
8 fols. Manuscript with emendations in the University of Texas Library.

J 88 The sportsmen: a parable.
4 pp. Typescript with MS corrections in the University of Texas Library.

J 89 Speech [on the educated man].
Carbon copy of the typescript with pencilled MS corrections in Yale University Library. Partially published in *Yale daily news*, 6 March 1941, and *Yale alumni magazine*, 21 March 1941.

J 90 Squares and oblongs.
31 fols. Manuscript with typescript fair copy in the Lockwood Memorial Library.

J 91 [A review of] *Towards a philosophy of history* [by] Ortega y Gasset.
4 fols. Manuscript in the files of the magazine *Decision* in Yale University Library.

J 92 [A review of] *Where do we go from here?* [by] H. Laski.
8 fols. Manuscript in the files of the magazine *Decision* in Yale University Library.

J 93 Note [to Joan Murray, "Orpheus"].
1 p. Manuscript in the files of the magazine *Decision* in Yale University Library.

J 94 A joyful and a pleasant thing it is to be thankful.
6 pp. Manuscript in Dartmouth College Library. Partially printed as "The giving of thanks."

J 95 The guilty vicarage.
18 pp. Typescript with MS corrections in the University of Texas Library.

J 96 The enchafèd flood.
110 pp. Carbon copy of the typescript with MS corrections in the Alderman Library, University of Virginia.

J 97 The public versus the late Mr W. B. Yeats.
9 pp. Manuscript in Harvard College Library.

J 98 Reply [to the symposium on "A change of air" in *Kenyon review*].
7 pp. Typescript in Kenyon College Library.

Manuscripts of unpublished work

J 99 Ballad: He offered her his paucity . . .
1 p. Typescript with MS corrections in the possession of the College of S. Mark and S. John.

J 100 [Chart on human experience.]
1 p. Manuscript in Swarthmore College Library. Published in *Connecticut review*, I, 2 (April 1968), 44.

J 101 Daydreams of a tourist: Across the waste to Northward, go . . .
1 p. Manuscript in the Berg Collection, New York Public Library.

J 102   The evolution of the dragon: Your shoulder stiffens to my kiss . . .
2 pp. Manuscript in the Berg Collection, New York Public Library, including other poems.

J 103   First meeting: A wind felt for the breastbone . . .
1 p. Manuscript in the possession of the College of S. Mark and S. John.

J 104   The happy tree: The blossoms burgeon sumptuously . . .
1 p. Manuscript in the Lockwood Memorial Library.

J 105   Here Marie Antoinette the fair French queen . . .
3 pp. Manuscript [from a dramatic scene?] in the Lockwood Memorial Library.

J 106   The last of the old year: My latest love appeared to me . . .
1 p. Typescript with MS addition in the possession of the College of S. Mark and S. John.

J 107   Poem: 'Sweet is it', say the doomed, 'to be alive though wretched . . .
3 pp. Typescript in the University of Texas Library.

J 108   Pride: When Little Claus met Big Claus in the road . . .
1 p. Manuscript in the Berg Collection, New York Public Library.

J 109   [Prologue:] Tyrone Guthrie who is tall and thin . . .
4 fols. Manuscript in the Berg Collection, New York Public Library.

J 110   Say yes!: They climbed a mountain in the afternoon . . .
1 p. Typescript with one MS correction in the Berg Collection, New York Public Library.

J 111   A song after Sappho: What's the loveliest thing in the eye . . .
1 p. Manuscript in the possession of Benjamin Britten.

J 112   This morning any touch is possible . . .
4 pp. Manuscript in the possession of Lester Littlefield.

J 113   Time flies, Cecil, hardly a week ago . . .
2 pp. Manuscript in the University of Texas Library.

J 114   Three fragments for films. [Pencil MS of "O lurcher loving collier"; 2 sections from the film *God's chillun*; a section of commentary to *Night mail*.]
6 fols. Typescript with MS emendations. The second section of the *God's chillun* draft contains an early version of "Acts of injustice done. . . ." In the University of Texas Library.

J 115   To Robert Russell.
Dedicatory poem on the flyleaf of a copy of *Continual dew* by John Betjeman (1937), in the New York Public Library.

J 116   Vocation and society.
12 pp. Typescript with MS corrections in Swarthmore College Library. Auden's Phi Beta Kappa address at Swarthmore, 15 January 1943.

J 117   What's the idea in looking so sad . . .
1 p. Manuscript in Harvard College Library.

J 118   When the postman knocks . . .
1 p. Manuscript in the possession of Benjamin Britten.

J 119   Winter afternoon: The office sunlight, edging back, protrudes . . .
1 p. Typescript with MS corrections in the possession of the College of S. Mark and S. John.

K

UNPUBLISHED AND UNFINISHED WORK

THIS section gathers Auden's unpublished plays, mimeographed texts, uncompleted work, and other projects. These lists cannot claim to be complete. For notes on Auden's film scripts and unpublished radio plays, see sections **L** and **M**.

Unpublished plays

In addition to the works listed below, five minor items should be noted. Auden prepared a brief prologue and epilogue for a production titled *The Group Theatre in songs, dances and a play* performed at the Croydon Repertory theatre, 24 July 1933. The prologue uses characters from the play which immediately followed it, *Lancelot of Denmark*, a fifteenth-century Danish play, and a 4-fol. manuscript survives in the Berg Collection, New York Public Library; the epilogue is apparently lost.

Auden adapted Cocteau's *Orphée* for a production at the Downs School Christmas songfest in 1933. His adaptation of the medieval mystery play *The deluge* was performed by the Group Theatre on a double bill with DD, 25 February and 4 March 1934, and again at the Downs School Easter songfest, 1934. Auden also wrote a topical "revue" for a performance at the Downs, 12 December 1934.[1] In *Rosina*, the Smith College faculty play, performed 17 April 1953, "the recitative of the Ghost [the character "Pa Greenseed," acted by Auden] was composed by the song team of W. H. Auden and W. A. Mozart" (from the programme); no manuscript of this topical farce has survived.

K 1 *The enemies of the bishop, or, die when I say when: a morality in four acts.* [1930?]
This play was Auden and Isherwood's first collaboration, and survives as a carbon-copy typescript in Isherwood's possession. Mardi Valgemae gives a brief description in *Huntington library quarterly*, XXI (August 1968), 373–75.

K 2 *The chase.* [1934]
Auden completed this play around Autumn 1934 and sent a fully revised carbon-copy

---

[1] Described by A. W. in *Badger* (Downs School magazine), III, 5 (Spring 1935), 19. Early drafts are in a notebook now in the University of Texas Library.

of the typescript to Isherwood, who suggested numerous changes, through which the play eventually became *The dog beneath the skin* (see notes to A9a). Auden gave another copy to Nevill Coghill, who in 1939 gave it to the library of Exeter College, Oxford. This copy has 98 leaves and includes corrections in Auden's hand; Breon Mitchell first called attention to its existence in *Oxford German studies*, 1 (1966), 170–71. A further revised copy of the same typescript, with two additional pages inserted, is now in the Berg Collection, New York Public Library; this copy had been used by Rupert Doone, apparently in planning a Group Theatre production. The play is described in detail by John Fuller in *A Reader's guide to W. H. Auden* (London: Thames and Hudson; New York: Farrar, Straus and Giroux, 1970), pp. 80–83. The process of revision from *The chase* to *The dog beneath the skin* is described by Mardi Valgemae in *Huntington library quarterly*, XXXI (August 1968), 373–83.[2]

K 3   *Paul Bunyan.* [1941]

This opera libretto, with music by Benjamin Britten, was performed at Columbia University, 5–10 May 1941, directed by Milton Smith. The work was later withdrawn by Britten, who used it as a quarry for later work. The text survives as a 47 fol. mimeographed libretto (a copy is in the Columbia University Music Library), as a line-copy vocal score containing the text of the songs (different parts are in the Columbia University Music Library and the music division of the Library of Congress), and as 24-side, 78 r.p.m. recording of one of the performances, including some material not in the libretto or score (the only copy is in the Brander Matthews Dramatic Museum at Columbia). The libretto was copyrighted 26 April 1941 (DU 3992; the copyright copy has not survived). The programme of the performance quotes a few words by Auden describing the work, and a full description appears in Daniel G. Hoffman, *Paul Bunyan: last of the frontier demigods* (Philadelphia: University of Philadelphia Press for Temple University Publications, 1952), pp. 143–53, and in Eric Walter White, *Benjamin Britten: his life and operas* (London: Faber, 1970), pp. 95–99, 234–35.

Contains:

The single creature leads a partial life... Reprinted in *Harper's bazaar*, April 1945, CP, CSP, and CSP2.

Gold in the North came the blizzard to say... Reprinted in CP and CSP.

You've no idea how dull it is... First printed in *New Yorker*, 24 August 1940 ("The glamour boys and girls have grievances too").

Carry her over the water... Reprinted in CP, CSP and CSP2.

Reviews:

O. Downes. *New York times*, 6 May 1941, p. 25.

R. A. Simon. *New Yorker*, XVII (17 May 1941), 65–66.

Time, XXXVIII (19 May 1941), 94.

K 4   *The Duchess of Malfi.* [1946]

This adaptation of Webster's play was begun by H. R. Hays and Bertolt Brecht in 1942–43, but about 1945 Auden joined the collaboration, and Hays dropped out. Auden copyrighted one version on 24 October 1945 (DU 95637; now in the Copyright Office of the Library of Congress); a photocopy of a carbon-copy of this version owned by Ruth Berlau, with notes in Auden's hand, is in the Bertolt-Brecht-Archiv in Berlin (BBA 1767/1–67+).[3] Another version was copyrighted by Auden

---

[2] Valgemae's article also mentions *The fronny*, described by Isherwood as an early draft of *The dance of death* (p. 376).

[3] Bertolt-Brecht-Archiv, *Bestandsverzeichnis des literarischen Nachlasses*, vol. 1: *Stücke* (Berlin: Der Aufbau, 1969), p. 181 (item 2078). The Archiv also owns a 3 fol. draft and a 7 p. draft in Auden's hand (BBA 1178/143–146+ and BBA 1178/147–157+; *ibid.*, pp. 204–5 [items 2372–73]).

and Brecht on 4 April 1946 (DU 2445; now in the Copyright Office). The final version, by Auden alone, opened in New York at the Barrymore Theatre on 15 October 1946, directed by George Rylands and with music by Benjamin Britten. For a note on the production, see *John Webster: a critical anthology,* ed. by G. K. and S. K. Hunter (Harmondsworth: Penguin, 1969), p. 309.
Reviews:
    B. Atkinson. *New York times,* 16 October 1946, p. 35.
    J. W. Krutch. *Nation,* CLXIII (2 November 1946), 510.
    M. McCarthy. *Partisan review,* XIV (January–February 1947), 64–65.
    S. Young. *New republic,* CXV (28 October 1946), 556–57.

K 5   *The rise and fall of the city of Mahagonny.* [1960]
This translation of Brecht's libretto, by Auden and Chester Kallman, was copyrighted on 1 September 1960 (DU 51627; now in the Copyright Office), but has apparently not been produced. Scenes 18 through the end were published in *Delos,* 4 (1970), 29–44.

K 6   *Arcifanfano, king of fools; or, it's always too late to learn.* [1965]
This translation by Auden and Kallman of the libretto by Goldoni was copyrighted on 8 January 1963 (DU 56852; now in the Copyright Office), and was first performed to the score by Dittersdorf at Town Hall, New York, on 11 November 1965, in the series of Clarion Concerts. The translation was partially printed on pp. [4–9] of the programme, and was reprinted in the programme of a repeat performance at Carnegie Hall, New York, 5 January 1966, pp. [5–10]. Fourteen lines are quoted by Raymond Ericson in "Dittersdorf's six 'mad' ones," *New York times,* 24 October 1965, section 2, pp. 19, 29.

Mimeographed texts

The mimeographed libretto of *Paul Bunyan* is described above; the mimeographed film scripts of *Runner* and *US* are mentioned in section **L**. Transcripts of radio and television broadcasts are not listed. The Swarthmore College Library has a copy of a mimeographed version of Auden's "Swarthmore chart" (see **G14**); this was prepared by Samuel Hynes and has no textual authority.

K 7   *Fate and the individual in European literature.* [Ann Arbor, Mich., 1941.]
A 2 fol. reading list for Auden's course at the University of Michigan, fall semester, 1941.

K 8   *Poetry and freedom.* [Charlottesville, Va.], 27 February 1948.
A 9 fol. leaflet containing Auden's address to the McGregor Room Seminar in Contemporary Poetry and Prose at the University of Virginia. Copies located are at the University of Virginia Library and the National Library of Scotland.

K 9   *Prime.* [Swarthmore, Pa., 9 March 1950.]
Auden distributed a 3 fol. leaflet containing the text of the poem and portions of earlier drafts at his lecture "Nature, history and poetry," at Swarthmore College. Spears quotes from the early versions in *The poetry of W. H. Auden,* pp. 317–18. Some copies of this leaflet were later included between pp. 4 and 5 of a mimeographed transcript of the entire lecture (7 fols., but 10 fols. with *Prime*), titled: *Transcript of a speech by W. H. Auden, under the auspices of the Cooper Foundation and the Department of English, at Swarthmore College on March 9, 1950.*

K 10 *Address of W. H. Auden, National Book Award.* New York, 7 February 1956.
The National Book Committee distributed this 3 fol. leaflet as a press release. There is a lengthy excerpt in *Publishers' weekly*, CLXIX, 7 (18 February 1956), 1016–17.

K 11 *The pattern and the way.* Venice, 16 September 1958.
This 9 fol. leaflet is a preprint of Auden's opening address to the round table discussions of tradition and innovation held under the sponsorship of the Fondazione Giorgio Cini and the Congress for Cultural Freedom, in collaboration with the Contemporary Music Festival of the Biennale. The cover title is given above; the title on the first page of the text reads *The model and the way.* A partial Italian translation appears in the course of an article by Piero Nardi in *L'Italia che scrive*, XLII, 1 (January 1959), 1–3.

K 12 *The seven deadly sins,* translated from the German text of Bert Brecht. [New York, 1959.]
This 9 fol. leaflet containing the translation by Auden and Kallman was used in rehearsals for the New York City Ballet production, which opened on 13 May 1959. The text was later published in *Tulane drama review*, September 1961 (C 590).

K 13 *Culture and leisure.* [Washington, D.C.], 26 February 1966.
A 12 fol. leaflet containing the text of Auden's lecture at the Catholic University of America under the auspices of UNESCO. The fullest excerpt from this lecture appears in *Ekistics*, November 1967; a briefer excerpt first appeared in *Unesco features*, August [II] 1966 (see C 688 for further details).

K 14 *Acceptance speech by W. H. Auden upon receipt of the 1967 National Medal for Literature.* New York, 30 November 1967.
This 4 fol. leaflet was distributed by the National Book Committee as a press release. The text was published in full in *Washington post*, 3 December 1967 (see C 720 for further details).

K 15 *Acceptance by Wystan Hugh Auden of the gold medal of the Institute for poetry.* [New York, 28 May 1968.]
A 6 fol. leaflet with Auden's address, which was read for him at a dinner meeting of the National Institute of Arts and Letters. Printed in *Proceedings of the American Academy of Arts and Letters and the National Institute of Arts and Letters*, 1969 (C 743).

Unfinished work

At least four uncompleted projects for books and plays have been mentioned in print: "a kind of travel book [on America], successor to their *Journey to a war*, to be called *Address not known*," planned briefly by Auden and Isherwood in Autumn 1938;[4] "a commentary on many things called *Thinks*," mentioned in 1952;[5] "a musical based on *Goodbye to Berlin*," planned with Isherwood and Chester Kallman;[6] and *Man of La Mancha*, a musical version of *Don Quixote*, for which Auden and Kallman prepared some lyrics in 1963–64, which were not used in the version eventually

---

[4] John Lehmann, *I am my brother* (London: Longmans, 1960), p. 14.
[5] [Notes on contributors], *Thought*, XXVII (Spring 1952), 2.
[6] Christopher Isherwood, "A conversation on tape," *London magazine*, n.s. I (June 1961). 51.

produced.[7] Auden was also commissioned by *Life* magazine to write the final article in a series "The Romans," published 3 March–17 June 1966;[8] this article was written but not published.

Two announced "works-in-progress" seem never to have been planned at all. Auden says he knows nothing of *La gran tenda verde,* mentioned in 1964 as a collaboration with Chester Kallman,[9] and that a newspaper report that he was translating Wagner's Ring cycle in 1966 was entirely in error.[10]

[7] *New York times,* 4 August 1963, section 2, p. 1; see also "Lady's man moves on," *Observer,* 24 January 1965, p. 22.

[8] See *Life,* LX (4 March 1966), 3.

[9] *Contemporary authors,* vols. 9–10 (Detroit: Gale Research, 1964), p. 27.

[10] *Evening standard,* 14 December 1966, p. 7.

L

FILMS

For six months in 1935–36 Auden worked with the G.P.O. Film Unit on a number of projects, some of them never completed. In addition to writing verse and commentary for the films listed below, Auden probably wrote part of the commentary for another called *Beside the seaside* (1935, produced by the Strand Film Company, directed by Marion Grierson, on behalf of the Travel Association of Great Britain and Ireland, and later distributed by Tida Films) although he is not listed in the credits, and for which the poem "On this island" was written,[1] although it is not used on the soundtrack. Auden also played Father Christmas in *Calendar of the year* (1936, produced by John Grierson for the G.P.O. Film Unit, music by Benjamin Britten).

For a showing of Dziga Vertov's film *Three songs of Lenin,* by the Film Society, London, 27 October 1935, Auden helped prepare a translation of the Uzbek songs.[2]

L 1 *Coal face.* 1935
Produced by John Grierson for the G.P.O. Film Unit, directed by Alberto Cavalcanti, music by Benjamin Britten, verse by W. H. Auden (published in *New verse,* Summer 1938). Reviewed by Arthur Vesselo, *Sight and sound,* IV, 16 (Winter 1935–36), 177. The text of the poem "O lurcher-loving collier, black as night…" appears in: *The film society programme,* 81st performance, 27 October 1935, p. [2], and is preceded by a paragraph of notes, not by Auden.

L 2 *Night mail.* 1936
Produced by John Grierson for the G.P.O. Film Unit, directed by Harry Watt and Basil Wright, music by Benjamin Britten, verse for the final section of the film by W. H. Auden (published in *GPO film library: notes and synopses, 1936* and *1937* and *1938,* as well as in *TPO: centenary of the Travelling Post Office* [1938], as a broadside, and in CSP2). Reviewed by Arthur Vesselo, *Sight and sound,* V, 17 (Spring 1936), 28–29.

L 3 *The way to the sea.* 1937
Produced by Paul Rotha for the Strand Film Company, directed by J. B. Holmes,

---

[1] *Janus,* May 1936, p. 12, reports that Auden contributed to a film titled *By the seaside,* which is probably this film. On a taped reading (23 March 1961) now in Yale University Library, Auden said that "On this island" was written for a film never completed; but an early draft of a commentary for *Beside the seaside* may have occasioned the poem.
[2] The programme mentions that Auden "kindly advis[ed] on the English rendering of many passages in the songs". The texts were not published.

music by Benjamin Britten. Verse for the final third of the film by W. H. Auden (unpublished) occupies most of the second reel and describes the train journey from Waterloo station to Portsmouth harbour. A print of the film is now in the National Film Archive, and the negative is held by George Humphries Ltd. Reviewed by Arthur Vesselo, *Sight and sound*, V, 20 (Winter 1936–37), 143.

L 4   *The Londoners.* 1939

Produced by John Grierson and the Realist Film Unit for the British Commercial Gas Association, directed by John Taylor, "Sections of commentary," by W. H. Auden (unpublished). The film is described and two lines of the commentary quoted in *Time*, XXXIII (24 April 1939), 66; reviewed by Arthur Rice, *Sight and sound*, VII, 29 (Spring 1939), 36.

L 5   *God's chillun.* 1939

Produced by the G.P.O. Film Unit, edited by Max Anderson, Rona Morrison, and Gordon Hales, words by W. H. Auden, music by Benjamin Britten. This brief film deals with the introduction of Negro slavery into the West Indies, its abolition, and the subsequent development of the islands. Auden's commentary is set to musical recitative by Britten. Britten has his musical drafts with Auden's words, and there is one page of typescript in the University of Texas Library. A brief note on the film appears in *Sight and sound*, VII, 28 (Winter 1938–39), 171. Further information on this and other films appears in: Basil Wright, "Britten and documentary," *Musical times*, CIV (November 1963), 779–80.

L 6   *Runner.* 1962

Produced by Tom Daly for the National Film Board of Canada, directed by Ronald Owen, narration by W. H. Auden (distributed as a 3 fol. mimeographed leaflet by the Commercial Division); describing Bruce Kidd. Published in CWW.

L 7   *US.* 1968

Produced by Francis Thompson Associates and directed by Theodore Holcomb for the U.S. Department of Commerce and shown at the U.S. Pavilion at Hemisfair '68, San Antonio, Texas. Music by David Amram, and narration by W. H. Auden (distributed as a 3 fol. mimeographed leaflet, and partially reprinted on pp. 14 and 16 of the exhibition leaflet *Confluence, U.S.A.*, by the U.S. Department of Commerce). Reviewed by Joseph Morgenstern, *Newsweek*, LXXI (20 May 1968), 96, 100; and by Richard Schickel, *Life*, LXIV (28 June 1968), 8.

M

RADIO AND TELEVISION PRODUCTIONS
AND APPEARANCES

THE first half of this section lists those works Auden devised especially for broadcasting. The BBC has produced adaptations of *The dog beneath the skin*, *The ascent of F 6*, and of Auden's translation of Cocteau's *The knights of the round table*, but none of these has any textual authority and they are not listed here. The second half of this section is devoted to an attempt at listing Auden's appearances before the microphone or on the small screen.

Productions

M 1   *Up the garden path.* 1937
A recital of bad music and bad poetry chosen by Benjamin Britten and W. H. Auden and broadcast in the BBC Regional programme on 13 June 1937.

M 2   *Hadrian's wall: an historical survey.* 1937
Produced by John Pudney and first broadcast in the Regional programme of the BBC from Newcastle on 25 November 1937. The incidental music was by Britten, and a transcript is held by the BBC. The poem "Roman wall blues" was written for this broadcast.

M 3   *The dark valley.* 1940
First broadcast in the CBS Columbia workshop on 2 June 1940. The music was by Britten. A secretarial transcript is held by CBS, and the published version is more fully described elsewhere in the bibliography (**B 25**).

M 4   *Pride and prejudice.*   1940
This "extraction" of the novel was prepared by Auden, but was greatly rewritten by John Houseman, to whom it was entirely attributed when broadcast by the CBS radio network in the Helen Hayes Theater, 24 November 1940.

M 5   *The rocking-horse winner.* 1940
This dramatization by Auden and James Stern of a short story by D. H. Lawrence was first broadcast in the CBS Columbia workshop on 6 April 1941. The music was by Britten. A secretarial transcript is held by CBS. "To CBS came a script hand-written in green ink—by W. H. Auden. It was about horse-racing. He got $100 for it, which he shared with a friend who had been able to provide him with information on betting procedures" (Eric Barnouw, *The golden web* [New York: Oxford University Press, 1968], p. 69).

M 6   *The magic flute.* 1956
This translation by Auden and Kallman was first broadcast on television by the NBC Opera Theatre on 15 January 1956. The piece is more fully described elsewhere in the bibliography (**A 37**).

M 7 *Don Giovanni.* 1960
This translation by Auden and Kallman was first broadcast on television by the NBC
Opera Theatre on 10 April 1960. The piece is more fully described elsewhere in the
bibliography (B 74).

Appearances

This list is principally compiled from information supplied by the BBC and
by networks and broadcasting stations in the United States. Broadcasts
about Auden, or in which his poems are read by others, have been excluded.
During his visit to Spain in 1937 Auden is believed to have broadcast on behalf of the Republican side, but no information seems to be available about
these broadcasts.

M 8 Poems I enjoy, chosen and introduced by W. H. Auden.   BBC
Regional programme, 11 November 1937.

M 9 In defence of gossip.   BBC National programme, 13 December 1937.
Published in *Listener,* 22 December 1937.

M 10 [Discussion with Christopher Isherwood on *The ascent of F6.*]
"Speaking personally," BBC television, 12 October 1938.

M 11 [Reading "In the square."]   "The modern muse," BBC National
programme, 18 October 1938.

M 12 A recent visit to China.   "Midland magazine," BBC Midland Home
service, 16 January 1939.
Published in *Listener,* 2 February 1939.

M 13 The function of the writer in the political crisis [a dialogue between Klaus Mann and W. H. Auden].   "Forum," WEVD [New York],
19 March 1941.
A copy of a 9 fol. spirit-duplicated transcript of this discussion entitled "Klaus Mann
and W. H. Auden | March 19, 1941" is among the papers of *Decision* in Yale Uni-
versity Library. Some edited excerpts from this transcript are quoted in Mann's
autobiography, *The turning point* (New York: L. B. Fischer, [1942]), pp. 341–42.

M 14 [Discussion with Norman Corwin and Lawrence Thompson of
Vachel Lindsay's *Daniel Jazz.*]   "Invitation to learning," CBS radio network, 28 January 1945.

M 15 [Talk given during the intermission of a dramatization of Graham
Green's *The ministry of fear.*]   "University theatre," NBC radio network,
23 January 1949.
Published in *Wind and the rain,* Summer 1949.

M 16 The art of Thomas Hardy.   BBC Third Programme, 16 September
1949.
Not read by Auden.

M 17 Do we expect too much of our children? [Discussion with Robert
Gomberg and Helen Parkhurst.]   "It's a problem," WNBT-TV [New
York], 30 January 1952.

M 18 Should parents teach pre-school age children? [Discussion with Roma Gans.] "It's a problem," NBC television network, 10 March 1952.

M 19 *The rake's progress* [a talk on the libretto]. BBC Third programme, 28 August 1953.

M 20 Huck and Oliver. BBC Third programme, 27 September 1953.
Published in *Listener*, 1 October 1953.

M 21 The poetry of Dylan Thomas, introduced by W. H. Auden. WNBC [New York], 3 March 1954.

M 22 W. H. Auden (Writers of today, 4). Dynamic Films for the National Educational Television Film service.
An interview with Walter Kerr, filmed in 1955 and often broadcast in the United States.

M 23 [Reading from *The shield of Achilles*.] "Anthology," NBC radio network, 27 February 1955.

M 24 The dyer's hand. BBC Third Programme, 8, 15, and 22 June 1955.
Published in *Listener*, 16, 23, and 30 June 1955.

M 25 History, feigned and real. BBC Third programme, 16 November 1955.
A review of *The lord of the rings*, by J. R. R. Tolkien.

M 26 [Participating in a tribute to Ezra Pound on his seventieth birthday.] WYBC [New Haven], 5 December 1955.
A mimeographed transcript entitled *A tribute to Ezra Pound* is in the Beinecke Library, with Auden's contribution on pp. 14–15. One sentence is reprinted in *Ezra Pound at seventy* (Norfolk, Conn.: New Directions, 1956), p. [4].

M 27 Professor of poetry at Oxford. "Panorama," BBC-TV, 13 February 1956.

M 28 [Guest interview with Dr. Stanley Hopper.] "Frontiers of faith," NBC television network, 11 March 1956.

M 29 [Guest interview, and reading his poems.] "Home," NBC television network, 27 March 1956.

M 30 [Member of the panel.] "Brains trust," BBC-TV, 17 June 1956.

M 31 Making, knowing, and judging. BBC Third programme, 29 September 1956.
Published as a pamphlet (1956).

M 32 [Sermon delivered at Edinburgh University.] BBC Scottish service, 10 March 1957.
See *Scotsman*, 25 February 1957, p. 8.

M 33 How should we use our new [Liverpool] cathedral? [Discussion with J. Bronowski and F. W. Dillistone.] "Meeting point," BBC-TV, 26 May 1957.

M 34 [A two-part programme on Auden.] 1: The secret agent [a dramatization of *The age of anxiety* and other poems in which Auden did not appear]. 2: The search for the hero [in which Auden read and discussed several poems]. "Camera three," CBS television network, 2 and 9 March 1958.

M 35 Byron's *Don Juan* [lecture]. BBC Third programme, 14 May 1958.
A report by K. W. Gransden appeared in *Listener*, LIX (22 May 1958), 876.

M 36 Realism in opera [discussion with Norman dello Joio]. "Metropolitan Opera broadcast," CBS television network, 3 January 1959.

M 37 [Discussion with Siobhan McKenna and Anne Fremantle on problems of Christianity today.] "Look up and live," CBS television network, 1 March 1959.

M 38 Culture in conflict [discussion with Jacques Barzun and Lionel Trilling]. "Open end," WNTA television [New York], 8 November 1959.

M 39 [Reading "Refugee blues."] "All of a kind: refugees," BBC Home service, 15 December 1959.

M 40 [Interview with Philip Burton.] "Monitor," BBC-TV, 24 April 1960.
Partially printed in *Listener*, 5 May 1960.

M 41 [Reading his poems.] WBAI-FM [New York], 5 June 1960.

M 42 [Discussion on poetry and religion with the Rev. Sidney Lanier.] "Look up and live," CBS television network, 22 January 1961.

M 43 An amateur world. BBC Third programme, 29 April 1961.
Published in *Listener*, 8 June 1961.

M 44 Elegy for young lovers [discussion with Henze and Kallman]. BBC Third programme, 13 July 1961.

M 45 Appointment with Auden, Spender, Isherwood, and Connolly [interviews with Malcolm Muggeridge]. Granada television, 23 March 1962.
Mimeographed transcript in the possession of Granada television.

M 46 W. H. Auden on Robert Graves. BBC Third programme, 15, 22, and 26 March 1962.

M 47 Ein Engländer sieht Europa. "Europäisches Konzert," Bayerischer Rundfunk, 29 October 1962.
German text published in *Wort und Wahrheit*, December 1962.

M 48 The poet's voice [interview with A. Alvarez and William Empson]. "Bookstand," BBC-TV, 31 October 1962.

M 49 W. H. Auden reading a selection of his poems. BBC Third programme, 24 December 1962.

M 50 [Guest appearance.] "The Merv Griffin show," NBC television network, 24 December 1962.

M 51 [Tribute to Louis MacNeice, from the memorial service.] "Radio newsreel," BBC Light programme, 17 October 1963.
Published as a pamphlet (A 46).

M 52 [Participating in] Britten at fifty. BBC-TV 1, 22 November 1963.

M 53 [Interview with Kerstin Anér on his translation of *Markings*.] "Obs!", Sveriges Radio second programme, 17 April 1964.

M 54 Shakespeare's sonnets. BBC Third programme, 31 May, 7 June 1964.
Published in *Listener*, 2 and 9 July 1964.

M 55 [Contributions to] Under pressure: the problems of the artist. BBC Third programme, 3 June 1964.
A discussion by various American writers. A transcript appears in *Under pressure*, by A. Alvarez ([Harmondsworth]: Penguin, [1965]), with Auden's remarks on pp. 160, 165–66.

M 56 T. S. Eliot, O.M.: a tribute. "Radio newsreel," BBC Light programme, 4 January 1965.
Published in *Listener*, 7 January 1965.

M 57 Poets in public [reading his poems at the Edinburgh Festival]. BBC Third programme, 27 August 1965.

M 58 Schriftsteller unserer Zeit: Wystan Hugh Auden [a lecture by Horst Bienek, followed by an interview]. Deutschlandfunk, 9 September 1965. The interview was rebroadcast as "Ein Werkstattgespräch" by R.I.A.S [Berlin], 6 March 1966.

M 59 Kein Gedicht aus Liebe [reading "Dichtung und Wahrheit," with Elizabeth Mayer's translation read by Ernst Schnabel]. "Literarische Illustrierte," Norddeutscher Rundfunk III. Programm [also Radio Bremen and Sender Fries Berlin], 28 October 1965. Partially rebroadcast, in a programme on Auden, by Sender Fries Berlin, 20 February 1967.

M 60 Poet of disenchantment: W. H. Auden [interviews with Peter Duval Smith and others]. "Sunday night," BBC-TV 1, 28 November 1965. Broadcast in shortened form over National Educational Television channels in the United States as "The creative person: W. H. Auden," August 1967–February 1968.
The sound track of the NET version was commercially distributed, without indication of its origin, as a tape cassette under the title *An encounter with W. H. Auden* (Tucson: Motivational Programming Corp., 1969).

M 61 Nowness and permanence: tradition and the new [no. 8 in the series]. BBC Third programme, 24 February 1966.
Published in *Listener*, 17 March 1966.

M 62 Masters of arts: W. H. Auden [interview with Peter Porter]. "Study session," BBC network 3, 29 April 1966.

M 63 The masters: W. H. Auden [reading "First things first" and discussing his poems]. BBC World service, 17 May 1966. Also broadcast by the CBS, 13 November 1968.
Despite the similar title, not the same as the previous entry.

M 64 Christen und Heiden in einem Zeitalter der Angst. Bayerischer Rundfunk II. Programm, 11 August 1966.

M 65 [Participating in] Louis MacNeice (1907–1963): a radio portrait. BBC Third programme, 7 September 1966.

M 66 [Reading his poem to Nevill Coghill.] "The look of the week," BBC-TV 1, 9 October 1966.

M 67   [Talk with Peter Stadlen on writing opera libretti.]   BBC Third programme, 29 October 1966.

M 68   [Reading and discussing "Joseph Weinheber (1892–1945)."] "Auden at sixty," BBC Home service, 21 February 1967.

M 69   T. S. Eliot memorial lectures.   BBC Third programme, 2, 9, 15, and 25 January 1968.
Published as *Secondary worlds* (1968).

M 70   [Interviewed with Sir William Walton.]   "Workshop," BBC-TV 2, 26 May 1968.

M 71   [Interviewed on the publication of *Collected longer poems.*]   "Release," BBC-TV 2, 12 October 1968.

M 72   [Reading "On the circuit," "A New Year's greeting," and "Doggerel by a senior citizen."]   "Poetry international 69," BBC Third programme, 21 July 1969.

N

RECORDINGS

Published recordings

THIS list attempts to describe the first release of published recordings on which Auden reads his own poems or translations, with some notes on re-issues. Each entry includes a brief transcription of the record label, a physical description of the record itself, a list of contents, and some details of the circumstances of recording and publication. In the contents note, the titles or first lines are taken directly from the recording, not from the sleeve or label. Introductory comments by Auden are also noted here.

In addition to these recordings Auden also read the verse on *An evening of Elizabethan verse and its music*, W. H. Auden and the New York Pro Musica Antiqua, Columbia ML 5051 [1955] (One 12 in., 33⅓ r.p.m. disc; matrix XLP–30831/2). This record, with sleeve notes by Auden, was recorded 3 and 4 February 1954 and released on 31 October 1955, and was reissued in March 1968 as Odyssey 32 16 0171.

N 1   *In memory of W. B. Yeats* [and other poems], read by W. H. Auden. National Council of Teachers of English. Contemporary poets series, [23–24]. Produced by Walter C. Garwick. Rye, N.Y., [1940].
One 10 in., 78 r.p.m. disc. Matrix: W. H. Auden 23/24.
Contents: Side 1 begins "This is W. H. Auden reading from his poems, March the 14th, 1940," followed by "In memory of W. B. Yeats." Side 2: "Law like love," and "Casino."
Notes: Recorded 14 March 1940 and released *c.* June 1940. Also [after 1941?] issued with the series number indicated on the label and with the label on side 1 reading "...W. G. [*sic*] Yeats...," and with the label on side 2 listing the place of publication as Harrison, N.Y. A later issue lists Harrison, N.Y., on both sides of the label and gives Yeats's initials correctly. A rematrixed issue in 1949 has a label reading "W. H. Auden reading his poem In memory of W. B. Yeats [side 2: ... reading his own Law like love ...   Casino] ...," with no place of publication given, and the matrix number D9-CB-2012/3. This reissue was still available from the National Council of Teachers of English in 1968.

N 2   *W. H. Auden reading his own poems.* The Harvard Vocarium Records, associate professor F. C. Packard, Jr., editor. P–1052/3. Cambridge, Mass., 1941.
One 12 in., 78 r.p.m. disc. Matrix: HFS1271/2.
Contents: Side 1 begins with the title "Four sonnets from *Journey to a war*," followed

by "The traveller," "In hospital," "Exiles," and "Wandering lost upon the mountains of our choice...." Side 2: "Song from *Another time*" [As I walked out one evening...], and "Spring in wartime" [O season of repetition and return...].
Notes: Recorded 4 May 1940 at the Widener Library, Harvard University, and released *c.* July 1941.

The original master disc, now in the Poetry Room of the Lamont Library at Harvard, also contains: "To ask the hard question is simple...," "Since you are going to begin today...," "What's in your mind, my dove, my coney...," "May with its light behaving...," "Casino," "Song" [Now the leaves are falling fast...].

N 3 *Wystan Hugh Auden reading his own poems.* Library of Congress Recording Laboratory, twentieth century poetry in English. P3. [Washington, 1949].
One 12 in., 78 r.p.m. disc from an album of five discs. Matrix: LCM-1668/9. Printed texts laid in.
Contents: Side A begins "Poems by W. H. Auden, read by the author," followed by "Alonso to Ferdinand." Side B: "Musée des beaux arts," "Refugee blues."
Notes: Recorded 24 January 1948 at the Library of Congress (see Unpublished recordings, below) and released in this form 18 February 1949. The album title is *Twentieth century poetry in English*, Library Reference Department, album PL-1.

Most of this album, including Auden's contribution, was reissued in Fall 1954 as a 12 in., 33⅓ r.p.m. disc, *Katherine Garrison Chapin, Mark Van Doren, W. H. Auden, Richard Eberhart reading their own poems*, Library of Congress, P-L1. Auden's poems are on side B.

N 4 *Pleasure dome:* an audible anthology of modern poetry read by its creators and edited by Lloyd Frankenberg. Columbia ML 4259. [New York, 1949.]
One 12 in., 33⅓ r.p.m. disc. Matrix: XLP 1728.
Contents: Side 2 of the 33⅓ r.p.m. disc: "Oh what is that sound...," "Simultaneously, as soundlessly...."
Notes: Recorded 7 October 1949 and released 5 December 1949. "'Prime'...is as yet unpublished" (From the sleeve). Released simultaneously as an album of four 12 in., 78 r.p.m. discs, Columbia MM 877, with Auden's poems on side 6. Matrix: XCO-41453. Often reissued from new matrixes; the earliest pressing has a dark blue label lettered in metallic yellowish white.

N 5 *W. H. Auden reading from his works.* Caedmon TC–1019. New York, [1954].
One 12 in., 33⅓ r.p.m. disc. Matrix: TC 1019 A/B.
Contents: Side 1: "He disappeared in the dead of winter...," "If it form the one landscape that we the inconstant ones...," "Quarter of pleasures where the rich are always waiting...," "Here are all the captivities; the cells are as real...," "Wrapped in a yielding air...," "As I walked out one evening...," "Jumbled in the common box...," "Seen when night is silent...," "My dear one is mine as mirrors are lonely...," "Sing, Ariel, sing...," "Be patient, solemn nose...." Side 2: "Deep below our violences...," "Sylvan meant savage in those primal woods...," "I know a retired dentist who only paints mountains...," "A lake allows an average father, walking slowly...," "Old saints on millstones float with cats...," "I can imagine quite easily ending up...," "Dear water, clear water, playful in all your streams...."
Notes: Recorded 12 December 1953, in New York, and first released May (?) 1954. The sleeve includes notes on the poems by Auden.

This recording has often been rematrixed and reissued. The label on the first pressing omits the title "Precious five," as does at least one later pressing. The sleeve of the first pressing has a white label on the front lettered in black: 'W. H. AUDEN | reading | IN MEMORY OF W. B. YEATS | [four lines]'. An English issue was released in 1960 (Caedmon library series); and a later English issue was reprocessed and released in 1968 as Caedmon 4FP 9006. This disc was also issued as one of four in *The Caedmon library of 4 modern poets.*

Auden's reading of "He disappeared in the dead of winter..." from this disc was included on side 2 of a two-disc album, *The Caedmon treasury of modern poets reading*, TC-2006, released late Fall 1956; also released in Great Britain as TC-0995 in 1960.

N 6 *An album of modern poetry:* an anthology read by the poets, edited by Oscar Williams. The Library of Congress Recording Laboratory, twentieth century poetry in English. PL21. [Washington, 1960].

One 12 in., 33⅓ r.p.m. disc from an album of three discs. Matrix: LCM 2017 21A/B. Printed texts laid in.

Contents: Side A begins "This is W. H. Auden reading his poetry," followed by "Musée des beaux arts" and "The unknown citizen."

Notes: Recorded 24 January 1948 ("Musée des beaux arts") and 4 March 1946 ("The unknown citizen") at the Library of Congress Recording Laboratory (see Unpublished recordings, below); released in this form 6 March 1960. The full album consists of discs PL20-22. The album was reprocessed and reissued in 1964 as Gryphon GR 902–904, *An album of modern poetry*, with printed texts included. The three discs were also reissued separately in 1966 by Audio Arts; Auden's poems are on AA 3309, *An album of modern poetry*, II.

N 7 *W. H. Auden.* Argo RG 184. Recording first published [London], 1960.

One 12 in., 33⅓ r.p.m. disc. Matrix: ARG-2117/8.

Contents: Side 1: "Homage to Clio," "Sext," "Nones," "Vespers," "Compline." Side 2: "Metalogue to The Magic flute," "The hard question," "Song" [Lady weeping at the crossroads...], "The more loving one," "A walk after dark," "Chorus" [Doom is dark and deeper than any sea-dingle...], "First things first," "Alonso to Ferdinand."

Notes: Recorded 20 June 1957 and released May 1960 and reissued at least once. Title from the sleeve: *W. H. Auden reads a selection of his poems.* A later pressing omits the words "Recording first published 1960" from the label.

This recording was also released in the United States in November 1960 as Spoken Arts SA 780. Matrix: LO-8P-1947/8.

Four poems from this recording ("The hard question," "Song," "The more loving one," "Chorus") were included on *The poets speak*, vol. 7, Argo RG 517, released July 1967.

N 8 *A little treasury of 20th century British poetry*, vol. I, edited by Oscar Williams. Colpix PS–1002. [New York, 1963].

One 12 in., 33⅓ r.p.m. disc. Matrix: P5RM 3278. Texts on sleeve.

Contents: Side 1: "Autumn 1940," "Blessed event," "Refugee blues."

Notes: Recorded 4 March 1946 ("Autumn 1940," "Blessed event") and 24 January 1948 ("Refugee blues") at the Library of Congress Recording Laboratory (see Unpublished recordings below), and released in this form in November 1963.

N 9 *Antiworlds*, the poetry of Andrei Voznesensky. Read by the poet in Russian and [in translation] by W. H. Auden, William Jay Smith, Stanley Kunitz, Richard Wilbur. Columbia OL 6590. [New York, 1966].

One 12 in., 33⅓ r.p.m. disc. Matrix: XLP 11325/6.

Contents: Side 1: "Parabolic ballad." Side 2: "My Achilles heart," "Autumn in Sigulda."
Notes: Recorded by Auden 3 January 1966 and released 2 May 1966.
　　This recording was also issued in Great Britain as CBS LP 70026 in 1967.
　　The sleeve includes excerpts from Auden's foreword to *Antiworlds*.

N 10　*Selected poems by W. H. Auden,* read by W. H. Auden.　Spoken Arts SA 999. [New Rochelle, N.Y., 1968].
One 12 in., 33⅓ r.p.m. disc. Matrix: A 1395 A/B SA 999 A/B.
Contents: Side 1: "The wanderer," "Legend," "Alonso to Ferdinand," "The Shield of Achilles," "A walk after dark"; Six songs: " 'O where are you going?' said reader to rider...," "Now the leaves are falling fast...," "Jumbled in one common box...," "If I could tell you," "When rites and melodies begin," "Song of the Devil." Side 2: "River profile," "Vespers," "Cattivo tempo," "Fleet visit," "On the circuit," "After reading a child's guide to modern physics," "Prologue at sixty." Auden provides a brief comment before reading each poem.
Notes: Recorded 29 January 1968 at New Rochelle, N.Y., and released June 1968. The recording was directed by Arthur Luce Klein. Title from the sleeve: *W. H. Auden: selected poems read by the poet.*
　　A slightly altered version of this recording for use in high schools was issued as Spoken Arts SA 999 HS (matrix: A 1395 A/B SA 999 HS A/B). This disc is identical to the regular issue, except that "Song of the Devil" is omitted, and "Prologue at sixty" is replaced by "The cave of making."
　　Five poems from this recording (" 'O where are you going?', said reader to rider," "If I could tell you," "The wanderer," "River profile," and "After reading a child's guide to modern physics") were included in *The Spoken Arts treasury of 100 modern American poets reading their poems,* vol. [*i.e.,* disc] 9 [of 18], SA 1048, side 2, released in Autumn 1969. A "sampler" recording, released to publicize the larger set, contains "If I could tell you."

Unpublished recordings

This list is undoubtedly incomplete: other recordings probably exist in libraries and in the files of various broadcasting companies. The recordings in the BBC Sound Archives were described by the BBC, who specify: "There is no public access to the Sound Archives section of the BBC and recordings are not normally available except to broadcasters." Two recordings in the Library of Congress (4 June 1940 and 24 January 1948) are described from entries in *Literary recordings: a checklist of the archive of recorded poetry and literature in the Library of Congress* (Washington, 1966), p. 7, corrected by Donald L. Leavitt of the Library's Recorded Sound section.

Unless indicated otherwise these recordings belong to the organizations which made them.

N 11　Reading his poems: "Look, stranger, on this island now..." "In spring" [May with its light behaving...]. "A bride in the thirties." Selected by Auden and recorded by the BBC, 27 January 1936 but apparently not broadcast. (BBC Sound Archives 1497.) A copy of this recording is in the Poetry Room of the Lamont Library, Harvard University.

N 12 Discussion with Christopher Isherwood on *The ascent of F6*. From "Speaking Personally," BBC-TV, 12 October 1938. (Sound Archives 12119–20.)

N 13 In the square. From "The Modern Muse," BBC National Programme, 18 October 1938. (Sound Archives 1967.)

N 14 Talk: a recent visit to China. From "Midland magazine," BBC Midland Home Service, 16 January 1939. (Sound Archives 24741.)

N 15 Two poems from *Poems* 1930: "To ask the hard question is simple..." "Since you are going to begin today..." Recorded on a disc labelled "Test pressing... Columbia Recording Corporation." No information has been found about this recording, which occupies one side of a 12 in., 78 r.p.m. disc now in the Poetry Room of the Lamont Library at Harvard. It was presumably recorded shortly after Auden's arrival in America. Another test pressing, catalogued as "Two poems," was missing from the Lamont Library in 1968.

N 16 Reading at City College, New York, 4 June 1940: "Prologue" [O love, the interest itself in thoughtless heaven...]. "Musée des beaux arts." "The composer." "The riddle" [Underneath the leaves of life...]. The original recording of these poems is no longer at City College, but a copy was made for the Library of Congress, which then made a preservation copy (LWO 2048, reel 1). (See *Quarterly journal of speech*, XXVIII [1942], 315–23.)

N 17 Reading in the Library of Congress Recording Laboratory, 4 March 1946: "Prospero to Ariel." "Autumn 1940." "Blessed event." "Atlantis." "The unknown citizen." "What do you think?" The Library also recorded Auden's public reading at the Library on the same day: *The sea and the mirror*, pt. II, and a number of poems by other writers. The Library has made a preservation copy of these recordings (LWO 5389, reels 5 and 6).

N 18 Reading in the Library of Congress Recording Laboratory, 24 January 1948: "Musée des beaux arts." "Refugee blues." "Alonso to Ferdinand." The Library has made a preservation copy (LWO 2689, reel 1).

N 19 Reading his poems: "Kicking his mother until she let go of his soul..." "Here are all the captivities; the cells are as real..." "Wrapped in a yielding air..." "Though aware of our rank and alert to obey orders..." "Returning each morning from a timeless world..." "Orchestras have so long been speaking..." "Jumbled in the common box..." "As I walked out one evening..." "Warm are the still and lucky miles ..." "On and on and on..." "Being set on the idea..." "Dear son, when the warm multitudes cry..." No information has been found about this recording, which is on four 12 in., 78 r.p.m. discs in the poetry room at the Princeton University Library. It was presumably recorded around 1948.

N 20   Talk given during the intermission of a dramatization of Graham Greene's *The ministry of fear*. "University theatre," NBC radio network, 23 January 1949.

N 21   Nature, history, and poetry. Recorded 9 March 1950; in the Swarthmore College Library.

N 22   Religion and the intellectuals [forum on the *Partisan review* symposium, with Auden, Paul Tillich, and Peter Weiss]. Recorded at the Union Theological Seminary, New York, 19 February 1952; a copy is in the Yale Memorabilia Room at the Yale University Library.

N 23   Reading his poems at the 92nd street YM-YWHA, [New York], 8 January 1953.

N 24   Address at Smith College on the artist's imagination, 23 April 1953. Recording in the Archives, Smith College Library.

N 25   Talk: rereading Huckleberry Finn [Huck and Oliver]. Recorded 20th June 1953; broadcast on the BBC Third Programme, 27 September 1953. (Sound Archives 19304-5.)

N 26   Reading his poems at the 92nd street YM-YWHA, [New York], 22 January 1955.

N 27   Reading from *The shield of Achilles*. "Anthology," NBC radio network. Recorded 25 February 1955; broadcast 27 February 1955.

N 28   The dyer's hand: three lectures on poetry. Recorded 5–7 April 1955; broadcast on the BBC Third Programme, 8, 15, 22 June 1955. (Sound Archives 24269–70, 24309–10.)

N 29   Tribute to Ezra Pound on his 70th birthday. Broadcast by WYBC [New Haven], 5 December 1955. A copy is in the BBC. (Sound Archives 24688.)

N 30   Making, knowing and judging. Recorded at Oxford 11 June 1956; broadcast on the BBC Third Programme, 29 September 1956. (Sound Archives 24256–7.)

N 31   Reading in New York, 18 March 1959: "Good-bye to the Mezzogiorno" (1958). "On installing an American kitchen in lower Austria" (1958). "The journey of life" [final four sections of "Caliban to the audience"]. "The proof" (1954). "A permanent way" (1956). "Nocturne" (1956). "The more loving one" (1957). "Fleet visit" (1951). "The shield of Achilles" (1952). The original tape is in the Historical Sound Recordings section of the Yale University Library: a copy is at the Library of Congress (LWO 2946). The dates given above were written by Auden on the box containing the tape at Yale.

N 32   Reading his poems [in New York]: "Goodbye to the mezzogiorno." "On installing an American kitchen in lower Austria." "A permanent way." "The history of science." "Numbers and faces." "Dame kind." "The proof." "First things first." "The more loving one." "Friday's child." Broadcast on WBAI-FM, 5 June 1960. (Tape AL 2503.)

N 33 Reading [in New York?], 23 March 1961: " 'O where are you going?' said reader to rider . . ." "Doom is dark and deeper than any sea-dingle . . ." "Our hunting fathers told the story . . ." "A song" [Fish in the unruffled lakes . . .]. "Look, stranger, on this island now . . ." "Autumn song." "Wandering lost upon the mountains of our choice . . ." "Law like love." "Musée des beaux arts." "Alone, alone about a dreadful wood . . ." [from *For the time being*]. "Antonio" [from *The sea and the mirror*]. "There will be no peace." "Homage to Clio." "Three dreams." "Ode" [Though aware of our rank and alert to obey orders . . .]. "The aged catch their breath . . ." "The dead echo." "Song for St. Cecilia's day." "So from the years the gifts were showered; each . . ." "He turned his field into a meeting-place . . ." "The life of man is never quite completed . . ." "Nothing is given: we must find our law . . ." [From *For the time being:*] "My shoes were shined, my pants were cleaned and pressed . . ." "Advent" "If on account of the political situation . . ." Original tape in the Historical Sound Recordings section of the Yale University Library.

N 34 [Ronald Firbank and] an amateur world. Recorded in New York; broadcast on the BBC Third programme, 29 April 1961. (Sound Archives 29962.)

N 35 Discussion among Hans Werner Henze, Auden, and Chester Kallman on *Elegy for young lovers*. Recorded 10 July 1961; broadcast on the BBC Third Programme, 13 July 1961. (Sound Archives 26827.)

N 36 Introducing and reading a selection of his poetry: "Journey to Iceland." "No change of place." "One evening." "Seascape." "As he is." "The shield of Achilles." "The proof." "Reflections in a forest." "There will be no peace." "Friday's child." Recorded 12 July 1961; broadcast on the BBC Third Programme 24 December 1962. (Sound Archives 29471.) A copy is held in the British Institute of Recorded Sound.

N 37 Ein Engländer sieht Europa. [Broadcast in English?] "Europaisches Konzert," Bayerischer Rundfunk, 29 October 1962.

N 38 Interview with A. Alvarez. "Bookstand," BBC TV, 31 October 1962. (Sound Archives 28381.)

N 39 Guest interview. "The Merv Griffin show," NBC television network, 24 December 1962.

N 40 Reading his poems. Recorded by the Academy of American Poets, 12 March 1964.

N 41 Shakespeare's sonnets. Broadcast 31 May and 7 June 1964 on the

BBC Third programme. Recording held in the British Institute of Recorded Sound.

N 42 [A short defense of poetry.] Budapest P.E.N. club, 18 October 1964.

N 43 Reading his poems. Edinburgh Festival, 1965. Broadcast by the BBC Third programme, 27 August 1965. Recording held in the British Institute of Recorded Sound.

N 44 Talking about poetry with Peter Porter. Recorded 27 August 1965; broadcast on the BBC Third programme 29 April 1966. (Sound Archives 30578.)

N 45 Talking about his life and work with Peter Duval Smith, Chester Kallman, Christopher Isherwood, and Igor Stravinsky. Recorded 19 September 1965; broadcast on TV BBC-1, 28 November 1965. (Sound Archives 30206.)

N 46 Reading his poems. Recorded by the Academy of American Poets, 27 January 1966.

N 47 Nowness and permanence. Recorded in New York, February 1966; broadcast on the BBC Third programme, 24 February 1966. (Sound Archives 30578.) This and the recording of 27 August 1965 are both available on disc CN 514 for hire to other radio stations throughout the world, and are held in the British Institute of Recorded Sound.

N 48 Reading his poems. St. Mark's Church-in-the-Bouwerie. Recorded for WRVR radio, New York, 10 March 1966.

N 49 Talking about poetry with Stanley Kunitz. Recorded by the Academy of American Poets, 16 March 1966. (See *Atlantic*, August 1966, for an edited version.)

N 50 Christen und Heiden in einem Zeitalter der Angst. Recorded and broadcast by the Bayerischer Rundfunk on 11 August 1966.

N 51 Participating in "Louis MacNeice (1907–1963): a radio portrait." BBC Third programme, 7 September 1966. Also held in Columbia University Library.

N 52 Sermon in Westminster Abbey: A service for those engaged in science, medicine and technology. Recorded by the BBC 18 October 1966, but not broadcast. (BBC Sound Archives 30636.)

N 53 Talking with Peter Stadlen about writing libretti. Broadcast on the BBC Third Programme, 22 October 1966. (Sound Archives 30665.)

N 54 Reading his poems at the 92nd street YM-YWHA [New York], 6 November 1966.

N 55 Reading his poems. Poetry International Festival, [London], 13 July 1967. Recording held in the British Institute of Recorded Sound, copied from a BBC recording.

N 56 T. S. Eliot memorial lectures. Recorded at Eliot College, University of Kent, 20, 23, 25, 27 October 1967; broadcast on the BBC Third Programme, 2, 9, 15, 25 January 1968. In the BBC Sound Archives, and also held in the British Institute of Recorded Sound.

N 57   Reading his poems.   Poetry International Festival, [London], July 1969. Broadcast on the BBC Third Programme, 21 July 1969. Recording held in the British Institute of Recorded Sound.

R

ANTHOLOGIES

THIS list includes anthologies and other books reprinting, usually for the first time in book form, poems and essays by W. H. Auden previously published in periodicals. Auden's involvement with these books appears to have been limited to the granting of permission to reprint; books to which Auden contributed directly are listed and described in section B above.

Also mentioned in this list are anthologies which include complete texts of the plays and longer poems, and some anthologies with later printings of essays which Auden has not included in his own books. Some other out-of-the-way anthologies are also listed. Only the first appearances of these anthologies are listed here.

The first publication of a poem or essay in book form is indicated by an asterisk. Some titles are given in slightly abbreviated form.

R 1 *The best poems of 1926*, ed. by L. A. G. Strong. New York: Dodd, Mead, 1926.
Contains: *Portrait: The lips so apt for deeds of passion ... (p. 9)

R 2 *The European caravan*, ed. by Samuel Putnam [*et al.*]. New York: Brewer and Putnam, 1931.
Contains: Poem: It was Easter as I walked in the public gardens ... (pp. 462–67)

R 3 *Whips and scorpions*, collected by Sherard Vines. [London]: Wishart, 1932.
Contains: *Birthday ode to John Warner. (pp. 11–20)

R 4 *Recent poetry, 1923–1933*, ed. by Alida Monro. London: Gerald Howe & The Poetry Bookshop, [1933].
Contains: *The witnesses. (pp. 6–11)

R 5 *Modern prose style*, by Bonamy Dobrée. Oxford: Clarendon Press, 1934.
Contains: [Extracts from] Journal of an airman. (pp. 242–43)

R 6 *The year's poetry*, [1934], compiled by Denys Kilham Roberts, Gerald Gould, John Lehmann. London: John Lane, [1934].
Contains: Three poems: To ask the hard question is simple ... Hearing of harvest rotting in the valleys ... *Our hunting fathers told the story ... (pp. 96–100)

R 7 *Then and now: a selection from the first fifty numbers of* Now and then, *1921–1935*. London: Jonathan Cape, 1935.
Contains: *T. E. Lawrence. (pp. 21–23)

R 8   *Poems of tomorrow*, chosen from *The Listener* by Janet Adam Smith. London: Chatto & Windus, 1935.
Contains: The witnesses.   Our hunting fathers told the story ...   *A bride in the 30's. (pp. 5–16)

R 9   *The year's poetry, 1935*, compiled by Denys Kilham Roberts, Gerald Gould, John Lehmann. London: John Lane, [1935].
Contains: Chorus[es] from *The dog beneath the skin* [The summer holds ... *and* You with shooting sticks ...].   *In the square.   *Poem: May with its light behaving ... (pp. 98–107)

R 10   *The best poems of 1937*, selected by Thomas Moult. London: Jonathan Cape, [1937].
Contains: *Orpheus. (p. 111)

R 11   *The year's poetry, 1937*, compiled by Denys Kilham Roberts [and] Geoffrey Grigson. London: John Lane, [1937].
Contains: *Lay your sleeping head, my love ...   O who can ever look his fill ... Journey to Iceland.   O who can ever praise enough ...   *Song for the New Year. (pp. 63–75)

R 12   *Recognition of Robert Frost*, ed. by Richard Thornton. New York: Holt, [1937].
Contains: [Essay on Frost, reprinted from Frost's *Selected poems* (1936).] (pp. 293–98)

R 13   *In letters of red*, ed. by E. Allen Osborne. [London]: Michael Joseph, [1938].
Contains: *Dover. (pp. 11–15)

R 14   *TPO: centenary of the Travelling Post Office.* [London: General Post Office, 1938.]
Contains: Night mail. (pp. 15, 18)

R 15   *The year's poetry, 1938*, compiled by Denys Kilham Roberts [and] Geoffrey Grigson. London: John Lane, [1938].
Contains: *Song: As I walked out one evening ...   Dover.   *From the film "Coalface."   *Miss Gee.   *Blues: Stop all the clocks, cut off the telephone ... (pp. 51–62)

R 16   *Best short plays of the social theatre*, ed. by William Kozlenko. New York: Random House, [1939].
Contains: The dog beneath the skin. (pp. 339–456)

R 17   *Poems for Spain*, ed. by Stephen Spender & John Lehmann. London: Hogarth Press, 1939.
Contains: Spain. (pp. 55–58)
The accidentals of this text differ from those of all others, and it is possible that it was revised by Auden.

R 18   *The music of poetry*, [ed.] by Alfred H. Body. London: Thomas Nelson, [1939].
Contains: Night mail. (pp. 44–45 and 144–47)

R 19   *New verse: an anthology*, ed. by Geoffrey Grigson. London: Faber, [1939]
Contains: Dover: *Foxtrot from a play.   Poem: The fruit in which your parents hid you, boy ...   Song: I have a handsome profile ...   From the film "Coal-face." Ballad: O what is that sound which so thrills the ear ...   Poem: The earth turns

over; our side feels the cold ... The economic man.   To a writer on his birthday. The dream. (pp. 159–80)

R 20   *The best poems of 1939*, selected by Thomas Moult. London: Jonathan Cape, [1939].
Contains: *In memory of W. B. Yeats [pt. 1]. (pp. 109–10)

R 21   *The poet speaks*, selected by Marjorie Gullan and Clive Sansom. London: Methuen, [1940].
Contains: Night mail.   Chorus from *The dog beneath the skin*. (pp. 66–67, 130–32)

R 22   *Poetic drama*, ed. by Alfred Kreymborg. New York: Modern Age Books, [1941].
Contains: The dog beneath the skin. (pp. 757–805)

R 23   *New poems, 1942*, ed. by Oscar Williams. Mount Vernon, N.Y.: Peter Pauper, [1942].
Contains: Prologue [to DM].   *At the grave of Henry James.   Epilogue [to DM]. (pp. 38–49)

R 24   *New poems, 1943*, ed. by Oscar Williams. [New York]: Howell, Soskin, [1943].
Contains: *Mundus et infans.   The maze.   Musée des beaux arts.   *At the manger. (pp. 15–25)

R 25   *The poets speak*, with an introduction by May Sarton. New York: New York Public library, 1943.
Contains: *Canzone. (pp. 7–8)
The entire pamphlet is reprinted from the *Bulletin of the New York Public Library*, November 1943.

R 26   *New poems, 1944*, ed. by Oscar Williams. New York: Howell, Soskin, [1944].
Contains: Alonzo to Ferdinand.   *After Christmas, a passage from a Christmas oratorio.   Voltaire at Ferney. (pp. 28–36)

R 27   *The Partisan reader*, ed. by William Phillips and Philip Rahv. New York: Dial, 1946.
Contains: Canzone.   *The public v. the late Mr. William Butler Yeats. (pp. 267–68, 348–53)

R 28   *The stature of Thomas Mann*, ed. by Charles Neider. [New York]: New Directions, [1947].
Contains: *A toast. (p. 19)

R 29   *Criticism: the foundations of modern literary judgement*, ed. by Mark Schorer, Josephine Miles, [and] Gordon Mackenzie. New York: Harcourt Brace, [1948].
Contains: The public v. the late Mr. William Butler Yeats. (pp. 168–72)

R 30   *Twenty-five modern plays*, ed. by S. Marion Tucker, revised edition by Alan S. Downer. New York: Harper, [1948].
Contains: The ascent of F6. (pp. 925–60)

R 31   *A little treasury of American prose*, ed. by George Mayberry. New York: Scribners, 1949.
Contains: *The poet of the encirclement. (pp. 639–45)

R 32 *The permanence of Yeats*, ed. by James Hall and Martin Steinman. New York: Macmillan, 1950.
Contains: *[Yeats as an example.] (pp. 344–51)

R 33 *English masterpieces* [vol. 7]: *modern poetry*, ed. by Maynard Mack, Leonard Dean, [and] William Frost. New York: Prentice-Hall, 1950.
Contains: [Twenty poems]. For the time being. (pp. 159–245)

R 34 *Religion and the intellectuals.* [New York: Partisan Review, 1950]. (PR series, 3.)
Contains: *W. H. Auden [contribution to a symposium]. (pp. 22–31)
This volume gathers the complete text of a symposium which had been published in various numbers of *Partisan review*. Auden's contribution appeared in the number for February 1950.

R 35 *The Kenyon critics*, ed. by John Crowe Ransom. Cleveland: World, [1951].
Contains: Yeats as an example. (pp. 107–14)

R 36 *Literary opinion in America*, revised edition, ed. by Morton Dauwen Zabel. New York: Harper, [1951].
Contains: *A knight of the infinite. *Heretics. The poet of the encirclement. The public v. the late Mr. William Butler Yeats. (pp. 253–69)

R 37 *Modern essays*, ed. by Russel Nye. [Chicago: Scott Foresman, 1953].
Contains: *The guilty vicarage. (pp. 400–412)

R 38 *Women today*, ed. by Elizabeth Bragdon. Indianapolis: Bobbs-Merrill, [1953].
Contains: *The mythical sex. (pp. 225–33)

R 39 *New poems, 1953*, ed. by Robert Conquest, Michael Hamburger, and Howard Sergeant. London: Michael Joseph, [1953].
Contains: *Fleet visit. (p. 43)

R 40 *George Bernard Shaw: a critical survey*, ed. by Louis Kronenberger. Cleveland: World, [1953].
Contains: *The Fabian Figaro. (pp. 153–57)

R 41 *The new Partisan reader, 1945–1953*, ed. by William Phillips and Philip Rahv. New York: Harcourt Brace, [1953].
Contains: *A playboy of the western world. (pp. 603–7)

R 42 *Highlights of modern literature, a permanent collection of memorable essays from the New York times book review*, ed. by Francis Brown. [New York]: New American Library, [1954].
Contains: *The world that books have made. *The notebooks of Somerset Maugham. (pp. 13–15, 99–102)

R 43 Stanley Edgar Hyman. *The critical performance.* New York: Vintage Books, 1956.
Contains: The guilty vicarage. (pp. 301–14)

R 44 *American writing today*, ed. by Allan Angoff. [New York]: New York University Press, 1957.

Contains: *How cruel is April? (pp. 8–11)
The contents of this volume are reprinted from the *Times literary supplement,* 17 September 1954.

R 45   *Religious drama, 1,* ed. by Marvin Halverson. New York: Meridian Books, 1957.
Contains: For the time being. (pp. 11–68)

R 46   *Best poems of 1956: Borestone Mountain poetry awards 1957.* Stanford, Calif.: Stanford University Press, 1957.
Contains: *The song. (p. 3)

R 47   *The world treasury of grand opera,* ed. by George R. Marek. New York: Harper, [1957].
Contains: *Verismo opera [Cav and Pag]. (pp. 142–48)

R 48   Cleanth Brooks [and] Robert Penn Warren. *Modern rhetoric.* 2nd ed. New York: Harcourt, Brace & World, [1958].
Contains: The world that books have made. (pp. 592–95)

R 49   *The art of the essay,* ed. by Leslie Fiedler. New York: Crowell, [1958].
Contains: The guilty vicarage.   *Huck and Oliver. (pp. 598–603)

R 50   James Agee. *Agee on film.* [Vol. 1]. [New York]: McDowell-Obolensky, [1958].
Contains: *A letter to the editors of *The nation.* (p. [v])

R 51   *Best poems of 1957: Borestone Mountain poetry awards 1958.* Stanford, Calif.: Stanford University Press, 1958.
Contains: *An island cemetery.   The old man's road. (pp. 3–5)

R 52   *American literary essays,* ed. by Lewis Leary. New York: Crowell, [1960].
Contains: *The Anglo-American difference. (pp. 208–15)

R 53   *The comic in theory & practice,* ed. by John J. Enck, Elizabeth T. Forter, and Alvin Whitley. New York: Appleton, [1960].
Contains: *Notes on the comic. (pp. 109–15)

R 54   *Discovering modern poetry,* [ed. by] Elizabeth Drew [and] George Connor. New York: Holt, [1961].
Contains: *Making and judging poetry [the abridged version, from the *Atlantic*]. (pp. 324–44)

R 55   *Modern satire,* ed. by Alvin B. Kernan. New York: Harcourt Brace, [1962].
Contains: Letter to Lord Byron. (pp. 22–42)   The poem is extensively annotated by the editor.

R 56   *The Partisan review anthology,* ed. by William Phillips and Philip Rahv. New York: Holt, [1962].
Contains: *Keats in his letters. (pp. 428–32)

R 57   *Vogue's gallery.* London: Condé Nast Publications, [1962].
Contains: *Opera addict. (pp. 21–24)

R 58   *Hardy: a collection of critical essays,* ed. by Albert J. Guerard. Englewood Cliffs, N.J.: Prentice-Hall, [1963].
Contains: *A literary transference. (pp. 135–42)

R 59 *Tragedy: modern essays in criticism*, ed. by Laurence Michael [and] Richard B. Sewall. Englewood Cliffs, N.J.: Prentice-Hall, [1963].
Contains: *The Christian tragic hero. (pp. 234-38)

R 60 *Mark Twain: a collection of critical essays*, ed. by Henry Nash Smith. Englewood Cliffs, N.J.: Prentice-Hall, [1963].
Contains: Huck and Oliver. (pp. 112-16)

R 61 *T. E. Lawrence by his friends: a new selection of memoirs*, ed. by A. W. Lawrence. New York: McGraw-Hill, [1963].
Contains: T. E. Lawrence. (pp. 382-83)

R 62 *Shakespeare's tragedies: an anthology of modern criticism*, ed. by Laurence Lerner. [Harmondsworth]: Penguin, [1963, for 1964].
Contains: *Macbeth and Oedipus [extract from "The dyer's hand," *Listener*, 16 June 1955]. (pp. 217-23)

R 63 Oscar Wilde. *De profundis*. [New York]: Avon Books, [1964].
Contains: *An improbable life. (pp. 3-30)

R 64 *The contemporary poet as artist and critic*, ed. by Anthony Ostroff. Boston: Little Brown, [1964].
Contains: *A change of air. *[Reply by] W. H. Auden. (pp. 168-69, 183-87).
The symposium on Auden's poem is reprinted from *Kenyon Review*, Winter 1964.

R 65 *Half-way to the moon: new writers from Russia*, ed. by Patricia Blake and Max Hayward. London: Weidenfeld and Nicolson, [1964].
Contains: [Translations by W. H. Auden of:] *Parabolic ballad, by Andrei Voznesensky. *Every railway station..., by Evgeni Vinokurov. *Volcanoes, by Bella Akhmadulina. (pp. 40-43)
Most of the contents of this book, including Auden's translations, first appeared in *Encounter*, April 1963.

R 66 *The essence of opera*, ed. by Ulrich Weisstein. [New York]: Free Press of Glencoe; London, Collier-Macmillan, [1964].
Contains: Some reflections on music and opera. (pp. 354-60)

R 67 *Of poetry and power*, ed. by Erwin A. Glikes and Paul Schwaber. New York: Basic Books, [1964].
Contains: *Elegy for J. F. K. (p. 111)

R 68 *Tragedy: vision and form*, ed. by Robert W. Corrigan. San Francisco: Chandler, [1965].
Contains: The Christian tragic hero. (pp. 143-47)

R 69 *Sprints and distances*, compiled by Lillian Morrison. New York: Crowell, [1965].
Contains: *Runner [fragment]. (pp. 55-56)

R 70 *Hiroshima plus 20*, prepared by *The New York times*. New York: Delacorte Press, [1965].
Contains: *The bomb and man's consciousness. (pp. 126-32)
This book collects articles written for the *New York times* magazine section on the atomic bomb. Auden's contribution first appeared in the issue of 1 August 1965 ("The corruption of innocent neutrons"), and is revised here.

R 71 Christopher Isherwood. *Exhumations*. London: Methuen, 1966.
Contains: *Escales [by Auden and Isherwood]. (pp. 144-49)

R 72   *Poets for peace; poems from the fast.* [New York, 1967].
Contains: Fleet visit. (p. 87)
The accidentals of this text differ from those in all other printings, and it is possible that the poem was directly contributed by Auden.

R 73   *The lure of the limerick: an uninhibited history*, by William S. Baring-Gould. New York: Potter, [1967].
Contains: *The Marquis de Sade and Genet... (p. 78)

R 74   *Moderns on tragedy: an anthology*, ed. by Lionel Abel. Greenwich, Conn.: Fawcett, [1967].
Contains: The Christian tragic hero. (pp. 40–44)

R 75   *Perspectives in contemporary criticism*, ed. by Sheldon Norman Grebstein. New York: Harper and Row, [1968].
Contains: *The quest hero. (pp. 370–81)

R 76   *The bitch-goddess success*, [ed. by Leslie Katz]. New York: Eakins Press, [1968].
Contains: *[Nowness and permanence (fragment)]. (pp. 82–90)

R 77   *Yeats: Last poems: a casebook*, ed. by Jon Stallworthy. [London]: Macmillan, [1968].
Contains: In memory of W. B. Yeats.   *Yeats, master of diction. (pp. 25–27, 47–49)

R 78   *Word in the desert*, ed. by C. B. Cox and A. E. Dyson, London: Oxford, 1968.
Contains: *Good and evil in *The lord of the rings*. (pp. 138–42)
The contents of this volume are identical with those of *Critical quarterly*, Spring-Summer 1968.

R 79   George Kennan. *Democracy and the student left*. Boston: Atlantic–Little, Brown, [1968].
Conains: *[Letter to the *New York times*, 4 February 1968.] (pp. 105–7)

R 80   *Tolkien and the critics*, ed. by Neil D. Isaacs and Rose A. Zimbardo. Notre Dame [Ind.]: University of Notre Dame Press, [1968].
Contains: The quest hero. (pp. 40–61)

R 81   *A. E. Housman: a collection of critical essays*, ed. by Christopher Ricks. Englewood Cliffs, N.J.: Prentice-Hall, [1968].
Contains: A. E. Housman.   *Jehovah Housman and Satan Housman. (pp. 11, 32–34)

R 82   *Page 2*, ed. by Francis Brown. New York: Holt, Rinehart and Winston, [1969].
Contains: *A novel by Goethe [reprinted from the *New York times*, 18 October 1964]. (pp. 234–37)

R 83   *Twentieth century interpretations of Don Juan: a collection of critical essays*, ed. by Edward E. Bostetter. Englewood Cliffs, N.J.: Prentice-Hall, [1969].
Contains: *[The life of] A that-there poet [conclusion]. (pp. 16–20)

R 84   *Forty years on: an anthology of school songs*, compiled by Gavin Ewart. London: Sidgwick and Jackson, [1969].
Contains: *Raynes Park Grammar School, London [school song]. (sig. F16v)

R 85   *Oscar Wilde: a collection of critical essays*, ed. by Richard Ellmann. Englewood Cliffs, N.J.: Prentice-Hall, [1969].
Contains: An improbable life. (pp. 116–37)

R 86 *Cervantes: a collection of critical essays*, ed. by Lowry Nelson, Jr. Englewood Cliffs, N.J.: Prentice-Hall, [1969].
Contains: *The ironic hero: some reflections on Don Quixote [reprinted from *Horizon*, August 1949]. (pp. 73–81)

S

MUSICAL SETTINGS OF W. H. AUDEN'S VERSE

AUDEN has been interested in music from his school days and many of his poems have been set to music, principally by Benjamin Britten. Auden said that none of the poems were written for music, with the exception of parts of *Our hunting fathers, Hermit songs, Elegy for J. F. K.,* and *The twelve.*

Apart from the published song settings the contact with Britten was fruitful in other ways. Britten set Auden's "Four cabaret songs for Hedli Anderson" in 1938, and his setting of "O tell me the truth about love" was also used in the *Punch revue* for 1955. The opera *Paul Bunyan,* subsequently withdrawn, was a collaboration of their early days in America, and Britten wrote the incidental music for the plays *The ascent of F 6* and *On the frontier,* the films *Coal face, Night mail,* and *The way to the sea,* and the radio programmes *Hadrian's wall, The dark valley,* and *The rocking-horse winner.* They collaborated again in 1946 in the New York adapted production of *The Duchess of Malfi.*

Auden's interest and work in the operatic field is well known and is not dealt with in this Appendix. His poem *The age of anxiety* inspired Leonard Bernstein's symphony of the same name (1949, revised 1965), which in its turn was the music used for Jerome Robbin's ballet similarly titled and presented by the New York City Ballet on 26 February 1950. (The first version of Bernstein's symphony was recorded as Columbia ML 4325 [1949]; the revised version was recorded as Columbia ML 6285 / MS 6885 [1966], and issued in England as CBS [S]BRG 72503 [1967].)

The following is a brief list, with a few notes, of the musical settings of Auden's poems, excluding *Our hunting fathers, Hermit songs, Elegy for J. F. K.,* and *The twelve,* which are more fully described elsewhere in this bibliography. Recordings are listed within parentheses following the entries. A diagonal stroke separates monaural and stereophonic versions of the same recording; commas separate different issues of the same recording; and semi-colons separate different recordings of a work.

S 1 Richard Rodney Bennett. *One evening.* Unpublished; composed for a recording, *The Jupiter book of contemporary ballads,* JUR OA10 [1968].
S 2 William Douglas Bennett. *The quarry.* London: Boosey and Hawkes, [1967].

S 3   Luciano Berio. *Nones*. Milan: Suvini Zerboni, [1955].

S 4   Lennox Berkeley. *Night covers up the rigid land*. London: Boosey & Co., 1939. (Winthrop Rogers Edition.)

S 5   Lennox Berkeley. *Five poems* ["Lauds," "O lurcher-loving collier black as night...," "What's in your mind my dove, my coney...," "Eyes look into the well...," "Carry her over the water..."]. London: J. & W. Chester, [1960]. (HMV DLP 1209 [1960], HMV HQM 1609 [1967])

S 6   *Sir* Arthur Bliss. He is the way... [in] *The Cambridge hymnal*, ed. by David Holbrook and Elizabeth Poston. Cambridge: Cambridge University Press, 1967. pp. 50–51. Also published separately: [London]: Novello, [1968].

S 7   Benjamin Britten. *Two ballads* [includes "Underneath the abject willow"]. London: Boosey and Hawkes, [1937]. (WCFM LP-15 [1953], McIntosh Music MC-1003 [1955])

S 8   Benjamin Britten. *On this island* ["Let the florid music praise...," "Now the leaves are falling fast...," "Seascape," "Nocturne: Now through night's caressing grip...," "As it is plenty..."]. London: Winthrop Rogers, 1938. (WCFM LP-15 [1953], McIntosh Music MC-1003 [1955]; ["Let the florid music praise" only:] Decca LW 5241 [1956], London LL 1532 [1957], London 5234 [1957], Decca BR 3066 [1960], Decca VD 1063 [1962])
Issued as vol. 1 of a set, but vol. 2 was never published.

S 9   Benjamin Britten. *Ballad of heroes*. London: Hawkes and Son, 1939. (Winthrop Rogers Edition.)
Scherzo ["It's farewell to the drawing-room's civilized cry..."] by Auden; recitative and chorale [final chorus from *On the frontier:* "Europe lies in the dark..."] by Auden and Randall Swingler. The texts were edited by Britten from separate works; Auden and Swingler did not collaborate.

S 10   Benjamin Britten. *Hymn to St. Cecilia*. London: Winthrop Rogers, 1942; new ed., London: Boosey and Hawkes, [1967]. (Decca AK 1088–89 [1943]; Key records LP 14 [1951], Word 4001 [1954?]; WCFM LP-11 [1951], McIntosh Music MC-1004 [1956]; Brolga BXM 18 [c. 1958]; Oiseau Lyre OL 50206 / SOL 60037 [1961]; Kapp KCL 9057 / 9057S [1961], Decca ACL-R 254 [1965]; Argo ZRG 621 [1969])

S 11   Benjamin Britten. *Fish in the unruffled lakes*. London: Boosey and Hawkes, 1947. (WCFM LP-15 [1953], McIntosh Music MC-1003 [1955]; Jupiter jepoc 33 [1963])

S 12   Benjamin Britten. *Now thro' night's caressing grip*. London: Boosey and Hawkes, [1949?]
Separate publication of the "Nocturne" from *On this island*.

S 13   Benjamin Britten. *Spring symphony*. [Choral score. Part II: "Out on the lawn I lie in bed..."]. London; Boosey and Hawkes, 1949. (Decca LXT 5624 / SXL 2264 [1960], London 5612 / OS 25242 [1961], Eurodisc 70302 KK / 570303 KK [1963])

The piece was first performed on 9 July 1949 in Amsterdam. Full, pocket, and vocal scores were published in 1950.

S 14   Benjamin Britten. Chorale (after an old French carol) ["Our father whose creative will . . ." from FTB]. *The score*, 28 (January 1961), 47–51. (Argo RG 424 / ZRG 5424 [1964] with text on a separate sheet.)
Originally set for a BBC feature programme *Poet's Christmas* in 1944.

S 15   Benjamin Britten. Shepherd's carol. ["O lift your little pinkie . . ." Supplement to] *Musical times*, CIII, 1436 (October 1962). (Argo 424 / ZRG 5424 [1964], with text on a separate sheet.)
Written and set for a BBC feature programme *Poet's Christmas* in 1944. First publicly performed on 17 October 1962. Plate marked 19167.

S 16   Leonard Clair. *Cunarder waltz* ["You were a great Cunarder, I . . ."]. 1943. Unpublished.

S 17   James Myron Cohn. *Three phrases of love* ["Carry her over the water," "Underneath an abject willow," "Tell me the truth about love"]. 1969. Unpublished.

S 18   Lukas Foss. *Time cycle* [includes "Clocks cannot tell our time of day . . ."]. New York: Carl Fischer, [1962]; [Chamber version], Carl Fischer, [1964]. (Columbia ML 5680 / MS 6280 [1962]; [chamber version] Epic BC 1286 / LC 3886 [1964])

S 19   Norman Fulton. Round ["Released by love from isolating wrong . . ." in] *The Cambridge hymnal*, ed. by David Holbrook and Elizabeth Poston. Cambridge: Cambridge University Press, 1967. p. 374.

S 20   Alex Harvey. *Roman wall blues*. [Composed for a recording] Fontana TR 1063 [1969], Fontana STL 5334 [1969].

S 21   Philip James. *Chorus of shepherds and angels* [from FTB]. London: G. Ricordi, [1959].

S 22   Bryan Kelly. *The shield of Achilles*. London: Novello, [1967].

S 23   Randall B. Kreuger. *O what is that sound*. 1968. Unpublished.

S 24   Marvin David Levy. *For the time being: a Christmas oratorio*. London: G. Ricordi, [1959]; [revised score] New York: Boosey and Hawkes, [1967].
Set in 1959 and first performed in New York at Carnegie Hall on 7 December 1959 by the Collegiate Chorale. A German translation by S. Szekely is included in the revised score published by Boosey and Hawkes.

S 25   Elizabeth Lutyens. *Refugee blues* and *As I walked out one evening*. Unpublished.

S 26   Nicholas Maw. *Nocturne* [includes "Make this night lovable . . ."]. London: J. & W. Chester, [1960].

S 27   Wilfrid Mellers. *Lauds* [from *Ex nihilo and Lauds*]. [London]: Mills Music, [1961].

S 28   Vincent Persichetti. *Hymns and responses for the church year* [includes "Our father whose creative will . . ."]. Philadelphia: Elkan-Vogel, [1965].

S 29   Daniel Pinkham. *Sing agreeably of love* ["Carry her over the water ..."]. Boston: R. D. Row, (1949). Also published as part of *Three lyric scenes* (Boston: R. D. Row, [1949]).
First performed by the Music Department of Harvard University on 17 October 1948.

S 30   Michael B. Saffle. *Petition.* 1969. Unpublished.

S 31   Ned Rorem. *Poems of love and the rain* [includes "Stop all the clocks ..."]. London: Boosey and Hawkes, [1965]. (Composers records CRI 202 [1965]; Desto DC 6480 [1969])

S 32   Wallace Southam. *Poetry set in jazz* [includes "Underneath the abject willow ..." and "Stop all the clocks ..."]. London: Robbins Music, 1966. (Jupiter jepoc 39 [1966], Turret TRT 101 [1969])

S 33   Anthony Strilko. *Songs from "Markings"* [words by D. Hammarskjöld, tr. by Leif Sjöberg and W. H. Auden]. New York: Mercury Music, [1966].

S 34   Raymond Warren. *Song for St. Cecilia's day.* Belfast: Queen's University, 1967.

T

TRANSLATIONS

THIS list of translations is considerably more extensive than that in the first edition of the bibliography, and the more obvious sources have been searched, although it is not to be supposed that the list is exhaustive. Items are arranged under language and then in the three categories—books, anthologies, and periodicals. In listing the English title of the translated work, the form used in the publication itself has been preferred. Names and titles in Arabic, Bengali, Chinese, Greek, Gujarati, Hebrew, Hindi, Japanese, Korean, Russian, and Serbian have been romanized. Proper names in Hungarian and Japanese have generally been inverted, with the surname given last. Although Serbo-Croatian is a single language, Serbian and Croatian are listed separately as a convenient way of making the bibliographical distinction between items in the Roman alphabet (Croatian) and those in the Cyrillic alphabet (Serbian).

Albanian

Periodical

T 1   Dishepulli i Eliotit. *Flaka e vëllazërimit* (Skoplje), XXIII, 836 (22 June 1967), [supplement 24], p. 2.
Translations, by A. Karjagdiu, of "Always in trouble," "Law like love," and "Lady, weeping at the crossroads."

Arabic

Periodical

T 2   Min "Hādhā wa-dhāk." *Aswāt* (London), 3 (1961), 15–17.
A translation, by A. F., of excerpts from "Hic et ille."

Bengali

Anthology

T 3   *Sapta sindhu daś diganta,* ed. by Śaṅkha Ghoṣ and Alokrañjan Dāśgupta. Calcutta: Natun Sahitya Bhawan, 1963. [Not seen.]

Contains translations of "Miranda's song," by Sunil Gangopadhyay; "Carry her over the water," by Alokrañjan Dāśgupta; and "The lesson," by Tarapada Ray.

Catalan

Books with contributions

T 4   *Els escriptors anglesos es pronuncien sobre la guerra espanyola.* [Barcelona?]: Commissariat de Propaganda de la Generalitat de Catalunya, [1938?].
A translation of *Authors take sides on the Spanish war*, with Auden's contribution on p. 16.

T 5   Manent, Marià. *Versions de l'anglès.* Barcelona: Edicions de la Residència d'Estudiants, 1938.
Contains Manent's translation of "Chorus from a a play" (pp. 101–2).

Chinese

Anthologies

T 6   Yü Kuang-chung. *Ying shih i chu.* Taipei: Wen hsing shu tien, 1960. [Not seen.]
Contains Yü's translation of "In memory of W. B. Yeats [pt. 3]" (pp. 156–57).

T 7   Yü Kuang-chung. *Ying mei hsien tai shih hsüan.* Vol. 2. Taipei: Hsueh sheng shu tien, 1968. [Not seen.]
Contains Yü's translations of "Look, stranger," "Macao," "Musée des Beaux Arts," "In memory of W. B. Yeats," and "The maker" (pp. 297–316).

Periodicals

[It has not been possible to locate translations of Auden's poems which were reportedly published on mainland China, *c.* 1945–49.

T 8   [The world that books have made.] *Chung-yang jih-pao* (Taipei), [*c.* 1955?]. [Not seen.]
Translated by Yü Kuang-chung.

T 9   I shih san shou. *Wen hsüeh chi k'an* (Taipei), 4 (July 1967), 142–44. [Not seen.]
Includes a translation, by Chen Tsu-wen, of "Upon this line between adventure ...."

T 10   Ao-têng shih san shou. *Ta hsüeh tsa chih* (Taipei), 2 (February 1968), 24.
Translations, by Chen Tsu-wen, of "To settle in this village of the heart ..." and "To lie flat on the back with the knees flexed ...."

Croatian

Book

T 11   *Poezija.* Zagreb: Mladost, 1964 [for 1965]. (Biblioteka Orion.) 6⅝ x 4½ in., pp. [1–5] 6–101 [102–104].

Translations, by Tomislav Sabljak, of twenty-three poems. English and Croatian texts. Published 3 March 1965 in an edition of 1,485 copies at Din. 5.50. The book quotes a letter from Auden to the translator.

Anthologies

T 12 *Savremena engleska poezija (Antologija)*, izbor i prijevod Ivan Slamnig i Antun Šoljan, naslovna stranica Alfred Pal. Zagreb: Lykos, 1956. (Pjesnici i Narodi, 1.) [Not seen.]
Contains translations of poems.

T 13 *Antologija savremene engleske poezije (1900–1950)*, priredili Miodrag Pavlović i Svetozar Brkić. Belgrade: Nolit, 1957.
Contains translations of "The witnesses," "Rimbaud," "In time of war, XXVII," "Edward Lear," "Stop all the clocks...," "In memory of W. B. Yeats [pt. 1]," and Spain 1937," by Pavlović; "Their lonely betters" and "Memorial for the city," by Isídora Sekulić; "The unknown citizen," by Milica Mihajlović; and "Nones," by Sekulić (pp. 241–61).

Periodicals

T 14 U spomen grada. Svedočanstva. *Književne novine* (Belgrade), I, 30 (5 August 1954). [Not seen.]
Translations of "Memorial for the city," by Isídora Sekulić, and "The witnesses," by Miodrag Pavlović.

T 15 O kuda to ideš. *Studentski list* (Zagreb), X (6 December 1955), 10. [Not seen.]
A translation of "O where are you going...."

T 16 Stvaranje i ocenjivanje poezije. *Književne novine*, VIII, n.s. 35 (17 February 1957), 6.
A translation, by Ema Časar, of "Making and judging poetry."

T 17 Ahilejev štit. *Republika* (Zagreb), XV, 11–12 (November–December 1959), 20.
A translation, by Mira Šunjić, of "The shield of Achilles."

T 18 Šest pjesama. *Zadarska revija* (Zadar), XI, 3 (June 1962), 209–13.
Translations, by Darko Suvin, of "O where are you going...," "Let us honour, if we can...," "Acts of injustice done...," "O for doors to be open...," "O what is that sound...," and "Night falls on China."

T 19 None. *Republika*, XVIII, 8 (August 1962), 337.
A translation, by Tomislav Sabljak, of "Nones."

T 20 Suđenje V. B. Jejtsu. *Književne novine*, XV, n.s. 205 (6 September 1963), 8–9.
A translation, by Dušan Puvačić, of "The public v. the late Mr. W. B. Yeats."

T 21 Tajna je otkrivena. U zdenac gledaju oči. *Književne novine*, XVI, n.s. 215 (24 January 1964), 5.
Translations, by Tomislav Sabljak, of "At last the secret is out..." and "Eyes look into the well...."

T 22 Četiri pjesme. *Kolo* (Zagreb), n.s. II, 2 (February 1964), 175–80.
Translations, by Tomislav Sabljak, of "Journey to Iceland," "Atlantis," "As we like it," and "The ship."

T 23 Španjolska 1937. Pravda kao ljubav. Ispod vrbe tužne. *Republika*, XX, 2–3 (February–March 1964), 86–87.
Translations, by Tomislav Sabljak, of "Spain 1937," "Law like love," and "Underneath the abject willow...."

T 24 S rodom ljudskim. *Forum* (Zagreb), III, 7–8 (July–August 1964), 166–76.
Translations, by Tomislav Sabljak, of "Good-bye to the Mezzogiorno," "Streams," "The shield of Achilles," "Lady, weeping at the crossroads...," and "The witnesses."

T 25 Uvijek u nevolji. *Telegram* (Zagreb), V, 222 (24 July 1964), 10.
A translation, by Tomislav Sabljak, of "Always in trouble."

T 26 Sjećanje na Island. Elegija za Johna F. Kennedyja. *Republika*, XX, 11 (November 1964), 478.
Translations, by Tomislav Sabljak, of "Iceland revisited [stanzas 10–12]" and "Elegy for J. F. K."

T 27 T. S. Eliotu na njegov šezdeseti rođendan. *Telegram*, VI, 246 (15 January 1965), 13.
A translation, by Tomislav Sabljak, of "For T. S. Eliot on his sixtieth birthday."

T 28 Dug pjesniku T. S. Eliotu. *Telegram*, VI, 248 (29 January 1965), 13.
A translation, by Tomislav Sabljak, of "T. S. Eliot, O.M.: a tribute."

T 29 Nepoznati građanin. *15* [i.e., *Petnaest*] *dana* (Zagreb), VIII, 13–14 (1965), 31. [Not seen.]
A translation, by Ivo Dekanović, of "The unknown citizen."

T 30 Uspavanka. *Telegram*, VIII, 361 (31 March 1967), 10.
A translation, by Tomislav Sabljak, of "Lullaby."

T 31 Pjesnik i grad. *Revija* (Osijek), IX, 5 (September–October 1969), 73–83.
A translation, by Giga Gračan, of "The poet and the city."

Czech

Anthology

T 32 *Moderní anglická poezie*, antologii uspořádaní a předmluva napsal R. F. Willetts. Prague: Mladá Fronta, 1964. [Not seen.]
Contains translations, by Jan Zábrana, of "Danse macabre," "Spain 1937," "Lullaby," "Refugee blues," "September 1, 1939," and "The shield of Achilles" (pp. 56–73).

Periodicals

T 33 Nějaký možný sen. *Světová literatura* (Prague), VII, 1 (February 1962), 150–51.
Translations, by Stanislav Mareš, of "O for doors to be open...," "It's no use raising a shout...," "It is time for the destruction of error...," "Sir, no man's enemy...," "Happy the hare at morning...," "What's in your mind, my dove, my my coney...," "Who will endure...," and "O love, the interest itself...."

T 34 Emigrantské blues. Tot' sbohem salónu. *Plamen* (Prague), VI, 6 (1964), 18–20.
Translations, by Jan Zábrana, of "Refugee blues" and "Danse macabre."

T 35 Barvířova ruka. *Sešity pro mladou literatura* (Prague), II, 10 (April 1967), 43–48.
A translation, by Stanislav Mareš, of a section of "The poet and the city."

Danish

Anthologies

T 36 *Under månens skive*, poetisk postil, efter engelsk, fransk, spansk, tysk og svensk. Oversat og redigeret af Elsa Gress. [Copenhagen]: Spectator, [1964]. (Spectators Girafbøger.)
Contains Gress's translations of "Refugee blues" (pp. 94–95), "Who's who" (p. 103), "As I walked out one evening" (pp. 126–27), "The novelist" (p. 142), "Musée des Beaux Arts" (p. 143), and "Blessed event" (p. 151).

T 37 Hansen, Martin N. *Til glæden og andre gendigtninger*. Odense: Odense Amts Bogtrykkeri, 1967.
Contains Hansen's translation of "Make this night loveable . . ." (p. 38).

Periodicals

T 38 Befrieren. *Heretica* (Copenhagen), I, 1 (1948), 3–4.
A translation, by Thorkild Bjørnvig, of the opening chorus of Act II, scene 5, of *The ascent of F6*.

T 39 Af: Bestigningen af F.6: 2. Akt, 1. scene. *Heretica*, II, 2 (1949), 177–83.
A translation, by Bjørn Poulsen, of Act II, scene 1, of *The ascent of F6*.

T 40 James Honeyman. *Ekstra bladet* (Copenhagen), 26 July 1949, pp. 5–6.
Translated by Kai Friis Møller.

T 41 Det magtesløse sprog. *Perspektiv* (Copenhagen), III, 7 (April 1956), 16–18.
A translation, by Jørgen Rothenborg, of "The word and the machine."

T 42 Akilles's skjold. *Information* (Copenhagen), 24 July 1956, p. 4.
A translation, by Lorentz Eckhoff, of "The shield of achilles". An adjoining article includes Eckhoff's translations of "Their lonely betters" and "Barcarolle."

T 43 Ikaros. *Politiken* (Copenhagen), 27 December 1958, *Magasinet*, p. 2.
A translation, by Elsa Gress Wright, of "Musée des Beaux Arts."

T 44 Digte. *Vindrosen* (Copenhagen), VII, 1 (1960), 3–8.
Translations, by Elsa Gress Wright, of "As I walked out one evening," "Roman wall blues," "Refugee blues," "Musée des Beaux Arts," and "Blessed event."

T 45 Digteren som professor. *Jyllands-posten* (Aarhus), 8 February 1961, pp. 9–10.
A translation of "The poet as professor."

Dutch

Book

T 46 *Vier gedichten*, vertaald door C. Buddingh'. [Dordrecht]: Semaphore Pers, 1945. 9⅝ x 7¼ in., pp. [1–4] 5–12 [13–16].
Translations, by Buddingh', of "Hearing of harvests...," "Here on the cropped grass...," "O for doors to be open...," and "Journey to Iceland." Published clandestinely in the early part of 1945 in an edition of 275 numbered copies.[1]

Anthology

T 47 van der Plas, Michel [B. G. F. Brinkel]. *I hear America singing.* Amsterdam: Uitgeverij Vrij Nederland, [1948].
Contains van der Plas's translations of "Dear, though the night is gone...," "Lay your sleeping head, my love...," "Over the heather the wet wind blows...," "O what is that sound...," "Say this city has ten million souls...," "Underneath the abject willow...," "Nothing is given: we must find our law...," and "Here war is simple like a monument..." (pp. 11–21).

Periodicals

T 48 Sonnet. *Vrij Nederland* (Amsterdam), VIII, 13 (22 November 1947), 7.
A translation, by Michel van der Plas, of "Here war is simple like a monument...."

T 49 Song 28. *Vrij Nederland*, VIII, 17–18 (20 December 1947), 19.
A translation, by Michel van der Plas, of "Say this city has ten million souls...."

T 50 Advent. *Kroniek van kunst en kultuur* (Amsterdam), IX, 4 (April 1948), 102–3.
A translation, by Max Schuchart, of the opening chorus of *For the time being.*

T 51 Sonnet. Song 35. *Ad interim* (Utrecht), V. 7–8 (July–August 1948), 284–85.
Translations, by Michel van der Plas, of "Here war is simple like a monument..." and "Underneath the abject willow...."

T 52 Epiloog (uit het kerstoratorium "For the time being"). *Elseviers weekblad* (Amsterdam), VI, 52 (30 December 1950), 17.
A translation, by Michel van der Plas, of "Well, so that is that. Now we must dismantle the tree...."

T 53 Dichtung und Wahrheit, een ongeshcreven gedicht. *Randstad* (Amsterdam), 3 (August 1962), 57–72.
Translated by J. Bernlef.

Finnish

Book with contribution

T 54 *Igor Stravinskin keskusteluja Robert Craftin kanssa.* Helsinki: Kirjayhtymä, 1963. [Not seen.]

[1] See Peter Hopkirk, "Illicit wartime books," *Times,* 14 March 1970, p. 6.

A translation, by Riita Björklund, of *Memories and commentaries,* containing Auden and Stravinsky's scenario for *The rake's progress.*

Periodicals

T 55   I hminen ja atomi. *Valitut palat* (Helsinki), XXII, 1 (January 1966), 3–5. [Not seen.]
A translation of "Of man and the atom" from *Reader's digest.*

T 56   Hetkeisyys ja pysyvyys. *Parnasso* (Helsinki), [XVI], 4 (April 1966), 173–78.
A translation, by Eila Pennanen, of "Nowness and permanence."

Flemish

Anthology

T 57   Christiaens, A. G. *Onvindbaar land, gedichten 1937–1967.* Aude-narde: Drukkerij-uitgeverij Sanderus, [1968]. [Not seen.]
Contains Christiaens's translations of "Brussels in winter" and "Gare du Midi" (pp. 7, 9).

Periodicals

T 58   Musée des Beaux Arts. *Tijd en mens* (Antwerp), I, 6 (July–August 1950), 203.
Translated by Ben Cami.

T 59   Gare du Midi. *Dietsche warande en Belfort* (Antwerp), CXIV, 2 (February 1969), 140–41.
Translated by A. G. Christiaens.

T 60   Musée des Beaux-Arts. *Dietsche warande en Belfort,* CXIV, 5 (June 1969), 391.
Translated by A. G. Christiaens.

T 61   Matrozenlied. *Dietsche warande en Belfort,* CXIV, 7 (September 1969), 546–47.
A translation, by A. G. Christiaens, of "Master and Boatswain" from "The sea and the mirror."

French

Books

T 62   *Le libertin,* opéra en trois actes, sur une fable de W. H. Auden et Chester Kallman, musique par Igor Strawinsky, version française de André de Badet. London: Boosey and Hawkes, [1952]. 7⅞ x 5 in., pp. [1–4] 5–64.
A translation of *The rake's progress.* Published 1952 at 1/6d.

T 63   *Worte und Noten,* Rede zur Eröffnung der Salzburger Festspiele 1968. Salzburg: Festungsverlag, [1968]. (Salzburger Festreden, 5.)

Contains a translation, by Martha Eissler, of "Words and notes." This book is described elsewhere in the bibliography (A 60).

Anthologies and books with contributions

T 64 *On this island*, words by W. H. Auden, texte français by [*sic*] Maurice Pourchet. Vol. 1. London: Boosey & Hawkes, [1938]. (Winthrop Rogers Edition.)
The musical score contains the English and French texts of "Let the florid music praise...," "Now the leaves are falling fast...," "Seascape," "Nocturne" ["Now thro' night's caressing grip..."], and "As it is plenty...." The "Nocturne" was also published separately by Boosey and Hawkes [1949?].

T 65 Isherwood, Christopher. *Le lion et son ombre*, récit, traduit de l'anglais par Maurice-Ian Hilleret. Paris: Editions du Sagittaire, [1947].
Contains Hilleret's translations of "The traction engine," "The engine house," "Rain," and "The rookery" (pp. 176–79).

T 66 *Aspects de la littérature anglaise 1918–1945*, présentés par Kathleen Raine et Max-Pol Fouchet. Paris: Fontaine, [1947].
Contains translations, by M.-P. Fouchet and J.-M. Rivet, of "Lay your sleeping head, my love..." and "Refugee blues" (pp. 392–96). French and English texts.

T 67 *Anthologie de la poésie anglaise contemporaine*, poèmes choisis et présentés par G.-A. Astre. Paris: L'Arche, [1949].
Contains translations of "Doom is dark" and "Night falls on China," by Claudine Chonez; "The leaves of life," by Jacques Vallette; Look, stranger, at this island," by Chonez; and "Palais des Beaux Arts," by Jean-Jacques Mayeux (pp. 116–29). English and French texts.

T 68 *Un demi-siècle de poésie*. Tome II. Dilbeek: La Maison du Poète, [1954]. (Biennales Internationales de Poésie.)
Contains a translation, by L. G. Gros, of "In praise of limestone" (pp. 26–30).

T 69 Ginestier, Paul. *Les meilleurs poèmes anglais et américains d'aujourd'hui* (panorama bilingue), lettre-préface par Jean Cocteau. Paris: Société d'Editions d'Enseignement Supérieur, 1958.
Contains Ginestier's translations of "In memory of W. B. Yeats" (pp. 88–93), "In memory of Sigmund Freud" (pp. 116–23), "Lay your sleepy [*sic*] head, my love..." (pp. 274–77), and "The unknown citizen" (pp. 344–45). English and French texts.

T 70 *Ohne Hass und Fahne. No hatred and no flag. Sans haine et sans drapeu...*, herausgegeben von Wolfgang G. Deppe, Christopher Middleton, und Herbert Schönherr. Hamburg: Rowohlt, [1959].
Contains a translation, by Jacques E. David, of "Say this city has ten million souls..." (pp. 77–78). German, English, and French texts.

T 71 Stravinsky, Igor, and Robert Craft. *Souvenirs et commentaires*, traduit de l'anglais par Francis Ledoux. [Paris]: Gallimard, [1963].
A translation of *Memories and commentaries*, containing Auden and Stravinsky's scenario for *The rake's progress* (pp. 211–19).

T 72 Astre, Georges-Albert. *La poésie anglaise*, édition bilingue. [Paris]: Editions Seghers, [1964].
Contains translations of "Doom is dark," "Night falls on China," and "Look, stranger at this island," by Claudine Chonez; "Palais des Beaux Arts," by Jean-Jacques

Mayoux; and "As I walked out one evening...," by G.-A. Astre (pp. 365–73). French and English texts.

T 73 *Honneur à Saint-John Perse,* hommages et témoignages littéraires .... [Paris]: Gallimard, [1965].
Contains a translation, by Marie Tadié, of "A song of life's power to renew" (pp. 502–3).

Periodicals

T 74 Un poème ... de W. H. Auden. *Le journal des poètes* (Brussels), II, 3 (29 November 1931), 4.
A translation, by Edouard Roditi, of "Before this loved one...." Roditi's typescript, with Auden's MS suggestions and comments, is in the library of the University of California at Los Angeles.

T 75 Un inédit de V. W. [*sic*] Auden: A un jeune homme pour son vingt-et-unième anniversaire. *Le journal des poètes,* IV, 6 (29 April 1934), 4.
A translation, by George Sheridan and René Maurant, of "To a young man on his twenty-first birthday."

T 76 Le chien sous la peau. *Mesures* (Paris), III, 2 (15 April 1937), 13–42.
An abridged translation, by A. M. Petitjean, of *The dog beneath the skin.*

T 77 Espagne. *Commune* (Paris), IV, 48 (August 1937), 1437–40.
A translation, by Jacqueline Cartier, of "Spain".

T 78 Grande Bretagne. Fragment d'une scène de "The ascent of F-6." *Babel* (Cambridge), I, 3 (Summer 1940), 135–36.
Translations, by Clark Mills and André Cuisenier, of "Look, stranger" and of the chorus beginning "Turn off the wireless; we are tired of descriptions of travel..." from *The ascent of F6.*

T 79 Pose la tête endormie, mon amour .... La complainte du refugié. *Fontaine* (Algiers), 37–40 (1944), 412–16.
Translations, by J.-M. Rivet and M.-P. Fouchet, of "Lay your sleeping head, my love..." and "Refugee blues." French and English texts.

T 80 Le massacre des innocents: lamentations du roi Herode. *Choix* (London), II, 7 ([1945]), 61–65.
A translation of "Herod" from *For the time being.*

T 81 Comme je déambulais un soir. *Age nouveau* (Paris), 49–50 (May 1950), 60–62.
A translation, by G.-A. Astre, of "As I walked out one evening." French and English texts.

T 82 Reflexions sur la musique et l'opéra. *Revue musicale* (Paris), 215 (1952), 3–11.
A translation of "Some reflections on music and opera."

T 83 [A review of] *Short novels of Colette. Profils* (Paris), 3 (April 1953), 144–48.
Translated by J. F.

T 84 Le temps ne dira rien. *Le journal des poètes*, XXIV, 6 (June 1954), 2.
A translation, by Claire Goll, of "Time will say nothing but I told you so...."

T 85 Poèmes. *Profils*, 14 (Winter 1956), 70–79.
Translations, by Alain Bosquet, of "The old man's road," "Hunting season," and "Streams." English and French texts.

T 86 [Statement on the 10th anniversary of the Congress for Cultural Freedom]. *Congrès pour la liberté de la culture: informations* (Paris), June–July 1960, p. 5.

T 87 La lecture. *La table ronde* (Paris), 198–99 (July–August 1964), 7–17.
A translation, by Marcelle Sibon, of "Reading" from *The dyer's hand.*

T 88 [Notes to *The Bassarids.*] *Salzburger Festspiele 1966: Die Bassariden* [programme] (Salzburg), 6 August 1966, pp. [21–27].
An anonymous translation.

T 89 Le chien du Prince. *Preuves* (Paris), XVII, 198–99 (Summer 1967), 31–45.
A translation of "The prince's dog."

Record sleeves

T 90 Henze, Hans Werner. *Elegie für junge Liebende....Elégie pour de jeunes amants.* DGG LPM 18 876 *and* SLPM 138 876 [1964].
The libretto stapled to the record sleeve contains an anonymous translation of scenes from *Elegy for young lovers.*

T 91 Henze, Hans Werner. *Moralitäten....Moralités.* DGG SLPM 139 374 [1968].
The libretto stapled to the record sleeve contains an anonymous translation of *Moralities* (pp. 8–12).

Frisian

Periodical

T 92 Refugee blues. *It heitelân* (Sneek), XXVIII, 12 (December 1950), 238.
Translated by Dam Jaarsma.

German

Books

T 93 Strawinsky, Igor. *The rake's progress (Der Wüstling)*, Oper in 3 Akten, eine Fabel von W. H. Auden und Chester Kallman, ins Deutsche übertragen von Fritz Schröder. London: Boosey & Hawkes, [1951]. 7¾ x 5¼ in., pp. [1–3] 4–58 [59–60].

Published 17 August 1951 in an impression of 2,000 copies at DM 1.80, and reprinted in October 1951 (1,000 copies), November 1952 (1,000 copies), June 1962 (1,000 copies), May 1965 (1,000 copies), and April 1967 (2,500 copies). This text also appears in the full and vocal scores of the opera, described elsewhere in the bibliography (A 33), and in *Spectaculum: Texte moderner Opern*, herausgegeben von H. H. Stuckenschmidt (Frankfurt am Main: Suhrkamp, 1962), pp. 285–325.

T 94 *Das Zeitalter der Angst: ein barockes Hirtengedicht*, eingeleitet von Gottfried Benn. Wiesbaden: Limes Verlag, [1951]. 7½ x 4½ in., pp. [1–6] 7–116.

An abridged translation, by Kurt Heinrich Hansen, of *The age of anxiety*. Published 30 March 1951 in an edition of 2,800 copies at DM 6. A second edition, without Benn's introduction, was published in an edition of 7,000 copies in 1958 as *Das Zeitalter der Angst: ein dramatisches Gedicht...* (Munich: R. Piper & Co. Verlag, [1958]; Piper-Bucherei, 117).

T 95 *Der Wanderer*. Wiesbaden: Limes Verlag, [1955]. (Dichtung unserer Zeit, Heft 4.) 7¼ x 4¾ in., pp. [1–3] 4–31 [32].

Translations, by Astrid Claes and Edgar Lohner, of "Musée des Beaux Arts," "The voyage," "The wanderer," "The traveller," "O who can ever gaze his fill...," "The sphinx," "In memory of W. B. Yeats," "Rimbaud," "In time of war, XVII," and "In praise of limestone." English and German texts. Published October 1955 in an edition of 1,265 copies at DM 1.90.

T 96 *Hier und Jetzt: ein Weihnachtsoratorium*, ins Deutsche übertragen von Gerhard Fritsch. Salzburg: Otto Müller Verlag, [1961]. 7½ x 7¾ in., pp. [1–6] 7–88.

A translation of *For the time being*. Published 20 September 1961 in an edition of 2,000 copies at 65 öSch. This translation was broadcast by the Norddeutscher Rundfunk, Hamburg, 2 January 1962.

T 97 *Elegie für junge Liebende. Elegy for young lovers*, Oper in drei Akten von Wystan H. Auden und Chester Kallman, Musik von Hans Werner Henze, deutsche Fassung von Ludwig Landgraf unter Mitarbeit von Werner Schachteli und dem Komponisten. Mainz: B. Schott's Söhne, [1961]. 7¾ x 5⅛ in., pp. [1–7] 8–64.

Published 15 May 1961 [CCE 20 May 1961] in an impression of 3,000 copies at DM 2., and reprinted January 1963 (2,000 copies). This text also appears in the full and vocal scores of the opera, described elsewhere in the bibliography (A 43).

T 98 *The common life*, Deutsch von Dieter Leisegang. Darmstadt: J. G. Bläschke Verlag, [1964]. (Das neueste Gedicht, Band 5.)

Translations of "Ascension Day 1964" and "The common life." This book is described elsewhere in the bibliography (A 48).

T 99 *Shakespeare: Fünf Aufsätze*. [Frankfurt am Main]: Insel-Verlag, [1964]. (Insel-Bucherei, Nr. 811.) 7⅛ x 4½ in., pp. [1–4] 5–128 [129–132].

Translations, by Fritz Lorch, of "The Globe," "The prince's dog," "Brothers and others," "The joker in the pack," and "Music in Shakespeare." Published 1964 in an edition of 7,000 copies at DM 4.50.

T 100 *The cave of making*, Deutsch von Dieter Leisegang. Darmstadt: J. G. Bläschke Verlag, [1965]. (Das neueste Gedicht, Band 15.)

Translations of "The cave of making" and "A change of air." This book is described elsewhere in the bibliography (A 49).

T 101 *Des Färbers Hand und andere Essays.* [Gütersloh]: Sigbert Mohn Verlag, [1965]. 8⅛ x 5 in., pp. [1–10] 11–622 [623–624].
A translation, by Fritz Lorch, of *The dyer's hand.* Published Autumn 1965 in an edition of 2,000 copies at DM 44.

T 102 *Die Bassariden,* Opera seria mit Intermezzo in einem Akt, nach den "Bacchanten" des Euripides, von W. H. Auden und Chester Kallman, Musik von Hans Werner Henze. Mainz: B. Schott's Söhne, [1966]. 7¾ x 5⅛ in., pp. [1–5] 6–55 [56].
A translation, by Maria Bosse-Sporleder, of *The bassarids.* Published 20 July 1966 in an edition of 4,000 copies at DM 2. This text also appears in the vocal score of the opera, described elsewhere in the bibliography (A 54).

T 103 *Worte und Noten,* Rede zur Eröffnung der Salzburger Festspiele 1968. Salzburg: Festungsverlag, [1968]. (Salzburger Festreden, 5.)
Contains a translation, by Max Kaindl-Hönig, of "Words and notes." This book is described elsewhere in the bibliography (A 60).

Anthologies and books with contributions

T 104 *Englische Horn,* Anthologie angelsächischer Lyrik von den Anfängen bis zur Gegenwart, übertragen von Georg von der Vring. [Cologne]: Phaidon, [1953].
Contains von der Vring's translations of "Villanelle" and "But I can't" (pp. 246–47).

T 105 *Gedichte aus der neuen Welt,* amerikanische Lyrik seit 1910, eingeleitet und übertragen von Kurt Heinrich Hansen. Munich: R. Piper & Co. Verlag, [1956].
Contains Hansen's translations of "Musée des Beaux Arts" (p. 9), "The unknown citizen" (pp. 26–27), "The ship" (p. 37), "Spain 1937" (pp. 42–45), and "If on account of the political situation..." from *For the time being* (pp. 61–63).

T 106 *Englische Gedichte aus sieben Jahrhunderten,* Englisch-Deutsch, herausgegeben von Levin L. Schücking. Bremen: Carl Schünemann Verlag, [1956]. (Sammlung Dieterich, Band 109.)
Contains a translation, by Kurt Erich Meurer, of "Sir, no man's enemy" (pp. 340–41). English and German texts.

T 107 *Ohne Hass und Fahne. No hatred and no flag. Sans haine et sans drapeau...* herausgegeben von Wolfgang G. Deppe, Christopher Middleton, und Herbert Schönherr. Hamburg: Rowohlt, [1959].
Contains a translation, by Schönherr, of "Say this city has ten million souls..." (p. 76). German, English, and French texts.

T 108 *Löwe und Einhorn,* englische Lyrik der Gegenwart, ausgewählt und ins Deutsche übertragen von Waltraud Maschke, mit Einleitung und Anmerkungen von Herbert Foltinek. Göttingen: Vandenhoeck & Ruprecht, [1959]. (Kleine Vandenhoeck-Reihe, 86/87.)
Contains Maschke's translations of "Lay your sleeping head, my love..." (pp. 68–69), "In time of war, XVIII," and "The shield of Achilles" (pp. 88–91). English and German texts.

T 109 *Museum der modernen Poesie,* eingerichtet von Hans Magnus Enzensberger. Frankfurt am Main: Suhrkamp Verlag, 1960.

Contains translations of "Musée des Beaux Arts," by Kurt Heinrich Hansen (pp. 72–73); "In memory of W. B. Yeats [pt. 1]" (p. 169), and "Culture" (p. 343), by Enzensberger; and "Spain 1937," by Hansen (pp. 354–57). German and English texts.

T 110 *Panorama moderner Lyrik*, Gedichte des 20. Jahrhunderts in Übersetzungen, herausgegeben von Gunther Steinbrinker in Zusammenarbeit mit Rudolf Hartung. [Gütersloh: Sigbert Mohn, 1960].
Contains translations of "The composer," by A. Claes and E. Lohner (p. 16); "In memory of Sigmund Freud," by Elizabeth Mayer (pp. 96–99); and "Now we must dismantle the tree..." from *For the time being*, by W. Reimerschmid (pp. 214–15).

T 111 *Von Hopkins bis Dylan Thomas*, englische Gedichte und deutsche Prosaübertragungen, herausgegeben und übertragen von Ursula Clemen und Christian Enzensberger. [Frankfurt am Main]: Fischer Bücherei, [1961].
Contains Clemen and Enzensberger's translations of "Sir, no man's enemy," "1st January 1931," "Taller to-day," "Epilogue" to *The double man*, "Legend," and "Eyes look into the well" (pp. 122–33). German and English texts.

T 112 *Gedichte gegen den Krieg*, herausgegeben von Kurt Fassmann. [Munich]: Kindler, [1961].
Contains translations of "Spain 1937," by Kurt Heinrich Hansen (pp. 157–59); and "If on account of the political situation..." from *For the time being*, by Gerhard Fritsch (pp. 257–58).

T 113 Strawinsky, Igor. *Gespräche mit Robert Craft*. [Zurich]: Atlantis-Verlag, [1961].
A translation, by Manfred Gräter, *et al.*, of *Memories and commentaries*, including Auden and Stravinsky's scenario for *The rake's progress* (pp. 155–66).

T 114 *Geistliche Lyrik des Abendlandes*, herausgegeben von Edgar Hederer. Salzburg: Otto Müller Verlag, [1962].
Contains translations of "O shut your bright eyes..." from *For the time being*, by Hederer; and "Sir, no man's enemy...," by Kurt Erich Meurer (pp. 497–98).

T 115 *Documenta poetica*, englisch, amerikanisch im Original und im deutscher Übertragung, herausgegeben von Hans Rudolf Hilty. [Munich]: Kindler, [1962].
Contains translations of "On writing poetry today," by Ursula Clemen (abridged from *Merkur*, November 1955) (pp. 5–11); "Musée des Beaux Arts," by Kurt Heinrich Hansen (pp. 258–59); "Say this city," by Herbert Schönherr (pp. 260–63); and "Funeral song, from *Age of anxiety*," by Hansen (pp. 263–65). English (for the poems only) and German texts.

T 116 *Europa heute*, Prosa und Poesie seit 1945, eine Anthologie ausgewählt und herausgegeben von Hermann Kesten. Band I. [Munich]: Kindler, [1963].
Contains a translation, by Franz Peter Künzel, of "Exiles" (p. 1026).

T 117 Malik, Rudolf. *Ein erwachender Zweig*, Grundfragen des Menschen in der modernen Literatur. Munich: Verlag J. Pfeiffer, [1964].
Contains a translation, by Kurt Heinrich Hansen, of "The ship" (p. 186).

T 118 Höllerer, Walter. *Theorie der modernen Lyrik*, Dokumente zur Poetik, I. [Hamburg]: Rowohlt, [1965]. (Rowohlts deutsche Enzyklopädie, 231–33.)

Contains a translation, by Eva Hesse, of excerpts from "Squares and oblongs" from *Poets at work* (pp. 390–92).

T 119 Levy, Marvin David. *For the time being*, Christmas oratorio ... from the poem by W. H. Auden, German translation by Suzanne Szekely. Vocal score.... [New York]: Boosey and Hawkes, [1967].
A revised edition of the score. The German translation was not in the first edition (London: G. Ricordi, [1959]).

T 120 *Ensemble*, Lyrik, Prosa, Essay. [Munich]: R. Oldenbourg Verlag, [1969].
Contains a translation, by Hans Egon Holthusen, of "Ode to Terminus" (pp. 50–55). English and German texts.

T 121 Henze, Hans Werner. *Moralitäten*, drei szenische Spiele von W. H. Auden nach Fabeln des Äsop, deutsche Übersetzung von Maria Bosse-Sporleder.... Mainz: B. Schott's Söhne, [1969].
The score contains Maria Bosse-Sporleder's translation of *Moralities*. This book is described elsewhere in the bibliography (**B 12**). The German translation was included in the libretto stapled to the record sleeve of the recording, DGG SLPM 139 374 [1968].

Periodicals and theatre programmes

T 122 Spanien. *Internationale Literatur* (Moscow), VIII, 12 ([December] 1938), 8–10.
A translation, by Klara Blum, of "Spain."

T 123 Eines Abends. Die Ballade von James Honeyman. *Mass und Wert* (Zurich), III, 4 (May–July 1940), 519–25.
Translations, by Berthold Viertel, of "As I walked out one evening..." and "James Honeyman."

T 124 Carl Sandburg: *Abraham Lincoln*. *Mass und Wert*, III, 4 (May–July 1940), 532–34.
A translation of the review published in *Common sense*, March 1940.

T 125 Weihnachtsausklang. *Die amerikanische Rundschau* (Munich), III, 11 (January 1947), 3–4.
A translation of "After Christmas." English and German texts.

T 126 Aus dem "Weihnachtsoratorium": die Betrachtung Simeons. Der Bethlehemitische Kindermord. *Wort und Wahrheit* (Vienna), II, 12 (December 1947), 739–47.
Translations, by Hubert Greifeneder, of "The meditation of Simeon" and "The massacre of the innocents" from *For the time being*.

T 127 Der Versuchungen des Schriftstellers: Henry James als Vorbild. *Das neue Auslese* (Munich), III, 10 (October 1948), 73–80.
A translation of "Henry James and the artist in America."

T 128 Dem Andanken Sigmund Freuds. *Die Wandlung* (Heidelberg), III 7 (November 1948), 600–605.
A translation, by Elizabeth Mayer, of "In memory of Sigmund Freud." English and German texts.

T 129 W. B. Yeats als Vorbild. *Der Monat* (Berlin), I, 4 (January 1949), 113–19.

A translation of "Yeats as an example," followed by the English text, and a translation by Karl Berisch of the last five stanzas of "In memory of W. B. Yeats" (pp.
120–21).

T 130   Spanien 1937. *Thema* (Munich), 7 (January 1950), 14–15.
A translation, by Kurt Heinrich Hansen, of "Spain 1937." German and English texts.

T 131   "Ich mag keine Gedichte": Aphorismen von Wystan Hugh Auden.
Die neue Zeitung (Munich), 15 March 1950, p. 7.
Translations, by Eva Hesse, of four excerpts from "Squares and oblongs" from *Poets
at work*.

T 132   Das Zeitalter der Angst. *Merkur* (Baden-Baden), IV, 5 (May
1950), 512–26.
An abridged translation, by Kurt Heinrich Hansen, of *The age of anxiety*.

T 133   Der ironische Held: Reflektionen über "Don Quixote." *Wort und
Wahrheit*, V, 7 (July 1950), 518–25.
A translation, by Hubert Greifeneder, of "The ironic hero."

T 134   Musée des Beaux Arts. *Rheinischer Merkur* (Cologne), VI, 4 (20
January 1951), 7.
Translated by Kurt Heinrich Hansen.

T 135   Reflexionen über die Oper. *Musik der Zeit* (Bonn), [1] (1952),
59–64.
A translation (by Ursula Richter?) of "Reflections on opera."

T 136   Einige Gedanken über die Oper als Kunstgattung. *Melos* (Mainz),
XIX, 1 (January 1952), 1–6.
A translation, by Willi Reich, of "Some reflections on opera as a medium."

T 137   Natur, Geschichte und Poesie. *Merkur* (Munich), VI, 4 (April
1952), 342–51.
A translation, by Eva Rechel, of "Nature, history and poetry."

T 138   Gedenkmal für die Stadt. *Wort und Wahrheit*, VII, 8 (August
1952), 594–98.
A translation, by Karl August Horst, of "Memorial for the city."

T 139   [A review of] *Short novels of Colette. Perspektiven* (Frankfurt
am Main), 3 (May 1953), 134–37.

T 140   Aus dem Weihnachtsoratorium. *Wort und Wahrheit*, VIII, 12
(December 1953), 922–23.
A translation, by Werner Reimerschmid, of "Now we must dismantle the tree. . . ."
German and English texts. Reimerschmid's translation of *For the time being*, "Für
diese Zeit: ein Weihnachtsoratorium," was broadcast by the Bayerischer and Öster-
reichischer Rundfunk, 25 December 1953, with music by Paul Kont.

T 141   Wort und Maschine. *Merkur*, VIII, 6 [for 7] (July 1954), 697–
99.
A translation, by Hermann Stresau, of "The word and the machine."

T 142   Der Schild des Achilles. *Wort und Wahrheit*, X, 9 (September
1955), 664–66.
A translation, by Karl August Horst, of "The shield of Achilles." German and English texts.

T 143   Drei Gedichte. *Merkur*, IX, 10 (October 1955), 906–9.

Translations, by Astrid Claes and Edgar Lohner, of "Oh stretch your hands across the sea...," "The wanderer," and "Musée des Beaux Arts."

T 144 Dichten heute. *Merkur*, IX, 11 (November 1955), 1010–23.
A translation, by Ursula Clemen, of "On writing poetry today."

T 145 Drei Gedichte. *Perspektiven*, 14 (Winter 1956), 64–71.
Translations, by Astrid Claes and Edgar Lohner, of "The traveller," "Prime," and "Lay your sleeping head, my love...."

T 146 Vesper. *Der Monat*, VIII, 92 (May 1956), 16–19.
A translation, by Karl Berisch, of "Vespers." English and German texts.

T 147 Musik bei Shakespeare. *Forum* (Vienna), V, 50 (February 1958), 74–76, and V, 51 (März 1958), 111–13.
A translation of "Music in Shakespeare."

T 148 Eine neue englische Übersetzung der "Zauberflöte": Vorrede zur Buchausgabe. *Merkur*, XII, 5 (May 1958), 438–43.
Reprinted in *Neue Zeitschrift für Musik* (Mainz), CXIX, 19 (October 1958), 571–74.
A translation of the "Preface" to *The magic flute*.

T 149 Glückwünsche aus aller Welt. W. H. Auden. *Kongress für die Freiheit der Kultur: Nachrichten* (Paris), June 1960, pp. 2–3.
A translation of Auden's statement on the tenth anniversary of the Congress for Cultural Freedom.

T 150 Dichtung und Wahrheit: ein ungeschreibenes Gedicht. *Merkur*, XIV, 11 (November 1960), 1007–20.
Translated by Isabella Levitin.

T 151 Geburt eines Librettos. *Neue Zeitschrift für Musik*, CXXII, 5 (1961), 179–80.
A translation, by Ken W. Bartlett, of "Genesis of a libretto." Four pages of Henze's score for *Elegy for young lovers* are printed between pp. 198–99.

T 152 Pfingstsonntag in Kirchstetten. *Wort und Wahrheit*, XVIII, 5 (May 1963), 336–38.
A translation, by Claus Pack, of "Whitsunday in Kirchstetten." German and English texts.

T 153 Drei Gedichte zu Shakespeares "Sturm." *Das Inselschiff* (Frankfurt am Main), N.F. 7 (March 1964). [Not seen.]
Translations of "Miranda's song," "Invocation to Ariel," and "Stephano's song."

T 154 Shakespeares Welttheater. *Merkur*, XVIII, 4 (April 1964), 301–10.
A translation, by Fritz Lorch, of "The Globe."

T 155 Aus der Budapester PEN-Diskussion über Tradition und Moderne: W. H. Auden. *Sinn und Form* (Berlin), XVII, 5 (1965), 785–86.
A translation, by Stephan Hermlin, of Auden's address to the P.E.N. conference in Budapest, October 1964. This translation was made from a mimeographed transcript of Auden's address, and differs from the revised version published as "A short defense of poetry" (B 103). No copy of the mimeographed transcript has been located.

T 156 Anmerkungen zu Musik und Oper. *Neue deutsche Hefte* (Gütersloh), XII, 104 (March–April 1965), 45–56.
A translation, by Fritz Lorch, of "Notes on music and opera."

T 157 Josef Weinheber. *Neue Rundschau* (Berlin), LXXVI, 3 (1965), 398–405.

Translated by Herbert Heckmann. English and German texts.

T 158   Kultur. *Neue Literatur* (Bucharest), XVI, 5 (October 1965), 56–57.
A translation, by Hans Magnus Enzensberger, of "Culture."

T 159   Des Färbers Hand. *Melos*, XXXIII, 3 (March 1966), 73–75.
A translation, by Fritz Lorch, of "The dyer's hand."

T 160   Brief an eine Wunde. *Merkur*, XX, 5 (May 1966), 443–45.
A translation, by Isabella Levitin, of "Letter to a wound."

T 161   Die Bombe und das menschliche Buwusststein. *Merkur*, XX 8 (August 1966), 705–9.
A translation, by Elizabeth Mayer, of "The corruption of innocent neutrons."

T 162   [Notes on *The bassarids*. Programme of the] *Salzburger Festspiele 1966: Die Bassariden*, 8 August 1966, pp. [5–11].
This translation also appears in the full score of the opera, described elsewhere in the bibliography (**A 54**).

T 163   Gedichte. *Merkur*, XXI, 1 (January 1967), 31–34.
Translations, by Hans Egon Holthusen, of "Friday's child" (with English text), "Master and Boatswain," and "Elegy for J. F. K."

T 164   But I can't. *Merkur*, XXI, 2 (February 1967), 157–59.
The English text, followed by three translations, by Kurt Hoffman (from a broadcast by the Bayerischer Rundfunk, May 1955), by Georg von der Vring, and by Hans Egon Holthusen.

T 165   Rockhope [*sic*]. *Frankfurter allgemeine Zeitung* (Frankfurt am Main, 21 February 1967, p. 24.
A translation, by Kurt Hoffman, of 16 lines from "New year letter."

T 166   Tal der Finsternis. *Neue Rundschau*, LXXVIII, 3 (1967), 443–53.
This translation, by Hanns A. Hammelmann, of "The dark valley" had previously been broadcast by the Bayerischer and Norddeutscher Rundfunk, 1964, and again by R.I.A.S., Berlin, 18 August 1965, spoken by Tilla Durieux.

T 167   Prolog mit sechzig Jahren. *Neue deutsche Hefte* (Berlin), XIV, 4 (1967), 15–18.
A translation of "Prologue at sixty." "Die Übersetzung . . . stammt (unter Mitwirkung und Autorisierung des Autors) von Ingo Seidler."

T 168   Mondlandung. *Wort und Wahrheit*, XXIV, 6 (November–December 1969), 506–7.
A translation, by Herbert Zand, of "Moon landing." English and German texts.

Greek

Periodicals

T 169   Prosphygiko blioyz. *Eleuthera grammata* (Athens), n.s. 2 (1 July 1947), 41.
A translation, by Kleitos Kyrou, of "Refugee blues."

T 170   [Hearing of harvests . . . . Look, stranger . . . .] *Prosperos* (Corfu), 2 (1950), 38–40. [Not seen.]

T 171   [Poem.] *Epochē* (Volos), 1 (January–February 1952), 13–14. [Not seen].

A translation, by Kleitos Kyrou, of "O what is that sound."

T 172 Merikes simeioseis stous Grimm kai ston Andersen. *Anglo-ellēnikē epitheōrēsē* (Athens), VII, 8 (Spring 1955), 332–40. [Not seen.]
A translation, by Leon Karapanayiotis, of "Some notes on Grimm and Andersen."

T 173 [Poems.] *Endochōra* (Ioannina), IV, 20 ([November–December 1962]), 1050–51.
Translations, by Kleitos Kyrou, of "The unknown citizen," "Who's who," and "Epitaph on a tyrant."

T 174 Nomos, lene oi kēpoura. *Endochōra*, IV, 23 (May–June 1963), 1174–76.
A translation, by Stairos Thepsanithi, of "Law like love."

T 175 To epikairo kai to pantoteino stēn technē. *Aktines* (Athens), XXX, 277 (January 1967), 17–21.
A translation, by I. A. Papageorgiou, of "Nowness and permanence."

Gujarati

Book with contribution

T 176 Toller, Ernst. *Kāyāpalat*. Ahmadabad: Ravani, [1961.] [Not seen.]
A translation, by "Sundaram" [Tribhuvan Das Luhar] of Toller's *Transformation*, preceded by a translation of Auden's "In memory of Ernst Toller" (pp. 30–31), along with the English text (pp. 28–29).

Hebrew

Anthologies

T 177 Avinoam, Reuben. *Mivḥar shirat Angliyah* . . . . Tel Aviv: Massadah, 1956. [English title: *A Hebrew anthology of English verse*.]
Contains Avinoam's translations of "Look, stranger . . . ," "Canzone," "In memory of W. B. Yeats [pt. 3]," "September 1, 1939," "If on account of the political situation . . ." from *For the time being*, and "The unknown citizen" (pp. 632–42).

T 178 *Luaḥ ha-ohavim* . . . [ed. by] Leah Goldberg. [Tel Aviv]: Amyaḥi, [1956].
Contains Goldberg's translation of "As I walked out one evening" (pp. 130–31).

Periodical

T 179 Ha-nokhri veha-ʻir: ketsat hirhurim ʻal "Otelo." *Molad* (Tel Aviv), XIX, 157 (July–August 1961), 343–54.
A translation of "The alienated city: reflections on *Othello*."

Hindi

Anthology

T 180 *Deśāntar*, [compiled and translated by] Dharmvīr Bhārati. Benares: Bharatiya Gyanpith, 1960. [Not seen.]
Contains a translation of "Musée des Beaux Arts" (p. 117).

Hungarian

Book

T 181   *Achilles pajzsa*, válogatott versek. Budapest: Európa Könyviadó, 1968. 6⅛ x 6⅜ in., pp. [1–6] 7–163 [164–168].
Translations, by András Fodor, Ágnes Gergely, *et al.*, of thirty-five poems, selected and with an afterword by András Fodor. Published August 1968 in an edition of 2,100 copies at Ft. 11.50.

Anthologies

T 182   *Szerelmes versek*, világirodalmi antológia két ezredév költészetéből; Képes, Géza [*et al.*], műfordításai. Budapest: Szukits-kiadás, [1941].
Contains Képes's translation of "O what is that sound…" (pp. 109–10).

T 183   *A sziget énekel*, angol költők, Képes, Géza, műfordításai. Budapest: Parnasszus, 1947.
Contains Képes's translations of "I have a handsome profile…" and "O what is that sound…" (pp. 136–39). English and Hungarian texts.

T 184   Szabó, Lőrinc. *Örök barátaink*, kisebb lírai versfordítások második gyűjteménye. [Vol. 2]. [Budapest]: Egyetemi Nyomda, 1948.
Contains Szabó's translations of "The novelist" (p. 143) and "Look, stranger…" (p. 165). An enlarged second edition ([Budapest]: Szépirodalmi Könyvkiadó, 1958), contains the same poems (pp. 499–500, 595).

T 185   *Szabó Lőrinc válogatott műfordításai*. [Budapest]: Franklin Könyvkiadó N.V., [1950].
Contains Szabó's translation of "Look, stranger…" (pp. 396–97).

T 186   *Énekek éneke*, a világirodalom szerelmes verseiből, [válogatta Vas, István]. Budapest: Európa Könyvkiadó, 1957.
Contains a translation, by Géza Képes, of "O what is that sound…" (pp. 610–11).

T 187   *Az angol líra kincsesháza*, [vol. 8], huszadik század, válogatta és szerkesztette Bartos, Tibor. Budapest: Európa Könyvkiadó, 1958. [Not seen.]
Contains translations, by Géza Képes, of "O what is that sound…" and "I have a handsome profile…."

T 188   *Angol költők angológiája*, [ed. by Miklós Vajda, selection begun by Lőrinc Szabó]. [Budapest]: Móra Ferenc Könyvkiadó, [1960].
Contains translations of "Look, stranger…," by Szabó; "Epitaph on a tyrant," by Ernő Hárs; "The unknown citizen," by László Kálnoky; "The novelist," by Szabó; "I have a handsome profile…," by Géza Képes; "At last the secret is out…" by István Vas; "This lunar beauty…" by Sándor Weöres; and "Sir, no man's enemy…," by Kálnoky (pp. 663–74).

T 189   Végh, György. *Modern Orfeusz*, válogatott műfordítások. Budapest: Magvető Könyvkiadó, 1960.
Contains Végh's translation of "Musée des Beaux Arts" (pp. 153–54).

T 190   *Költők színei–színek költői*, válogatta: Földes, Anna [és] Mihályi, Gábor. Budapest: Képzőművészeti Alap Kiadóvállalata, 1961. [Not seen.]

Contains a translation, by György Végh, of "Musée des Beaux Arts" (p. 82).

T 191 *Guernica,* a spanyol polgárháború költészete. Budapest: Magvető Könyvkiadó, 1963. [Not seen.]
Contains a translation, by Ágnes Nemes Nagy, of "Spain" (p. 158 ff.).

T 192 Nemes Nagy, Ágnes. *Vándorévek.* Budapest: Magvető Könyvkiadó, 1964.
Contains Nemes Nagy's translation of "Spain" (pp. 351–55).

T 193 *Szerelmes arany kalendárium* ... [Kormos, István, válogatta]. [Budapest]: Kosmosz Könyvek, 1965.
Contains a translation, by István Tótfalusi, of "Lady, weeping at the crossroads..." (pp. 434–35).

T 194 Kálnoky, László. *Évgyűruk,* műfordítások. Budapest: Szépirodalmi Könyvkiadó, 1967.
Contains Kálnoky's translation of "The unknown citizen" (pp. 267–68).

T 195 *Szerelmes ezüst kalendárium* ... [Kormos, István, válogatta]. [Budapest]: Kozmosz Könyvek, 1967.
Contains a translation, by István Tótfalusi, of "As I walked out one evening" (pp. 210–12).

T 196 *A líra ma,* vallomások, esszék; az antológiát szerkesztette és a bevezetőt írta: Hajnal, Gábor. Budapest: Gondolat, 1968.
Contains a translation, by Júlia Kada, of "The poet and the city" (pp. 409–17).

T 197 Szemlér, Ferenc. *Változott egekben,* válogatott műfordítások. [Budapest]: Európa Könyvkiadó, 1969.
Contains Szemlér's translations of "It's no use raising a shout...," "In memory of W. B. Yeats [p. 3]," and "Chorus from a play" (pp. 335–39).

Periodicals

T 198 Ballada. *Új idők* (Budapest), LI, 7 (15 September 1945), 197.
A translation, by Géza Képes, of "O what is that sound...."

T 199 [Two poems.] *Válasz* (Budapest), VII, 1 (January 1947), 102.
Translations, by Laszló Fazekas, of "It's no use raising a shout..." and "We made all possible preparations...."

T 200 [Two poems.] *Új idők,* LII (1947), 128. [Not seen.]
Translations, by Pál Tábori, of "Say this city has ten million souls..." and "In memoriam Ernst Toller."

T 201 Versek. *Nagyvilág* (Budapest), III, 2 (February 1958), 202–3.
Translations, by Ágnes Gergely, of "One evening" and "The unknown citizen."

T 202 Wystan Hugh Auden verseiből. *Vigilia* (Budapest), XXIV, 7 (July 1959), 413–17.
Translations with an introductory note, by Kálmán Lakatos, of "Lauds," "Look, stranger..." and "Metalogue to The magic flute."

T 203 A nagy titok. *Nagyvilág,* IV, 9 (September 1959), 1380.
A translation, by István Vas, of "At last the secret is out...."

T 204 1939 szeptember 1. *Alföld* (Debrecen), XI, 3 (May–June 1960), 78–80. [Not seen.]
A translation, by Ferenc Pákozdy, of "September 1, 1939."

T 205 Dal. Utónang. *Új irás* (Budapest), V, 2 (February 1965), 167–70.
Translations, by Géza Kepes, of "I have a handsome profile..." and "Certainly our city...."

T 206 Elégia J. F. K.–hez. *Igaz szó* (Bucharest), XIII, 3 (March 1965), 460–1. [Not seen.]
A translation, by János Szász, of "Elegy for J. F. K."

T 207 Erdők. *Nagyvilág*, XIII, 11 (November 1968), 1724–25.
A translation, by András Fodor, of "Woods."

Icelandic

Anthologies

T 208 Ásgeirsson, Magnús. *Þýdd ljóð, V*. Reykjavík: Bókadeild Menningarsjóðs, 1936.
Contains Ásgeirsson's translation of "Journey to Iceland" (pp. 67–69).

T 209 Ásgeirsson, Magnús. *Siðustu þýdd ljóð*, Guðmundur Böðvarsson bjó til prentunar. Reykjavík: Bókaútgáfa Menningarsjóðs, 1961.
Contains Ásgeirsson's translation of stanzas 8 and 9 of "Letter to Lord Byron" (pp. 65–66).

Periodicals

T 210 Njála í enskri útgáfu. *Tímarit máls og menningar* (Reykjavík), XVII, 2–3 (December 1956), 258–62.
A translation, by Gísli Asmundsson, of "Concrete and fastidious."

T 211 [The world that books have made.] *Nýtt helgafell* (Reykjavík), II, 1 (January–April 1957), 48.

T 212 Lít gestur. *Lesbók morgunlaðsins* (supplement of *Morgunblaðið*) (Reykjavík), XXXIX, 14 (19 April 1964), 3.
A translation, by Sigurður A. Magnússon, of "Look, stranger...."

T 213 Iceland revisited. *Lesbók morgunblaðsins*, XXXIX, 20 (31 May 1964), 3.
Icelandic and English texts.

Italian

Books

T 214 *Carriera d'un libertino* (The rake's progress), favola in tre atti, di W. H. Auden & Chester Kallman, musica di Igor Strawinsky, versione ritmica italiana di Rinaldo Küfferle, con prefazione di Guglielmo Barblan. London: Boosey and Hawkes, 1951. 7¾ x 5¼ in., pp. [1–2] 3–55 [56]. Printed by Carisch S. A., Milan, 1951.
Published 3 December 1951 in an edition of 2,000 copies at L.400.

T 215 *Poesie di W. H. Auden,* introduzione, versione e note di Carlo Izzo. [Parma]: Guanda, [1952]. (Collezione Fenice, 18.) 8⅝ x 5½ in., pp. [I–VII] VIII–XXXVI, 1–254 [255–256].
Translations, by Carlo Izzo, of ninety poems. English and Italian texts. Published May 1952 in an impression of 1,500 copies at L.1200, and reprinted June 1961 (2,000 copies). The book quotes some letters from Auden to the translator.

T 216 *Good-bye to the Mezzogiorno,* poesia inedita e versione italiana di Carlo Izzo. Milan: All'Insegna del Pesce d'Oro, 1958.
This book is described elsewhere in the bibliography (A 41).

T 217 *Per il tempo presente,* oratorio di Natale, traduzione di Aurora Ciliberti. Milan: All'Insegna del Pesce d'Oro, 1964. (Acquario, n. 25.) 6¾ x 4¾ in., pp. [1–7] 8–170 [171–176].
A translation of *For the time being.* English and Italian texts. Published December 1964 in an edition of 1,000 copies at L.1500.

T 218 *Opere poetiche,* di W. H. Auden, volume primo .... Milan: Lerici Editori, [1966]. (Poeti Europei, 22.) 8¼ x 5 in., pp. [1–8] 9–559 [560–570].
Translations of "The quest," "Sonnets from China," "Letter to a wound," and "Depravity, a sermon," by Aurora Ciliberti; "New year letter," by Giovanni Fattorini; *For the time being* and *The sea and the mirror,* by Aurora Ciliberti. English and Italian texts. The English texts of "The quest" and "Sonnets from China" are similar to, but not entirely identical with, the revised texts published in CSP2 later the same year; this volume also quotes a letter from Auden to Aurora Ciliberti and contains a facsimile manuscript of "The door." Published February 1966 in an edition of 3,000 copies at L.4800.
     The second volume of this collection contains translations by Aurora Ciliberti of *The orators,* "Letter to Lord Byron," and the shorter poems of 1927–38 (with slight changes by Auden in the English text of the shorter poems); there is also a facsimile manuscript of "Autumn song." Rome: Lerici Editore, [1969]; (Poeti Europei, 26); 8¼ x 5 in., pp. [1–8] 9–533 [534–44]. Published February 1969 in an edition of 2,500 copies at L.6000.

T 219 *L'età dell'ansia,* egloga barocca, a cura di Antonio Rinaldi. [Milan]: Arnoldo Mondadori Editore, [1966]. (Lo Specchio.) 7⅜ x 4⅞ in., pp. [1–8] 9–277 [278–284].
A translation, by Lina Dessí and Antonio Rinaldi, of *The age of anxiety,* English and Italian texts. Published October 1966 in an edition of 1,800 copies at L.2800.

T 220 *Saggi,* prefazione di Enzo Siciliano. [Milan]: Garzanti, [1968]. (Collezione Saggi.) 8¼ x 4⅜ in., pp. [1–4] 5–223 [224–226].
A translation, by Gabriella Fiori Andreini, of *The dyer's hand,* from the "Foreword" through "The well of Narcissus." Published May 1968 in an edition of 2,400 copies at L.3000.

T 221 *Dall'Età dell'ansia,* egloga barocca, di Wystan Hugh Auden. [Verona: Corubolo e Castiglioni, 1969]. 11 x 8 in., pp. [i–iv, 1–6] 7–34 [35–36].
A separate edition of part 5 of Lina Dessí and Antonio Rinaldi's translation of *The age of anxiety.* Privately printed August 1969 in an edition of 70 numbered copies, of which 20 are accompanied by a portfolio of lithographs by Valerio Adami.

Anthologies with contributions

T 222 *Poesia inglese contemporanea*, da Thomas Hardy agli apocalittici, introduzione, versione e note di Carlo Izzo. [Modena]: Guanda, [1950]. (Collezione Fenice, 13.)
Contains Izzo's translations of "A shilling life will give you all the facts...," "Law like love," "Edward Lear," "The capital," "Petition," "As well as can be expected," "But I can't," "Look, stranger...," "Refugees blues," "It's no use raising a shout," and "No, nothing that matters will ever happen..." from Act I of the "*The ascent of F6* (pp. 354–75). English and Italian texts.

T 223 *Guida a The rake's progress....* [Venice: Biennale d'Arte, 1951].
Contains a translation, by Carlo Izzo, of "Some reflections on opera as a medium," from *Tempo* (pp. 13–21).

T 224 Isherwood, Christopher. *Leoni e ombre*, romanzo, unica traduzione autorizza dall'inglese di Manlio Eocci. Milan, Verona: A. Mondadori, 1953. [Not seen.]
Contains Eocci's translations of "The traction engine," "The engine house," "Rain," and "The rookery."

T 225 *Poeti stranieri del '900*, tradotti da poeti italiani, a cura di Vanni Scheiwiller. Milan: All'Insegna del Pesce d'Oro, 1956. (Strenna del Pesce d'Oro, [5].)
Contains a translation, by Sergio Solmi, of "At last the secret is out..." (p. 100).

T 226 *Poesia straniera del novecento*, a cura di Attilio Bertolucci. [Milan]: Garzanti, [1958].
Contains translations, by Augusto Gaudi, of "In memory of W. B. Yeats," "As I walked out one evening," "Musée des Beaux Arts," "Their lonely betters," and "It was Easter as I walked in the public gardens..." (pp. 348–63). English and Italian texts.

T 227 *Poeti del novecento*, italiani e stranieri, antologia a cura di Elena Croce. [Turin]: Einaudi, [1960].
Contains translations of "But I can't," by Carlo Izzo; "Reflections in a forest," by Elemire Zolla; and "Good-bye to the Mezzogiorno," by Carlo Izzo (pp. 70–83). English and Italian texts.

T 228 Puccini, Dario. *Romancero della resistenza spagnola (1936–1959)*. Milan: Feltrinelli Editore, [1960]. (Antologia, 2.)
Contains a translation of "Spain" (pp. 378–87). English and Italian texts.

T 229 *Poeti inglesi del 900*, teste, traduzioni e introduzione a cura di Roberto Sanesi. [Milan]: Bompiani, [1960].
Contains Sanesi's translations of "Musée des Beaux Arts," "Easy knowledge," "In memory of W. B. Yeats," "Spain 1937," "Underneath the abject willow," an extract from the "Commentary" to "In time of war," the "Prologue" to "New year letter," and part I of "New year letter" (pp. 372–417). English and Italian texts.

T 230 *Antologia della critica americana del novecento*, a cura di Morton Dauwen Zabel. [Vol.] II. Rome: Edizioni di Storia e Letteratura, 1961.
Contains translations, by Augusto Gaudi, of "A knight of the infinite," "Heretics," "The poet of the encirclement," and "The public v. the late Mr William Butler Yeats" (pp. 129–54).

T 231 *Il Natale*, antologia di poeti del '900, a cura di Mary de Rachewiltz

e Vanni Scheiwiller. Milan: All'Insegna del Pesce d'Oro, 1961. (Strenna del Pesce d'Oro, [10].)
Contains a translation, by Carlo Izzo, of the first stanza of "Advent" from *For the time being* (pp. 14–15). English and Italian texts.

T 232   *Poesia americana del '900* con testo a fronte, introduzioni e note biobibliographiche a cura di Carlo Izzo. [Parma]: Guanda, [1963]. (Collana Fenice, nuova serie, sezione antologie, 4.)
Contains Izzo's translations of "Good-bye to the Mezzogiorno," "Streams," "Sext," and "Walks" (pp. 476–503). English and Italian texts.

T 233   Solmi, Sergio. *Versioni poetiche da contemporanei.* Milan: All'-Insegna del Pesce d'Oro, 1963. (Acquario, n. 15.)
Contains Solmi's translations of "At last the secret is out...," "Let the florid music praise...," and "Look, stranger..." (pp. 62–67). English and Italian texts.

T 234   *La fortuna di Shakespeare (1593–1964),* a cura di Gabriele Baldini. Vol. 2. [Milan]: Casa Editrice Il Saggiatore, [1965].
Contains a translation, by Wanda Colosimo d'Addio, of "The fallen city: some reflections on Shakespeare's *Henry IV*" (pp. 668–93).

T 235   di Salvo, Tommaso, and Giuseppe Zagarrio. *Tavola rotonda,* antologia di letture italiane e straniere. Florence: La Nuova Italia Editrice, [1969].
Contains translations, by Carlo Izzo, of "Refugee blues" (pp. 1156–57) and "No, nothing that matters will ever happen..." from Act I of *The ascent of F6* (pp. 1243–44).

Periodicals

T 236   Poesia. *Poesia* (Rome), 1 (1945), 178–86.
A translation, by Augusto Gaudi, of "It was Easter as I walked in the public gardens...." Italian and English texts.

T 237   Landfall. *Inventario* (Florence), I, 3–4 (Autumn–Winter 1946–47), 29.
English and Italian texts.

T 238   Ischia. *Botteghe oscure* (Rome), II ([Autumn] 1948), [supplement of translations of] *Poeti inglesi e americani,* pp. 3–5.
Translated by Salvatore Rosati.

T 239   Yeats, un esempio. *La rassegna d'Italia* (Milan), IV, 5 (May 1949), 469–75.
A translation, by Marta Bini, of "Yeats as an example."

T 240   Guarda, straniero. *La fiera letteraria* (Rome), IV, 24 (12 June 1949), 5.
A translation, by Romeo Lucchese, of "Look, stranger."

T 241   Poesie. *Archi* (Bologna), 5–6 ([1951]), 38–45.
Translations, by Carlo Izzo, of "Musée des Beaux Arts," "If on account of the political situation..." from *For the time being,* and "Nursery rhyme." English and Italian texts.

T 242   [A review of] *Short novels of Colette. Prospetti* (Florence), 3 (Spring 1953), 174–77.

Translated by Eugenio Vaquer.

T 243 Le notti scendono.... *La fiera letteraria*, VII, 4 (27 January 1952), 3.
A translation, by Romeo Lucchese, of "Taller to-day."

T 244 Guarda ora a quest'isola. *La fiera letteraria*, VII, 6 (10 February 1952), 3.
A translation, by Leone Traverso, of "Look, stranger."

T 245 Commento alla collana di sonnetti scritti "In tempo di guerra." *La fiera letteraria*, VII, 16 (20 April 1952), 5–6.
A translation, by Carlo Izzo, of the "Commentary" to "In time of war."

T 246 Herman Melville. *La fiera letteraria*, VIII, 10 (8 March 1953), 4.
Translated by Alfredo Rizzardi.

T 247 Frammente dal New Year letter. *La fiera letteraria*, IX [for X], 39 (25 September 1955), 6.
Fragments translated by Roberto Sanesi.

T 248 Ischia. *La fiera letteraria*, IX [for X], 42 (16 October 1955), 1.
Translated by Glauco Cambon.

T 249 Tre poesie. *Prospetti*, 14 (Winter 1955), 18–27.
Translations, by E. B. and C. T., of "The old man's road," "Hunting season," and "Streams." English and Italian texts. A passage in Italian from a letter by Auden concerning "The old man's road" appears as a footnote on pp. 24–25.

T 250 Poesie. *Il veltro* (Rome), I, 3–4 (June–July 1957), 10–14.
Translations, by M. Carpitella, of "Look, stranger," "O unicorn among the cedars ..." from "New Year letter," and "In youth the panting slave pursues..." from *The rake's progress*. English and Italian texts.

T 251 Del fare e del giudicare. *Il tempo presente* (Rome), III, 2 (February 1958), 96–108.
A translation, by Vittorio Guerrini, of "Making and judging poetry," from *Atlantic*.

T 252 Cattivo tempo. Herman Melville. *Galleria* (Rome), VIII, 5–6 (September–December 1958), 257–61.
Translated by Alfredo Rizzardi. English and Italian texts.

T 253 La parrocchia delittuosa: observazioni sul romanzo poliziesco. *Paragone* (Florence), VII, 84 (December 1956), 19–31.
A translation, by Giorgio Manganelli, of "The guilty vicarage."

T 254 La mano del tintore: la poesia e il processo poetico. *Questioni* (Turin), VII, 1–2 (January–April 1959), 23–32. Continued as: Lo scienziato e l'artista. *Questioni*, VII, 3 (maggio 1959), 4–16.
A translation, by Livia Magliano, of "The dyer's hand."

T 255 Dalla *New Year letter*. *Inventario* (Milan), XIV, 1–6 (January–December 1959), 186–197.
Translations, by Roberto Sanesi, of the "Prologue" to "New Year letter" and part I of "New Year letter."

T 256 De "L'età dell'ansia." *L'approdo letterario* (Rome, n.s. X, 26 (April–June 1964), 57–85.
Selections from *The age of anxiety*, translated by Lina Dessí and Antonio Rinaldi. English and Italian texts.

T 257 Ode a Terminus. *Conoscenza religiosa* (Florence), 1 (January–March 1969), 62–68.
A translation, by Carlo Izzo, of "Ode to Terminus." English and Italian texts.

Japanese

Books

T 258 *Ōden shishū.* [Tokyo]: Chikuma Shobō, [1955]. 7 x 4¾ in., pp. [i–vi, 1–2] 3–196, (English text) [i–iv], 1–70.
Translations, by Motohiro Fukase, of forty-two poems from CSP. Published 1 June 1955 in an edition of 2,200 copies at ¥650. An enlarged edition was published January 1968 at ¥900. [Tokyo]: Serika Shobō, [1968]; 8¼ x 5 in., pp. [1–10] 11–250, (English text) [1–2] 3–68. [Not seen.]

T 259 *Ikareru umi,* roman shugi no umi no imēji; sōsho, *Fuan no jidai.* Tokyo: Nan'undo, [1962]. 7¼ x 4½ in., pp. [1–8] 9–244. [Not seen.]
Translations, by Jun'nosuke Sawasaki, of *The enchafèd flood* and *The age of anxiety.* Published 10 June 1962 in an edition of 500 copies at ¥580.

T 260 *Wakai koibito-tachi e no erēji....* [Tokyo]: Ongakunotomosha, [1966]. (Opera Taiyaku Shīrīzu, 9.) 6¾ x 4¼ in., pp. [1–7] 8–159 [160].
A translation, by Kei'ichi Uchigaki, of *Elegy for young lovers.* German [*sic!*] and Japanese texts. Published 1 October 1966 in an edition of 3,000 copies at ¥350.

Anthologies and books with contributions

T 261 *Zoku watashi wa shinzuru.* Tokyo: Shakai Shisō Kenkyū-kai Shuppan-bu, 1953. [Not seen.]
A translation, by Yoshio Nakano *et al.,* of *I believe,* including Auden's essay.

T 262 Uchimura, Naoya. *Gendai sekai gikyoku senshū, 11: Igirisu.* Tokyo: Hakusuisha, 1954.
Contains a translation, by Kazuo Nakahashi, of *The dance of death* (pp. 73–96).

T 263 Ando, Ichiro, and Katsuji Takamura. *Ei-bei gendaishi no kanshō.* Tokyo: Kenkyusha, 1956. [Not seen.]
Contains translations of "Schoolchildren" and "Look, stranger" (pp. 202–15).

T 264 Isherwood, Christopher. *Raion to kage.* Tokyo: Nan'undo, 1958. [Not seen.]
A translation, by Minoru Hashiguchi, of *Lions and shadows,* containing "The traction engine," "The engine house," "Rain," and "The rookery."

T 265 *Sekai meishishū taisei, 10: Igirisu....* [Tokyo]: Heibonsha, [1959].
Contains translations, by Hideo Kano, of *Look, stranger!* (the complete book), and, by Minoru Hashiguchi, of "Spain," "Refugee blues," "In memory of Ernst Toller," and "September 1, 1939" (pp. 329–52).

T 266 *Waga shinjō.* Tokyo: Taishūkan Shoten, 1960. (Taishūkan Kosumosu Raiburari.) [Not seen.]
Contains an annotated translation, by Yoshitaka Sakai, of Auden's contribution to *I believe* (pp. 1–20).

T 267 *Sekai jinseiron zenshu, 7.* [Tokyo]: Chikuma Shobō [1962].

Contains a translation, by Yūichi Takamatsu, of "Anger" from *The seven deadly sins* (pp. 146–54).

T 268   Kirkup, James, and Chozo Kokunaga. *Shijin no koe.* Tokyo: Kenkyusha, 1967. [Not seen.]
Contains translations and discussions of "The unknown citizen," "Fleet visit," and "Islands."

T 269   *Seikai meishishū 4: Eliot*, Arechi; *Auden*, Miyo, tabibito yo!; *Spender*, Shishū. [Tokyo]: Heibonsha, [1968].
Contains a translation, by Hideo Kano, of *Look, stranger!* (the complete book) (pp. 55–152).

T 270   *Sekai shijin zenshū, 19: Auden, Spender, Thomas, shishū....* [Tokyo]: Shinchōsha, [1969].
Contains translations, by Masao Nakagiri, of thirty-one poems, with English texts of "The wanderer" and "Autumn song" (pp. 5–106).

T 271   Narita, Shigehisa. *Eigo saijiki: natsu.* Tokyo: Kenkyusha, 1969.
Contains a translation of the first stanza of "A summer night" (p. 46). English and Japanese texts. A similar volume, *Eigo saijiki: fuyu*, published the same year, contains English and Japanese texts of the first stanza of "In memory of W. B. Yeats" (p. 9).

Periodicals

T 272   Ode. *Shinryodo* (Tokyo), I, 1 (May 1937). [Not seen.]
A translation, by Shin Abiru, of "January 1, 1931."

T 273   Zatsueika. *Shinryodo*, III, 13 (May 1938). [Not seen.]
A translation, by Tetsuo Nagiri, of "As I walked out one evening."

T 274   Shina ni te. *Shinryodo*, IV, 21 (January 1939). [Not seen.]
A translation, Tetsuo Nagiri, of "Far from the heart of culture he was used...."

T 275   Gasshō. *Shinryodo*, IV, 24 (April 1939). [Not seen.]
A translation, by Tamotsu Ueda, of the chorus beginning "The summer holds..." from *The dog beneath the skin.*

T 276   [Spain]. *Shinryodo*, V, 27 (July 1939).
Translated by Shigeru Adachi.

T 277   Ōden shisho. *Shinryodo*, V, 29; VI, 31, 32, 34 (September, November, December 1939, and February 1940). [Not seen.]
Translations, by Tetsuo Nagiri, of the first thirteen poems in *Poems* (1933), published in four instalments (poems numbered 1–3, 4–5, 6–9, and 10–13).

T 278   [September 1, 1939.] *Shinryodo*, V, 34 (February 1940). [Not seen.]
Translated by Tetsuo Nagiri.

T 279   [So from the years the gifts were showered....] *Kaizo* (c. 1939–40?). [Not seen.]
Translated by Tamotsu Ueda.

T 280   Kotoba to kikai. *Gendaishi kenkyū* (February 1955). [Not seen.]
A translation, by Toshio Inagaki, of "The word and the machine."

T 281   Sōsaku no shōdō. *Eigo seinen (The rising generation)* (Tokyo), CIII, 1 (January 1957), 12–14, *and* CIII, 2 (February 1957), 68–69.
An annotated translation, by Hiroshi Miyake, of excerpts from *Making, knowing and judging*, under the title "The impulse to create." English and Japanese texts.

T 282 Hon'yaku to dentō. *Gendaishi kenkyū*, 91 (1958), 14–15, *and* 92 (1958), 13–15. [Not seen.]
A translation, by Toshio Inagaki, of "Translation and tradition."

T 283 [Poems.] *Shigaku* (Tokyo), XIII, 4 (March 1958), 71–75. [Not seen.]
Translations, by Shigehisa Narita, of "Hunting season," "The truest poetry is the most feigning," and "The shield of Achilles."

T 284 Ballad XXIV. *Eigo Kenkyū*, X, 10 (October 1958), 28–29. [Not seen.]
An annotated translation, by Shōzō Kajima, of "O what is that sound which so thrills the ear...." English and Japanese texts.

T 285 Victor. *Direction* (Nagoya), 4 (1961). [Not seen.]
Translated by Harunori Hisada.

T 286 Tankyū. *Direction*, 5 (1962). [Not seen.]
A translation, by Shūji Iwasaki, of "The quest."

T 287 Tenchi. *Shigaku*, XVII, 10 (November 1962). [Not seen.]
A translation, by Masao Nakagiri, of "A change of air."

T 288 Furoito no omoideni. *Direction*, 6 (1963). [Not seen.]
A translation, by Shūji Iwasaki, of "In memory of Sigmund Freud."

T 289 Rōma joheki no blues. *Shi to hihyo*, III, 6 (June 1968). [Not seen.]
A translation, by Shozo Kajima, of "Roman wall blues."

Korean

Anthologies

T 290 Kim Chong-gil. *Isipsegi yong sisŏn*. Taegu: Sinsaeng Munhwasa, 1954. [Not seen.]
Contains Kim's translations of "Musée des Beaux Arts" and "Spain 1937" (pp. 127–36).

T 291 Song Uk. *Sihak p'yongjŏn*. [Seoul]: Ilchogak, [1963].
Contains Song's translation of, and commentary on, "Law like love" (pp. 72–86). Korean and English texts.

T 292 Yi Ch'ang-bae. *Isipsegi Yŏng-Mi si ŭi ihae*. [Seoul]: Minjung Sogwan, [1968].
Contains Yi's translations of, and commentaries on, "Look, stranger," "Our hunting fathers told the story," "As I walked out one evening," "Schoolchildren," and "September 1, 1939" (pp. 387–425). English and Korean texts.

T 293 Yi Ch'ang-bae. *Isipsegi segye sisŏn*. Seoul: Ŭryu Munhwasa, 1969. [Not seen.]
Contains Yi's translations of "Look, stranger," "September 1, 1939," "O what is that sound...," "The unknown citizen," "Petition," "Lay your sleeping head, my love...," "In memory of W. B. Yeats," "As I walked out one evening," "Schoolchildren," "Our hunting fathers told the story...," and "The wanderer" (pp. 125–43).

Periodicals

T 294 Si wa kigye. *Munhak yaesul*, II, 1 (June 1955). [Not seen.]
A translation, by Yi Su-sok, of "The word and the machine."

T 295 Herrit wang: ch'amsi t'ongan man e so. *Si wa pip'yŏng* (February 1956). [No seen.]
A translation of "Herod" from *For the time being*.

T 296 P'yorangja. *P'ipyŏng* (February 1956). [Not seen.]
A translation of "The wanderer."

T 297 Yimbo munhwa. *Hyŏndae*, II, 2 (February 1958). [Not seen.]
A translation, by Yi Pŏm-gu, of "Limbo culture."

T 298 Anyŏng ŭn ŭpsŭrira. *Chayu munhak*, VI, 11 (1961), 187–88.
A translation, by Kim Sa-mok, of "There will be no peace."

T 299 Hakkyo aedŭl. *Si munhak*, 15 (June 1966). [Not seen.]
A translation, by Yi Ch'ang-bae, of "Schoolchildren."

Norwegian

Anthology

T 300 *Framande dikt frå fire tusen år*, ein antologi redigert av Hartvig Kiran, Sigmund Skard, og Halldis Moren Vesaas. Oslo: Det Norske Samlaget, 1968. [Not seen.]
Contains a translation, by Sigmund Skard, of "The more loving one" (p. 481).

Periodical

T 301 Til minne om Sigmund Freud. *Syn og segn* (Oslo), LXXV, 7 (1969), 387–90.
A translation, by Ragnvald Skrede, of "In memory of Sigmund Freud."

Broadcast

T 302 *Erobringen av F.6*, et vers-drama av W. H. Auden og Christopher Isherwood, musikk av Benjamin Britten, oversatt av Inger Hagerup.
This translation was broadcast by Norsk Rikskringkasting, 2 November 1954, and a mimeographed text is in the Universitetsbiblioteket, Oslo.

Polish

Anthologies

T 303 *Czas niepokoju*, antologia współczesnej poezji Brytyjskiej i Amerykańskiej, wybrał i opracował Paweł Mayewski.... New York: Criterion Books, The East Europe Institute, 1958.
Contains translations of "Musée des Beaux-Arts," by Mayewski; "Voltaire at Ferney," by Czesław Miłosz; "Law, say the gardeners is the sun," by Marian Pankowski; "Petition," by Mayewski; "Taller to-day," by Pankowski; and "Say this city has ten million souls," by Józef Wittlin (pp. 308–29). English and Polish texts. A second edition (New York: Perspectives in Culture, 1965) prints revised versions of these translations, without the English texts (pp. 181–95).

T 304 Szewczyk, Wilhelm. *Zima boi się drzew, wiersze*. Katowice: Wydawnictwo "Śląsk," 1959.

Contains Szewczyk's translation of "Lay your sleeping head, my love..." (pp. 45–46).

T 305 Sito, Jerzy S. *W pierwszej i trzeciej osobie.* [Warsaw]: Pánstwowy Instytut Wydawniczy, [1967].
Contains Sito's translations of "In memory of Sigmund Freud," "Dover 1937," and "The shield of Achilles" (pp. 301–10).

Periodicals

T 306 Musée des Beaux-Arts. *Kronika* (Łódź), III, 2 (16–31 January 1957), 5. [Not seen.]
Translated by Lech Budrecki and Mirosław Ochocki.

T 307 Droga starego człówieka. *Współczesność* (Warsaw), [II], 6 (May 1957), 8. [Not seen.]
A translation, by W. Krysiński and T. Mongird, of "The old man's road."

T 308 Recitativo. *Życie literackie* (Cracow), VII, 39 (22 September 1957), 7.
A translation, by Leszek Elektorowicz, of the recitative from "Advent" in *For the time being.*

T 309 To miasto.... *Nowa kultura* (Warsaw), X, 44 (1 November 1959), 8.
A translation, by Marji Kureckiej, of "Refugee blues."

T 310 To miasto.... *Tygodnik powszechny* (Cracow), XIV, 5 (31 January 1960), 1.
A translation, by Jósef Wittlin, of "Refugee blues."

T 311 Petycja. *Tygodnik powszechny*, XV, 33 (13 August 1961), 5.
A translation, by Paweł Mayewski, of "Petition."

T 312 Ach co to za głos. *Kultura* (Paris), 168 (October 1961), 46–47.
A translation, by Zygmunt Haupt, of "O what is that sound...."

T 313 Blues rzymskiego legionisty. *Odgłosy* (Łódź), IV, 47 (26 November 1961), 7. [Not seen.]
A translation, by Jarosław Marek Rymkiewicz, of "Roman wall blues."

T 314 Poeta i polis. *Tematy* (New York), II, 5 (Winter 1963), 14–42.
A translation, by Tymon Terlecki, of "The poet and the city."

T 315 Hiszpania 1937. *Życie literackie*, XIII, 44 (3 November 1963), 7.
A translation, by Leszek Elektorowicz, of a fragment of "Spain 1937."

T 316 Jerzy S. Sito prezentuje W. H. Audena. *Współczesność*, VIII, 24 (16–31 December 1963), 5.
Translations, by Sito, of "Dover 1937," "The unknown citizen," "In memory of Sigmund Freud," and "The shield of Achilles."

T 317 [Reading.] *Kierunki* (Warsaw), IX, 35 (30 August 1964), 8.
An abridged translation, by M. Tazbir, of the French translation in *La table ronde,* 1964.

T 318 1 września 1939. *Życie literackie*, XIV, 35 (30 August 1964), 1.
A translation, by Leszek Elektorowicz, of "September 1, 1939."

T 319 Musée des Beaux-Arts. *Świat* (Warsaw), XIV, 38 (20 September 1964), 11.

Translated by Artur Międzyrzecki.

T 320 Paysage moralisé. *Życie literackie*, XV, 1 (3 January 1965), 7.
Translated by Bolesław Taborski.

T 321 Pamięci W. B. Yeatsa. *Glosy* (Wrocław), 3 (March–May 1965), 34–35. [Not seen.]
A translation, by M. Orski, of a fragment of "In memory of W. B. Yeats."

T 322 [Poems.] *Tematy*, V, 19 (Autumn 1966), 7–18.
Translations, by Jerzy S. Sito, of "Dover 1937," "The unknown citizen," "We all make mistakes," "In memory of Sigmund Freud," "Lullaby," and "The shield of Achilles."

T 323 Pan Pickwick w raju i przedsionku piekiel. *Kultura* (Warsaw), V, 8 (19 February 1967), 3, 8.
A translation, by Marek Milenaj, of excerpts from "Dingley Dell and the Fleet."

T 324 Canzone. *Kultura* (Warsaw), V, 13 (26 March 1967), 3.
Translated by Tadeusz Ross.

T 325 [Poems.] *Poezja* (Warsaw), III, 5 (May 1967), 63–73.
Translations of "Consider," "The epigoni," "The old man's road," and "Nones," by Jarosław Marek Rymkiewicz; "Musée des Beaux Arts," by Artur Międzyrzecki; "Certainly our city..." and "The exiles," by Bolesław Taborski; "Invocation to Ariel" and "In father's footsteps," by Leszek Elektorowicz. These poems are followed by the English text of Auden's translation of Mickiewicz's "The romantic," reprinted from *About the house* (pp. 74–75).

T 326 O czytaniu. *Poezja*, III, 5 (May 1967), 76–82.
A translation, by Henryk Krzeczkowski, of "Reading."

T 327 Pierwszego września 1939. *Kultura* (Warsaw), V, 36 (3 September 1967), 1.
A translation, by Tadeusz Ross, of "September 1, 1939."

T 328 Ku pamięci W. B. Yeatsa. *Kultura* (Paris), 250–251 (August–September 1968), 55–57.
A translation, by Wacław Iwaniuk, of "In memory of W. B. Yeats."

T 329 Poeta a społeczeństwo. *Twórczość* (Warsaw), XXIV, 8 (August 1968), 67–69.
A translation, by Anna Bartling, of "The poet and the city."

T 330 Muzyka u Szekspira. *Res facta* (Warsaw), [XIII], 3 (1969), 148–65. [Not seen.]
A translation, by Wiesław Juszczak, of "Music in Shakespeare."

Portuguese

Periodicals

T 331 Canção. *Confronto* (Coimbra), 1 (1946), 82–87.
A translation, by Jorge Emílio, of "Say this city has ten million souls...." English and Portuguese texts.

T 332 Pousa a cabeça adormecida. *Jornal de letras* (Rio de Janeiro), IV, 36 (June 1952), 13.
A translation, by P[aulo] M[endes] C[ampos], of "Lay your sleeping head my love."

Rumanian

Periodicals

T 333 Aici războiu-i simplu.... *Secolul 20* (Bucharest), [IV], 7–8 (1964), 162.
A translation, by Petro Solomon, of "Here war is simple like a monument...."

T 334 *La table ronde:* W. H. Auden despre lectură. *Secolul 20*, [V], 1 (1965), 175.
A translation, by Alexandru Baciu, of the French translation of "Reading" in *La table ronde*, 1964.

T 335 Cetațeanul necunoscut. *Luceafărul* (Bucharest), IX [for VIII], 1 (2 January 1965) 12.
A translation, by Toma Pavel, of "The unknown citizen."

T 336 În memoria lui W. B. Yeats. *Secolul 20*, [V], 12 (1965), 127–28.
A translation, by Sorin Mărculescu, of "In memory of W. B. Yeats [pt. 1]."

T 337 Plimbîndu-mă într-o seară. *Tribuna* (Cluj), X 30 (28 July 1966), 8. [Not seen.]
A translation, by Mircea Crainic, of "As I walked out one evening."

T 338 Destinu-i negru. *Luceafărul*, XII, 48 (29 November 1969), 8.
A translation, by Ştefan Aug. Doinaş, of "The wanderer."

Russian

Anthology

T 339 *Antologiia novoi angliiskoi poezii*, vstupitel'naia stat'ia i kommentarii M. Gutnera [*i.e.*, ed. by M. Gutner]. Leningrad: Gosudarstvennoe izdatel'stvo "Khudozhestvennaia literatura," 1937.
Contains translations of "Doom is dark..." and "It's no use raising a shout...," by E. Tarasov; "Who stands, the crux left of the watershed..." and "What's in your mind, my dove, my coney...," by I. Romanovich; "We made all possible preparations...," by Tarasov; "The strings' excitement, the applauding drum...," by Romanovich; "Who will endure...," by Vl. Zukkau-Nevskoi; "Dear, though the night is gone..." and "Sir, no man's enemy...," by Romanovich (pp. 398–405).

Periodicals

T 340 Ispaniia. *Internatsional'naia literatura* (Moscow), [XI], 5 (1938), 135–36.
A translation, by M. Zenkevich, of "Spain."

T 341 "Vechernii chas. Zavyl gudok...." *Znamia* (Moscow), [IX], 3 (March 1939), 201–3.
A translation, by M. Mendel'son, of "Brothers, who when the sirens roar...."

T 342 Angliiski pisateli kitaiskomu narodu. *Internatsional'naia literatura*, [XII], 9–10 (1939), 274–75.
A translation of Auden and Isherwood's message on China printed in *Far eastern magazine*, April 1939.

Serbian

Periodicals

T 343   Renbo. U doba rata, XXVII. *NIN: nedeljne informativne novine*
(Belgrade), IV, 188 (8 August 1954). [Not seen.]
Translations, by Miodrag Pavlović, of "Rimbaud" and "In time of war, XXVII."

T 344   Stvaranje i ocenjivanje poezije. *Politika* (Belgrade), LIV, 15734
(1 March 1957), *Godine*, p. 4107 [*i.e.*, p. 9 of this number].
A translation of "Making and judging poetry."

T 345   "Svet koji su knjige stvorile." *NIN: nedeljne informativne novine*,
X, 503 (28 August 1960), *Izbor*, I, 35, p. 17. [Not seen.]
Apparently a translation of an excerpt from "The world that books have made."

T 346   Parohija greha. *Knijiževnost* (Belgrade), XVI, 3 (March 1961),
244–53.
A translation, by J. D., of "The guilty vicarage."

Slovene

Anthology

T 347   *Svetovna književnost*, izbrana dela in odlomki, druga knjiga. [Iz-
brali in uredili Janko Kos . . . .] [Ljubljana]: Mladinska Knjiga, 1964. [Not
seen.]
Contains translations, by Veno Taufer, of "The unknown citizen" and "Musée des
Beaux Arts."

Periodical

T 348   Pesmi W. H. Audena. *Perspektive* (Ljubljana), II, 18 (1961–62),
972–78.
Translations, by Veno Taufer, of "The unknown citizen," "It's no use raising a
shout . . . ," "Law like love," "Musée des Beaux Arts," and "Nones."

Spanish

Anthologies

T 349   Shand, William, and Alberto Girri. *Poesía inglesa de la guerra es-
pañola*, prólogo de Guillermo de Torre. Buenos Aires: Libreria y Editorial
"El Ateneo," [1947.]
Contains Shand and Girri's translation of "Spain" (pp. 36–45). English and Spanish
texts.

T 350   *La poesía inglesa: los contemporáneos*, selección, traducción y pró-
logo de M[ariano] Manent. [Barcelona]: Ediciones Lauro, 1948.
Contains Manent's translations of "As I walked out one evening," "Palais des Beaux
Arts," and "Miranda" (pp. 298–307). English and Spanish texts.

T 351 *Poesía británica moderna*, selección y prólogo de E. L. Revol. [Buenos Aires: Ediciones Continental, 1948]. (Pequeña Enciclopedia Poética Universal.)
Contains Revol's translations of "Musée des Beaux Arts," "The unknown citizen," "Michael, you shall be renowned..." from *The ascent of F6*, and "The fall of Rome" (pp. 75–80).

T 352 Shand, William, and Alberto Girri. *Poesía inglesa contemporánea; contemporary English poetry*, prólogo de Patrick O. Dudgeon, dibujos de Luis Seoane. [Buenos Aires]: Editorial Nova, [1948].
Contains Shand and Girri's translations of "Look, stranger...," "Who will endure...," and "Hearing of harvests..." (pp. 72–79). English and Spanish texts.

T 353 *Antología de la poesía Norteamericana contemporánea*, selección, traducción y estudio preliminar de Eugenio Florit. Washington: Unión Panamericana, [1955]. (Pensiamento de America.)
Contains Florit's translations of "In memory of W. B. Yeats [pt. 1]," "Musée des Beaux Arts," and a fragment of the "Commentary" to "In time of war" (pp. 119–25 *bis*). English and Spanish texts.

T 354 *Antología de poetas ingleses modernos*, introducción de Dámaso Alonso. [Madrid]: Editorial Gredos, [1962].
Contains translations of "Musée des Beaux Arts," by Jaime Gil de Biedma; "In memory of W. B. Yeats [pt. 3]," by J. R. Wilcock; and "Miranda," by Mariano Manent (pp. 200–205). English and Spanish texts.

Periodicals

T 355 En memoria de W. B. Yeats. *Sur* (Buenos Aires), XVI [for XVII], 153–156 (July–October 1947), 388–91.
A translation, by J. R. Wilcock, of "In memory of W. B. Yeats [pt. 3]." English and Spanish texts.

T 356 Algunas notas sobre D. H. Lawrence. *Orígenes* (Havana), IV, 15 (Autumn 1947), 28–32.
A translation, by José Rodríguez Feo, of "Some notes on D. H. Lawrence."

T 357 [Statement on the 10th anniversary of the Congress for Cultural Freedom]. *Congreso por la libertad de la cultura: informaciones* (Paris), June 1960. [Not seen.]

T 358 En memoria de Sigmund Freud. *Revista de la Universidad de México* (Mexico City), XVII, 5–6 (January–February 1963), 11–12.
A translation, by José Rodríguez Feo, of "In memory of Sigmund Freud."

T 359 Yago o el bromista. *Eco* (Bogotá), VIII, 6 (April 1964), 549–83.
A translation of "The joker in the pack."

T 360 Elefentes insignificantes. *Dialogos* (Mexico City), III, 5 (September–October 1967), 3–4.
A translation, by Isabel Fraire, of "Insignificant elephants."

T 361 Metalogo a "La flauta mágica." *Los papeles de son armadans* (Madrid, Palma de Mallorca), LV, 165 (December 1969), 313–17.
A translation, by Edgardo Cozarinsky, of "Metalogue to The magic flute."

Swedish

Books

T 362 *En rucklares väg*, opera i tre akter, libretto av W. H. Auden och
Chester Kallman, musik av Igor Stravinskij, Svensk text av Östen Sjöstrand.
Stockholm: Albert Bonniers Förlag, [1961]. (Bonniers Operabibliotek.)
7½ x 4½ in., pp. [1–4] 5–77 [78–80].
A translation of *The rake's progress*. Published February 1961 in an edition of 800
copies at 9.50 Kr. This translation includes an introduction by Folke H. Törnblom
(pp. 5–11) and an afterword by the translator (pp. 77–78).

T 363 *Färgarens hand och andra essayer.* Stockholm: Albert Bonniers
Förlag, [1965]. 8¼ x 5¼ in., pp. [1–6] 7–231 [232–236].
A translation, by Erik Sandin and Torsten Blomkvist, of the following essays from
The dyer's hand: "Reading," "Writing," "Making, knowing and judging," "The
poet and the city," "Robert Frost," "Balaam and his ass," "The American scene,"
"Notes on music and opera," "Don Juan," and "Genius and apostle." Published May
1965 in an edition of 2,000 copies at 29.50 Kr.

T 364 *Och i vår tid*, dikter i urval och tolkning av Petter Bergman, in-
ledning av översättaren. Stockholm: Albert Bonniers Förlag, [1965]. (Svalans Lyrikklubb, 8.) 7⅞ x 5 in., pp. [1–6] 7–98 [99–104].
Translations, by Petter Bergman, of thirty-two poems. Published May 1965 in an
edition of 7,000 copies at 14.50 Kr.

T 365 *Bestigningen av F6*, tragedi i två akter, Svensk tolkning, Erik Lindegren. Stockholm: Albert Bonniers Förlag, [1969]. (Panacheserien.) 7⅞ x
4½ in., pp. [1–6] 7–99 [100–104].
A translation, by Erik Lindegren, of *The ascent of F6*. Published September 1969 in
an edition of 1,500 copies at 19.50 Kr. An earlier version of this translation was broadcast by Radiojänst, Stockholm, 19 November 1948.

Anthologies and books with contributions

T 366 *Min tro*, en bok om livsåskådningar, med förord av Alf Ahlberg.
[Stockholm]: Bokförlaget Natur och Kultur, [1941].
Contains Ahlberg's translation of Auden's untitled essay in *I believe* (pp. 105–19).

T 367 *Nya tolkningar*, av Johannes Edfelt. [Stockholm]: Bonniers,
[1945].
Contains Edfelt's translation of "At last the secret is out..." from *The ascent of F6*
(pp. 85–87).

T 368 *Artur Lundkvist, 3 mars 1956*, [ed. by Stig Carlson]. Stockholm:
Tidens Förlag, [1956].
Contains a translation, by Folke Isaksson, of "Air port" (pp. 133–35).

T 369 *100 dikter ur världslyriken*, en antologi av Erik Blomberg....
Stockholm: FIB:s Lyrikklubb, 1959. (FIB:s Lyrikklubbs Bibliotek, nr
D 10.)
Contains a translation, by Erik Lindegren, of "Though he believe it, no man is
strong..." (p. 137).

T 370 Ekelöf, Gunnar. *Valfrändskaper*, omdiktningar. Stockholm: Albert Bonniers Förlag, [1960].
Contains Ekelöf's translation of "Musée des Beaux Arts" (p. 51).

T 371 *Världens bästa lyrik i urval*, redigerad av Johannes Edfelt. Stockholm:Natur och Kultur, [1961]. (Världens Bästa i Urval.)
Contains translations of "Miranda's song," by Göran Printz-Påhlson; and "Musée des Beaux Arts," by Sven Collberg (pp. 273–75).

T 372 *Engelsk lyrik*, urval av Petter Bergman. Stockholm: Albert Bonniers Förlag, [1968]. (Svalans Lyrikklubb, nr 21; All Världens Lyrik.)
Contains translations of "Musée des Beaux Arts," by Gunnar Ekelöf; "Though he believe it, no man is strong . . ." by Erik Lindegren; "Barcarolle," by Östen Sjöstrand; and "Deftly, Admiral, cast your fly . . . ," by Petter Bergman (pp. 104–7).

Periodicals

T 373 Ur The orators, *Horisont* (Stockholm), 2 (Autumn 1941), 19–26.
Translations, by Thorsten Jonsson, of "Address for a prize-day" and "Statement."

T 374 Musée des Beaux Arts. *Ord och bild* (Stockholm), LV, 11 (1946), 514.
Translated by Gunnar Ekelöf.

T 375 Hermann Melville. *Röster i radio* (Stockholm), XX, 46 (15–21 November 1948), 4.
Translated by Folke Isaksson.

T 376 Barnamordet i Betlehem. *Prisma* (Stockholm), III, 1 (1950), 23–26.
A translation, by E[rik] L[indegren], of "Herod" from *For the time being*.

T 377 Resa till Island. *Vox* (Lund), 3 (1951), 14–16.
A translation, by Bengt Holmström, of "Journey to Iceland."

T 378 Frågan och svaret. *All världens berättare* (Stockholm), VIII, 3 (March 1952), 183–84.
A translation, by Erik Lindegren, of "The hard question."

T 379 Under Sirius. *BLM: Bonniers litterära magasin* (Stockholm), XXIV, 1 (January 1955), 23–24.
Translated by Kjell Espmark.

T 380 Den poetiska processen. *Samtid och framtid* (Stockholm), XII, 10 (December 1955), 459–63.
A translation of "The poetic process" ("The dyer's hand," part II).

T 381 Barkaroll ur The rake's progress. *Dagens nyheter* (Stockholm), 17 March 1957, p. 3.
A translation, by Östen Sjöstrand, of "Barcarolle."

T 382 Musée des Beaux Arts. *Sydsvenska dagbladet snällposten* (Malmö), 7 July 1957, p. 13.
Translated by Sven Collberg.

T 383 Två dikter, *Lyrikvännen* (Stockholm), VII, 5–6 (1960), 23.
Translations, by Göran Printz-Påhlson, of "Nursery rhyme" and "Hunting season."

T 384 Brev till ett sår. *Svenska dagbladet* (Stockholm), 21 May 1961, p. 5.
A translation, by Marianne Höök, of "Letter to a wound."

T 385   Roms fall. *Sydsvenska dagbladet snällposten*, 8 April 1962, p. 23.
A translation, by Lars Bjurman, of "The fall of Rome."

T 386   Mirandas sång. *Dagens nyheter*, 1 March 1964, p. 4.
A translation, by Petter Bergman, of "Miranda's song."

T 387   Romanförfattaren. *Svenska dagbladet*, 16 August 1964, p. 5.
A translation, by Petter Bergman, of "The novelist."

T 388   Sex dikter. *BLM: Bonniers litterära magasin*, XXXIII, 9 (November 1964), 659–66.
Translations, by Petter Bergman, of "A walk after dark," "The fall of Rome," "Music ho!," "Memorial for the city [fragment]," "The love feast," and "Secrets."

T 389   Dag Hammarskjöld. *Arsbok för kristen humanism* (Lund), 27 (1965), 55–67.
A translation, by Kerstin Wentz and Margaret Tornborg, of the "Foreword" to *Markings*.

T 390   Atomkraften och människan. *Det bästa ur Reader's digest* (Stockholm), XXIV, 1 (January 1966), 32–34.
A translation of "Of man and the atom."

T 391   Flod i profil. *Svenska dagbladet*, 18 December 1966, p. [19].
A translation, by Caj Lundgren, of "River profile."

T 392   Vesper. *Vår lösen* (Sigtuna), LXIX, 1 (1968), 38–40.
A translation by Petter Bergman, of "Vespers."

Turkish

Anthologies

T 393   Nutku, Özdemir and Tarık Darsun K. . . . *Çağdaş Amerikan şiirleri* –Robert H. Ball'un bir öndeyişi ile. [Dinar]: Şairler Yaprağı Yayınları, [1956].
Contains Nutku and Darsun K.'s translations of "Look, stranger . . . ," "In Schrafft's," and "Petition" (pp. 12–14.)

T 394   Meriçelli, Anıl. *Çağdaş İngiliz-Amerikan şiiri*. Istanbul: Gün Matbaası, 1968. [Not seen.]
Contains Meriçelli's translation of an unidentified poem ("Gözlerinde yangın") (pp. 53–54).

Periodical

T 395   Roma sularında düşünceler. Bir zorbanın mezar taşına. İsimiz. *Yeni ufuklar* (Istanbul), II, 6 (March 1954), 306–7.
Translations, by Halit Cakir, of "Roman wall blues," "Epitaph on a tyrant," and the first stanza of "Lay your sleeping head, my love . . . ."

Appendices

APPENDIX I

BIBLIOGRAPHY AND CRITICISM
OF W. H. AUDEN'S WORK

THE volume of criticism on Auden and his work has grown enormously since the years covered by the first edition of this bibliography, and this classified list attempts to impose some order on a large amount of material. Although this is not an exhaustive list of everything ever published about Auden, no critical commentary with any substance has knowingly been omitted. Every item listed in the annual bibliographies published by the Modern Humanities Research Association (covering items published through 1967) and the Modern Language Association (through 1969) has been included either in this appendix or in the lists of reviews in section A. Some items published early in 1970 are also included here.

Criticism published in languages other than English has been listed in detail, both for its own value and to indicate the extent of Auden's reputation. Free translations of Japanese titles are provided. Some biographical material has been included, but not parodies, poems addressed to Auden, and so on.[1]

The list is divided into the following categories:

Bibliography
General studies: books
General studies: articles and parts of books
Studies of individual poems: the shorter poems
Studies of individual poems: the longer poems, *The orators* and *Letters from Iceland*
Studies of the plays, libretti, films, and musical settings
Studies of Auden's criticism
Theses and dissertations

Within each section, items are listed chronologically by year and alphabetically within each year. Reviews of books entirely about Auden are included; some of these are important critical articles in their own right, and the titles of these reviews are given in parentheses. In the lists of articles and parts of books an asterisk indicates an item which the compilers consider to be of special interest.

---

[1] Many poems about Auden, or addressed to him, may be found in *Sunday times*, 19 February 1967, p. 28, and in *Shenandoah*, XVIII (Winter 1967).

This is a short-title list, and square brackets are used only for information supplied by the compilers.

Bibliography

1. Writings by W. H. Auden [1924–1937]. *New verse*, 26–27 (November 1937), 32–46.
Compiled by Ruthven Todd. Earlier manuscript and typescript versions, the latter with some notes in Auden's hand, are in the University of Texas Library.

2. Clancy, Joseph P. A W. H. Auden bibliography 1924–1955. *Thought*, XXX (Summer 1955), 260–70.

3. Callan, Edward. *An annotated check list of the works of W. H. Auden* [1924–1957]. Denver: Alan Swallow, 1958.
An earlier version appeared in *Twentieth century literature*, IV (April–July 1958), 30–50. Continued as "W. H. Auden: annotated checklist II (1958–1969)," *ibid.*, XVI (January 1970), 27–56.

4. Bloomfield, B. C. W. H. Auden's first book. *Library*, 5th ser., XVII (June 1962), 152–54.

5. ——. *W. H. Auden: a bibliography: the early years through 1955.* Charlottesville: University Press of Virginia, 1964. Foreword by W. H. Auden.
Reviews: Lee Ash, *Publications of the bibliographical society of America*, LXIX (1965), 331–32; [A. R. A. Hobson], *Times literary supplement*, 1 July 1965, p. 568; R. J. Roberts, *Book collector*, XIV (Autumn 1965), 389–90, 393; Robert Scholes, *Philological quarterly*, XLIV (July 1965), 423–24; Julian Symons, *London magazine*, n.s. V (November 1965), 103–4; William White, *American book collector*, XV (Summer 1965), 4.

6. Tolley, A. T. The printing of Auden's *Poems* (1928) and Spender's *Nine experiments*. *Library*, 5th ser., XXII (June 1967), 149–50.

General Studies: Books

Pamphlets on individual works are listed in the appropriate sections, below.

7. Scarfe, Francis. *W. H. Auden.* Monaco: Lyrebird Press, 1949. (Contemporary British poets.)

8. Hoggart, Richard. *Auden: an introductory essay.* London: Chatto & Windus; New Haven: Yale University Press, 1951.
Reviews: Helen Bevington, *South Atlantic quarterly*, LI (July 1952), 461–62; Hayden Carruth ("Understanding Auden"), *Nation*, CLXXIII (22 December 1951), 550–51; Stanley K. Coffman, Jr., *Books abroad*, XXVII (Spring 1953), 194; Babette Deutsch, *New York herald tribune*, 17 February 1952, section 6, p. 12; Francis Fergusson, *Partisan review*, XIX (July–August 1952), 483–87; Rolfe Fjelde, *New republic*, CCXXVI (28 April 1952), 20; Geoffrey Grigson, *Observer*, 12 August 1951, p. 7; *Listener*, XLVI (2 August 1951), 191; Martin Price, *Yale review*, XLI (Spring 1952), 460–61; V. S. Pritchett, *New stateman & nation*, XLII (4 August

1951), 130, 132; Seldon Rodman, *New York times*, 30 December 1951, section 7, p. 4; Henry Savage ("Auden as moralist"), *Poetry review*, XLIII (January–February 1952), 24–29; *Times literary supplement*, 10 August 1951, p. 495.

9. Beach, Joseph Warren. *The making of the Auden canon*. Minneapolis: University of Minnesota Press, 1957.
Reviews: Bernard I. Duffey, *American literature*, XXX (May 1958), 261–62; A. J. Farmer, *Études anglaises*, XII (October–December 1959), 362; Joe M. Ferguson, Jr., *New Mexico quarterly*, XXIX (Spring 1959), 124–25; Dorothy V. Fuller, *Arizona quarterly*, XIV (Autumn 1958), 273–75; L. D. Lerner, *Modern language review*, LIV (January 1959), 107; Mordecai Marcus, *Journal of English and Germanic philology*, LVII (April 1959), 315–18; John H. Raleigh, *Books abroad*, XXXII (Spring 1958), 186; A. E. Rodway and F. W. Cook ("An altered Auden"), *Essays in criticism*, VIII (July 1958), 303–19; Karl Shapiro, *Prairie schooner*, XXXII (Spring 1958), 73–75; Grover Smith, Jr., *South Atlantic quarterly*, LVII (Summer 1958), 380–81. *See also:* B. C. Bloomfield, "Notes and corrections on 'The making of the Auden canon,' by J. W. Beach," *Notes and queries*, n.s. VI (June 1959), 227–28.

10. Hoggart, Richard. *W. H. Auden*. London: Longmans for the British Council, 1957. (Writers and their work, no. 93.)
Reprinted in *British writers and their work*, 5 (Lincoln, Neb., 1965), pp. 71–118, with a revised bibliography by J. W. Robinson. The original pamphlet appeared in slightly revised editions in 1962 (dated 1961) and 1966, and the entire text was reprinted as "The long walk: the poetry of W. H. Auden" in Hoggart's *Speaking to each other*, vol. 2 (London: Chatto & Windus, 1970), pp. 56–94. Translated into Polish by Halina and Bolesław Taborscy in *Portrety pisarzy angielskich*, 1st ser. (London: B. Świderski, 1962), pp. 11–53.
Reviews: Times literary supplement, 17 January 1958, p. 31; Harriet Zinnes, *Books abroad*, XXXIII (Summer 1959), 351.

11. Spears, Monroe K. *The poetry of W. H. Auden: the disenchanted island*. New York: Oxford University Press, 1963.
A corrected impression, with a new preface, was published in 1968 (Galaxy books, GB 229).
   The section on *For the time being* is reprinted in Spears's *Auden: a collection of critical essays* (1964), pp. 160–71; the chapter on the longer poems is reprinted in *Modern poetry: essays in criticism*, ed. John Hollander (New York: Oxford University Press, 1968), pp. 359–94.
Reviews: James Boatright, *English language notes*, II (September 1964), 74–76; Cleanth Brooks, *Sewanee review*, LXXII (Spring 1964), 300–306; R. G. Cox, *Modern language review*, LX (April 1965), 271–72; Gavin Ewart, *London magazine*, n.s. III (February 1964), 81–83; *John Fuller ("Early Auden: an allegory of love"), *Review* (Oxford), 11–12 ([1964]), 83–90; Geoffrey Grigson, *New statesman*, LXVI (6 December 1963), 846; Barbara Hardy ("Spears on Auden"), *Essays in criticism*, XV (April 1965), 230–38; Richard Hoggart, *Listener*, LXX (5 December 1963), 951; Peter Levi, *Tablet*, CCXVII (7 December 1963), 1321–22; Frederick P. W. McDowell, *Philological quarterly*, XLIV (July 1965), 417–23; Dom Moraes, *Spectator*, CCXII (24 January 1964), 114–15; Richard M. Ohmann, *Commonweal*, LXXIX (10 January 1964), 437–38; Pál Soós, *Helikon* (Budapest), XII (1966), 220; John Thompson, *New York review of books*, I (23 January 1964), 13–14; *Times literary supplement*, 20 August 1964, p. 746; Richard Wasson, *Journal of English and Germanic philology*, LXIII (July 1964), 541–42; George T. Wright, *American literature*, XXXVI (May 1964), 231–32.

12. Everett, Barbara. *Auden*. Edinburgh: Oliver & Boyd, 1964. (Writers and critics.)

Reviews: *Alistair Elliott ("Auden is good"), *Essays in criticism,* XV (October 1965), 462–70; *Times literary supplement,* 17 December 1964, p. 1146.

13.   Spears, Monroe K., ed.   *Auden: a collection of critical essays.* Englewood Cliffs, N.J.: Prentice-Hall, 1964. (Twentieth century views.)
The contents of this volume are listed separately, below.

14.   Blair, John G.   *The poetic art of W. H. Auden.* Princeton: Princeton University Press, 1965.
Reviews: Frederick P. W. McDowell, *Philological quarterly,* XLV (July 1966), 624–26; Justin Replogle, *Western humanities review,* XX (Autumn 1966), 359–61; Howard Sergeant, *English,* XVI (Autumn 1966), 113; A Kingsley Weatherhead, *Modern philology,* LXV (November 1967), 186–88.

15.   Dewsnap, Terence.   *The poetry of W. H. Auden.* New York: distributed by Monarch press, 1965. (Monarch notes and study guides, 791–4).

16.   Binni, Francesco.   *Saggio su Auden.* Milan: U. Mursia, 1967.

17.   Greenberg, Herbert.   *Quest for the necessary: W. H. Auden and the dilemma of divided consciousness.* Cambridge: Harvard University Press, 1968. Prefatory note by Stephen Spender.
Reviews: Robert Bloom, *Journal of modern literature,* I (1970), 119–22; Samuel Hynes, *Contemporary literature,* XI (Winter 1970), 98–103; Monroe K. Spears, *South Atlantic quarterly,* LXIX (Spring 1970), 291–92.

18.   Nelson, Gerald.   *Changes of heart: a study of the poetry of W. H. Auden.* Berkeley: University of California Press, 1969. (Perspectives in criticism, 21.)

19.   Replogle, Justin.   *Auden's poetry.* Seattle: University of Washington Press; London: Methuen, 1969.
Reviews: Robert Bloom, *Western humanities review,* XXIV (Winter 1970), 89–90; John Fletcher, *Spectator,* CCXXIII (13 December 1969), 827–28; Samuel Hynes, *Contemporary literature,* XI (Winter 1970), 98–103; Peter Porter, *New statesman,* LXXIX (23 January 1970), 121; Monroe K. Spears, *Yale review,* LX (Autumn 1970), 98–100; Robert D. Spector, *Saturday review,* LII (21 June 1969), 55.

20.   Wright, George T.   *W. H. Auden.* New York: Twayne Publishers, (Twayne's United States authors series, 144.)

21.   Bahlke, George W.   *The later Auden: from "New Year letter" to About the house.* New Brunswick: Rutgers University Press, 1970.

22.   Davison, Dennis.   *W. H. Auden.* London: Evans Brothers, 1970. (Literature in perspective.)

23.   Fuller, John.   *A reader's guide to W. H. Auden.* London: Thames & Hudson; New York: Farrar, Straus & Giroux, 1970.
Reviews: Peter Porter, *New statesman,* LXXIX (23 January 1970), 121; *Times literary supplement,* 16 April 1970, p. 403; John Whitehead, *London magazine,* n.s. X (May 1970), 97–100.

24.   Stoll, John E.   *W. H. Auden: a reading.* Muncie, Ind.: Ball State University, 1970. (Ball State monograph no. 18; Ball State University publications in English, no. 12.)

General Studies: Articles and Parts of Books

In addition to separately published articles, this section lists the contents of three collective works: the "Auden double number" of *New verse*, November 1937;[2] *Auden: a collection of critical essays*, ed. Monroe K. Spears (1964, see item 13, above); and "A tribute to Wystan Hugh Auden on his sixtieth birthday," *Shenandoah*, Winter 1967.

25. Grigson, Geoffrey. Notes on contemporary poetry. *Bookman*, LXXXII (September 1932), 287–89.

26.* Spender, Stephen. Five notes on W. H. Auden's writing. *Twentieth century* (Promethean Society), III (July 1932), 13–15.

27. Porteus, Hugh Gordon. W. H. Auden. *Twentieth century* (Promethean Society), IV (February 1933), 14–16.

28. Stonier, G. W. *Gog Magog and other essays*. London: Dent, 1933. "New poets." (pp. 171–76)

29. Bullough, Geoffrey. *The trend of modern poetry*. Edinburgh: Oliver & Boyd, 1934. (pp. 160–2)
In the second edition (1941), pp. 165–69; in the third edition (1949), pp. 188–96.

30. Burgum, Edwin Berry. Three English radical poets. *New masses*, XII (3 July 1934), 33–36. Replies by Horace Gregory, Obed Brooks, Robert Gessner, and Stanley Burnshaw, *ibid.* (21 August 1934), 26–28.
Burgum's article is reprinted in *Proletarian literature in the United States*, ed. Granville Hicks *et al.* (New York: International Publishers, 1935), pp. 330–39.

31. Burnham, James. W. H. Auden. *Nation*, CXXXIX (8 August 1934), 164–65.

32. Day Lewis, C. *A hope for poetry*. Oxford: Blackwell, 1934. (*passim*)

33. Foxall, Edgar. The politics of W. H. Auden. *Bookman* (London), LXXXV (March 1934), 474–75.

34. Powell, Dilys. *Descent from Parnassus*. London: Cresset Press, 1934. (pp. 173–94)

35. Sitwell, Edith. *Aspects of modern poetry*. London: Duckworth, 1934. (pp. 238–45)

36. Deutsch. Babette. *This modern poetry*. New York: Norton, 1935 (pp. 241–48); London: Faber, 1936 (pp. 259–67).

37. Maynard, Theodore. When the pie was opened. *Commonweal*, XXII (2 August 1935), 339–41.

38.* Spender, Stephen. *The destructive element*. London: Jonathan Cape, 1935. "The airman, politics and psychoanalysis." (pp. 251–77)

[2] In a letter "to a friend," February 1938, Kenneth Allott wrote: "Costs of Auden no. were £60—returns £63. We sold out 2,500 copies..." (Bertram Rota, Ltd., catalogue 163 [Spring 1970], p. 2).

39.* Lehmann, John. Some revolutionary trends in English poetry: 1930–1935. *International literature* (Moscow), [VI] (April 1936), 60–83 (especially 69–74).

40. Turnell, G. M. Two notes on English poetry: I. Hopkins to W. H. Auden. *Colosseum*, III (June 1936), 120–25.

41. Antifashistskie pisateli mira: U. Oden. *Internatsional'naia literatura* (Moscow), [X] (November 1937), 220–21.

42.* Close, H. M. The development of Auden's poetry. *Cambridge review*, LVIII (9 June 1937), 478–79.

43. Glicksberg, Charles I. Poetry and Marxism: three English poets take their stand. *University of Toronto quarterly*, VI (April 1937), 309–25.

44. Gregory, Horace. The liberal critics and W. H. Auden. *New masses*, XXIII (20 April 1937), 25–27.

45. Grigson, Geoffrey. Auden as a monster. *New verse*, 26–27 (November 1937), 13–17.

46.* Isherwood, Christopher. Some notes on Auden's early poetry. *New verse*, 26–27 (November 1937), 4–8.
Reprinted in *Auden: a collection of critical essays*, ed. Monroe K. Spears (1964), pp. 10–14, and, with introductory comments, in Isherwood's *Exhumations* (London: Methuen, 1966), pp. 11–12, 17–22 (and see also pp. 141–42).

47. MacNeice, Louis. Letter to W. H. Auden. *New verse*, 26–27 (November 1937), 11–12.

48. Rickword, Edgell. Auden and politics. *New verse*, 26–27 (November 1937), 21–22.

49. Sixteen comments on Auden. *New verse*, 26–27 (November 1937), 23–30.
By Edwin Muir, George Barker, Frederic Prokosch, David Gascoyne, Dylan Thomas, Berthold Viertel, C. Day Lewis, Allen Tate, Bernard Spencer, Charles Madge, Herbert Read, Ezra Pound, John Masefield, Graham Greene, *Sir* Hugh Walpole, W. J. Turner.

50. Spender, Stephen. Oxford to Communism. *New verse*, 26–27 (November 1937), 9–10.

51. Traversi, D. A. Marxism and English poetry. *Arena*, I (October–December 1937), 199–211.

52. Weygandt, Cornelius. *The time of Yeats*. New York: Appleton, 1937. "Of poetry and propaganda." (pp. 429–33)

53. Drummond, John. The mind of Mr. W. H. Auden. *Townsman*, I (July 1938), 23–26.

54. Dudman, George, and Patrick Terry. *Challenge to Tom Harrisson*. [Oxford, 1938?]. (*passim*)

55. Engle, Paul. New English poets. *English journal*, college edition, XXVII (February 1938), 89–101.

56. Flint, F. Cudworth. New leaders in English poetry. *Virginia quarterly review*, XIV (Autumn 1938), 502–18.

57.   Glicksberg, C. I.   Poetry and social revolution. *Dalhousie review*, XVII (January 1938), 493–503.

58.   Hewett, Peter.   W. H. Auden. *University forward*, IV (5 February 1938), 5.

59.*   Isherwood, Christopher.   *Lions and shadows*. London: Hogarth Press, 1938. (*passim*)
Auden is caricatured as "Hugh Weston," who also appears briefly in Isherwood's *Down there on a visit* (New York: Simon & Schuster, 1962), p. 142.

60.   Iyengar, K. R. Srinvasa.   Mr. W. H. Auden, the King's poetry medalist. *Bombay University journal*, May 1938, pp. 1–11.

61.   MacNeice, Louis.   *Modern poetry: a personal essay*. London: Oxford University Press, 1938. (*passim*)

62.   Nagata, Subetaro.   W. H. Auden. *Shinryodo* (Tokyo), II (January 1938). [Not seen.]

63.*   Southworth, James G.   Wystan Hugh Auden. *Sewanee review*, XLVI (April–June 1938), 189–205.
Reprinted in Southworth's *Sowing the spring* (Oxford: Blackwell, 1940), pp. 128–48.

64.   W. H. Auden. *Wilson bulletin*, XII (January 1938), 362.

65.   Bailey, Ruth.   *A dialogue on modern poetry*. London: Humphrey Milford, Oxford University Press, 1939. (*passim*)

66.*   Brooks, Cleanth.   *Modern poetry and the tradition*. Chapel Hill: University of North Carolina Press, 1939. (pp. 125–35).
Excerpts appear as "Auden's imagery" in *Auden: a collection of critical essays*, ed. Monroe K. Spears (1964), pp. 15–25.

67.*   Daiches, David.   W. H. Auden: the search for a public. *Poetry*, LIV (June 1939), 148–56.

68.   Eberhart, Richard.   W. H. Auden. In *We moderns: Gotham Book Mart 1920–1940*, catalogue 42 [1939], p. 12.

69.   Hausermann, H. W.   Left-wing poetry: a note. *English studies*, XXI (October 1939), 203–13.

70.   Henderson, Philip.   *The poet and society*. London: Secker & Warburg, 1939. "The age of Auden." (pp. 202–15)

71.*   Lehmann, John.   *New writing in England*. New York: Critics Group Press, 1939. (*passim*)

72.   Schwartz, Delmore.   The two Audens. *Kenyon review*, I (Winter 1939), 34–45.
Reprinted in *Selected essays of Delmore Schwartz* (Chicago: University of Chicago Press, 1970), pp. 143–52.

73.   Spender, Stephen.   The importance of W. H. Auden. *London mercury*, XXXIX (April 1939), 613–18.

74.*   Daiches, David.   *Poetry in the modern world*. Chicago: University of Chicago Press, 1940. "Poetry in the 1930's: II. W. H. Auden and Stephen Spender." (pp. 214–39)

75. Lehmann, John. *New writing in Europe.* Harmondsworth: Penguin, 1940. (*passim*)

76. Wells, Henry W. *New poets from old.* New York: Columbia University Press, 1940. (pp. 46–49, 63–70 *et passim*)

77. Brenner, Rica. *Poets of our time.* New York: Harcourt, Brace, 1941. "Wystan Hugh Auden." (pp. 245–77)

78.* Jarrell, Randall. Changes of attitude and rhetoric in Auden's poetry. *Southern review*, VII (Autumn 1941), 326–49.
Reprinted in Jarrell's *The third book of criticism* (New York: Farrar, Straus & Giroux, 1969), pp. 115–50.

79. Scarfe, Francis. *Auden and after.* London: Routledge, 1942. "Aspects of Auden." (pp. 10–34)
Cf. "Poets at school and war," *Times literary supplement*, 15 August 1942, pp. 402, 405.

80. Lindegren, Erik. W. H. Audens diktning. *Ord och bild*, LII (February 1943), 104–8.

81. Savage, D. S. *The personal principle.* London: Routledge, 1944. "The strange case of W. H. Auden." (pp. 155–82)

82. ———. The poet's perspectives. *Poetry*, LXIV (June 1944), 148–58.

83. Hamm, Victor M. W. H. Auden: pilgrim's regress? *America*, LXXII (26 May 1945), 156–57.

84.* Jarrell, Randall. Freud to Paul: the stages of Auden's ideology. *Partisan review*, XII (Fall 1945), 437–57.
Reprinted in Jarrell's *The third book of criticism* (New York: Farrar, Straus & Giroux, 1969), pp. 153–87.

85. Mason, Eudo C. Die Stellung von W. H. Auden und seiner Gruppe in der neueren englische Dichtung. *Schweizer Annalen*, II (December 1945), 495–501.

86. Shapiro, Karl. *Essay on rime.* New York: Reynal & Hitchcock, 1945. (pp. 18–19, 41–44)

87. The faith of W. H. Auden. *Christian century*, LXII (16 January 1946), 71–73.

88. Gregory, Horace, and Marya Zaturenska. *A history of American poetry, 1900–1940.* New York: Harcourt, Brace, 1946. (pp. 487–89)

89. Miles, Josephine. Major adjectives in poetry: from Wyatt to Auden. *University of California publications in English*, XII, 3 (1946), 305–426 (especially pp. 398–99).

90.* Stauffer, Donald A. *Which side am I supposed to be on?*: the search for beliefs in W. H. Auden's poetry. *Virginia quarterly review*, XXII (Autumn 1946), 570–80.

91. Brooks, Benjamin Gilbert. The poetry of W. H. Auden. *Nineteenth century and after*, CXLI (January 1947), 30–40.

92. Griffin, Howard. The idiom of W. H. Auden. *New quarterly of poetry*, II (Fall 1947), 6–10.

93. Hennecke, Hans. Wystan Hugh Auden und die jüngste anglo-amerikanische Dichtung. *Fähre*, II, 2 (1947), 99–104.
Reprinted in Hennecke's *Dichtung und Dasein* (Berlin: Henssel, 1950), pp. 194–200.

94. Jameson, Storm. W. H. Auden, the poet of *Angst*. *Gate* (Oxford), I (December 1947), 2–9.
Reprinted in the Bremen edition of *Gate*, II, 1 ([1948]), 17–24, and in Jameson's *The writer's situation* (London: Macmillan, 1950), pp. 83–101.

95. Praz, Mario. Poeti inglesi dei nostri giorni: Spender, Auden, Mac-Neice. *La fiera letteraria*, II (23 January 1947), 3.
Reprinted as "Tre poeti inglesi moderni" in Praz's *Cronache letterarie anglosassoni*, vol. 2 (Rome: Edizioni di Storia e Letteratura, 1951), pp. 84–90.

96. Bradbury, John M. Auden and the tradition. *Western review*, XII (Summer 1948), 223–29.

97. Coghill, Nevill. Sweeney agonistes. In *T. S. Eliot: a symposium*, compiled by Richard March and Tambimuttu (London: Poetry London, 1948), p. 82.
On Auden's early response to Eliot's poems.

98. Duncan, Chester. W. H. Auden. *Canadian forum*, XXVIII (September 1948), 131–32.

99. Greenberg, Samuel. W. H. Auden: poet of anxiety. *Masses and mainstream*, I (June 1948), 38–50.

100.* Kermode, Frank. The theme of Auden's poetry: I. *Revista di letterature moderne*, III (March–June 1948), 1–14.
The second part of this article was never published.

101. Mason, Ronald. W. H. Auden. In *Writers of to-day*, 2, ed. Denys Val Baker (London: Sidgwick & Jackson, 1948), pp. 105–16.

102. Anderson, D. M. Aspects of Auden. *Landfall*, III (September 1949), 270–9.

103. Beach, Joseph Warren. The poems of Auden and the prose diathesis. *Virginia quarterly review*, XXV (Summer 1949), 365–83.

104. Frankenberg, Lloyd. *Pleasure dome*. Boston: Houghton Mifflin, 1949. "W. H. Auden." (pp. 301–15)

105. Hamilton, G. Rostrevor. *The tell-tale article*. London: Heinemann, 1949. (pp. 40–50)

106. Morawski, Stefan. Kipling–Yeats–Auden. *Twórczość*, V (June 1949), 84–99.

107. Astre, Georges Albert. Zum dichterischen Werk von W. H. Auden. *Merkur*, IV (May 1950), 526–30.

108. Fraser, G. S. *Post-war trends in English literature*. Tokyo: Hoku-seido, 1950. "Notes on the achievement of Auden." (pp. 51–63)

109.   Hansen, Kurt Heinrich.   Wystan Hugh Auden. *Thema*, 7 (January 1950), 13.

110.   Leavis, F. R.   *New bearings in English poetry*. New ed. London: Chatto & Windus, 1950. (pp. 226–29)

111.   V[allette], J[acques].   État actuel de l'oeuvre de W. H. Auden. *Mercure de France*, CCCX (1 December 1950), 714–18.

112.   Izzo, Carlo.   Consapevolezza moderna di W. H. Auden. *Archi* (Bologna), 5–6 ([1951]), 46–48.

113.   Kavanagh, Patrick.   Auden and the creative mind. *Envoy*, V (June 1951), 33–39.

114.*   Roth, Robert.   The sophistication of W. H. Auden: a sketch in Longinian method. *Modern philology*, XLVIII (February 1951), 193–204.

115.*   Spears, Monroe K.   The dominant symbols of Auden's poetry. *Sewanee review*, LIX (Summer 1951), 392–425.

116.*   ——.   Late Auden: the satirist as lunatic clergyman. *Sewanee review*, LIX (Winter 1951), 50–74.

117.*   Spender, Stephen.   *World within world*. London: Hamish Hamilton, 1951. (*passim*)
Biographical. Some material on Auden not included in the published book may be found in earlier versions: "The life of literature: I," *Partisan review*, XV (November 1948), 1204–11; and "W. H. Auden at Oxford," *World review*, n.s. 6 (August 1949), 45–49.

118.   Vallette, Jacques.   W. H. Auden: aspects d'une inquiétude. *Langues modernes*, XLV, 2 (1951), 153–65.

119.   Allen, Walter.   W. H. Auden: "the most exciting living poet." *Listener*, XLVII (17 April 1952), 640–41.

120.   Braybrooke, Neville.   Auden: an interim view. *Books: the journal of the National Book League*, 275 (December 1952), 136–38.

121.   Deutsch, Babette.   *Poetry in our time*. New York: Holt, 1952. (pp. 378–92 *et passim*)

122.   Enright, D. J.   Reluctant admiration: a note on Auden and Rilke. *Essays in criticism*, II (April 1952), 180–95.
Reprinted in Enright's *The apothecary's shop* (London: Secker & Warburg, 1957), pp. 187–205.

123.   Farmer, A. J.   Où va W. H. Auden? *Études anglaises*, V (November 1952), 346–49.

124.   Hutchinson, Pearse.   W. H. Auden: the search for happiness. *Litterair paspoort*, VII (October 1952), 180–82.

125.   Izzo, Carlo.   W. H. Auden. *La fiera letteraria*, VII (20 April 1952), 5, 7.

126.   Lombardo, Agostino.   Dalla scuola di Eliot a quella di Auden: la "realtà americana" nella tradizione. *La fiera letteraria*, VII (18 May 1952), 1–2.

Reprinted as "Dalla scuola di Eliot alla scuola di Auden" in Lombardo's *Realismo e simbolismo* (Rome: Edizioni di Storia e Letteratura, 1957), pp. 151–63.

127. Moore, Geoffrey. Three who did not make a revolution. *American Mercury*, LXXIV (April 1952), 107–14.

128. Rizzardi, Alfredo, Il poeta dell'età dell'angoscia. *La fiera letteraria*, VII (20 April 1952), 6.

129. Wilder, Amos N. *Modern poetry and the Christian tradition*. New York: Scribner's, 1952. "Mr. W. H. Auden: towards a new Christian synthesis." (pp. 196–204) "Recovery of the tradition: Mr. Auden's 'Christmas oratorio.'" (pp. 251–56)

130. Braybrooke, Neville, W. H. Auden: the road from Marx. *America* LXXXVIII (21 March 1953), 680–81.

131. Christie, Erling. W. H. Auden og angstens tidsalder. *Kirke og kultur*, LVIII (June 1953), 364–82.
Reprinted in Christie's *Tendenser og profiler* (Oslo: Aschchoug, 1955), pp. 68–92.

132. Cooley, John K. W. H. Audens Weg zur Humanität. *Wort und Wahrheit*, VIII (December 1953), 965–67.

133.* Fraser, G. S. *The modern writer and his world*. London: Derek Verschoyle, 1953. (pp. 232–43 *et passim*)

134. Nakagiri, Masao. Auden no shi to shisō [Auden's poems and thoughts]. *Shigaku*, VIII (December 1953), 18–28. [Not seen.]

135. ———. *Kiki no shijin: Ōden, Spenda, Ruisa, nado* [Poets of crisis: Auden, Spender, Lewis *et al.*]. Tokyo: Hayakawa Shobō, 1953. [Not seen.]

136. Spender, Stephen. *The creative element*. London: Hamish Hamilton, 1953. "The theme of political orthodoxy in the 'thirties" (pp. 140–58).

137.* ———. W. H. Auden and his poetry. *Atlantic*, CXCII (July 1953), 74–79.
Reprinted in *Auden: a collection of critical essays*, ed. Monroe K. Spears (1964), pp. 26–38.

138. Andō, Ichiro, and Katsuji Takamura. W. H. Auden: gendai shi gappyō [W. H. Auden: criticism of a modern poem]. *Eigo seinen* (Tokyo), C (February 1954), 72–75. [Not seen.]

139. Duncan, Chester. The compassion of W. H. Auden. *Canadian forum*, XXXIV (April 1954), 12–13.

140. Gerevini, Silvano. Note su Auden. *Letterature moderne*, V (September–December 1954), 647–51.

141. Sato, Hiroshi. Auden no sekai [Auden's world]. *Nihon daigaku setagaya kyōyō-bu kiyō* (Tokyo), 2 (1954), 29–49. [Not seen.]

142. Seif, Morton. The impact of T. S. Eliot on Auden and Spender. *South Atlantic quarterly*, LIII (January 1954), 61–69.

143.* Southworth, James G. *More modern American poets*. Oxford: Blackwell, 1954. "W. H. Auden: 1940 and after." (pp. 120–36)

144. Weisgerber, Jean. Het dualisme in de poëzie van W. H. Auden. *Kroniek van kunst en kultuur*, XIV (September 1954), 156–58.

145. ——. W. H. Auden as critic (1930–1941). *Revue des langues vivantes*, XX, 2 (1954), 116–25.
On the poems as social criticism.

146. Graves, Robert. These be your gods, O Israel! *Essays in criticism*, V (April 1955), 145–47.
Reprinted in *New republic*, CXXIV (5 March 1956), 17–18, and in Graves's *The crowning privilege* (London: Cassell, 1955), pp. 130–32, and (New York: Doubleday, 1956), pp. 136–38.

147. Hauge, Ingvar. Freud, Marx eller Kristus: en linje i W. H. Audens diktning. *Samtiden*, LXIV, 5 (1955), 335–45.

148. Kranz, Gisbert. Der amerikanische Dichter Wystan Hugh Auden. *Die Kirche in der Welt*, VIII, 3 (1955–56), 357–60.

149. Lehmann, John. *The whispering gallery*. London: Longmans, Green, 1955. (*passim*)
Biographical. See also Lehmann's *I am my brother* (London: Longmans, Green, 1960), pp. 14–15, 288–91, *et passim;* both books are collected in his *In my own time* (Boston: Little, Brown, 1969).

150. Magnússon, Sigurður A. Skáldið W. H. Auden er af íslenzku kyni í foðuraett. *Lesbók morgunblaðsins* (supplement to *Morgunblaðið*, Reykjavik), XXX (18 September 1955), 511–13.

151.* Moore, Marianne. *Predilections*. New York: Viking Press, 1955. "W. H. Auden." (pp. 84–102)

152. Spender, Stephen. It began at Oxford. *New York times*, 13 March 1955, section 7, pp. 4–5.

153.* The dog beneath the gown. *New statesman and nation*, LI (9 June 1956), 656–57.
Reprinted in *New statesman profiles* (London: Phoenix House, 1957), pp. 211–16. An important biographical sketch.

154.* Kalow, Gert. *Zwischen Christentum und Ideologie*. Heidelberg: Wolfgang Rothe, 1956. "W. H. Auden: der Christ und die Gesellschaft." (pp. 110–27)

155. Maanen, W. van. Voorspel tot volmaaktheid. *De gids*, CXIX (May 1956), 355–62.
Mostly on *The shield of Achilles*.

156. Martin, W. B. J. W. H. Auden and the preacher. *Congregational quarterly*, XXXIV (October 1956), 354–60.

157. Profile of a poet. *Observer*, 9 December 1956, p. 5.
Cf. letters to the editor from George A. Auden and "Ex-House Captain," *ibid.*, 23 December 1956, p. 8. The profile is reprinted on the sleeve of the recording *W. H. Auden* (Argo RG 184, London, 1960).

158. Thompson, John. Auden at the Sheldonian. *Truth*, CLVI (15 June 1956), 690.

159.* Wilson, Edmund. W. H. Auden in America. *New statesman and nation*, LI (9 June 1956), 658–59.
Reprinted in Wilson's *The bit between my teeth* (New York: Farrar, Straus & Giroux, 1965), pp. 355–63, and in *Auden: a collection of critical essays*, ed. Monroe K. Spears (1964), pp. 54–59.

160.* Bayley, John. *The romantic survival*. London: Constable, 1957. "W. H. Auden." (pp. 127–85; *cf.* pp. 36–39)
Excerpts appear in *Auden: a collection of critical essays*, ed. Monroe K. Spears (1964), pp. 60–80.

161. Brewer, D. S. Dualism in the poetry of W. H. Auden. *Eigo eibungaku kenkyū* (Hiroshima), IV (July 1957). [Not seen.]

162. Karlsson, Kristján. W. H. Auden. *Nýtt helgafel*, II (January–April 1957), 29–33.

163. Moore, Gerald. Luck in Auden. *Essays in criticism*, VII (January 1957), 103–8.

164. Thwaite, Anthony. *Essays on contemporary English poetry.* Tokyo: Kenkyusha, 1957. "W. H. Auden." (pp. 65–81) Also in the English edition, *Contemporary English poetry* (London: Heinemann, 1959), pp. 65–78.

165.* Alvarez, A. *The shaping spirit*. London: Chatto & Windus; New York: Scribner's, 1958 (as *Stewards of excellence*). "W. H. Auden: poetry and journalism." (pp. 87–106)

166. Kamei, Toshisuke. Auden to Rilke [Auden and Rilke]. *Rōman guntō*, 16 (1958). [Not seen.]

167. Kato, Yashuhide. W. H. Auden tembyō [The profile of W. H. Auden]. *Rikkyō daigaku eibei bungakkai kaiho*, 26 (1958). [Not seen.]

168. Nakagiri, Masao. Auden zakkan [Thoughts on Auden]. *Shigaku*, XIII (March 1958), 65–70. [Not seen.]

169. Ōsawa, Minoru. W. H. Auden no mondaiten: Thwaite-shi no shoron [Some questions about Auden: opinions of Mr. Thwaite]. *Shigaku*, XIII (March 1958), 56–65. [Not seen.]

170. Clancy, Joseph P. Auden waiting for his city. *Christian scholar*, XLII (Fall 1959), 185–200.

171.* Fraser, G. S. *Vision and rhetoric*. London: Faber, 1959. "Auden as the young prophet," "Auden in midstream," *and* "Auden's later manner." (pp. 149–78)
Excerpts appear as "The career of W. H. Auden" in *Auden: a collection of critical essays*, ed. Monroe K. Spears (1964), pp. 81–104.

172. Gorlier, Claudio. Auden, protagonista e testimone. *Questioni*, VII (January–April 1959), 19–23.

173. Magnússon, Sigurður A. *Nýju fötin keisarans*. Akureyri: Odds Björnssonar, 1959. "Blaðamaður í bundnu máli." (pp. 53–58)
Reprinted in *Lesbók morgunblaðsins* (supplement to *Morgunblaðið*, Reykjavik), XXXIX (19 April 1964), 5–6.

174. Martin, W. B. J. Significant modern writer: W. H. Auden. *Expository times*, LXXI (November 1959), 36–38.

175. Scott, Nathan A., Jr. The poetry of Auden. *Chicago review*, XIII (Winter 1959), 53–75.
Reprinted in *London magazine*, VIII (January 1961), 44–63; revised and shortened as "Auden's subject: 'the human clay'—'the village of the heart,' " in *Four ways of modern poetry*, ed. Nathan A. Scott, Jr. (Richmond: John Knox, 1965), pp. 71–92.

176. Beach, Joseph Warren. *Obsessive images*. Minneapolis: University of Minnesota Press, 1960. (*passim*)

177. Cook, F. W. The wise fool: W. H. Auden and the management. *Twentieth century*, CLXVIII (September 1960), 219–27.

178. Day Lewis, C. *The buried day*. London: Chatto & Windus; New York: Harper, 1960. (pp. 25, 176–79, 185–86, 216–17)

179. Jóhannesson, Ragnar. Í fylgd með Auden. *Andvari*, n.s. II (Autumn 1960), 245–58.
Biographical; on Auden's visit to Iceland.

180. Lerner, Laurence. *The truest poetry*. London: Hamish Hamilton, 1960. (pp. 204–7)

181. Nakagiri, Masao. W. H. Auden no shiron [Essay on Auden]. *Shigaku*, XV (May 1960). [Not seen.]

182. Peel, Marie. Modern poets: W. H. Auden. *Writing today*, 10 (December 1960), 7–8.

183. Pudney, John. *Home and away*. London: Michael Joseph, 1960. (pp. 45–49, 97–98, 206).
Portions were printed as "Auden as a schoolboy," *Guardian*, 21 May 1960, p. 6.

184. Quinn, Sister M. Bernetta. Auden's city of God. *Four quarters*, IX (March 1960), 5–8.

185. ——. Persons and places in Auden. *Renascence*, XII (Spring 1960), 115–24, 148.

186. Replogle, Justin. Social philosophy in Auden's early poetry. *Criticism*, II (Fall 1960), 351–61.

187. Rosenthal, M. L. *The modern poets*. New York: Oxford University Press, 1960. "Auden and the thirties." (pp. 182–96)

188. Schulte, E[dvige]. *Profilo storico della metrica inglese*. Naples: Istituto Universitario Orientale, 1960. "W. H. Auden." (pp. 204–8)
On Auden's metrics.

189. Shapiro, Karl. *In defense of ignorance*. New York: Random House, 1960. "The retreat of W. H. Auden." (pp. 115–41)
For a reply, *see:* Thomas R. Thornburg, "The man with the hatchet: Shapiro on Auden," *Ball State University forum*, XI (Summer 1970), 25–34.

190. Symons, Julian. *The thirties*. London: Cresset Press, 1960. (*passim*)

191. Thompson, E. P. Outside the whale. In *Out of apathy*, ed. E. P. Thompson (London: Stevens, 1960), pp. 141–94 (especially pp. 147–56).

192. Wright, Elsa Gress. Auden, digter og intellektuel atlet. *Vindrosen*, VII, 1 (1960), 9–11.

193. Andō, Ichiro. Auden no kingyō [Recent works of Auden]. *Gakutō* (Tokyo), LVIII (February 1961). [Not seen.]

194. Blackburn, Thomas. *The price of an eye*. London: Longmans, 1961. "W. H. Auden." (pp. 85–98)

195. Cox, R. G. The poetry of W. H. Auden. In *The modern age: the Pelican guide to English literature*, vol. 7, ed. Boris Ford (Harmondsworth: Penguin, 1961), pp. 373–93.

196.* Hoggart, Richard, ed. *W. H. Auden: a selection*. London: Hutchinson Educational, 1961. "Introduction." (pp. 13–41)
Partially reprinted as "Introduction to Auden's poetry" in *Auden: a collection of critical essays*, ed. Monroe K. Spears (1964), pp. 105–24.

197. Joost, Nicholas. English poetic satire and the modern Christian temper. *Delta Epsilon Sigma bulletin* (Effingham, Ill.), VI (May 1961), 40–48.

198. Kudo, Akio. W. H. Auden to seiji [W. H. Auden and politics]. *Oberon*, 17 (October 1961). [Not seen.]

199. Mander, John. *The writer and commitment*. London: Secker & Warburg, 1961. "Must we burn Auden?" (pp. 24–70)

200. Schrickx, W. W. H. Auden, virtuoos en dichter van de vervreemding. *De vlaamse gids*, XLV (1961), 115–29.

201. Spears, Monroe K. Auden in the fifties: rites of homage. *Sewanee review*, LXIX (Summer 1961), 375–98.

202. Tanaka, Seitarō. Auden no shi ni okeru seijisei to geijutsusei [Political nature and artistic nature in Auden's poems]. *Oberon*, 17 (October 1961). [Not seen.]

203. Berry, Francis. *Poetry and the physical voice*. London: Routledge, 1962. (pp. 185–88)

204.* Bullough, Geoffrey. *Mirror of minds*. Toronto: University of Toronto Press; London: Athlone Press, 1962. (pp. 234–42)

205. Davidson, Michael. *The world, the flesh and myself*. London: Arthur Barker, 1962. (pp. 126–30)
Biographical.

206. Demetillo. Ricaredo. *The authentic voice of poetry*. Diliman: University of the Philippines, 1962. "The high game of poetry in W. H. Auden." (pp. 195–211)

207. Kudo, Akio. *Hametsu no shogen* [The testimony of destruction]. Tokyo: Nan'undo, 1962. (pp. 7–105) [Not seen.]

208. McDowell, Frederick P. W. "The situation of our time": Auden in his American phase. In *Aspects of American poetry*, ed. Richard M. Ludwig (Columbus: Ohio State University Press, 1962), pp. 223–55.

An excerpt concerning *The sea and the mirror* appears in *Auden: a collection of critical essays*, ed. Monroe K. Spears (1964), pp. 142–51.

209. ——. Subtle, various, ornamental, clever: Auden in his recent poetry. *Wisconsin studies in contemporary literature*, III (Fall 1962), 29–44.

210. Replogle, Justin. The gang myth in Auden's early poetry. *Journal of English and Germanic philology*, LXI (July 1962), 481–95.

211. Spears, Monroe K. W. H. Auden at Swarthmore. *Swarthmore College bulletin*, LIX (March 1962), 1–6.

212. Suvin, Darko. Želimo li živjeti. *Zadarska revija*, XI (June 1962), 205–8.

213. Chittick, V. L. O. Angry young poet of the thirties. *Dalhousie review*, XLIII (Spring 1963), 85–97.

214. Empson, William. Early Auden. *Review*, 5 (February 1963), 32–34.

215. Dasgupta, N. *Modern English poetry (1920–1960)*. Delhi: Kitab Mihal, 1963. "Auden." (pp. 58–73)

216. Nakagiri, Masao. Somemonoya Auden no te [The dyer Auden's hand]. *Eigo seinen*, CIX (July 1963), 392–93.

217. Ohmann, Richard M. Auden's sacred awe. *Commonweal*, LXXVIII (31 May 1963), 279–81.
Reprinted in *Auden: a collection of critical essays*, ed. Monroe K. Spears (1964), pp. 172–78.

218. Replogle, Justin. Auden's homage to Thalia. *Bucknell review*, XI (March 1963), 98–117.

219. Stravinsky, Igor and Robert Craft. *Dialogues and a diary*. Garden City, N.Y.: Doubleday, 1963; London: Faber, 1968. (*passim*)
Biographical.

220. Ayukawa, Nobuo. Shi to taiken no kakudai: Auden to Yevtushenko ni furete [Magnification of poetry and experience: regarding Auden and Yevtushenko]. *Gendaishi*, XI (March 1964), 27–33. [Not seen.]

221.* Fraser, G. S. Auden: the composite giant. *Shenandoah*, XV (Summer 1964), 46–59.

222. Gross, Harvey. *Sound and form in modern poetry*. Ann Arbor: University of Michigan Press, 1964. "W. H. Auden." (pp. 249–61)

223.* Hardy, Barbara. The reticence of W. H. Auden. *Review*, 11–12 ([1964]), 54–64.

224. Izzo, Carlo. The poetry of W. H. Auden. In *Auden: a collection of critical essays*, ed. Monroe K. Spears (1964), pp. 125–41.
Translated and abridged from Izzo's introduction to *Poesie di W. H. Auden* (Parma: Guanda, 1952), and from his *Storia della literatura inglese* [vol. 2] (Milan: Nuova Accademia, 1963).

225. Jóhannesson, Ragnar. Auden heimsækir Ísland. *Alþýðublaðið* (Reykjavik), 8 April 1964, pp. 5, 10.

226. Kleinstück, Johannes. *Mythos und Symbol in englischer Dichtung*. Stuttgart: Kohlhammer, 1964. "Paradies und Stadt in der Dichtung W. H. Audens." (pp. 134–57)

227. Kuna, F. M. W. H. Auden, der subtile "Poeta doctus." *Die neueren Sprachen*, n.s. XIII (February 1964), 57–65.

228. Magnússon, Sigurður A. Auden in Iceland. *Iceland review*, II, 3 (1964), 20.

229. Replogle, Justin. The Auden group. *Wisconsin studies in contemporary literature*, V (Summer 1964), 133–50.

230. Sabljak, Tomislav. Portret pjesnika W. H. Audena. *Republika* (Zagreb), XX (November 1964), 477–78.
Includes an account of Auden's visit to Zagreb. Sabljak published other notes on Auden in *Forum* (Zagreb), III (July–August 1964), 164–65, and in *Kolo* (Zagreb), n.s. II (February 1964), 279–84.

231. Weatherhead, A. Kingsley. The good place in the latest poems of W. H. Auden. *Twentieth century literature*, X (October 1964), 99–107.

232. Bain, Carl E. W. H. Auden. *Emory University quarterly*, XXI (Spring 1965), 45–58.

233. Blair, John G. W. H. Auden: the poem as performance. *Shenandoah*, XVI (Spring 1965), 55–66.

234. Eknar, Reidar. Äntligen Auden. *BLM: Bonniers litterära magasin*, XXXIV (November 1965), 672–74.

235. Fowler, Helen. The faces and places of Auden. *Approach*, 57 (Fall 1965), 6–14.

236. Grubb, Frederick. *A vision of reality*. London: Chatto & Windus, 1965. "English Auden and the 30's ethos." (pp. 137–57; *et passim*)

237. Gustafson, Richard. The paragon style: Frost and Auden. *Poet and critic*, II (Fall 1965), 35–42.

238. Harris, Henry. The symbols and imagery of hawk and kestrel in the poetry of Auden and Day Lewis in the thirties. *Zeitschrift für Anglistik und Amerikanistik*, XIII (July 1965), 276–85.

239.* Morgan, Kathleen E. *Christian themes in contemporary poets*. London: SCM Press, 1965. "The analysis of guilt: poetry of W. H. Auden." (pp. 92–122)

240. Replogle, Justin. Auden's intellectual development 1950–1960. *Criticism*, VII (Summer 1965), 250–62.

241.* ——. Auden's Marxism. *PMLA*, LXXX (December 1965), 584–95.

242. Rodway, Allan. Logicless grammar in Audenland. *London magazine*, n.s. IV (March 1965), 31–44.

243. Ungvári, Tamás. Beszélgetés W. H. Audennel. *Új irás*, V (February 1965), 166–67.

244. Wallace-Crabbe, Chris. Auden revisited. *Dissent* (Melbourne), 14 (Winter 1965), 22–26.

245.* Whitehead, John. Auden: an early poetical notebook. *London magazine*, n.s. V (May 1965), 85–91, 93, and plate facing p. 74.

246. Wright, George T. A general view of Auden's poetry. *Tennessee studies in literature*, 10 (1965), 43–64.

247.* Bloom, Robert. W. H. Auden's bestiary of the human. *Virginia quarterly review*, XLII (Spring 1966), 207–33.

248. Harris, Henry. The symbol of the frontier in the social allegory of the 'thirties. *Zeitschrift für Anglistik und Amerikanistik*, XIV (April 1966), 127–40.

249. Kudo, Akio. W. H. Auden, *Ie ni tsuite:* igirisu bungaku [W. H. Auden, *About the house*]. *Bungakukai*, XX (August 1966), 103–6.

250. Mortimer, Anthony. *Modern English poets: five introductory essays*. Milan-Varese: Instituto Editoriale Cisalpine, 1966. "W. H. Auden." (pp. 115–42)
Reprinted in Mortimer's *Modern English poets: seven introductory essays* (Toronto: Forum House, 1968), pp. 113–40.

251.* Replogle, Justin. Auden's religious leap. *Wisconsin studies in contemporary literature*, VII (Winter–Spring 1966), 47–75.

252. Schauder, Karlheinz. W. H. Auden. *Hochland*, LVIII (April 1966), 376–79.

253. Stravinsky, Igor, and Robert Craft. *Themes and episodes*. New York: Knopf, 1966; London: Faber, 1968. (*passim*)
Biographical.

254.* Weimer, David R. *The city as metaphor*. New York: Random House, 1966. "Rome sacked." (pp. 123–46)

255. Woodhouse, A. S. P. *The poet and his faith*. Chicago: University of Chicago Press, 1965. (pp. 286–93).
Also printed as "W. H. Auden and his faith," *Midway*, 25 (Winter 1966), 50–57.

256. Binni, Francesco. Auden: il dissenso della "ragione." *Letteratura*, XXXI, 88–90 (1967), 206–20.

257.* Bloom, Robert. Auden's essays at man: some long views in the early poetry. *Shenandoah*, XVIII (Winter 1967), 23–43.

258.* Callan, Edward. Auden's goodly heritage. *Shenandoah*, XVIII (Winter 1967), 56–68.

259.* ——. W. H. Auden: the farming of a verse. *Southern review*, n.s. III (April 1967), 341–56.

260. Dobrée, Bonamy. W. H. Auden. *Shenandoah*, XVIII (Winter 1967), 18–22.

225. Jóhannesson, Ragnar. Auden heimsækir Ísland. *Alþyðublaðið* 1924–36. *Shenandoah*, XVIII (Winter 1967), 6–11.

262.* Ellmann, Richard. *Eminent domain.* New York: Oxford University Press, 1967. "Gazebos and gashouses." (pp. 97–126)
Portions were printed in *Irish times*, 10 June 1965, supplement, p. iii.

263. Fauderau, Serge. Auden, poète anglais. *Critique*, XXII (November 1967), 974–76.

264. FitzGerald, David. Auden's city. *Dublin magazine*, VI (Summer 1967), 3–17.

265. Five [comments on Auden]. *Shenandoah*, XVIII (Winter 1967), 45–47.
By Robert Lowell, Louise Bogan, M. F. K. Fisher, John Betjeman, and Leonard Bernstein.

266. Fremantle, Anne. Anima naturaliter Christiana. *Shenandoah*, XVIII (Winter 1967), 69–77.
Also published, with slight changes, as "Auden and the Incarnation," *Month*, n.s. XXXVII (May 1967), 292–300.

267. Hollander, John. Auden at sixty. *Atlantic*, CCXX (July 1967), 84–87.

268. Kutsuki, Toshiki. Auden ni okero chokuyu no kōzō: *Another time* o chūshin ni [Structure of Auden's similes: mainly in *Another time*]. *Fukui daigaku kyōikugakubu kiyo*, 17 (October 1967), 23–35. [Not seen.]

269.* Le Breton, Georges. Auden. *Preuves*, XVII (Summer 1967), 27–30.

270. Mitchison, Naomi. Young Auden. *Shenandoah*, XVIII (Winter 1967), 12–15.

271. Nagata, Hiroshi. "Ai" (W. H. Auden) ["Love"]. *Gendaishi techō*, X (September 1967), 70–77.

272. Sarang, Vilas. Personal pronouns in the poetry of W. H. Auden. *Literary criterion* (Mysore), VII (Summer 1967), 51–63.

273.* Serpieri, Alessandro. Auden, lo specchio e il caos. *Il ponte*, XXIII (June 1967), 770–786.
Enlarged and revised in Serpieri's *Hopkins—Eliot—Auden* (Bologna: Riccardo Pàtron, 1969), pp. 163–208.

274. Sito, Jerzy. S. *W pierwszej i trzeciej osobie.* Warsaw: Państwowy Instytut Wydawniczy, 1967. "Gra wiedzy." (pp. 290–310)

275. Symons. Julian. Early Auden. *Shenandoah*, XVIII (Winter 1967), 48–50.

276. Yü Kuang-Chung. Ch'ien ch'iao ti liang hsin [A conscience of many eyes]. *Shun wên hsüeh* (Taipei), II, 6 (December 1967), 60–75. [Not seen.]

277.* Bloom, Robert. The humanization of Auden's early style. *PMLA*, LXXXIII (May 1968), 443–54.

278. Fairchild, Hoxie Neale. *Religious trends in English poetry*, vol. 6. New York: Columbia University Press, 1968. (pp. 134–44, 299–301, 443–45 *et passim*)

279. Fink, Guido. Auden: l'eccezione e la regola. *Paragone*, XIX (October 1968), 81–99.

280. Goetsch, Paul. W. H. Auden und Amerika. *Jahrbuch für Amerikastudien*, 13 (1968), 215–227.

281. Jurak, Mirko. Zapis o književnem ustvarjanju W. H. Audena. *Dialogi* (Maribor), IV, 7–8 (1964), 395–405.

282.* Lewars, Kenneth. Auden's Swarthmore chart. *Connecticut review*, I (April 1968), 44–56.
An account, with a facsimile, of a chart of human experience which Auden prepared in 1943.

283. Moraes, Dom. *My son's father*. London: Secker & Warburg, 1968. (pp. 190–92, 205–6)
Biographical.

284.* Panaro, Cleonice. L'arte inclusiva di W. H. Auden. *Convivium*, XXXVI (July–August 1968), 206–26.

285. Tolley, A. T. The thirties poets at Oxford. *University of Toronto quarterly*, XXXVIII (July 1968), 338–58.

286. Furomoto, Taketoshi. W. H. Auden ne tabi: sanjūnen no ichimen [The voyage in Auden: an aspect of the thirties]. *Kōbe daigaku kyōyō-bu jimbungakkai ronshū*, VI (March 1969), 41–78. [Not seen.]

287.* Hardy, Barbara. W. H. Auden, thirties to sixties: a face and a map. *Southern review*, n.s. V (July 1969), 655–72.

288.* Holloway, John. The master as joker. *Art international*, XIII (January 1969), 17–20.

289.* Hoskins, Katharine Bail. *Today the struggle*. Austin: University of Texas Press, 1969. (pp. 165–82, 207–18 *et passim*)
Includes a general account of Auden's work in the thirties.

290. Jäger, Dietrich. Das Haus als Raum des lyrischen Geschehens und als Gengenstand der lyrischen Meditation: das Thema der nächsten Umwelt des Menschen in Audens *About the house* und bei deutschen und angelsächsischen Zeitgenossen. *Literatur in Wissenschaft und Unterricht*, II, 4 (1969), 238–57.

291. Mandle, W. F. Auden and the failure of the left. *ANU historical journal*, 6 (November 1969), 3–9.

292. Masuno, Masae. Shijin no shinnen: W. H. Auden o chūshin ni [Poets' faith: with emphasis on Auden]. *Kōnan daigaku bungakkai ronshū*, XL (March 1969), 1–30. [Not seen.]

293. Masutani, Sotoyoshi. Auden no me: gendaishi to shinwa [Auden's eye: modern poems and myth]. *Hitotsubashi ronsō*, LXI (February 1969), 33–43.

294.* Maxwell, D. E. S. *Poets of the thirties*. London: Routledge, 1969. "W. H. Auden: the island and the city." (pp. 127–72)

295. Press, John. *A map of modern English verse*. London: Oxford University Press, 1969. "W. H. Auden." (pp. 186–98)
Includes reprinted writings by and about Auden, in addition to Press's commentary.

296. Reeves, James, ed. *The poets and their critics* [vol. 3]: *Arnold to Auden*. London: Hutchinson, 1969. "W. H. Auden." (pp. 242–73)
A selection of criticism by and about Auden.

297. Stravinsky, Igor, and Robert Craft. *Retrospectives and conclusions*. New York: Knopf, 1969. (pp. 145–49, 160–5, 173–79)
Biographical.

298. Bowen, C. Pardon for writing well. *Poetry magazine* (Sydney), XVIII, (June 1970), 3–12.

299. Faulkner, Peter. W. H. Auden: then and now. *Humanist* (London), LXXXV (March 1970), 80–82.

300.* Kermode, Frank. The poet in praise of limestone. *Atlantic*, CCXXV (May 1970), 67–71.

301.* Stravinsky, Igor. A maker of libretti. *Harper's magazine*, CCXL (April 1970), 112–14.

Studies of Individual Poems: The Shorter Poems

Only separately published studies are listed here; individual poems are of course also discussed in the general studies listed above. It should be noted that cricticism from *Explicator*, through volume XX (1962), is collected in *The explicator cyclopedia*, vol. 1 (Chicago: Quadrangle Books, 1964), pp. 2-18.

Poems in *Collected Shorter Poems 1927–1957* and Later Poems

The letter
302. Ishiguro, Masayuki, *et al.* Shimpojūm: W. H. Auden's "The love letter" [Symposium: W. H. Auden's "The love letter"]. *Eigo eibungaku kenkyū*, VI (December 1959). [Not seen.]
For a reply *see*: Tadashi Oda, "Symposium kōki to hihan: W. H. Auden i 'The love letter' ni tsuite," [Criticism of a symposium on W. H. Auden's "The love letter"], *Kyūshū shōka daigaku shōkei ronshū*, III (January 1963). [Not seen.]

Family ghosts
303. Cleophas, Sister M. Auden's *Family ghosts* (or *The strings' excitement*). *Explicator*, VII (October 1948), item 1.

The questioner who sits so sly
304. Chatman, Seymour. Auden's *The questioner who sits so sly*. *Explicator*, XXVIII (November 1969), item 21.

1929

305. Emerson, Dorothy. Poetry corner. *Scholastic*, XXVII (11 January 1936), 14.

"O where are you going" said reader to rider ...

306. Ricks, Christopher. "O where are you going?": W. H. Auden and Christina Rossetti. *Notes & queries*, n.s. VII (December 1960), 472.

Have a good time

307. Philbrick, F. A. Auden's *Have a good time. Explicator*, IV (December 1945), item 21.

The wanderer

308.* Bloomfield, Morton W. "Doom is dark and deeper than any sea-dingle": W. H. Auden and "Sawles warde." *Modern language notes*, LXIII (December 1948), 548–52.

309. Robertson, Duncan. Auden's *The wanderer. Explicator*, XXVIII (April 1970), item 70.

Ode

310. Long, Richard, A. Auden's *Ode to my pupils. Explicator*, VI (April 1948), item 39.

311. LeCompte, Calvin B., Jr. *Which side am I supposed to be on?* (or *Ode to my pupils*). *Explicator*, VIII (December 1949), item 21.

Paysage moralisé

312. Meller, Horst. W. H. Auden: paysage moralisé. *Die neueren Sprachen*, n.s. XIV (January 1965), 23–31.

O what is that sound

313. Ahern, Eckoe M. There may be many answers. *English journal*, LI (December 1962), 657–58.

314. Haeffner, Paul. Auden and Ella Wheeler Wilcox. *Notes & queries*, n.s. IX (March 1962), 110–11.

Our hunting fathers

315. Tate, Allen. *Reason in madness*. New York: Putnam, 1941. (pp. 97–98)

316. Flint, F. Cudworth. Auden's *Our hunting fathers told the story. Explicator*, II (October 1943), item 1.

Schoolchildren

317. Long, Richard A. Auden's *Schoolchildren. Explicator*, VII (February 1949), item 32.

On this island

318. Barnes, T. R. *Poetry appreciation*. London: Faber, 1968. (pp. 31–35)

Night mail

319. Stebner, Gerhard. Whitman, Liliencron, W. H. Auden: Betrachtung und Vergleich motivähnlichter Gedichte. *Die neueren Sprachen*, n.s. IX (March 1960), 105–18.

As I walked out one evening

320. Mason, Ellsworth. Auden's *As I walked out one evening*. *Explicator*, XII (May 1954), item 43.

321. McAleer, Edward C. As Auden walked out. *College English*, XVIII (February 1957), 271–72.

322.* Brooks, Cleanth, and Robert Penn Warren. *Understanding poetry*. 3rd ed. New York: Holt, Rinehart & Winston, 1960. (pp. 330–35)
This discussion is not in the earlier editions.

Fish in the unruffled lakes

323. Bauerle, Ruth H. Auden's *Fish in the unruffled lakes*. *Explicator*, XXVI (March 1968), item 57.

Now the leaves are falling fast . . .

324. Warner, Alan. W. H. Auden's "Autumn song." *Critical survey*, I (Summer 1964), 203–5.

Lullaby

325.* Goetsch, Paul. W. H. Auden: *Lay your sleeping head, my love*. In *Die moderne englische Lyrik: Interpretationen*, ed. Horst Oppel (Berlin: Erich Schmidt, 1967), pp. 193–206.

326. Caswell, Robert W. Auden's *Lay your sleeping head my love*. *Explicator*, XXVI (January 1968), item 44.

Miss Gee

327. Irwin, John T. MacNeice, Auden, and the art ballad. *Contemporary literature*, XI (Winter 1970), 58–79.

Victor

328. Iwasaki, Shūji. W. H. Auden no "Victor" ni tsuite [About "Victor" by W. H. Auden]. *Direction* (Nagoya), 4 (1961). [Not seen.]

329. Friedman, S. Auden and Hardy. *Notes & queries*, n.s., XIII (November 1964), 419.

See also item 327.

Musée des Beaux Arts

330. Hyams, C. Barry, and Karl H. Reichert.   A test lesson on Brueghel's "Icarus" and Auden's "Musée des Beaux Arts." *Die neueren Sprachen*, n.s. VI (May 1957), 228–32.

331. Charney, Maurice.   Sir Lewis Namier and Auden's "Musée des Beaux Arts." *Philological quarterly*, XXXIX (January 1960), 129–31.

332.* Bluestone, Max.   The iconographic sources of Auden's "Musée des Beaux Arts." *Modern language notes*, LXXVI (April 1961), 331–36.

333. Haas, Rudolf.   *Wege zur englischen Lyrik in Wissenschaft und Unterricht*. Heidelberg: Quelle & Meyer, 1962. "Bemerkungen zu Audens 'Musée des Beaux Arts.' " (pp. 173–82)

334. Kinney, Arthur F.   Auden, Bruegel, and "Musée des Beaux Arts." *College English*, XXIV (April 1963), 529–31.

335. Werlich, Egon.   *Poetry analysis*. Dortmund: Lambert Lensing, 1967. "Musée des Beaux Arts." (pp. 223–28)

Sonnets from China

336. Stanley, F. R.   Today the struggle (a critical commentary on Auden's sonnet-sequence *In time of war*). *Literary half-yearly* (Mysore), VI (January 1965), 74–88.

337. Wheeler, Charles B.   *The design of poetry*. New York: Norton, 1966. (pp. 131–36)
On "And an age ended, and its last deliverer died . . . ."

In memory of W. B. Yeats

338.* Fraser, G. S.   Auden: In memory of W. B. Yeats. In *Master poems of the English language*, ed. Oscar Williams (New York: Trident Press, 1966), pp. 1017–21.

339. Rosenheim, Edward W., Jr.   The elegiac act: Auden's "In memory of W. B. Yeats." *College English*, XXVII (February 1966), 422–25.

340.* Otten, Kurt.   W. H. Auden: In memory of W. B. Yeats. In *Die moderne englische Lyrik: Interpretationen*, ed. Horst Oppel (Berlin: Erich Schmidt, 1967), pp. 207–19.

Voltaire at Ferney

341. Lindenberg, E.   Twee digters—twee Voltaire's. *Kriterium* (Kaapstad), II (January 1965), 8–11.

Anthem for St. Cecilia's Day

342. Hough, Ingeborg.   Auden's *Song for St. Cecilia's Day. Explicator*, XVIII (March 1960), item 35.

343. Warren, Raymond.   *Song for St. Cecilia's Day: an inaugural lec-*

ture . . . . Belfast: The Queen's University, 1967. (Queen's University of Belfast, new lecture series, no. 45.)
A pamphlet containing a lecture (pp. 1–17) and a musical setting (pp. 18–43).

Diaspora
344. Knoll, Robert E. The style of contemporary poetry. *Prairie schooner*, XXIX (Summer 1955), 118–25 (especially pp. 122–24).

In sickness and in health
345.* Chase, Richard Volney. *Quest for myth*. Baton Rouge: Louisiana State University Press, 1949. (pp. 127–31)

Mundus et infans
346. Highet, Gilbert. *The powers of poetry*. New York: Oxford University Press, 1960. "Auden on the baby: kicking his mother." (pp. 167–73)
347. Thornburg, Thomas. Auden's *Mundus et infans*, [lines] 46–56. *Explicator*, XXVII (January 1969), item 33.
348. Barnes, T. R. *Poetry appreciation*. London: Faber, 1968. "Mundus et infans." (pp. 24–30)

A healthy spot
349. Satterwhite, J. N. Auden's *A healthy spot*. *Explicator*, XXI (March 1963), item 57.

The fall of Rome
350.* Wheelwright, Philip. *Metaphor and reality*. Bloomington: Indiana University Press, 1962. (pp. 86–87)

In praise of limestone
351. Hagopian, John V. Exploring Auden's limestone landscape. *Die neueren Sprachen*, n.s. XI (June 1962), 255–60.
352.* Parkin, Rebecca Price. The facsimile of immediacy in W. H. Auden's "In praise of limestone." *Texas studies in language and literature*, VII (Autumn 1965), 295–304.

Metalogue to The magic flute
353. Cozarinsky, Edgardo. Desencantar, desintoxicar: nota sobre W. H. Auden y W. A. Mozart. *Los papeles de son armadans*, LV (December 1969), 306–12.

Their lonely betters
354. Hooper, A. G., and C. J. D. Harvey. *Talking of poetry*. Cape Town: Oxford University Press, 1961. "Commentary." (pp. 183–86)

The shield of Achilles

355. Westlake, John H. J.   W. H. Auden's "The shield of Achilles": an interpretation. *Literatur in Wissenschaft und Unterricht*, I, 1 (1968), 50–58.

The epigoni

356. Poggioli, Renato.   Decadence in minature. *Massachusetts review*, IV (Spring 1963), 531–62 (especially pp. 537–41).

Woods

357. Fodor, András.   Egy Auden versről. *Nagyvilág*. XIII (November 1968), 1724–27.

Good-bye to the Mezzogiorno

358. Izzo, Carlo.   "Goodbye to the Mezzogiorno". *Shenandoah*, XVIII (Winter 1967), 80–82.

A change of air

359.* Elliott, George P., Karl Shapiro, Stephen Spender; reply by W. H. Auden.   A symposium on W. H. Auden's "A change of air." *Kenyon review*, XXVI (Winter 1964), 190–208.
Reprinted in *The contemporary poet as artist and critic*, ed. Anthony Ostroff (Boston: Little, Brown, 1964), pp. 167–87.

Uncollected Poems

It's no use raising a shout . . .

360. Rowan, Mark, John H. Sutherland, and George MacFadden.   Auden's *It's no use raising a shout*. *Explicator*, XV (November 1956), item 12.

Petition

361. Brown, Wallace Cable.   Auden's *Sir, no man's enemy, forgiving all*. *Explicator*, III (March 1945), item 38.
Cf. D. A. Robertson, Jr., W. K. Wimsatt, Jr., and Hallett Smith III, *ibid.*, (May 1945), item 51.
362. Williams, Melvin G.   Auden's "Petition": a synthesis of criticism. *Personalist*, XLVI (Spring 1965), 222–32.

Foxtrot from a play

363. Power, William.   Auden's *Foxtrot from a play*. *Explicator*, XVI (March 1958), item 32.

Spain 1937

364. Wall, Bernard.   W. H. Auden and Spanish civilization. *Colosseum*, III (September 1937), 142–49.

365. "Orwell, George." *Inside the whale*. London: Gollancz, 1940. (pp. 169–70)

366. Mori, Kiyoshi. "Spain": Auden to sono mure ["Spain": Auden and his group]. *Sakka to seiji*, July 1958. [Not seen.]

367. Cox, C. B., and A. E. Dyson. *Modern poetry*. London: Edward Arnold, 1963. "W. H. Auden: Spain 1937." (pp. 90–97)

368. Ford, Hugh D. *A poet's war*. Philadelphia: University of Pennsylvania Press, 1965. (pp. 206–15, 288)

369. Muste, John M. *Say that we saw Spain die*. Seattle: University of Washington Press, 1966. (pp. 56–59)

370. Nakagiri, Masao. Spain, 1966. *Eigo seinen*, CXII (October 1966), 666–67.
In Japanese.

371.* Stead, C. K. Auden's "Spain." *London magazine*, n.s. VII (March 1968), 41–54.

372. Weintraub, Stanley. *The last great cause*. New York: Weybright & Talley, 1968. (pp. 65–71)

September 1, 1939

373.* Bartlett, Phyllis, and John A. Pollard. Auden's *September 1, 1939*, stanza 2. *Explicator*, XIV (November 1955), item 8.

374. Bennett, Daphne Nicholson. Auden's "September 1, 1939": an interpreter's analysis. *Quarterly journal of speech*, XLII (February 1956), 1–13.

375. Fujimoto, Reiji. W. H. Auden no "September 1, 1939" ni tsuite: kaishaku oboegaki [An explanation of "September 1, 1939"]. *Hiroshima shōdai ronshū*, V (March 1965). [Not seen.]

376. Schorer, Mark. Auden: September 1, 1939. In *Master poems of the English language*, ed. Oscar Williams (New York: Trident Press, 1966), pp. 1025–28.
Includes an account of the text of the poem.

Crisis

377. Morland, Harold. Auden's *Crisis*. *Explicator*, V (November 1946), item 17.
Cf. F. A. Philbrick, *ibid.*, V (April 1947), item 45.

Studies of Individual Poems: The Longer Poems, *The Orators*
and *Letters from Iceland*

Paid on both sides

378.* Empson, William. A note on Auden's "Paid on both sides." *Experiment*, 7 (Spring 1931), 60–61.

379.* Cook, F. W. Primordial Auden. *Essays in criticism,* XII (October 1962), 402–12.

380.* Hazard, Forrest E. The Father Christmas passage in Auden's "Paid on both sides." *Modern drama,* XII (September 1969), 155–64.

The orators

381. La Drière, J. Craig. People we are living with. *Fleur de lis,* XXXIII (May 1934), 29–35.

382. Sparrow, John. *Sense and poetry.* London: Constable, 1934. (pp. 145–55)

383.* Fraser, G. S. The young prophet. *New statesman & nation,* LI (28 January 1956), 102–3.

384. Reed, John R. *Old school ties.* Syracuse: Syracuse University Press, 1964. (pp. 107–9, 206–7)

385.* Sellers, W. H. New light on Auden's *The orators.* PMLA, LXXXII (October 1967), 455–64.

386. Mendelson, Edward. The coherence of Auden's *The orators. ELH,* XXXV (March 1968), 114–33.

Letters from Iceland

387. Jóhannesson, Ragnar. Auden, MacNeice og *Bréf frá Íslandi. Lesbók morgunblaðsins* (supplement to *Morgunblaðið*), XXXIX (9 February 1964), 1, 12–14.

388.* Porter, Peter. The assent of '36: an encomium of Auden and MacNeice's *Letters from Iceland. Ambit,* 27 (1966), 18–23.

New Year letter

389.* Sanesi, Roberto. Nota per la "New Year letter" di W. H. Auden. *Aut-aut,* III (March 1953), 145–49.

390. Wallace-Crabbe, Chris. Auden's "New Year letter" and the fate of long poems. *Melbourne critical review,* 5 (1962), 128–36.

391.* Callan, Edward. Auden's "New Year letter": a new style of architecture. *Renascence,* XVI (Fall 1963), 13–19.
Reprinted in *Auden: a collection of critical essays,* ed. Monroe K. Spears (1964), pp. 152–59.

For the time being

392. Wasson, S. Carson. A descant on W. H. Auden's Christmas oratorio. *Crozer quarterly,* XXIII (October 1946), 340–49.

393. Plas, Michel van der. Triomf der liefde: Auden's "For the time being." *Elseviers weekblad,* IV (25 December 1948), 13–17. [Not seen.]

394. Frost, William. Auden's *Fugal-chorus. Explicator,* XI (December 1952), item 21.
Cf. Frederick A. Pottle, *ibid.,* XI (April 1953), item 40.

395. Shepherd, T. B. "For the time being": W. H. Auden's Christmas oratorio. *London quarterly & Holborn review,* CLXXVII (October 1952), 277–84.

396. Popma, S. J. Toen de dagen vervuld waren. *Horizon* (Kampen), XX (December 1957), 302–8.

397. Janet, Sister M., S.C.L. W. H. Auden: two poems in sequence. *Renascence,* XIII (Spring 1961), 115–18.

398. Reschke, Rudolf Helmut. Auden–wieder Falsch gedeutet. *Neue deutsche Hefte,* IX (November–December 1962), 114–20.

399. Driver, Tom F. Auden's view of history in "For the time being." *Journal of Bible and religion,* XXI (January 1963), 3–8.

400.* Callan, Edward. Auden and Kierkegaard: the artistic framework of "For the time being." *Christian scholar,* XLVIII (Fall 1965), 211–23.

401. Kont, Paul. Prima l'arte, dogo la techniza. *Die Zukunft* (Vienna), [XXII], 6 (end of March 1967), 24–27.

402. Matsubara, Kazuo. "Warui kisetsu no tameni": Auden no shi to sono kikikan ["For the time being": Auden's poem and its critical feeling]. *Eibungaku,* 28 (1967). [Not seen.]

403. Morse, Donald E. The nature of man in Auden's "For the time being." *Renascence,* XIX (Winter 1967), 93–101.

404. ——. "For the time being": man's response to the incarnation. *Renascence,* XIX (Summer 1967), 190–97.

405. Woodbery, Potter. *Redeeming the time: the theological argument of Auden's* For the time being. Atlanta: Georgia State College, 1968. (Georgia State College, School of Arts and Sciences, research paper no. 18.)

406. Morse, Donald E. Meaning of time in Auden's *For the time being. Renascence,* XXII (Spring 1970), 162–68.

407. ——. Two major revisions in W. H. Auden's "For the time being." *English language notes,* VII (June 1970), 294–97.
Cf. correction, *ibid.,* VIII (December 1970), 139–40.
See also item 129.

The sea and the mirror

408.* Sunesen, Bent. "All we are not stares back at what we are": a note on Auden. *English studies,* XL (December 1959), 439–49.

409.* Callan, Edward. Auden's ironic masquerade: criticism as morality play. *University of Toronto quarterly,* XXXV (January 1966), 133–43.

410. Whitehead, Lee M. Art as communication: Auden's "The sea and the mirror." *Perspective,* XIV (Spring 1966), 171–78.

411. Thornburg, Thomas R. *Prospero, the magician-artist: Auden's* The sea and the mirror. Muncie, Ind.: Ball State University, 1969. (Ball State

monograph no. 15; Ball State University publications in English, no. 10.)
See also item 397.

The age of anxiety

412. Schuur, Koos. Een barok herdersgedicht van Auden. *Het woord,*
Winter 1948–49, pp. 170–75.

413. McCoard, William B. An interpretation of the times: a report on
the oral interpretation of W. H. Auden's "Age of anxiety." *Quarterly
journal of speech,* XXXV (December 1949), 489–95.

414. Benn, Gottfried. Das Zeitalter der Angst: eine Einführung in
W. H. Audens grosse Gedicht. *Literarische Deutschland,* II (20 January
1951), 4.
Reprinted with the translation *Das Zeitalter der Angst* (Wiesbaden: Limes Verlag,
1951), pp. 7–19, and in Benn's *Gesammelte Werke,* vol. 4 (Wiesbaden: Limes, 1961),
pp. 364–76 (also in a 1968 edition, vol. 7, pp. 1820–32).

415. Takahashi, Genji. Urei no jidai: Auden ni tsuite [Age of anxiety:
about Auden]. *Meiji gakuin daigaku ryōshi,* June 1952. [Not seen.]

416. Busch, Günther. Aufzeichnungen zu W. H. Auden's "Zeitalter der
Angst." *Begegnung,* XI (15 October 1956), 309–11.
This periodical was also published as a supplement to *Anregung,* VIII (15 October
1956).

417. Yi Ch'ang-bae. [On Auden's Age of anxiety.] *Sin sajo* (Seoul),
November 1962, pp. 264–70. [Not seen.]

418.* Brooke-Rose, Christine. Notes on the metre of Auden's "The age
of anxiety." *Essays in criticism,* XIII (July 1963), 253–64.

419. Galinsky, Hans. The expatriate poet's style: with reference to
T. S. Eliot and W. H. Auden. *English studies today,* 3rd ser. (1964), pp.
215–26.
Reprinted, with the subtitle altered to "T. S. Eliot's and W. H. Auden's use of
American-British speech differentiations," in Galinsky's *Amerika und Europa* (Ber-
lin: Langenscheit, 1968), pp. 102–10.

420.* Callan, Edward. Allegory in Auden's "The age of anxiety."
Twentieth century literature, X (January 1965), 155–65.

Studies of the Plays, Libretti, Films
and Musical Settings

General studies

421. Allott, Kenneth. Auden in the theatre. *New verse,* 26–27 (November 1937), 17–21.

422.* Spender, Stephen. The poetic dramas of W. H. Auden and Christopher Isherwood. *New writing,* n.s. 1 (Autumn 1938), 102–8.

423.* Symons, Julian. Auden and poetic drama 1938. *Life and letters
today,* XX (February 1939), 70–79.

424. White, Eric Walter. *Benjamin Britten.* London: Boosey & Hawkes, 1949. "Collaboration with W. H. Auden." (pp. 8–12)
The revised edition (London: Faber, 1970) also includes a chapter on *Paul Bunyan* (pp. 22–27, 95–99).

425.* Doone, Rupert. The theatre of ideas. *Theatre newsletter,* VI (29 September 1951), 5.
Includes an account of the origin of *The dance of death.*

426. Ozu, Jirō. Auden to Isherwood [Auden and Isherwood]. In *Engeki kōza,* vol. 3: *Engeki no shimpu,* ed. Kumo no Kai (Tokyo: Kawade Shobō, 1951), ch. 27. [Not seen.]

427. Mitchell, Donald, and Hans Keller, eds. *Benjamin Britten.* London: Rockliff, 1952. (*passim*)

428. Williams, Raymond. *Drama from Ibsen to Eliot.* London: Chatto & Windus, 1952. "Auden and Isherwood." (pp. 247–56)
Revised in his *Drama from Ibsen to Brecht* (London: Chatto & Windus, 1968), pp. 199–206.

429.* Greenwood, Ormerod. It was something like this .... *Ark* (London), 15 ([1955]), 35–38.
On the Group Theatre.

430. Steinberg, Erwin R. Poetic drama in general and Auden and Isherwood in particular. *Carnegie studies in English,* 2 (1955), 43–58.

431. Donoghue, Denis. *The third voice.* Princeton: Princeton University Press, 1959. "*Drame à thèse:* Auden and Cummings." (pp. 62–69)

432. Maes-Jelinek, Hena. The knowledge of man in the works of Christopher Isherwood. *Revue des langues vivantes,* XXVI, 5 (1960), 341–60 (especially pp. 348–51).

433. Isherwood, Christopher. A conversation on tape [with Stanley Poss]. *London magazine,* n.s. I (June 1961), 41–58.

434. Gerstenberger, Donna. Poetry and politics: the verse drama of Auden and Isherwood. *Modern drama,* V (September 1962), 123–32.

435. Khan, B. A. *The English poetic drama.* Aligarh: Muslim University, 1962. (pp. 47–51)

436.* Wright, Basil. Britten and documentary. *Musical times,* CIV (November 1963), 779–80.

437. Wickes, George. Interview with Christopher Isherwood. *Shenandoah,* XVI (Spring 1965), 23–52.

438.* Mitchell, Breon. W. H. Auden and Christopher Isherwood: the "German influence." *Oxford German studies,* 1 (1966), 163–72.

439. Chaturvedi, B. N. *English poetic drama of the twentieth century.* Gwalior: Kitab Ghar, 1967. (pp. 76–85)

440. Salus, Peter H. Auden and opera. *Quest* (New York), II (Spring 1967), 7–14.

441. Geitel, Klaus. *Hans Werner Henze.* Berlin: Rembrandt Verlag, 1968. (*passim*)

442.* Jurak, Mirko. English political verse drama in the thirties: revision and alteration. *Acta neophilologica,* 1 (1968), 67–78.
An account of the variations between the published texts and the production texts of the plays.

443. ———. *Glavna problemska območja v angleški poetično-politični dramatiki v letih 1930–1940: the main spheres of the problems in the English politico-poetic drama (1930–1940).* Ljubljana: Univerza v Ljubljani, 1968. (*passim*)
In Slovene, with summary in English.

444.* ———. The Group Theatre: its development and significance for the modern English theatre. *Acta neophilologica,* 2 (1969), 3–43.
A detailed history of the Group Theatre; the footnotes include lists of reviews of the productions.

445. Hahnloser-Ingold, Margrit. *Das englische Theater und Bert Brecht.* Bern: Francke Verlag, 1970. (Schweizer anglistische Arbeiten, Band 61.) "W. H. Auden: Brechtschüler in den dreissiger Jahren?" (pp. 84–124)

The dog beneath the skin

446. Nakagiri, Masao. W. H. Auden, C. Isherwood, *Inu ni natta otoko:* shigekiron no ichibu [*The dog beneath the skin:* on a poetic drama]. *Shigaku,* VII (April 1952), 60–74. [Not seen.]

447.* Valgemae, Mardi. Auden's collaboration with Isherwood on *The dog beneath the skin. Huntington library quarterly,* XXI (August 1968), 373–83.
A detailed account of the genesis of the play.

The ascent of F6

448.* Humphreys, A. R. The ascent of F6. *Cambridge review,* LXIII (30 April 1937), 353–55.

449.* Cavanaugh, William C. "Coriolanus" and "The ascent of F6": similarity in theme and supporting detail. *Drama critique,* IV (February 1961), 9–17.

450. Stebner, Gerhard. W. H. Auden: The ascent of F6: Interpretation eines Dramas. *Die neueren Sprachen,* n.s. X (September 1961), 397–413. Reprinted as "Wystan H. Auden und Christopher Isherwood: *The ascent of F6*" in *Das moderne englische Drama: Interpretationen,* ed. Horst Oppel (Berlin: Erich Schmidt, 1963), pp. 203–19.

451. Markan, Ronald. Power and conflict in "The ascent of F6." *Discourse,* VII (Summer 1964), 277–82.

452. Ghosh, Prabodh Chandra. *Poetry and religion as drama.* Calcutta: World Press Private, 1965. "The ascent of F6 and Fry." (pp. 185–96)

453.* Bruehl, William J. *Polus naufrangia:* a key symbol in *The ascent of F6. Modern drama,* X (September 1967), 161–64.

On the frontier

454. Nakagiri, Masao. W. H. Auden, C. Isherwood saku *Kokkyo nite* [*On the frontier*]. *Shigaku*, VII (June 1952), 58–65, and (July 1952), 54–62. [Not seen.]

455. Takagi, Narahide. *On the frontier* no seijiteki fūshi: W. H. Auden to Christopher Isherwood no gassaku shigeki ni tsuite [Political satire of *On the frontier*]. *Eigo kenkyu*, IV (May 1952), 20–23. [Not seen.]

Paul Bunyan

456.* Hoffman, Daniel G. *Paul Bunyan: last of the frontier demigods.* Philadelphia: University of Pennsylvania Press for Temple University Publications, 1952. "Auden's American demigod." (pp. 143–53)
See also item 424.

The rake's progress

457. *Guida a The rake's progress.* [Venice: Biennale d'Arte, 1951].

458. See, Max. *Igor Strawinsky: The rake's progress: Einführung.* London, Bonn: Boosey & Hawkes, 1951.

459. Mason, Colin. Stravinsky's opera. *Music and letters*, XXXIII (January 1952), 1–9.

460.* Kallman, Chester. New Stravinsky opera: "The rake's progress" to have its American première on Saturday. *New York herald tribune*, 8 February 1953, section 4, p. 6.

461. Kerman, Joseph. Opera à la mode. *Hudson review*, VI (Winter 1954), 560–77.
Reprinted in *Opera* (London), V (July 1954), 411–15; revised in Kerman's *Opera as drama* (New York: Knopf, 1956), pp. 234–49.

462.* MacFadden, George. *The rake's progress:* a note on the libretto. *Hudson review*, VIII (Spring 1955), 105–12.
For a reply, apportioning the authorship of the libretto between Auden and Kallman, *see:* Alan Ansen, "A communication," *ibid.*, IX (Summer 1956), 319–20.

463.* Stravinsky, Igor, and Robert Craft. *Memories and commentaries.* Garden City, N.Y.: Doubleday, 1960. "The rake's progress." (pp. 144–67) Also in the English edition (London: Faber, 1960), pp. 154–76.

464.* Kallman, Chester. Looking and thinking back. In the booklet accompanying the recording of *The rake's progress* (Columbia M3S 710 / M3L 310, New York, 1964), pp. 33–34.
This booklet also includes Vera Stravinsky's account of the opening night, "La prima assoluta," p. 8; reprinted in Igor Stravinsky and Robert Craft, *Themes and episodes* (New York: Knopf, 1966), pp. 51–54, and in *London magazine*, n.s. VI (January 1967), 80–82.

465.* White, Eric Walter. *Stravinsky: the composer and his works.* London: Faber, 1966. "The rake's progress." (pp. 412–28, *et passim*) "Elegy for J. F. K." is discussed on pp. 493–94.

The magic flute

466. Kerman, Joseph. Auden's "Magic flute." *Hudson review*, X (Summer 1957), 309–16.

467. Einseidel, Wolfgang von. Eine neue englische Übersetzung der "Zauberflöte": kritische Gedanken zu einem meisterlichen Experiment. *Merkur*, XII (May 1958), 444–48.
Reprinted in *Neue Zeitschrift für Musik*, CXIX (October 1958), 574–77.

468.* W[eisstein], U[lrich]. Sarastro's brave new world, or *Die Zauberfloete* transmogrified. *Your musical cue* (Bloomington, Ind.), II (December 1965–January 1966), 3–9.

Elegy for young lovers

469.* Kallman, Chester. Ein persönlicher Kommentar. *Schloss Schwetzingen 1961* [Schwetzingen Festspiele programme], Stuttgart, 1961, pp. 21–24.

470. Henze, Hans Werner. *Essays.* Mainz: Schott, 1964. (pp. 95–101)
Reprinted from *Blatter der Bayerischen Staatsoper München*, Festspiele, 1961 [not seen].

The bassarids

471.* Spears, Monroe K. Auden and Dionysus. *Shenandoah*, XVIII (Winter 1967), 85–95.

Studies of Auden's Criticism

472. Darlington, W. A. A theorist in the theatre. *Discovery*, XVI (December 1935), 349–51.
On "I want the theatre to be...."

473. Uekesa, Jin'ichi. Shijin Auden no tantei shōsetsu-ron [Auden's study of detective stories]. *Ondori tsūshin*, IV (November 1948), 22–23.
On "The guilty vicarage."

474. Donahue, Charles. Auden on romanticism. *Thought*, XXVI (Summer 1951), 283–87.
On *The enchafèd flood.*

475. Gruenter, Rainer. Vom Wesen des Romantischen: eine Traumdeutung W. H. Audens. *Merkur*, VIII (February 1954), 193–95.
On *The enchafèd flood.*

476. Weales, Gerald. A little faith, a little envy: a note on Santayana and Auden. *American scholar*, XXIV (Summer 1955), 340–47.
On Auden's review of Santayana in *New Yorker*, 2 May 1953.

477. Whittemore, Reed. Auden on Americans. *Sewanee review*, LXV (Winter 1957), 146–51.
On *The Criterion book of modern American verse.*

478. Arbasino, Alberto. La poesia onorata a Oxford. *Paragone*, IX (March 1958), 131–48.
On *Making, knowing and judging.*

479. Callan, Edward. The development of W. H. Auden's poetic theory since 1940. *Twentieth century literature*, IV (October 1958), 79–91.

480. Musulin, Stella. In Oxford Dichtung lehren. *Wort und Wahrheit*, XVI (April 1961), 318–20.

481. Shinoda, Kazushi. Auden no Beethoven ron [Auden's essay on Beethoven]. *Bungakukai*, XVI (May 1962), 144–46.
On "The untruth about Beethoven."

482.* Brooks, Cleanth. W. H. Auden as a critic. *Kenyon review*, XXVI (Winter 1964), 173–89.
Mostly on *The dyer's hand.*

483. Binni, Francesco. Definizione di poetica per W. H. Auden. *Letteratura*, XXIX, 76–77 (1965), 109–21.

484. Holthusen, Hans Egon. Auden als Prosaist. *Merkur*, XX (May 1966), 469–78.
Reprinted in Holthusen's *Plädoyer für den Einzelnen* (Munich: Piper, 1967), pp. 107–18.

485. Binni, Francesco. Su Auden critico. *Letteratura*, XXXII, 94–96 (1968), 212–17.

486.* Weisstein, Ulrich. Reflections on a golden style: W. H. Auden's theory of opera. *Comparative literature*, XXII (Spring 1970), 108–24.

Theses and Dissertations

This list is undoubtedly incomplete, and the compilers will welcome any additions or corrections. Authors' middle names have been reduced to initials. Published abstracts are noted; *Dissertation abstracts*, later *Dissertation abstracts international*, is abbreviated *DA*, later *DAI*.

487. Householder, Samuel B. Some modern tendencies in English poetry as illustrated in the works of Auden, Spender and Day Lewis. M.A., Texas, 1938.

488. Schiller, Sister Mary B., O.S.F. Trends in modern poetic drama in English, 1900–1938. Ph.D., Illinois, 1939. (pp. 230–42)

489. Zeiger, Arthur. Wystan Hugh Auden. M.A., Columbia, 1941.

490. Church, Margaret. For this is Orpheus: or, Rilke, Auden and Spender. M.A., Columbia, 1942.

491. Marcuse, Katharine L. The poetry of W. H. Auden. M.A., British Columbia, 1943. [Not seen.]
Abstracted in *Canadian graduate theses* ... (Ottawa, 1951), p. 107.

492. Fogel, Ephim G. The influence of Homer Lane on W. H. Auden. M.A., New York University, 1947.

493. Hinkel, Cecil E. A production study and text of the Auden and Isherwood *The ascent of F6* as presented at Catholic University. M.F.A., Catholic University, 1947.

494. Lewars, Kenneth. The quest in Auden's poems and plays. M.A., Columbia, 1947.

495. Murphy, Irma E. No man's enemy. M.A., New York University, 1947.

496. Brown, Abigail. The benign wizard: a study in the cosmology and later poetry of W. H. Auden. M.A., Columbia, 1948.

497. Cross, Margaret R. An aspect of the poetry of W. H. Auden. M.A., University of the Witwatersrand, 1948. [Not seen.]

498. Hoffman, Dan G. Paul Bunyan: last of the frontier demigods. M.A., Columbia, 1949. (pp. 178–87)

499. Ward, R. B. Genesis and nature of the social, political and historical content of English poetry between two world wars, with particular reference to the works of Pound, Eliot and Auden. M.A., Adelaide, 1950. [Not seen.]

500. McKenty, Betty J. The critical attitudes of W. H. Auden. M.A., Manitoba, 1952. [Not seen.]

501. Hobbs, Joe K. The coterie playwright then and now: a study of John Lyly and W. H. Auden. M.A., Columbia, 1953.

502. Aney, Edith T. British poetry of social protest in the 1930's: the problem of belief in the poetry of W. H. Auden, C. Day Lewis, "Hugh MacDiarmid," Louis MacNeice, and Stephen Spender. Ph.D., Pennsylvania, 1954.
Abstracted in *DA*, XIV, 11 (1954), 2061.

503. Benstock, Bernard. Illusion and disillusion: the political aspects of the poetry of W. H. Auden. M.A., Columbia, 1954.

504. Williams, Haydn M. The poetry of Auden, Spender, and Day Lewis in relation to the thought of the period 1930–1940. M.A., Wales, 1954. [Not seen.]

505. Wingate, Gifford W. Poetic drama in the 1930's: a study of the plays of T. S. Eliot and W. H. Auden. Ph.D., Cornell, 1954. [Not seen.]

506. Greico, Michael F. X. A bibliography of W. H. Auden's critical prose. M.A., Columbia, 1956.

507. Kuna, Franz. Die Entwicklung des sozialen und politischen Denkens bei W. H. Audens. D.Phil., Vienna, 1956.

508. Replogle, Justin M. The Auden group: the 1930's poetry of W. H. Auden, C. Day Lewis, and Stephen Spender. Ph.D., Wisconsin, 1956.
Abstracted in *DA*, XVI, 11 (1956), 2169.

509. Bloomfield, Barry C. W. H. Auden: a trial checklist with some bibliographical notes. Diploma in Librarianship, London, 1957.

510. Matsubara, Kazuo. A study of W. H. Auden. M.A., Waseda Daigaku, 1957. [Not seen.]

511. Linebarger, James M. W. H. Auden's "The sea and the mirror." M.A., Columbia, 1957.

512. Moss, Leonard S. "New signatures," 1932: a study of the aims and poetic methods of the contributors with special reference to their previous writings and later work to 1935. M.A., London, 1957.

513. Rowan, Mark. Politics in the early poetry of W. H. Auden, 1930–1945. Ph.D., Cornell, 1957.
Abstracted in *DA*, XVII (December 1957), 3023-24.

514. Gerstenberger, Donna L. Formal experiments in modern verse drama. Ph.D., Oklahoma, 1958.
Abstracted in *DA*, XIX (January 1959), 1757-58.

515. Nelson, Hugh A. Individuals of a group: the 1930's poetry of W. H. Auden, C. Day Lewis and Stephen Spender. Ph.D., Northwestern, 1958.
Abstracted in *DA*, XIX (December 1958), 1389.

516. Simone, Roberta A. Structural metaphors in the short poetry of W. H. Auden, 1928–1945. M.A., Bowling Green State University, 1958. [Not seen.]
Abstracted in Bowling Green State University, *Abstracts of masters' theses*, VII (1957–58), 52.

517. Callan, Edward T. O'D. A study of the relationship of structure and meaning in W. H. Auden's major poems, 1940–1955; together with an annotated checklist of W. H. Auden's published writings, 1924–1957. D.Litt., University of South Africa, 1959. [Not seen.]

518. Katō, Yasuhide. On W. H. Auden's "The sea and the mirror." M.A., Rikkyō Daigaku, 1959. [Not seen.]

519. Olsen, Marilyn J. A study of "The age of anxiety" by W. H. Auden. M.A., Columbia, 1959.

520. Bahlke, George W. The poetry of W. H. Auden, 1941–1955. Ph.D., Yale, 1960.

521. Bloomfield, B. C. W. H. Auden: a bibliography (to the end of 1955). M.A., London, 1960.

522. Lohmann, Barbara. Gestalt und Funktion des Bildes in W. H. Audens und Edith Sitwells Dichtung zwischen 1940 und 1948: ein Beitrag zum Bild als Form der Aussage in moderner englischer Dichtung. D. Phil., Münster, 1960.

523. Muste, John M. The Spanish Civil War in the literature of the United States and Great Britain. Ph.D., Wisconsin, 1960. (pp. 149–55)
Abstracted in *DA*, XXI (December 1960), 1568-69.

524. Ford, Hugh D. British poetry of the Spanish Civil War. Ph.D., Pennsylvania, 1961. (pp. 336–47)
Abstracted in *DA*, XXIII (September 1962), 1017-18.

525. Villgradter, Rudolf F.   Über Grundzuge der Dichtungstheorie der Lyriker Wystan Hugh Auden, Cecil Day Lewis und Stephen Spender. D. Phil., Berlin, 1961.

526. Blair, John G.   W. H. Auden: his characteristic poetic mode. Ph.D., Brown, 1962.
Abstracted in *DA*, XXIV (December 1963), 2473–74.

527. Dodd, John T.   The influence of left-wing political theories on English poetry in the nineteen thirties. M.A., London, 1962. [Not seen.]

528. Rosen, Aaron H.   The critical prose of W. H. Auden. Ph.D., California, Berkeley, 1962.
Abstracted in *DA*, XXIV (May 1964), 4703.

529. Cook, Frederick W.   The allotropy of the Auden group. Ph.D., Nottingham, 1963.

530. Helland, Claire E.   An analysis of W. H. Auden's *For the time being* and its relationship to Kierkegaardian philosophy and the medieval mystery plays. M.A., Columbia, 1963.

531. Loose, John H.   W. H. Auden's poetic: a study of the relationship between his aesthetic theory and his theological point of view. Ph.D., Chicago (Divinity School), 1963.

532. Stevens, Peter S.   The development of W. H. Auden, 1930 to 1945. M.A., McMaster, 1963. [Not seen.]

533. Crabbe, C. K. W.   The later poetry of W. H. Auden, M.A., Melbourne, 1964. [Not seen.]

534. Greenberg, Herbert S.   Quest for the necessary: a study of the poetry of W. H. Auden. Ph.D., Wisconsin, 1964.
Abstracted in *DA*, XXIV (June 1964), 5407.

535. Hazard, Forrest E.   The Auden group and the Group Theatre: the dramatic theories and practices of Rupert Doone, W. H. Auden, Christopher Isherwood, Louis MacNeice, Stephen Spender, and Cecil Day Lewis. Ph.D., Wisconsin, 1964.
Abstracted in *DA*, XXV (September 1964), 1913–14.

536. McLaughlin, Franklin B., Jr.   The outsider viewed through modern poetry: a study of the alienated individual as reflected in the poetry of T. S. Eliot, W. H. Auden, Conrad Aiken, Robinson Jeffers, and Archibald MacLeish. M.A., Villanova, 1964. [Not seen.]

537. Matthews, S. Jerry.   Twentieth-century romanticism: W. H. Auden. M.A., North Texas State University, 1964. [Not seen.]

538. Morgan, Kathleen E.   Christian themes in English poetry of the twentieth century. Ph.D., Liverpool, 1964. [Not seen.]

539. Povey, John F.   The Oxford group: a study of the poetry of W. H. Auden, Stephen Spender, C. Day Lewis and Louis MacNeice. Ph.D., Michigan State University, 1964.
Abstracted in *DA*, XXV (May 1965), 6633–34.

540. West, William C. Concepts of reality in the poetic drama of W. B. Yeats, W. H. Auden, and T. S. Eliot. Ph.D., Stanford, 1964.
Abstracted in *DA*, XXV (April 1965), 6120–1.

541. Greenfield, Miriam T. The rebellion against the duality of mind and matter in W. H. Auden's poetry. M.A., Florida, 1965. [Not seen.]

542. Hooker, Peter J. The ideology of W. H. Auden's early poetry. M.A., Southampton, 1965. [Not seen.]
Abstracted in University of Southampton, *Abstracts of theses . . .*, 1964–65, p. 7.

543. Hoskins, Katharine B. Today the struggle: a study of literature and politics in England during the Spanish Civil War. Ph.D., Columbia 1965. (pp. 294–301)
Abstracted in *DA*, XXVI (October 1965), 2214–15.

544. Johnson, Richard A. A reading of W. H. Auden's poetry. Ph.D., Cornell, 1965.
Abstracted in *DA*, XXVIII (August 1967), 680A.

545. Lawlor, Mary B. The influence of Thomas Hardy on the poetry of W. H. Auden. M.A., John Carroll University, 1965. [Not seen.]

546. McNeely, James T. W. H. Auden and the drama. M.A., Alberta, 1965. [Not seen.]

547. Wolfe, Marian S. W. H. Auden and the neurotic dread. M.A., Texas Technological College, 1965. [Not seen.]

548. Bruehl, William J. The Auden/Isherwood plays. Ph.D., Pennsylvania, 1966.
Abstracted in *DA*, XXVII (November 1966), 1361A. Includes a transcript of a telephone interview with Isherwood.

549. Haines, Victor Y. Notes on prosody with notes on W. H. Auden's prosody. M.A., Carleton (Ottawa), 1966. [Not seen.]

550. Morse, Donald E. "Darning and the eight-fifteen": artistry and thought in W. H. Auden's "For the time being." Ph.D., Connecticut, 1966.
Abstracted in *DA*, XXVII (April 1967), 3465A.

551. Owen, Elsie E. A critical analysis of the religious ideology reflected in the poetry written by Wystan Auden since 1940. M.A., University of Miami, 1966. [Not seen.]

552. Panahi, M. M. The ethic of love: the philosophical development of W. H. Auden's poetry, 1922–1960. Ph.D., Exeter, 1966.

553. Park, Lea G. Poet of perspectives: the style of W. H. Auden. Ph.D., Northwestern, 1966.
Abstracted in *DA*, XXVII (May 1967), 3967A.

554. Shea, Daniel R. Art in the religious world: an interpretation of W. H. Auden's *The sea and the mirror*. M.A., Boston College, 1966. [Not seen.]

555. Twining, Edward S. Love and politics in the early poetry of W. H. Auden. Ph.D., Connecticut, 1966.
Abstracted in *DA*, XXVII (June 1967), 4268A.

556. Connors, James J.   Poets and politics: a study of the careers of C. Day Lewis, Stephen Spender and W. H. Auden in the 1930's. Ph.D., Yale, 1967.
Abstracted in *DA*, XXVIII (April 1968), 4085–86A.

557. DeMott, Robert J.   Anti-romantic tendencies in the poetic practice and theory of W. H. Auden and T. S. Eliot. M.A., John Carroll University, 1967. [Not seen.]

558. Jurak, Mirko.   Angleška poetično-politična drama v letih 1930–1940. Ph.D., Ljubljana, 1967.   [Not seen.]

559. Lepack, Gary W.   W. H. Auden and Kierkegaard: the religious background of *For the time being*. M.A., Duke, 1967. [Not seen.]

560. Morgan, Ronald E.   The definition of Kierkegaard's aesthetic, ethical, and religious categories in Auden's ideas of poetry from 1940. M.A., Duke, 1967. [Not seen.]

561. Nelson, Gerald B.   The problem of persona in the poetry of W. H. Auden, 1940–1966. Ph.D., Columbia, 1967.
Abstracted in *DA*, XXIX (July 1968), 269A.

562. Rivers, James C. S.   Astronomy and physics in British and American poetry, 1920–1960. Ph.D., South Carolina, 1967. (pp. 217–26)
Abstracted in *DA*, XXVIII (November 1967), 1826A. On *New Year letter*.

563. Shaughnessy, Eileen M.   Auden's use of landscape symbolism. M.A., Niagara University, 1967. [Not seen.]

564. Walsh, William F.   The heel of Achilles: dialectic in the long poems of W. H. Auden. Ph.D., Columbia, 1967.
Abstracted in *DA*, XXVIII (June 1968), 5075–76A.

565. Zulich, Olga M.   The birds and the beasts in Auden: a study of the use of animal imagery in the non-dramatic poetry of W.H. Auden from 1930 to 1965. M.A., Ball State University, 1967. [Not seen.]

566. Arnold, Leslie E.   The motif of the "quest" in the early works of W. H. Auden. Ph.D., Simon Fraser, 1968. (Canadian theses on microfilm, no. 1973)

567. Davidson, Edward J.   W. H. Auden's "New Year letter" and its relationship to the rest of his work. Ph.D., London (Birkbeck College), 1968.

568. Horne, B. L.   Christian doctrines in the poetry of T. S. Eliot and W. H. Auden: an investigation of the religious ideas of these writers in relation to modern sensibility. M.Litt., Durham, 1968. [Not seen.]

569. McLeod, Craig C.   The ideological background of W. H. Auden's "In time of war." M.A., New Brunswick, 1968. (Canadian theses on microfilm, no. 3652)

570. Boyer, Robert H.   Anglo-Saxon and Middle English influences in the poetry of W. H. Auden. Ph.D., Pennsylvania, 1969.
Abstracted in *DAI*, XXXI (September 1970), 1262–63A.

571. Clark, Vera F. W. **The rhetoric of W. H. Auden's verse plays.** Ph.D., University of Washington, 1969.
Abstracted in *DAI*, XXX (December 1969), 2651A.

572. Mendelson, Edward. **Auden's landscape.** Ph.D., Johns Hopkins, 1969.

573. Pak Chong-mi. A study of W. H. Auden. M.A., Seoul Taehakkyo, 1969. [Not seen.]

574. Sarang, Vilas. The verbal contraption: technique and style in the poetry of W. H. Auden. Ph.D., Bombay, 1969. [Not seen.]

575. Song In-kap. The meaning of landscape in W. H. Auden's poetry. M.A., Koryo Taehakkyo (Seoul), 1969. [Not seen.]

576. Stiehl, Harry C., Jr., Auden's artists: portraits of the artist in the poetry of W. H. Auden. Ph.D., Texas (Austin), 1969.
Abstracted in *DAI*, XXX (October 1969), 1576–77A.

577. Quesenbery, William D., Jr. Variant readings in W. H. Auden's poetry: *Collected shorter poems 1927–1957* and *Collected longer poems.* Ph.D., Columbia, 1970. [Not seen.]

APPENDIX II

A POEM ATTRIBUTED TO W. H. AUDEN

ACCORDING to persistent rumour the poem generally known as "The Platonic blow" was written by Auden in 1948 under the stylistic influence of Charles Williams. The poem appears to have circulated in typescript copies, one of which came into the hands of Mr. Ed Sanders, who printed it in his magazine *Fuck you / a magazine of the arts* (no. 5, vol. 8 [*sic*], March 1965, [4 fol., various paging]), and in so doing transposed the first and fifth stanzas. The poem is untitled but is described as "A gobble poem snatched from the notebooks of W. H. Auden," and the original manuscript is stated to be in the Pierpont Morgan Library, New York. The misplacing of the first stanza, and the two statements regarding the title and the whereabouts of the manuscript, characterize texts which derive from this first magazine printing. The notoriety attaching to this first appearance led Mr. Sanders to issue the following separate edition:

THE PLATONIC BLOW | © 1965 The Dietrich Von Buttfükel Gobble | Grope Fellowship | designed and published, zapped & ejaculated | by two legendary | editors and poets | at a secret location | in the Lower East Side, | New York City, U.S.A. | printed | by the FUCK YOU/® press |⌐FUCKPRESS⌐| for the world | GOBBLE GROPE FELLOWSHIP | [device] | "dicks around the world"
Collation: 8½ x 7 in. One unsigned gathering of six leaves, pp. [1–12].
   [1]: title page. [2]: blank. [3–10]: text. [11]: blank. [12]: '[eight lines] | printed in four editions: | – – – A Trade edition of 300 copies | – – – A Rough Trade Edition of 5 numbered copies, | each with beautiful slurp drawings by the artist | Joe Brainard | – – – An edition of 3 numbered copies, each with a sealed | packet sewn in, containing secret gobble relics | from the body of W. H. Auden | – – – The Turkey Edition, 2 copies which reveals the names of the publishers, both evil young poets, | Toe Queens, and cocksmen, scandalously freaking | in the Lower East Side. | [five lines]'.
Binding and paper: Stapled twice in a plain white wrapper lettered across the front cover in black: 'THE PLATONIC BLOW | W. H. AUDEN.' White laid paper with a pearly uneven finish.

   The text of this printing is rearranged into the clearly more sensible order and the first line reads "It was a Spring day, a day for a lay, when the air . . . ." The usual title of the poem first appears in this printing, but there is no evidence that the title and the text are the work of the same author. There may well have been two undifferentiated impressions in the Trade edition, and it is perhaps possible that the second is printed on smoother paper than the pearly paper found in early copies. The whole pamphlet is produced by offset duplication from a typewritten master.

The trade edition was originally priced at $2 a copy. The Rough Trade edition is identical with the Trade edition except that a drawing by Brainard is stapled in facing the verso of the title page with the stub projecting between pages [10] and [11]. Inside the rear wrapper, written by a felt-tipped pen in red, is the following statement: 'Copy [copy number] | Rough Trade Edition | [ornament].' However, there appear to be more than one set of this limited issue, for there are at least two copies of number 5 of the Rough Trade edition, in the second of which the statement of limitation runs as follows in Indian ink: 'THE ROUGH TRADE EDITION | THIS IS NO. [copy number in red upper-case written by a felt-tipped pen and underlined in black]'. In this second number 5 the Brainard drawing, which is alleged to be different in each copy of this issue, is tipped in before the title page with a shortened stub. Other limited issues probably exist, probably made up of the Trade edition with added illustrations. (A copy of a "very special edition" of six copies was catalogued by the Houghton Library in 1967 but could not recently be found.) There appears to be no evidence for the existence of the last two editions described in the pamphlet itself.

The poem soon reached England, where the first publication appears to be the following:

[No title page.]
Collation: Two sheets 14 x 8¾ in. folded once and stapled within a cover. Xeroxed on one side of the paper only.
[1]: blank. [2]: text. [3]: blank. [4–5]: text. [6]: blank. [7]: '[twenty lines of text] | Said to be taken from a notebook of W. H. Auden | now in the Morgan library. This text taken from | Fuck You Magazine Volume 8 Number 5 [*sic*], New York | City, March 1965 [*sic*] and includes the first four | lines left out of the Fuck You press edition. | This first British edition published in London | in the Charing Cross Road, October 1966 in two | editions: One of 150 copies duplicated and a | special edition Xeroxed from typewritten mss | lettered A–Z. Of the special edition this is: [letter of the copy in white Gothic transfer lettering]'. [8]: blank.
Binding and paper: The two sheets are folded once and stapled twice in ordinary buff or grey card wrappers. White wove paper.

It appears that the duplicated edition was never issued and the publisher's claim to completeness of text does not bear examination.

This edition was followed by another which is briefly described as follows:

[All across the caricature of the torso and legs of a naked man: the title in hollow upper-case, the rest in cursive script] A | GOBBLE POEM | snatched from the note-books of w. h. auden & | now believed to be in the morgan library | w. h. auden | fuck books unlimited—london 1967. | first english printing.
Collation: 10 x 7½ in. Six single sheets printed on rectos only, pp. [i, 1] 2–5.
[i]: title page, verso blank. [1]–5: text, versos blank.

Binding and paper: Stapled twice in a card cover lettered across the front cover in green: 'The | Gobble | Poem | [ornament] | W. H. Auden'. Copies which were put together first have light violet (210) card covers, but when this stock was exhausted vivid green (139) card covers were used. White wove paper.

This edition was produced by offset duplication from typewritten masters by Mr. Bill Butler in Brighton in March 1967 in an edition variously stated to be between 250 and 400 copies. The edition was not priced, and the text follows that of the first magazine printing.

Needless to say, all printings are without authority, and Auden denies any association with the poem.[1] However, the poem goes on propagating itself; it appears under the title "The gobble poem" in *Suck: the first European sex-paper* (Amsterdam), 1 (October 1969), p. 8, and as "A day for a lay" in *Avant garde* (New York), 11 (March 1970), pp. 46–47. This last text adds a third line to stanza eleven which had been missing in previous printings. A separate pamphlet edition with illustrations was published by the Guild Press, Washington, D.C., in 1970 at $3.50. No doubt surreptitious editions will proliferate and provide work for future bibliographers. However, to lighten the load somewhat, we should say that Mr. Herbert Cahoon, of the Pierpont Morgan Library, denies that the Library has the original manuscript, or indeed ever had. No manuscript of the poem is known to exist.

Copies of the Trade edition and that described as the "first english printing" are in the British Museum and the Bodleian libraries, but we do not know of any copies of the other printings in public collections in England. American locations can be gleaned from the National Union Catalog.

[1] But see the account of an interview with Auden in *Daily telegraph magazine*, 201 (9 August 1968), p. 22, reprinted in *Holiday*, XLV (June 1969), 67.

APPENDIX III

SIX PAMPHLETS PRINTED FOR FREDERIC PROKOSCH

On 20 May 1959 and again on 16 July 1960 Frederic Prokosch wrote to Bloomfield stating that he had printed four pamphlets containing poems by Auden and he enclosed brief descriptions of them. (These pamphlets are described elsewhere in this bibliography as items A6, A8, A10, and A11.)

However, when Sotheby & Co. published the catalogue of their book sale held on 8 and 9 December 1969, it included two items (numbered 756 and 757) which were described as "first separate edition[s]" of the poems printed in *Two poems* (A8). These two pamphlets, both printed in sans serif, may be described as follows:

Separate edition of *The latest ferrule*

THE LATEST FERRULE | [star] | W. H. | AUDEN | CHRISTMAS | 1934

Collation: 3 x 2¼ in. One unsigned gathering of four leaves.
  [1–2]: blank. [3]: title page. [4]: blank. [5]: text. [6]: 'Five special miniature copies of this | poem were printed: four on white | Normandie and bound in red Batik, | numbered alpha, beta, gamme [*sic*], delta; | and one on gray Fabriano and bound | in gold, numbered omega. | This is number | [in black ink] delta | [followed by a note in pencil] Printed simultaneously | with the larger-sized | "Two Poems." | F. P.' [7–8]: blank.
Binding: Stitched with a black thread in a vivid reddish orange (34) batik-patterned wrapper, with a gold label on the front cover lettered across in black: 'THE LATEST FERRULE | [star] | W. H. AUDEN'. A duplicate label is tipped in inside the rear wrapper.
Contents: The latest ferrule now has tapped the curb...
Notes: See above. A "special copy on blue vellum" with a coloured frontispiece was sold at Sotheby's on 11 May 1971, and copy "gamma" at the sale on 1 May 1972.

Separate edition of *Sleep on beside me*

SLEEP ON BESIDE ME | [star] | W. H. | AUDEN | CHRISTMAS | 1934

Collation: As *The latest ferrule*, with the substitution on p. [6] of 'blue Batik' for 'red Batik'; the copy number on the same page is 'delta', followed by a note in pencil: 'Printed simultaneously | with "Two Poems" | (in a larger format) | which includes this | sonnet. | F. P.'
Binding: Stitched with a black thread in a moderate blue (182) and dark blue (183) batik-patterned wrapper, with a gold label on the front cover lettered across in

black: 'SLEEP ON BESIDE ME | [star] | W. H. AUDEN'. A duplicate label is tipped in inside the rear wrapper.
Contents: Sleep on beside me though I wake for you...
Notes: See above. Copy "beta" was sold at Sotheby's on 1 May 1972.

The publication by Sotheby & Co. of the catalogue of the book sale held on 1 and 2 May 1972 brought to light no fewer than four more similar pamphlets containing poems by Auden, all of them previously unrecorded. (The catalogue also listed five "illuminated manuscripts" written out by Prokosch in 1932 of five poems by Auden: "Chorus," "This lunar beauty," "Before this loved one," "Sir, no man's enemy," and "The summer quickens all." As these were not set in type and claim no textual authority we do not describe them here.) The four pamphlets, items numbered 238, 247, 252, and 267 in the sale catalogue, may be described as follows:

Sonnet

SONNET | [star] | W. H. | AUDEN | CHRISTMAS | 1935

Collation: 3 x 2¼ in. One unsigned gathering of six leaves.
   [1–4]: blank, with frontispiece tipped in on p. [4]. [5]: title page. [6–7]: text. [8]: 'Six tiny illustrated copies of this | poem were printed: two on white | paper and bound in red Cockerell, | numbered I and II; two on gray | paper and bound in blue marble, | numbered A and B; one on red | paper and bound in silver, numbered | *alpha;* and one on blue paper and | bound in gold, numbered *omega*. | This is number | [in black ink] II'. [9–12]: blank.
Binding: Stitched with a black thread in a marbled Cockerell wrapper (dominant colour strong reddish brown 40; reference KO2B) folded round the first and last blank leaves with a gold label on the front cover lettered across in black: 'SONNET | [star] | W. H. AUDEN'. A duplicate label is tipped in inside the rear wrapper.
Contents: The fruit in which your parents bred you, boy...
Notes: A pencil note on p. [3] in Prokosch's hand reads: 'Printed by the Cambridge | University Press in | November, 1935. | F. P. | This poem was sent to | me in manuscript by | Auden in the Summer of | 1935. | F. P.'

Sonnet

SONNET | [star] | W. H. | AUDEN | GHENT | Easter | 1936

Collation: 6¼ x 4¼ in. One unsigned gathering of six leaves.
   [1–4]: blank, with frontispiece tipped in on p. [4]. [5]: title page. [6]: blank. [7]: text. [8]: 'Of this poem three copies, each with an original drawing, | were printed: one on Arches, numbered *zeta;* one on | Johannot, numbered *eta;* and one on Imperial Japan | vellum, numbered *theta*. | This is number | [in black ink] theta'. [9–12]: blank.
Binding: Stitched with a gold thread in a bluish grey (191) wrapper speckled with gold, folded round the first and last blank leaves, and with a gold label on the front cover lettered across in black: 'SONNET | [star] | W. H. AUDEN'. A duplicate label is tipped in inside the rear wrapper.
Contents: Just as his dream foretold, he met them all...
Notes: A recent [1972?] bibliographical note in Prokosch's hand is loosely inserted in this copy and reads: 'Printed by J. de Mulder in Ghent, Belgium, in March,

1936. After I had sent him the pamphlet "Poem" for Christmas, 1933, Auden suggested to me the possibility of printing privately a sequence of sonnets which he was then writing (or had just written). He sent me the manuscripts of five sonnets, but no others, and the "sequence-pamphlet" never materialized. However these five were printed separately: "The latest ferrule..." and "Sleep on beside me..." in Bryn Mawr, Pennsylvania, in November, 1934, both separately and together as "Two Poems" in a larger format; "On the provincial lawn..." and "The fruit in which..." were printed by the Cambridge University Press in November, 1935, along with the poem "Our Hunting Fathers"; and the fifth, the present sonnet, was done in Ghent in March, 1936. In addition to the three regular copies there were also a proof copy and a printer's trial copy. F. P.'

Sonnet

SONNET | [star] | W. H. | AUDEN | Venice | 1939

Collation: 3 x 2¼ in. One unsigned gathering of six leaves.
    [1–4]: blank, with frontispiece tipped in on p. [4]. [5]: title page. [6–7]: text. [8]: 'Ten hand-illustrated copies of this | poem were printed: three on Arches, | numbered 1–3; three on Ingres, num- | bered a–c; three on Canson, numbe- | red A–C; and one on Italian vellum, | numbered X. | This is number | [in black ink] 2'. [9–12]: blank.
Binding: Stitched with a black thread in a dark purplish pink (251) and greyish green (150) wrapper folded round the first and last blank leaves, with a white paper label on the front cover lettered across in black: 'SONNET | [star] | W. H. AUDEN'. A duplicate label is tipped in inside the rear wrapper.
Contents: He looked in all His wisdom from the throne...
Notes: A recent [1972?] bibliographical note in Prokosch's hand is loosely inserted in this copy and reads: 'Printed by Mario Conti in Venice in August 1939, just before the outbreak of World War II. Most of the copies were lost in the subsequent chaos and turmoil of transit. The drawings were done in Cernobbio in June–July 1939. F. P.'

The sphinx

THE | SPHINX | [star] | *W. H.* | *AUDEN* | *LISBON* | *Christmas* | *MCMXL*

Collation: 3 x 2¼ in. One unsigned gathering of six leaves.
    [1–4]: blank, with frontispiece tipped in on p. [4]. [5]: title page. [6]: blank. [7]: text. [8]: '*Of this poem nine hand-illustrated* | *copies were printed: two on* *old* | *Florentine paper, numbered 1 and 2;* | *two on old Castilian paper, num-* | *bered I and II; two on old French* | *paper, numbered a and b; two on* | *old Flemish paper, numbered A and* | *B; and one on old Portuguese* | *parchment, numbered X.* | *This is number* | [in black ink] 1'. [9–12]: blank.
Binding: Stitched with a black thread in a marbled wrapper (dominant colours moderate yellowish green 136, light yellowish brown 76, and strong reddish brown 40) folded round the first and last blank leaves, with a gold label on the front cover lettered across in black: '*THE SPHINX* | [star] | *W. H. AUDEN*'. A duplicate label is tipped in inside the rear wrapper.
Contents: Did it once issue from the carver's hand...
Notes: A recent [1972?] bibliographical note in Prokosch's hand is loosely inserted in this copy and reads: 'Printed in Lisbon at the Sociedade Tipografica in November 1940. The drawings were done during the same month at the Hotel Palacio in Estoril, where I lived from October 1939 to September 1941. F. P.'

Research by Mr. Nicolas Barker, editor of the *Book collector*, and Professor Arthur Freeman, of Boston University, to whom we are indebted for permission to publish this information, has apparently demonstrated "that the first and second items described above are set in Folio [sans serif] type, which was introduced into general use by the Bauersche Giesserei in 1958; the third and fifth items are set in Aster type, which was introduced into general use by Simoncini Officine S.p.A. in 1957; while the sixth item is set in Aster italic which was introduced at the same time as the main face. The fourth item however is set in Bodoni, as issued by the Mergenthaler Linotype Company." The detailed results of these investigations are to be published shortly.

Index

INDEX

References in this index are to item numbers in the bibliography. The titles of Auden's works are capitalized. The titles of books which Auden reviewed, the titles of periodicals carrying reviews of his work, and the titles of critical studies are not indexed. Sections **M** and **T** are only indexed selectively. No titles like "Poem," "Song," or "Sonnet" have been indexed unless a work is definitely known by such a name. Initial definite and indefinite articles in titles or first lines are here disregarded in alphabetization; "*n*" indicates a reference to a footnote.

W. H. Auden: A Bibliography

was composed, printed, and bound by
Kingsport Press, Inc., Kingsport, Tennessee.
The types are Janson and Garamond Bold
and the paper is Warren's Olde Style.
Design is by Edward G. Foss.